PRACTICAL DIGITAL VIDEO WITH PROGRAMMING EXAMPLES IN C

PRACTICAL DIGITAL VIDEO WITH PROGRAMMING EXAMPLES IN C

Phillip E. Mattison

John Wiley & Sons, Inc.

New York • Chichester • Brisbane • Toronto • Singapore

Trademark List

Windows is a trademark of Microsoft Corporation.
Video for Windows is a trademark of Microsoft Corporation.
QuickTime is a trademark of Apple Computer, Inc.
Smart Video Recorder is a trademark of Intel Corporation.
Indeo is a trademark of Intel Corporation.
Pro Movie Studio is a trademark of Media Vision, Inc.
Video Spigot is a trademark of Creative Labs, Inc.
Corel Draw is a trademark of Corel Systems Corporation.

Publisher: Katherine Schowalter
Editor: Diane D. Cerra
Managing Editor: Angela Murphy
Editorial Production & Design: Impressions

Library of Congress Cataloging-in-Publication Data
Mattison, Phillip E.
    Practical digital video programming with examples in C / Phillip
  E. Mattison
      p.   cm.
    Includes bibliographical references.
    ISBN 0–471–31016–6 (paper/disk : acid-free paper). —ISBN
  0–471–31015–8 (paper : acid-free paper)
    1. Digital television. 2. Interactive video. 3. C (Computer
program language) I. Title.
TK6678.M38 1994
005.362—dc20   93–49734
Printed in the United States of America.

10 9 8 7 6 5 4 3 2 1

Acknowledgments

I would like to dedicate this book to my lovely wife Carol, without whose hyper-speed typing I probably would have died of carpal-tunnel syndrome, and to my two kids, Christian and Rachel, who (usually) waited patiently for me to get through my book-writing workaholic phase.

Thanks also to the helpful people at Intel Corporation and Microsoft, Benita Kenn at Creative Labs, Kim Federico at Media Vision, and Debbie Miani Gordon at Apple Computer for their help in securing the necessary hardware, software, and technical documentation to make most of the current-information sections possible.

Preface

To many people, motion video on a PC is more a curiosity than anything else. It may be fun to show movies from a TV receiver or VCR in a window on a PC, but there is not much utility in this. It's cheaper (and easier) just to watch a regular TV. The real value in PC motion video is the ability to transmit and manipulate information that cannot be easily handled by other means. For example, it might be difficult or impossible to adequately describe the appearance and behavior of a physical object, while a motion-video demonstration could do it well in a matter of seconds. Through image processing or image enhancement it is possible to illustrate things that are not obvious even to a first-hand observer, things that would constitute a dissertation if described in words. Up to now, the transmission of most visual information has been on a mass-distribution basis only. Just as the development of personal computers has produced an explosion in the volume of transmitted written information, enhancing the ability of *individuals* to communicate with each other, the evolution of the PC will continue to increase the volume of information traffic, allowing visual communication on a point-to-point basis. Taking this perspective, the more obvious applications will be video telephony, non-real-time messages or documents incorporating video information, editing of visual information, and storage or processing. Each of these imposes different constraints on the equipment used to do the job.

The purpose of this book is to provide enough insight into the workings of digital video to allow the reader to talk intelligently on the subject without getting terminal math-anxiety, while also providing enough depth to satisfy the reader who wants more than a superficial understanding of the technology. It is also to provide a foundation for further study, and a clue where to look for more in-depth information for those determined to become experts. It is a good first book on the subject, but probably not suited to someone without a technical background in computers or electronics. The principles and techniques involved in processing digital video images do rely on some fairly intensive mathematics, but rigorous proofs are not necessary to an intuitive understanding of the mechanics of image transformation in practice. For math majors who want to see proofs of the theorems this technology relies on, those proofs are well documented in numerous academic texts.

The information in this book is organized around the basic elements required to understand video information as used on personal computers. If the reader is already proficient in any of these areas, it is a simple matter to skip those sections. An attempt is made to present information in a context of practical application wherever possible. The book covers video cameras, display systems, color representation, data formats and relevant digital information storage technologies, programming environments, commercial video digitizing hardware, and digital compression standards for the sake of completeness and to give insight into the practical problems faced by developers. Each topic is discussed first from an intuitive perspective, followed by specific detail and information designed to allow the reader to assess the relative complexity and difficulty of each area, as well as providing some handy reference data.

Given the rapid evolution of the technology and the industry, every attempt is made to include up-to-date information reflecting the current state of affairs. However, it should be noted that the basic intent is to provide a foundation, and that the speed of change requires almost daily insight to remain current. At the time of this writing, there is still a great deal of uncertainty in the industry; who will dominate the markets, will committee standards be accepted by the public, will digital video really revolutionize the information society; these and many other questions remain unanswered.

This book does not attempt to provide a complete, exhaustive reference incorporating the full text of the various standards (JPEG, MPEG, H.261, etc.) Nor does it presume to be a final source for information on any of the collateral elements of digital video technology. Digital signal processing has been a science in itself for many years, as have video broadcasting, display technology, data processing, and many others. There is a vast amount of information available in each area. The problem is not availability, but finding the "needle in the haystack." It is the synthesis of these previously disparate specialties that has the computer industry scrambling to be first, in the face of often bewildering complexity. While it may not be clear yet who will win, or even what the game is, it seems there is little doubt there is a prize to be won. It is hoped this book will at least get you to the starting line.

Contents

Four pages of full-color illustrations follow page 224.

1   The Evolution of Information   **1**
Memory Aids   2
Communication   5
Television   6
Information Processing   6
Digital Technology   8
Who Needs Moving Pictures?   10
    Special Effects   10
    Advertising   10
    Insurance   11
    Education   12
    Engineering   13
    Medicine   14
    Law Enforcement   14
    Entertainment   15

2   Video Fundamentals   **16**
How Video Cameras Used to Work   16
How (Most) Video Cameras Work Now   21
Color CCD Image Sensors   24
National Television System Committee (NTSC)   31
Synchronization   35
PAL and SECAM   37
Analog versus Digital Image Data   41
Quantization   43
Resolution   44

Filtering   49
Two-Dimensional Filtering   52
Conversion Devices   53
    Brooktree Bt812   53
    Motorola MC44011   54
    Brooktree Bt858   55
Bandwidth Requirements   55
Graphics versus Natural Image Data   56
Display Frame Buffer Organization   58
    PAL_EDIT Program Listing   **61**

3   Computer Display Systems   71
How Computer Displays Work   71
    Digital Cathode Ray Tubes (CRT)   71
    Analog Cathode Ray Tubes (CRT)   75
    Liquid Crystal Displays (LCD)   80
    Passive Matrix LCD   81
    Active Matrix LCD   85

4   Color Representation   88
CIE Standard   88
Conversion to RGB Color Space   93
    CIE_PLOT Program Listing   **95**
Additive versus Subtractive Primaries   101
YUV Color Space   104
Color Space Conversions   109
    Color Space Conversion Software   112
    RGB_DEMO Program Listing   **112**

5   Data Compression Techniques   123
Color Subsampling   123
    CCIR 601 Chroma Subsampling   124
    Bidirectional Chroma Subsampling   125
    Color Subsampling Demonstration Software   125
    SUB_SAMP Program Listing   **126**
Luma Subsampling   132
    2:1 Luma Subsampling Example Program   **132**
    4:1 Luma Subsampling Example Program   **134**
Run Length Encoding   136
Huffman Encoding   137
    Building a Huffman Code Table   138
    Huffman Encode Programming Example   138
    HUFFDEMO Program Listing   **140**
Vector Quantization   143
    Vector Quantization Programming Example   147

VQ_DEMO Program Listing   **148**
Simple Quantization Programming Example   150
SQ_DEMO Program Listing   **150**
Four Square Transform (FST) Encoding   152
Differential Pulse Code Modulation (DPCM)   153
Application to Natural Images   154
DPCM Compression Programming Example   155
PCM_DEMO Program Listing   **156**
Discrete Cosine Transform (DCT)   158
Two-Dimensional DCT   160
Computation Efficiency   162
Example 8x8 Block Encode and Decode   166
Example 8x8 Block Encode and Decode Program   **168**
DCT Image Compression Programming Example   **173**
Motion Estimation   178
Factors Affecting Choice of Image Compression Technique   181
Compatibility   181
Multiple Coding   181
Progressive Transmission   181
Image Artifacts   182
Encode/Decode Symmetry   182
Error Tolerance   182
Source Image Quality and Characteristics   182
Transmission Data Rate   182
Implementation Limitations   183

6   Video Data Storage   **184**
Compact Disk Optical Storage   184
Theory of Operation   185
Diffraction   187
Polarization   189
CD Optics   189
Focus and Tracking   190
Data Formats   194
CCIR-656 Serial Video Code   196
Fixed Disk Drives   196
Defect Handling   201
Video Disk Fragmentation   202
Helical-Scan Magnetic Tape   203
Digital Tape Formats   208
D1 Format   208
D2 Format   209

7   Motion Video Capture Hardware   **212**
Video Spigot   212

Media Vision Pro Movie Studio   217
Intel Smart Video Recorder   220
Capture Resolution and Image Quality   222

8   Motion Video Software Environment   226
Programming Under DOS   226
Microsoft Windows   228
Dynamic Link Libraries (DLLs)   229
Video for Windows   233
    Media Control Interface   235
    Installable Compression Manager   236
    Video Compression and Decompression Drivers 237
    Example Program Code for Video Driver **245**
    AVI File Format   248
    RIFF AVI File Structure   **248**
    AVI2VID Source Code   **252**
    VIEW_VID Source Code   **255**
    VID_FILE.CPP Source Code   **257**
QuickTime for Windows   263
    Conceptual Model   264
    QuickTime Application Programmer Interface 264
    MCDoAction()   264
    Writing a Decompressor Component   264
Conclusion   269

9   Video Image Processing Techniques   271
Filtering   271
    Low-Pass Spatial Filter   272
    High-Pass Spatial Filter   272
    Filter Demonstration Programs   274
    LPF_DEMO.CPP Listing   **274**
    HPF_DEMO.CPP Listing   **277**
Scaling   279
    Scaling Up   280
    Scaling Down   281
    DDA_DEMO Scaling Demonstration Program   282
    DDA_DEMO.CPP Listing   **282**
Contrast Enhancement   287
    CON_DEMO Contrast Adjustment Demonstration
    Program   288
    CON_DEMO.CPP Listing   **288**
Negative Transformation   292
    NEG_DEMO Image Negative Demonstration Program 293
    NEG_DEMO.CPP Listing   **293**

Feature Extraction   296
    EDG_DEMO Edge Detection Demonstration Program   298
    EDG_DEMO.CPP Listing   **299**
Threshold Representation   302
    THD_DEMO Threshold Demonstration Program   303
    THD_DEMO.CPP Listing   **303**
Graphics and Video   307
    G_V_DEMO Image Negative Demonstration Program   308
    G_V_DEMO.CPP Listing   **308**

10   JPEG Image Compression Standard   313

Compressed Data Formats   316
Frame Header   318
    Start of Frame (SOF)   318
    Frame Header Length (Lf)   318
    Sample Precision (P)   318
    Number of Lines (Y)   318
    Number of Samples per Line (X)   318
    Number of Image Components in a Frame (Nf)   319
    Component Identifier (Ci)   319
    Horizontal Sampling Factor (Hi)   319
    Vertical Sampling Factor (Vi)   319
    Quantization Table Selector (Tqi)   319
Scan Header Syntax   320
    Scan Header Length (Ls)   320
    Number of Image Components (Ns)   320
    Start of Spectral Selection (Ss)   321
    End of Spectral Selection (Se)   321
    Successive Approximation Bit Positions
    High and Low (Ah & Al)   321
Quantization Table Specification Syntax   321
Huffman Table Specification Syntax   323
    Table Class (Tc)   324
    Table Identifier (Th)   324
    Huffman Code Counts (Li)   324
    Huffman Code Table (Vij)   324
Restart Interval Definition Marker Syntax   325
Application Data Segment   325
Encoding Procedures   325
Magnitude Range Categories   330
Predefined Huffman Code Tables   331
    AC Code Tables   331
    DC Code Tables   340
Predefined Quantization Tables   342

JPEG Demonstration Software   342
    Source File JPEG_CMP.CPP   **343**
    Source File JPEG_UNC.CPP   **346**
    Source File JPEG_SUB.CPP   **350**
    Source File JPEG_DEF.H   **371**

11   MPEG Video Compression Standard   373
Overview   373
Target Image Characteristics   376
Encoded Bit-Stream Syntax   378
    Sequence Header   379
    Picture Group   381
    Encoded Image   383
    Image Slice   385
    Macro Block   385
    Block Encoding   389
Summary   393

12   H.261 Video Compression Standard   395
Encoder Structure   395
Picture   398
Group of Blocks   399
Macro Blocks   400
Forward Error Correction   406
Summary   408

Appendix A   Motion Video and Still Image File Formats   409
Eight-Bit and 24-Bit AVI Files   410
VID File Format   414
    Compressed Color Index Format   415
    YCrCb Format   416
    JPEG File Format   416
Alternate AVI-to-VID Conversion Program Source Code   417
Still Image File Formats   431
AVI-to-PIC File Conversion Program Source Code   432

Appendix B   DOS-Based C++ Source Files   436
Include File Source Code Listings   440
    AVI_RIFF.H Source Code   440
    MOUSE.H Source Code   440
    CONTROL.H Source Code   444
    DISPLAY.H Source Code   445
    MOUSE256.H Source Code   446

CTRL_256.H Source Code 448
DISP_256.H Source Code 450
C++ Library Source Code Listings 451
MOUSE.CPP Source Code 451
CONTROL.CPP Source Code 455
DISPLAY.CPP Source Code 457
MOUSE256.CPP Source Code 461
CTRL_256.CPP Source Code 464
DISP_256.CPP Source Code 466
Assembly Language Module Source Code Listings 469
SETVMODE.ASM Source Code 469
VPALETTE.ASM Source Code 470
DRAW_BLK.ASM Source Code 475
DRWASCII.ASM Source Code 478
WRITEBLK.ASM Source Code 482
Utility Program Source Code Listings 484
VIEW_PIC.CPP Source Code 484
VIEW_ERR.CPP Source Code 485
MONO_PIC.CPP Source Code 487
CLUT2YUV.CPP Source Code 488
YUV2CLUT.CPP Source Code 491
COMPRESS.CPP Source Code 494
DECMPRES.CPP Source Code 497
MONO_VID.CPP Source Code 499
WRP_DEMO.CPP Source Code 501
DOSSHELL.CPP Source Code 505
SHELL256.CPP Source Code 507

Appendix C **About the Software** **511**

Further Reading **514**

Index **517**

1

The Evolution
of Information

In prehistoric times, information usually took a more direct form than it does today. For example, if you felt hunger pangs, it meant the time had come to hunt or gather. Distant drums meant there might be a raid from a rival tribe. A feeling of wetness; it's raining. A growling dog; better stay away. A sharp blow to the head; someone is trying to get your attention. Of course, many of us still recognize some of these information types even now. As difficult as it is to imagine, there is contemporary evidence that a society *can* exist without the benefit of spoken language, much less written. We see it in the community of chimpanzees, gorillas, lions, and many other gregarious or herd animals. It is certainly conceivable humans could have lived this way at some time in the remote past. Without getting into the debate over Creation versus Darwin, we can still surmise an evolutionary path for the creation and use of information. A lowest common denominator as near as possible to the animal realm is useful because there is massive evidence that abstraction of information is one of the key differences between humans and animals. If there is an evolutionary process it is reasonable to assume it started at that level or somewhere near it.

That said, let us imagine a primitive character living in the remote past, differing from animals more in potential than in anything else. Because there is no spoken language he has no name, but we will call him Oog, since that sounds prehistoric and is easier to use than repeatedly drawing pictures of his face. Oog lives in a cave (how cliché) and has a female friend who has given birth to a couple of children since they met. Oog tolerates them and even shares his food with them because he has found comfort in their companionship. They live in a relatively temperate climate, but lately Oog has found himself waking up occasionally in the middle of the night shivering from cold. One night as he lay awake, shivering, a connection occurred in his dimly lit mind: this is not the first time this has happened. It always happens on nights when the thing he can't look at in the sky doesn't climb all the way up over his head during the day. For many days he pondered this amazing realization, remembering more and more nights when the same thing had happened. Oog didn't like being cold at night, and he had a gnawing urge to do something, though he didn't know what or why. Then one day as he stood squinting at the thing in the sky, feeling its warmth on his face, he knew. He would follow the thing in the sky. He was never cold when it was over his head. He grabbed all the food from the cave, and started out. Because he had all the food, his companions followed. Often they wanted to follow an easier way, but Oog was driven by his newfound enlightenment. Whenever they would stray he would point to the thing in the sky and say, "Oog, Oog!" and they would follow again. After many days of travel the nights started getting warmer. Spring had returned. Oog and his family were comfortable, so they rested. Whenever Oog would find himself shivering every night they would travel again, always following the thing in the sky, always directed by Oog's pointing finger and his insistent "Oog, Oog!" Eventually, after many seasons, they had traveled far enough so the nights were comfortable, even in winter. By now the children were grown, and had acquired companions of their own, but had never forgotten about the thing in the sky. For now it was no longer simply a place they couldn't look, it was Oog. When the night was unusually chilly they would murmur longingly to each other, "Oog." Now each evening as Oog sets in the west, you can hear them quietly chanting, "Oog, Oog, Oog," acknowledging their dependence on Oog, and their hope for its return in the morning. So might the first spoken word have been invented.

Of course, if one cave person can invent a word, another can invent a better one, or maybe even two. Carry this on long enough and eventually you have network news. But we're getting ahead of ourselves. Along with language, maybe before, maybe after, came symbolism. Actually, language *is* symbolism, just auditory instead of visual. We've all seen the caveman hand outlines on the walls of caves discovered by Leaky and his ilk. Maybe this was a sign of ownership. If your hand doesn't fit the outline you'd better not be caught walking out with the television. Then there were the crude drawings of a beast with a spear sticking out of it, caveman with a silly grin standing by. This may have been the first financial statement, or maybe, "how I got this spiffy fur tunic." With the combination of auditory symbolism and visual symbolism we had the makings for mass confusion. That is, civilization. Lucky for us, though, it was also the means to dominion.

Historians generally agree that for an unknown period of time history and genealogy were passed from generation to generation by word of mouth. Particularly noteworthy deeds may have been occasionally immortalized in cave drawings, but language and random visual symbolism existed long before any systematic visual symbolism (written language). The key advantage humans now had over animals was the ability for one generation to learn from the experience of the previous. One may ask why it was important to track genealogy. It is good to remember this was still a very physical environment. While you may have been smarter than the predators and your own prey, in many cases they were both faster and stronger than you, so your competitive edge was limited at best. Heroes were those who were best at the business of survival. Close association with a hero improved your own chances for survival, and what better association than blood relations? Besides, language was probably much better suited at first to people, places, and things than to arcane discussions of technique. Think about it, what does an infant or a student of a foreign language learn first? Names. Next come verbs. Go. Stop. Run. Jump. Hide. Throw. From these can be built an entire mythology. Names and deeds are the stuff of history. It is only recently anyone has cared about when or how or why.

Memory Aids

Again, no one knows exactly how long it took, but it was inevitable. Sooner or later the list of names, and the stories attached to them, would get so long they would be hard to remember. People who could cram it all into their heads would come to be seen as pretty extraordinary individuals in their own right. Even our own culture tends to equate age with wisdom, and senility with loss of wisdom. Priesthoods were created. It was no use, though. The advent of symbolic memory would guarantee that eventually no one could retain it all. Even with specialization, the growing populations of villages and towns would create more history and genealogy than anyone could remember. This may have been the necessity that drove the creation of written language. At first it took the form of mnemonics. The most primitive drawing or carving could be used to jog the memory and bring forth an entire story attached to it. Eventually a system of classification was developed for these mnemonics, as demonstrated by Egyptian hieroglyphics and Asian ideograms. Evidently these worked fairly well at the time, as attested to by the fact that they reach back thousands of years to some of the earliest known recorded history. For example, the earliest Egyptian dynasties (Menes, Aha, Zer, Zet, etc.) are believed to date as far back as 3200 B.C. Over time this system was refined more and more, and is still used in some cultures.

Throughout most of this period, however, the basic content of recorded information didn't change drastically. It was not until phonetic encoding of language was developed that the groundwork for modern civilization was laid. Even then, for many years the keepers of written records were the elite of whatever society they served. The existence of such records enabled rulers of the people to maintain an advantage over the average person, because not everyone had access to the information. Even if they had, they would not have known what to do with it. Already information was power. This situation dominated the world into the current millennium.

True to its nature, the volume of information suitable for recording continued to increase unabated. Soon even legions of scribes could not keep up with the need to record new events and maintain the crumbling records of the past. Pressure for a solution grew along with the value of information. Great thinkers and philosophers were molding the moral fabric of whole civilizations. The megalomaniacs of the world were having a hard time creating the kinds of changes they wanted to see within one lifetime. A major dissertation took a king's ransom to reproduce in enough copies to influence a significant number of people. Intolerable. None the less, books were made in relatively large quantities up to the fall of the Roman Empire. After that, most of the rich patrons of literature were either dead or had fled for their lives, and their libraries were largely destroyed by the Gothic invaders. Fearing the remaining literature might be lost forever, St. Benedict at Monte Cassino and Cassiodorus at Beneventum instituted a program requiring monks to copy religious and classic writings. The situation persisted for hundreds of years. It wasn't until there was a prolonged moral outrage at abuses by the clerical community in disseminating religious information that someone thought up the printing press. It is still a matter of debate exactly who invented printing and when. There is evidence someone in Holland printed on paper using movable type in the fifteenth century. The earliest dated specimens of printing are reputed to have been made by Johann Gutenberg, who supposedly began his experiments at Strasbourg in about 1436, producing a Latin grammar by Donatus. Unfortunately, he did not place his name on any of his work. Johann Fust, Gutenberg's partner, foreclosed on a mortgage and took over Gutenberg's printing business in Mainz, Germany, with a partner, Peter Schöffer. Fust and Schöffer identified their work with their names and trademark, and Fust claimed to have invented printing. Workmen who had been taught by Gutenberg, Fust, and Schöffer dispersed to Strasbourg, Bamberg, and Cologne when Mainz was sacked in 1462. There were printers in Italy by 1465, and in Paris by 1470. It didn't take long before printing was employed throughout the entire civilized world.

What an idea. Now the average guy didn't have to rely on the church or the government for spiritual enlightenment. Of course, most people still couldn't read, but at least now those who could were more likely to find something on which to practice their skill. The general effect was to produce more open debate on issues, and a more educated society. With a wider availability of printed material there was more incentive to learn how to read and write. Now you could find out for yourself what ancient scholars had thought, what was going on in other parts of the world, how a distant friend or relative was doing, and any number of other things. Obviously this didn't happen overnight. Most people were too busy plowing their fields to be bothered with reading and writing. For hundreds of years more, an education was still mostly the province of royalty or wealthy families. It wasn't until the advent of public education that a majority of people in a population could learn to read and write. But with printing presses operating around the world, the volume of current and stored information continued to rise exponentially, regardless of whether the masses could read or not. The introduction of public education simply accelerated the demand for printed material. The concept of public education is generally believed to have been introduced in the United States in the first half of the nineteenth century. Evolution of educational norms combined with massive economic and social changes in a growing nation created an environment where such a new and radical idea could find root. Notable leaders of the time who were instrumental in bringing this about were Horace Mann in Massachusetts, and Henery Barnard in Connecticut. In 1837 a state board of education was organized in Massachusetts, with Mann as secretary. The same thing happened in Connecticut in 1838, with Barnard as secretary. These two systems served as a model for the rest of the country. As the United States grew in size and power, it gradually began to dawn on the rest of the world that an educated population could produce a more robust economy, something national leaders are always interested in. Today the correlation between the average educational level of a population and the economic health of a nation is generally recognized.

At this point, the stage was set for an explosion in the volume and velocity of information transfer we find ourselves struggling to keep up with even now. General availability of printed books and the ability of a large segment of the population to read and write was great for improving the standard of living, but people were still having to send letters across the country by train or pony express. Notable as it was that such an ability to communicate had previously been available only to kings and emperors, it was still fundamentally no different. When the fastest thing known to man is a guy riding a horse, that's who you get to carry your mail when you're in a hurry. Actually, carrier pigeons were probably faster, but not nearly as reliable. Not only that, but a pigeon can't carry very much in one trip. Something was needed that didn't require the medium of communication (paper) to be carried from point to point. Some other medium was needed that could carry information over a distance *by itself*. The medium eventually chosen was electricity. A basic awareness of electricity had been around for a long time. We've all heard the story about Benjamin Franklin flying his kite in the thunderstorm and as a result, inventing the lightning rod in about 1746. He was lucky not to have *become* a lightning rod. Still, he is credited with the idea of electricity as a fluid. You may have heard of the Leyden jar, invented at the University of Leyden by a man named Musschenbroek in the same year. This was one of the first devices used to detect and measure the presence of electricity. In 1819 a Danish physicist named Oersted discovered a connection between electricity and magnetism. Over the next few years an American scientist named Joseph Henry refined the application of electromagnetism to the point where it was useful for more than a laboratory curiosity. Thus all the necessary elements were in place for the invention of telegraphy.

Communication

The first successful telegraph was demonstrated for President Martin Van Buren in 1838 by Samuel Morse. That's about a hundred years from a basic awareness of electricity to its application as a medium for information. A hundred years seems like a long time by our standards today, but it is a fraction of the time required for the transition, say, from ideograms to phonetic writing. As a result of the demonstration, Congress awarded Morse $30,000 for further study. A year later a forty-mile telegraph line was set up between Washington and Baltimore. Morse had a patent on the technology and offered to sell it to the government for $100,000, but they turned it down as too financially risky. By the time the Civil War broke out, over fifty telegraph companies had been formed using private venture capital. Apparently politicians came from the ranks of the "best and the brightest" even then. The existence of the telegraph during the Civil War facilitated a type of warfare never before seen. Generals could now gather intelligence faster and more efficiently than ever before. This might help explain the massive numbers of casualties suffered by the South during that war. Information was power now more than ever.

By now the nation knew we had a good thing going. All that was needed was to refine the technology. Who could tell how far it might go? In 1875 Alexander Graham Bell invented, almost by accident, the first speaking telephone. He was trying to develop a "harmonic" telegraph that could carry multiple messages over a single wire by using different carrier frequencies when he realized that if he could send different frequencies he could also send a voice or other sounds. Bell demonstrated the telephone a year later at the Philadelphia Centennial. A year after that there were 2,600 telephone sets in the United States. There were 228,000 by 1890, and over 1.3 million by 1900. By 1947 there were 11 million, and over 43 million by 1951. That's growth. But in spite of all the benefits bestowed by the telegraph and telephone, there was still a crucial limitation: The sets had to be connected by a physical wire. The longer the wire was the more power was required to transmit information over it. Repeater stations were needed at regular intervals in the transmission line to strengthen the signal. About the same time Bell was making the telephone a practical instrument for general use, a man named Clerk Maxwell was theorizing about yet another way to transmit and receive information.

In 1873 Maxwell published his theories under the title *Electricity and Magnetism*. Building on the work of Michael Faraday, he postulated that if magnetism could be thought of as a field of energy existing in the absence of any detectable supporting medium, it should also be capable of taking the form of *waves*. He developed an elaborate mathematical model that predicted the behavior and characteristics of these waves. In 1888, after Maxwell had died, a German physicist named Gustav Hertz demonstrated experimentally the magnetic waves Maxwell had predicted. Eight years later an Italian scientist named Guglielmo Marconi was the first to successfully demonstrate the use of electromagnetic waves for telegraphic communication. Yet another limitation to the flow of information had been removed. People in ships on the ocean could send and receive messages from people on land. People in remote locations could communicate with people in cities or other remote locations. The development of radar (*RA*dio *D*etection *A*nd *R*anging) during World War II proved a decisive advantage to those who had it. It provided its users advance information on the location of enemies. Elaborate encryption schemes were devised to protect sensitive information from the enemy. The art of warfare had advanced to a new level because of the amount and speed of information transfer. It could be argued the industrial revolution was the result of advances in information technology. In the stock market, then as now, those with the best information were generally winners, with the rest paying for their gains.

Television

With the advent of radio it seemed there was almost no limit to the nation's ability to communicate information. However, the benefits bestowed by access to information provide a strong motivation to find ever better ways to obtain and use it. The seeds of entirely new industries had already been planted, and had taken root. There were then, and still are, better ways to transmit and use information. In 1923 a man named Vladimir Zworykin invented what he called an *iconoscope*, which could convert images into electrical signals. Zworykin joined RCA in 1929 and developed the iconoscope into a product along with the television picture tube, then known as the *kinescope*. With the creation of these two devices it was possible to send visual information as well as sound over wires or via radio signals. Because of the low quality and large expense involved, however, there was little public interest in the technology before about 1939. By then, there were some regularly scheduled weekly programs and television receivers were commercially available. During World War II there was almost no regular programming because of the intense focus on the war effort. But military applications of the technology and private research and development had refined it to a point that allowed television broadcasting and manufacturing to grow into a billion-dollar industry almost overnight when the war was over. By 1951 there were 107 broadcast stations reaching three-fifths of the national population. The term *informed person* had already come to carry considerable prestige. Information was becoming more and more synonymous with knowledge.

Information Processing

Unfortunately this wonderful surplus of information created its own kinds of problems. There is such a thing as *too much* information. The problem was no longer only how to get adequate information, but also how to make the best use of it; how to sort through the massive piles of data to find the one piece you really needed, or to draw statistical conclusions from it. It was no longer enough just to send and receive information; some efficient way was needed to *process* it. The first mechanical devices for processing information were adding machines. It could be argued that the Chinese abacus was the first mechanical computing device, but the abacus is actually a memory aid, used to make it easier to accumulate sums. The adding machine actually performed calculations and provided a result to the user. Universities and government agencies used to employ large rooms full of mathematicians to perform statistical and complex mathematical calculations. The adding machine greatly improved their efficiency and reduced the number of workers required. In the mean time, scientists and engineers were busy refining the concept of information processing and finding better ways to implement it. While mechanical analog computers were constructed at Massachusetts Institute of Technology as early as 1931, the first digital electronic machines were not constructed until around 1940. The analog computers were relatively limited in the types of problems they could solve, and were used mainly for scientific research. The original concept for a large-scale digital computing machine was proposed in 1835 by Charles Babbage, but was never constructed because of the prohibitive cost and complexity of a mechanical implementation. The first practical electronic computer was the Electronic Numerical Integrator And Calculator (ENIAC), built in 1942 to solve ballistic calculations for the army. It contained about 18,000 vacuum tubes, cost about $90,000, and computed at the blazing speed of 5,000 additions per second. It was designed mainly to do relatively simple calculations repetitively on large volumes of similar information. It was also useful for calculations requiring successive approximation, as it could repeat operations very rapidly. It was essentially little more than an elaborate calculator with mechanical extensions that allowed it to automatically retrieve input data in sequence (punch card reader) and record results (printer or card punch). Nonetheless, this produced a revolution in the way information was used, and in the amounts of information that could be handled. Huge databases could now be compiled. Researchers could analyze volumes of data never before imagined. Universities, corporations, and government agencies could observe trends, track progress, and collect statistics like never before.

Of course, computers were very expensive to build and operate. They required special rooms where the temperature was carefully controlled. They took up a lot of space and used a lot of electrical power. Certainly room for improvement there. The technology for communicating and using information evolves as well as the nature of information itself. At about the same time, the science of information *theory* was beginning to develop. Now information was more than just a commodity, it was an object of study in its own right. The study of linguistics, semantics, abstract mathematics, and numerous other specialties focused on various types of information. As mechanical and electronic technology evolved so did myriad other sciences, all feeding off each other. Discoveries made by physicists were used to accelerate the development of new electronics. The equipment devised by electronics engineers help the physicists carry out their research. More and more companies grew up to support the transfer and processing of information. The flow and availability of information has become an ever more critical element in the competitiveness of business and society. Computers played a big part in this, still do, and will continue to do so. Because of their expense, for years computers were primarily the domain of governments and large corporations. As more people became aware of computers and their potential, opportunities began to arise for different ways of using computers. An executive at one of the largest business equipment manufacturers in the world is purported to have said there might be a need for as many as five computers in the world. He underestimated . . . slightly.

Most people old enough to be interested in this book probably remember those amazing little transistor radios. They were so small you could actually carry them around in your hand. They operated from a battery. It was quite a breakthrough. Little did most people know that the thing that made these radios different (the transistor) would also be the key to the next explosion in the evolution of information. The transistor was invented by the American physicists John Bardeen, Walter Brattain, and William Shockley in about 1948, and opened the door to what would become known as solid-state technology. This eventually led to the development of the *microprocessor*, which would revolutionize the way computers were built and used. The first signs of this change were the appearance of rudimentary microprocessor-based computers for electronics hobbyists. Before you knew it there were all sorts of young upstart technologists with no respect for the establishment building little computers in their garages. Most "real" computer engineers and manufacturers just scoffed at them. But these were not the kind of people who were easily discouraged by scoffers.

The first really commercial personal computers were introduced by a couple of guys named Jobs and Wozniack in the late 1970s under a company they had formed called Apple Computers. Their primary markets at the time were educational institutions and hobbyists. The scoffers continued to scoff. Eventually, however, it became obvious they were on to something. Other personal computer companies began to spring up. You might recall names like Osborn, Kaypro, Digital Research, and so forth. Some did better than others. As more of a sideline than anything else, International Business Machines (IBM) decided to build a personal computer. Of course they took a slightly different approach than most of the others because of their mainframe computer background. However, it was probably their massive existing distribution channels more than their technology that allowed them to be as successful with their personal computer as they were. They were able to gain the lion's share of the business personal computer market before anyone else. The fact that they provided full documentation of their hardware and software laid the groundwork for a situation almost all personal computer developers are aware of today: About 80 percent of the personal computers in use today are compatible with that original machine introduced by IBM, though they are not necessarily made by IBM. The intense price competition created by massive numbers of personal computer "clone" manufacturers served to accelerate the acceptance of personal computers in general. It also created a de facto standard for a new industry that would spring up around it. The information processing capability of computers would soon be in the hands of almost any individual who really wanted it.

The kinds of work done using computers would be revolutionized as well. *Word processing* became a generic term that replaced the word "typing." Soon everyone knew what a spreadsheet was, a previously unheard of concept. Computer-aided drafting, sophisticated accounting, graphic design, and many other activities could now be done faster and more efficiently than before, on an *individual* basis. Note that all these involve the creation and use of information. Take word processing, for example. Just a few years ago if someone wanted to produce a document for distribution it had to be typed and edited and then sent to a printing specialist. The specialist would do the typesetting and graphic artwork to produce what was called camera-ready copy. Now with a personal computer and a laser printer almost anyone can produce documents of equal quality in a fraction of the time and at a fraction of the expense. It was a major shift in the way things were done, with massive implications for the typesetting and printing industries. It involved a fundamental change from specialists producing written documents for mass distribution to individuals being able to do nearly the same thing for themselves. This did not eliminate the need for specialists and mass distribution. It simply brought the basic capability to a much wider group of people. With the advent of what is now commonly called multimedia we may be seeing a similar revolution in the way visual and auditory information is created and distributed.

Digital Technology

The engineering and scientific communities have probably been more aware than most of the change taking place in many areas from analog to digital technology. Whether or not this is a good thing is often the subject of heated debate. But there is little doubt it is happening. One of the first traditionally analog technologies to make the switch was telephony. It is clear there was much to be gained by the telephone companies themselves in this transition because it has not been easy for them. In fact they have yet to make a complete transition. While it is true virtually all central office equipment and local and long distance communication channels have been converted to digital technology, the wire that connects to the phone in most people's homes is still an analog current loop. This was the one expense too huge for the phone companies to undertake even when they had a monopoly. How ironic that now the monopolies have been broken up and people rarely buy their telephones from their telephone company anyway. The analog connections to millions of homes are the weakest links in what is otherwise an all-digital telecommunications infrastructure. Gradually, however, even this last barrier is coming down. The installation of digital telecommunication channels has enabled the phone companies to operate much more efficiently, and when digital subscriber equipment connections become commonplace, the average person will have access to services and information most people can't imagine now.

Another area where this transition is very evident is in the production and distribution of music and other auditory information. First we saw magnetic tape displace plastic phonograph records. Now we are seeing compact disk (CD) technology gradually displacing magnetic tape. There is also a feverish effort underway to convert magnetic tape from an analog to a digital standard medium. There are two critical advantages to digital technology in both cases. First, digital information is generally more reliable, more precise, and less subject to signal degradation than the analog equivalent. Second, information stored in digital format can be manipulated and processed in a much wider variety of ways using the same basic equipment than analog information can. For example, most professional recording studios today use digital recording and mixing equipment. Digitally recorded sound can be copied and mixed without *any* loss in fidelity. In any analog electronics–based system, the signal-to-noise ratio is a critical element in every part of the system. In a digital sound system, this is only a factor up to the point where the signal is converted to digital format, or after it is converted back to analog format.

There are many other areas where the conversion from an analog to a digital approach has yielded similar advantages, too numerous to mention here. Usually the existence of an entrenched analog-based industry creates certain barriers to the transition to digital technology, and the video information industry is no exception. Shortly after the invention of television the National Television Systems Committee (NTSC) was formed to set standards to ensure equipment manufactured by different companies would work together. These standards defined levels of image quality and broadcast methods that have survived to the present. Most people still would consider them adequate but, unfortunately, they are not very well suited for conversion into a digital domain. For some time now there have been research and development efforts underway to implement certain phases of television broadcasting in digital technology. For example, practically all satellite broadcasts are digital. Studio equipment is increasingly digital. Laser disks store video information in digital format. Certain types of video cassette recorders (VCRs) incorporate digital processing of video to facilitate special effects and advanced editing capabilities. A lot of activity is underway in international standards committees to define a new high definition television (HDTV) standard, which will almost certainly be digital. Still, virtually all the television receivers in the United States are designed in a way that would allow them to receive and display broadcasts in the same format used thirty to forty years ago.

Just as the conversion of the telephone system from analog to digital technology has and will provide advantages that more than offset its cost, so will the same conversion do for video information. One of the more interesting aspects of this trend is the migration of digital video information to the desktop personal computer. As a result of this there is a possibility the same type of phenomenon that occurred in the printed material publishing industry could happen in the motion picture publishing industry. Already some of the features previously only available to film industry professionals are coming out in PC-compatible software packages. One example is *morphing*, probably one of the newest types of special effects. There are almost no limits to the kinds of processing that can be done to visual information once it is in digital format. The ability to store, process, and communicate motion pictures within the personal computer environment has the potential to revolutionize the way computers are used.

Who Needs Moving Pictures?

A question that frequently arises in discussions about PC motion video is, "What would I use it for?" This is certainly a valid question. Handling motion video on a PC requires considerably more processing power than do other forms of data. It is natural to hesitate to adopt a new data type if there are no clear advantages to justify the cost. You have probably heard the old adage, "A picture is worth a thousand words." If that is true, then full motion video should be worth about 30,000 words per second. Now *that's* fast talking. Specialized hardware to capture and display still images is already commercially available for the PC, and fairly common. If motion pictures can be made available at a comparable price, there is little reason to believe the technology would not be accepted at least as well; probably better. It is certainly possible the pioneers of PC motion video are wrong about what the predominant applications will be. There can be little doubt, though, that simply bringing it into the realm of possibility will evoke yet-to-be imagined innovation. This will happen in both the hardware and software industries. The remainder of this chapter is devoted to describing possible uses for computer-based motion video as a data type. No attempt is made to stay within the current realm of feasibility, as that is the antithesis of innovation.

Special Effects

One application we are already seeing is animation and special effects. A number of recent full-length animated feature films have contained stunning scenes created by computers using solids modeling and three-dimensional image rendering techniques. This combined with conventional animation sequences or natural images can produce truly amazing results. Another technique mentioned earlier, called "morphing," involves the transition from one image to another in a way that can be arbitrarily dictated by the producer. Certain elements of the original image can appear to transform themselves into some other object while the rest of the scene remains intact. The illusion created is very convincing if done properly. The technique is possible because the image comprising each frame of the motion picture is converted to digital format, which allows the computer to analyze and modify color, intensity, and spatial relationships of the various regions that make up the total image. The editor can identify an arbitrary region of an image, and specify that it is to metamorphose into some other arbitrary region of another image. The computer then interpolates between the two regions and generates the intermediate frames required to create the illusion of metamorphosis over the specified time. It is essentially a very sophisticated version of what is called a "fade," where one image fades away while another takes its place.

Advertising

There are many potential applications for computer motion video in the form of sales aids or advertising. It is possible even now to see a "video kiosk" in some places, where you can select from a menu of choices for information, and get motion pictures with sound on command. The cable broadcast industry is working feverishly to develop what is commonly called *interactive multimedia*, or the ability to program your own viewing schedule and respond in real time to advertisements. There is a great deal of uncertainty over what impact this would have on existing conventional methods of advertising. Many products are currently sold through salespeople calling on customers in person. A very simple improvement on this theme would be the ability to show video demonstrations or testimonials on the spot, using a portable computer. To carry the concept further, the number of on-site sales calls (and corresponding required travel time) could be drastically reduced by the availability of video telecommunication. The existing division between items readily sold through mail order and those that are not could be radically changed by the advent of widespread video communication. Many articles that cannot be sold in this way have that restriction because people want to *see* what they are buying. It is reasonable to assume this restriction would be removed in at least some cases. The classified advertising industry could be revolutionized as well. It is not hard to imagine a classified advertising database containing motion pictures of every item to be sold, and accessible to subscribers via their computers. This would provide two major benefits. First, it is much easier to sell something with pictures than with a written description. Remember a thousand words each? How many newspaper column inches is that? Second, the subscriber would never have to look at advertising that holds no interest. The computer can do the searching for you. It could even, conceivably, search for a certain type of *picture*. Imagine looking for that mint-condition 1954 red Corvette, finding an ad for it, and being able to look at it from all angles *and* hear the engine before you ever call the seller.

Insurance

The insurance industry could probably find more applications for computerized motion video than any engineer could ever think of. Visualize a minor fender-bender: The police are on the scene making their reports while the vehicle owners are at the nearest phone booth (no injuries) calling their insurance agents. The insurance company dispatches a claims assessor to the scene, who arrives carrying a video-enabled portable computer with cellular telecommunication capability. The assessor talks to the police, talks to the vehicle owners, takes pictures of the accident scene, and transmits a report to the local office. By the time the tow trucks arrive, a damage assessment and arrangements with the nearest authorized auto body shop have been made. Shortly after that, a courier arrives with a rental car for the accident victim. Sure, this may be just a pipe dream, but if it doesn't happen that way it is not because the technology isn't available.

It also works in the medical insurance world, both for health care and malpractice insurance. Imagine every surgical procedure paid for by insurance (in other words, just about all of them) being recorded and archived in an insurance company database. There would never be any question about exactly what services were or were not provided. Patient monitoring data could be saved as well, just as telemetry data is stored for a space mission. It would virtually eliminate insurance fraud, and would either convict or vindicate doctors accused of malpractice, in most cases. Records of standard procedures could be recalled instantly for comparison.

There are possibilities for homeowner's insurance as well. While it is true that already in some cases people videotape their possessions, with a system of compressed digital video stored on computers it would be feasible for insurance companies to establish a policy of always videotaping the possessions and the property of homeowners they insure. Because of the random access possible with computerized data storage it would be a relatively simple matter for claims processors to verify the existence of items claimed in a loss claim. In the event of total loss, for example as in a fire, the records would probably be much more complete and would be easier to keep up to date.

Education

The range of uses for PC motion video in the training and education field are almost limitless. It is significant that the beginnings of the whole PC revolution were in the classroom. Education is always a matter of great debate because of the cost of providing a good education as well its importance. Computers are already used in schools for much more than simply learning about computers. For very young children, learning sometimes takes a form similar to a video game. The advantage this provides is a high degree of familiarity because most children have played some sort of video game before they ever get into school. The quality of the video game's visual impact and the degree to which it engages the attention has a direct impact on its effectiveness as an educational tool. For older students, a great deal more can be conveyed by motion pictures combined with reading material than by reading material alone, even if still pictures are used as they are commonly in textbooks. Most of us can remember much more clearly things that were *demonstrated* in the classroom by the teacher than things we read in a textbook. Educational films used several years ago or videotapes used nowadays are much preferred by students over a lecture or reading a book.

Obviously there can never be any really adequate substitute for direct hands-on learning as in lab experiments and so forth, but the use of computer-based video can do a great deal to accelerate the remaining portions of the learning process. There are at least two ways in which this would be superior to the methods commonly used today. First, the idea of self-paced learning would be more practical than ever using this type of approach. It would be true interactive learning; the closest thing to having a private tutor without actually having one. Through the use of natural language algorithms currently being developed, and possibly even speech recognition, the training software could anticipate commonly asked questions and make answers available to students in direct response to questions. This would be a supplement to the core material provided and could be used to round out the student's understanding in the event there are any problems or gaps in his or her learning, but would not require students to wade through a lot of material they already understand. Written tests would be almost totally automated and paperless. Instructors would be relieved of a great deal of mundane and repetitive work and be able to focus on the really critical elements of teaching, concentrating on the areas where students need help the most. Second, the content of the training material itself could be greatly enhanced and kept up-to-date much more easily. When textbooks are published a lot of production work is involved and the number of textbooks to be printed must be accurately anticipated. Textbooks are quite expensive to produce. When a new edition comes out the old edition is rendered practically useless. A CD-ROM, on the other hand, can be produced at a small fraction of the cost of a textbook.

This kind of technology is already beginning to appear in commercial form. For example, even now you can get an entire set of encyclopedias and several other reference documents on a single CD-ROM. These include animated sequences and narrated explanations. By the time this book is published there will probably be CD-ROM applications of this type that also contain natural video sequences. The big difference between computer-based educational material of this type and ordinary tape or film productions is the fact that computer-based video is much easier to produce and update. It is not necessary to produce an entire program as you would with a videotape, for example. The video sequences can be very short, illustrating very specific points. They can be easily intermixed with still graphics, computer-generated animation, text, and audio. It is possible to imagine entire libraries of material stored on CD-ROM.

Even today it is possible to go into some libraries and use a computerized on-line index system. Imagine being able to find your author, title, or subject matter and then view it without ever leaving the terminal. Library materials could then be checked out by copying them to a data cartridge supplied by the library. There would never then be a situation where a book is checked out and not available. Copyright issues would be addressed by the fact that the copy is temporary, on a medium authorized and owned by the library to be returned by the borrower for reuse.

The same principles apply to training of almost any type. Specialized job training could be accelerated and its cost reduced by using this type of media. The cost of producing and maintaining training materials in an up-to-date form would be greatly reduced relative to ordinary text-based or videotape production methods because of the fact that sections that need to be changed, added, or deleted can be handled without affecting the remainder of the content. Currently only relatively large organizations can afford a production staff to develop training materials of their own involving videotape. With low-cost computer-based video production editing tools, the threshold for entering this field would be much lower, enabling a vast number of smaller companies to benefit from increased or improved training capabilities.

Engineering

There are so many distinct engineering disciplines that if a person was familiar enough with all of them it would be possible to fill an entire book just with the potential applications of computer-based motion video to engineering. That won't happen here. One fundamental capability of the medium, which creates a lot of potential in this area, is the ability to enhance images to bring out particular features of interest or deemphasize others. This is already routinely done for satellite photographs and radar weather maps. The ability to do it frame by frame on a motion video sequence intelligently applied over a period of time enhances the ability even further. This combined with cameras containing image sensor elements sensitive to different bands of the frequency spectrum can provide insights previously not available. For example, a camera with an image sensor array sensitive to the infrared spectrum, taking time lapse photography that is then enhanced by the computer, could be used to analyze traffic patterns in a city, or energy utilization patterns in a city or in a building. Multiple-image sensors simultaneously focused on the sun, each sensitive to a different band of radiation, could be used to monitor and analyze sun spot activity, probably providing as-yet unknown insights.

If you ever saw the movie "Blade Runner" you might remember this scene: Harrison Ford is analyzing a picture trying to find clues. He inserts it into a machine that shows the picture on a display. By giving voice commands he's able to focus on different parts of the picture, magnify them, enhance the image, and perform various other operations. It is possible to imagine an instant camera that produces pictures with a visual image not only in the surface emulsion but also recorded in a digital format on a magnetic medium embedded in the paper. This could then be viewed as a conventional picture simply by looking at the picture. Or it could be viewed in detail, edited, modified, enhanced or whatever when used in conjunction with a machine. It is possible to imagine paper with similar qualities. Someone could hand you an ordinary-looking report that contains graphics and natural images. You could read the report as you read any other printed material. You could also pass the pages through a special scanner that would allow you to edit the text or view animated graphics and motion video of natural images with audio. This could conceivably be implemented with any combination of the features mentioned above.

In biological or genetic engineering it would be possible to do microscopic time-lapse photography with image enhancement and the ability to automatically detect certain fundamental changes in the subject matter, automatically adjust environmental factors, or automatically record the time and date when certain events happen.

For electronic circuits at a board level or semiconductor level, thermal stress or other factors could be analyzed under a range of operating conditions. In general, there are many processes in both engineering and scientific endeavors that are time consuming, difficult, tedious, or require a lot of expensive apparatus, which could be greatly simplified or automated by using this technology.

Medicine

In the medical field there have already been significant advances in the areas of noninvasive surgical techniques, endoscopic examination, and the use of computerized metabolic monitoring devices. A lot of work has been done in the area of digitizing X-ray or cat-scan images, for example, to allow image enhancement or compression or rapid storage and retrieval. The medical instrumentation field has been quite innovative in using up-to-date technology. Equipment and supplies generally tend to be on the expensive side, however, because of the kinds of liability involved. The general availability of relatively low-cost computer-based motion video recording, processing, and storage capabilities could greatly enhance the record-keeping process for a wide range of general practitioners. The family doctor, for example, could then easily compare your general appearance, the sound of your voice, the sound of your pulse, and other factors to previous visits. An ophthalmologist could easily store a visual record of each retina examination. There is quite a wide range of possibilities. You would probably have to be an expert in the field to really do justice to the potential here.

Law Enforcement

Law enforcement and security is another area where this technology could find many applications. A lot of publicity has been given to a few recent incidents videotaped by private citizens. One obvious way to prevent this kind of problem is for the police themselves to videotape every confrontation. Of course, using conventional equipment this really isn't practical because it would require a cameraperson to accompany a police officer everywhere. With advances in camera and digital recording technology, however, it will soon be feasible to have a video camera mounted in a policeman's helmet connected to recording equipment that is small enough and light enough to be used in the field. Cameras could easily be mounted on cars or motorcycles to record the actions of a suspect vehicle in a pursuit. By recording all this information in digital format it would be readily processed by image enhancement software to extract the kind of information necessary to make a determination of what happened. It is fairly common for bank security systems, for example, to have multiple video cameras focused on all the teller windows. A problem with this kind of arrangement is each camera requires a separate videotape recorder and all of them record linearly. In other words, in order not to miss anything each camera and recorder has to be operating all day long. With a digital camera being monitored by an intelligent software package, it is possible for the computer to detect when nothing is happening (in other words if there's no motion) and not record those periods that are of no interest. Recording does not have to be linear because the computer can keep track of the time and stamp each frame of recorded information with the time it was recorded.

The cost of this type of system is likely to be much less than a conventional system with similar capabilities. Therefore, it becomes practical to use it in many other applications such as home security or other types of businesses. Home and small business security systems often utilize monitoring services where a central office manned by security guards is notified automatically by a phone signal or some other means if there is an intrusion or panic alarm or some other event requiring attention. With the availability of compressed digital video it would be possible in the event of an intrusion to have local automatic security systems take pictures of events automatically, detecting where there is activity and where there is not, and send these pictures over conventional phone lines to monitoring stations. The security officers at the monitoring station would then be able to make a much more informed decision about the severity of the situation and what kind of response they should make. This would also work well for automobile security systems. A hidden camera could be mounted in the dashboard of the car or some other location. If somebody breaks into the car it would be possible to send their picture automatically over a cellular telephone network to a security monitoring station. Using global positioning satellite technology (which is already available) the location of the car could be transmitted as well in the event of an emergency.

Entertainment

Last but not least, of course, is the entertainment field. Much has already been done, as previously mentioned, using digital image technology in this area. Computerized special effects and digital editing stations are already in use by entertainment industry professionals. In the Far East, and increasingly in the United States, a popular form of entertainment called "karaoke" is currently being implemented in many places through the use of digital video technology. Over time the trend will probably be for the price and availability of this type of equipment to move more and more into general business use and eventually to consumer availability. It is not hard to imagine in the near future a home-movie enthusiast being able to record the kid's birthday party with background music, special effects, and voice-overs. Particularly noteworthy scenes might be captured as still images, printed on paper, and stored in the family photo album or made into a Christmas or birthday card or greeting card to be sent to all the relatives. Cable companies are hard at work on digital video technology pursuing the possibility that they might be able to transmit ten times as many programs over the same cable infrastructure. Instead of "57 channels and nothing on" it would be 570 channels. Probably still nothing worth watching, but so what? The potential effect on efficiency and profit margins tends to make this very attractive. The ability to so easily record, store, manipulate, copy, and transmit visual information is likely to have a profound impact on the existing system of copyright laws. Ultimately though, whether the overall effect is beneficial or detrimental will depend on the intentions of those who use the technology. In the meantime, there's much to be gained just by making the technology available, because it is almost certain to be popular in one way or another.

2

Video Fundamentals

How Video Cameras Used to Work

When television was invented, just about everything electronic was based on vacuum tubes. Believe it or not, there are still people alive today who remember this. In fact, the television itself is one of the few remaining electronic devices that still uses vacuum tube technology (the picture tube), although it too may soon be replaced by solid state electronics such as *light emitting diode* (LED) displays. Television cameras as well, including the image sensor, used vacuum tube technology. The basic premise was to focus an image on an image sensor, and using a scanning electron beam, generate a signal that represents the picture sliced into a series of lines. To display the picture remotely, another scanning electron beam repaints the image slices on the inside surface of the television picture tube, which is coated with a phosphor compound that glows when struck by the electron beam. During live broadcast, the beam in the picture tube is synchronized with the beam in the camera. Figure 2.1 shows these relationships for closed circuit and broadcast video pictures.

Within the camera, the image sensor was a special kind of vacuum tube called an *iconoscope*, invented by Vladimir Zworykin in 1923. Zworykin joined RCA in 1929 and developed the iconoscope into a product along with the television picture tube, then known as the *kinescope*. The iconoscope had a hot cathode to generate free electrons that formed an electron beam when biased properly, and a set of deflection coils similar to those in a television picture tube to control the direction of the beam. The beam was directed at a two-dimensional array of photosensitive silver-cesium elements deposited on a flat mica anode with a conductive coating at the opposite end of the tube. For each element, the electron beam striking it would cause more or less electrons to be released depending on how much light was striking it. The deflection coils caused the beam to repeatedly scan across each row of photo elements in sequence, from top to bottom. Each complete set of row scans is called a *field*. This created a flow of electrons from the anode proportional to the amount of light striking the photosensitive element the beam was focused on at the time. Figure 2.2 shows the internal construction of the iconoscope tube. Later a new type of image sensor tube called the *vidicon* was

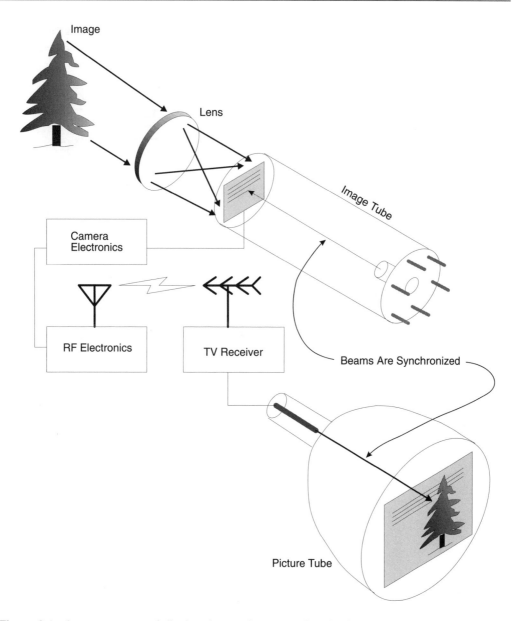

Figure 2.1 Image sensor and display electron beam synchronization.

developed, which replaced the photoemissive elements with photoconductive materials, increasing efficiency. This was followed by further refinements on the theme, with names like Newvicon, Saticon, and Trinicon (reminiscent of the old Disney characters Omicron and Nudnicron).

The signal from the iconoscope (or whatever) was conditioned electronically and combined with synchronization pulses to allow the receiver to determine when to start a new scan or field of

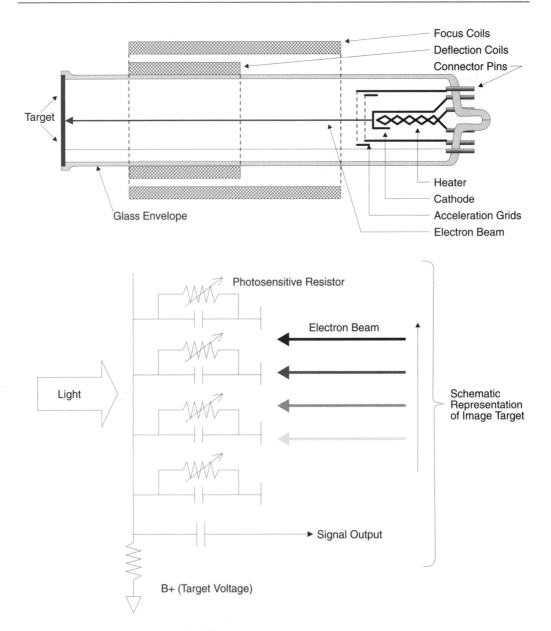

Figure 2.2   Iconoscope internal construction.

scans. It was this method of converting images into electrical signals that drove the creation and adoption of the various broadcast standards. These standards are discussed in detail later in this chapter. The standards allowed multiple, independent companies to develop cameras, broadcast equipment, and televisions that all worked together. They have evolved somewhat over time, but still reflect the same basic method of image transmission. Because of their age, and the huge volume of existing and new equipment, these standards have rarely been questioned. But as we will see, current broadcast standards may not be the best solution to the problem now that digital computers have become so common. Signs of this trend are becoming more and more visible with the emergence of international committees to establish new standards for digital television and high definition television (HDTV).

Color capability was added to the vacuum tube image sensor by applying a *stripe filter* to the surface of the sensor. This filter consists of an extremely fine grid of transparent colored material that separates the light striking the sensor into the primary colors. These can then be encoded and recombined with the luminance signal and sync signals to form the standard NTSC composite video signal. Figure 2.3 shows how the stripe filter is physically organized. The filter is composed of diagonal *yellow* and *cyan* stripes that overlap in some areas, and leave other areas unfiltered.

The spacing of the stripes is such that each pair of scan lines produces a set of signals corresponding to four different color values. Figure 2.4 shows how scan lines, N, N+1, N+2, and so on, intersect the stripe filter. Scan line N intersects the filter stripes where they do not overlap. Where the beam intersects the yellow filter, blue light is filtered out, so the signal corresponds to the red-plus-green content of the image. Where the beam intersects the cyan filter, red light is filtered out, so the signal corresponds to the blue-plus-green content of the image. Scan line N+1 intersects the filter stripes where they do overlap. Where the beam intersects the filter, red light is filtered out by the cyan stripe and blue light is filtered out by the yellow stripe, so the signal corresponds to the green content of the image. The remaining area is not covered by any filter, so the signal indicates the full luminance value of the image. Note that because of the diagonal orientation of the filter stripes, the timing of the components of alternate lines is effectively *interleaved*. Figure 2.5 shows the relationship between color components on adjacent scan lines. One line consists of R+G, B+G, R+G, and so on, while the next line consists of G, Y, G, Y, and so on. Note that Y is the composite luminance value derived from all three primary colors in specific proportions. The sweep frequency of the beam and the spacing of the filter stripes is such that the time from one Y to the next

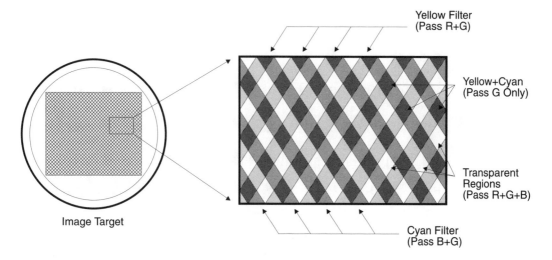

Figure 2.3   Detail of image sensor stripe filter.

Figure 2.4 Electron beam intersection with stripe filter.

is related to the color burst frequency, 3.579545 MHz. The phase relationship between color components on adjacent lines therefore is plus or minus 90°. This is instrumental in recombining the components to form the luminance (Y), R−Y, and B−Y signals used in the final NTSC signal.

As shown in Figure 2.6, the signal from the image sensor is first run through a preamplifier, a band pass filter (BPF), and into a color separator. The band pass filter effectively separates the color components from the luminance components of the signal. The color signals are then applied to a 90° phase-shift network and a 1H delay network. The red signal (R) is created by adding the 1H and 90° signals. The blue signal (B) is created by subtracting the 1H and 90° signals. Figure 2.7 shows how the Y, R, and B signals are combined to form the Y, R−Y, and B−Y signals. The total brightness at any point in the image is proportional to the Y component. The color at each point is encoded in the R−Y and B−Y components. Note that these are *color difference* signals. This concept is covered in more detail in Chapter 4.

Note that the luminance signal is split into two components, YL and YH. YL is in the frequency range of 0.5 MHz and below. YH incorporates frequencies up to 3.7 MHz. YL is used to generate the color difference signals, while YH is the full bandwidth luminance signal. The R−Y and B−Y signals are modulated with two 3.579545 MHz carrier signals separated by 90°, and then

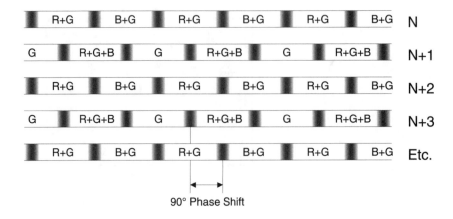

Figure 2.5 Phase relationship of alternating scan lines.

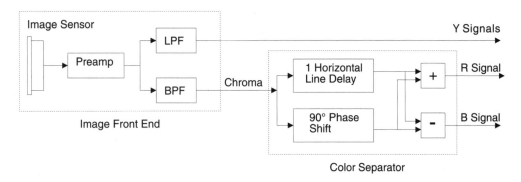

Figure 2.6   Color separation processing sequence.

combined in a signal mixer. This process is called *quadrature modulation*, and results in a signal where the color value (hue) corresponds to the *phase angle* of the signal. Again, this concept is covered in more detail in Chapter 4, as well as later in this chapter in the section on NTSC.

How (Most) Video Cameras Work Now

The most commonly used image sensor today is the *charge coupled device* (CCD) array. This replaces the vidicon tube, allowing much smaller cameras that use much less power. The CCD array is a solid state device consisting of a two-dimensional array of photosensitive cells deposited on a substrate of silicon. Each cell contains metal oxide semiconductor (MOS) transistors to create depletion layers that act as capacitors. One of these is built as a photosensitive diode, so that it becomes electrically charged when exposed to light. The others are used for transfering the charge for later processing. Between the rows and columns of cells are circuits that allow the stored charges to be sequentially transferred out of the CCD array for processing, and to control the accumulation and transfer of electrical charges. One technique for creating the photosensitive cells is to

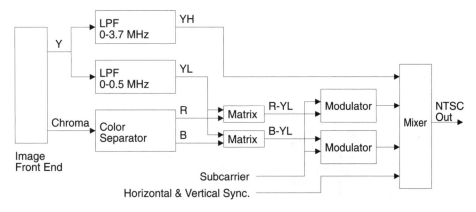

Figure 2.7   Color recombination and color difference signal generation.

construct a diode barrier region that coincides with a standing wave pattern at the desired radiation wavelength. This is defined by controlling the thickness of the various semiconductor materials used to create an "optical cavity," that is, a region between the surface of the cell and an aluminum reflector. Figure 2.8 shows how the semiconductor layers are arranged for a single pixel. The radiation penetrating the surface is reflected by the aluminum layer and creates a standing wave interference pattern that coincides with the photosensitive material sandwiched between the substrate and the dielectric layers. This generates free electrons (and "holes") that are accumulated in a capacitive storage layer.

There are two switches connected to the accumulating capacitor. One allows the accumulated charges to be transferred to a second storage capacitor, and the other allows the charges to be shunted to ground. The second storage capacitor is connected with other cells in a sort of analog shift register arrangement. This allows the stored charges to be sequentially transferred to one or more output pads on the device. The grounding switch controls the charge accumulation time of the first capacitor. While the switch is closed, there is effectively no charge accumulated. In normal operation an external timing controller holds the shunt switch closed until the beginning of a frame or field time. The shunt switch is then opened, and charges begin to accumulate in each cell at a rate dependent on the incident radiation. Charge accumulation continues for a predetermined period of time, and then the transfer switch is opened, allowing the accumulated charge to dump into the second capacitor. The transfer switch is then closed, and the shunt switch reopened until the next field or frame integration time. While waiting for the next field integration period, or possibly during field integration, the charges stored in the second-level capacitors are shifted out of the device for processing. Figure 2.9 shows how the signals used to control accumulation, transfer, and shifting of charges can be timed relative to each other. Another method is to continuously cycle the charges out of the cells at a fixed frequency established by the physical construction of the device. Figure 2.10 shows how the charges are transferred from one depletion region to another to create the shift register effect.

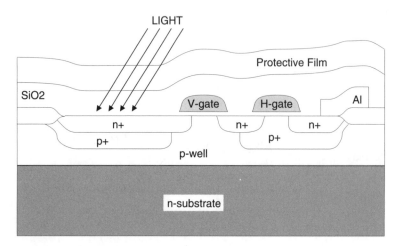

Figure 2.8   Simplified cross-section of photosensitive diode construction.

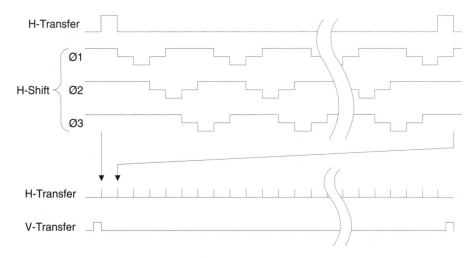

Figure 2.9   Relative timing of CCD control signals.

Of course, a capacitor with a given size and dielectric constant can store only a certain amount of electrical charge. Exposed continuously to radiation of the appropriate wavelength, assuming the shunt switch was open, all the cells would eventually reach saturation and the circuit would be in a kind of equilibrium. The length of time this takes depends on the intensity of the radiation and the physical characteristics of the CCD array. This fact can result in a couple of visual artifacts in the final image as displayed on a CRT. These were generally more of a problem in older vacuum-tube image sensors, and can still occur in CCD sensors if not properly designed or fabricated. The first is called *blooming*, and is fairly common in cameras using vacuum tube image sensors. If a spot of high-intensity radiation is focused on the image sensor, it may cause the cells involved to reach saturation before the field integration time has elapsed. If this happens, the excess charge being generated may leak into adjacent cells. This creates the illusion that a spot of intense light is growing larger, or blooming. It may also exceed the capacity of the shunt switch to drain off the total charge between integration times. If this happens, and the image sensor remains focused on the intense light source, the spot can appear to continue to grow until it floods the entire image. Most modern CCD arrays are very resistant to this type of artifact, however, and the semiconductor fabrication technology used in making the CCD arrays themselves has been refined to a high degree of accuracy and reliability. The second artifact is *streaking*. This is the result of essentially the same physical conditions, but the high-intensity spot is moving across the image array, rather than fixed in one place.

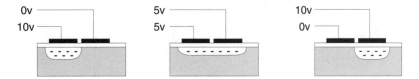

Figure 2.10   Analog charge shift register operation.

Generally, streaking is an indication of an inability of the shunt to drain the accumulated charges within one interfield time. In other words, an intense level of radiation strikes a number of cells momentarily, driving them into saturation, and it takes several field intervals to completely drain off the accumulated charge. As the spot moves across the array it appears to leave a trail because the accumulated charges cannot be immediately dissipated when the radiation is removed.

Color CCD Image Sensors

Producing color from a solid state CCD image sensor is similar to the method used for the vacuum tube image sensor except that the color filter is arranged a little bit differently. Each picture element, or pixel, of the solid state device is actually made up of four distinct photosensitive cells. Three out of the four cells have a transparent color filter applied to the surface in the manufacturing process. The three colors are yellow, cyan, and green. The fourth cell has no color filter and therefore produces a signal corresponding to the total illumination. The basic operation of the photosensitive cells is the same as in a monochrome camera except that instead of having one output signal that represents only the luminance of the scanned image there are now four parallel outputs that represent the luminance and three separate color values. Figure 2.11 shows how a single photosensitive cell is constructed in silicon layers. Note the transparent color filter in the silicon oxide protective film on the surface of the structure.

Similar to the monochrome image sensing device, a vertical scanning pulse opens the vertical gate in the cell allowing the charge to be transferred from the photosensitive diode into a horizontal analog shift register. Subsequent horizontal synchronization pulses cause the charges in the horizontal analog shift registers to be moved one position with each pulse. Figure 2.12 shows the arrangement of the yellow, cyan, green, and white photosensitive diodes in the matrix and the transistors that move these charges into the horizontal shift registers.

As the four color signals for each pixel are shifted through the analog shift register matrix, appearing on the output pins of the CCD, they are mixed in an electronic matrix to produce the final

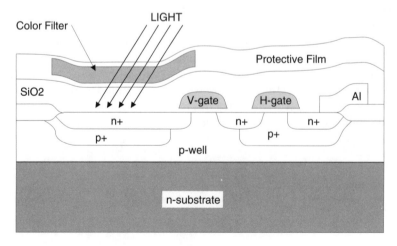

Figure 2.11   Color CCD photosensitive cell construction.

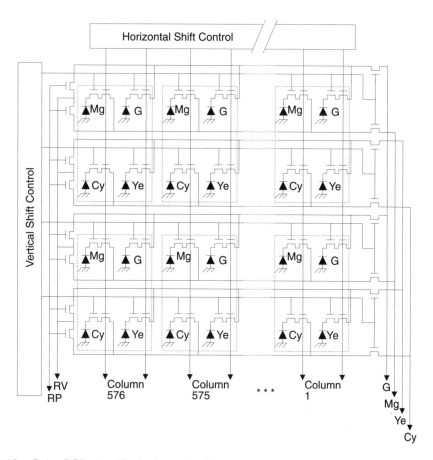

Figure 2.12 Color CCD simplified schematic diagram.

luminance and chrominance output signals. As in the monochrome CCD image sensor, each photo diode is charged during the integration period by light striking the sensor. The integration period is the time of one field minus the vertical blanking interval. A CCD image sensor requires a specialized controlling circuit that generates the required voltages and timings in order to facilitate the transfer from one cell to another in the analog shift registers. It also generates the appropriate horizontal and vertical synchronization timings for the required optical integration period and generates a sampling clock for the receiving device. The analog shift registers work by creating depletion wells in the substrate of the silicon on which the image sensor is built. The capacity of the depletion wells is proportional to the amount of voltage applied to the gate of the analog shift register's cell. Figure 2.13 shows how the gates for the analog shift register are arranged in sequence to allow the transfer of charge from each cell to an adjacent cell. To transfer a charge from one cell to the next, the cell downstream from the one holding a photoelectric charge is activated by applying a voltage potential to its gate. This creates a depletion well that is shared between two adjacent charge cells. The photoelectric charge then diffuses evenly between the two cells. After this, the gate voltage of the upstream cell is removed, allowing the depletion region to collapse, transferring

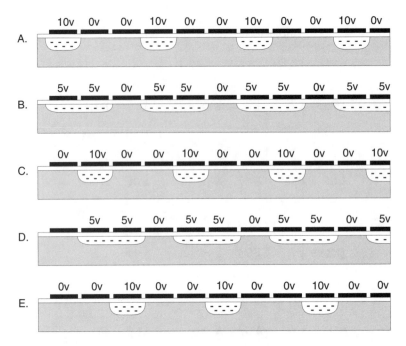

Figure 2.13   Operating sequence of linear analog charge shift register.

the remainder of the photoelectric charge into the downstream cell. By generating the appropriate voltages at the appropriate times in adjacent groups of three cells, the controller can create a transfer of charge in the required direction down the row of cells.

There is one such analog shift register for each vertical row of photo diodes in the CCD image sensor. These feed into a horizontal analog shift register that works in a similar manner and transfers the charges to the final output stages of the device. There is one such network of analog shift registers for each of the four color signals generated by a color CCD. Figure 2.14 shows how the vertical and horizontal shift registers are arranged to transfer the charges to the device output pins.

Low-cost commercial CCD arrays are designed to support the NTSC interlaced field format. This divides each frame into two fields, one with all the even pixel rows, and the other with all the odd rows. Color information is further interlaced within each field, alternating (R−Y) on one row, (B−Y) on the next, etc. This was done for historical reasons having to do with RF modulation bandwidth limitations, and so forth, described later in this chapter. The CCD is an array of tiny photocells, each with a color filter. There are four different color filters, arranged as shown in Table 2.1.

The filter colors, and their effects in terms of the primary colors R, G, and B are:

    Ye (Yellow),   filters out B,   leaving R+G.
    G (Green),   filters out B+R, leaving G.
    Cy (Cyan),   filters out R,   leaving B+G.
    Mg (Magenta), filters out G,   leaving R+B.

The array can then be redrawn labeling each cell with the primary colors it senses, as shown in Table 2.2.

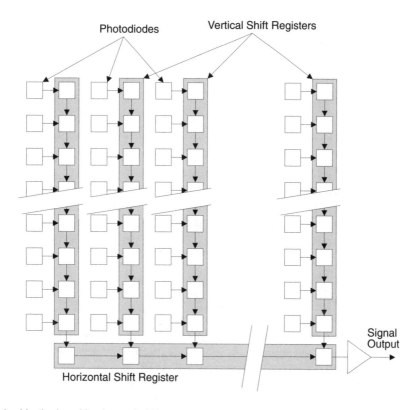

Figure 2.14 Vertical and horizontal shift register organization.

For each field, vertically adjacent pairs of cells are combined to produce a charge signal proportional to different combinations of colors. Field zero combines rows 0&1, 2&3, and so on, while field one combines rows 1&2, 3&4, and so on. For either field then, the output signal is proportional to:

(2G+B), (2R+G+B), (2G+B), (2R+G+B), (2G+B), (2R+G+B), ... for line 0.
(R+G+2B), (R+2G), (R+G+2B), (R+2G), (R+G+2B), ... for line 1.
(2G+B), (2R+G+B), (2G+B), (2R+G+B), (2G+B), ... for line 2, and so on.

This arrangement allows the same cells to be used for both odd and even fields, and creates the correct physical offset for interlaced scan lines. The horizontal timing from one cell to the next

Table 2.1 CCD Color Filter Organization

Cy	Ye	Cy	Ye	Cy	
G	Mg	G	Mg	G	
Cy	Ye	Cy	Ye	Cy	Etc.
Mg	G	Mg	G	Mg	
Cy	Ye	Cy	Ye	Cy	
		Etc.			

Table 2.2   CCD Color Sensitivity

Field 0, Row 0	B+G	R+G	B+G	R+G	B+G	
Field 1, Row 0	G	R+B	G	R+B	G	
Field 0, Row 1	B+G	R+G	B+G	R+G	B+G	Etc.
Field 1, Row 1	R+B	G	R+B	G	R+B	
	B+G	R+G	B+G	R+G	B+G	
		Etc.				

is, incidentally, proportional to the NTSC color burst frequency. Taken in pairs horizontally, each pair from each line carries the same information:

from line 0, (2G+B)+(2R+G+B) = (2R+3G+2B), and

from line 1, (R+G+2B)+(R+2G) = (2R+3G+2B).

This signal is fed into an analog color separation matrix that calculates the YUV components as follows:

$$Y = 1/2(2R+3G+2B)$$
$$(R-Y) = (2R+G+B)-(2G+B) = (2R-G)$$
$$-(B-Y) = (R+2G)-(R+G+2B) = -(2B-G)$$

Each color component, therefore, is the difference of sums from two adjacent scan lines, effectively subsampling chroma by 2:1 vertically. The apparent divergence from the classical formula for luminance given by (Y= .299R + .587G + .114B) is actually an illusion, because the spectral response of each filtered photocell produces a very close approximation of the classical formula. That is, the spectral response is not linear. The output from the imager, therefore, is very similar to that from older vacuum-tube imagers, except that there is no 90° phase shift between adjacent pixel rows. Imagers that operate this way are said to operate in *field integration mode*, because the imager automatically integrates the necessary color components. The color separation matrix uses a technique called *correlated double sampling* (CDS). This simply means that vertically adjacent signal values are sampled simultaneously.

CCD image sensors use both analog and digital techniques to generate the required video signals. The charges produced in each photosensitive diode cell are proportional to the amount of light striking the diode cell. The sequencing of signals to transfer the charges through the analog shift registers is a digital function even though the shift registers themselves carry analog charges. Figure 2.15 is a simplified block diagram of how a typical CCD controller is connected with the CCD as a receiving device. The controller circuit contains elements necessary to create a type of phase-locked loop clocking scheme. For precise frequency control it generates correction voltages that are applied to external veractor diodes connected with an inductive and capacitive filter network. This arrangement controls a frequency of an external 16 MHz oscillator that is tuned to operate at a precise frequency.

Vertical clocking signals are fed into an external amplifier in order to generate the correct voltages required by the CCD array. The external amplifier generates the three voltage levels required to drive the analog shift registers. The controller circuit also generates horizontal synchronization signals that are inverted and amplified to control the horizontal shift registers. It generates a four-phase vertical drive signal, signals V1–V4, and a two-phase horizontal drive signal, signals

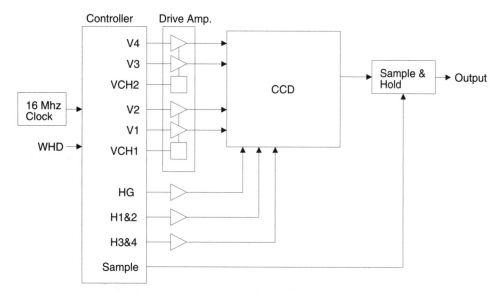

Figure 2.15 Simplified block diagram of CCD controller connection.

H1 and H2. It also generates bias voltages for the CCD element. H1 and H2 control the transfer timing for charges from the horizontal register to the output circuit during the horizontal scan period. The precharge gate (PG) is applied to the output circuit and times the reset charge, which remains in the output circuit after the previous scan but before charge is transferred from the horizontal register to the output circuit. V1–V4 control the timing of transfer charges from the vertical register to the horizontal registers inside the CCD during the horizontal blanking period. They also control the timing of transfers from the photosensitive diodes into the vertical shift registers and the mixing of charges during the vertical blanking period. The output voltages of signals V1 and V3 can take three values; 15 volts, 0 volts, and −10 volts.

The controller generates a horizontal gate signal that controls the timing of the transfer of photoelectric charges from the CCD array to the receiving device. Overall frame synchronization for the circuit is generated externally and fed into the controller via the wide horizontal drive signal (WHD on the diagram). During each horizontal scan period one horizontal row of photoelectric charges is fed out of the CCD array into a sample and hold circuit that is controlled by a sample timing signal generated by the controller. The sampled photoelectric charge is then fed through a noise removal filter before being applied to the final processing circuits.

CCD image sensor arrays are manufactured in a wide range of sizes and configurations. The Zenith VM6150 CCD has a vertical resolution of 270 lines with a total of 223,368 pixels. The Pentax PV-C850A 8mm CCD image sensor array has 510 horizontal and 492 vertical lines with a total of 250,920 pixels. This device also has an integration time as low as 1/1200 of a second. This is equivalent to the shutter speed on a film camera. The realistic HE98245 MOS color image sensor has an image size of 8.8 by 6.5 mm. This is suitable for a two-third inch optical system. It has 570 rows by 485 columns for a total of 276,450 pixels. Specific image array circuits or families of image array circuits generally have corresponding controller circuits manufactured by the same producer. For example, the Pentax PV-C850A 8mm synchronization signal generator produces fifteen synchronization and clock signals to control the Pentax CCD image array mentioned earlier. Figure 2.16 shows a diagram of the Pentax PV-C850A synchronization signal generator circuit. The signals generated by the circuit are described as follows: The horizontal burst flag (HBF) determines when to insert the subcarrier signal. The camera horizontal drive (CHD) generates timing signals for the horizontal drive of the image sensor. The chrominance blanking pulse (BLKC) times the blanking of the chroma signal. The window gate pulse (WGP) determines the sampling time for automatic gate control and iris detector circuits. The vertical drive pulse (VD) creates timing for vertical drive of the image sensor. The luminance blanking pulse (BLKY) generates timing for the clamping of the luminance signal. The luminance optical block pulse (YOBP) times the sampling of optical block levels from the image sensor outputs. Chrominance optical block pulse (COBP) times the sampling of RGB signals.

The Pentax PV-C850A 8mm CCD image drive circuit controls the corresponding Pentax CCD mentioned earlier. The reference voltages control certain parameters for operation of the CCD. The voltage overflow drain (VODF) determines the overflow drain voltage. If excess charge occurs on a heavily illuminated image it's possible for some of the excess to leak into adjacent cells, which would cause blooming as mentioned before. The CCD array is able to detect this and drain off the excess charge in advance to control blooming. The reference signal (VODF) determines the charge level at which this would occur. The voltage precharge drain (VFD) determines the reset level for precharge drain in the output circuits. If there are any charges remaining in the photosensitive cells from the previous scanning period, these will be drained by applying this voltage to the output circuit. The sensor gate voltage reference (VSG) determines the depth of the potential wells in the storage and transfer sections of the sensor. This effectively controls how much charge can be accumulated and transferred through the horizontal and vertical analog shift registers. Table 2.3 summarizes the part numbers and some of these parameters for the CCD image sensors.

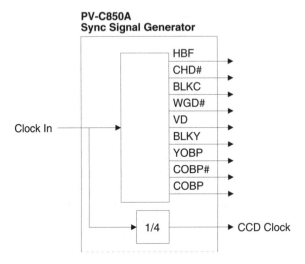

Figure 2.16   Pentax PV-C850A synchronization signal generator circuit.

Table 2.3 Summary of CCD Image Sensors

Part Number	Vertical	Horizontal	Total Pixels
VM6150	413	540	223,020
PV-C850A	492	510	250,920
HE98245	485	570	276,450

National Television System Committee (NTSC)

Black-and-white transmission of television pictures actually began in the United States and England in about 1926. These were based on a rotating disk with a spiral arrangement of holes, invented by Paul Nipkow. By 1930 there was regularly scheduled TV programming broadcast from various stations on the East Coast. The first public service broadcasts were in 1939 by NBC. A few years earlier in 1935, a man named David Sarnoff was carrying on field tests of receivers and transmitters with 343 scan lines at 30 frames per second. These were interlaced images with a video bandwidth of about 1.5 MHz. By 1939 they had improved this to 441 lines with 4.2 MHz of bandwidth. By this time virtually all television transmission was totally electronic. No more spinning perforated disks. Progress was slowed heavily by World War II, but by 1949 almost four million receivers had been manufactured and 108 television stations were broadcasting. In 1949 and 1950 the Federal Communications Commission (FCC) received a massive response from industry to its investigation into the feasibility of developing color television in the United States. The first companies to propose systems were CBS, RCA, and Color Television, Inc. CBS proposed a system involving a revolving disk composed of three color filters synchronized between the camera and the television. Figure 2.17 shows how the disk was arranged in front of the camera and the television. The idea was that each field and sequence was filtered by a different color on the camera and on the final display. It produced reasonably acceptable results because of the tendency of the human eye to integrate rapid sequences over time. There were some reliability problems because of the mechanical nature of the system and rapid motion in the image tended to produce a separation of colors.

The CBS proposal was selected because of its simplicity and rapid implementation but was never widely utilized because of mechanical problems. It turned out not to be compatible with standard black-and-white television receivers because of the fact that the sequential frames were in groups of three, corresponding to the three basic colors. The field transmissions of standard television images were in pairs, odd and even fields. In the meantime, RCA had started transmitting color broadcasts in 1949 on its NBC station in Washington DC. These were compatible with the CBS color television system but used a different technique. RCA used three image orthicon tubes in the camera to generate three separate images each filtered with the primary colors. The receivers had three picture tubes and the images were merged with dichroic mirrors. These were housed in a large cabinet and reflected from a mirror into the viewers' eyes. By 1950 RCA had developed a prototype of the color television picture tube that is still in use today. This consisted of a 16-inch metal cone cathode ray tube with three electron guns and a shadow mask to allow the separation of the electron beams directed at the front surface of the screen. The screen was coated with phosphor of three different types arranged in a triangular pattern of dots to produce the three primary colors. Even with

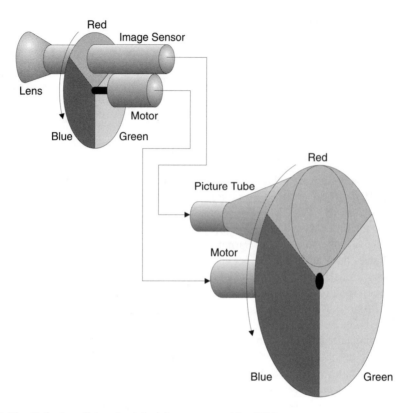

Figure 2.17   Spinning disk color television proposed by CBS.

these improvements, however, the FCC adopted the CBS system. RCA sued but lost in the courts. Between 1950 and 1953 a number of different companies demonstrated various improvements and breakthroughs in color television technology. It was during this period that the idea of separate high-frequency luminance and two lower-frequency color difference signals relative to the luminance was introduced. In 1953, the second NTSC color standard specification was published. The color subcarrier frequency was set at 3.579545 MHz, which is still in use today. The chroma bandwidth proposal from RCA was approved. Compatibility with current monochrome television broadcast standards was considered absolutely essential in order to avoid rendering existing receivers obsolete. It not only had to be compatible, but also could not produce any noticeable visual artifacts. The color encoding scheme as specified did have the result of producing slightly more contrast in a black-and-white only receiver but this was deemed acceptable. The other difficult problem was how to fit the new color information into the existing broadcast spectrum for television. Video color information had to be modulated onto the various carrier frequencies that had been allocated for television broadcast between 54 MHz and 806 MHz, channels 2 through 69. Monochrome video television signals contain frequency components ranging from about 30 Hz up to about 4 MHz. The horizontal sync and blanking pulses occur at 15.734 KHz, and the vertical sync and blanking occur at 59.94 Hz. Each scan line of information tends to be highly correlated to the previous one because of spatial correlation in the image. Therefore, a spectral analysis of a video signal tends to show the energy clustered around multiples of the line scanning frequency of 15.734 KHz. Figure 2.18 shows how a spectral diagram of the video signal might look as measured from zero Hz up to the full bandwidth of the video signal, about 4.2 MHz on the Y (mono) chart. Note that each cluster of energy bands is separated from the previous by the horizontal scanning frequency and that there are 267 clusters, which when multiplied by the horizontal scanning frequency gives the overall bandwidth of the video signal. Note also that there are regions between the clusters where there is little or no energy.

By interleaving color information between clusters of monochrome video information the entire signal can still be modulated on the same video broadcast carrier. This is done by modulating the color information on a subcarrier that generates energy at multiples of one-half the line scanning frequency. If the horizontal scan rate of 15.73464 KHz is multiplied by 455 and divided by 2 the color subcarrier frequency of 3.579545 MHz results. This has a harmonic relationship to both vertical and horizontal frequencies. In transmission the 3.579545 MHz subcarrier is canceled by ballast modulators. Only chroma information is transmitted on the subcarrier. The color information is encoded onto the color subcarrier as follows: The color is divided into two elements, hue and saturation. Hue (or tint) is the element that distinguishes between colors (green, red, blue, yellow, etc.). The hue information is contained in the phase angle of the 3.579545 MHz color subcarrier. The three primary colors, red, blue, and green are separated by a phase angle of 270° each. A phase shift of this color subcarrier through 360° will produce every hue in the rainbow by changing combinations of the primary colors. Saturation is the amount of color such that 100 percent saturation means there is no white component in the color. Less than 100 percent saturation tends to produce lighter

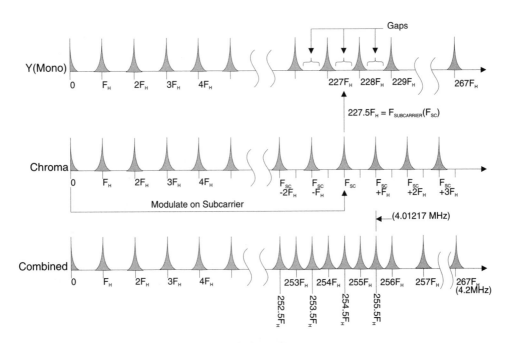

Figure 2.18 Monochrome video signal spectral diagram.

and lighter colors like pastel. The saturation level of the color is indicated by the amplitude of the color subcarrier. It should be noted that a change in phase angle of a frequency is effectively a momentary change in the frequency itself. Because of the limited available bandwidth for the total video signal the rate of phase angle change of the 3.579545 MHz color subcarrier has to be limited to plus or minus 0.5 MHz. This prevents the color subcarrier from interfering with the luminance carrier information. The combination of hue and saturation is called chroma, or chrominance. This information appears in the video signal as a 3.579545 MHz sine wave. The phase shift of the sine wave at any given moment indicates the hue of the current pixel. The amplitude of the sine wave indicates the saturation of the current pixel, and the average level relative to zero of the overall video signal indicates luminance. Figure 2.19 shows an approximation of how a common color bar test signal for one horizontal scan line would look if viewed on an oscilloscope. There is no oscillation of the color subcarrier in the regions that are white, black, or any shade of gray because color saturation is at zero. Therefore, the amplitude of the subcarrier is zero. The signal level is at its maximum for white and its minimum for black. In between, where color information is shown, the subcarrier amplitude is at its maximum, indicating maximum saturation of color.

The color values themselves cannot really be observed in the diagram because the phase shift information would require more precision than can be conveyed in a diagram like this. As a reference, to allow the receiver to determine the phase angle of the chroma subcarrier, approximately eight to nine cycles of the subcarrier frequency are included in each horizontal blanking interval. A continuous color subcarrier reference frequency inside the receiver is phase-locked to this reference

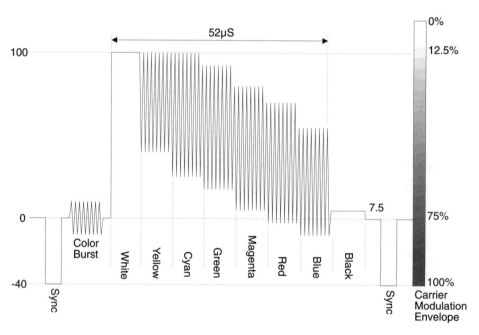

Figure 2.19   Single horizontal scan NTSC color bar test signal.

burst at the beginning of each scan line. This burst of eight or nine cycles is where the term *color burst* comes from. To effectively separate the luminance and chrominance information, in the 1970s Magnavox developed what is known as a *comb filter*. The name probably comes from the idea that throughout the available spectrum for the video signal luminance and chrominance information are effectively interleaved, and something that could extract the chrominance and leave the luminance would probably look something like a comb. To facilitate the separation of color information from the luminance component a mathematical model was developed that defines two elements to represent the color component. These are called *I* and *Q*. The I stands for *in-phase* and the Q stands for *quadrature modulation*. The term *quadrature* is used presumably because it represents the component of color information that is 90° out of phase from the in-phase portion, and 90° is one quarter of a cycle. If you assume that both I and Q can take both positive and negative values, the combination of the two can produce a signal that has any phase angle. Effectively I and Q represent the polar model of chrominance in a Cartesian coordinate system. Because the primary colors are red, green, and blue, the color vectors I and Q have to be derived from red, green, and blue. Because the two vectors represent color without any luminance information, luminance information has to be subtracted in the process. To understand how these are derived, it is useful first to understand how luminance information is derived. An idealized formula for luminance (denoted Y) is given by the following equation:

$$Y = (0.299 \times Red) + (0.587 \times Green) + (0.114 \times Blue)$$

The reasons for these particular coefficients are described in Chapter 4. Once Y has been calculated, I and Q can be calculated according to the following formulas:

$$I = \cos 33°[0.877(R-Y)] - \sin 33°[0.493(B-Y)]$$
$$Q = \sin 33°[0.877(R-Y)] - \cos 33°[0.493(B-Y)]$$

Again, the reasons for these coefficients are described in Chapter 4. Because I incorporates the sine of the chrominance subcarrier and Q incorporates the cosine of the chrominance subcarrier, if the two signals are added together using vector addition, the resulting signal is equal in frequency to the chrominance subcarrier but with a phase angle that indicates a specific color, and an amplitude that indicates its saturation.

Synchronization

To allow the receiver to maintain line and frame synchronization with the transmitter, a system of synchronization signals was developed for the NTSC standard. These are similar in technique for the European PAL and SECAM television standards as well, although as we will see, they are different in a few specific parameters. To put synchronization signals in context with the rest of the video transmission already described, a brief description of IRE (Institute of Radio Engineers) units is in order. An NTSC standard composite video signal is one volt peak-to-peak. That is, the maximum potential voltage swing from the highest level ,which is equivalent to 100 percent white, to the lowest level, which is reached during a sync pulse, is one volt. This one-volt signal swing is divided into 140 equal parts called IRE units. The range is defined as +100 maximum and −40 as a minimum. The zero reference level is considered the blanking level. That is, there is no luminance output when the NTSC signal is at zero IRE. The active video signal is defined to range from 7.5 IRE units up to 100 IRE units. Anything in between represents various shades of gray. It is critical that the ratio between the sync pulse and the video be maintained even if the overall voltage swing of the video signal exceeds one volt peak to peak. Thirty percent for the sync pulse and 70 percent for the video signal must be maintained. For broadcast, the video signal is modulated on an RF carrier using amplitude modulation. In order to minimize the effects of noise at low signal levels, *negative modulation* is used. The lowest video signal level, which is the sync pulse at −40 IRE units, produces the maximum peak-to-peak amplitude of the modulated carrier signal, or 100 percent modulation. The maximum video signal level, which is +100 IRE units, produces the minimum amplitude of the modulation envelope, or 12.5 percent modulation. The advantage of this is that the minimum modulation levels, where signal noise or other types of interference could corrupt the signal, correspond to the white level of video. Therefore, any noise that does get injected into the signal is likely to be masked by the display, which is already white, rather than showing up as white snow or sparkles on a dark background. As mentioned earlier, the blanking level is zero IRE units, which is 7.5 IRE units below the voltage that corresponds to black on the display. Thus the term *blacker than black*. The horizontal synchronization signal is a pulse that goes from zero to −40 IRE units. In the receiver this triggers a reset of the horizontal deflection circuits to move the electron beam into position for the next horizontal scan line. The horizontal retrace sequence is divided into three parts known as the front porch, the horizontal sync pulse, and the back porch. The front porch is a 1.47 microsecond period during which the video signal is at the blanking level or zero IRE units. This is followed by a 4.89 microsecond horizontal sync pulse in which the video signal is at −40 IRE units. The back porch is a 4.40 microsecond period during which the video signal is again at the blanking level of zero IRE units. If the video signal is carrying color information, 0.56 microseconds after the end of the horizontal synchronization pulse there are 8 to 9 cycles of the color burst frequency, which is 3.579545 MHz. Figure 2.20 shows the timings and voltage levels of the horizontal sync pulse and blanking interval for both monochrome and color NTSC television signals.

Vertical synchronization signals the end of a field. There are two fields in a frame. A frame is considered a complete video image as seen on a television screen. Each field contains 262.5 lines for a total of 525 lines in a frame. The field frequency is 59.94 Hz for a total frame rate of approximately 30 Hz. The half of a scan line in each field is responsible for creating the line interlace between fields. Even though it is not visible to the casual observer, the scan lines that make up each field are not exactly horizontal. As the beam sweeps across the screen horizontally to create a scan line, it is also sweeping down the screen vertically to create the frame. This creates a very shallow slope for the scan line. If the last line of the first field goes only halfway across the screen and the first line of the second field starts halfway across the screen, then the lines of each field will be interleaved or interlaced. Figure 2.21 illustrates this.

Between vertical fields, the vertical blanking interval is equal to several horizontal lines. This prevents any illumination of the picture tube while the vertical sweep circuits reset the electron beam back to the top of the screen. During this time the horizontal sweep circuits continue to function. This can be observed in most CRT displays (either television or computer displays) by adjusting the intensity to a very high level, overriding the ability of the blanking signal to shut it off. You can then actually see the beam sweeping back and forth as it retraces back up to the top of the screen. Vertical synchronization is actually triggered by a *series* of synchronization pulses. The sequence of events during the vertical blanking interval is as follows: The sequence begins with six equalization pulses that are half the width of a normal horizontal synchronization pulse but twice the frequency

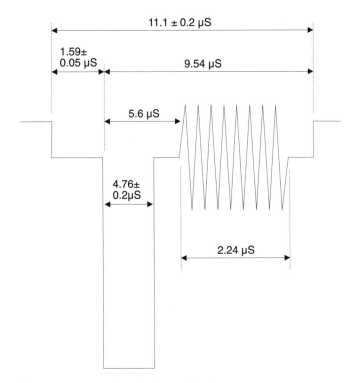

Figure 2.20   NTSC horizontal synchronization pulse diagram.

for a total of three horizontal line periods. The vertical synchronization pulse sequence consists of another three horizontal line periods in which there are six vertical synchronization pulses of 27.1 microseconds each, again at twice the horizontal frequency. This is followed by another equalization pulse sequence similar to the first. Following this are 13 normally timed horizontal sync pulses with the video signal held at the blanking level. There is no color burst information during the equalizing pulses or vertical blanking pulses. The last line of the odd field is only half the duration of a normal scan line. This generates the line interlace between even and odd fields as illustrated in Figure 2.21. Figure 2.22 shows the sequence of equalization and synchronization pulses during the vertical blanking interval.

PAL and SECAM

The differences between NTSC video standards and the European standards, PAL and SECAM, from Germany and France respectively, are mainly driven by differences in power distribution standards. In the United States electrical power is generally delivered at 120VAC 60 Hz, while in Europe, it is normally 220 or 240VAC and 50 Hz. The television field rate is designed to match the frequency of the AC power source. Therefore, while the effective frame rate for NTSC broadcast video is 30 frames per second, it is 25 frames per second for PAL and SECAM. PAL stands for *phase alternation line* and SECAM stands for *sequential color with memory*. You probably need to

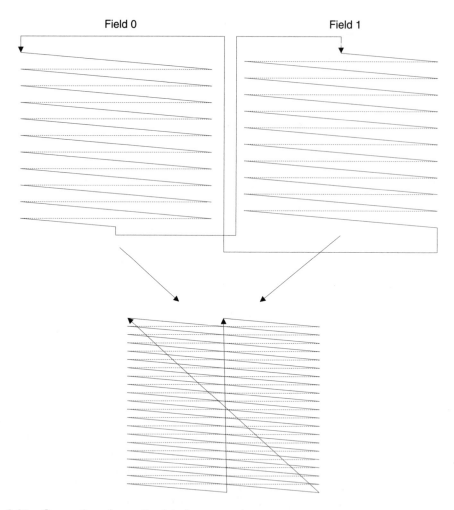

Figure 2.21   Generation of scan line interleave spacing.

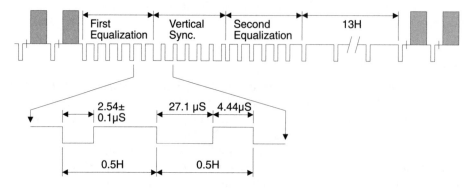

Figure 2.22   NTSC vertical blanking and synchronization sequence.

speak French to understand how you get SECAM from that. Actually, it is *SEquential Couleur Avec Memoire*. As a result of the slower frame rate, the European standards generate 625 scan lines instead of 525. Otherwise the standards are quite similar, differing mostly in the timing of signals. For example, under PAL and SECAM the vertical equalization and synchronization pulse sequences last for only two and a half horizontal line times rather than three as in NTSC. The horizontal line period is nearly identical for all three standards. Figure 2.23 is an illustration of the horizontal blanking and synchronization sequence for PAL and SECAM video signals. Figure 2.24 is an illustration of the vertical synchronization sequence for PAL and SECAM.

Table 2.4 gives a comparison of timing parameters for NTSC, PAL, and SECAM. One of the most significant differences is the fact that under NTSC the video signal is amplitude modulated on

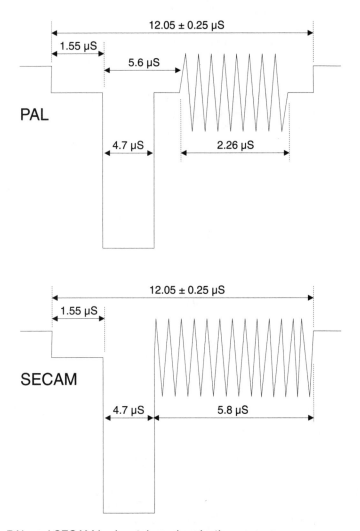

Figure 2.23   PAL and SECAM horizontal synchronization sequence.

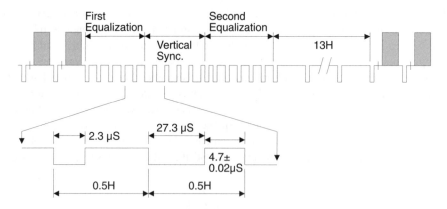

Figure 2.24   PAL and SECAM vertical synchronization sequence.

the RF carrier, whereas under SECAM, it is frequency modulated. Under PAL the color subcarrier is 4.443 MHz with side bands 1.7 MHz below and 1.3 MHz above for color difference signals, and the phase of the color burst is reversed on alternating scan lines. This effectively gives better color resolution. SECAM transmits its color difference signals for $R-Y$ and $B-Y$ in sequence, one with each line. Therefore, frequency interlace is not part of the system as it is in NTSC, and memory is needed to store at least one line of color information.

Table 2.4   Summary of PAL, SECAM, and NTSC Parameters

Parameter	NTSC	PAL	SECAM
Line Period	63.5 µS	64 µS	64 µS
Line Blanking Interval	11.1 ± 0.2 µS	12.05 ± 0.25 µS	12.05 ± 0.25 µS
Front Porch	1.59 ± 0.05 µS	1.55 ± 0.25 µS	1.55 ± 0.25 µS
Sync Pulse Width	4.76 ± 0.2 µS	4.7 ± 0.2 µS	4.7 ± 0.2 µS
Rise Time (Blank to Peak)	0.64 µS	0.3 ± 0.1 µS	0.3 ± 0.1 µS
Rise Time (Line Sync)	0.25 µS	0.3 ± 0.1 µS	0.3 ± 0.1 µS
Color Burst Duration	2.24 µS	2.26 ± 0.23 µS	Entire Back Porch
Field Period	16.667 mS	20 mS	20 mS
Field Blanking Period	(19.5-21)H+ 11.1 µS	(18-22)H+ 12 µS	(18-22)H+ 12 µS
First Equalization Duration	3H	2.5H	2.5H
Field Sync Sequence Duration	3H	2.5H	2.5H
Second Equalization Duration	3H	2.5H	2.5H
Equalizing Pulse Width	2.54 ± 0.1 µS	2.3 ± 0.1 µS	2.3 ± 0.1 µS
Field Sync Pulse Width	27.1 µS	27.3 µS	27.3 µS
Field Sync Pulse Interval	4.44 ± 0.45 µS	4.7 ± 0.2 µS	4.7 ± 0.2 µS

Analog versus Digital Image Data

There are at least two problems inherent in the existing international analog-based television standards that are likely to be solved by the transition from analog to digital. First is the inflexibility of the current standards. Screen sizes, transmission bandwidths, information content and many other factors are fixed by the standards. No real provision is made for varying levels of quality or transmission bandwidth requirements, image size, or any number of other factors dictated by the application. For example, medical imaging or military requirements tend to far exceed the capabilities of NTSC or the other standards. On the other hand, the requirements for video games, kiosks, and a whole range of other applications are much less than the NTSC standard, driven more by cost than by quality. The inability of the NTSC standard to fit the lower cost or higher quality requirements of various applications places significant technical difficulties on engineers who wish to use video in their products. The other problem is that the NTSC analog signals are not well suited to processing or manipulation. They are essentially linear and sequential in nature and have to be delivered as a synchronous stream of information. The requirements when the standards were developed were much different than today. When television was first invented its primary application was real-time remote vision. Hence the name *tele*vision. The equipment that has evolved from this original invention, however, is used in a much wider range of applications. Probably one of the most significant developments likely to arise out of the transition from analog to digital video technology on a wide scale is the ability of a far wider number of people to be able to create and use motion video information in their day-to-day activities. There are, of course, certain disadvantages to the use of digital formats for video information and in the interest of fairness these should be discussed as well. For one thing, the quality of an image, once converted into digital format, can never really be improved above the level established at the time of conversion. Generally the higher the quality level required, the more digital data required to store each image. This can very easily overwhelm conventional digital storage and transmission mediums. This is essentially the downside of the ability to scale digital video. Another disadvantage is in digital filtering and other types of processing where an attempt is made to emulate equivalent analog functions. There is a tendency to introduce nonlinearity errors and other artifacts. For example, a digital filter is very precise. However, if there is even the slightest error introduced in the filtering process, it will be precisely reproduced every time the filter is used. This tends to produce deterministic error patterns that show up as visual artifacts. These errors can be compounded if the filter is used multiple times on the same data. While it is true that transmission and reproduction of digital data is error-free by definition the same does not hold for processing of digital data when it represents analog information. Cameras and displays are usually analog devices, so conversions to and from the digital domain are required at each end of any digital process. Currently, sources of video input are almost universally in the form of one of the international broadcast standards. This may not always be so, but for the time being it places certain constraints on the ability to translate in and out of the digital domain. The actual conversion from an analog to a digital signal involves a procedure known as *sampling*. The analog NTSC video signal is essentially a continuously varying voltage representing the illumination of the picture in the horizontal direction. The video bandwidth of about 4 MHz places an effective limit on how much information can be extracted from a single horizontal scan line of a video image. The amount of color information available in the video signal is effectively reduced further by the fact that it is modulated on the color subcarrier. The essential analog nature of the video signal does not really hold for the vertical dimension of the picture. This is because an imaginary line drawn vertically through the television image is effectively divided into a number of discrete samples equivalent to the number of scan lines in the picture. It also provides a clue to the appropriate sampling rate to be used horizontally. While it is tempting simply to sample the horizontal signal at a rate determined by the aspect ratio and the effective vertical sampling, there are other factors that need to be taken into consideration. For an arbitrary waveform with a frequency component up to a maximum of N the Nyquist theorem states that the sampling frequency must be at least 2N. This is illustrated in Figure 2.25. Figure 2.25(a) shows a waveform sampled at several times its frequency. It is fairly obvious that a reconstructed waveform will be a reasonable facsimile of the original. Figure 2.25(b) shows a waveform that approaches the sampling frequency.

Upon reconstruction it can be seen that the apparent frequency is much different from the original. This is known as *aliasing*. The example shown illustrates an alias frequency lower than the original, but frequencies higher than the original can also be generated. To further illustrate this principle, it is useful to view it in terms of a spectral analysis. The range of frequencies comprising the original analog signal is called the *baseband*. Because the sampling frequency is essentially an impulse signal, it shows up on a spectral diagram as narrow bands of energy at multiples of the sample frequency. Figure 2.26 illustrates a spectrum showing the baseband frequencies with a sample frequency at greater than 2× the baseband.

The baseband is simply shown as a gray area with no indication of energy levels at the various component frequencies other than a gradual rolloff at higher frequencies. Because of the impulse nature of the sampling signal, the frequency components of the baseband are effectively reflected on both sides of the sample frequency and all of its harmonics. Figure 2.27 illustrates this.

If the baseband frequencies include elements above one half the sample frequency the original and reflected frequencies begin to overlap. This overlap region is where aliasing occurs. For any

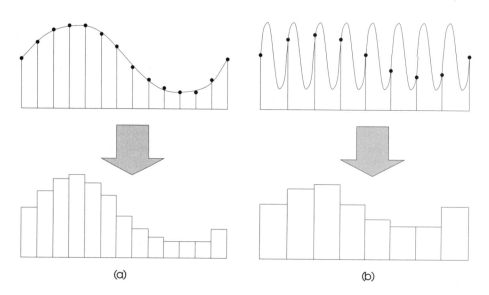

(a)   (b)

Figure 2.25 Sampling illustration.

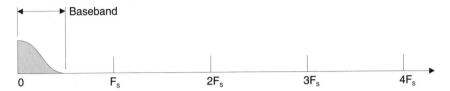

Figure 2.26   Baseband and sampling frequency spectrum illustration.

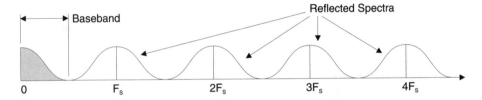

Figure 2.27   Reflected baseband components of a sampling impulse signal.

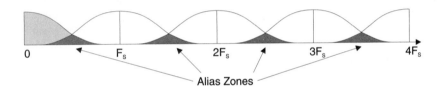

Figure 2.28   Spectral diagram of frequency overlap causing aliasing.

energy band in the overlapped region it becomes impossible to determine whether it is relative to the baseband or to the sample frequency. Figure 2.28 shows the overlapping frequency spectrum in a case where the baseband exceeds one half the sample frequency. The degree to which this introduces errors depends on the energy levels of the bands within the overlapping regions.

Quantization

Another factor that affects the accuracy of the conversion from analog to digital is *quantization*. Because the original signal is continuously variable within some range, the precise value measured at any given moment (at sampling for example) depends entirely on the accuracy of the measuring device. Analog-to-digital conversion devices divide the input signal range into a number quantizing intervals. For certain applications such as pulse code modulation used in telephones, these intervals may not be uniform. However, for digitizing video signals it is generally preferable to use a digitizing device with uniform quantizing intervals. This simplifies processing and filtering after the conversion process. For any given input value, the quantizer will generate a numerical value equivalent to the quantizing interval in which the input signal falls. While this does introduce errors, the error can never exceed one half the quantizing interval. A random input signal that generates values throughout the range of the quantizer will produce an overall quantizing error between -0.5 and $+0.5$ of the quantizing interval with uniform probability. Figure 2.29 shows the probability distribution of quantizing errors.

These errors should be distinguished from conventional noise found in analog electronic equipment, which has a Gaussian distribution. It is therefore not sufficient to calculate the signal-to-noise ratio for a digitizer simply based on the number of bits in the word it generates. The mathematics of the calculation work only if the probability distribution of the quantizing error is uniform. At low signal levels the quantizing error is no longer random. It becomes a function of the input signal. If the noise signal is a deterministic function of the input signal it should be referred to as *distortion* rather than noise. For smaller signal levels on the analog input, quantizing error becomes more and more significant and less random. The harmonics caused by these deterministic quantization error functions can introduce aliasing within the baseband spectrum. Figure 2.30 illustrates the harmonic frequencies generated by a deterministic quantization error function. In practice this seldom happens because of imperfections in the quantizing device and real noise in the input signal. This tends to randomize the quantization error and reduces the distortion.

In fact, many analog to digital conversion devices intentionally introduce noise into the input signal to randomize quantization errors and smooth the transfer function. This technique is known as *dithering*. Figure 2.31 shows the transfer function for an input signal with a uniform slew rate using a theoretically perfect conversion process. The resulting output signal values look like a stairstep. The effect of dithering is essentially to produce a horizontal jitter in the quantized values. Figure 2.32 shows that this tends to average the output transfer function. When the dithering is sufficient the averaging produces a transfer function that is nearly linear.

Resolution

The number of quantizing intervals that can be generated by an analog to digital converter depends on the number of bits in the output word. Generally an 8-bit quantizer is considered sufficient for video signals. Probably the most common analog-to-digital converter is known as the *flash converter*. Its operation is very simple. It consists of an array of comparators, one for each quantization interval. One input of each comparator is connected to a resistor ladder. The resistor ladder creates a series of different voltages that correspond to the range of levels anticipated from the input signal. The range of voltages produced by the resistor ladder can be varied by controlling the reference volt-

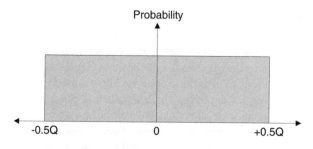

Figure 2.29   Probability distribution of quantization errors.

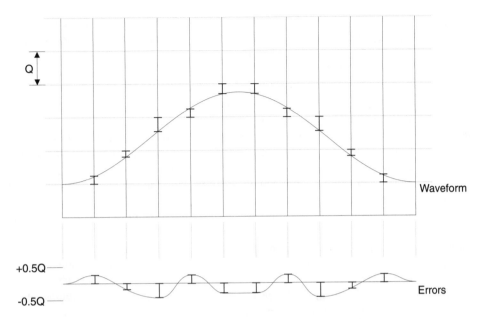

Figure 2.30   Harmonic frequencies generated by deterministic quantization errors.

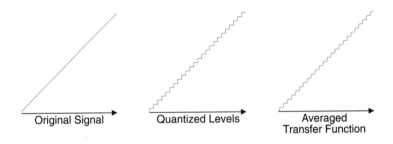

Figure 2.31   D/A transfer function without dithering.

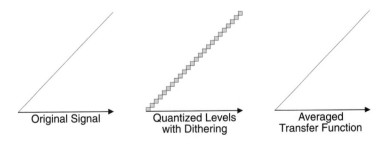

Figure 2.32   Dithering to average a D/A transfer function.

age or current that drives the ladder. The other input of each comparator is connected in parallel with all the others and driven by the input signal. Figure 2.33 shows the general arrangement of the comparators and the resistor ladder. The outputs of the comparators switch depending on which portion of the resistor ladder most closely corresponds to the input signal. Figure 2.34 shows how the outputs of the comparators relate to a changing input signal.

The outputs of the comparators are then connected to a priority encoder that generates the final binary encoded word corresponding to the level of the input signal. The least significant bit (LSB) of the output word then corresponds to one step in the resistor ladder, assuming all steps are equal. The advantage of this type of circuit is that it is very fast. No sample and hold circuitry is required and quantizing takes place continuously in real time. The outputs of the priority encoder can be stored in a register latched by the sample clock for later transfer and processing by a receiving device, as shown in Figure 2.35.

For digital-to-analog conversion a common technique is to employ a series of current sources. Each current source is controlled by one bit of the digital word driving the converter. The current sources are weighted in a binary arrangement with each current source providing twice the current of the next less significant bit. Figure 2.36 shows a series of current sources with corresponding switches to add the currents.

Consider the case of a binary rollover where several less significant switches are closed, and then opened while the next most significant switch closes. The net change in output current is equal

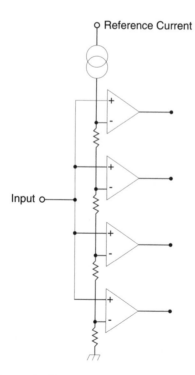

Figure 2.33   General A/D organization.

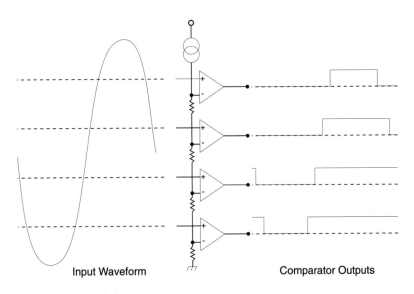

Figure 2.34   Output signals generated by A/D comparators.

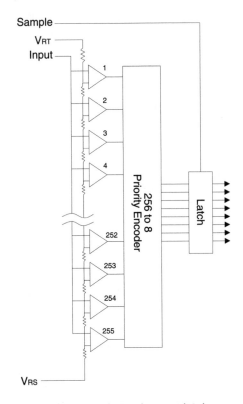

Figure 2.35   A/D converter with priority encoder and output latch.

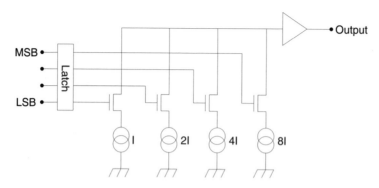

Figure 2.36   Current sources used in D/A converter.

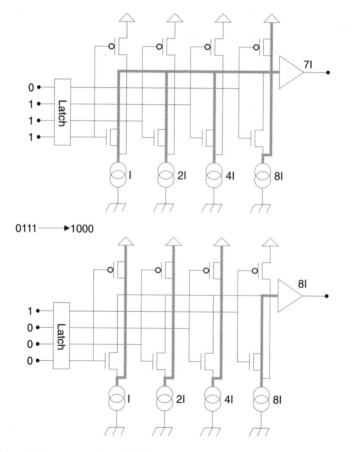

Figure 2.37   Current mirrors used to minimize switching noise in D/A converter.

to the amount provided by the least significant bit. It should be noted, however, that at high output currents the switching noise can be significant. For this reason a fairly common technique is to use what is known as *current mirrors*, shown in Figure 2.37. This involves placing an extra switch on each current source that shunts the current to another drain when it is not being sent to the output. This allows current to flow continuously at the same rate through each current source and eliminates ringing and other problems associated with switching electrical currents. To further reduce switching errors, the switches are generally fabricated in different sizes proportional to the current sources they control. Each binary bit of resolution added to a converter built in this way effectively doubles its size, as each more significant bit must be equal in size to all less significant bits combined.

Filtering

It is critical to perform filtering both before converting an analog video signal into digital format and after any scaling processes or any other operations that affect the signal mix of the image in digital format. Filtering before conversion to digital format is important because the analog signal must be conditioned to make it compatible with the limitations of the digital encoding system being used. For example, if the frequency spectrum of the input signal exceeds the Nyquist frequency of the sampling device signal, aliasing will occur. This can result in visible artifacts in the final image. To prevent this a band-pass filter should be used to eliminate any frequencies above the acceptable limit. In a compression process any noise or signal distortion introduced during the digitization phase has to be compressed. In other words, the compression process cannot distinguish between valid signal data and noise data and must compress all of it. This can greatly reduce the effectiveness of the compression process. For this reason the signal to noise ratio, distortion levels, and other factors related to the analog portion of the input side of a digital video system are very critical. One of the most common filtering techniques used for digital video information is the finite impulse response (FIR) filter. The advantage of an FIR filter for digital image processing is that its response is fixed and predictable. When applied to a video image, the space over which the filter responds is well defined. An FIR filter can be implemented in either the analog or the digital domain but tends to be simpler and more reliable when implemented in a digital format. In analog filters there is a tendency for different frequencies to be delayed by different amounts in the filtering process. This is known as *group delay* error and is particularly unacceptable in video because it tends to blur sharp edges, or produce spatial color separation in color images. An FIR filter works by explicitly constructing the impulse response for each input frequency. The coefficients for the correct impulse response have to be determined mathematically when constructing the filter. The impulse response of a perfect low pass filter is a sin $(X)/X$ curve where the time between the two central zero crossing points is the reciprocal of the cutoff frequency. Figure 2.38 shows a diagram of an impulse response function that implements a low pass filter that cuts off at one fourth of the sampling rate. Note that a sin $(X)/X$ curve effectively extends indefinitely in both directions, so a decision needs to be made how much of the curve to use in implementing an FIR filter. Therefore, for practical application, it is necessary to truncate the ends of the impulse response.

This introduces a delay in the filter equal to one-half the duration of the truncated impulse. For a linear sequential signal in the time domain this delay can be critical. However, for a two-dimensional image the filter delay translates into spatial considerations. That is, for each pixel to be

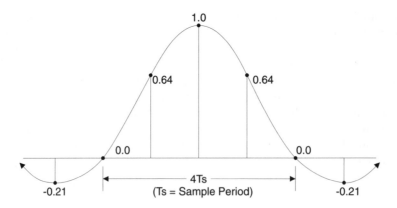

Figure 2.38 Impulse response function curve sin (*X*)/*X*.

properly filtered it must be surrounded by other pixels in the two-dimensional signal space. The sampling rate used to apply the impulse response function must be the same as the sampling rate for which the filter is being designed. In practice the filter coefficients are calculated in advance and generally implemented as integer numbers. The accuracy of the coefficients has to be a compromise between cost and performance. In other words, the more digital bits used to represent the filter coefficients, the more accurate the filter will be but the more transistors will be required to implement the registers and the math units involved. Another critical factor is the number of coefficients used to represent the impulse response function. Generally, the more coefficients, the more accurate the filter is, but the trade-off is again complexity of implementation. By simply truncating the impulse response function an abrupt transition is created between samples that matter and those that do not. This creates a tendency for the filter response to peak just before the cutoff frequency. Figure 2.39 shows the response curves of filters implemented with differing numbers of impulse response function coefficients. It can be seen that by using more coefficients the amount of ripple and the accuracy of the filter window is improved.

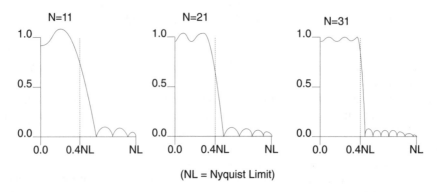

Figure 2.39 Response curves of filters implemented with differing numbers of impulse response function coefficients.

In order to reduce the effect of truncation on the impulse response function a common technique is to multiply the coefficients by another function that reduces their effect linearly at increasing distances from the center of the impulse response function. Figure 2.40 shows the original impulse response function with the linear reduction function, and then the resulting function when they are multiplied together. This final function gives the actual coefficients to be used in a real filter implementation. The linear reduction function is known as a *Bartlett* window function.

Applying the filter digitally to a linear input signal such as an audio waveform is relatively straightforward. It can be created by implementing a serial shift register through which the sampled values of the original waveform are shifted. From each stage of the shift register the signal train is tapped and multiplied by the impulse response coefficients. These products are then summed to create the filtered output. Figure 2.41 shows how such a filter could be implemented in hardware.

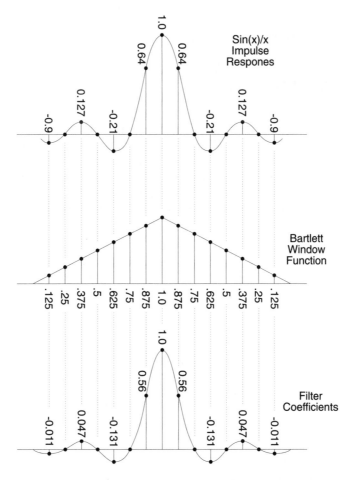

Figure 2.40   Adjusting impulse response function with a Bartlett window function.

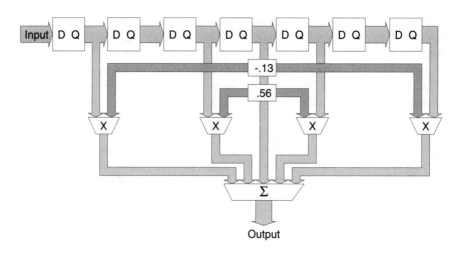

Figure 2.41   Linear FIR filter design example.

Two-Dimensional Filtering

For effective filtering of a video image, taking into account the two-dimensional nature of the data, this approach is not always adequate. When the finite impulse response function is plotted in two dimensions the result looks something like the circular ripple patterns created by a droplet falling onto a smooth surface of water. Assuming that each pixel in a video image represents one sample in a two-dimensional sample space it is fairly simple to calculate the values of filter coefficients in the horizontal and vertical directions relative to the target pixel. Figure 2.42 illustrates how the impulse response function would be applied in the horizontal and vertical directions.

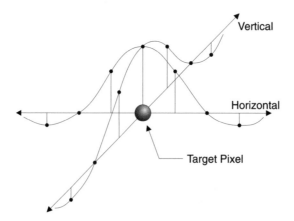

Figure 2.42   Two-dimensional application of FIR filter response curve.

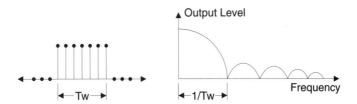

Figure 2.43 Response curve for a simple averaging filter.

For other pixels in the immediate vicinity of the target pixel the filter coefficient is calculated by determining the distance of the pixel in question from the target pixel and using that distance to calculate the appropriate coefficient based on the impulse response function. For example, to determine the filter coefficient for the pixels located at 45-degree angles from the horizontal and vertical planes relative to the target pixel assuming that the pixel displacements is equal to one, the standard distance formula for a hypotenuse yields value of 1.414 (approximately). If this value is then fed into the sin $(X)/X$ impulse response function and multiplied by the appropriate value from the Bartlett window function, the resulting value is the appropriate coefficient to be used for a two-dimensional FIR filter. Of course, the cost of implementing an FIR filter either in hardware or software using a complicated impulse shape is often prohibitive. In such cases it may be acceptable to use slightly degenerate versions of the theoretically perfect FIR function. One such approach is to use integer approximations for the filter coefficients. These are selected in a way that allows the math to be accomplished by simple add and shift operations. For example, if the target pixel is multiplied by four (which can be accomplished by shifting left two bit positions) and the four horizontally and vertically adjacent pixels are added to that value the result can then be divided by eight (which again simply involves shifting to the right three bit positions), producing a simple approximation of two-dimensional FIR function. Probably the easiest degenerative case of the FIR filter is a simple averaging of immediately adjacent samples. This produces a filter response that can be represented as the absolute value of a sin $(X)/X$ curve. This is illustrated in Figure 2.43. It may or may not be practical to implement two-dimensional filtering on video images in the analog-to-digital conversion process. Two-dimensional filtering generally requires that each frame be stored in memory while the filtering process takes place, which tends to be prohibitively expensive. It is highly desirable, however, that horizontal filtering at least be implemented in the analog to digital conversion process.

Conversion Devices

Brooktree Bt812

There are a number of VLSI devices commercially available for digitally encoding video signals that are compliant with the international broadcast standards. One such device is the Bt812 digital video decoder manufactured by Brooktree Corporation. This device is capable of decoding either NTSC or PAL video signals and generating a digital data stream that is compliant with the CCIR601 digital video format. The CCIR standard is discussed in more detail in Chapter 5. The device is designed to handle a range of input signal conditions including the case where the NTSC or PAL signal is coming from a video cassette recorder in fast forward mode. This mode of operation tends to create special problems for decoding devices because the magnetic tape is moving through the machine at a faster rate than normal. This causes the mechanical tape heads to jump tracks in the middle of video frames affecting the line rate and creating tracking problems. The device contains analog-to-digital converters, chroma separation circuitry, and a digitally synthesized genlock implementation. Genlock refers to the generation of synchronization signals that are phase-locked to the incoming video signal. This allows the device to properly recognize and process the appropriate portions of the incoming signal. Ordinarily, genlock is implemented as a phase-locked loop circuit that locks to the incoming horizontal synchronization pulse. The horizontal frequency is then used to generate a higher frequency sampling clock, which generates a constant number of pixels for every video scan line. If there are any variations in the length of the video scan line the frequency of the sampling clock is adjusted accordingly. This is generally difficult to accommodate when connecting to a digital computer system because the clocks in a computer system run at a fixed frequency. The Brooktree device is designed to operate with a fixed frequency sampling clock for the receiving device and automatically compensate for any nonlinearities in the input signal. This is accomplished through a technique called *adaptive linear interpolation*. This involves monitoring the input signal for aberrations and adjusting a set of interpolation coefficients internally to automatically compensate for the errors. If the number of video pixels does not match the number of sample clocks for a horizontal scan line period, the device can insert dummy pixels in order to maintain a fixed sampling frequency for the receiving device. The Bt812 image digitizer accepts NTSC and PAL inputs and generates either RGB or YCrCb digital video data output at rates anywhere from 8 MHz to 16.5 MHz. The digital outputs are in the form of a 24 bit bus that can supply 24-bit RGB, 16-bit RGB, 15-bit RGB, 24-bit YCrCb, or 16-bit YCrCb in subsampled format. It incorporates a built in four-to-one multiplexer that allows up to four separate video signals to be selected under program control. The analog-to-digital conversion is accomplished by a pair of 8-bit flash A/D converters and incorporates automatic gain control. Figure 2.44 is a simplified block diagram showing the major functional units and data flows in the device. A significant advantage of the Bt812 is the fact that it incorporates both NTSC/PAL decoding and analog to digital conversion in a single device. The decoding and processing of information internally is all done in the digital format.

Motorola MC44011

Another approach is taken by the Motorola MC44011 NTSC/PAL decoder. This is an analog device that decodes the NTSC or PAL video signal and generates analog RGB outputs, which can then be converted from analog to digital. The basic functionality is similar, although accomplished in a different way, and it requires external A/D converters. The MC44011 generates a pixel clock to set the sampling rate for the external A/D converters. The pixel clock is phase locked to the incoming video sync signals. After decoding the NTSC or PAL input video signal and separating the chroma from the luminance the Y, $R-Y$, and $B-Y$ signals are available on output pins. These can then be processed externally or fed back into the device through a set of Y, $R-Y$, and $B-Y$ input pins. There are also a set of RGB input pins. The device converts the Y, $R-Y$, and $B-Y$ input signals into RGB output signals. It also incorporates an analog multiplex circuit to allow the luminance and chrominance signals to be multiplexed with the input RGB signals under program control. External program control is facilitated through an I2C interface. The recommended analog-to-digital con-

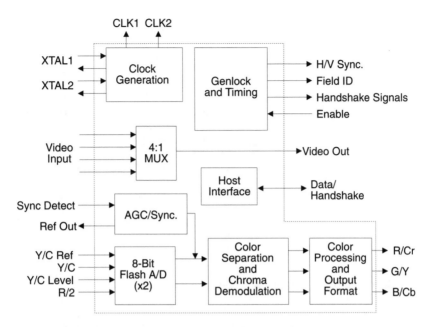

Figure 2.44 Simplified block diagram of Bt812.

verter for use with the MC44011 is the MC44250 triple 8-bit video A/D. This device supports sample rates up to 15 MHz and incorporates automatic dithering.

Brooktree Bt858

For conversion of digital RGB or YCrCb signals back into NTSC or PAL format the Bt858 from Brooktree Corporation is useful. It is designed to be compatible with the digital output of the Bt812. The device incorporates three independent 8-bit lookup tables to facilitate color correction. It also incorporates an automatic color bar generator for creating a test pattern on the output display device. Figure 2.45 is a simplified block diagram showing the internal functions and data paths of the Bt858.

Bandwidth Requirements

The standard for full screen NTSC video in digital format is 640 x 480 pixels. This is referred to as an SIF image size. At this resolution, assuming 24 bits-per-pixel and 30 frames per second, the bandwidth required is approximately 27.6 megabytes per second. This may seem high when compared to the 4 to 6 MHz overall bandwidth of the original NTSC analog signal but it should be remembered that this data rate represents carrying color information at the same resolution as the luminance information, which is not the case in the modulated analog signal. It should also be remembered that the NTSC bandwidth numbers represent an analog frequency spectrum, not a data rate. Generally, digital circuits can operate at far higher frequencies than analog circuits using

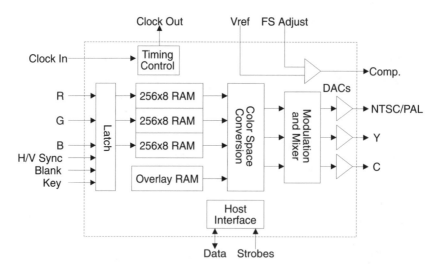

Figure 2.45 Simplified block diagram of Bt858.

equivalent technology because of the high noise immunity of the digital circuits. Furthermore, the range of possibilities for chroma subsampling, image processing and enhancement, filtering, and so on is much wider in the digital format than it is in the original NTSC analog format. This, combined with the rapidly expanding availability of low-cost computing equipment, makes the synthesis of video, audio, and computing technologies very attractive and probably accounts for a great deal of the activity along those lines.

Graphics versus Natural Image Data

One of the fundamental problems involved in merging video and computer technologies is the difference between the displays ordinarily used for the two applications. Television displays are completely optimized for displaying images consistent with the NTSC or other international video signal standards. Computer graphics displays, on the other hand, have evolved to meet a completely different set of requirements. To really understand the graphics architecture currently used in personal computers today, it is helpful to understand a little of the history that led to the current state of affairs. For purposes of this discussion the evolution of IBM PC–compatible graphics displays will be covered. When the IBM PC was first introduced in the early 1980s there were two types of display adapters available. The monochrome display adapter (MDA) was a text-only display controller driving a digital CRT. The display data was stored in the form of eight-bit extended ASCII codes and the screen image generated by translating these codes through a ROM-based character generator. The color graphics adapter (CGA) supported the same display modes and capabilities as the MDA but also added graphics extensions. It also was designed for use with a digital CRT and supplied three bits of color information and one bit of intensity information. The CRT, therefore, was capable of displaying eight different colors at two different intensities simultaneously on the screen. Unfortunately the CGA did not take advantage of this capability for graphics modes, only supporting four colors maximum in low-resolution graphics mode (320×200) and two colors in high-resolution graphics mode (640×200). Another shortcoming was that it was not designed to generate square pixels. In other words, the aspect ratio of the logical pixel map did not correspond to the physical aspect ratio of the display screen, so if a circle or a square was drawn in the graphics memory with equal width and height in number of pixels, it did not appear perfectly square or round on the display. Compensating for this tended to be a headache for graphics programmers. It didn't take long before third-party manufacturers began making compatible display adapters that improved on the theme. The most notable of these was the Hercules display adapter, which added graphics to the MDA display and extended the resolution for graphics modes beyond that available from the CGA. In response, IBM introduced their next generation display controller, the *enhanced graphic adapter* (EGA). This device supported graphics displays up to 640×380 resolution, again with a digital monitor, but now driven by six bits of information. The CRT therefore was capable of displaying 64 colors simultaneously on the screen, although the EGA only supported 16 simultaneously. Any of the 16 displayed, however, could be selected from the 64 available. The display memory was organized in the form of a planar bitmap as opposed to packed-pixel arrangement as in the CGA, but also supported all display modes of the CGA and MDA. The next-generation display controller introduced by IBM was the *video graphics array* (VGA), so named because the VLSI controller was implemented in a gate array. It also maintained hardware compatibility with each of the earlier display controllers as well as adding a few more display modes. It was the first display adapter to solve the aspect ratio problem, which greatly simplified programming for graphics applications. Probably the most significant advancement over earlier graphics controllers was the fact that the VGA used an analog display instead of digital. This meant there was virtually no limit to the number of colors that CRT was capable of displaying simultaneously. The VGA includes one display mode that supports 256 colors on the screen simultaneously, although at a reduced resolution from the maximum available. Presumably the rationale behind this was to conserve memory components, because for any given amount of memory a trade-off can be made between display resolution and the number of bits-per-pixel. This trade-off is still very evident in the display modes supported by virtually all PC display adapters even today.

When third-party PC graphics vendors began competing by offering VGA compatible devices, IBM took steps to raise the entry barriers by offering the 8514A display controller. This was the first display controller offered by IBM that broke from the tradition of offering backward hardware compatibility with earlier versions. It supported display resolutions up to 1024×768 with 256 colors. IBM did not publish the register programming specifications for the device, presumably hoping that this would delay any clone manufacturers in their attempts to enter the market. In response, third-party graphics hardware manufacturers developed their own extensions to the VGA standard, introducing the concept of Super VGA. Some of the Super VGA controllers were able to meet or exceed the display resolution and color capabilities of the 8514A. However, the 8514A did have one critical advantage: an intelligent graphics drawing engine. A number of third-party Super VGA makers reverse-engineered the 8514A and introduced compatible products. These didn't really meet with much more success than the 8514A but did create potential for new advances in the Super VGA arena. A number of companies incorporated drawing engines similar to that in the 8514A into their Super VGA graphics adapters. This allowed them to exceed the 8514A performance in resolution, color capacity, and speed. IBM did introduce another graphics controller called the XGA, which is essentially an 8514A controller with VGA compatibility added plus a few other features, but by this time many Super VGA features had achieved the status of industry de-facto standards through the development of an organization called the Video Electronics Standards Association (VESA).

Display Frame Buffer Organization

Graphics display memories (otherwise known as *frame buffers*) can be essentially divided into two classifications. One is a packed-pixel organization and the other is a bit-planar organization. A bit-planar memory map effectively represents each pixel in the image with one memory bit in contigu-

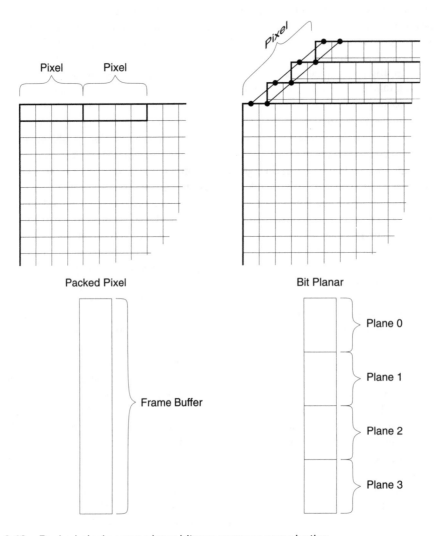

Figure 2.46   Packed pixel versus planar bitmap memory organization.

ous memory. If multiple bits-per-pixel are needed, multiple memory maps are employed. Packed-pixel organization has meaning only in cases where more than one bit-per-pixel is required. Each pixel is composed of contiguous bits in memory. Figure 2.46 illustrates the difference in memory organization between packed-pixel and bit-planar display memory for an implementation using four bits-per-pixel.

Probably the most commonly used display mode for VGA controllers is 640x480 resolution (or higher) with 16 colors. This requires four bits per pixel, which are organized in memory as four planar bitmaps as established by the EGA display controller. Figure 2.47 illustrates how these four bits-per-pixel were used in the EGA controller to select colors on the digital CRT. For each pixel, one bit from each bit plane was used to form a four-bit pixel value, which was then used as an address into a 16-location color palette lookup table RAM memory. The output of this memory was a six-bit value divided into three groups of two bits each. Each pair of bits drove one of the three electron guns in the CRT, so for each gun four different intensity levels could be selected.

The VGA improved on the scheme by switching to an analog CRT and adding another stage of color lookup tables to allow a wider selection of colors and finer control. Figure 2.48 illustrates how this was done. The six bits from the EGA color palette RAM are combined with two bits from a color select register to form an eight-bit value used as an address into three color lookup tables with 256 locations each. Each of the three tables produces a six-bit value that is used to drive a digital to analog converter that generates an analog value to drive the electron gun in the analog CRT. This means that 18 bits of resolution are available for each color displayed on the CRT, so each of the 16 colors displayed can be any of 262,144 (256K) different colors.

In practice, however, the lookup tables are programmed to produce the same colors that were produced in the digital monitor of the EGA in almost all cases. For motion video applications, however, this display mode is not really useful anyway because there are not enough distinct colors to render a realistic looking natural image. The real advantage of the VGA for motion video applications is its ability to display 256 colors on the screen simultaneously. Unfortunately, a standard

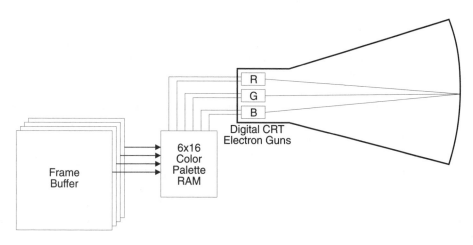

Figure 2.47 EGA digital display output data flow.

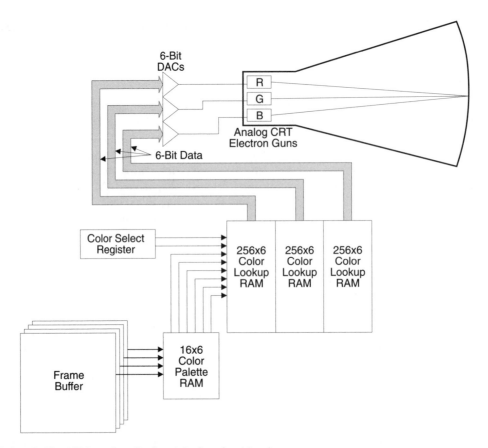

Figure 2.48   VGA analog display data flow for 16 colors.

VGA can do this only at a resolution of 320×200 pixels, which is not supported by popular user interfaces such as Microsoft Windows. To display 256 or more colors at resolutions higher than this requires a Super VGA. To display 256 colors, memory is organized in a packed-pixel configuration using eight bits-per-pixel. These eight bits directly drive the color lookup tables for conversion into analog format. Figure 2.49 illustrates this.

For the 320×200 display mode, the graphics display memory starts at address A0000(hex) in the PC address space, and is 64,000 bytes long. The first byte of this region corresponds to the upper-left pixel on the display, and the first 320 bytes correspond to the first pixel row on the display. This arrangement makes address calculation for pixel drawing considerably simpler than it is for 640×480 or other modes. Assuming a (0,0) coordinate at the upper-left corner of the screen, any (x,y) coordinate can be calculated as A0000(hex) + y*320 + x. To illustrate the default color arrangement for 256-color mode, a program named PAL_EDIT is provided. This allows the user to select any of the 256 colors provided by the hardware palette and modify the RGB components to produce a different color. Any color beyond the first sixteen can be modified without affecting the appearance of the user interface screen. If any of the colors that are used in the user interface screen

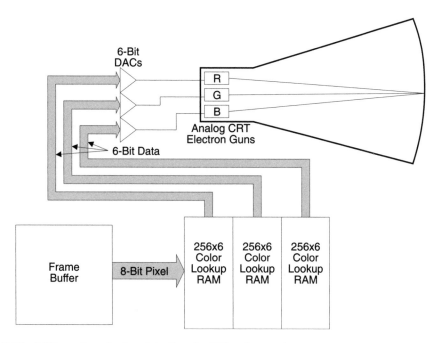

Figure 2.49 VGA analog display data flow for 256 color mode.

(from the first sixteen) are modified, the result will be immediately apparent in the appearance of the display. The following is a source code listing for the main program segment:

PAL_EDIT Program Listing

```
// =================================================
// VGA Hardware Palette Editor Demonstration Program
// =================================================
// This program demonstrates the organization and operation
// of the VGA hardware color palette. The program is
// built on a C++ DOS application programming shell
// provided in file SHELL256.CPP. It uses class
// definitions from include files CTRL_256.H and
// DISP_256.H to provide user interface functions for
// mouse control. Low level display functions are
// provided in assembly language files DRAW_BLK.ASM,
// DRWASCII.ASM, SETVMODE.ASM, and VPALETTE.ASM.
// To run, type "PAL_EDIT".
//
// Compiler: Borland Turbo C++ Version 1.01
// Author:   Phil Mattison
// Date:     5/20/93
// Revision: 1.0
// =================================================
```

```
#define APP_TITLE   "Palette Editor Demonstration"
#define PALETTE_X   10
#define PALETTE_Y   20
#define SHOW_X      140
#define SHOW_Y      20
#define TAG_X       7
#define TAG_Y       6
#define C1          140
#define C2          200
#define C3          260
#define R1          80
#define R2          100
#define R3          120
#define R4          140
#define R5          160
#define W_SIZE      40,12
#define B_SIZE      20,12

#include <stdio.h>
#include <conio.h>
#include <dos.h>
#include "ctrl_256.h"
#include "disp_256.h"

extern "C" void SetVmode(int);
extern "C" void WriteBlock(int,int,int,int,unsigned char far *);
extern "C" void DrawBlock(int,int,int,int,int);
extern "C" void DrawASCII(int,int,int,int);
extern "C" void ReadEntry(int,unsigned char far *);
extern "C" void WriteEntry(int,int,int,int);
extern "C" void ReadPalette(unsigned char far *);
extern "C" void WritePalette(unsigned char far *);

TControl *Mouse;
int      palette_index;
TDisplay *index,*rw,*gw,*bw;

void SignOn(void)
  {
  DrawBlock(0,0,320,200,WHITE);          // White background
  DrawBlock(0,0,320,10,LIGHTBLUE);       // Title Bar
  DrawString(160-strlen(APP_TITLE)*4,2,APP_TITLE,WHITE); // Title
  DrawBlock(0,10,320,1,BLUE);            // Title Bar Outline
  DrawBlock(319,0,1,10,BLUE);
  DrawBlock(0,0,320,1,CYAN);
  DrawBlock(0,0,1,10,CYAN);

  DrawBlock(0,186,320,14,LIGHTGRAY);     // Message Bar
  DrawBlock(2,198,220,1,WHITE);
  DrawBlock(222,187,1,12,WHITE);
  DrawBlock(2,187,221,1,DARKGRAY);
  DrawBlock(2,187,1,12,DARKGRAY);
```

```
  }

int EscExit()  //Exit via Escape key (process KB input)
  {
  int st;
  st=kbhit();
  if(st!=0)
    {
    st=getch();
    if(st==27)return(RUN_DISABLED);
    }
  return(RUN_ENABLED);
  }

int Quit()      //Exit via mouse click
  {
  return(RUN_DISABLED);
  }

void UserMessage(char *message)
  {
  DrawBlock(3,189,218,10,LIGHTGRAY);
  DrawString(6,189,message,WHITE);
  DrawBlock(2,198,220,1,WHITE);
  }

//****************************************************
// Process mouse input
//****************************************************

int Palette()        // Update selected palette entry color display
  {
  int color,x,y;
  unsigned char rgb_data[3];
  x=Mouse->GetPositionX();
  y=Mouse->GetPositionY();
  color=(x-PALETTE_X)/TAG_X+((y-PALETTE_Y)/TAG_Y)*16;
  palette_index=color;
  DrawBlock(SHOW_X,SHOW_Y,100,40,color);
  index->Show(color);
  ReadEntry(color,rgb_data);
  rw->Show((int)rgb_data[0]);
  gw->Show((int)rgb_data[1]);
  bw->Show((int)rgb_data[2]);
  return(RUN_ENABLED);
  }

int RI() // Increase Red
  {
  unsigned char rgb_data[3];
  ReadEntry(palette_index,rgb_data);
  rgb_data[0]++;
```

```
  if(rgb_data[0]>63)rgb_data[0]=63;
  rw->Show((int)rgb_data[0]);
  WriteEntry(palette_index,
    (int)rgb_data[0],
    (int)rgb_data[1],
    (int)rgb_data[2]);
  return(RUN_ENABLED);
  }

int RD() // Decrease Red
  {
  unsigned char rgb_data[3];
  ReadEntry(palette_index,rgb_data);
  rgb_data[0]--;
  if(rgb_data[0]>63)rgb_data[0]=0;
  rw->Show((int)rgb_data[0]);
  WriteEntry(palette_index,
    (int)rgb_data[0],
    (int)rgb_data[1],
    (int)rgb_data[2]);
  return(RUN_ENABLED);
  }

int GI()
  {
  unsigned char rgb_data[3];
  ReadEntry(palette_index,rgb_data);
  rgb_data[1]++;
  if(rgb_data[1]>63)rgb_data[1]=63;
  gw->Show((int)rgb_data[1]);
  WriteEntry(palette_index,
    (int)rgb_data[0],
    (int)rgb_data[1],
    (int)rgb_data[2]);
  return(RUN_ENABLED);
  }

int GD()
  {
  unsigned char rgb_data[3];
  ReadEntry(palette_index,rgb_data);
  rgb_data[1]--;
  if(rgb_data[1]>63)rgb_data[1]=0;
  gw->Show((int)rgb_data[1]);
  WriteEntry(palette_index,
    (int)rgb_data[0],
    (int)rgb_data[1],
    (int)rgb_data[2]);
  return(RUN_ENABLED);
  }

int BI()
  {
```

```
  unsigned char rgb_data[3];
  ReadEntry(palette_index,rgb_data);
  rgb_data[2]++;
  if(rgb_data[2]>63)rgb_data[2]=63;
  bw->Show((int)rgb_data[2]);
  WriteEntry(palette_index,
     (int)rgb_data[0],
     (int)rgb_data[1],
     (int)rgb_data[2]);
  return(RUN_ENABLED);
  }

int BD()
  {
  unsigned char rgb_data[3];
  ReadEntry(palette_index,rgb_data);
  rgb_data[2]--;
  if(rgb_data[2]>63)rgb_data[2]=0;
  bw->Show((int)rgb_data[2]);
  WriteEntry(palette_index,
     (int)rgb_data[0],
     (int)rgb_data[1],
     (int)rgb_data[2]);
  return(RUN_ENABLED);
  }

//****************************************************

void main(void)
  {
  int x,y;
  unsigned char palette_data[3*256];
  SetVmode(0x13);
  SignOn();
  Mouse=new TControl;
  index=new TDisplay(260,SHOW_Y,W_SIZE,WHITE,BLACK,BORDER);
  index->Show(0);
  DrawString(260,SHOW_Y+14,"Index",BLACK);
  rw=new TDisplay(C1,R1,W_SIZE,WHITE,BLACK,BORDER);
  gw=new TDisplay(C2,R1,W_SIZE,WHITE,BLACK,BORDER);
  bw=new TDisplay(C3,R1,W_SIZE,WHITE,BLACK,BORDER);
  DrawString(C1,R1-10,"Red",BLACK);
  DrawString(C2,R1-10,"Green",BLACK);
  DrawString(C3,R1-10,"Blue",BLACK);
  rw->Show(0);
  gw->Show(0);
  bw->Show(0);

  Mouse->SetStandardCallback(&EscExit);
  Mouse->CreateButton(&Quit,226,187,90,11,"[Esc] Quit");
  DrawBlock(C1-2,R2-1,164,15,LIGHTGRAY);
  Mouse->CreateButton(&RI,C1-1, R2,B_SIZE,"\x18");
  Mouse->CreateButton(&RD,C1+20,R2,B_SIZE,"\x19");
```

```
Mouse->CreateButton(&GI,C2-1, R2,B_SIZE,"\x18");
Mouse->CreateButton(&GD,C2+20,R2,B_SIZE,"\x19");
Mouse->CreateButton(&BI,C3-1, R2,B_SIZE,"\x18");
Mouse->CreateButton(&BD,C3+20,R2,B_SIZE,"\x19");
Mouse->CreateButton(&Palette,PALETTE_X,PALETTE_Y,112,96," ");
DrawBlock(PALETTE_X-1,PALETTE_Y-1,114,98,DARKGRAY);
DrawBlock(SHOW_X-1,SHOW_Y-1,102,42,LIGHTGRAY);
DrawBlock(SHOW_X,SHOW_Y,100,40,BLACK);

for(y=0;y<16;y++)             // Display the palette
   {
   for(x=0;x<16;x++)
     {
     DrawBlock(PALETTE_X+TAG_X*x,PALETTE_Y+TAG_Y*y,
     TAG_X,TAG_Y,x+y*16);
     }
   }
Mouse->Run();
SetVmode(3);
}
```

A range of 256 colors is enough to produce a recognizable video image. However, this arrangement presents certain difficulties for the processing of color information. The color lookup tables effectively isolate the color information stored in the pixel map from the actual colors displayed on the screen. A better graphics organization for natural images and motion video is to use at least 15 bits-per-pixel. Each pixel can then be divided into three fields to directly drive the analog-to-digital converters for the red, green, and blue values going to the CRT. This is sometimes referred to as *direct color* mode. Figure 2.50 illustrates how memory is organized in this case. This arrangement allows either 32,768 (32K) or 65,536 (64K) colors to be displayed on the screen simultaneously and produces quite good color resolution for motion video, although it is considered by some to be inadequate for high-resolution color still images.

The highest color resolution generally used in PC graphics adapters uses 24 bits-per-pixel. This is generally referred to as *true color*. The memory organization scheme is essentially the same as that for 15 or 16 bits-per-pixel except that 8 bits each are used for red, green, and blue.

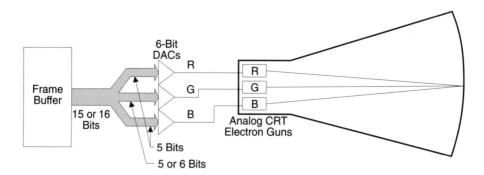

Figure 2.50   Direct color display data flow for 15-bit color or higher.

This gives a total range of 16,777,216 colors, which can theoretically all be displayed simultaneously on the screen. However, in practice this cannot really be done at VGA resolutions because even if every pixel on the screen had a different color it still would not be possible to display 16,777,216 colors because there are not that many pixels on the screen. The display would have to be 4,096x4,096 pixels in order to do this. It goes without saying that 24 bits-per-pixel is generally considered adequate for motion video applications. In the real world, of course, it is usually necessary to make trade-offs among cost, quality, and other factors. The more bits-per-pixel used for generating the display images, the more difficult it is to process and move the data around through the system. It also requires more memory. The reason 16-color display systems have predominated until now is that 16 colors are generally adequate for the bulk of applications currently running on PCs. Word processing, spreadsheets, computer-aided design applications, and many other types of software really don't need much more than 16 colors. For most conventional PC applications the spatial resolution of the display is generally a much more critical consideration than the ability to display a large number of unique colors. A general priority is to display large amounts of graphical information on the screen. This graphical information tends to be very high contrast. For example, a word processing or a spreadsheet application generally uses a white background with black foreground, text, figures, etc. Each transition from white to black or black to white represents a swing from one extreme to the other of the total range of values that can be displayed. In a natural image the spatial variations tend to be much more gradual. If the average intensity levels for a single scan line of a graphical image (say, for example, from a word processing application) is compared with an equivalent scan line from a natural image and each are analyzed for their frequency content, the graphical image will generally be found to have a much higher spatial frequency content than the natural image. Figure 2.51 illustrates a comparison between how a typical graphics versus natural image intensity profile might look when charted in the spatial domain and then in the spatial frequency domain. It can be seen from this that there is a great deal more frequency energy in the graphics image than in the natural image. The reason for this is that graphics images tend to be composed primarily of the equivalent of digital impulse signals. A spectral analysis of a digital impulse signal shows up as multiple bands of high energy at multiples of the impulse frequency.

The frequency content of a natural image tends to show up as a relatively random distribution of frequency energy typically tapering off at the high end of the spectrum and not mathematically related to the pixel size. It could be stated that the natural image, therefore, contains less information if it were not for the fact that a much higher color resolution is required in order for the image to actually look natural. The point of all this is that the evolutionary path taken by computer graphics display devices tends to be fundamentally incompatible with that taken by television and other natural image display devices. The emerging synthesis of these two previously disparate technologies requires a great deal of ingenuity to overcome the inherent difficulties. There are two primary functions carried out by a graphics display controller such as the VGA. One is to maintain the screen refresh data flow for the display device, usually the CRT. This generally means supplying a pixel stream from the frame buffer at a rate fast enough to meet the requirements of the CRT. This places certain data transfer bandwidth requirements on the frame buffer memory. The other is to coordinate access to the frame buffer memory by the CPU and possibly carry out drawing operations in the case of an advanced VGA controller that contains a drawing engine. It is clear then that the frame buffer memory is really the focus of graphic controller activity. Frame buffer memory is generally imple-

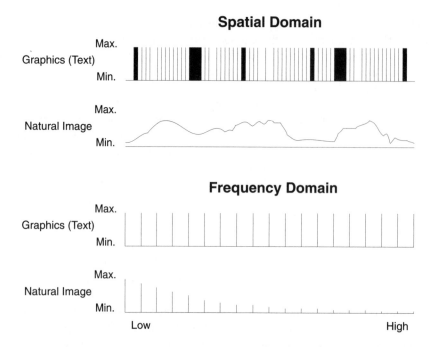

Figure 2.51   Comparison of graphics versus natural image frequency content.

mented with one of two types of memory, DRAM or VRAM. VRAM is generally used in graphic systems where performance is more critical than cost. VRAM is essentially a DRAM with a built-in shift register that allows rows of data from the memory array to be shifted out of the device independently of access through the normal random access port. Figure 2.52 is a simplified block diagram showing how a VRAM is internally organized. In graphic controller applications, generally the serial shift register port of the VRAM is the path through which screen refresh data flows. This allows practically unrestricted access for the host CPU into the frame buffer memory.

Unfortunately, the cost of VRAM makes its use prohibitive for a large majority of VGA controllers. In these cases DRAM is used, forcing CPU access and display refresh access to share the same random access memory port. Figure 2.53 illustrates the differences in the data flow paths between DRAM and VRAM display controller implementations.

For a DRAM-based graphic controller the restrictions on access to the frame buffer tend to create significant problems in achieving the data rates necessary to implement motion video. Table 2.5 summarizes for a number of different pixel sizes and display sizes what data rates are required to sustain display refresh on a 70 Hz screen.

The available remaining bandwidth into the DRAM frame buffer for the CPU and other types of access then depends on the width of the data path and the manner in which it is constructed. Various VGA controller devices support quite a wide range of data path configurations for memory interface. Some VGA controllers also employ elaborate memory arbitration and buffering schemes to better utilize the available memory bandwidth, particularly for DRAM implementations. The memory interface itself, however, is not the only consideration. By far the majority of

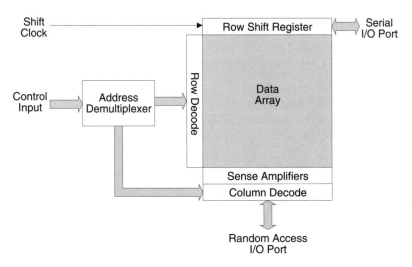

Figure 2.52   Internal organization of VRAM.

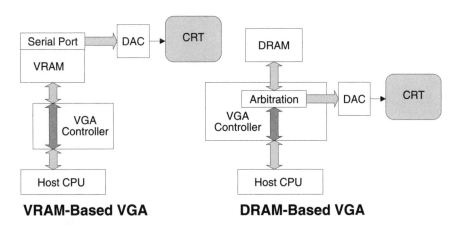

VRAM-Based VGA   **DRAM-Based VGA**

Figure 2.53   Comparative data flows for DRAM versus VRAM frame buffers.

Table 2.5   Display Refresh Data Rates (Megabytes per Second)

Screen Size	8 Bits-per-Pixel	16 Bits-per-Pixel	24 Bits-per-Pixel
640x480	21.504	43.008	64.512
800x600	33.600	67.200	100.800
1024x768	55.050	110.100	165.150
1280x1024	91.750	183.500	275.250

Table 2.6   Motion Video Data Rates (Megabytes per Second)

Image Size	Frame Rate	Pixel Size	Data Rate	
160x120	15 Frames/Sec.	8-Bits	288	Kb/S
160x120	30 Frames/Sec.	8-Bits	576	Kb/S
160x120	30 Frames/Sec.	16-Bits	1.152	Mb/s
320x240	15 Frames/Sec.	8-Bits	1.152	Mb/s
320x240	30 Frames/Sec.	8-Bits	2.304	Mb/s
320x240	30 Frames/Sec.	16-Bits	4.608	Mb/s
640x480	15 Frames/Sec.	8-Bits	4.608	Mb/s
640x480	30 Frames/Sec.	8-Bits	9.216	Mb/s
640x480	30 Frames/Sec.	16-Bits	18.432	Mb/s
800x600	15 Frames/Sec.	8-Bits	7.2	Mb/s
800x600	30 Frames/Sec.	8-Bits	14.4	Mb/S
800x600	30 Frames/Sec.	16-Bits	28.8	Mb/S
1024x768	15 Frames/Sec.	8-Bits	11.796	Mb/S
1024x768	30 Frames/Sec.	8-Bits	23.592	Mb/S
1024x768	30 Frames/Sec.	16-Bits	47.185	Mb/S
1280x1024	15 Frames/Sec.	8-Bits	13.107	Mb/S
1280x1024	30 Frames/Sec.	8-Bits	26.214	Mb/S
1280x1024	30 Frames/Sec.	16-Bits	52.428	Mb/S

VGA controllers currently installed or on the market are designed to plug into the standard expansion slot in the PC. This is generally the major source of restrictions on the ability to transfer data in and out of the frame buffer. The best transfer rate that can reasonably be achieved over this channel is about eight megabytes per second. When arbitration latencies and other factors are taken into account, this bandwidth can decline by as much as 50 percent or more. This has a direct and significant impact on the ability to display motion video pictures. Table 2.6 shows the data rates required to display motion video picture at various frame rates, pixel sizes, and image sizes. It is not difficult to see the majority of these configurations exceed the ability of the standard PC expansion slot to deliver the data.

Computer Display Systems

How Computer Displays Work

The evolution of computer displays has been driven by a different set of requirements from those that drove the evolution of television displays. The cathode ray tube (CRT) has been used in numerous applications beyond both television and computer displays. For example, oscilloscope displays, radar displays, and medical monitoring equipment all use CRTs designed differently based on the application requirements. For television the principle requirement was to produce a display that could be synchronized well with an image sensing device and which had enough resolution to produce an acceptable image to the viewer. Historically, television has been used primarily for leisure and entertainment and consequently the viewer tends to be relatively far away from the screen and not concentrating heavily on the image. The images themselves are generally designed to carry a strong emotional impact rather than a large information content and are supplemented heavily in this mission by the accompanying audio. In fact, television can be thought of as a new and improved type of radio that uses motion pictures to enhance the message that was already being delivered by sound. Computers, on the other hand, have historically been focused more on the processing and manipulation of information. The stereotypical concept of a computer or somebody heavily involved in computers is one totally devoid of emotional content. Look at *Star Trek's* Mr. Spock, made famous by his unwavering preference for logic and reason over emotion—the quintessential computer nerd if ever there was one.

Digital Cathode Ray Tubes (CRT)

CRTs used as computer displays were originally designed primarily to display letters and numbers otherwise known as alphanumeric information. To create this kind of display a common technique is to use a character generator. This involves storing a series of binary patterns in a read-only memory (ROM) and then supplying these patterns in a serial digital bit stream to the

CRT so several scan lines of the image combine to form a row of characters. The CRT electronics could be simplified somewhat because it was no longer necessary to produce a linear response to an analog input signal. A typical display terminal for a large computer contained a small amount of memory to hold character codes, a character generator, a CRT, and a keyboard. It was capable of displaying only a fixed set of characters with a certain number of rows and columns. Figure 3.1 is a simplified block diagram showing how the major functional units of such a display terminal are organized.

Display terminals of this type were typically referred to as *dumb terminals* because they could only receive and display data and could not generate any output other than what came from the keyboard, and could not process the information in any way. For graphics displays a fairly common approach in the early days was something known as a *vector graphics* display. These were similar to conventional CRTs except that the beam deflection coils were not designed to generate a repetitive series of scan lines organized into fields and frames. Instead, the beam could be controlled to move to any point on the display at any time. To create a line on the screen the control electronics would simply turn the electron beam off, adjust the deflection circuits to point to one endpoint of the line, turn the beam on, and then move it smoothly from one endpoint to the other. For the CRT this meant the horizontal and vertical deflection circuits had to be able to respond at the same speed rather than having a high horizontal frequency and a low vertical frequency as in a conventional CRT. The display memory in this case was organized as a series of X and Y endpoints for lines to be displayed on the screen. These coordinate pairs would then feed into a pair of A/D converters to generate the start and stop values for a pair of horizontal and vertical sweep generators. The sweep generators could be as simple as a pair of capacitors charged to one set of values for the beginning endpoint and then charged or drained to another set of values for the other endpoint. The voltage from the capacitors would then be fed into an amplifier to generate a proportional current to drive the electron beam deflector coils. The fact that a fixed charging current does not generate a fixed rate of voltage change over time for a charging capacitor generally doesn't create a problem because the charging curves are the same for both X and Y capacitors. Control of the electron beam intensity,

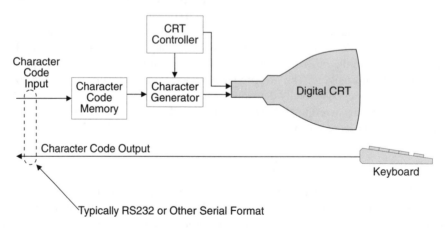

Figure 3.1   Organization of common display terminal functions.

however, was essentially digital. Figure 3.2 is a simplified diagram illustrating how the coordinate memory and sweep generators would be organized in a vector scope to create lines of any length and any angle on the display screen.

In both types of display terminals the primary function of the terminal was to display information. All computing was assumed to be carried out somewhere else. The first personal computers were little more than a display terminal with a microprocessor, some memory, and a floppy disk drive attached. In fact, some hobbyists constructed their own personal computers by buying small single-board microprocessor units and installing them inside previously "dumb" terminals. Eventually, it became common to use a separate CRT so different display devices could be used with different computing devices. In a digital CRT, the electron beam intensity is controlled by one or more digital inputs. The simplest monochrome displays used with early PCs had two digital beam control inputs and could display two levels of intensity. One input controlled whether the beam was on or off and the other controlled whether it was high or low intensity when it was on. This allows certain characters on the screen to be highlighted. Digital monitors use an input signal ranging from zero to five volts and thus are often referred to as transistor-transistor logic (TTL) monitors because TTL

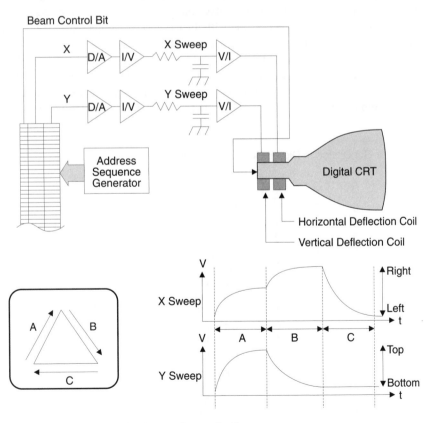

Figure 3.2 Vector graphic display internal organization.

has a five-volt operating range. The development of color CRTs for personal computers required more digital inputs, but the same basic approach was used. Monitors for use with the color graphics adapter (CGA) had four digital inputs, one each for the three primary colors and an extra for intensity control. This allowed for eight basic colors ranging from white to black, which could be displayed at two levels of intensity. Of course, this was advertised as 16-color capability even though it really wasn't. The fact that the range of eight colors was actually duplicated with two levels of intensity resulted in four of the 16 so-called colors being allocated to different shades of white and black. This led to a rather strange situation where two of the "colors" would have to be called either light black or dark white. Rather than do this, they were named light gray and dark gray. Table 3.1 shows how the binary control bits combined to form the 16 colors in the CGA display. It can be seen from the table that there are in fact six colors at two levels of intensity.

All six colors at both levels of intensity are effectively fully saturated. This fact tends to make the CGA color set not well suited for natural image production. Natural images tend to have relatively low levels of color saturation. They also tend to have a relatively low contrast ratio. The color set selected for computer displays was intentionally designed to produce very high contrast images with high levels of color saturation. Even the transition to the *enhanced graphics adapter* (EGA) did not really solve this problem. Although the EGA monitor is capable of displaying 64 colors simultaneously on the screen, the EGA display controller is only capable of generating 16, and those 16 are selected to match the 16 possible with the CGA. To obtain a reasonable range of color saturation and intensity levels using a digital monitor such as the EGA, it is necessary to use a technique known as *spatial dithering*. This involves combining several physical pixels on the display to create each effective pixel of the natural image. It allows the effective range of colors for each virtual pixel to be multiplied by the number of actual pixels used to represent it. For example, if each image pixel is composed of a 2x2 matrix of display pixels (which is 4 pixels) on an EGA display,

Table 3.1   Color Generation in Digital CGA Graphics Monitor

Intensity	R	G	B	Color
0	0	0	0	Black
0	0	0	1	Blue
0	0	1	0	Green
0	0	1	1	Cyan
0	1	0	0	Red
0	1	0	1	Magenta
0	1	1	0	Dark Yellow
0	1	1	1	Light Gray
1	0	0	0	Dark Gray
1	0	0	1	Light Blue
1	0	1	0	Light Green
1	0	1	1	Light Cyan
1	1	0	0	Light Red
1	1	0	1	Light Magenta
1	1	1	0	Light Yellow
1	1	1	1	White

each virtual pixel can then display 64 different colors. Remember, the EGA display is only capable of actually showing 16 different colors simultaneously on the screen. The technique depends on a certain limitation of the human visual system. That is, the human eye is only capable of detecting spatial variations down to a certain level; beyond that, any differences tend to be averaged. A number of studies have been conducted to determine the limitations of the human visual system and these limitations can be taken advantage of in compressing visual information. This is discussed further in Chapter 5. In general, the human eye is capable of detecting finer details at high levels of luminance contrast and is not as sensitive to color variations. This sensitivity is measured in cycles per degree and is generally two to five cycles per degree for the average human eye at maximum contrast levels. Figure 3.3 illustrates the meaning of cycles per degree as related to the human visual system. This sensitivity tends to decline as contrast is reduced; however, recall that a digital display system for a computer is specifically designed to produce very-high-contrast graphic images.

A 14-inch EGA monitor with a horizontal resolution of 640 points can display 320 cycles of contrast across approximately 11 inches of horizontal space. At a normal viewing distance of about 18 inches, this corresponds to a spatial frequency of about eight cycles per degree. This is not much above the eye's ability to detect detail, so a natural image created using the dithering technique mentioned earlier will tend to look very grainy. It is necessary to move away from the display in order to get a pleasing image.

Analog Cathode Ray Tubes (CRT)

For natural images and motion video the big advantage of an analog CRT is that it much more closely emulates the function of an ordinary television than a digital CRT does. Analog CRTs are also available in very high resolutions and therefore can display amazingly clear pictures. Much effort is underway currently to take advantage of this fact with the development of international standards for High Definition Television (HDTV). For computer applications, this means it is possible to display multiple television images on one computer display simultaneously. An analog col-

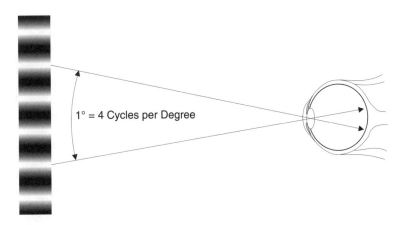

Figure 3.3   Measurement of human visual acuity.

or CRT allows the beam intensity for each of its three electron guns to be controlled proportionally to an analog input signal. Recall in the earlier discussion of NTSC that the voltage swing for the input signal was one volt peak-to-peak divided into 140 IRE units. The RGB analog monitors used in today's personal computers also conform to this protocol. Except for differences in timing, adaptation of an NTSC video signal to an analog RGB computer monitor is relatively straightforward. Of course, the differences in timing can present a significant technical hurdle in themselves. For one thing, computer monitors support quite a wide range of horizontal and vertical frequencies. Displaying an NTSC signal with a frame rate of 59.94 Hz on a computer monitor with, say, a 72 Hz refresh rate creates a vertical frequency interaction that can result in visual artifacts known as *tearing*. In this particular frequency relationship, for example, the NTSC vertical frequency is approximately five-sixths of the display frequency. The fact that NTSC uses two interlaced fields for each frame where computer displays generally use a noninterlace display also creates significant difficulty. This is often overcome by using only the even or odd fields from the NTSC signal, which explains the often-quoted 30 frames per second generally associated with PC motion video. A common technique used to solve the problems caused by differences in the vertical frequency between the NTSC and the computer display is to store the video frames in memory and "paint" them on the display screen as needed. In the case of a 72 Hz display refresh rate versus a 60 Hz NTSC frame rate, every fifth motion video frame would simply be left on the screen for two display refresh cycles. Table 3.2 shows some fairly common PC display monitor timings for computer displays at various resolutions and refresh rates.

The color CRT design used in virtually all commercial applications uses what is known as a *shadow mask*. This takes two forms. The first form is a metal plate with approximately 400,000 tiny perforations arranged in a triangular pattern. The second version, which was an improvement for color televisions, is a similar metal plate but with vertical slots rather than round perforations. Both types of CRT use three electron guns, one each for red, green, and blue signals. The physical arrangement of the guns, however, is different for the two types of CRTs in order to take advantage

Table 3.2 Typical PC Display Monitor Timings

Resolution	640×480	640×480 (72 Hz)	800×600 (72 Hz)	1024x×768 (70 Hz)	1280×1024 (74 Hz)
Horizontal Frequency	31.469 KHz	37.860 KHz	48.077 KHz	56.476 KHz	78.855 KHz
Horizontal Period	31.778 µS	26.413 µS	20.800 µS	17.707 µS	12.861 µS
Horizontal Pulse Width	3.813 µS	1.270 µS	2.400 µS	1.813 µS	1.067 µS
Horizontal Back Porch	1.589 µS	4.603 µS	1.280 µS	1.920 µS	1.896 µS
Horizontal Active Area	26.058 µS	20.317 µS	16.000 µS	13.653 µS	9.481 µS
Horizontal Front Porch	0.318 µS	0.762 µS	1.120 µS	0.320 µS	0.237 µS
Vertical Frequency	59.940 Hz	72.809 Hz	72.010 Hz	70.069 Hz	74.117 Hz
Vertical Period	16.683 mS	13.735 mS	13.887 mS	14.272 mS	13.492 mS
Vertical Pulse Width	0.064 mS	0.079 mS	0.124 mS	0.106 mS	0.038 mS
Vertical Back Porch	0.793 mS	0.740 mS	0.479 mS	0.513 mS	0.496 mS
Vertical Active Area	15.762 mS	12.678 mS	12.479 mS	13.599 mS	12.985 mS
Vertical Front Porch	0.064 mS	0.238 mS	0.772 mS	0.053 mS	0 mS

of the different shadow mask arrangements. The perforated shadow mask design is generally better for large-screen displays because the mask is stronger and more stable. It is, however, more difficult to align. The aperture grille shadow mask is easier to align and produces a brighter picture but doesn't work well for large screen CRTs. Figure 3.4 shows the differences in the perforation patterns between the two types of shadow masks.

A CRT using a perforated shadow mask has the three electron guns arranged in a triangular pattern separated by 120 degrees of rotation from each other. The beams are directed so they all strike the shadow mask at the same point. The separation of the guns causes the beams to strike the shadow mask at different angles. Figure 3.5 shows the arrangement of the electron guns inside the CRT glass envelope. The phosphor deposited on the inside surface of the glass envelope at the front of the CRT is formulated in three different types to produce the three primary colors, red, green, and blue, when excited by an electron beam.

The three types of phosphor are deposited in a honeycomb pattern so that as the three electron beams pass through the shadow mask they're each directed at the appropriate type of phosphor. Figure 3.6 illustrates how the angle of the electron beams passing through the shadow mask results in the beams striking the appropriate phosphor dots, and how the holes in the shadow mask are arranged relative to the phosphor dots. The size of the holes in the shadow mask does not necessarily have any relation to the resolution of the display other than the fact that they must be equal to or smaller than the desired pixel size. The pitch of the phosphor dots is really a function of how small they can be made and still be deposited accurately over the entire surface of the display screen. A typical television screen, for example, has phosphor dots quite a bit smaller than the spot formed by the electron beam. This can be easily verified by closely examining a television screen (while it is on) using a magnifying glass.

The electron beams can be large enough to pass through several holes in the shadow mask and will still only strike the correct phosphor dots. It is the angle of the beams that is critical and not the size. Modern CRTs generally contain some combination of electrostatic and/or electromagnetic deflection devices placed in strategic points around the glass envelope to compensate for the angle of the beam as it sweeps across the surface of the display. The increased effectiveness of these compensation schemes with advances in technology have allowed CRTs to be manufactured with flat display surfaces. Early CRT displays had a curved screen that matched the curvature of the electron

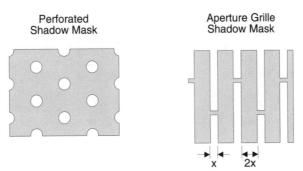

Figure 3.4   Two types of CRT shadow masks.

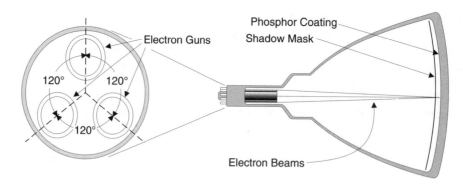

Figure 3.5   Triangular CRT electron gun arrangement.

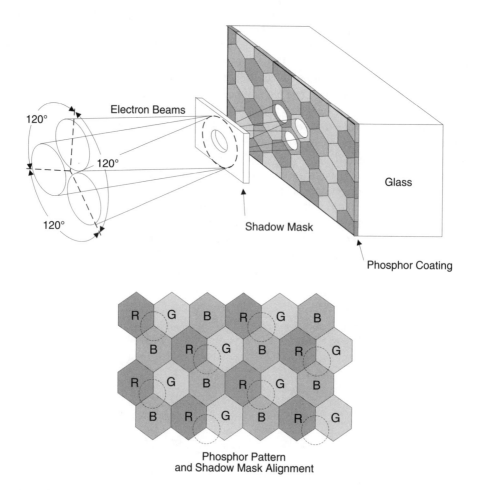

Figure 3.6   Shadow mask operation illustrated.

beam radius. Figure 3.7 illustrates the need for compensation when the curvature of the screen does not match the radius of the electron beam.

In an aperture grille shadow mask CRT design, the three electron guns are arranged side by side horizontally. The apertures in the shadow mask consist of vertical slots. Approximately two-thirds of the shadow mask is solid and one-third consists of open slots. This allows a greater amount of energy to pass through the mask than in a perforated type. The phosphor coating is arranged in parallel vertical bands of red, green, and blue phosphor. Again, this supports a brighter image because there are fewer gaps between differing types of phosphor. Figure 3.8 illustrates how the aperture grille shadow mask directs the three electron beams to the appropriate phosphor stripes.

Another type of CRT-based display often used in computer applications is the projection display system. This actually employs three separate CRTs, one for each of the primary colors. The CRTs are relatively small and coated with a special type of phosphor that generates high-intensity light. The images from the three CRTs are then focused through large lenses and converged on a reflective or translucent display screen. Figure 3.9 illustrates how the three CRTs are arranged in the system.

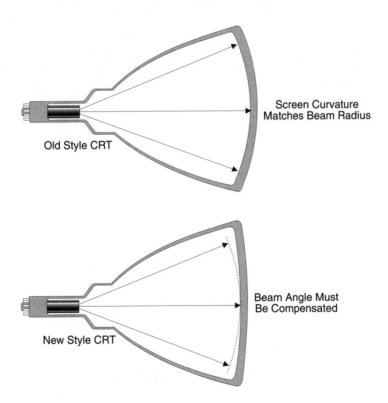

Figure 3.7   Electron beam curvature compensation.

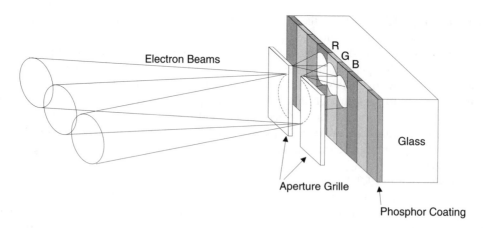

Figure 3.8   Aperture grille shadow mask operation.

Liquid Crystal Displays (LCD)

A display technology that has helped popularize portable computers is the *liquid crystal display* (LCD). The main advantages of this type of display are small size relative to a CRT, and low power consumption. LCDs can be generally categorized into two types: passive matrix and active matrix. Both types of display use a special crystalline compound known as *twisted nematic liquid crystal*. This material is sensitive to electrostatic fields and has optical characteristics that can be modified by the presence or absence of such a field. In the absence of any electrical field, the molecules of the crystal substance are in a generally disorganized state. In this state the liquid crystal

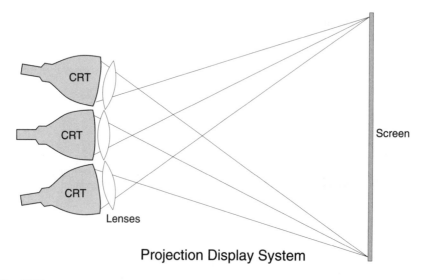

Figure 3.9   CRT arrangement in projection TV.

tends to pass light with no particular polarization. In the presence of an electrostatic field the crystalline molecules align themselves with the field to an extent dependent on the field strength. As more and more molecules are aligned with the field, the crystal becomes more and more light polarized, so that any light passing through has its polarity *twisted* by 90° (hence the name). Figure 3.10 illustrates the operation of a typical liquid crystal display. Polarizing filters on the front and back of the panel are rotated 90° from each other, so that ordinarily light is prevented from passing through. At any point where an electrostatic field exists, the liquid crystal twists the polarized light from the first filter by 90° so that it can pass through the second filter.

The fact that the alignment of crystal molecules is responsible for the reflection or transmission of light tends to make the material very directional when it does transmit light. This accounts for the phenomena of not being able to see a portable computer display from the side. Anyone who has ever worn an LCD watch in very cold weather may have noticed that the numbers seem to change very slowly or not at all when it is really cold. This is because the viscosity of the liquid crystal is affected by temperature. The crystal can, in fact, be frozen, which prevents the display from operating. Another property some users may have noticed is that in a relatively large LCD graphics display used in a vertical position over a long period of time the crystal will tend to pool at the bottom, affecting the brightness and contrast relative to the top of the screen.

Passive Matrix LCD

The passive matrix LCD is more widely used in portable computing applications because it is cheaper to make than active matrix displays. In a passive matrix display the electrodes for any particular display element on the screen are effectively charge coupled. That is, they store a capacitive charge and are not continuously driven by an electrical source. There are a number of factors that affect the quality of visual display. First, the frequency with which the charges on

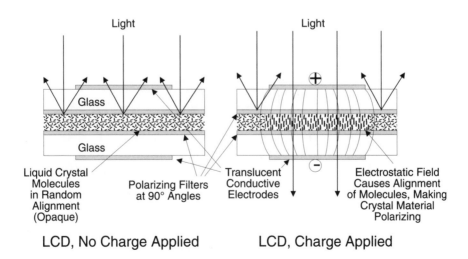

Figure 3.10 Operation of typical passive matrix LCD.

each display element are refreshed determines whether or not there's any noticeable flicker. Second, the size and spacing of the display elements determine how grainy the display looks. Third, the method of lighting used has an impact on the contrast ratio that can be achieved. The refresh frequency also has an affect on this. The most common form of passive matrix 640x480 LCD display for VGA use is known as the *dual scan* variety. This divides the screen horizontally in half and refreshes the top and bottom portions simultaneously. The VGA LCD panel is a synchronous device. Each half of the display receives a four-bit binary value on each clock. Each bit of the input corresponds to one pixel on the display. Figure 3.11 illustrates how the display is organized. The data is loaded into a shift register that is daisy-chained through a series of column drivers. When enough data has been loaded for an entire pair of rows, one for the top half and one for the bottom half, the entire two rows of pixel electrodes are refreshed according to the binary pattern loaded.

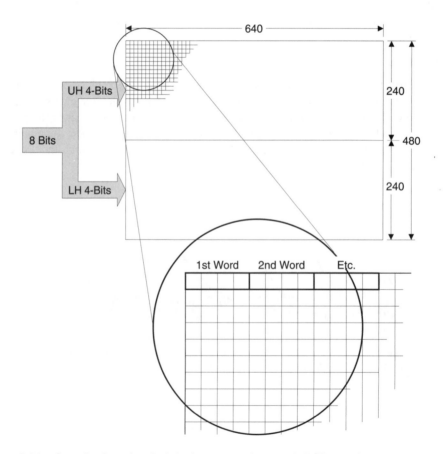

Figure 3.11   Organization of typical dual-scan passive matrix LCD panel.

A typical VGA LCD panel uses row-and-column driver devices that support 80 rows or columns each. Figure 3.12 illustrates how the row-and-column drivers are connected to the liquid crystal display panel and to the input data stream.

One curious property of the LCD is that the polarity of the pixel electrodes has to be reversed periodically, otherwise the liquid crystal molecules become electrically polarized and cease to return to their disorganized opaque state. This is generally done once per frame and is controlled by an external input signal. Figure 3.13 shows how the data and clock and other input signals are synchronized. Each pixel electrode is recharged once per frame.

The display is divided into two halves because this allows the horizontal frequency to be half of what it would be otherwise. The entire display then can be refreshed in half the time, reducing the delay between refreshing the top half and the bottom half of the screen. Simply refreshing each row one at a time from top to bottom of the entire display would be much more likely to produce visible flickering effects. This is because between refresh pulses the charge on each pixel electrode gradually decays due to internal leakage currents. This accounts for the relationship between refresh frequency and contrast ratio. It also makes it possible to generate gray-scale images on what would otherwise be a plain black-and-white digital display. Figure 3.14 illustrates for one pixel electrode how the charge gradually leaks down between refresh pulses. By omitting a certain percentage of

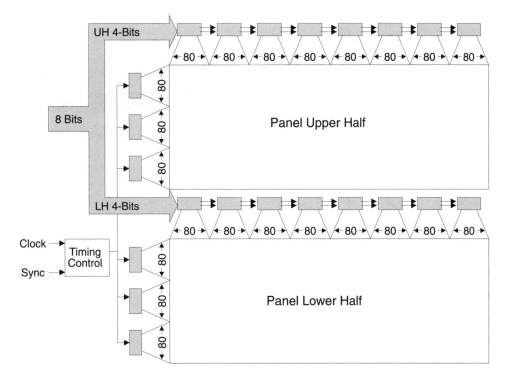

Figure 3.12 Row-and-column drivers in LCD panel.

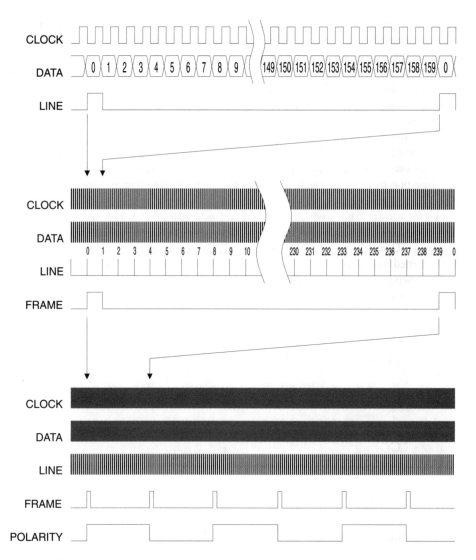

Figure 3.13   Data and clock synchronization in LCD panel.

Figure 3.14   Illustration of LCD pixel charge leakage.

refresh pulses to a pixel electrode that would otherwise be turned on, the average charge of that electrode can be maintained at some level between full off and full on.

Of course, the longer the interval between refresh pulses, the more likely there will be visible flickering. Also, the harmonic interaction between the effective refresh rate of gray-scale pixels and the normal refresh rate, combined with the vertical scanning motion of the display, can create standing wave patterns visible to the user. Therefore, manufacturers of LCD controller devices often incorporate complex spatial and temporal dithering algorithms into their devices for generating gray-scale display. The effect of this is to stagger the refresh timing of adjacent pixels that are being maintained at the same gray-scale intensity level. While this is fairly effective in most cases, it is virtually impossible to eliminate all such visual artifacts. These can be observed on the LCD panels of even the best portable computers by creating a gray-scale test pattern on the display that shows all the possible gray scales supported by the machine and then adjusting the brightness and contrast controls until the interference patterns become visible. Another factor that affects the display quality of the LCD panel is the lighting method used. Some older systems used simple reflective lighting where the LCD panel was backed by a black material that absorbed light. When a display element was turned on the light would simply pass through the panel and be absorbed creating a dark area. Otherwise the light would be reflected from the surface of the LCD. This tends to produce very poor contrast ratios, however, because the surface of the liquid crystal is not especially reflective. A much better system, which is quite common today, is the use of backlighting. This technique involves placing a thin fluorescent tube along one or more edges of the LCD. The tube is completely enclosed in a housing on the back side of a panel. The housing contains a special reflective material that distributes the light as evenly as possible over the surface behind the LCD. When a display pixel is turned on, the light shows through. Figure 3.15 illustrates the LCD backlighting cavity. Of course, the LCD material is not perfectly opaque so some light shows through, even when no pixels are turned on.

Active Matrix LCD

The primary difference between an active matrix and passive matrix LCD is the fact that each pixel electrode may be continuously driven to one state or another in an active matrix LCD. This required the development of thin film transistors that could be deposited on the surface of an LCD panel. Active matrix displays are therefore sometimes called TFT (thin film transistor) displays. The advantage of this approach is that there is less charge decay on the pixel electrodes due to the relatively long interval between refresh pulses as in the passive matrix system. This allows a much high-

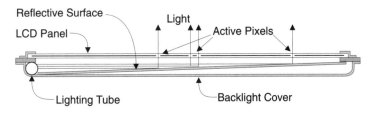

Figure 3.15   LCD backlighting cavity.

er contrast ratio and creates a much sharper looking display. Recall that the ability of the human eye to perceive spatial variation is heavily dependent on contrast. Most color LCD panels are built using active matrix technology. For a color LCD, the input data interface operates about the same as for a passive matrix display, except that there are more digital inputs and the display is not split. Each color pixel actually consists of three charge electrodes, each with a transparent color filter deposited on the surface. These color filters represent the three primary colors. Rather than an 8-bit input split into two 4-bit values there is a 12-bit input split into three 4-bit values. The three 4-bit values represent the red, green, and blue binary control bits for each of four pixels. In its simplest form, this scheme can generate white, black, and six colors in between just like the EGA or CGA digital CRT displays. Figure 3.16 illustrates a typical arrangement for the three primary color electrodes and a color active matrix LCD panel. To generate more than eight colors, the same techniques that are used in the passive matrix LCD panel for gray-scale can be used in the color active matrix LCD panel.

The total number of colors that can be displayed using this technique generally depends on the construction of the controlling device rather than on the panel itself. This is also true for the passive

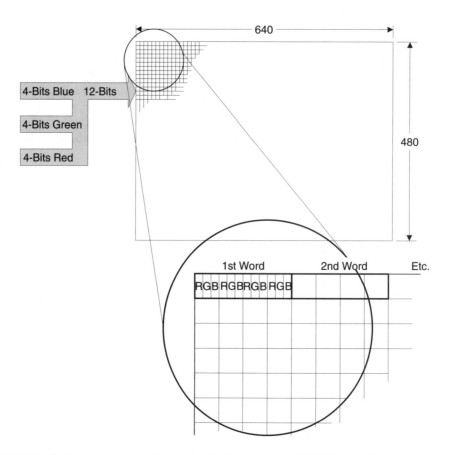

Figure 3.16   Color electrode and filter organization for color TFT LCD panel.

matrix panels regarding the total number of gray-scale levels that can be displayed. In practice there is an upper limit on the number of colors that can be displayed because of the total possible contrast ratio of the display. There is a point of diminishing returns in adding finer color quantization to the display controller because at some point the step from one color to the next becomes too small to be perceived by the viewer. For motion video display, quite acceptable results can be achieved with an active matrix LCD provided the display controller is capable of generating a wide enough range of color values for the display. This is generally not as true for a passive matrix LCD because the response time of the passive matrix panel tends to be considerably slower than that of the active matrix panel. This tends to produce smearing or trails when there is rapid motion in a video image. This, combined with the lower contrast ratio and lack of color, makes it difficult to discern what is happening in the motion video image. From a programming perspective LCD panels can be treated the same as any other PC display. The controlling devices are designed to emulate all the functions of an ordinary VGA display. Any program that works with a standard VGA adapter and CRT should work the same way on a portable system using an LCD panel.

Color Representation

Visible light is a form of electromagnetic radiation, part of the same spectrum as radio waves, microwaves, X-rays, and gamma rays. The portion of this spectrum visible to the human eye is a very narrow band from approximately 400 to 700 nM in wavelength. That's equivalent to a range between 16 and 28 millionths of an inch. Note that the total range includes only about 300 nM of difference. This would mean that if the human eye were capable of perceiving variations in color represented by only 1 nM change we would be able to perceive only about 300 different colors. Obviously, this is not so. Therefore, the human eye is capable of perceiving color variations represented by wavelength changes of less than one billionth of a meter. When white light is passed through a prism it appears to split into a range of colors. This is because the index of refraction is different for glass than it is for air. We all know that if you put one end of a pencil into a bowl of water it makes the pencil look as though it is bent. This works only if the pencil is not perpendicular to the surface of the water, otherwise it just makes the pencil look shorter. Different wavelengths are refracted by different amounts as they pass from one medium into another. This accounts for the separation of colors created by a prism. It is interesting to note that, depending on the source, a beam of white light may contain other frequencies of radiation beyond the visible spectrum and that these are refracted as well by the prism. Figure 4.1 illustrates a portion of the electromagnetic radiation spectrum. It should be noted that this diagram represents a logarithmic scale, so each major increment on the scale represents ten times the previous increment. The visible portion of the spectrum is found between infrared and ultraviolet radiation.

CIE Standard

The most commonly used standard for the measurement and specification of color is that defined by the International Commission on Illumination in 1931. This is referred to as the CIE standard. CIE stands for the French phrase *Commission Internationale de l'Eclairage*. The method used by the CIE was to define a spectral energy distribution for each of the three primary colors in the visible

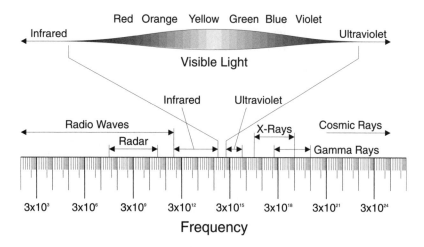

Figure 4.1   Electromagnetic spectrum with visible portion defined.

spectrum. From these a formula was derived that could be used to define any visible color in terms of the three primary colors. By taking a physical measurement of the spectral energy distribution in a color it is possible to calculate the amount of the three primaries to obtain a visual match with the color measured. Figure 4.2 shows the spectral distributions for the CIE-defined primary colors in terms of wavelength.

The spectral distributions for the three primary colors defined by the CIE are used to derive a two-dimensional coordinate space that comprehends all visible colors in the human visual system at all levels of saturation. This is referred to as the CIE chromaticity diagram. The chromaticity diagram is defined within a coordinate space between zero and one in both the x and y axis. It is derived from the spectral distributions by the following formulas:

$x = X/(X + Y + Z)$
$y = Y/(X + Y + Z)$

In the spectral distribution diagrams the capital letters X, Y, and Z correspond to the three primary color spectra for red, green, and blue. It should be noted that the three curves in the spectral distribution diagram represent relative intensities at each wavelength. The spectral distributions can be represented as a table of numbers as shown in Table 4.1. If the x and y coordinates in the chromaticity diagram are calculated for each discrete wavelength in the table, the resulting curve is the outline of the chromaticity diagram. This curve is referred to as the locus of pure spectral colors. It effectively represents pure monochromatic light at all the wavelengths within the visible spectrum.

In the one-by-one coordinate space the chromaticity diagram fits underneath the asymptote defined by $X + Y = 1$. Obviously the two ends of the curve represent the limits of the visible spectrum. If a straight line is drawn between the two extreme ends of the curve, the interior of the resulting figure represents all possible colors and saturation levels visible to the human eye. The

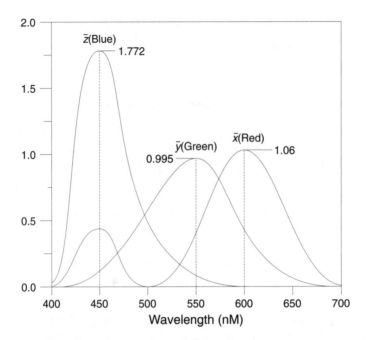

Figure 4.2 CIE spectral distributions for primary additive colors.

straight line is referred to as the locus of pure nonspectral colors. These are the colors resulting from various combinations of red and blue to produce purple and violet in various shades. If the x and y coordinates for the chromaticity diagram are calculated using the sum of all the values for each of the primary colors in the spectral distributions the resultant coordinates are approximately 0.3333 for both x and y. This point on the diagram represents white light because it contains elements at every wavelength in the visible spectrum. The color saturation at this point is said to be zero. This point on the diagram is referred to as the Illuminant C. It approximately represents what you might call average daylight. Any straight line passing through point C will obviously intersect the locus of pure colors at two points. These points are said to be contrasting colors. Each point on the outer curve of the chromaticity diagram is calculated by multiplying the CIE spectral distributions by a theoretically perfect narrow band spectrum consisting of one frequency. When this is done for each frequency within the visible spectrum the chromaticity diagram outline is the result, as illustrated by Figure 4.3.

If one dominant wavelength is selected for a reference spectrum and multiplied by the CIE spectra with a range of spectral distributions around the dominant wavelength in the reference spectrum the resulting points on the chromaticity diagram create a line that converges with the Illuminant point C. This is illustrated in Figure 4.4 for a wavelength in the green region. It is clear that a broader spectral distribution results in a less saturated color with white being represented by all wavelengths in the visible spectrum.

Table 4.1 Values for CIE Spectral Distribution Curves

Wavelength$_\lambda$ (nM)	x_λ	y_λ	z_λ
380	0.0014	0.0000	0.0065
390	0.0042	0.0001	0.0201
400	0.0143	0.0004	0.0679
410	0.0435	0.0012	0.2074
420	0.1344	0.0040	0.6456
430	0.2839	0.0116	1.3856
440	0.3483	0.0230	1.7471
450	0.3362	0.0380	1.7721
460	0.2908	0.0600	1.6692
470	0.1954	0.0910	1.2876
480	0.0956	0.1390	0.8130
490	0.0320	0.2080	0.4652
500	0.0049	0.3230	0.2720
510	0.0099	0.5030	0.1582
520	0.0633	0.7100	0.0782
530	0.1655	0.8620	0.0422
540	0.2904	0.9540	0.0203
550	0.4334	0.9850	0.0087
560	0.5945	0.9950	0.0039
570	0.7621	0.9520	0.0021
580	0.9163	0.8700	0.0017
590	1.0263	0.7570	0.0011
600	1.0622	0.6310	0.0008
610	1.0026	0.5030	0.0003
620	0.8544	0.3810	0.0002
630	0.6424	0.2650	0.0000
640	0.4479	0.1750	0.0000
650	0.2835	0.1070	0.0000
660	0.1649	0.0610	0.0000
670	0.0874	0.0320	0.0000
680	0.0468	0.0170	0.0000
690	0.0227	0.0082	0.0000
700	0.0114	0.0041	0.0000
710	0.0058	0.0021	0.0000
720	0.0029	0.0010	0.0000

It is also clear that the color content of any visible combination of wavelengths corresponds to exactly one point on the chromaticity diagram. For this reason, the CIE chromaticity diagram is widely used throughout industry as a common reference for color specification. It is possible, for example, to physically measure the spectral distribution of a given color and find its coordinates on the chromaticity diagram. These coordinates can then be communicated and used to exactly duplicate the original color. The CIE chromaticity diagram is the basis for the color model used in NTSC television.

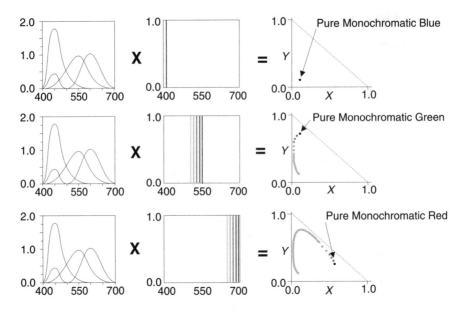

Figure 4.3   Process for plotting CIE chromaticity diagram outline.

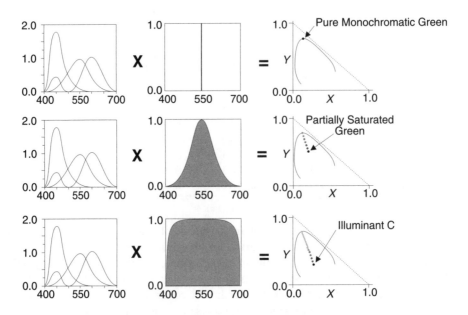

Figure 4.4   Process for plotting CIE chromaticity diagram interior points.

Conversion to RGB Color Space

Of course, it is fine to create two-dimensional diagrams from spectral distributions but it begs the question, "How do you recreate the necessary spectral distributions from a point on a two-dimensional diagram?" It is important to note that the chromaticity diagram represents all theoretically visible colors, not necessarily all colors that can be reproduced using currently available technology. For example, the phosphors used in the construction of cathode ray tubes produce colors that lie somewhere inside the boundaries of the CIE diagram. Using three primary colors thus plotted on the chromaticity diagram, the colors that can be represented will all fall within a triangle formed by the three points on the diagram, as illustrated by Figure 4.5.

To find the coordinates for a particular phosphor in the chromaticity diagram the spectral distribution of the phosphor is measured. This is then multiplied by each of the CIE spectral distributions and used to calculate the coordinates used on the chromaticity diagram. For example, Figure 4.6 illustrates how this might be done for a blue phosphor.

If this is done for each primary phosphor the effective result is a set of modified CIE spectral distributions. The modified spectral distributions can then each be multiplied by a scale factor that represents the range of values possible in the physical implementation to determine the effective points on the chromaticity diagram that will be produced by each combination of physical primary colors. Figure 4.7 illustrates how the coordinates of a specific color might be calculated for an arbitrary set of RGB values assuming a digital-to-analog converter with 256 quantization steps. Note that the X, Y, and Z used in the divisor for these calculations are the spectral distributions sums for the original CIE distributions.

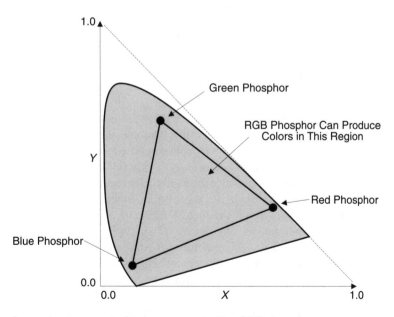

Figure 4.5   Approximate gamut of colors supported by CRT phosphor.

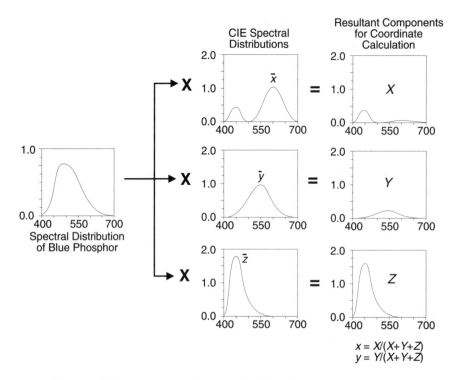

Figure 4.6 Example CIE coordinate calculation for blue phosphor.

The demonstration program named CIE_PLOT.EXE illustrates how the colors from a 256-color VGA system can be mapped onto the chromaticity diagram. The program works by dividing each of the primary color ranges into eight equal steps. The value eight is chosen because all the colors displayed have to fit into a palette of 256 possible colors, and the objective is to display as many colors as possible at full intensity with varying hue and saturation levels, not wasting any palette entries on shades of gray or low-intensity colors. It is also necessary to leave at least 16 palette entries unused so as not to disturb the basic VGA color set. The color set for the demonstration is defined such that at least one of the primary colors is always at full intensity. This creates two possible ways to vary the primary colors to produce the various combinations: The first is to set one color at a time to each of the possible values in its range. Because there are eight steps for each color, and there are three different colors, this will produce 24 different colors. The second is to vary a pair of primary colors throughout their ranges. This results in eight times eight, or 64 different colors for each pair. Because there are three pairs, this generates 192 different colors. This scheme therefore yields 216 distinct colors, which is a small enough number to fit into the VGA color palette without disturbing the standard 16 VGA colors. Because white is the unique case where all three primaries are at full intensity, only one entry in the palette is needed for white. Therefore, the eight color values used in generating the various color combinations can actually represent the first eight of nine different values for the primaries. To produce the diagram on the screen, a square coordinate space

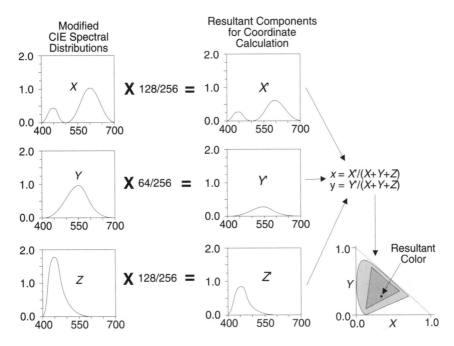

Figure 4.7   Example CIE coordinate calculation for digitized primary colors.

is defined representing the values zero to one in both X and Y directions. The outline of the chromaticity diagram is then plotted in the space by calculating the various points along the locus of pure spectral color. To plot the colors, a range of values is selected from each CIE spectral distribution to simulate the physical spectral distribution, and then the resulting spectral distribution is scaled so that the largest component is equal to the full-scale intensity level of one of the physical primary colors. The same scale factor is applied to the other two components used in the VGA card to program the RGB levels for each color entry in the palette. The coordinates for each point in the chromaticity diagram are then calculated using the methods described earlier and the point is plotted on the screen using the color defined in the palette that most closely matches that calculated from the spectral distribution. Of course, this doesn't fill every point in the diagram because of the limited number of distinct colors available in the VGA color palette. However, it does give an indication of how the colors are distributed throughout the chromaticity diagram. The main program module listing is shown here:

CIE_PLOT Program Listing

```
//=================================================
// VGA CIE Diagram Plotting Demonstration Program
//=================================================
//
// This program demonstrates the mathematics involved
```

```
// in deriving the CIE color model diagram. The program is
// built on a C++ DOS application programming shell
// provided in file SHELL256.CPP. It uses class
// definitions from include files CTRL_256.H and
// DISP_256.H to provide user interface functions for
// mouse control. Low level display functions are
// provided in assembly language files DRAW_BLK.ASM,
// DRWASCII.ASM, SETVMODE.ASM, and VPALETTE.ASM.
// To run, type "CIE_PLOT".
//
// Compiler:  Borland Turbo C++ Version 1.01
// Author:    Phil Mattison
// Date:      6/6/93
// Revision:  1.0
//================================================

#define APP_TITLE "CIE Diagram Plotting Demonstration"
#define X_LOC  60
#define Y_LOC  15

#include <stdio.h>
#include <conio.h>
#include <dos.h>
#include "ctrl_256.h"
#include "disp_256.h"

extern "C" void SetVmode(int);
extern "C" void DrawBlock(int,int,int,int,int);
extern "C" void DrawPixel(int,int,int);
extern "C" int  ReadPixel(int,int);
extern "C" void DrawASCII(int,int,int,int);
extern "C" void ReadEntry(int,unsigned char far *);
extern "C" void WriteEntry(int,int,int,int);

void SignOn(void)
  {
  DrawBlock(0,0,320,200,WHITE);          // White background
  DrawBlock(0,0,320,10,LIGHTBLUE);       // Title Bar
  DrawString(160-strlen(APP_TITLE)*4,2,APP_TITLE,WHITE); // Title
  DrawBlock(0,10,320,1,BLUE);            // Title Bar Outline
  DrawBlock(319,0,1,10,BLUE);
  DrawBlock(0,0,320,1,CYAN);
  DrawBlock(0,0,1,10,CYAN);
  DrawBlock(0,186,320,14,LIGHTGRAY);     // Message Bar
  DrawBlock(2,198,220,1,WHITE);
  DrawBlock(222,187,1,12,WHITE);
  DrawBlock(2,187,221,1,DARKGRAY);
  DrawBlock(2,187,1,12,DARKGRAY);
  }

int EscExit()           //Exit via Escape key (process KB input)
  {
```

```
   int st;
   st=kbhit();
   if(st!=0)
     {
     st=getch();
     if(st==27)return(RUN_DISABLED);
     }
   return(RUN_ENABLED);
   }

int Quit()          //Exit via mouse click
   {
   return(RUN_DISABLED);
   }

void UserMessage(char *message)
   {
   DrawBlock(3,189,218,10,LIGHTGRAY);
   DrawString(6,189,message,WHITE);
   DrawBlock(2,198,220,1,WHITE);
   }

//****************************************************
// Process mouse input
//****************************************************

float cie_table[140]=
   {
   380.0 ,0.0014 ,0.0000 ,0.0065,
   390.0 ,0.0042 ,0.0001 ,0.0201,
   400.0 ,0.0143 ,0.0004 ,0.0679,
   410.0 ,0.0435 ,0.0012 ,0.2074,
   420.0 ,0.1344 ,0.0040 ,0.6456,
   430.0 ,0.2839 ,0.0116 ,1.3856,
   440.0 ,0.3483 ,0.0230 ,1.7471,
   450.0 ,0.3362 ,0.0380 ,1.7721,
   460.0 ,0.2908 ,0.0600 ,1.6692,
   470.0 ,0.1954 ,0.0910 ,1.2876,
   480.0 ,0.0956 ,0.1390 ,0.8130,
   490.0 ,0.0320 ,0.2080 ,0.4652,
   500.0 ,0.0049 ,0.3230 ,0.2720,
   510.0 ,0.0099 ,0.5030 ,0.1582,
   520.0 ,0.0633 ,0.7100 ,0.0782,
   530.0 ,0.1655 ,0.8620 ,0.0422,
   540.0 ,0.2904 ,0.9540 ,0.0203,
   550.0 ,0.4334 ,0.9850 ,0.0087,
   560.0 ,0.5945 ,0.9950 ,0.0039,
   570.0 ,0.7621 ,0.9520 ,0.0021,
   580.0 ,0.9163 ,0.8700 ,0.0017,
   590.0 ,1.0263 ,0.7570 ,0.0011,
   600.0 ,1.0622 ,0.6310 ,0.0008,
   610.0 ,1.0026 ,0.5030 ,0.0003,
```

```
620.0 ,0.8544 ,0.3810 ,0.0002,
630.0 ,0.6424 ,0.2650 ,0.0000,
640.0 ,0.4479 ,0.1750 ,0.0000,
650.0 ,0.2835 ,0.1070 ,0.0000,
660.0 ,0.1649 ,0.0610 ,0.0000,
670.0 ,0.0874 ,0.0320 ,0.0000,
680.0 ,0.0468 ,0.0170 ,0.0000,
690.0 ,0.0227 ,0.0082 ,0.0000,
700.0 ,0.0114 ,0.0041 ,0.0000,
710.0 ,0.0058 ,0.0021 ,0.0000,
720.0 ,0.0029 ,0.0010 ,0.0000
};

int index,x,y,R,G,B;
int local_palette[3][256];

void FindCoordinates(int size) // Calculate chart coordinates and RGB value
  {
  float x_sum,y_sum,z_sum,xyz_sum,r_max;
  int i_tmp;

  i_tmp=index;
  x_sum=0.0;
  y_sum=0.0;
  z_sum=0.0;

  while(size>0)
    {
    x_sum+=cie_table[index+1];
    y_sum+=cie_table[index+2];
    z_sum+=cie_table[index+3];
    size--;
    index+=4;
    if(index>136)index=0;
    }
  xyz_sum=x_sum+y_sum+z_sum;
  x=(int)(200.0*x_sum/xyz_sum);
  y=(int)(150.0*y_sum/xyz_sum);

  r_max=x_sum;
  if(r_max<y_sum)r_max=y_sum;
  if(r_max<z_sum)r_max=z_sum;
  r_max=63.0/r_max;
  R=(int)r_max*x_sum;
  G=(int)r_max*y_sum;
  B=(int)r_max*z_sum;

  index=i_tmp;
  }

int FindMatch(int r,int g,int b) // Return index of nearest palette match.
  {
  int i,err,prev_err=192,idx=0;
```

```
    for(i=0;i<256;i++)
      {
      err=abs(local_palette[0][i]-r)+
          abs(local_palette[1][i]-g)+
          abs(local_palette[2][i]-b);
      if(err<prev_err)
        {
        idx=i;
        prev_err=err;
        }
      }
    return(idx);
    }

int CIE_Plot() // Plot points for various wavelengths and distributions
    {
    int size,color_index;
    UserMessage("Plotting.");
    DrawBlock(X_LOC,Y_LOC,200,152,BLACK);
    for(size=1;size<35;size++)
      {
      for(index=0;index<136;index+=4)
        {
        FindCoordinates(size);
        if(ReadPixel(x+X_LOC,Y_LOC+150-y)==0)
          {
          color_index=FindMatch(R,G,B);
          DrawPixel(x+X_LOC,Y_LOC+150-y,color_index);
          if(ReadPixel(x+X_LOC+1,Y_LOC+150-y+1)==0) // Splatter a little
            DrawPixel(x+X_LOC+1,Y_LOC+150-y+1,color_index);
          if(ReadPixel(x+X_LOC-1,Y_LOC+150-y-1)==0) // for better
            DrawPixel(x+X_LOC-1,Y_LOC+150-y-1,color_index);
          if(ReadPixel(x+X_LOC+1,Y_LOC+150-y-1)==0) // visibility.
            DrawPixel(x+X_LOC+1,Y_LOC+150-y-1,color_index);
          if(ReadPixel(x+X_LOC-1,Y_LOC+150-y+1)==0)
            DrawPixel(x+X_LOC-1,Y_LOC+150-y+1,color_index);
          }
        }
      }
    UserMessage("");
    return(RUN_ENABLED);
    }

//****************************************************

void main(void)
    {
    int i,j;
    unsigned char rgb_pal[3];
    SetVmode(0x13);
    SignOn();
    TControl Mouse;
    Mouse.SetStandardCallback(&EscExit);
```

```
Mouse.CreateButton(&Quit,226,187,90,11,"[Esc] Quit");
for(i=0;i<256;i++) // Get original hardware palette data
  {
  ReadEntry(i,rgb_pal);
  local_palette[0][i]=(int)rgb_pal[0];
  local_palette[1][i]=(int)rgb_pal[1];
  local_palette[2][i]=(int)rgb_pal[2];
  }
index=16;
for(i=0;i<8;i++)   // Load local palette with saturated color gamut
  {
  for(j=0;j<8;j++)
    {
    local_palette[0][index]=56-i*7;        //Red
    local_palette[1][index]=56-j*7;        //Green
    local_palette[2][index]=56;            //Blue
    local_palette[0][index+64]=56;         //Red
    local_palette[1][index+64]=56-j*7;     //Green
    local_palette[2][index+64]=56-i*7;     //Blue
    local_palette[0][index+128]=56-i*7;    //Red
    local_palette[1][index+128]=56;        //Green
    local_palette[2][index+128]=56-j*7;    //Blue
    index++;
    }
  }
for(i=16;i<208;i++) // Save new colors to hardware palette
  {
  WriteEntry(i,local_palette[0][i],
               local_palette[1][i],
               local_palette[2][i]);
  }
Mouse.CreateButton(&CIE_Plot,100,170,120,12,"Plot Diagram");
Mouse.Run();
SetVmode(3);
}
```

To derive the physical primary colors from the chromaticity diagram, if the physical properties of the color-generating device are known, a chromaticity diagram can be constructed for which each set of coordinates on the diagram has a corresponding set of primary color values to generate the known color. An independent source can then specify a position in the chromaticity diagram, and if the diagram was set up properly the coordinates can be used to extract a set of physical color generation parameters that should very nearly reproduce the original color as specified by the coordinates. It also gives an immediate indication whether the physical device is even capable of reproducing the precise color. If the required coordinates don't exactly match a point in the physically defined chromaticity diagram, the nearest point can be found by interpolation. The CIE chromaticity diagram, therefore, provides a relatively simple and effective way to measure and communicate information that would otherwise be very subjective. Probably everyone has heard an argument over whether or not something was blue or green at one time or another. With the CIE system it is no longer necessary to name the colors; they can be specified mathematically.

Additive versus Subtractive Primaries

The color primaries used in the CIE system are referred to as *additive primaries*. This means that when all the primaries are added together into equal quantities the result is white light. Colors other than the primary colors are then formed by adding the primary colors in various ratios. The color primaries used for printing and painting are called *subtractive primaries* because they create color by reflecting only a certain amount of light and absorbing (or subtracting) the rest. The subtractive primary colors are magenta, yellow, and cyan. The subtractive nature of these primaries can be easily demonstrated by observing a magenta object in a nearly pure green light. It becomes impossible to tell that the object is magenta; it appears black. The magenta object only reflects magenta, so when light that is mostly green wavelengths strikes it, most of the light is absorbed and the object appears black, just as a black object absorbs light at all wavelengths. A key difference between the two color-primary systems is the use of yellow instead of green in the subtractive system. The eye tends to be most sensitive to wavelengths in the yellow region, so yellow as a subtractive primary absorbs the least amount of light visible to the human eye. When subtractive primary colors are mixed, they form the new color by subtracting more than the primaries individually. This can be illustrated by considering white light as a combination of all visible light. Yellow paint, for example, absorbs blue wavelengths and reflects yellow wavelengths. This is illustrated in Figure 4.8.

If the yellow pigment is mixed with a red pigment the red pigment now tends to absorb both yellow and blue light so the total amount of reflected light is reduced, shifting the dominant wavelength toward the red into the orange region. This is illustrated in Figure 4.9.

The absorption property of pigments can be easily observed by noting that as more and more colors of paint are mixed together the resulting color becomes more and more murky and dark. For additive primaries, green makes a good center primary because it is not a color the eye is most sensitive to yet it is still near the center of the visible spectrum. Green light and red light (if they are not pure monochromatic light) for example, each represent a spectral distribution with the dominant wavelength near green or red, respectively. Because under normal circumstances they are spectral *distributions*, when they are added together the distributions tend to overlap considerably. This overlap creates a region between the two dominant wavelengths where both primary sources are

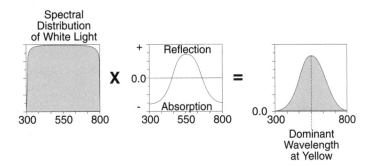

Figure 4.8   Absorption of red and blue wavelengths resulting in yellow dominant wavelength.

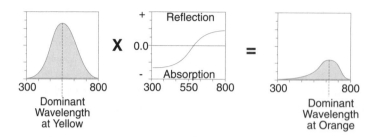

Figure 4.9   Absorption of yellow and blue wavelengths resulting in orange dominant wavelength.

contributing light at the same wavelengths. This results in a new distribution with a new dominant wavelength between the two primary wavelengths as illustrated in Figure 4.10. In the case of green and red the new dominant wavelength is in the region of yellow and the total light energy transmitted is greater than either of the primaries at the dominant frequency.

The subtractive primaries are yellow, which absorbs mostly blue; magenta, which absorbs mostly green; and cyan, which absorbs mostly red. These can be mixed in pairs to produce red, blue, and green. The additive primaries, of course, are red, green and blue, which can be mixed in pairs to produce yellow, magenta, and cyan. Figure 4.11 illustrates this. Note that when all three additive primaries are mixed the resulting color is white light.

When all three subtractive primaries are mixed, theoretically, the resulting color is black, but because of the imperfect absorption powers of most subtractive primary pigments, the actual color is not black but sort of a gray or brown. This is why most printing processes use a four-color process rather than three because the fourth color is black to compensate for the inability of the primary colors to produce black. A color model using cyan, magenta, and yellow, referred to as the CMY model, can be conceptualized as a three-dimensional space with cyan on one axis, magenta on another axis, and yellow on the third axis. White is at the origin representing zero pigment and black is at the opposite corner of the cube. Figure 4.12 illustrates this three-dimensional model.

Another commonly used color model often used in the interior design industry is known as the *Munsell Color Space*. The normal method of using the system is to match the desired color against a standard set of paint chips known as the *Munsell Book of Color*. A number is assigned to each color. The system uses three parameters known as *hue*, *value*, and *chroma*. Hue refers to the actual color and

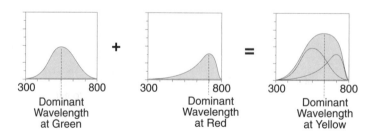

Figure 4.10   Addition of red and green wavelengths resulting in yellow dominant wavelength.

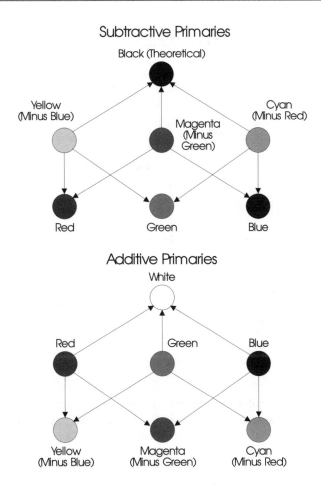

Figure 4.11   Additive and subtractive primary color relationships.

is defined as five basic colors: purple, blue, green, yellow, and red; and five intermediate colors: purple-blue, blue-green, green-yellow, yellow-red, and red-purple. The transition from each color to the next is defined on a ten-point scale so that effectively there are a hundred different hues defined in the system. Value refers to the lightness of a color and has a range of values from zero, which is very dark, to ten, which is very light. Intuitively this could be thought of as how much black is mixed with the color; zero being the maximum amount of black. Chroma refers to the saturation, or purity, of the color. This ranges from zero, which means no color, to 14, which means fully saturated, or pure color. Any color in the system can be specified using a letter code and two numbers specifying value and chroma. To get an accurate match with the paint chips and the *Munsell Book of Color*, it is generally necessary to do the match under controlled lighting conditions. Figure 4.13 illustrates the three-dimensional model used for the Munsell Color Space. The conceptual model is in the form of a cylinder with hue defined as various points on the perimeter, value defined along the vertical axis of the perimeter, and chroma, or saturation, defined as the distance from the center.

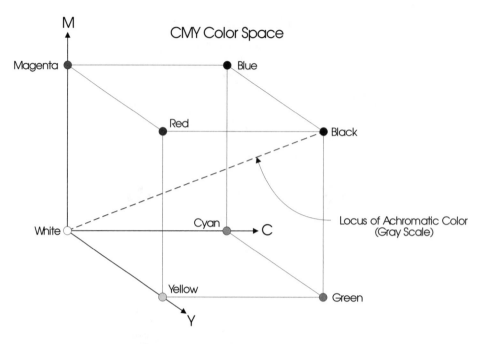

Figure 4.12 Conceptual model of the CMY color space.

Another fairly common color space model is the *HSV model*. HSV stands for *hue, saturation,* and *value*. It is conceptually similar to the Munsell Color Space except that it uses three primary and three secondary colors defined at specific angles around the vertical axis. These are defined as 0° for red, 60° for yellow, 120° for green, 180° for cyan, 240° for blue, and 300° for magenta. Contrasting colors are 180° apart, similar to the CIE chromaticity diagram. Saturation is defined in a way similar to the Munsell Color Space, ranging from a minimum value of zero to a maximum of one. It refers to the radial distance from the vertical axis of the model. Value is defined along the vertical central axis of the model and also ranges from zero to one. An interesting difference between this and the Munsell Color Space is that the possible range of saturation levels decreases uniformly as the color approaches a value of zero, which is black. A value of one with a saturation of zero is defined as white. Figure 4.14 illustrates the conceptual model of the HSV color space. There are no basic limitations on the accuracy of color specification built into the model. Note that if value equals zero, the other two parameters, hue and saturation, have no meaning. Also, if saturation equals zero then hue has no meaning.

YUV Color Space

The YUV color space is used in the British PAL broadcast television standard. *YUV* is not an acronym. The letters stand for the three components that define colors as derived from the red, green, and blue primary colors. The Y component represents luminance or total illumination. It is defined as a weighted sum of the red, green, and blue components. The scale factors for the prima-

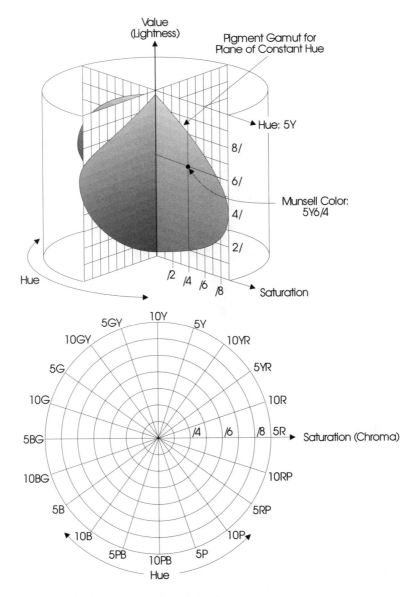

Figure 4.13   Conceptual model for Munsell Color Space.

ry colors in Y are 0.299 for red, 0.587 for green, and 0.114 for blue. Note that these three-scale factors add up to a value of one. The different percentages of red, green, and blue used in the formula reflect the differences in the human eye's response to different wavelength of light. The U and V components are coordinates that define hue and saturation in a coordinate space similar to that defined in the CIE chromaticity diagram. U and V are known as color difference values and repre-

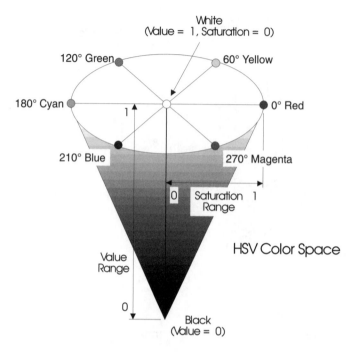

Figure 4.14   Conceptual model for HSV Color Space.

sent a relative distance from a zero saturation point in a color coordinate space along two perpendicular axes. U is defined as 0.493(B − Y), where B refers to Blue. V is defined as 0.877(R − Y), where R stands for Red. Because the coefficients for Y are known, it is a simple matter to calculate a new set of coefficients to derive U and V based on red, green, and blue. Substituting the formula for Y into the term (R − Y) results in

$$1.0R − 0.299R − 0.587G − 0.114B$$

Combining the red terms gives

$$(R-Y) = 0.701R − .587B − .114B$$

Applying the scale factor for V (0.877) across the three coefficients results in

$$V = 0.615R − 0.515G − 0.1B$$

A very similar process is used to calculate the U coefficient:

$$U = 0.493(B − Y)$$
$$U = 0.493(1.0B − 0.299R − 0.587G − 0.114B)$$
$$U = 0.493(0.886B − 0.299R − 0.587G)$$
$$U = 0.463B − 0.147R − 0.289G$$

The color definition system used for NTSC video is called YIQ. Y means the same thing as in the YUV system in this case, and the I and the Q stand for in-phase and quadrature, respectively. The in-phase and quadrature terminology reflect the modulation techniques used to transmit color information in the NTSC signal as described in Chapter 2. The I and Q components are actually derived from the U and V components in the YUV system. I and Q are defined as:

$$I = V\cos 33° − U\sin 33°$$
$$Q = V\sin 33° + U\cos 33°$$

Of course, the sine and cosine terms have meaning only in the context of a modulated signal. Yet another color system, referred to as YDrDb, is used for the French SECAM broadcast system. This is calculated very similarly to the YUV color system except that different coefficients are used in calculating the Dr and Db components. Dr refers to difference in red and Db refers to difference in blue. Again, the Y component is calculated in the same way as in the previous two systems. Dr and Db are calculated as:

$$Dr = −1.902(R − Y)$$
$$Db = 1.505(B − Y)$$

In response to increasing demands for digital methods for handling video information, the CCIR has defined a digital color system known as YCrCb. CCIR stands for *International Consultative Committee on Broadcasting* (another acronym for foreign words). This specification is spelled out in CCIR recommendation 601-2 and is sometimes referred to as the CCIR 601 color space. The definition is essentially the same as the YUV color space without the coefficients for U and V (this refers to the 0.493 for U and 0.877 for V), plus a few other minor modifications to allow integer math. The Cr component is equivalent to (R − Y), and the Cb component is equivalent to (B − Y). The coefficients used in the matrix multiplication to transform RGB values into Y, Cr, and Cb values are defined as fractions each having a divisor of 256. This allows a simple multiply-and-shift operation to approximate the real number values used in the other systems. The fractional coefficients applied to (R − Y) and (B − Y) in the PAL, NTSC, and SECAM systems are not used in the YCrCb system. These coefficients were necessary to compensate for certain physical characteristics of the broadcast and reception electronics used with the respective systems and are not necessary for a digital system.

It is important to understand the meaning of the terms (R − Y) and (B − Y). These are known as color difference signals and as such carry no brightness information. It would be natural to assume, for example, that (R − Y) controls the amount of redness in the image. Actually, however, that wouldn't be totally accurate. A positive (R − Y) corresponds to a purplish-red color, whereas a negative (R − Y) corresponds to bluish-green. The (B − Y) axis is perpendicular to (R − Y) so that a positive (B − Y) corresponds to purplish-blue and a negative (B − Y) corresponds to greenish-yellow. Mapped to the CIE chromaticity diagram the (R − Y) and (B − Y) axes cross at the Illuminant C. Figure 4.15 illustrates how the (R − Y) and (B − Y) axes are mapped to the CIE chromaticity diagram. It is clear from the diagram that when (R − Y) and (B − Y) are zero, color saturation is zero and the Y value simply creates various shades of gray.

To facilitate manipulation in an unsigned integer number system, the YCrCb color system offsets the (R − Y) and (B − Y) components by 128. Thus, numbers below 128 represent negative values and numbers above 128 represent positive values. The application of the sine and cosine of

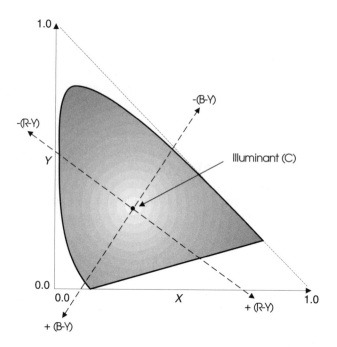

Figure 4.15   Orientation of (R − Y) and (B − Y) axes on CIE chromaticity diagram.

33 degrees to the (R − Y) and (B − Y) values transforms them into a polar coordinate space resulting in a color model very similar to the HSV color space. Figure 4.16 illustrates the relative positions of (B − Y), (R − Y), I and Q in a polar coordinate space.

The orientation of the I and Q axes was specifically chosen to take advantage of differences in the sensitivity of the human eye to different colors. The human visual system is more sensitive to colors in the orange-blue color axis where flesh tones are found than in the purple-green range. In the NTSC signal, more bandwidth is allocated to the I axis ,which is the orange-blue axis, than to the Q axis. This effectively allows a finer quantization of color variations in the range where the eye is most sensitive. Table 4.2 illustrates the relative bandwidths allocated to Y, I, and Q for the NTSC signal.

It is interesting to note that this optimization is lost in the conversion to YCrCb color space, which makes no provision for asymmetric color resolution. Of course, it could be argued that the sampling frequency for digital video easily exceeds the bandwidth of either the I or Q components in NTSC video. It should be remembered, though, that no matter how high the sampling rate for digital video is it cannot in any way carry more information than the original signal. It certainly does not make sense to have a sampling frequency higher than the color burst frequency, because in an analog system the color burst frequency effectively *is* the color sampling frequency. Of course, to decode a composite NTSC signal it is *necessary* to have a sampling frequency higher than the subcarrier frequency. A digital NTSC color TV frame (active image area) is defined as 640 × 480 pixels. Taking into account blanking and retrace times, this works out to a sampling frequency of about 14.3 MHz or four times the color burst frequency. Given the bandwidth of the basic color signals

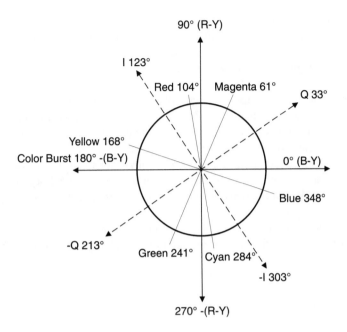

Figure 4.16   Relative orientation of I and Q to (R − Y) and (B − Y).

Table 4.2   Relative Bandwidths of Y, I, and Q Parameters

	Maximum Frequency		
Signal	*MHz*	*Cycles/Pixel*	*Cycles/Line*
Y	4.2	1/3.4	267
I	1.5	1/9.5	96
Q	0.55	1/26	35

this represents significant oversampling of color information. As will be seen in Chapter 5, this fact can be taken advantage of by subsampling the color information to increase compression ratios.

Color Space Conversions

Conversion from any of the color systems that use a separate luminance component (i.e., Y) into HSV color space is fairly straightforward. It has already been shown that the YUV, YIQ, and YDrDb color spaces are all quite similar to each other, involving mostly differences in coefficients and slight translations in the coordinate space used for color information. All of these calculate the Y component from RGB in exactly the same way. All of them use a two-dimensional coordinate system to define color in a space very similar to the CIE chromaticity diagram. Conversion from any of these systems into HSV simply involves scaling the Y value to a range of zero to one and converting the Cartesian coordinates of the color components into polar coordinates using the phase angle to define hue and the magnitude to define saturation. The magnitude is, of course, scaled to a range from zero to one.

Once the mathematical relationships between color systems are understood, it is a fairly straightforward matter to convert from one to another. We've already demonstrated how to derive each of the broadcast color standards from RGB color coordinates. Converting from any of these back into RGB is simply a matter of reversing the formula. Because the method in each case (with the possible exception of YIQ) is so similar, each of the conversions can be shown as a simple matrix multiplication with a set of coefficients derived from the constants defined for each color space discussed above. Table 4.3 summarizes the matrix multiplication coefficients for each of the broadcast color spaces.

Conversion to HSV color space is most easily accomplished from YCrCb because the (B − Y) value is defined on an axis coincident with the zero degree phase angle of the HSV model.

Table 4.3   Summary of Color Space Conversion Coefficients

PAL

Y = 0.299R + 0.587G + 0.114B	
U = 0.463B − 0.147R − 0.289G	NOTE: U = 0.493(B − Y)
V = 0.615R − 0.515G − 0.100B	NOTE: V = 0.877(R − Y)

NTSC

Y = 0.299R + 0.587G + 0.114B	
I = 0.596R − 0.271G − 0.322B	NOTE: I = Vcos33° − Usin33°
Q = 0.211R − 0.522G + 0.311B	NOTE: Q = Vsin33° + Ucos33°

SECAM

Y = 0.299R + 0.587G + 0.114B	
Db = 1.333B − 0.450R − 0.883G	NOTE: Db = 1.505(B − Y)
Dr = 0.217B − 0.133R + 1.116G	NOTE: Dr = 1.902(R − Y)

CCIR 601(YCrCb)

Y = 77R/256 + 150G/256 + 29B/256	
Cr = [131R/256 − 110G/256 − 21B/256] + 128	NOTE: Cr = (R − Y)+128
Cb = [131B/256 − 44R/256 − 87G/256] + 128	NOTE: Cb = (B − Y)+128

Therefore, the (B − Y) and (R − Y) values can be used as simple *x-y* coordinates in the conversion into polar coordinate space. Recall in Figure 4.16 that (B − Y) and (R − Y) can be either positive or negative. The YCrCb color space offsets these by 128 so that values below 128 represent negative values. To convert to polar notation the offset must be removed. Recall from trigonometry that the tangent of an angle can be derived from polar coordinates by the formula:

$$\tan\theta = \text{opposite/adjacent}$$

where opposite is the vertical axis (R − Y) and adjacent is horizontal (B − Y). Therefore, the color angle for HSV can be calculated from YCrCb by:

$$\text{color}\theta = \arctan((Cr - 128)/(Cb - 128)).$$

Of course, there is a danger of dividing by zero in this approach, which tends to make computers complain bitterly. This can be avoided by using an alternate form:

$$\sin\theta = \text{opposite/hypotenuse}$$

where the hypotenuse can be calculated by:

$$\text{hyp} = \text{square\_root}((Cr - 128)^2 + (Cb - 128)^2)$$

An extra benefit of this approach is that the hypotenuse corresponds to saturation in the HSV color space, so it doesn't have to be calculated in a separate step. Because the values in HSV have a range from zero to one, the results of these calculations must be scaled accordingly. The final equations then, are:

$$V = Y/256$$
$$S = \text{square\_root}((Cr - 128)^2 + (Cb - 128)^2)/128$$
$$H = \arcsin(((Cr - 128)/128)/S)$$

Conversion back into RGB is simplest for the YCrCb color model because of the lack of any special coefficients to compensate for physical electronic properties. The red and blue values can be reconstructed very simply by adding Y to Cr and Cb, which are (R − Y) + 128 and (B − Y) + 128 respectively. The value for green can then be reconstructed using red, blue, and Y. Recall that:

$$Y = 0.299R + 0.587G + 0.114B$$

Rearranging, to isolate Green:

$$0.587G = Y - 0.114B - 0.299R$$
$$G = (Y - 0.299R - 0.114B)/0.587$$
$$G = Y - 0.509R - 0.194B$$

The equations for conversion from YCrCb to RGB, therefore, are:

$$R = Y + Cr - 128$$
$$B = Y + Cb - 128$$
$$G = Y - 0.509R - 0.194B$$

Converting to RGB from YUV or YDrDb requires first multiplying the color components by the reciprocal of the coefficients used to compensate for physical device characteristics. After that, the conversion proceeds in the same way as for YCrCb. Conversion from YIQ is a little more complex because it involves a trigonometric translation to convert from YIQ into YUV color space before applying the rest of the conversion process as defined for YUV. The translation of I and Q back into U and V is as follows:

$$V = I\sin 33° + Q\cos 33°$$
$$U = I\cos 33° - Q\sin 33°$$

Color Space Conversion Software

Once the mathematical relationships between the various color space representations are well understood, software can be developed that will perform conversions from one space to another in the most efficient manner. Because this book deals with video image compression and real-time motion video display, it is critical that all phases of computation be performed as efficiently as possible to maximize image quality and frame rate. To do this, a common technique is to avoid multiply and divide operations wherever possible or to implement them as simple shift operations. This is done by arranging numerical operations such that anything involving a multiply or divide has one of the components as a power of two. The conversion coefficients for YCrCb color space are intentionally defined in this manner. A program named RGB_DEMO provided with this book illustrates the relationships between RGB and YCrCb color spaces as well as a programming technique for doing the conversions. The program displays a color on the screen along with its numeric representation in both RGB and YCrCb color spaces. The components of the color can be modified in real time by the user in either color space. The program immediately updates the color displayed and the numeric representation in the other color space to reflect the one modified. The source code for the main program module is listed here:

RGB_DEMO Program Listing

```
//===============================================
//   RGB vs YCrCb Color Space Demonstration Program
//===============================================
//
// This program demonstrates the relationship between
// RGB and YCrCb (YUV) color systems. The program is
// built on a C++ DOS application programming shell
// provided in file DOSSHELL.CPP. It uses class
// definitions from include files CONTROL.H and
// DISPLAY.H to provide user interface functions for
// mouse control. To run, type "RGB_DEMO".
//
// Compiler:  Borland Turbo C++ Version 1.01
// Author:    Phil Mattison
// Date:      4/25/93
// Revision:  1.0
//===============================================

#include "control.h"
```

```c
#include "display.h"
#include <stdio.h>
#include <string.h>
#include <graphics.h>
#include <conio.h>

#define APP_TITLE "RGB/YCrCb Demonstration"

#define C1              70
#define C2              170
#define C3              270
#define C4              370
#define C5              470
#define R1              200
#define R2              240
#define R3              280
#define R4              330
#define R5              370
#define R6              410
#define BUTTON_SIZE     80,24
#define LBL_SIZE        32,24
#define BOX_POSITION    70,50
#define BOX_END         550,170

TDisplay                *R,*G,*B,*Y,*Cr,*Cb;
struct palettetype      palette;
int                     Rv,Gv,Bv,Yv,Crv,Cbv;

void SignOn(void)
  {
  setfillstyle(SOLID_FILL,WHITE);
  bar(0,0,639,479);                             // White background
  setfillstyle(SOLID_FILL,LIGHTBLUE);
  setcolor(BLUE);
  setlinestyle(SOLID_LINE,0,THICK_WIDTH);
  bar3d(0,0,639,20,0,0);                        // Title Bar
  setcolor(WHITE);                              // Title
  settextjustify(CENTER_TEXT,CENTER_TEXT);
  outtextxy(320,10,APP_TITLE);
  setcolor(CYAN);                               // Title Bar Outline
  line(0,0,639,0);
  line(0,0,0,20);
  setfillstyle(SOLID_FILL,LIGHTGRAY);
  setcolor(BLACK);
  setlinestyle(SOLID_LINE,0,NORM_WIDTH);
  bar3d(0,455,639,479,0,0);                     // Message Bar
  rectangle(4,457,532,476);
  setcolor(WHITE);
  line(4,476,532,476);
  line(532,457,532,476);
  setfillstyle(SOLID_FILL,LIGHTGRAY);
  setcolor(BLACK);
```

```
  setlinestyle(SOLID_LINE,0,THICK_WIDTH);
  }

int EscExit() //Exit via Escape key (process KB input)
  {
  int st;
  st=kbhit();
  if(st!=0)
    {
    st=getch();
    if(st==27)return(RUN_DISABLED);
    }
  return(RUN_ENABLED);
  }

int Quit()        //Exit via mouse click
  {
  return(RUN_DISABLED);
  }

void UserMessage(char *message)
  {
  setfillstyle(SOLID_FILL,LIGHTGRAY);
  bar(5,458,530,474);
  setcolor(WHITE);
  settextjustify(LEFT_TEXT,CENTER_TEXT);
  outtextxy(12,468,message);
  }

//****************************************************
// User functions here (Process mouse input)
//****************************************************

void ShowColor(void)
  {
  R->Show(Rv);
  G->Show(Gv);
  B->Show(Bv);
  Y->Show(Yv);
  Cr->Show(Crv);
  Cb->Show(Cbv);
  setrgbpalette(palette.colors[LIGHTMAGENTA],Rv>>2,Gv>>2,Bv>>2);
  }

//****************************************************
// Here we translate from RGB into YCrCb. For the
// sake of simplicity, this routine does not scale
// the YCrCb values to the official range of 220
// LSB's, but rather retains the full swing of 256.
// Note the temporary variables are unsigned integers,
// and the RGB values are cast to unsigned integer
// values to prevent math overflow errors. The
```

```
// constants used in this function are derived as
// follows:
//                     0.299 ~=  77/256
//                     0.587 ~= 150/256
//                     0.114 ~=  29/256
//                     0.701 ~= 180/256
//                     0.886 ~= 227/256
//
// The conversion formula used is:
//
//        Y  = 0.299R + 0.587G + 0.114B
//        Cr = 0.701R - 0.587G - 0.114B
//        Cb = 0.886B - 0.587G - 0.299R
//****************************************************
void CalculateYCrCb(void)
  {
  unsigned int Rc,Gc,Bc,Rx,Bx;
  Rc=((unsigned int)Rv*77)/256;
  Gc=((unsigned int)Gv*150)/256;
  Bc=((unsigned int)Bv*29)/256;
  Rx=((unsigned int)Rv*180)/256;
  Bx=((unsigned int)Bv*227)/256;
  Yv=Rc+Gc+Bc;
  Crv=Rx-Gc-Bc+128;
  Cbv=Bx-Gc-Rc+128;
  if(Yv>255)Yv=255;
  if(Crv>255)Crv=255;
  if(Cbv>255)Cbv=255;
  if(Yv<0)Yv=0;
  if(Crv<0)Crv=0;
  if(Cbv<0)Cbv=0;
  }


//****************************************************
// Here we translate from YCrCb to RGB. This is simply
// the inverse of the matrix calculation performed
// above. Note that because the Cr and Cb values can
// be negative, unsigned integers cannot be used.
// Therefore, The Cr constant multiplication (which
// could cause an overflow) is split into two smaller
// operations. The constants are derived as follows:
//
//        0.509 ~= 130/256 (or 65/256 + 65/256)
//        0.194 ~=  50/256
//
// The conversion formula used is:
//
//        R == Y + Cr
//        G == Y - 0.509Cr - 0.194Cb
//        B == Y + Cb
//****************************************************
void CalculateRGB(void)
```

```
    {
    int Crc,Cbc;
    Crc=Crv-128;
    Cbc=Cbv-128;
    Rv=Yv+Crc;
    Gv=Yv-(65*Crc)/256-(65*Crc)/256-(50*Cbc)/256;
    Bv=Yv+Cbc;
    if(Rv>255)Rv=255;
    if(Gv>255)Gv=255;
    if(Bv>255)Bv=255;
    if(Rv<0)Rv=0;
    if(Gv<0)Gv=0;
    if(Bv<0)Bv=0;
    }

int ButtonRP16()
    {
    Rv+=16;
    if(Rv>255)Rv=255;
    CalculateYCrCb();
    ShowColor();
    return(RUN_ENABLED);
    }

int ButtonRP04()
    {
    Rv+=4;
    if(Rv>255)Rv=255;
    CalculateYCrCb();
    ShowColor();
    return(RUN_ENABLED);
    }

int ButtonRM04()
    {
    Rv-=4;
    if(Rv<0)Rv=0;
    CalculateYCrCb();
    ShowColor();
    return(RUN_ENABLED);
    }

int ButtonRM16()
    {
    Rv-=16;
    if(Rv<0)Rv=0;
    CalculateYCrCb();
    ShowColor();
    return(RUN_ENABLED);
    }

int ButtonGP10()
```

```
    {
    Gv+=16;
    if(Gv>255)Gv=255;
    CalculateYCrCb();
    ShowColor();
    return(RUN_ENABLED);
    }

int ButtonGP01()
    {
    Gv+=4;
    if(Gv>255)Gv=255;
    CalculateYCrCb();
    ShowColor();
    return(RUN_ENABLED);
    }

int ButtonGM01()
    {
    Gv-=4;
    if(Gv<0)Gv=0;
    CalculateYCrCb();
    ShowColor();
    return(RUN_ENABLED);
    }

int ButtonGM10()
    {
    Gv-=16;
    if(Gv<0)Gv=0;
    CalculateYCrCb();
    ShowColor();
    return(RUN_ENABLED);
    }

int ButtonBP10()
    {
    Bv+=16;
    if(Bv>255)Bv=255;
    CalculateYCrCb();
    ShowColor();
    return(RUN_ENABLED);
    }

int ButtonBP01()
    {
    Bv+=4;
    if(Bv>255)Bv=255;
    CalculateYCrCb();
    ShowColor();
    return(RUN_ENABLED);
    }
```

```
int ButtonBM01()
  {
  Bv-=4;
  if(Bv<0)Bv=0;
  CalculateYCrCb();
  ShowColor();
  return(RUN_ENABLED);
  }

int ButtonBM10()
  {
  Bv-=16;
  if(Bv<0)Bv=0;
  CalculateYCrCb();
  ShowColor();
  return(RUN_ENABLED);
  }


int ButtonYP16()
  {
  Yv+=16;
  if(Yv>255)Yv=255;
  CalculateRGB();
  ShowColor();
  return(RUN_ENABLED);
  }

int ButtonYP04()
  {
  Yv+=4;
  if(Yv>255)Yv=255;
  CalculateRGB();
  ShowColor();
  return(RUN_ENABLED);
  }

int ButtonYM04()
  {
  Yv-=4;
  if(Yv<0)Yv=0;
  CalculateRGB();
  ShowColor();
  return(RUN_ENABLED);
  }

int ButtonYM16()
  {
  Yv-=16;
  if(Yv<0)Yv=0;
  CalculateRGB();
  ShowColor();
```

```c
  return(RUN_ENABLED);
  }

int ButtonCrP10()
  {
  Crv+=16;
  if(Crv>255)Crv=255;
  CalculateRGB();
  ShowColor();
  return(RUN_ENABLED);
  }

int ButtonCrP01()
  {
  Crv+=4;
  if(Crv>255)Crv=255;
  CalculateRGB();
  ShowColor();
  return(RUN_ENABLED);
  }

int ButtonCrM01()
  {
  Crv-=4;
  if(Crv<0)Crv=0;
  CalculateRGB();
  ShowColor();
  return(RUN_ENABLED);
  }

int ButtonCrM10()
  {
  Crv-=16;
  if(Crv<0)Crv=0;
  CalculateRGB();
  ShowColor();
  return(RUN_ENABLED);
  }

int ButtonCbP10()
  {
  Cbv+=16;
  if(Cbv>255)Cbv=255;
  CalculateRGB();
  ShowColor();
  return(RUN_ENABLED);
  }

int ButtonCbP01()
  {
  Cbv+=4;
  if(Cbv>255)Cbv=255;
```

```
   CalculateRGB();
   ShowColor();
   return(RUN_ENABLED);
   }

int ButtonCbM01()
   {
   Cbv-=4;
   if(Cbv<0)Cbv=0;
   CalculateRGB();
   ShowColor();
   return(RUN_ENABLED);
   }

int ButtonCbM10()
   {
   Cbv-=16;
   if(Cbv<0)Cbv=0;
   CalculateRGB();
   ShowColor();
   return(RUN_ENABLED);
   }
//****************************************************
void main(void)
   {
   int         gdriver=VGA;
   int         gmode=VGAHI;
   TDisplay    *LR,*LG,*LB,*LY,*LCr,*LCb;
   initgraph(&gdriver,&gmode,"");
   SignOn();
   TControl Mouse;
   Mouse.SetStandardCallback(&EscExit);
   Mouse.CreateButton(&Quit,536,457,98,20,"[Esc] Quit");

   Mouse.CreateButton(&ButtonRM16,C1,R1,BUTTON_SIZE,"<<");
   Mouse.CreateButton(&ButtonRM04,C2,R1,BUTTON_SIZE,"<");
   Mouse.CreateButton(&ButtonRP04,C4,R1,BUTTON_SIZE,">");
   Mouse.CreateButton(&ButtonRP16,C5,R1,BUTTON_SIZE,">>");

   Mouse.CreateButton(&ButtonGM10,C1,R2,BUTTON_SIZE,"<<");
   Mouse.CreateButton(&ButtonGM01,C2,R2,BUTTON_SIZE,"<");
   Mouse.CreateButton(&ButtonGP01,C4,R2,BUTTON_SIZE,">");
   Mouse.CreateButton(&ButtonGP10,C5,R2,BUTTON_SIZE,">>");

   Mouse.CreateButton(&ButtonBM10,C1,R3,BUTTON_SIZE,"<<");
   Mouse.CreateButton(&ButtonBM01,C2,R3,BUTTON_SIZE,"<");
   Mouse.CreateButton(&ButtonBP01,C4,R3,BUTTON_SIZE,">");
   Mouse.CreateButton(&ButtonBP10,C5,R3,BUTTON_SIZE,">>");

   Mouse.CreateButton(&ButtonYM16,C1,R4,BUTTON_SIZE,"<<");
   Mouse.CreateButton(&ButtonYM04,C2,R4,BUTTON_SIZE,"<");
   Mouse.CreateButton(&ButtonYP04,C4,R4,BUTTON_SIZE,">");
```

```
Mouse.CreateButton(&ButtonYP16,C5,R4,BUTTON_SIZE,">>");

Mouse.CreateButton(&ButtonCrM10,C1,R5,BUTTON_SIZE,"<<");
Mouse.CreateButton(&ButtonCrM01,C2,R5,BUTTON_SIZE,"<");
Mouse.CreateButton(&ButtonCrP01,C4,R5,BUTTON_SIZE,">");
Mouse.CreateButton(&ButtonCrP10,C5,R5,BUTTON_SIZE,">>");

Mouse.CreateButton(&ButtonCbM10,C1,R6,BUTTON_SIZE,"<<");
Mouse.CreateButton(&ButtonCbM01,C2,R6,BUTTON_SIZE,"<");
Mouse.CreateButton(&ButtonCbP01,C4,R6,BUTTON_SIZE,">");
Mouse.CreateButton(&ButtonCbP10,C5,R6,BUTTON_SIZE,">>");

R=  new TDisplay(C3,R1,BUTTON_SIZE,WHITE,BLACK,BORDER);
G=  new TDisplay(C3,R2,BUTTON_SIZE,WHITE,BLACK,BORDER);
B=  new TDisplay(C3,R3,BUTTON_SIZE,WHITE,BLACK,BORDER);
Y=  new TDisplay(C3,R4,BUTTON_SIZE,WHITE,BLACK,BORDER);
Cr= new TDisplay(C3,R5,BUTTON_SIZE,WHITE,BLACK,BORDER);
Cb= new TDisplay(C3,R6,BUTTON_SIZE,WHITE,BLACK,BORDER);

LR= new TDisplay(15,R1,LBL_SIZE,WHITE,BLACK,NOBORDER);
LG= new TDisplay(15,R2,LBL_SIZE,WHITE,BLACK,NOBORDER);
LB= new TDisplay(15,R3,LBL_SIZE,WHITE,BLACK,NOBORDER);
LY= new TDisplay(15,R4,LBL_SIZE,WHITE,BLACK,NOBORDER);
LCr=new TDisplay(15,R5,LBL_SIZE,WHITE,BLACK,NOBORDER);
LCb=new TDisplay(15,R6,LBL_SIZE,WHITE,BLACK,NOBORDER);

R->Show(255);
G->Show(255);
B->Show(255);
Y->Show(255);
Cr->Show(128);
Cb->Show(128);

LR->Show("R");
LG->Show("G");
LB->Show("B");
LY->Show("Y");
LCr->Show("Cr");
LCb->Show("Cb");

Rv=255; Gv=255; Bv=255;
Yv=255; Crv=128; Cbv=128;

// NOTE: The color indexed as LIGHTMAGENTA is used as the
// variable color modified by adjusting the VGA palette,
// because it is not used for any of the user interface
// functions. The normal color is automatically restored
// on exit at the execution of closegraph().

setfillstyle(SOLID_FILL,LIGHTMAGENTA);
setcolor(BLACK);
getpalette(&palette);
```

```
setrgbpalette(palette.colors[LIGHTMAGENTA],255,255,255);
setlinestyle(SOLID_LINE,0,THICK_WIDTH);
bar3d(BOX_POSITION,BOX_END,0,0);   // Color Bar
Mouse.Run();                       // Start processing user input
closegraph();
}
```

5

Data Compression Techniques

There are many ways to reduce the amount of stored or transmitted digital data. Which way is best depends on the data and the application. Almost all types of data compression rely on a principle known as *entropy*. Webster's dictionary defines entropy as "The logarithm of the probability of occurrence of a given state, i.e. arrangement of constituent particles, which in turn depends upon the relative energies of the possible states." In general, entropy can be thought of as a measure of randomness. For relatively large data sets, entropy can be increased by consolidating redundant data patterns and substituting small patterns for large recognizable ones. The net result is that the amount of data is reduced but its randomness is increased. There are many data encoding techniques that can be classified as entropy coding. Several of these will be discussed here along with other techniques that do not rely as much on the principle of entropy. Several programming examples showing various compression techniques are provided. Each of these works on gray-scale still images. The intent is to illustrate the types of visual artifacts introduced by each type of compression scheme.

The image files may be compressed and decompressed, and viewed using a program called VIEW_PIC.EXE. To compare the fidelity of original and reconstructed images, a program called VIEW_ERR.EXE is provided, which gives a visual representation of the difference between two images. To do this, the difference between each corresponding pixel in the reference image and reconstructed image is calculated, and the relative magnitude shown as a deviation from a neutral gray level. If two identical image files are compared, the screen will show a featureless gray matte. Differences show up as light or dark areas. A root mean square error (RMSE) value for the entire image area is also calculated, and shown after the visual representation is dismissed. Source code for these programs is included in Appendix B.

Color Subsampling

One of the non-entropy-based data compression techniques is as simple as eliminating data that will not be missed. In conventional binary computer systems, traditionally every bit of data has been critical. Computers have for a long time employed complicated error detection and correction schemes because of this. The processing and transmission of what could be called natural data types, on the other hand, does not necessarily require such strict adherence to accuracy and repeatability. For visual data types a certain property of the human visual system can be taken advantage of to reduce the amount of data processed and transmitted. That is, the human eye is less sensitive to variations in color than it is to variations in light intensity. The eye's sensitivity to various spatial frequencies is illustrated in Figure 5.1.

Given this fact it is not necessary to reproduce the colors in an image with as much frequency information as that needed for light intensity. This fact has been well known for many years and the technique is used in all three major broadcast standards (NTSC, PAL, and SECAM; see Chapter 2). It is the basis of a technique known as *color subsampling*. The need to do this is one of the reasons color systems with a separate luminance component were developed.

CCIR 601 Chroma Subsampling

The CCIR, in recommendation 601-2, has defined several methods of subsampling color information for digital picture data. Each of these is identified by a sequence of three digits separated by colons (:). The digits represent the relative number of samples from each image component. The first digit represents Y (luminance), the second digit represents Cr (Red minus Y), and the third digit represents Cb (Blue minus Y). Two of the more commonly used subsampling ratios are 4:2:2 and 4:1:1. Format 4:2:2 means that for every four luminance samples there are two of each type of chrominance sample. In other words, for every two luminance samples there are one of each chrominance sample. Format 4:1:1 means that for every four luminance samples there are one of each chrominance sample. In both cases, the color is subsampled horizontally only. All brightness and color information needed to produce one scan line of a video frame is present in the same scan line. Figure 5.2 illustrates how the image components are related horizontally for 4:2:2 and 4:1:1 color subsampling.

Assuming a sample size of eight bits for each image component, the average number of bits per pixel in 4:2:2 subsampling is $8 \times 4/2$, or 16 bits per pixel. For 4:1:1 subsampling, it is $8 \times 6/4$, or 12 bits per pixel on average. The values of subsampled pixels are typically calculated as averages of the full resolution pixels they represent.

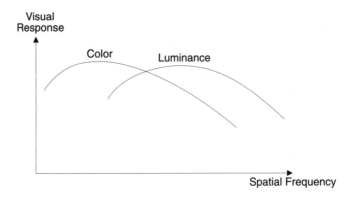

Figure 5.1   Human visual response to spatial frequencies.

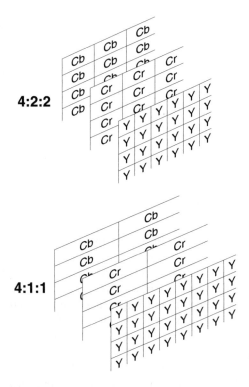

Figure 5.2 Sample relationships for 4:2:2 and 4:1:1 subsampling.

Bidirectional Chroma Subsampling

Another method of subsampling involves reducing the sample frequency in both horizontal and vertical directions. Using this technique it is possible to achieve the same subsampling ratio as in the CCIR-601 4:1:1 subsampling by using a subsample factor of two in both horizontal and vertical directions. This produces a more uniform distribution of sampling errors and, therefore, tends to result in fewer visual artifacts. The logical arrangement of image component samples in this case is illustrated in Figure 5.3.

Using this technique just about any ratio of subsampling of one component relative to another can be achieved. Of course, the more the amount of color information in an image is reduced, the more likely it is that visual artifacts will result. In general, images with high spatial energy content tend to produce more visual artifacts when compressed than images with a low energy level. The term *energy level* refers to the amount of information in the picture and the degree of contrast. An image with a lot of sharp edges and a high contrast ratio is said to have a higher energy level than one with smooth variations in texture and color.

Color Subsampling Demonstration Software

To illustrate the effects of color subsampling, a program called SUB_SAMP.EXE is provided. Because all software provided with this book is designed to work with a standard VGA graphics

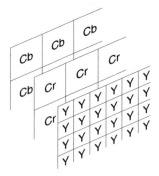

Figure 5.3   Bidirectional color subsampling.

adapter it is not practical to demonstrate the effects of color subsampling over a large image area. The restriction to a maximum of 256 distinct colors displayed on the screen simultaneously requires some special techniques to produce natural-looking images. Because the subsampling demonstration requires precise control over the color value of each individual pixel which makes up an image, a small 16 × 15 pixel segment is cropped from a larger image for use in the demonstration. This allows a separate color palette entry to be dedicated to each pixel in the sample image while leaving 16 remaining for use as standard display screen colors. The demonstration magnifies the original image segment by four both horizontally and vertically to make it easier to distinguish the boundaries between individual pixels. The critical fact demonstrated by this program is that while color content may be reduced, the resolution of luminance information is not reduced. The program shows how pixel color values are changed after subsampling and reconstruction using linear or bilinear interpolation. The following source code is stored in file SUB_SAMP.CPP:

SUB_SAMP Program Listing

```
#define  APP_TITLE "Color Sub-sampling Demo"
#include <stdio.h>
#include <conio.h>
#include <dos.h>
#include "ctrl_256.h"
#include "disp_256.h"

extern "C" void SetVmode(int);
extern "C" void DrawBlock(int,int,int,int,int);
extern "C" void DrawPixel(int,int,int);
extern "C" void DrawASCII(int,int,int,int);
extern "C" void WriteEntry(int,int,int,int);
//
// Define RGB data for a small (16x15) section of an image.
// This data was extracted from file BALOONS.PIC.
//
int original_image[768]=
  {
```

```
0x2c,0x5b,0xa2,  0x2c,0x5b,0xa2,  0x29,0x45,0x87,  0x23,0x25,0x48,
0x2a,0x24,0x3a,  0x52,0x1e,0x1f,  0x99,0x2e,0x22,  0xcd,0x5f,0x34,
0xcd,0x5f,0x34,  0xc6,0x57,0x32,  0xcd,0x5f,0x34,  0xcd,0x5f,0x34,
0xcd,0x5f,0x34,  0xbb,0x83,0x2f,  0xd0,0x9e,0x44,  0xe0,0xab,0x4d,
0x32,0x54,0x9a,  0x2a,0x53,0x9b,  0x25,0x2b,0x53,  0x42,0x1c,0x2c,
0x6b,0x1b,0x16,  0x72,0x22,0x1e,  0xb4,0x43,0x3c,  0xc6,0x57,0x32,
0xcd,0x5f,0x34,  0xcd,0x5f,0x34,  0xc2,0x8b,0x2d,  0xd0,0x9e,0x44,
0xe8,0xc0,0x56,  0xe8,0xd0,0x59,  0xfb,0xe6,0x6d,  0xfb,0xe6,0x6d,
0x2a,0x53,0x9b,  0x2a,0x3a,0x68,  0x52,0x24,0x37,  0x72,0x22,0x1e,
0x72,0x22,0x1e,  0x7c,0x24,0x19,  0xcd,0x5f,0x34,  0xc4,0x92,0x33,
0xe0,0xab,0x4d,  0xe8,0xc0,0x56,  0xf1,0xda,0x5f,  0xfb,0xe6,0x6d,
0xfb,0xe6,0x6d,  0xf1,0xda,0x5f,  0xe8,0xd0,0x59,  0xf1,0xda,0x5f,
0x29,0x45,0x87,  0x63,0x29,0x3d,  0x72,0x22,0x1e,  0x72,0x22,0x1e,
0x7c,0x24,0x19,  0x97,0x5f,0x24,  0xe8,0xc0,0x56,  0xf1,0xda,0x5f,
0xf1,0xda,0x5f,  0xf1,0xda,0x5f,  0xe8,0xd0,0x59,  0xf1,0xda,0x5f,
0xe8,0xd0,0x59,  0xe8,0xc0,0x56,  0xe8,0xd0,0x59,  0xe8,0xd0,0x59,
0x5b,0x31,0x54,  0x72,0x22,0x1e,  0x7c,0x24,0x19,  0x9b,0x35,0x31,
0xbe,0x4e,0x2f,  0xbc,0x79,0x2b,  0xf1,0xda,0x5f,  0xf1,0xda,0x5f,
0xe8,0xd0,0x59,  0xe8,0xd0,0x59,  0xe8,0xd0,0x59,  0xe8,0xd0,0x59,
0xe8,0xd0,0x59,  0xd7,0xca,0x79,  0xd7,0xca,0x79,  0xd7,0xca,0x79,
0x63,0x29,0x3d,  0x89,0x26,0x1b,  0xb4,0x43,0x3c,  0xc6,0x57,0x32,
0xc6,0x57,0x32,  0xbb,0x83,0x2f,  0xf1,0xda,0x5f,  0xe8,0xd0,0x59,
0xe8,0xd0,0x59,  0xe8,0xd0,0x59,  0xd7,0xca,0x79,  0xd7,0xca,0x79,
0xc5,0xb5,0xad,  0xad,0xb2,0xbe,  0xad,0xb2,0xbe,  0xa6,0xa9,0xb2,
0x85,0x3c,0x45,  0xc6,0x57,0x32,  0xc6,0x57,0x32,  0xc6,0x57,0x32,
0xc6,0x57,0x32,  0xbc,0x79,0x2b,  0xe8,0xd0,0x59,  0xd7,0xca,0x79,
0xd5,0xb3,0x84,  0xc5,0xb5,0xad,  0xba,0xa4,0xa1,  0xad,0xb2,0xbe,
0xa6,0xa9,0xb2,  0xad,0xb2,0xbe,  0xa6,0xa9,0xb2,  0xad,0xb2,0xbe,
0xc6,0x57,0x32,  0xc6,0x57,0x32,  0xc6,0x57,0x32,  0xc6,0x57,0x32,
0xbb,0x83,0x2f,  0xd0,0x9e,0x44,  0xd5,0xb3,0x84,  0xc5,0xb5,0xad,
0xa6,0xa9,0xb2,  0xad,0xb2,0xbe,  0xad,0xb2,0xbe,  0xad,0xb2,0xbe,
0xad,0xb2,0xbe,  0xad,0xb2,0xbe,  0xad,0xb2,0xbe,  0xad,0xb2,0xbe,
0xc6,0x57,0x32,  0xc6,0x57,0x32,  0xb3,0x73,0x27,  0xd0,0x9e,0x44,
0xe8,0xd0,0x59,  0xfb,0xe6,0x6d,  0xa3,0xaa,0x8b,  0xc5,0xb5,0xad,
0xad,0xb2,0xbe,  0xad,0xb2,0xbe,  0xad,0xb2,0xbe,  0xad,0xb2,0xbe,
0xad,0xb2,0xbe,  0xad,0xb2,0xbe,  0xad,0xb2,0xbe,  0xba,0xa4,0xa1,
0xc6,0x57,0x32,  0xbb,0x83,0x2f,  0xe8,0xc0,0x56,  0xf1,0xda,0x5f,
0xf1,0xda,0x5f,  0xf1,0xda,0x5f,  0xb4,0xa2,0x73,  0xad,0xb2,0xbe,
0xad,0xb2,0xbe,  0xad,0xb2,0xbe,  0xad,0xb2,0xbe,  0xba,0xa4,0xa1,
0xba,0xa4,0xa1,  0xae,0x93,0x93,  0xa1,0x84,0x8a,  0xc1,0x5d,0x7d,
0xd2,0xaa,0x53,  0xe8,0xd0,0x59,  0xf1,0xda,0x5f,  0xe8,0xd0,0x59,
0xe8,0xd0,0x59,  0xf1,0xda,0x5f,  0xb4,0xa2,0x73,  0xa6,0xa9,0xb2,
0xba,0xa4,0xa1,  0xae,0x93,0x93,  0xc8,0x6d,0x8a,  0xa4,0x69,0x81,
0xb8,0x54,0x76,  0xb8,0x54,0x76,  0xb8,0x54,0x76,  0xc1,0x5d,0x7d,
0xf1,0xda,0x5f,  0xe8,0xd0,0x59,  0xe8,0xc0,0x56,  0xe8,0xc0,0x56,
0xe8,0xc0,0x56,  0xd7,0xca,0x79,  0xa8,0x8c,0x8d,  0xa4,0x69,0x81,
0xb8,0x54,0x76,  0xb8,0x54,0x76,  0xb8,0x54,0x76,  0xb8,0x54,0x76,
0xc1,0x5d,0x7d,  0xc1,0x5d,0x7d,  0xc1,0x5d,0x7d,  0xc1,0x5d,0x7d,
0xe8,0xc0,0x56,  0xda,0xbc,0x55,  0xda,0xbc,0x55,  0xda,0xbc,0x55,
0xc3,0xaf,0x76,  0x98,0x9b,0xae,  0xa1,0x84,0x8a,  0xa7,0x4a,0x69,
0xb8,0x54,0x76,  0xc1,0x5d,0x7d,  0xc1,0x5d,0x7d,  0xc1,0x5d,0x7d,
0xc1,0x5d,0x7d,  0xc1,0x5d,0x7d,  0xc1,0x5d,0x7d,  0xc1,0x5d,0x7d,
```

```c
    0xe8,0xc0,0x56,  0xda,0xbc,0x55,  0xc3,0xaf,0x76,  0x98,0x9b,0xae,
    0x90,0x93,0xa2,  0x98,0x9b,0xae,  0xa6,0xa9,0xb2,  0x96,0x58,0x71,
    0xb8,0x54,0x76,  0xc1,0x5d,0x7d,  0xc1,0x5d,0x7d,  0xc1,0x5d,0x7d,
    0xb8,0x54,0x76,  0xa7,0x4a,0x69,  0x8a,0x41,0x5c,  0x63,0x29,0x3d,
    0xe8,0xd0,0x59,  0xb4,0x9c,0x99,  0x96,0x9d,0x91,  0x90,0x93,0xa2,
    0x98,0x9b,0xae,  0x98,0x9b,0xae,  0xad,0xb2,0xbe,  0xa4,0x69,0x81,
    0xb8,0x54,0x76,  0xc1,0x5d,0x7d,  0x9c,0x47,0x69,  0x72,0x34,0x52,
    0x52,0x24,0x37,  0x21,0x1d,0x2d,  0x1b,0x14,0x1c,  0x14,0x13,0x19,
    0xe8,0xd0,0x59,  0xb4,0x9c,0x99,  0x96,0x9d,0x91,  0x90,0x93,0xa2,
    0x98,0x9b,0xae,  0x98,0x9b,0xae,  0xad,0xb2,0xbe,  0xa4,0x69,0x81,
    0xb8,0x54,0x76,  0xc1,0x5d,0x7d,  0x9c,0x47,0x69,  0x72,0x34,0x52,
    0x52,0x24,0x37,  0x21,0x1d,0x2d,  0x1b,0x14,0x1c,  0x14,0x13,0x19,
    };
int y_map[16][16],cr_map[16][16],cb_map[16][16];

void SignOn(void)
  {
  DrawBlock(0,0,320,200,WHITE);        // White background
  DrawBlock(0,0,320,10,LIGHTBLUE);     // Title Bar
  DrawString(160-strlen(APP_TITLE)*4,2,APP_TITLE,WHITE); // Title
  DrawBlock(0,10,320,1,BLUE);          // Title Bar Outline
  DrawBlock(319,0,1,10,BLUE);
  DrawBlock(0,0,320,1,CYAN);
  DrawBlock(0,0,1,10,CYAN);
  DrawBlock(0,186,320,14,LIGHTGRAY); // Message Bar
  DrawBlock(2,198,220,1,WHITE);
  DrawBlock(222,187,1,12,WHITE);
  DrawBlock(2,187,221,1,DARKGRAY);
  DrawBlock(2,187,1,12,DARKGRAY);
  DrawBlock(5,15,310,122,DARKGRAY);   // SignOn Message Bar
  DrawBlock(6,16,308,120,LIGHTGRAY);
  }

int EscExit() //Exit via Escape key (process KB input)
  {
  int st;
  st=kbhit();
  if(st!=0)
    {
    st=getch();
    if(st==27)return(RUN_DISABLED);
    }
  return(RUN_ENABLED);
  }

int Quit()    //Exit via mouse click
  {
  return(RUN_DISABLED);
  }

void UserMessage(char *message)
  {
  DrawBlock(3,189,218,10,LIGHTGRAY);
```

```
    DrawString(6,189,message,WHITE);
    DrawBlock(2,198,220,1,WHITE);
    }

int Saturate(int i) // Make sure RGB values don't over- or under-flow.
    {
    if(i>255)i=255;
    if(i<0)i=0;
    i=i>>2;
    return(i);
    }

int Original() // Program the VGA palette with original image colors.
    {
    int i,r,g,b;
    UserMessage("Original Image");
    for(i=0;i<720;i+=3)
        {
        r=original_image[i]>>2;
        g=original_image[i+1]>>2;
        b=original_image[i+2]>>2;
        WriteEntry(i/3+16,r,g,b);
        }
    return(RUN_ENABLED);
    }

int CCIR_422() // Program the VGA palette with subsampled colors.
    {
    int x,y,r,g,b,cr[8][16],cb[8][16];
    UserMessage("CCIR 4:2:2 Sub-sampling");
    for(y=0;y<16;y++)for(x=0;x<8;x++)    // First, subsample by 2:1
        {
        cr[x][y]=(cr_map[x*2][y]+cr_map[x*2+1][y])/2;
        cb[x][y]=(cb_map[x*2][y]+cb_map[x*2+1][y])/2;
        }
    for(y=0;y<16;y++)for(x=0;x<16;x++)  // Then reconstitute the image
        {
        r=cr[x/2][y]+y_map[x][y];
        b=cb[x/2][y]+y_map[x][y];
        g=(int)((float)y_map[x][y]*1.7-(float)r*0.509-(float)b*0.194);
        r=r>>2;
        g=g>>2;
        b=b>>2;
        if(y<15)WriteEntry(y*16+x+16,r,g,b);
        }
    return(RUN_ENABLED);
    }

int CCIR_411() // Program the VGA palette with subsampled colors.
    {
    int x,y,r,g,b,cr[4][16],cb[4][16];
    UserMessage("CCIR 4:1:1 Sub-sampling");
    for(y=0;y<16;y++)for(x=0;x<4;x++) // First, subsample by 4:1
```

```
      {
      cr[x][y]=(cr_map[x*4][y]+  cr_map[x*4+1][y]+
               cr_map[x*4+2][y]+cr_map[x*4+3][y])/4;
      cb[x][y]=(cb_map[x*4][y]+  cb_map[x*4+1][y]+
               cb_map[x*4+2][y]+cb_map[x*4+3][y])/4;
      }
   for(y=0;y<16;y++)for(x=0;x<16;x++) // Then reconstitute the image
      {
      r=cr[x/4][y]+y_map[x][y];
      b=cb[x/4][y]+y_map[x][y];
      g=(int)((float)y_map[x][y]*1.7-(float)r*0.509-(float)b*0.194);
      r=Saturate(r);
      g=Saturate(g);
      b=Saturate(b);
      if(y<15)WriteEntry(y*16+x+16,r,g,b);
      }
   return(RUN_ENABLED);
   }

int Bidir_4() // Program the VGA palette with subsampled colors.
   {
   int x,y,r,g,b,cr[8][8],cb[8][8];
   UserMessage("Bidirectional, 4:1");
   for(y=0;y<8;y++)for(x=0;x<8;x++) // First, subsample by 2:1 in X & Y
      {
      cr[x][y]=(cr_map[x*2][y*2]+  cr_map[x*2+1][y*2]+
               cr_map[x*2][y*2+1]+cr_map[x*2+1][y*2+1])/4;
      cb[x][y]=(cb_map[x*2][y*2]+  cb_map[x*2+1][y*2]+
               cb_map[x*2][y*2+1]+cb_map[x*2+1][y*2+1])/4;
      }
   for(y=0;y<16;y++)for(x=0;x<16;x++) // Then reconstitute the image
      {
      r=cr[x/2][y/2]+y_map[x][y];
      b=cb[x/2][y/2]+y_map[x][y];
      g=(int)((float)y_map[x][y]*1.7-(float)r*0.509-(float)b*0.194);
      r=Saturate(r);
      g=Saturate(g);
      b=Saturate(b);
      if(y<15)WriteEntry(y*16+x+16,r,g,b);
      }
   return(RUN_ENABLED);
   }

int Bidir_16() // Program the VGA palette with subsampled colors.
   {
   int x,y,x1,y1,r,g,b,cr[4][4],cb[4][4],cr_tmp,cb_tmp;
   UserMessage("Bidirectional, 16:1");
   for(y=0;y<4;y++)for(x=0;x<4;x++) // First, subsample by 4:1 in X & Y
      {
      cr_tmp=0L;
      cb_tmp=0L;
      for(y1=0;y1<4;y1++)for(x1=0;x1<4;x1++)
```

```
          {
      cr_tmp+=cr_map[x+x1][y+y1];
      cb_tmp+=cb_map[x+x1][y+y1];
          }
     cr[x][y]=cr_tmp/16;
     cb[x][y]=cb_tmp/16;
        }
  for(y=0;y<4;y++)for(x=0;x<4;x++)  // Then reconstitute the image
     {
     for(y1=0;y1<4;y1++)for(x1=0;x1<4;x1++)
        {
        r=cr[x][y]+y_map[x*4+x1][y*4+y1];
        b=cb[x][y]+y_map[x*4+x1][y*4+y1];
        g=(int)((float)y_map[x*4+x1][y*4+y1]*1.7-
                (float)r*0.509-(float)b*0.194);
        r=Saturate(r);
        g=Saturate(g);
        b=Saturate(b);
        if(y*4+y1<15)WriteEntry(y*64+y1*16+x*4+x1+16,r,g,b);
        }
     }
  return(RUN_ENABLED);
  }
//****************************************************

void main(void)
  {
  int x,y;
  float y_val,rf,gf,bf;
  SetVmode(0x13);
  SignOn();
  TControl Mouse;
  Mouse.SetStandardCallback(&EscExit);
  Mouse.CreateButton(&Quit,226,187,90,11,"[Esc] Quit");
  DrawBlock(196,56,118,100,LIGHTGRAY);
  Mouse.CreateButton(&Original,200,60, 110,12,"Original");
  Mouse.CreateButton(&CCIR_422,200,80, 110,12,"CCIR 4:2:2");
  Mouse.CreateButton(&CCIR_411,200,100,110,12,"CCIR 4:1:1");
  Mouse.CreateButton(&Bidir_4, 200,120,110,12,"Bilinear 4:1");
  Mouse.CreateButton(&Bidir_16,200,140,110,12,"Bilinear 16:1");
  Original();
  for(y=0;y<16;y++)for(x=0;x<16;x++)  // Calculate YCrCb representation
     {
     rf=(float)original_image[(y*16+x)*3];
     gf=(float)original_image[(y*16+x)*3+1];
     bf=(float)original_image[(y*16+x)*3+2];
     y_val=0.299*rf+0.587*gf+0.114*bf;
     y_map[x][y]=(int)y_val;
     cr_map[x][y]=(int)(rf-y_val);
     cb_map[x][y]=(int)(bf-y_val);
     }
  DrawBlock(20,20,88,68,BLACK);        // Draw black frames
```

```
DrawBlock(118,22,20,19,BLACK);
for(y=0;y<15;y++)for(x=0;x<16;x++)
  {
  DrawBlock(x*5+24,y*4+24,5,4,y*16+x+16);  // Plot the image magnified
  DrawPixel(x+120,y+24,y*16+x+16);         // Plot the image normal
  }
Mouse.Run();
SetVmode(3);
}
```

Luma Subsampling

The same basic technique can be applied to luminance information, with the effective result being a reduction of image resolution. For small reductions, such as 2:1 horizontally and vertically, the loss of resolution may or may not be objectionable depending on the original resolution. The still images provided with the sample software have an overall resolution of 320×200 pixels, and reduction to 160×100 gives fairly good results at viewing distances of about two feet or more. Two programs are provided to compress images using this method, one called SS2_DEMO.EXE, which compresses the image by 2:1 horizontally and vertically, and one called SS4_DEMO.EXE, which compresses the image by 4:1 horizontally and vertically. The results can be viewed by decompressing the images and viewing them with the program named VIEW_PIC.EXE. Source code for the two sub-sample compression programs is provided in the following:

2:1 Luma Subsampling Example Program (SS2_DEMO.CPP)

```
#include <stdlib.h>
#include <stdio.h>
#include <conio.h>
#include <dos.h>

void main(int argc, char* argv[])
  {
  FILE *fi,*fo;
  unsigned char image[2][320],coded_image[160];
  int row,size,pel,tmp;

  printf("4:1 Spatial Sub-sampling Image Compression Demo Program\n\n");
  printf("Copyright (c) John Wiley & Sons, Inc., 1994.\n\n");
  if(argc<4)
    {
    printf
    ("Please provide two file names: <input_file> <output_file>\n");
    printf("followed by /c for compress or /u for uncompress.\n");
    printf("Example: SS2_DEMO picture.pic picture.out /c\n\n");
    exit(0);
    }
  if(argv[3][1]!='c' && argv[3][1]!='u')
    {
    printf("Please specify /c for compress or /u for uncompress.\n");
    exit(0);
```

```
      }

    fi=fopen(argv[1],"rb");
    fo=fopen(argv[2],"wb");
    if(fi==NULL)
      {
      printf("Could not open input file %s.\n",argv[1]);
      exit(0);
      }
    if(fo==NULL)
      {
      printf("Could not open output file %s.\n",argv[2]);
      exit(0);
      }
//----------------------------------------------------------
    if(argv[3][1]=='c')                 // User wants to compress
      {
      printf("Compressing.\n");
      for(row=0;row<100;row++)          // Compress two rows at a time
        {
        fread(&image[0][0],320,1,fi); // Read a row
        fread(&image[1][0],320,1,fi); // Read a row
        for(pel=0;pel<160;pel++)
          {
          tmp =(int)image[0][2*pel];
          tmp+=(int)image[0][2*pel+1];
          tmp+=(int)image[1][2*pel];
          tmp+=(int)image[1][2*pel+1];
          coded_image[pel]=(unsigned char)(tmp/4);
          }
        fwrite(coded_image,160,1,fo);
        }
      }
//----------------------------------------------------------
    if(argv[3][1]=='u')               // User wants to uncompress
      {
      printf("Uncompressing.\n");

      for(row=0;row<100;row++)     // Uncompress two pixel rows at a time
        {
        fread(coded_image,160,1,fi);  // Read a row
        for(pel=0;pel<320;pel+=2)
          {
          image[0][pel]=  coded_image[pel/2];
          image[0][pel+1]=coded_image[pel/2];
          image[1][pel]=  coded_image[pel/2];
          image[1][pel+1]=coded_image[pel/2];
          }
        fwrite(&image[0][0],320,1,fo);
        fwrite(&image[1][0],320,1,fo);
        }
      }
    fclose(fi);
```

```
    fclose(fo);
    printf("Done.\n");
    }
```

4:1 Luma Subsampling Example Program (SS4_DEMO.CPP)

```cpp
#include <stdlib.h>
#include <stdio.h>
#include <conio.h>
#include <dos.h>

void main(int argc, char* argv[])
  {
  FILE *fi,*fo;
  unsigned char image[4][320],coded_image[80];
  int row,size,pel,tmp;

  printf
  ("16:1 Spatial Sub-sampling Image Compression Demo Program\n\n");
  printf("Copyright (c) John Wiley & Sons, Inc., 1994.\n\n");
  if(argc<4)
    {
    printf
    ("Please provide two file names: <input_file> <output_file>\n");
    printf("followed by /c for compress or /u for uncompress.\n");
    printf("Example: SS4_DEMO picture.pic picture.out /c\n\n");
    exit(0);
    }
  if(argv[3][1]!='c' && argv[3][1]!='u')
    {
    printf("Please specify /c for compress or /u for uncompress.\n");
    exit(0);
    }

  fi=fopen(argv[1],"rb");
  fo=fopen(argv[2],"wb");
  if(fi==NULL)
    {
    printf("Could not open input file %s.\n",argv[1]);
    exit(0);
    }
  if(fo==NULL)
    {
    printf("Could not open output file %s.\n",argv[2]);
    exit(0);
    }
//-------------------------------------------------------
  if(argv[3][1]=='c')  // User wants to compress
    {
    printf("Compressing.\n");

    for(row=0;row<50;row++)  // Compress four rows at a time
      {
```

```
       fread(&image[0][0],320,1,fi);          // Read a row
       fread(&image[1][0],320,1,fi);          // Read a row
       fread(&image[2][0],320,1,fi);          // Read a row
       fread(&image[3][0],320,1,fi);          // Read a row
       for(pel=0;pel<80;pel++)
         {
         tmp =(int)image[0][4*pel];
         tmp+=(int)image[0][4*pel+1];
         tmp+=(int)image[0][4*pel+2];
         tmp+=(int)image[0][4*pel+3];
         tmp+=(int)image[1][4*pel];
         tmp+=(int)image[1][4*pel+1];
         tmp+=(int)image[1][4*pel+2];
         tmp+=(int)image[1][4*pel+3];
         tmp+=(int)image[2][4*pel];
         tmp+=(int)image[2][4*pel+1];
         tmp+=(int)image[2][4*pel+2];
         tmp+=(int)image[2][4*pel+3];
         tmp+=(int)image[3][4*pel];
         tmp+=(int)image[3][4*pel+1];
         tmp+=(int)image[3][4*pel+2];
         tmp+=(int)image[3][4*pel+3];
         coded_image[pel]=(unsigned char)(tmp/16);
         }
       fwrite(coded_image,80,1,fo);
       }
     }
//-----------------------------------------------------------
   if(argv[3][1]=='u')              // User wants to uncompress
     {
     printf("Uncompressing.\n");
     for(row=0;row<100;row++)  // Uncompress two pixel rows at a time
       {
       fread(coded_image,80,1,fi);  // Read a row
       for(pel=0;pel<320;pel+=4)
         {
         image[0][pel]=  coded_image[pel/4];
         image[0][pel+1]=coded_image[pel/4];
         image[0][pel+2]=coded_image[pel/4];
         image[0][pel+3]=coded_image[pel/4];
         image[1][pel]=  coded_image[pel/4];
         image[1][pel+1]=coded_image[pel/4];
         image[1][pel+2]=coded_image[pel/4];
         image[1][pel+3]=coded_image[pel/4];
         image[2][pel]=  coded_image[pel/4];
         image[2][pel+1]=coded_image[pel/4];
         image[2][pel+2]=coded_image[pel/4];
         image[2][pel+3]=coded_image[pel/4];
         image[3][pel]=  coded_image[pel/4];
         image[3][pel+1]=coded_image[pel/4];
         image[3][pel+2]=coded_image[pel/4];
         image[3][pel+3]=coded_image[pel/4];
         }
```

```
        fwrite(&image[0][0],320,1,fo);
        fwrite(&image[1][0],320,1,fo);
        fwrite(&image[2][0],320,1,fo);
        fwrite(&image[3][0],320,1,fo);
        }
    }
fclose(fi);
fclose(fo);
printf("Done.\n");
}
```

Run Length Encoding

Another technique commonly used for compressing graphics images is called *run length encoding* (RLE). This is simply a matter of detecting a series of identical values and representing them as a single instance of that value along with a count. Upon reconstruction, the value is simply repeated the number of times indicated by the count. The technique is applicable only to linear sequences of symbols. Therefore, when applied to two-dimensional image data the image is usually broken up into a series of scan lines. Figure 5.4 illustrates how run length encoding might be applied to a simple binary image.

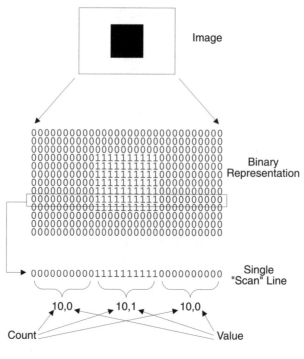

Figure 5.4   Run length encoding of binary image data.

A possible modification on the basic theme of run length encoding is to use variable length codes to represent symbol values as well as run lengths. This can be done by calculating the probability distribution of run lengths and symbol values. It is basically a combination of run length encoding with statistical encoding. Run length encoding is not directly suitable for continuous-tone natural images encoded with a linear digitizing process. The reason is that in order for RLE to be effective the data set to be compressed must contain relatively large runs of data that are all the same. While continuous-tone images may contain relatively low spatial frequency information, the chances of large areas completely filled with identical pixel values are relatively small. However, by mapping pixel values to a gray-code table and applying run length encoding bitwise on a plane-by-plane basis it is possible to achieve reasonable compression ratios. This way, run length encoding is applied only to runs of binary ones or zeros. Translation to gray code increases correlation among pixels in a single-bit plane because any change equivalent in delta value to one least significant bit in the original sample space will affect no more than one bit plane in the gray-code sample space. The number of bit planes affected by pixel value differences tends to be proportional to the size of the difference. Contrast this with linear coding where, for example, a transition from 127 to 128 can cause all eight bits of an eight-bit sample to change. Generating a gray-code sequence is fairly simple: Starting with the first two table entries of zero and one, no further entries can be generated without adding the next more significant bit. This generates a value of three. Scanning backwards up the list, using each possible combination of less significant bits combined with the most significant bit just introduced, the size of the table can be doubled. In the case of a most significant bit with a value of two, there is only one remaining lower combination, which is zero. Thus, the first four entries are zero, one, three, and two. Repeating the process adds the next most significant bit, which has a value of four. Combined with the last entry up to that point the resulting table entry has a value of six. Scanning backwards up the list for less significant bit combinations produces three more values, which are seven, five, and four. The process can be repeated indefinitely until the number of table entries required have been generated. For the natural images used with this book, even when using gray-code techniques, RLE by itself did not provide significant compression levels. In some cases the data is actually enlarged due to high spatial energy levels in the image. Therefore, no software example is provided for simple RLE compression. RLE is used, however, in conjunction with several other techniques in the H.261, JPEG, and MPEG compression standards. In these cases, RLE is applied to quantized frequency coefficients rather than directly to image data.

Huffman Encoding

Huffman encoding is commonly referred to as entropy encoding or statistical encoding. The basic idea behind the technique is to use variable-length codes to represent image data, using shorter codes to represent data that has a higher probability of occurrence and longer codes to represent data with a lower probability. The result is that a large percentage of the coded data consists of very short codes, thereby reducing the overall amount of data. Huffman coding is distinguished from other variable-length coding techniques in the algorithm used to generate the codes. The distinctive characteristics of the code-generating algorithm are as follows:

1. No two code words may consist of identical sequences of code bits.
2. No information beyond the code itself is required to specify the beginning and end of any code value.

3. For a given number of symbols arranged in descending order of probability, the length of their associated code values will be such that the code associated with any given symbol will be less than or equal to the length of the code associated with the next less probable symbol.
4. No more than two code words of the same length are alike in all but their final bits.

Building a Huffman Code Table

The algorithm for generating Huffman codes is as follows: First, the relative probability of occurrence of each symbol within the data set to be encoded is calculated. The symbols are then sorted in decreasing order of probability. Because the set of symbols represents all possible symbols which can be used in the image, the sum of their probabilities equals one. The next stage of the algorithm involves recursion. Each step in the recursion assigns a binary code bit to two or more of the symbols in the data set. The recursive procedure is as follows: The symbol with the lowest probability in the list is assigned a bit value of one. The symbol of the next higher probability is assigned a bit value of zero. The bit value assignments are recorded and the two probabilities are added together. The resulting probability is inserted into the list in the appropriate position. Of course, this new probability value is no longer associated with a single symbol from the original data set, so the fact that it resulted from the addition of two other probabilities is also recorded. This effectively creates a tree structure where the terminal nodes correspond to symbols from the original data set and intermediate nodes correspond to the sums of probabilities. Figure 5.5 illustrates the creation of the first branch in the tree structure.

The process is repeated until only two values remain in the list. Each probability will correspond to a tree structure that leads to all the other symbols from the original list. Figure 5.6 illustrates the rest of the tree construction procedure for the small data set of seven symbols illustrated in Figure 5.5.

Once the tree structure has been created, the Huffman codes can be generated simply by tracing the tree structure to each terminal node, collecting the one and zero bits along the way. Table 5.1 illustrates the resulting Huffman codes generated for the seven-symbol data set originally introduced in Figure 5.5.

Huffman Encode Programming Example

The following program example illustrates the Huffman encode and decode processes. The program operates on gray-scale images by calculating the statistical distribution of pixel values and generating a separate Huffman code for each value. The Huffman codes are then written to an output file

Symbol	Probability (P)
A	0.4
B	0.17
C	0.15
D	0.12
E	0.08
F	0.06
G	0.02

(0)F 0.06 ─┐
           ├─ Z
(1)G 0.02 ─┘

Symbol	P
A	0.4
B	0.17
C	0.15
D	0.12
E	0.08
Z	0.08

Figure 5.5   First branch of a Huffman code generation tree.

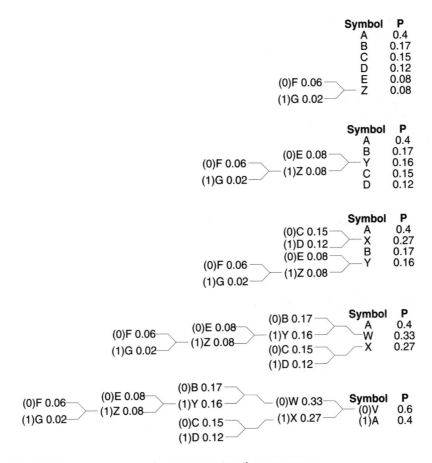

Figure 5.6 Huffman code generation tree construction sequence.

Table 5.1 Example Sample Set with Huffman Codes

Symbol	P	Code
A	.4	1
B	.17	000
C	.15	010
D	.12	011
E	.08	0010
F	.06	00110
G	.02	00111

instead of the original eight-bit pixel values. A table showing the correspondence between the Huffman codes and the original pixel values is also written to the file. The decoding process simply reads bits from the file and concatenates them until a match is found with one of the Huffman codes, and writes the corresponding pixel value to the output file. Ordinarily, Huffman encoding is used in conjunction with other compression techniques such as run length encoding in order to achieve a higher overall compression ratio. The sample program is command-line driven and requires the name of an input file and an output file. It does not display the images; it simply compresses them or decompresses them. The following source code is stored in file HUFFDEMO.CPP:

HUFFDEMO Program Listing

```cpp
#include <stdlib.h>
#include <stdio.h>
#include <conio.h>
#include <dos.h>

#include "huffdemo.h"

//----------------------------------------------------------
// Program:  Huffman Encode Compression Demostration Program
// Author:   Phil Mattison
// Compiler: Borland Turbo C++ v1.01
//----------------------------------------------------------

void main(int argc, char* argv[])
  {
  FILE          *fi,*fo;                  // File pointers
  Node          *head;                    // Symbol list head
  Node          *tail;                    // Symbol list tail
  Node          *node0;                   // 0 Node temp pointer
  Node          *node1;                   // 1 Node temp pointer
  Node          *pointer_table[NSYMBOLS]; // Cross reference table
  Node          *ntmp;                    // Temporary Node pointer
  int           row;                      // row index
  int           pel;                      // pixel index
  int           entries;                  // code table entry count
  int           code_table[NSYMBOLS];     // huffman code table
  int           symbol_table[NSYMBOLS];   // symbol cross reference
  int           decode_table[NSYMBOLS];   // symbol cross reference
  int           symbol;                   // symbol variable
  float         stat[NSYMBOLS];           // symbol statistics table
  float         ftmp;                     // temporary float variable
  Encoder       Encode;                   // Encoder object
  unsigned char image[IW];                // Image pixel row buffer
  unsigned char code_length[NSYMBOLS];    // Code length tags

  for(pel=0;pel<NSYMBOLS;pel++)           // Initialize tables
    {
    stat[pel]=0.0;
    code_table[pel]=0;
    code_length[pel]=0;
```

```
      symbol_table[pel]=0;
      decode_table[pel]=0;
      pointer_table[pel]=NULL;
      }

  printf("Huffman Encoding Image Compression Demo Program\n\n");
  printf("Copyright (c) John Wiley & Sons, Inc., 1994.\n\n");
  if(argc<4)
    {
    printf
    ("Please provide two file names: <input_file> <output_file>\n");
    printf("followed by /c for compress or /u for uncompress.\n");
    printf("Example: HUFFDEMO picture.b_w picture.out /c\n\n");
    exit(0);
    }
  if(argv[3][1]!='c' && argv[3][1]!='u')
    {
    printf("Please specify /c for compress or /u for uncompress.\n");
    exit(0);
    }
  fi=fopen(argv[1],"rb");
  fo=fopen(argv[2],"wb");
  if(fi==NULL)
    {
    printf("Could not open input file %s.\n",argv[1]);
    exit(0);
    }
  if(fo==NULL)
    {
    printf("Could not open output file %s.\n",argv[2]);
    exit(0);
    }
//--------------------------------------------------------
  if(argv[3][1]=='c')  // User wants to compress
    {
    printf("Calculating image statistics.\n");
    for(row=0;row<IH;row++)          // Collect image statistics first
      {
      fread(image,IW,1,fi);          // Read a row, truncate LSBs
      for(pel=0;pel<IW;pel++)stat[(int)(image[pel]>>QUANTIZER)]+=1.0;
      }
    for(pel=0;pel<NSYMBOLS;pel++)stat[pel]/=64000.0;
    head=new Node(0,stat[0],NULL,NULL,NULL,NULL);
    tail=head;
    for(pel=1;pel<NSYMBOLS;pel++)   // Transfer stats to list/tree
      {
      tail->succ=new Node(pel,stat[pel],NULL,NULL,tail,NULL);
      tail=tail->succ;
      }
    head->Sort();                   // Sort by probability
    while(head->pred!=NULL)head=head->pred;  // Find list head again
    tail=head;
    pel=0;
```

```
    while(pel<NSYMBOLS && tail!=NULL && tail->probability>0.0)
      {
      pointer_table[pel]=tail;       // Pointers for cross reference
      symbol_table[tail->symbol]=pel;
      decode_table[pel]=tail->symbol;
      tail=tail->succ;
      pel++;
      }
    entries=pel;                     // Save # of table entries
    tail=head;
    while(tail->succ!=NULL)tail=tail->succ;    // Find list tail again
    while(tail->probability==0.0 && tail!=NULL) // Delete unused symbols
      {
      ntmp=tail->pred;
      delete tail;
      tail=ntmp;
      }
    while(tail!=NULL)                // Build Huffman tree
      {
      node1=tail;                    // Take the last two entries
      node1->state=1;
      tail=tail->pred;
      node0=tail;
      node0->state=0;
      tail=tail->pred;
      ftmp=node0->probability+node1->probability;   // Add probability
      ntmp=new Node(-1,ftmp,node0,node1,tail,NULL); // Make new node
      node0->parent=ntmp;      // Attach branches to new node
      node1->parent=ntmp;

      if(tail!=NULL)
        {
        tail->succ=ntmp;        // Attach new node to list end
        ntmp->Sort();           // Insert new node in list
        while(tail->succ!=NULL)tail=tail->succ; // Find list tail again
        }
      }

    for(pel=0;pel<entries;pel++) // Generate Huffman Code Table
      {
      code_length[pel]=(unsigned char)pointer_table[pel]->Length();
      code_table[pel]=pointer_table[pel]->Encode(0);
      }
    delete ntmp;  // Delete the tree
//-------------------------------------------------------
    printf("Compressing.\n");
    rewind(fi);
    fwrite(&entries,sizeof(int),1,fo); // Write # of table entries
    fwrite(code_length,entries,1,fo);  // Write length and code tables
    fwrite(code_table,entries*sizeof(int),1,fo);
    fwrite(decode_table,entries*sizeof(int),1,fo);
    for(row=0;row<IH;row++)    // Compress one row at a time
      {
```

```
        fread(image,IW,1,fi);    // Read a row
        for(pel=0;pel<IW;pel++)
          {
          symbol=symbol_table[(int)(image[pel]>>QUANTIZER)];
          Encode.AddCode(code_table[symbol],(int)code_length[symbol]);
          }
        Encode.WriteBuffer(fo);
        }
      }
//---------------------------------------------------------
    if(argv[3][1]=='u')   // User wants to uncompress
      {
      printf("Uncompressing.\n");

      fread(&entries,sizeof(int),1,fi);   // Read # of table entries
      fread(code_length,entries,1,fi);    // Read length and code tables
      fread(code_table,entries*sizeof(int),1,fi);
      fread(decode_table,entries*sizeof(int),1,fi);

      for(row=0;row<IH;row++)   // Uncompress one pixel row at a time
        {
        Encode.ReadBuffer(fi); // Read a row
        for(pel=0;pel<IW;pel++)
          {
          symbol=Encode.GetSymbol(entries,code_length,code_table);
          image[pel]=(unsigned char)decode_table[symbol]<<QUANTIZER;
          }
        fwrite(image,IW,1,fo);
        }
      }
    fclose(fi);
    fclose(fo);
    printf("Done.\n");
    }
```

Vector Quantization

Vector quantization is basically a means of reducing the resolution with which a set of data is represented. The essential method is to represent groups of values from the original data set as single values in the new data set, effectively reducing the total amount of information. The exact method of grouping values from the original data set is the key to minimizing the amount of information lost. Vector quantization is by definition a *lossy* compression technique. That is, some of the original data is lost. Described in simplest terms, vector quantization consists of gathering the data values from the original data set into groups and then representing each group as a vector. Quantization occurs in reconstructing the original data set because all of the values that made up each group can no longer be distinguished and each is replaced by a new value, which approximates as closely as possible the group as a whole. The process is similar to rounding the numbers 1.1, 1.2, and 1.3 to the nearest integer. After rounding, the three values can no longer be distinguished from each other. The selection criteria for gathering values into groups depends on the degree of correlation among the values as well as their statistical distributions. As a simple example, imagine a data set in which all elements are integers with values ranging from 0 to 1023. The exact number of points in the data set is not relevant. What is relevant, however, is the relative frequency of occurrence of each of the possible 1023 values. Assume we want to represent this data set using only 128 symbols. A value from 0 to 1023 can be represented as a ten-bit integer. A value from 0 to 127 can be represented as a seven-bit integer. This saves three bits per element. The most obvious approach would be to simply truncate the least significant three bits of each data element. This has the effect of uniformly decreasing the resolution with which values can be represented across the entire data set. If the probability of occurrence is the same for all possible values within the range this is the best we can do. However, if the probability distribution is uneven, the degree of quantization can be varied to allow higher accuracy in the areas where it is most necessary, further reducing the accuracy of values which are used seldom or not at all, to achieve the same overall reduction in total information content. Figure 5.7 illustrates a histogram for a range of values from 0 to 1023 where all values have an equal probability of occurrence.

Simple quantization from a ten-bit value to a seven-bit value is also illustrated in this figure. Figure 5.8 illustrates a similar case where the probability of distribution is not flat. In this case, it is desirable to more accurately represent those values that occur more often than those which occur seldom or not at all.

It can be seen that quantization is finer in areas where probability is higher and coarser in areas where probability is lower. In this case, there is no obvious mathematical relationship between the original data set and the quantized data set. From the original data set, each group of symbols that corresponds to a single element in the quantized data set is referred to as a *vector*. A table showing the correspondence between the quantized values and the nearest approximations to the original val-

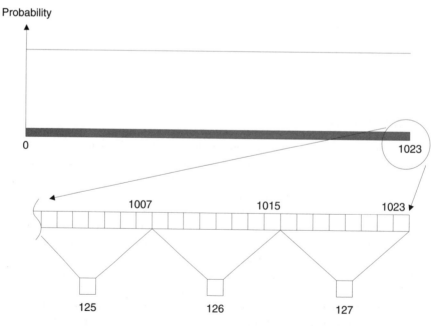

Figure 5.7   Flat probability distribution and corresponding equal quantization.

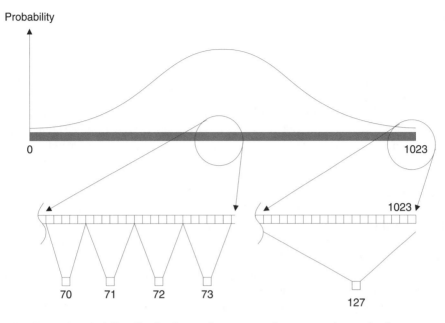

Figure 5.8 Normal probability distribution and corresponding unequal quantization.

ues is referred to as a *code book*. Volumes have been written debating the relative merits of various techniques for arriving at the optimal code book for a given data set; that is, how to find the best way to group values from the original data set into vectors. The intent here is not to delve into that discussion, but simply to illustrate the basic concepts involved. To increase the efficiency of the technique (and provide mathematicians with something to do) vectors can be defined with multiple dimensions. This introduces the concept of *correlation* among elements in a data set. Expanding on our previous example, imagine if values from the original data set were taken in pairs. Instead of 1024 possible values, there are now over a million possible combinations. This makes the collection of statistics considerably more time consuming, but at the same time increases the opportunities for optimization. The example just cited would be referred to as vector quantization in two dimensions. There is no theoretical limit on the number of dimensions that could be used although there are definite practical limitations. For example, a three-dimensional system using eight bit values would result in a number of cases given by 2^{8+8+8}, or approximately 16 million possibilities. Each time a dimension is added, the complexity of statistical analysis increases exponentially.

To illustrate the case of a two-dimensional system, consider an example involving a stream of digital samples taken from an audio waveform. The degree of correlation from one sample to the next will be a function of the sampling frequency. The largest differences from one sample to the next will occur only during periods of the highest frequencies within the audio spectrum. As the input frequency decreases, the differences between adjacent samples tend to decrease as well. This means that the probability of sample pairs with a small delta is higher than that of sample pairs with a large delta. If all the possible combinations of a pair of samples are plotted on a two-dimensional chart using the range of values for one sample as the X axis and the range of values for the other sample as the Y axis, the probabilities will tend to cluster around the line defined by $(X = Y)$. This is illustrated in Figure 5.9.

By partitioning this two-dimensional space into regions, each of which contains more than one sample pair, and assigning a symbol to each region, the overall number of symbols can be reduced from a million to some more manageable number. It should be remembered that points above the diagonal line represent $(Y>X)$ and points below represent $(X>Y)$. These differences must be preserved. Otherwise, when the data stream is reconstructed each vector would produce a pair of equal samples. This would introduce large sampling errors into the reconstituted output stream. The code table therefore must associate each vector symbol with a *pair* of output samples. Each sample in the output pair should approximate the values of the original group of samples, thereby preserving the relative difference. Figure 5.10 illustrates how the two-dimensional sample space might be partitioned to reflect the higher probability of small differences between samples.

This is, of course, a very simplistic partitioning scheme and any sophisticated quantizer would likely produce a different pattern, perhaps something looking more like a honeycomb. The example used here is a sequence of audio samples but the same principles can be applied to a digitized video image as well. Because of the relatively low spatial frequency content of most natural images there is a relatively high degree of correlation among closely spaced pixels. Groups of four pixels quantized together then, for example, would represent a four-dimensional vector quantization scheme. It is important not to confuse vector dimensions with sample space dimensions. We saw that a digitized audio stream, which is essentially a one-dimensional sample space, can be quantized using

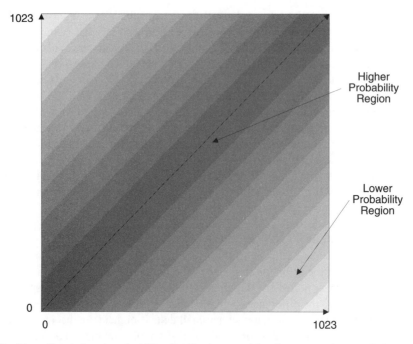

Figure 5.9   Two-dimensional probability distribution resulting from sample correlation.

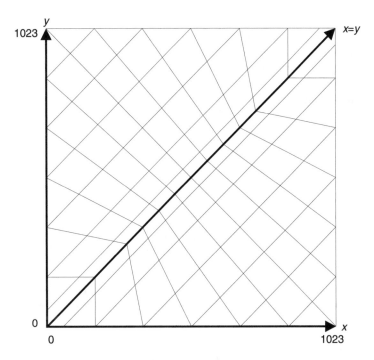

Figure 5.10   Two-dimensional sample space partitioning for vector quantization.

two-dimensional vectors by taking samples in pairs. Quantizing a two-dimensional sample space such as a natural image does not imply anything about the number of dimensions in the quantization vectors. It is the number of discrete samples that make up each quantization vector that determine its dimensions, regardless of the logical organization of the original sample space. The logical organization of the original sample space, on the other hand, will have some impact on its statistical characteristics, which in turn will affect the way sample groups are quantized.

Vector Quantization Programming Example

A sample program is provided, called VQ_DEMO.EXE, which compresses gray-scale images using a simple one-dimensional vector quantization scheme. This uses a very rudimentary quantizer that first calculates the statistical distribution of pixel values and then quantizes pixels in groups of two or more depending on their relative probabilities. The objective is to reduce the original range of values, which is 240, down to 16 unique values, representing the most-often-used pixels with more accuracy than those that are used less often. The resulting compression ratio is therefore 2:1. The quantizer works by first creating a histogram of the original pixel values, giving the number of occurrences of each value. Since there will be 16 symbols in the quantized symbol set the probabilities of each of the 16 should be approximately equal. In other words, the probability should be approximately 1/16 (0.0625) for each vector. The probabilities of adjacent values are accumulated until the sum exceeds 1/16th. The weighted average of all pixels in the resulting set is then calculated to derive the quantized reconstruction pixel value. This procedure is repeated for all 16 quantization vectors. The resulting data is then written to a file. Images may be compressed and decompressed and the results viewed using the picture viewer program provided, named VIEW_PIC.EXE. The following program source code is stored in file VQ_DEMO.CPP:

VQ_DEMO Program Listing

```
#include <stdlib.h>
#include <stdio.h>
#include <conio.h>
#include <dos.h>

void main(int argc, char* argv[])
  {
  FILE *fi,*fo;
  unsigned char image[320],coded_image[160];
  int row,size,pel,index,tag,above,below,toggle,flag;
  int code_table[256],code_book[16];
  float stat[256],max,avg;
  printf("Vector Quantization Image Compression Demo Program\n\n");
  printf("Copyright (c) John Wiley & Sons, Inc., 1994.\n\n");
  if(argc<4)
     {
     printf
     ("Please provide two file names: <input_file> <output_file>\n");
     printf("followed by /c for compress or /u for uncompress.\n");
     printf("Example: VQ_DEMO picture.b_w picture.out /c\n\n");
     exit(0);
     }
  if(argv[3][1]!='c' && argv[3][1]!='u')
     {
     printf("Please specify /c for compress or /u for uncompress.\n");
     exit(0);
     }
  fi=fopen(argv[1],"rb");
  fo=fopen(argv[2],"wb");
  if(fi==NULL)
     {
     printf("Could not open input file %s.\n",argv[1]);
     exit(0);
     }
  if(fo==NULL)
     {
     printf("Could not open output file %s.\n",argv[2]);
     exit(0);
     }
//-------------------------------------------------------------
  if(argv[3][1]=='c')   // User wants to compress
     {
     printf("Calculating image statistics.\n");
     for(pel=0;pel<256;pel++)  // Initialize tables
        {
```

```
                stat[pel]=0.0;
                code_table[pel]=(-1);
                }
        for(row=0;row<200;row++)   // Collect image statistics first
            {
            fread(image,320,1,fi);   // Read a row
            for(pel=0;pel<320;pel++)stat[(int)image[pel]]+=1.0;
            }
        for(pel=0;pel<256;pel++)stat[pel]/=64000.0;
        pel=0;
        for(index=0;index<16;index++) // Find remaining 8 categories
            {
            max=0.0;
            avg=0.0;
            below=pel;
            while(code_table[pel]==(-1) && max<0.0625 && pel<255)
                {
                max+=stat[pel];
                avg+=(float)pel;
                code_table[pel]=index;
                pel++;
                }
            if(pel>below)code_book[index]=(int)(avg/(float)(pel-below));
            else code_book[index]=pel;
            }
        while(pel<256)     // Fill any unused entries
            {
            if(code_table[pel]==(-1))code_table[pel]=15;
            pel++;
            }
        for(index=8;index<16;index++)   // Check limits
            {
            if(code_book[index]<16)code_book[index]=16;
            }
//----------------------------------------------------------
        printf("Compressing.\n");
        fwrite(code_book,16*sizeof(int),1,fo); // Codebook for decompress
        rewind(fi);
        for(row=0;row<200;row++)              // Compress one row at a time
            {
            fread(image,320,1,fi);            // Read a row
            index=0;
            for(pel=0;pel<320;pel+=2)
                {
                coded_image[index]=(unsigned char)(code_table[image[pel]]<<4);
                coded_image[index++]|=(unsigned char)(code_table[image[pel+1]]);
                }
            fwrite(coded_image,160,1,fo);
            }
        }
//----------------------------------------------------------
    if(argv[3][1]=='u')  // User wants to uncompress
        {
```

```
      printf("Uncompressing.\n");
      fread
      (code_book,16*sizeof(int),1,fi); // Codebook for decompress

      for(row=0;row<200;row++)  // Uncompress one pixel row at a time
        {
        fread(coded_image,160,1,fi);   // Read a row
        index=0;
        for(pel=0;pel<320;pel+=2)
          {
          image[pel]=(unsigned char)
            (code_book[(int)(coded_image[index]>>4)]);
          if(image[pel]<16)image[pel]=16;
          image[pel+1]=(unsigned char)
            (code_book[(int)(coded_image[index]&0xf)]);
          if(image[pel+1]<16)image[pel+1]=16;
          index++;
          }
        fwrite(image,320,1,fo);
        }
      }
  fclose(fi);
  fclose(fo);
  printf("Done.\n");
  }
```

Simple Quantization Programming Example

To contrast with the vector quantization technique, a second program is provided, called SQ_DEMO.EXE, which simply truncates each pixel value to four bits. The visual result is similar in some cases, but not in others. Taking the BALLOONS.PIC image file for example, a large portion of the image is sky, which uses relatively few distinct pixel values, but needs small intensity changes. Under vector quantization, this area is more finely quantized than the rest of the image, which detracts from the appearance of the hot-air balloons. When compressed using simple quantization, the sky is more heavily quantized, resulting in easily visible steps between intensity levels, but the balloons look better. Images may be compressed and decompressed, and the results viewed using the picture viewer program provided, named VIEW_PIC.EXE. The following program source code is stored in file SQ_DEMO.CPP:

SQ_DEMO Program Listing

```
  #include <stdlib.h>
  #include <stdio.h>
  #include <conio.h>
  #include <dos.h>

  void main(int argc, char* argv[])
    {
    FILE *fi,*fo;
    unsigned char image[320],coded_image[160];
```

```
    int row,size,pel,index;
    printf("Simple Quantization Image Compression Demo Program\n\n");
    printf("Copyright (c) John Wiley & Sons, Inc., 1994.\n\n");
    if(argc<4)
      {
      printf
      ("Please provide two file names: <input_file> <output_file>\n");
      printf("followed by /c for compress or /u for uncompress.\n");
      printf("Example: SQ_DEMO picture.b_w picture.out /c\n\n");
      exit(0);
      }
    if(argv[3][1]!='c' && argv[3][1]!='u')
      {
      printf("Please specify /c for compress or /u for uncompress.\n");
      exit(0);
      }
    fi=fopen(argv[1],"rb");
    fo=fopen(argv[2],"wb");
    if(fi==NULL)
      {
      printf("Could not open input file %s.\n",argv[1]);
      exit(0);
      }
    if(fo==NULL)
      {
      printf("Could not open output file %s.\n",argv[2]);
      exit(0);
      }
//----------------------------------------------------------
  if(argv[3][1]=='c')                  // User wants to compress
      {
      printf("Compressing.\n");
      for(row=0;row<200;row++)  // Compress one row at a time
        {
        fread(image,320,1,fi);  // Read a row
        index=0;
        for(pel=0;pel<320;pel+=2)
          {
          coded_image[index]=image[pel]&0xf0;
          coded_image[index++]|=(image[pel+1]&0xf0)>>4;
          }
        fwrite(coded_image,160,1,fo);
        }
      }
//----------------------------------------------------------
  if(argv[3][1]=='u')            // User wants to uncompress
      {
      printf("Uncompressing.\n");
      for(row=0;row<200;row++)  // Uncompress one pixel row at a time
        {
        fread(coded_image,160,1,fi); // Read a row
        index=0;
        for(pel=0;pel<320;pel+=2)
```

```
        {
        image[pel]=coded_image[index]&0xf0;
        image[pel+1]=(coded_image[index]&0xf)<<4;
        index++;
        }
      fwrite(image,320,1,fo);
      }
    }
  fclose(fi);
  fclose(fo);
  printf("Done.\n");
  }
```

Four Square Transform (FST) Encoding

The FST is a class of compression algorithms that takes advantage of the reduced need for spatial resolution in color information for natural images. The FST allows this fact to be taken advantage of without converting from RGB color space into one of the separate luminance and chrominance color spaces. The basic concept involves operating on blocks of pixels, dividing each block into four sections, once horizontally and once vertically. Hence, the name *four square*. Figure 5.11 illustrates all possible ways a 3×3 group of pixels can be divided into 4 blocks.

The basic assumption behind FST compression algorithms is that color information need not be represented at as high a spatial frequency as light intensity information. The basic premise is that any 3×3 block of pixels (or larger) can be represented with reasonable accuracy using only two colors, dividing the 3×3 block of pixels into four regions as illustrated in Figure 5.11 to statistically

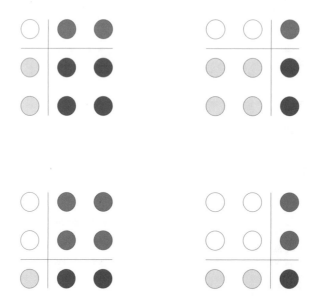

Figure 5.11   Block division in four square transform encoding.

determine the closest approximation for the two selected colors. Each 3×3 block of pixels is then represented as a bitmap with one bit per pixel rather than a full color representation for each pixel. The bitmap then selects one of the two approximate colors for each pixel in the block upon reconstruction. The number of pixels used for the basis block in the FST technique may be more than 3×3 or as little as 2×2. The more pixels used in the basic block, the more likely there will be significant distortions in color when reduced to two colors. The basis blocks need not be symmetrical (i.e., 3×2 or 2×3 or some other aspect ratio can be used). Determining which two colors best approximate any color transition that occurs in the basis pixel block is simply a matter of statistical analysis of the original colors. Note that each of the cases illustrated in Figure 5.11 comprises one group of four pixels, two groups of two pixels each, and a single pixel. Using this arrangement a maximum of four unique colors could be displayed. If this is reduced to two colors, it means two of the original four will be distorted. Selecting which two are appropriate for distortion is a matter of calculating which are predominant and what the relative differences are from one color to the next. Each 3×3 block of pixels can therefore be represented as a single bitmap consisting of nine bits, and two colors. If each color is represented using 15-bit representation, the total is 39 bits per block. This works out to a little less than four-and-a-half bits per pixel on average and creates a fairly good approximation of a natural image using 15 bits per pixel uncompressed. This compression ratio can be further improved by representing each frame in the video sequence as a bitmap where each bit indicates whether or not the corresponding 3×3 pixel block has changed from the previous frame. Pixel block information needs to be transmitted only for blocks that have changed because motion tends to be localized within an image. Frame bitmaps will tend to have long runs of zeros or ones, and can therefore be further compressed using run length encoding as discussed in the first section of this chapter. For each 3×3 pixel block, after determining the nearest two-color approximation for the block, if the difference between the two colors is small enough, the block can be represented with only one color. This further reduces the amount of data to be transmitted for that block. The probability of this occurring is fairly high because the spatial frequency in the immediate vicinity only needs to be lower than the sampling frequency of the block, which is fairly high. A programming example for FST compression is not provided because the FST algorithm is optimized for component color images, and all the compression program examples provided here use gray-scale images, because of the assumed standard VGA display limitation.

Differential Pulse Code Modulation (DPCM)

Pulse code modulation (PCM) is a technique commonly used for digital telephone signal transmission. It is a method of digitizing analog signals with a nonlinear correspondence between the original analog signal and the digital codes assigned. The technique takes advantage of the fact that large-amplitude signals are less sensitive to quantization errors than small-amplitude signals. Therefore, the delta between adjacent low-amplitude code values is much smaller than between high-amplitude code values. This is illustrated in Figure 5.12, which shows the range of amplitude levels assigned to each of the 16 possible values of a four-bit code word.

This allows absolute coding of every sample at some threshold above zero. *Differential pulse code modulation* (DPCM) uses a similar technique but encodes each sample relative to the previous sample. That is, each pulse code represents a plus or minus delta from the previous sample. The advantage of this technique is that delta values tend to be much smaller than absolute values and,

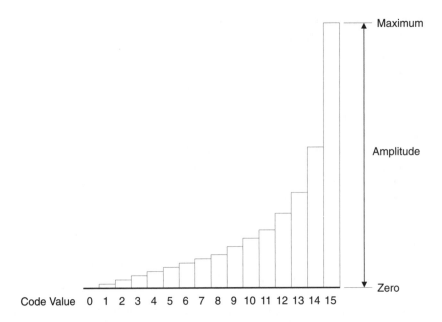

Figure 5.12   Relative sample amplitudes in typical PCM code book.

therefore, can be encoded using fewer bits. There are two main disadvantages. One is that significant quantization errors can be introduced in cases where the original signal makes large amplitude swings that the coding scheme is inadequate to represent. This is known as *slope overload*. The other is that errors in the digital domain tend to be propagated endlessly upon reconstruction of the original signal unless some method of error detection and correction is incorporated. Of course, DPCM requires the digital code set to represent both positive and negative values. A possible scheme for assigning delta values to digital codes is illustrated in Figure 5.13.

Note that there is no zero value in the code set. This means that for a flat input signal at any amplitude the nearest reconstructed approximation will carry a low-level ripple equal to one-half the sample frequency and equal in magnitude to twice the smallest code delta value. If these delta values are sufficiently small the unwanted ripple can be removed by subsequent filtering, especially if a finite impulse response filter is used, which is optimized for this case. Figure 5.14 illustrates a typical input signal and the corresponding unfiltered DPCM encoded output signal.

Application to Natural Images

For continuous-tone natural images, this technique can be applied to successive rows of pixels with fairly good results. It is a good idea to begin each row with an absolute value and encode the remaining pixels on the row with delta values. This restricts any digital bit errors to the row in which they occur. It also eliminates any fringe effects caused by slope overload at the image boundaries. Because of the fact that, upon reconstruction, each pixel value is calculated relative to the previous, the *reconstructed* value of each previous pixel must be used in calculating the delta value to be encoded during image compression. That is, the encoder must emulate the operation of the decoder,

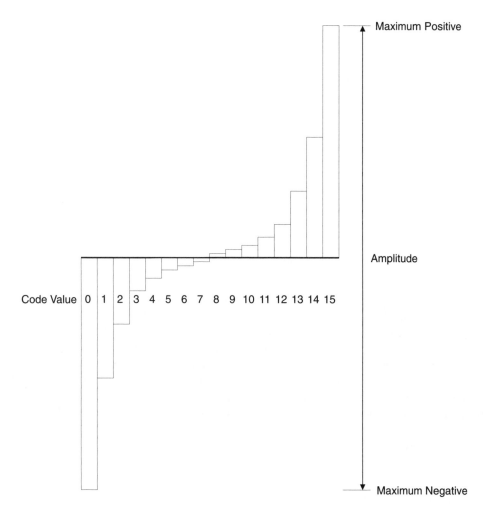

Figure 5.13   Relative sample amplitudes in typical DPCM code book.

otherwise cumulative errors will cause visible horizontal streaks in the reconstructed image. To verify this, try removing the line that has the comment

```
// Recode to emulate decode
```

from the example program provided, recompile, and compress one of the sample images. Upon reconstruction and viewing, the visual artifacts should be obvious.

DPCM Compression Programming Example

A program called PCM_DEMO.EXE is provided to illustrate the programming technique and visual results of DPCM encoding. This program encodes the differential between adjacent pixels as a

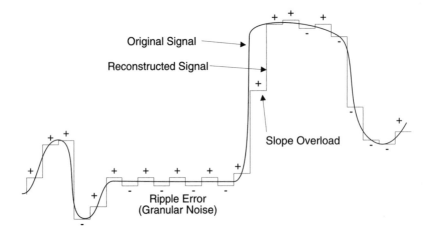

Figure 5.14   Typical DPCM quantization errors.

four-bit value, resulting in approximately 2:1 compression. The ratio is actually slightly less than that due to the need to have a full-resolution pixel at the start of each line, as a reference. Using the VIEW_ERR.EXE program to compare the reconstructed image with the original will show that the biggest errors tend to be along very sharp, high-contrast edges in the image. Slope overload performance could possibly be improved by increasing the maximum delta values in the DPCM code set from +/− 32 to maybe +/− 64 or more. A little experimentation with the code table will show how the compression process can be optimized for one type of image at the expense of others. The following program source code is stored in file PCM_DEMO.CPP:

PCM_DEMO Program Listing

```
#include <stdlib.h>
#include <stdio.h>
#include <conio.h>
#include <dos.h>

void main(int argc, char* argv[])
  {
  FILE *fi,*fo;
  unsigned char image[320],coded_image[162];
  int q1,q2,delta1,delta2,pcm1,pcm2,row,size,pel,index;
  printf("Differential Pulse Code Modulation Demo Program\n\n");
  printf("Copyright (c) John Wiley & Sons, Inc., 1994.\n\n");
  if(argc<4)
    {
    printf
    ("Please provide two file names: <input_file> <output_file>\n");
    printf("followed by /c for compress or /u for uncompress.\n");
    printf("Example: PCM_DEMO picture.b_w picture.out /c\n\n");
```

```
      exit(0);
      }
  if(argv[3][1]!='c' && argv[3][1]!='u')
    {
    printf("Please specify /c for compress or /u for uncompress.\n");
    exit(0);
    }
  fi=fopen(argv[1],"rb");
  fo=fopen(argv[2],"wb");
  if(fi==NULL)
    {
    printf("Could not open input file %s.\n",argv[1]);
    exit(0);
    }
  if(fo==NULL)
    {
    printf("Could not open output file %s.\n",argv[2]);
    exit(0);
    }
  int pcm[16]={-32,-16,-8,-6,-4,-3,-2,-1,1,2,3,4,6,8,16,32};
//-------------------------------------------------------
  if(argv[3][1]=='c')                // User wants to compress
    {
    printf("Compressing.\n");
    for(row=0;row<200;row++)    // Compress one pixel row at a time
      {
      fread(image,320,1,fi);    // Read a row
      coded_image[0]=image[0];  // Insert absolute start values
      coded_image[1]=image[1];
      size=2;
      for(pel=2;pel<320;pel+=2)
        {
        delta1=(int)image[pel]-(int)image[pel-1];
        q1=q2=256;
        for(index=0;index<16;index++)   // Find closest PCM code
          {
          if(abs(delta1-pcm[index])<q1)
            {
            q1=abs(delta1-pcm[index]);
            pcm1=index;
            }
          }
        q1=(int)image[pel-1]+pcm[pcm1];
        q1=(q1>255)?255:q1;
        q1=(q1<16)?16:q1;
        image[pel]=(unsigned char)q1;    // Recode to emulate decode
        delta2=(int)image[pel+1]-(int)image[pel];
        for(index=0;index<16;index++)
          {
          if(abs(delta2-pcm[index])<q2)
            {
            q2=abs(delta2-pcm[index]);
```

```
                    pcm2=index;
                    }
                }
            q2=(int)image[pel]+pcm[pcm2];
            q2=(q2>255)?255:q2;
            q2=(q2<16)?16:q2;
            image[pel+1]=(unsigned char)q2;   // Recode to emulate decode
            coded_image[size++]=(unsigned char)((pcm1<<4)|pcm2);
            }
        fwrite(coded_image,161,1,fo);
        }
    }
//-----------------------------------------------------------
  if(argv[3][1]=='u')                  // User wants to uncompress
    {
    printf("Uncompressing.\n");
    for(row=0;row<200;row++)        // Uncompress one pixel row at a time
        {
        fread(coded_image,161,1,fi);   // Read a row
        image[0]=coded_image[0];       // Insert absolute start values
        image[1]=coded_image[1];
        size=2;
        for(pel=2;pel<161;pel++)
            {
            pcm1=(int)(coded_image[pel]>>4);
            pcm2=(int)(coded_image[pel]&0xf);
            q1=image[size-1]+pcm[pcm1];
            q1=(q1>255)?255:q1;
            q1=(q1<16)?16:q1;
            image[size]=(unsigned char)q1;
            size++;
            q2=image[size-1]+pcm[pcm2];
            q2=(q2>255)?255:q2;
            q2=(q2<16)?16:q2;
            image[size]=(unsigned char)q2;
            size++;
            }
        fwrite(image,320,1,fo);
        }
    }
    fclose(fi);
    fclose(fo);
    printf("Done.\n");
    }
```

Discrete Cosine Transform (DCT)

The DCT is a mathematical operation that calculates the frequency components of a given signal sampled at a given sampling rate. The DCT must be applied to a finite number of samples. The mathematics can be simplified considerably if the number of samples used is an even power of two. The DCT is fairly easy to conceptualize. A one-dimensional DCT converts an array of numbers, which represent signal amplitudes at various points in time or space, into another array of numbers, each of which represents the amplitude of a certain frequency component from the original signal. The resulting array of numbers contains the same number of values as the original array. The first element in the result array is a simple average of all the samples in the input array and is referred to as the DC coefficient. The remaining elements in the result array each indicate the amplitude of a specific frequency component of the input array, and are known as AC coefficients. The frequency represented by each element in the result array is a function of the array index for that element. The frequency content of the sample set at each frequency is calculated by taking a weighted average of the entire set. The appropriate weight for each input sample is determined by multiplying the current index of the result array by the constant pi and the index of the input sample. This has the effect of producing a series of weight coefficients that approximate a *cosine* wave whose frequency is proportional to the result array index. Figure 5.15 illustrates the approximate relationships between weight coefficients as applied to each input sample for each result array index in a one-dimensional DCT operating on an array of eight input samples.

The maximum weight for any sample is one. Sample weights range from a maximum of one to a minimum of minus one. Inspection of Figure 5.15 reveals that each step of the result array

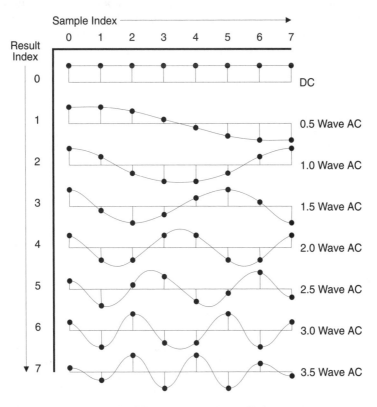

Figure 5.15   Relative magnitudes of DCT sample weight coefficients.

index corresponds to an increase of one-half cycle in the related frequency component. For an array of eight samples, the highest frequency is therefore 3.5 cycles. This closely approaches the maximum frequency that could be represented, which would be four cycles, or one-half the sampling rate. Table 5.2 gives the coefficients used to calculate the weighted averages for each frequency component. The equation for calculating the sample weight coefficients is given in Figure 5.16.

Inspection of this equation reveals that when the result array index is zero the numerator in the fraction will be zero. Taking the cosine of zero yields a value of one. Therefore, the weight factor will be the same for all samples in that case. Expanding this equation to generate weighted averages results in the equation shown in Figure 5.17. This is the equation for a one-dimensional DCT operating on a sample array of size N.

It is not necessary to calculate the entire equation for each element in the sample set. If the DCT is to be calculated for multiple sample sets the matrix of coefficients shown in Table 5.2 can be calculated once and applied to all subsequent sample sets. Figure 5.18 illustrates how the weight coefficients would be applied to the samples for the DC coefficient and the first AC coefficient when calculating the DCT for a set of eight samples.

Once a sample set has been transformed into a set of frequency coefficients, these can be selectively quantized to reduce the overall size of the data set while retaining the most critical information. Of course, if the frequency coefficients are quantized, the original data set cannot be perfectly restored. Restoration is performed simply by summing the products of the frequency coefficients and the weight coefficients for each sample. The equation for restoration of the sample set is referred to as an *inverse* DCT, or *IDCT,* and is illustrated in Figure 5.19 for a one-dimensional DCT. The forward DCT is also sometimes called the *FDCT.*

Two-Dimensional DCT

Now that the fundamental operation of a one-dimensional DCT has been described, we can consider a two-dimensional DCT. A common data set for this type of operation is an array of pixels. If we

Table 5.2   One-dimensional DCT Sample Weight Coefficients

Result Index ⇓	Sample Index ⇒ 0	1	2	3	4	5	6	7
0	+0.707	+0.707	+0.707	+0.707	+0.707	+0.707	+0.707	+0.707
1	+0.981	+0.831	+0.556	+0.195	-0.195	-0.556	-0.831	-0.981
2	+0.924	+0.383	-0.383	-0.924	-0.924	-0.383	+0.383	+0.924
3	+0.831	-0.195	-0.981	-0.556	+0.556	+0.981	+0.195	-0.831
4	+0.707	-0.707	-0.707	+0.707	+0.707	-0.707	-0.707	+0.707
5	+0.556	-0.981	+0.195	+0.831	-0.831	-0.195	+0.981	-0.556
6	+0.383	-0.924	+0.924	-0.383	-0.383	+0.924	-0.924	+0.383
7	+0.195	-0.556	+0.831	-0.981	+0.981	-0.831	+0.556	-0.195

$$\text{Coeff}_{(k,m)} = C(k) \cos\left[\frac{(2m+1)k\pi}{2N}\right]$$

Where: $C(k) = \dfrac{1}{\sqrt{2}}$ when $k = 0$, 1 otherwise

k = Result Array Index
m = Sample Array Index
N = Sample Array Size

Figure 5.16   Equation for sample weight coefficients.

consider a two-dimensional 8x8 array of pixels, it can be logically subdivided into eight rows of eight pixels or eight columns of eight pixels each. If the one-dimensional DCT is applied separately to each row of eight pixels, the result will be eight rows of frequency coefficients. If these eight rows of frequency coefficients are then taken as eight columns, the first column will contain all DC coefficients, the second column will contain the first AC coefficient from each row, and so on. The important thing to note about this arrangement is that even though the array represents frequency information in the horizontal direction it still represents spatial information in the vertical direction. Therefore, the one dimensional DCT can again be applied to the columns individually. Each element of the resulting two-dimensional array of frequency components will then represent a two-dimensional frequency component. The element in the upper-left corner is the DC coefficient for the entire two-dimensional array, and all the remaining coefficients contain frequency information. Each frequency coefficient, when applied through the inverse two-dimensional DCT, will produce a different pattern of light and dark areas with a contrast ratio defined by the amplitude of the coefficient. Figure 5.20 illustrates the patterns produced by each of the frequency coefficients in an 8×8 DCT result, assuming each coefficient is at its maximum value.

Note that the upper-left block is a solid gray, indicating an average intensity for the entire 8×8 block. The lower-right block looks like a checkerboard because it indicates the maximum frequency component both horizontally and vertically. The upper-right and lower-left blocks show vertical and horizontal stripes respectively because they show the maximum horizontal frequency and zero vertical frequency or vice-versa. The integrated equations for a two-dimensional DCT are shown in Figure 5.21.

$$X(k) = \sqrt{\frac{2}{N}}\, C(k) \sum_{m=0}^{N-1} x(m) \cos\left[\frac{(2m+1)k\pi}{2N}\right]$$

Where: $C(k) = \dfrac{1}{\sqrt{2}}$ when $k = 0$, 1 otherwise

$X()$ = Result Array
$x()$ = Sample Array
N = Array Size
k = Result Array Index
m = Sample Array Index

Figure 5.17   Equation for one-dimensional DCT.

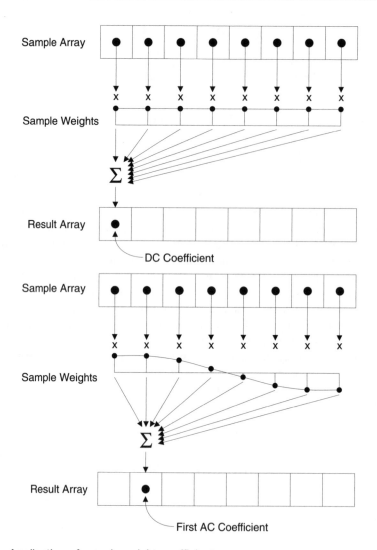

Figure 5.18   Application of sample weight coefficients.

Inspection of this equation reveals that there is a sum of cosine terms for horizontal and vertical directions for each element in the result array. The equation is simply a combination of two one-dimensional DCT equations, one for horizontal frequencies and one for vertical frequencies.

Computation Efficiency

Transforming a two-dimensional array of pixels into corresponding frequency components by itself does nothing to compress the data. The real advantage of the DCT is that it allows selective quanti-

$$x(m) = \sqrt{\tfrac{2}{N}} \sum_{k=0}^{N-1} X(k)\, C(k)\, \cos\left[\tfrac{(2m+1)k\pi}{2N}\right]$$

Where: $C(k) = \dfrac{1}{\sqrt{2}}$ when $k = 0$, 1 otherwise

$X()$ = Result Array
$x()$ = Sample Array
N = Array Size
k = Result Array Index
m = Sample Array Index

Figure 5.19   Equation for inverse one-dimensional DCT.

zation of the various frequency components that make up a given block of pixels. There is no theoretical or mathematical limit on the size of the input array for a DCT. The basic equation would be the same for transforming an entire image, although the computation time required for that large an array would be prohibitive. The number of multiplication operations required for each element of the result array for a one-dimensional DCT is proportional to the square of the number of elements in the sample array, on the order of $[N \log_2 (N)]^2$. For a two-dimensional DCT it is proportional to the sum of the squares of the horizontal and vertical dimensions of the sample array. By dividing the original image into smaller blocks the number of computations required is reduced significantly. The disadvantage of this approach is that after image reconstruction there may be visible boundaries between the blocks of pixels upon which DCT operations were performed. Figure 5.22 illustrates an original image next to a reconstructed image using an 8×8 DCT to transform and reconstruct the image.

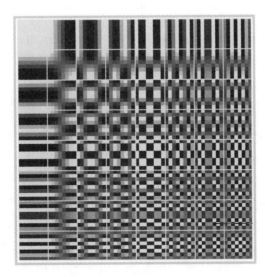

Figure 5.20   Two-dimensional DCT sample weight intensity patterns.

Forward DCT $\quad F_{[U,V]} = \frac{1}{N^2} C_U C_V \sum\limits_{m=0}^{N-1} \sum\limits_{n=0}^{N-1} f[m,n] \cos\left[\frac{(2m+1)U\pi}{2N}\right] \cos\left[\frac{(2n+1)V\pi}{2N}\right]$

Inverse DCT $\quad f[m,n] = \sum\limits_{U=0}^{N-1} \sum\limits_{V=0}^{N-1} C_U C_V F_{[U,V]} \cos\left[\frac{(2m+1)U\pi}{2N}\right] \cos\left[\frac{(2n+1)V\pi}{2N}\right]$

Where:

C_U and C_V = 1 when v,u = 0,0 (DC Component)

C_U and C_V = 2 in all other cases

$F_{[U,V]}$ = Target cell for DCT coefficient

$f[m,n]$ = Target cell for original or reconstructed pixel

Figure 5.21 Forward and inverse DCT equations.

Close inspection reveals some visible artifacts as a result of boundary conditions between 8×8 blocks of pixels. The dimensions of the image in this case are 272×272. This results in 34, 8×8 pixel blocks horizontally and vertically. The result of quantization in the frequency domain is usually a slight softening or blurring or reduction of contrast of features within each 8×8 block. This tends to exaggerate any differences at the boundaries between blocks. The net result is a less well-defined image and more visual artifacts. Figure 5.23 shows the original picture from Figure 5.22 with the reconstructed image after significant quantization of higher frequency elements.

In practice, the degree of quantization which can be applied to any particular frequency component depends on a number of factors including the characteristics of the image, the desired compression ratio, and the quality required in the reconstructed image. For color images it is usually acceptable to quantize color components more heavily than luminance components for perceptual reasons described earlier. When calculating the DCT for image blocks, it is generally preferable to use integer math rather than floating point because floating point math is more time consuming. A

Figure 5.22 Original and reconstructed image after DCT encoding without filtering.

Figure 5.23   Original and reconstructed image after DCT encoding with quantization.

reasonable approximation of the sample weight factors can be achieved by scaling each value by a factor of 1024 or more. This retains accuracy to three or four significant digits, which is no less than the accuracy shown in Table 5.2. If the sample weight factors are all multiplied by $2 \div 2$ before scaling to an integer approximation, the resulting frequency coefficients will be eight times larger than they would have been otherwise. This is because each one-dimensional DCT effectively squares this term and the two-dimensional DCT squares that result. Dividing an integer by eight is a simple matter of shifting right by three bits. This greatly simplifies scaling the result values back to the original scale factor. The initial scaling of the weight factors need only be done once, so computation time is not a critical factor. The real potential for data compression using the DCT comes as a result of quantization. The majority of frequency components in a natural image tend to be at the low end of the spectrum. This means that the frequency coefficients derived by the DCT at the high end of the spectrum tend to have low amplitudes. Quantization reduces many of the smaller values to zero. This results in a relatively large portion of the DCT result array being filled with zero values. By encoding runs of zeros using run length encoding, thereby reducing or eliminating redundancy, significant data compression can be achieved. This is the technique used by both the JPEG and MPEG compression standards. These standards combine DCT and run length encoding with several other techniques to achieve even greater compression and image quality. The degree of quantization that can be imposed on image blocks depends on the frequency content of the blocks. Images with large amounts of fine detail are more likely to be degraded by this technique than images with smooth contours. Figure 5.24 illustrates an approximation of frequency content distribution in a two-dimensional DCT result array.

It is easy to see that the majority of the array is composed of various combinations of frequency components in the mid-range for vertical and horizontal frequencies. There are two elements that contribute to the reduction of transmitted data in the quantization process: The first, as mentioned earlier, is quantization of low amplitude frequency coefficients to zero. The second is overall amplitude reduction of all nonzero coefficients as a result of quantization. The combination of zero runs and reduced-amplitude frequency coefficients allows the nonzero frequency coefficients to be encoded using a minimum number of data bits if variable-length encoding techniques are used. An optimum set of quantization coefficients can be determined based on the compression ratio required, image quality required, and a statistical analysis of the image or images to be encod-

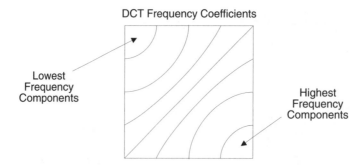

Figure 5.24   Approximate distribution of frequency content in two-dimensional DCT result.

ed. A statistical analysis consists of determining the relative probability of each frequency component having a significant amplitude. Exactly what constitutes a significant amplitude depends on the required quality of the reconstructed image. This gives an indication of which frequency components can be safely reduced or eliminated without seriously compromising image quality. If the indicated quantization does not produce adequate compression then a decision must be made whether to trade off compression ratio or image quality. Generally it is not possible to maximize both. Figure 5.25 illustrates how the degree of quantization of frequency components varies from maximum to minimum frequency levels in a typical application.

Example 8×8 Block Encode and Decode

As an example, consider the following 8×8 block of pixels taken from an actual image file. The 8×8 block represents the upper-left corner of the image file named BALLOONS.PIC. These values, shown in Table 5.3, are eight-bit luminance samples. After the two-dimensional DCT as shown in Figure 5.18 is applied, the resulting frequency coefficients are as shown in Table 5.4.

It is obvious that the majority of energy in the block is concentrated in a few relatively low frequency coefficients. Dividing each by its corresponding quantization coefficient, as shown in Table 5.5, results in many of the smaller frequency coefficients being reduced to zero.

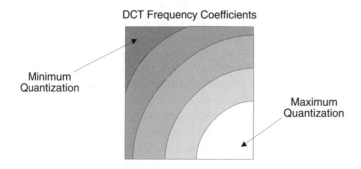

Figure 5.25   Relative amplitude distribution of quantization coefficients.

Table 5.3 Initial Pixel Values

97	97	97	102	102	102	102	102
88	88	97	97	97	97	102	97
88	88	97	88	88	97	88	88
88	88	88	88	88	88	88	88
80	92	88	88	88	88	88	88
80	88	83	88	82	88	88	88
80	83	80	86	88	86	86	86
80	80	83	83	80	80	83	88

Table 5.4 Frequency Coefficients

+2853	−47	−20	−16	−14	0	0	−10
+ 166	−4	−14	+10	−7	+11	+14	+12
+43	−23	+1	0	+21	+12	0	+6
+45	−13	−3	+2	+2	−7	−29	−16
+8	+12	+12	−6	+12	−7	−8	+1
+2	+11	+1	+21	+12	−4	+1	−4
−5	+15	+10	−3	−11	−1	+18	−13
+4	+7	−11	+3	−9	−14	+7	0

Table 5.5 Quantization Coefficients

1	8	8	8	8	8	8	8
8	8	8	8	8	8	8	8
8	8	8	8	256	256	256	256
8	8	8	256	256	256	256	256
8	8	256	256	256	256	256	256
8	8	256	256	256	256	256	256
8	8	256	256	256	256	256	256
8	8	256	256	256	256	256	256

After quantization, the frequency coefficient array is as shown in Table 5.6. Note how non-zero values are clustered at the upper-left corner of the array.

This presents an excellent opportunity to eliminate zero values using run length encoding techniques, especially if the coefficients are ordered in a nonorthogonal arrangement. See Chapter 10 for a description of zig-zag ordering of quantized coefficients. When the pixel block is reconstructed by multiplying the quantized frequency coefficient array with the quantization coefficient array and then performing an inverse DCT, the resulting set of pixel values is as shown in Table 5.7.

The errors introduced as a result of compression and decompression can be calculated by subtracting each pixel value in the reconstructed array from the corresponding pixel value in the origi-

Table 5.6 Quantized Frequency Coefficients

+2853	−5	−2	−2	−1	0	0	−1
+20	0	−1	+1	0	+1	+1	+1
+5	−2	0	0	0	0	0	0
+5	−1	0	0	0	0	0	0
+1	+1	0	0	0	0	0	0
0	+1	0	0	0	0	0	0
0	+1	0	0	0	0	0	0
0	0	0	0	0	0	0	0

Table 5.7 Reconstructed Pixel Values

95	96	101	100	100	103	102	100
88	89	95	95	96	99	99	98
88	89	92	91	90	91	90	88
86	88	89	89	87	88	87	87
84	87	87	88	87	88	88	88
80	85	84	86	85	86	87	88
79	84	82	85	83	85	86	88
78	83	80	83	81	82	83	85

Table 5.8 Error Values

+2	+1	−4	+2	+2	−1	0	+2
0	−1	+2	+2	+1	−2	+3	−1
0	−1	+5	−3	−2	+6	−2	0
+2	0	−1	−1	+1	0	+1	+1
−4	+5	+1	0	+1	0	0	0
0	+3	−1	+2	−3	+2	+1	0
+1	−1	−2	+1	+5	+1	0	−2
+2	−3	+3	0	−1	−2	0	+3

nal array. Table 5.8 gives the errors resulting from the compression and decompression in the previous example.

Example 8×8 Block Encode and Decode Program

The following C++ source code was used to generate the example block coefficients shown above. The program reads the image file BALLOONS.PIC, and writes a text file named DCT_FGEN.TXT. It operates on only one 8×8 pixel block, and therefore, even though the DCT calculations are done with floating point arithmetic, it is fairly fast. However, the DCT image encode/decode program example shown later in this chapter is derived from this program, and may be rather slow

depending on the speed of the machine running it. The following program source is in file
DCT_FGEN.CPP:

```c
#include <stdlib.h>
#include <stdio.h>
#include <conio.h>
#include <math.h>
#include <dos.h>


//--------------------------------------------------------
// Program:  DCT Image Compression Demostration Program
// Author:   Phil Mattison
// Compiler: Borland Turbo C++ v1.01
//--------------------------------------------------------

void main(void)
  {
  FILE *fi,*fo;                 // I/O file pointers
  unsigned char image[8][320];  // 8-row image buffer
  char coded_block[64];         // Buffer for coded pixel block
  int band;                     // Counter for 8-row bands
  int row;                      // Counter for rows
  int size;                     // Encoded block size
  int pel;                      // Pixel counter
  int index;                    // General index
  int block;                    // Block counter
  int coeff;                    // DCT coefficient counter
  int x,y,i;                    // General index
  float dct_tmp1[8][8];         // Intermediate block buffer
  float dct_tmp2[8][8];         // Intermediate block buffer
  float dct_coeff[8][8];        // DCT coefficient buffer
  double f1,f2,tmp;             // General real number variables
  char q[8][8]=                 // Quantization control array
    {                          // 1=Keep, 0=Eliminate
    1,1,1,1,1,1,1,1,
    1,1,1,1,1,1,1,1,
    1,1,1,1,0,0,0,0,
    1,1,1,0,0,0,0,0,
    1,1,0,0,0,0,0,0,
    1,1,0,0,0,0,0,0,
    1,1,0,0,0,0,0,0,
    1,1,0,0,0,0,0,0
    };
  fi=fopen("balloons.b_w","rb");
  fo=fopen("dct_fgen.txt","w");
  if(fi==NULL)
    {
    printf("Could not open input file.\n");
    exit(0);
    }
  if(fo==NULL)
    {
```

```c
      printf("Could not open output file\n");
      exit(0);
      }
  f1=2.0*atan(1.0)/8.0;   // Calculate DCT coefficients
  for(y=0;y<8;y++)
    {
    f2=(double)y*f1;
    for(x=0;x<8;x++)
      {
      tmp=cos((double)(2*x+1)*f2);
      if(y==0)dct_coeff[y][x]=(float)(1.0/sqrt(2.0));
      else    dct_coeff[y][x]=(float)tmp;
      }
    }
//-----------------------------------------------------------
  fprintf(fo,"1-Dimensional DCT Coefficients.\n");
  for(y=0;y<8;y++)
    {
    for(x=0;x<8;x++)
      {
      fprintf(fo,"%+1.3f,",dct_coeff[y][x]);
      }
    fprintf(fo,"\n");
    }
  fprintf(fo,"\n\n");
//-----------------------------------------------------------
  for(row=0;row<8;row++)
    {
    fread(&image[row][0],320,1,fi);           // Read a row
    }
//-----------------------------------------------------------
  fprintf(fo,"Original Pixel Values.\n");
  for(y=0;y<8;y++)
    {
    for(x=0;x<8;x++)
      {
      fprintf(fo,"%3d,",(int)image[y][x]);
      }
    fprintf(fo,"\n");
    }
  fprintf(fo,"\n\n");
//-----------------------------------------------------------
  for(y=0;y<8;y++)        // Do 1-dimensional row DCTs
    {
    for(coeff=0;coeff<8;coeff++)
      {
      dct_tmp1[y][coeff]=0.0;
      for(x=0;x<8;x++)
        {
        dct_tmp1[y][coeff]+=
        ((float)image[y][x])*(float)dct_coeff[coeff][x];
        }
      }
```

```
      }
    for(x=0;x<8;x++)        // Do 1-dimensional column DCTs
      {
      for(coeff=0;coeff<8;coeff++)
        {
        dct_tmp2[coeff][x]=0.0;
        for(index=0;index<8;index++)
          {
          dct_tmp2[coeff][x]+=dct_tmp1[index][x]*dct_coeff[coeff][index];
          }
        }
      }
//----------------------------------------------------------
  fprintf(fo,"DCT Frequency Components.\n");
  for(y=0;y<8;y++)
    {
    for(x=0;x<8;x++)
      {
      fprintf(fo,"%+5d,",(int)dct_tmp2[y][x]);
      }
    fprintf(fo,"\n");
    }
  fprintf(fo,"\n\n");
//----------------------------------------------------------
  for(y=0;y<8;y++)          // Quantize AC coefficients
    {
    for(x=0;x<8;x++)
      {
      if(x!=0 || y!=0)
        {
        dct_tmp2[y][x]=dct_tmp2[y][x]/8.0;
        if(dct_tmp2[y][x]> 127.0)dct_tmp2[y][x]= 127.0;// Saturate AC
        if(dct_tmp2[y][x]<-127.0)dct_tmp2[y][x]=-127.0;
        }
      if((x!=0 || y!=0) && q[y][x]==0)
          {
          dct_tmp2[y][x]=0.0;
          }
      }
    }
  if(dct_tmp2[0][0]> 32767.0)dct_tmp2[y][x]= 32767.0; // Saturate DC
  if(dct_tmp2[0][0]<-32767.0)dct_tmp2[y][x]=-32767.0;
//----------------------------------------------------------
  fprintf(fo,"Quantized DCT Frequency Components.\n");
  for(y=0;y<8;y++)
    {
    for(x=0;x<8;x++)
      {
      fprintf(fo,"%+5d,",(int)dct_tmp2[y][x]);
      }
    fprintf(fo,"\n");
    }
  fprintf(fo,"\n\n");
```

```
//---------------------------------------------------------
  for(y=0;y<8;y++)    // Dequantize AC coefficients
    {
    for(x=0;x<8;x++)
      {
      if(x!=0 || y!=0)
        {
        dct_tmp2[y][x]=dct_tmp2[y][x]*8.0;
        }
      }
    }
//---------------------------------------------------------
  for(x=0;x<8;x++)    // Do 1-dimensional column IDCT
    {
    for(coeff=0;coeff<8;coeff++)
      {
      dct_tmp1[coeff][x]=0.0;
      for(index=0;index<8;index++)
        {
        dct_tmp1[coeff][x]+=dct_tmp2[index][x]*dct_coeff[index][coeff];
        }
      }
    }

  for(y=0;y<8;y++)   // Do 1-dimensional row IDCT
    {
    for(coeff=0;coeff<8;coeff++)
      {
      dct_tmp2[y][coeff]=0.0;
      for(index=0;index<8;index++)
        {
        dct_tmp2[y][coeff]+=dct_tmp1[y][index]*dct_coeff[index][coeff];
        }
      dct_tmp2[y][coeff]/=16.0;
      if(dct_tmp2[y][coeff]>255.0)dct_tmp2[y][coeff]=255.0;
      if(dct_tmp2[y][coeff]<16.0) dct_tmp2[y][coeff]=16.0;
      }
    }
//---------------------------------------------------------
  fprintf(fo,"Reconstructed Pixel Values.\n");
  for(y=0;y<8;y++)
    {
    for(x=0;x<8;x++)
      {
      fprintf(fo,"%3d,",(int)dct_tmp2[y][x]);
      }
    fprintf(fo,"\n");
    }
  fprintf(fo,"\n\n");
//---------------------------------------------------------
  fprintf(fo,"Error Values.\n");
  for(y=0;y<8;y++)
    {
```

```
        for(x=0;x<8;x++)
          {
          fprintf(fo,"%+2d,",(int)image[y][x]-(int)dct_tmp2[y][x]);
          }
        fprintf(fo,"\n");
        }
      fprintf(fo,"\n\n");
      fclose(fi);
      fclose(fo);
      printf("\nDone.\n");
      }
```

A good measure of the relative fidelity of a given encoding and decoding process and related parameters is given by the root mean square error (RMSE). For 8×8 pixel image blocks this can be calculated as shown in Figure 5.26.

For the error figures shown in Table 5.8, the RMSE turns out to be 2.26. For eight-bit pixels this works out to less than one percent average error. Considerable work has been done to develop efficient ways to calculate the DCT. As explained earlier, the two-dimensional DCT can be implemented as a single computation or split into one-dimensional DCT operations, which are repeated. A one-dimensional eight-point DCT can be calculated with as little as 29 additions and 13 multiplication operations. To process an 8×8 block of pixels a total of 16 one-dimensional DCT operations are required resulting in a total of 464 additions and 80 multiplication operations per block. During quantization if a given frequency coefficient is less than one-half the corresponding quantization coefficient the result will be zero. This means that for coefficients that are likely to quantize to zero a comparison can more often than not eliminate the need for a multiplication.

DCT Image Compression Programming Example

The following program source code reads an image file and compresses it using DCT encoding with quantization of the frequency components. You can experiment with the quantization level by changing the pattern of ones and zeros in the quantization control array q[8][8]. Setting more elements to one will improve the quality of the reconstructed image but reduce the compression ratio, and vice-versa. The program code is in file DCT_DEMO.CPP:

```
#include <stdlib.h>
#include <stdio.h>
#include <conio.h>
#include <math.h>
#include <dos.h>

//---------------------------------------------------------
```

$$\text{RMSE} = \sqrt{\frac{1}{64}\sum_{j=0}^{7}\sum_{k=0}^{7} e^2(j,k)}$$

Figure 5.26 Equation for root mean square error calculation.

```
// Program:  DCT Image Compression Demostration Program
// Author:   Phil Mattison
// Compiler: Borland Turbo C++ v1.01
//-------------------------------------------------------

void main(int argc, char* argv[])
  {
  FILE *fi,*fo;                    // I/O file pointers
  unsigned char image[8][320];     // 8-row image buffer
  char coded_block[64];            // Buffer for coded pixel block
  int band;                        // Counter for 8-row bands
  int row;                         // Counter for rows
  int size;                        // Encoded block size
  int pel;                         // Pixel counter
  int index;                       // General index
  int block;                       // Block counter
  int coeff;                       // DCT coefficient counter
  int x,y,i;                       // General index
  float dct_tmp1[8][8];            // Intermediate block buffer
  float dct_tmp2[8][8];            // Intermediate block buffer
  float dct_coeff[8][8];           // DCT coefficient buffer
  double f1,f2,tmp;                // General real number variables
  char q[8][8]=                    // Quantization control array
    {                              // 1=Keep, 0=Eliminate
    1,1,1,1,1,1,1,1,
    1,1,1,1,1,1,1,1,
    1,1,1,1,0,0,0,0,
    1,1,1,0,0,0,0,0,
    1,1,0,0,0,0,0,0,
    1,1,0,0,0,0,0,0,
    1,1,0,0,0,0,0,0,
    1,1,0,0,0,0,0,0
    };

  printf("DCT Encoding Image Compression Demo Program\n\n");
  printf("Copyright (c) John Wiley & Sons, Inc., 1994.\n\n");
  if(argc<4)
    {
    printf
    ("Please provide two file names: <input_file> <output_file>\n");
    printf("followed by /c for compress or /u for uncompress.\n");
    printf("Example: DCT_DEMO picture.b_w picture.out /c\n\n");
    exit(0);
    }
  if(argv[3][1]!='c' && argv[3][1]!='u')
    {
    printf("Please specify /c for compress or /u for uncompress.\n");
    exit(0);
    }
  fi=fopen(argv[1],"rb");
  fo=fopen(argv[2],"wb");
  if(fi==NULL)
    {
```

```
        printf("Could not open input file %s.\n",argv[1]);
        exit(0);
        }
    if(fo==NULL)
        {
        printf("Could not open output file %s.\n",argv[2]);
        exit(0);
        }
    f1=2.0*atan(1.0)/8.0;   // Calculate DCT coefficients
    for(y=0;y<8;y++)
        {
        f2=(double)y*f1;
        for(x=0;x<8;x++)
          {
          tmp=cos((double)(2*x+1)*f2);
          if(y==0)dct_coeff[y][x]=(float)(1.0/sqrt(2.0));
          else    dct_coeff[y][x]=(float)tmp;
          }
        }
//--------------------------------------------------------
// The compression routine divides the 320x200 image onto
// 25 horizontal bands of 8 rows each. These are further
// subdivided into 40 8x8 blocks. Each block is processed
// by application of horizontal and vertical 1-dimensional
// DCT operations, resulting in a 2-dimensional 8x8 array
// of frequency components. The DC coefficient is stored
// as a signed int, and each of the AC coefficients is
// divided by 8, limited to a range of +/- 127, and stored
// as a char type if the quantization array (q) has a 1 in
// the corresponding position. All other AC coefficients
// are omitted.
//--------------------------------------------------------
  if(argv[3][1]=='c')              // User wants to compress
    {
    printf("Compressing.");

    for(band=0;band<25;band++)  // Divide image into 25 bands
      {
      printf(".");
      for(row=0;row<8;row++)      // Compress 8 pixel rows at a time
        {
          fread(&image[row][0],320,1,fi);  // Read a row
        }
      for(block=0;block<40;block++) // Divide the band into blocks
        {
        for(y=0;y<8;y++)                // Do 1-dimensional row DCTs
          {
          for(coeff=0;coeff<8;coeff++)
            {
            dct_tmp1[y][coeff]=0.0;
            for(x=block*8,index=0;index<8;x++,index++)
              {
              dct_tmp1[y][coeff]+=
```

```
                  ((float)image[y][x])*(float)dct_coeff[coeff][index];
                  }
                }
              }
        for(x=0;x<8;x++)   // Do 1-dimensional column DCTs
            {
            for(coeff=0;coeff<8;coeff++)
                {
                dct_tmp2[coeff][x]=0.0;
                for(index=0;index<8;index++)
                    {
                    dct_tmp2[coeff][x]+=
                      dct_tmp1[index][x]*dct_coeff[coeff][index];
                    }
                }
            }
        index=0;
        for(y=0;y<8;y++)   // Quantize AC coefficients
            {
            for(x=0;x<8;x++)
                {
                if((x!=0 || y!=0) && q[y][x]==1)
                    {
                    dct_tmp2[y][x]=dct_tmp2[y][x]/8.0;
                    if(dct_tmp2[y][x]> 127.0)dct_tmp2[y][x]= 127.0;
                    if(dct_tmp2[y][x]<-127.0)dct_tmp2[y][x]=-127.0;
                    coded_block[index]=(char)dct_tmp2[y][x];
                    index++;
                    }
                }
            }
        if(dct_tmp2[0][0]> 32767.0)dct_tmp2[y][x]= 32767.0;
        if(dct_tmp2[0][0]<-32767.0)dct_tmp2[y][x]=-32767.0;
        i=(int)dct_tmp2[0][0];
        fwrite(&i,sizeof(int),1,fo);        // Write DC coefficient
        fwrite(coded_block,index,1,fo); // Write AC coefficients
        }
      }
    }
//-----------------------------------------------------------
// The uncompression routine performs the inverse of the
// compression routine. For each block, the DC coefficient
// and corresponding AC coefficients are read from the
// input file and stored at the appropriate locations in an
// 8x8 array, under control of the quantization template
// (q). The horizontal and vertical inverse 1 dimensional
// DCT operations are then applied, resulting in values
// 16 times larger than the original. Each is then divided
// by 16, and the results stored in the pixel rows. When
// a complete band of 40 blocks has been processed, the
// 8 rows it comprises are written to the output file.
//-----------------------------------------------------------
  if(argv[3][1]=='u')   // User wants to uncompress
```

```
{
printf("Uncompressing.");
size=0;
for(y=0;y<8;y++)for(x=0;x<8;x++)
  if((x!=0 || y!=0) && q[y][x]==1)size++;
for(band=0;band<25;band++)   // Divide image into 25 bands
  {
  printf(".");
  for(block=0;block<40;block++) // Divide the band into 40 blocks
    {
    fread(&i,sizeof(int),1,fi);   // Read DC coefficient
    fread(coded_block,size,1,fi); // Read a block of AC coefficients

    index=0;
    for(y=0;y<8;y++)                  // Order by quantization control
      {
      for(x=0;x<8;x++)
        {
        if((x!=0 || y!=0) && q[y][x]==1)
          {
          dct_tmp2[y][x]=8.0*(float)coded_block[index];
          index++;
          }
        else dct_tmp2[y][x]=0.0;
        }
      }
    dct_tmp2[0][0]=(float)i;   // Store DC coefficient
    for(x=0;x<8;x++)              // Do 1-dimensional column IDCTs
      {
      for(coeff=0;coeff<8;coeff++)
        {
        dct_tmp1[coeff][x]=0.0;
        for(index=0;index<8;index++)
          {
          dct_tmp1[coeff][x]+=
          dct_tmp2[index][x]*dct_coeff[index][coeff];
          }
        }
      }
    for(y=0;y<8;y++)             // Do 1-dimensional row IDCTs
      {
      for(coeff=0;coeff<8;coeff++)
        {
        dct_tmp2[y][coeff]=0.0;
        for(index=0;index<8;index++)
          {
          dct_tmp2[y][coeff]+=
          dct_tmp1[y][index]*dct_coeff[index][coeff];
          }
        dct_tmp2[y][coeff]/=16.0;
        if(dct_tmp2[y][coeff]>255.0)dct_tmp2[y][coeff]=255.0;
        if(dct_tmp2[y][coeff]<16.0) dct_tmp2[y][coeff]=16.0;
        }
```

```
        }
    for(y=0;y<8;y++)   // Copy data into pixel rows
      {
      for(x=block*8,index=0;index<8;x++,index++)
        {
        image[y][x]=(unsigned char)dct_tmp2[y][index];
        }
      }
    }
  for(row=0;row<8;row++) // Write 8 pixel rows at a time
    {
    fwrite(&image[row][0],320,1,fo);
    }
  }
 }
fclose(fi);
fclose(fo);
printf("\nDone.\n");
}
```

Motion Estimation

Just as the data compression process takes advantage of correlation between pixels within a signal image, it can also take advantage of correlation from one frame to the next. In motion pictures the illusion of motion is very often created by having some object appear in different positions in successive frames of the video sequence. For example, in the case of a car driving across a fixed scene, the shape of the car does not alter significantly as it moves through the scene. Taking a pair of images from the video sequence and dividing each into a series of subimages, for example, 8×8 blocks of pixels, it is possible to determine which blocks represent parts of the picture that have moved and which have remained static. Figure 5.27 illustrates this.

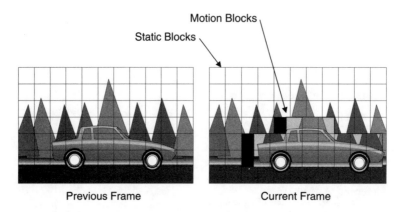

Figure 5.27   Pixel block motion tracking image object motion.

Determining which pixel blocks contain information representing parts of the image that have moved and how far they have moved is called *motion estimation.* The process of reconstructing an image using image segments from the previous image along with information about motion is called *motion compensation.* The motion estimation and compensation processes are conceptually quite simple although they may be fairly expensive in terms of computation time. Consider a single block of pixels from the illustration shown in Figure 5.27. If the part of the picture represented by this block of pixels has moved by some relatively small amount, say, less than the width of the block, and has not become significantly distorted in the process, say, by changing shape or orientation, there should be a fairly close match between the block of pixels from the previous image and an equivalent block in the next image. By mapping the block from the previous image to various positions on the new image and calculating the mathematical difference at each position it is possible to determine mathematically whether the difference at a given location is low enough to constitute a match. If a match is found, the new block can be represented as a displacement of the previous block rather than actually transmitting the entire block of pixels. To maintain image quality, a block of error values can also be transmitted, which allows correction of the newly constructed block to make it more closely match the new block which was *not* transmitted. The displacement of motion vectors is usually limited to less than or equal to the block size for two reasons: First, it would be very time consuming to search a large area of the image for each motion vector calculated. Second, moving blocks by large displacements would create a problem determining what to put in the space vacated by the moved block. The use of motion estimation and compensation places two requirements on the encode/decode system. First, the decoder must store the previous image while reconstructing the next image. Second, the encoder must reconstruct each image after encoding it to predict how the decoder will reconstruct the image. This is necessary because the decoder does not have any of the original images available for reconstructing motion-compensated blocks. A conceptual illustration of the block matching process is shown in Figure 5.28.

A variety of techniques can be used to detect block matches. One of the most accurate is the root mean square error method shown in Figure 5.26. This may, however, require too much computation time for a given application, so other approaches can be used. For example, the error calculation might be subsampled by using only every other pixel horizontally and vertically or by using every other row or every other column. Another technique is to take a simple sum of differences. By the same token there are a variety of possible approaches to the search algorithm. Assuming displacement vectors will be no larger than the block size horizontally or vertically, the search region for a particular pixel block would consist of the equivalent block in the current image surrounded by portions of the eight adjacent blocks as illustrated in Figure 5.29.

The most accurate but most expensive approach is the exhaustive search. This calculates the pixel matching error at every possible position within a search region. The accuracy of the motion vector thus determined can be further improved by further searching the immediate vicinity of the best available match using fractional-pixel resolution. This is done by interpolating among pixels in the search region to develop a set of new search pixels and performing a block match to see if this produces a lower error coefficient than the original match. Another technique is to check for the error level at predetermined points in all possible directions from the original position and then select one of these as the best candidate for a potential motion vector direction. The search is then concentrated along that axis using smaller and smaller displacement vectors until the best match is

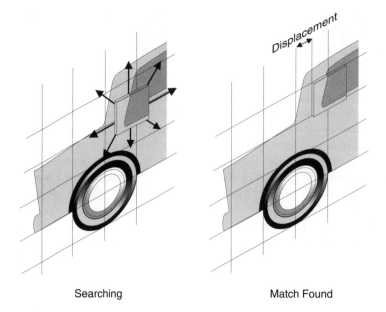

Searching   Match Found

Figure 5.28   Conceptualization of block matching process for motion estimation.

found. This is less expensive than an exhaustive search but more prone to errors due to local minima. The fact that image objects tend to be larger than individual pixel blocks indicates that once the displacement vector has been determined for a given pixel block there is a high probability that other pixel blocks in the same vicinity will have a similar or identical motion vector. An intelligent

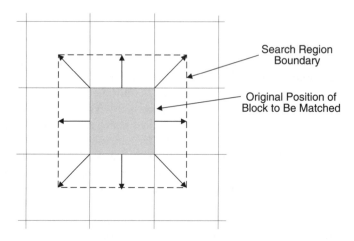

Figure 5.29   Relative orientation of search range to search block.

motion estimation algorithm will use this historical information to provide clues on where to begin the search process in cases where an exhaustive search is not being performed.

Factors Affecting Choice of Image Compression Technique

The wide range of applications for video compression technology dictate an equally wide range of compression techniques in actual practice. The choice depends on a number of factors. In real-time image transmission for video teleconference, for example, the encode and decode process must be performed in real time. If the entire encode transmission and decode process takes more than a fraction of a second it will introduce annoying round-trip delays and significant *lip-sync* problems. Lip-sync refers to the motion of a speaker's lips not matching the voice. By contrast, if compression is performed to reduce storage requirements there probably is no need for real-time compression, although it may be required for decompression. In this case, image quality and compression ratio are probably the most important. Error rates and the ability to recover from errors in the compressed data stream are also critical factors. A number of areas for consideration in the choice of compression technique are discussed in the following paragraphs.

Compatibility

For applications such as video telephony, video teleconference, or distribution of broadcast-quality entertainment media, it may be necessary to follow some de-facto or internationally recognized standard. Some examples of such standards are H.261, developed by the CCITT, or JPEG or MPEG, developed by the ISO (International Standards Organization).

Multiple Coding

In some applications it may be necessary to compress and decompress a given image or sequence of images multiple times. If the same compression and decompression technique is used in every case, successive applications are generally unlikely to produce cumulative image degradation even if the initial application does significantly degrade the image. This is because the reconstructed image tends to be optimized for the particular technique used. If, however, the image is modified in some way, such as by scaling or other processing, between successive compression and decompression stages, image degradation probably will be cumulative. This tends to eliminate compressed storage formats as a good medium for electronic editing and special effects of video entertainment media.

Progressive Transmission

Progressive transmission allows a complete, although relatively low-quality, image to be transmitted using a very low data rate in a relatively small amount of time. The purpose is to allow the recipient to recognize the image early in the reconstruction process to enable a decision to be made whether to continue the image recovery before the entire image has been processed. This is generally more relevant in applications using high-resolution still images than it is for motion video, because motion video requires very rapid sequential reconstruction of images to produce the illusion of motion.

Image Artifacts

Various compression techniques create different visual artifacts. The nature and degree of visual artifacts may also depend on the mode in which a given compression algorithm is operating and the parameters with which it is working. Exactly what level of visual artifacts is acceptable tends to be a highly subjective decision dependent on the application.

Encode/Decode Symmetry

Applications that require real-time transmission and decode of video information tend to require symmetrical encode and decode computation complexity. For example, if it takes significantly more computing power to encode than to decode, cost versus performance issues are likely to become a problem. Other applications such as those that require large amounts of stored content for mass distribution may require a very low-complexity playback capability but might be much less sensitive to the requirements of compression. The MPEG compression standard is a good example of this.

Error Tolerance

Various compression techniques are more or less susceptible to transmission errors. Block coding techniques can generally restrict errors to relatively small portions of an image. The DCT is a good example of this. Progressive techniques such as DPCM or FST may show errors as streaks across the image. For high-entropy variable-length coding schemes such as Huffman coding, transmission errors can be catastrophic, causing the loss of an entire image unless special error recovery mechanisms are incorporated in the data stream.

Source Image Quality and Characteristics

The differences between graphical and continuous-tone natural images were discussed in Chapter 2. Compression techniques well suited for continuous-tone images are generally not well suited for graphical images. This discussion assumes natural images. Even within this category there may be wide variations in contrast ratio, resolution, and signal-to-noise ratio. The effects of rapid motion in the source image and the ability to transmit necessary levels of image detail need to be taken into consideration. These factors may dictate an ability to dynamically adjust image encoding parameters.

Transmission Data Rate

Certain applications may be highly sensitive to maximum acceptable data rates. An example of this would be video teleconference via standard analog telephone lines. Current modem technology is limited to a maximum of about 28.8 kilobits per second over conventional telephone lines. This is due primarily to limitations of the transmission medium. Effective data rates and transmission error rates vary significantly from region to region. Other applications may be less sensitive to data transmission rates but require very high levels of image quality. The techniques required to optimize one image parameter may be mutually exclusive of those required for another.

Implementation Limitations

The anticipated application may impose certain restrictions on the type of computing equipment used. For example, video content intended for playback on personal computers would have to be decoded using no more computation power than is available in the majority of personal computers currently available. It may also be desirable to take into account the type of display device used.

Video Data Storage

Since the early days of broadcast television numerous ways of recording and replaying video information have been devised. Virtually all of these methods have been *linear* in nature, under the assumption that television programs are to be watched rather than manipulated. While this assumption has worked well up until now, it did not anticipate the eventual intersection of television and computer technology. Already it is possible to outfit a complete television production studio with all digital equipment, and this capability is gradually making its way into lower-cost markets. Some traditional industry diehards may worry that this will result in lower production standards (although a few hours viewing network television make it hard to imagine how standards could get any lower) but this is no more likely than a reduction in typesetting standards due to the advent of WYSIWYG word processors. The unique capabilities of the personal computer call for a different form of storage and retrieval, with random access being a key advantage. This chapter covers a few of the storage devices relevant to the use of video information on computers.

Compact Disk Optical Storage

The compact disk or CD, also known as CD-ROM when used in computer applications, is a read-only laser disk. No new information can be recorded on CDs, which are designed for mass production using stamping equipment. Digital information is recorded on CDs by means of microscopic indentations in the plastic material from which CDs are made. The surface upon which these indentations are made is coated with a thin layer of aluminum which makes the CD reflective. This is then covered by another layer of plastic to protect it from scratches. Without the indentations which record data, a CD would be nothing more than an expensive mirror. With the indentations, the CD is a digital storage device capable of carrying in the neighborhood of 600 to 800 megabytes of information. This section will discuss the physics upon which CDs are based, the mechanics of recording and reading data from CDs, and the logical organization of CD data.

Theory of Operation

The indentations which represent the digital data recorded on a CD are made on the opposite side from which the information is read. Therefore, to the device reading the data the indentations appear as microscopic bumps on the surface of a mirror. Laser light is used to detect the bumps on the recording surface of the CD because lasers have a well-defined polarization and wavelength. The height of the bumps is one-quarter the wavelength of the light used, so that light reflected from the surface of the bumps is 180° out of phase, and therefore creates destructive interference. The effect of this is that the bumps appear to reflect less light than the surrounding surface. The edges of the bump also scatter the light, further reducing the amount reflected back into the detector. The wavelength of the scanning laser is on the order of half a micron; therefore, the height of the data bumps has to be in the neighborhood of one-eighth micron. Figure 6.1 illustrates the approximate proportions and dimensions of the data bumps on the CD. It is clear from this that the dimensions involved are in the same category as those used for the manufacture of high-density large-scale integrated circuits.

There are two predominant theories to explain the behavior of light. One is the *particle theory* and the other is the *wave theory*. This discussion will proceed in the context of the wave theory. The wave theory explains the existence of a planar wavefront by postulating that light emanating from an infinite number of point sources is in the form of an infinite number of spherical waves. These combine in various forms of destructive interference except in the plane in which they are all in the same phase. Figure 6.2 illustrates this graphically.

As with other wave propagation phenomena, the velocity of propagation is dependent on the density of the medium. The propagation velocity of light through a medium such as a brick wall seems to be about zero. The velocity in a vacuum is very fast, of course, which would indicate that

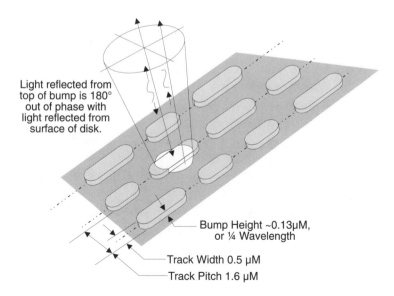

Light reflected from top of bump is 180° out of phase with light reflected from surface of disk.

Bump Height ~0.13µM, or ¼ Wavelength

Track Width 0.5 µM

Track Pitch 1.6 µM

Figure 6.1   Illustration of data bumps recorded on compact disk.

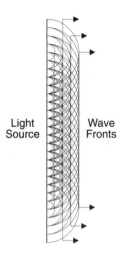

Figure 6.2   Development of planar wavefront resulting from point light sources.

outer space is actually composed of some medium which is simply far too rare for any human instrumentation to detect, if we assume the wave theory. This medium is often called *ether*, as in "ethereal." When a light wavefront passes through an interface between two media with different densities the velocity of propagation is changed accordingly. If the wavefront is not parallel to the interface, the change in velocity results in a change in the angle of the wavefront, as shown in Figure 6.3.

This change in velocity is referred to as *refraction*. The ratio of the velocity of light in a vacuum to its velocity in some propagating medium is the *refractive index* of the medium. The refractive index of a given medium is not necessarily constant for all wavelengths. This explains the

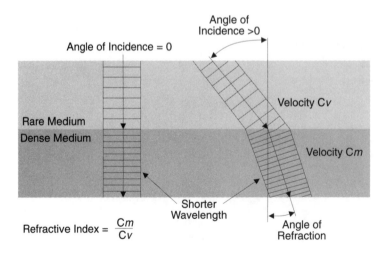

Figure 6.3   Change in light wave propagation velocity resulting in refraction.

behavior of a glass prism, which changes the angle of long wavelengths more than that of short wavelengths. Other types of glass are specifically formulated to have as uniform as possible a refractive index across the visible spectrum. Lenses manufactured from this type of glass are said to be *achromatic*.

Diffraction

The wave propagation theories used to explain the diffraction property of light can be easily observed using water. If the body of water is separated into two parts by a relatively thin barrier with an opening smaller than the wavelength of any waves propagating through the water, the waves appearing on the other side of the opening will be circular, as illustrated in Figure 6.4.

The same phenomenon is said to occur with planer light wavefronts. If the apertures are round, the resulting wavefronts will be spherical. If the apertures are linear slots, the resulting wavefronts will be cylindrical. It is the linear diffraction grating which is of interest here. Just as wavefronts were created as a result of constructive reinforcement from theoretical point sources, so they are created by the same process when light passes through a regular pattern of diffraction apertures. As shown in Figure 6.5, the angle of diffraction depends on the spacing of the apertures and the wavelength of the incident light. It is clear that the angle of diffraction is greater for longer wavelengths. Or conversely, for a given wavelength, the smaller the diffraction feature size the greater the angle of diffraction.

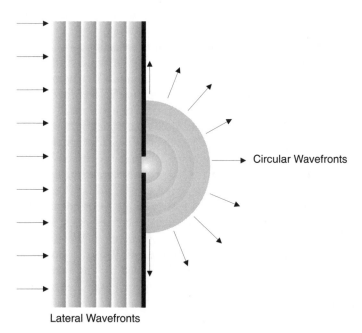

Lateral Wavefronts

Figure 6.4   Illustration of the conversion of linear wavefronts to circular wavefronts.

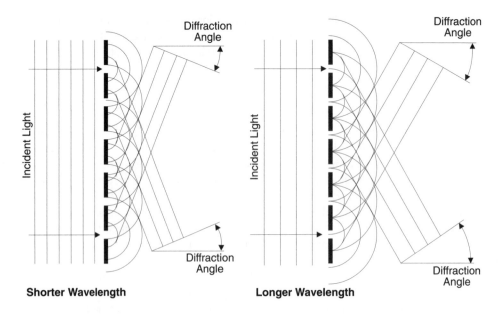

Figure 6.5   Illustration of the mechanics of light wave diffraction.

If white light is passed through a diffraction grating with an aperture spacing approaching the wavelength of infrared, the diffraction grating splits the light into a spectrum of colors very much the way a prism does. The same phenomenon can occur in reflection as well as transmission. This accounts for the rainbow colors often seen reflected from the surface of a CD. Recall that the lower end of the visible spectrum comprises wavelengths of around 700 nanometers. That's about 0.7 microns. The CD data track pitch of 1.6 microns indeed approaches the wavelength of infrared light. So what is the point of all this? It is that due to the diffraction of light caused by regular patterns with very small feature sizes there is a physical limitation on the dimensions of objects which can be detected optically. The combination of the focal length of a given lens and the diffraction angle of a given light source determine the minimum feature size which can be resolved by the lens. Figure 6.6 shows how, if the diffraction angle of an object of interest is too great, the light which carries information about the detail cannot be captured by the lens.

Light traveling along the optical axis of a lens (which is perpendicular to the lens) carries *average* brightness information. The sine of the angle between the optical axis and the wavefronts which carry the finest detail in the image defines the *numerical aperture* of the lens. Of course, manufacturing tolerances can also affect the performance of a lens. If aberrations introduced by the lens have variance less than the square of the wavelength divided by 180 there is essentially nothing more that can be done to improve the lens, because at that point it is limited more by diffraction than by physical aberrations. This level of accuracy is referred to as the *Maréchal criterion*. It is the combination of the laser wavelength and diffraction properties of the optics used in a CD system that limit feature size and, therefore, data capacity of CDs.

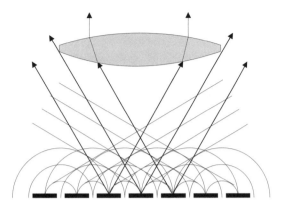

Figure 6.6   Mechanics of diffraction limiting on lens resolution.

Polarization

Certain techniques used in laser optics require polarization of light. To understand the physics of light polarization it is useful to imagine an electrical field content in light waves. Ordinarily these field components propagate at all angles. Light is said to be polarized when all but specific field angles have been filtered out. The polarizing filter was invented by Edwin Land, namesake of the Polaroid Land Camera. The filter is made by stretching vinyl while it is hot, causing the polymer molecules which make up the vinyl to align along the axis of stretching. Soaking the vinyl in iodine causes the molecules to become conductive so that they short out electric field components that are aligned with the molecules, effectively blocking those fields. Fields at right angles to the molecules are not absorbed and pass through. Certain types of plastic have a wave propagation velocity which varies with the angle of polarization. These materials are capable of rotating the angle of polarized light by 90°. A light filter made from this material is known as a *quarter-wave plate*.

CD Optics

Data is read from a CD by focusing a laser beam on the reflective surface which carries information encoded in the form of bumps. The reflected light is passed back through the same lens and directed into an optoelectric detector. The optical read-back system of a CD-ROM drive takes into account the refractive index of the transparent plastic from which the CD is manufactured. The light must be focused to a very small and precise spot which would tend to make the system susceptible to surface scratches and dust particles. However, the thickness of the disk is such that the diameter of the light beam entering at the surface is considerably larger than the spot focused on the data layer. Figure 6.7 illustrates this. It is clear this arrangement can tolerate surface defects much larger than the data track size and still read the data reliably.

The data track on a laser disk is typically organized as a continuous spiral rather than concentric circular tracks such as magnetic disks use. This allows continuous transfer of data once the optical pickup has locked onto the track. Because of the extremely narrow track width and the mass

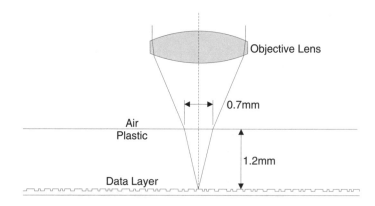

Figure 6.7   Relative spot size of light entering disk surface versus spot size at target.

of the optical data pickup mechanism, seeking and track locking operations generally cannot be performed as quickly as on magnetic hard disks. Once the pickup is locked onto a track the data transfer speed is a function of the rotational speed of the disk and the frequency at which the data was recorded. About 150 kilobytes per second is a common data transfer rate for commercially available CD-ROM drives, or 300 kilobytes per second for so-called double-spin drives. To achieve the extremely small pickup spot size a monochromatic light source is required. This requirement is usually met by the use of a small inexpensive semiconductor laser. Light from the laser is focused on the data surface of the CD-ROM and the reflected light is directed into a detector. To achieve the required spot size the angle of incidence must be perpendicular to the plane of the data surface. Therefore, reflected light is directed back to the source. One of two methods is used to deflect the reflected light into a detector. The first, illustrated in Figure 6.8, uses a partially silvered mirror to deflect the reflected light.

The disadvantage in this approach is that part of the light from the source is partially obstructed by the mirror and part of the reflected light is allowed to pass through rather than being deflected into the detector, resulting in a much reduced read-back signal amplitude. A more reliable, although more expense system, uses a polarizing prism and a quarter-wave plate. The source light is polarized and the polarization is rotated 90° on its way to the data surface. The reflected light is further rotated by another 90° as it passes back through the quarter wave plate so that the reflected light is now 180° out of phase with the source light and, therefore, deflected by the polarizing prism into the detector. This is illustrated in Figure 6.9.

Focus and Tracking

Because of the extremely small laser spot size involved, the focal depth of field is typically on the order of plus or minus one micron. As shown in Figure 6.1, the data track pitch is about 1.6 microns. CD-ROM disk planarity errors and spindle runout can easily exceed these parameters. Therefore, dynamic tracking and focus mechanisms are required. Focus is typically controlled by a voice coil actuator because of its low mass and rapid response time. Figure 6.10 illustrates the arrangement.

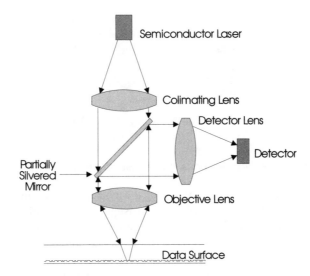

Figure 6.8   Arrangement of partially silvered mirror for CD optical read back.

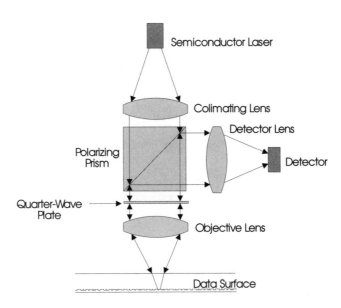

Figure 6.9   Arrangement of quarter-wave plate and polarizing prism beam splitter for CD optical read back.

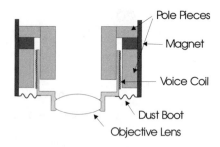

Figure 6.10   Illustration of dynamic focus lens adjustment mechanism.

A common feedback method for controlling the dynamic focus is to use an *astigmatic* lens on the reflected light beam focused on the detector. An astigmatic lens causes the focal length to be different in one plane than in another. Figure 6.11 shows a lens whose vertical focal length is shorter than the horizontal focal length. It can be seen from this diagram that a short focus produces a narrow horizontal spot of light while a long focus produces a narrow vertical spot of light.

By splitting the detector into four segments, the relative shape of the light spot can be used to generate an error signal to reposition the objective lens. This is illustrated in Figure 6.12.

Of course, this scheme allows only a fairly narrow range of control. If the objective lens gets too far out of focus the light spot on the detector will grow so large that it completely covers the detector array and generates an error signal of zero. This is illustrated in Figure 6.13.

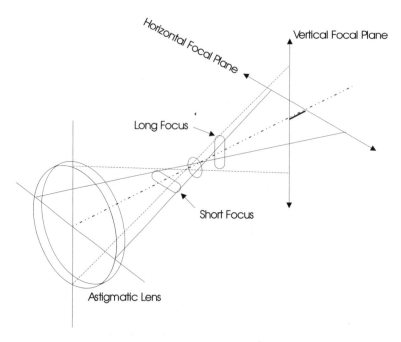

Figure 6.11   Illustration of the effects of an astigmatic lens on focus.

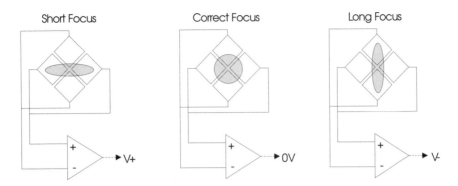

Figure 6.12   How a four-segment optical read-back detector doubles as a focus control.

To obtain correct focus, an initialization sequence is required which sweeps the focus control through its entire range and tracks the error signal for a zero crossing. Figure 6.14 illustrates the control range of a split-sensor focus control mechanism.

There are two primary anomalies which contribute to tracking error. These are disk warp and spindle runout. These parameters are controlled by manufacturing specifications, but remember the disk thickness is approximately 1.2 mm with a pickup spot size of half a micron. That means the distance from the surface of the disk to the recording layer is approximately 2400 times the spot size. Because of the refractive index of the plastic material from which CDs are made, it doesn't take very much warp to displace the pickup spot by more than one track. Spindle runout of even one-thousandth of an inch will displace the pickup spot by several tracks. Therefore, the pickup head must be dynamically repositioned during each rotation of the disk and some method of detecting tracking errors must be incorporated. A common method of generating a tracking error feedback signal is to intentionally vibrate the pickup head at a low frequency. This generates a predictable pat-

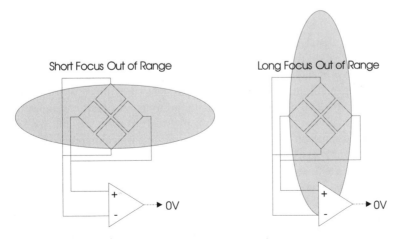

Figure 6.13   Out-of-range conditions for split-detector focus control.

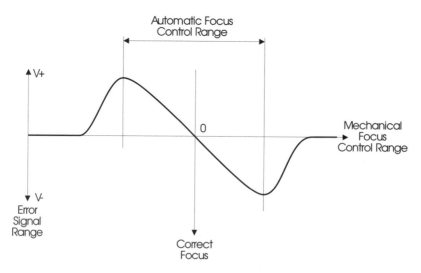

Figure 6.14   Control range for a split-sensor focus control detector.

tern of tracking errors on both sides of the target track. When the tracking spot begins to get off track, the result is a reduced amplitude signal coming from the data detector. Vibrating the pickup head effectively modulates a low-frequency sinusoid wave onto the high-frequency data signal. This low-frequency wave can be demodulated and rectified so that its phase can be monitored. Figure 6.15 shows how when the pickup spot path begins to move off-track the phase of the tracking error signal changes proportional to the direction and amplitude of the error. This vibration of the tracking beam can also be created by vibrating a small mirror in the optical path, which allows a higher frequency to be used, thereby improving tracking response time.

Data Formats

In a theoretical world of digital information there is never any ambiguity between binary states. Unfortunately, in the real world there is often more than enough ambiguity for everyone involved. Noise immunity has always been the major selling point for digital technology. However, when digital recording, processing, and transmission media are pushed to their physical limits, degenerative processes can begin to introduce errors into the digital information stream. Methods of encoding digital information to compensate for limitations of the physical channel are as much responsible for improvements in data transmission and storage capacities as are physical improvements. A common technique in digital systems is to use a clock signal which simply changes states in a predictable way at predictable times. The clock signal may be generated by a specialized component dedicated to that purpose, such as an oscillator, or may be derived from the data stream itself, which is usually the case in digital recording media. In an unconstrained digital data stream it is theoretically possible to have frequencies ranging all the way from one-half the sample rate down to DC. If a modulated tracking technique is used, such as the one described earlier, it is necessary to encode the data stream such that random occurrences of DC levels are prevented. Also, if the clock is derived from

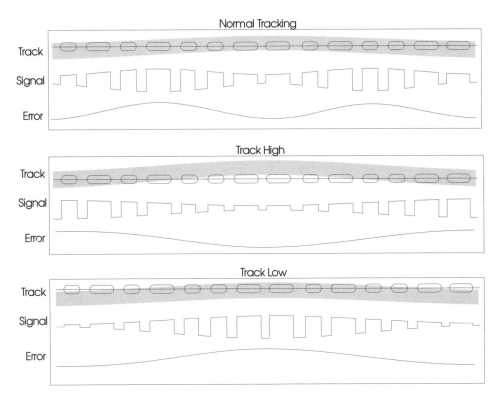

Figure 6.15   Mechanics of signal-modulation tracking error signal generation.

the data stream, the longest period without any transition must not exceed the ability of the clock synthesizer to maintain its synchronization and phase-lock. Floppy disks have a clock signal directly embedded into the data stream. Data bits are interleaved with clock bits. This limits the data rate to one-half the maximum frequency provided by the medium but provides a reliable synchronization source which is not overly sensitive to spindle-speed variations. For more highly optimized storage media, such as fixed disk or CD-ROM, other techniques have been devised. A simple serial stream of digital data is sometimes referred to as *non-return to zero* (NRZ). This simply means that when the digital state goes to a logical one it does not return to zero for the duration of the period in which it is defined as one. In totally random data streams, this can result in long periods where the signal remains at either one or zero. Figure 6.16 illustrates how the physical channel state directly corresponds with the logical signal state.

To eliminate the possibility of a steady state in the physical channel, a technique known as *Manchester coding* was developed, also sometimes called FM coding. This uses physical channel transitions rather than states to represent the logical data states. The scheme specifies that one channel transition within a data clock period indicates a logical one, whereas two channel transitions within a data period indicate a logical zero. This tends to limit bandwidth because the physical channel must support twice the data frequency. The scheme was modified to allow only one transition per data cycle, distinguishing between logical one and zero by the phase of the transition. The

Figure 6.16   Correspondence between logical data state and physical signal state for NRZ.

modified scheme is known as MFM. MFM effectively doubled the data capacity over FM using the same physical media. Figure 6.17 illustrates FM and MFM coding schemes.

Decoding MFM data requires a phase-locked loop with a slow enough locking time so that missing clock transitions don't cause significant changes in synthesized clock frequency. Improvement beyond MFM coding requires recognizing and converting undesirable data bit patterns into patterns more optimized for the physical channel. A common technique for this is to use a *code book,* which is effectively nothing more than a translation table. For example, if data is logically organized as bytes of eight bits each then the number zero is represented by eight binary zeros and the number 255 is represented by eight binary ones. The number of contiguous bits all of the same state is known as the run length. Coding schemes which translate undesirable run lengths into more optimized code sequences are known as *run length limited* (RLL).

CCIR-656 Serial Video Code

The CCIR developed a coding scheme specifically to support storage and transmission of digital video signals sampled in the 4:2:2 format. The scheme uses nine channel bits to represent each set of eight data bits. Using nine bits there are 213 possible combinations which have either four or five zero-bits per symbol. This leaves 43 symbols which must be encoded with more than five zero-bits. Each of these 43 symbols is assigned a *pair* of complimentary channel symbols. Successive occurrences of any of these 43 symbols use alternating channel codes. This mitigates the effect of the relatively long zero runs in these particular codes because the unbalancing effect of the occurrence of one symbol from this set is always reversed by the next occurrence of a symbol from this set. Table 6.1 gives the code table for CCIR-656 translation.

Fixed Disk Drives

The development of hermetically sealed hard disk drives has greatly increased the speed and capacity over earlier technology. Hark disk drives use what is known as *flying* read-write heads. This means that an air gap is maintained between the recording head and the oxide surface. The air gap is a result of aerodynamic lift imparted by a boundary layer of air rotating with the surface of the disk. Recording heads for magnetic media are constructed as electromagnetic devices with a very

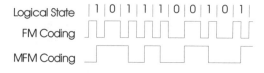

Figure 6.17   Illustration of FM and MFM coding of logical signal states.

Table 6.1 CCIR-656 Code Translation

8-Bit	9-Bit	9-Bit'	8-Bit	9-Bit	9-Bit'	8-Bit	9-Bit	9-Bit'
00	01E	101	2D	057		5A	09B	
01	027		2E	09B		5B	164	
02	1D8		2F	059		5C	09D	
03	033		30	1A6		5D	162	
04	1CC		31	05B		5E	0A3	
05	037		32	05D		5F	15C	
06	1C8		33	1A4		60	0A7	
07	039		34	065		61	158	
08	1C6		35	19A		62	025	1DA
09	03B		36	069		63	0A1	15E
0A	1C4		37	196		64	029	1D6
0B	03D		38	026	1D9	65	091	16E
0C	1C2		39	08C	173	66	045	1BA
0D	14D		3A	02C	1D3	67	089	176
0E	0B4		3B	098	167	68	049	1B6
0F	14B		3C	032	1CD	69	085	17A
10	1A2		3D	0BE	141	6A	051	1AE
11	0B6		3E	034	1CB	6B	08A	175
12	149		3F	0C2	13D	6C	0A4	15B
13	0BA		40	046	1B9	6D	054	1AB
14	145		41	0C4	13B	6E	0A2	15D
15	0CA		42	04C	1B3	6F	052	1AD
16	135		43	0C8	137	70	056	
17	0D2		44	058	1A7	71	1A9	
18	12D		45	0B1		72	05A	
19	0D4		46	14E		73	1A5	
1A	129		47	0B3		74	06A	
1B	0D6		48	14C		75	195	
1C	125		49	0B9		76	096	
1D	0DA		4A	06B		77	169	
1E	115		4B	194		78	0A9	
1F	0EA		4C	06D		79	156	
20	0B2		4D	192		7A	0AB	
21	02B		4E	075		7B	154	
22	1D4		4F	18A		7C	0A5	
23	02D		50	08B		7D	15A	
24	1D2		51	174		7E	0AD	
25	035		52	08D		7F	152	
26	1CA		53	172		80	155	
27	04B		54	093		81	0AA	
28	1B4		55	16C		82	055	
29	04D		56	097		83	1AA	
2A	1B2		57	168		84	0D5	
2B	053		58	099		85	12A	
2C	1AC		59	166		86	095	

Table 6.1 *continued*

8-Bit	9-Bit	9-Bit'	8-Bit	9-Bit	9-Bit'	8-Bit	9-Bit	9-Bit'
87	16A		B0	11A		D9	0CE	
88	0B5		B1	0E9		DA	133	
89	14A		B2	116		DB	0D8	
8A	09A		B3	02E		DC	131	
8B	165		B4	1D1		DD	0DC	
8C	0A6		B5	036		DE	127	
8D	159		B6	1C9		E1	0E2	
8E	0AC		B7	03A		E0	123	
8F	153		B8	1C5		E1	0E4	
90	0AE		B9	04E		E2	11D	
91	151		BA	1B1		E3	0E6	
92	02A	1D5	BB	05C		E4	11B	
93	092	16D	BC	1A3		E5	0E8	
94	04A	1B5	BD	05E		E6	119	
95	094	16B	BE	1A1		E7	0EC	
96	0A8	157	BF	066		E8	117	
97	0B7	148	C0	199		E9	012	
98	015	10A	C1	06C		EA	113	
99	0BB	144	C2	193		EB	014	
9A	0ED	112	C3	06E		EC	10D	
9B	0BD	142	C4	191		ED	076	
9C	0EB	114	C5	072		EE	10B	
9D	0D7	129	C6	18D		EF	0C7	
9E	0DD	122	C7	074		F0	13C	
9F	0DB	124	C8	18B		F1	047	
A0	146		C9	07A		F2	1B8	
A1	0C5		CA	189		F3	067	
A2	13A		CB	08E		F4	19C	
A3	0C9		CC	185		F5	071	
A4	136		CD	09C		F6	198	
A5	0CB		CE	171		F7	073	
A6	134		CF	09E		F8	18E	
A7	0CD		D0	163		F9	079	
A8	132		D1	0B8		FA	18C	
A9	0D1		D2	161		FB	087	
AA	12E		D3	0BC		FC	186	
AB	0D3		D4	147		FD	0C3	
AC	12C		D5	0C6		FE	178	
AD	0D9		D6	143		FF	062	190
AE	126		D7	0CC				
AF	0E5		D8	139				

small gap between the pole pieces. This creates a magnetic field which extends outward from the pole pieces and can be used to magnetize the oxide coating of the tape or disk. Figure 6.18 illustrates the relationship between the recording head and the recording media.

The strength of the magnetic field is inversely proportional to the distance from the pole pieces. Therefore, any gap at all between the head and the medium tends to reduce the effectiveness of the recording and read-back processes. The advantage of Winchester sealed-disk technology is that the environment in which the disk and the heads operate can be kept free of contamination. This allows the air gap to be much smaller than would be possible otherwise. The air gap cannot be eliminated entirely because friction between the head and the oxide surface of the disk resulting from the high rotational speed would create excessive wear. During startup and shutdown the recording heads are positioned over special landing tracks in which no data is recorded. In order to minimize wear during starting and stopping, a high-torque motor is used to accelerate the disk rapidly during startup and a braking mechanism is used to stop it quickly during shutdown. The brake is usually spring-operated and released by an electrical solenoid so that braking will occur even during a power failure. Today's high-density disk drives typically use *thin-film* read-write heads, which means that the magnetic coil is formed by photolithography techniques. Figure 6.19 illustrates how a typical thin film read-write head is constructed.

The physical shape of the head is designed to produce the desired air gap with a given head pressure and disk rotational speed. Disk platters are commonly made from aluminum, although some very small hard disk drives manufactured for portable systems have platters made from glass. Although glass is more brittle, it has better thermal characteristics and wears better than aluminum. For very small disk platters in the range of 1.8 to 1.5 inches in diameter, mechanical stresses due to shock and vibration are within tolerable limits for glass platters. Disk capacity of several hundred megabytes is almost a prerequisite for working with digital motion video even if it is compressed before being stored on the hard drive. The storage capacity and bandwidth requirements for various compressed and uncompressed digital video formats are discussed at the end of Chapter 2. The advantage of using a hard drive for digital video is a faster seek time and higher data transfer rates relative to CD-ROM. Factors that affect seek time and data transfer rates will be discussed here. A hard-disk drive may comprise multiple disk platters, each of which records data on both sides. Each

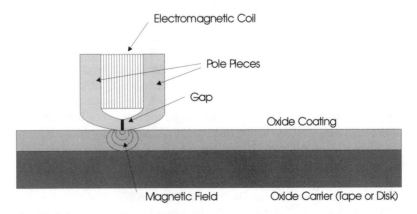

Figure 6.18 Magnetic field produced by recording head magnetizes oxide layer.

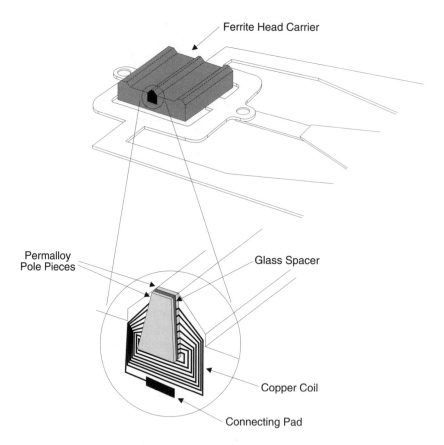

Figure 6.19   Physical design of thin-film disk read-write head.

platter is divided into tracks, which are concentric circles on the surface of the disk where data is recorded. If multiple platters are used, a data track at a given position is generally available on all platters. Therefore, a track is sometimes also referred to as a *cylinder*. Each track is further subdivided into *sectors*. A sector is nothing more than a logical division of the track perimeter. The number of tracks and their positions are determined by the physical location of the read-write heads over the recording media. The number of sectors and their positions are determined by format markers recorded on the disk. Typically, there is an index mark which notifies the drive control each time the disk has completed a full rotation. Sectors are positioned relative to this index mark. The disk controller tracks the rotational position of the disk and can therefore determine when the read-write heads are approaching a given sector. The process of writing sector marks on the disk is referred to as a *low-level format*. Often a given hard disk can be configured for different capacities and characteristics by selecting different low-level format parameters. Typical disk sector format information consists of a number of distinct fields as illustrated in Figure 6.20.

The address mark is a special area that the read circuit can detect to determine that the read-write head is about to enter the next sector. The header preamble is a pattern of transitions designed

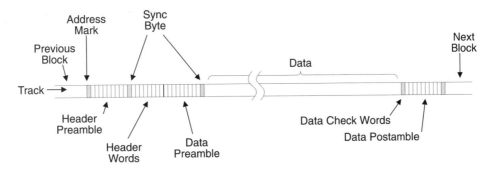

Figure 6.20 Organization of disk sector low-level format marks.

to allow the data separator to lock to the data frequency. The first sync-byte resets a counter which determines the boundaries between bytes along the track. The header words typically contain the cylinder number, sector number, and potentially other information such as bad-block flags or defect-skipping information. It also contains a cyclic redundancy check number to verify that the header information was read correctly. The data preamble and second sync-byte resynchronize the data separator in preparation for the actual data transfer. The data check words at the end of the data block allow data integrity to be verified and the data postamble prepares the controller to detect the next address mark. During a read function, clock synchronization and block structure information are derived directly from the data read from the disk. During write functions the physical block structure must be locked to the angular position of the disk. This is accomplished by having the controller simultaneously read servo information from a special servo track. The servo track has a dedicated read head and provides continuous information on the angular position of the disk. This is critical during write operations so that a sector being written does not overwrite part of the following sector.

Defect Handling

Practically all hard drives have defects, especially if they have a large data capacity. Rather than attempt to totally eliminate defects, it is more economical to develop ways to tolerate them. Numerous ways have been developed to deal with disk defects, and which method is used will have an impact on a given disk's suitability for motion video applications. Probably the most common technique is the bad-block map. This technique allocates one sector on the disk to contain pointers identifying all other sectors on the disk which contain defects. When a *high-level format* is performed on a disk these bad sectors are simply not made available to the system. High-level formatting refers to building a *file access table* (FAT), basically making a map of all the disk space that will be used by the operating system. The disadvantage of using the bad-block mapping technique is that under MS-DOS disk space is allocated in *clusters*. A cluster is a contiguous sequence of disk sectors. Disk sectors are sometimes also referred to as *blocks*. The operating system maps the beginning of each cluster into the FAT. There is no way to tell the operating system that a given cluster contains one or more bad blocks, so a bad block actually renders useless all blocks between the end of the last cluster and itself. The number of blocks per cluster varies depending on disk type, but four or eight blocks per cluster are not uncommon. This means that during a file transfer if a bad block is encountered it may be necessary to skip over several blocks before the next cluster is encountered. This temporarily slows down the data transfer rate and is not generally reflected in disk hardware specifications. The implication is that some leeway should be allowed between the anticipated maximum required data transfer rate and the rated transfer rate of the hard drive to be used.

Another technique is called *sector skipping*. This involves reserving a spare block at the end of each track. If a bad block is encountered during low-level formatting it is marked as such and the spare block is added to the end of the set of logical blocks, thereby apparently retaining track integrity. The skipping of the bad block can then be automatically handled by the disk controller and is, therefore, transparent to the operating system software. This does introduce a single sector delay into a contiguous data transfer but the bandwidth impact is minimal. An even more sophisticated technique, used only in more expensive disk drives, is known as *defect skipping*. This involves simply writing over any track defects with a preamble code and a sync pattern to allow the data separator to regain synchronization after passing the bad section. The block header contains a map of any defects in each block so the controller can be prepared to resynchronize the data separator when they are encountered. The presence of defects lengthens the physical block in which they occur by some defined amount. This means that disk sectors will not necessarily all be radially aligned with each other. The disk controller therefore must be considerably more intelligent and able to respond rapidly enough to handle variable length sectors in real time as the disk rotates.

Video Disk Fragmentation

When a new hard disk is installed in a computer system and software loaded into it, the disk sectors and tracks are filled in an orderly, contiguous manner. However, as disk files are added and deleted during the course of normal use, cluster utilization can become fragmented. This simply means that used and unused disk clusters are no longer necessarily contiguous. For example, if ten short files are added to a new disk and then three of them (not the last three) subsequently deleted, there will be empty spaces between some of the files on the disk. This is illustrated in Figure 6.21.

If a new file is then loaded which is larger than any of the available fragments, the operating system will first attempt to find contiguous space large enough to hold the file. Failing that, the file will be broken up and placed into whatever clusters are available. If a disk is operated near capacity over a long period of time this fragmentation of files tends to get worse and worse. When capturing motion-video frames to be stored on a hard disk drive, it is generally necessary to have contiguous tracks and sectors available in sufficient quantity to store the incoming data. If the disk drive has to seek further than adjacent tracks or skip many sectors per track, the data transfer rate may not be

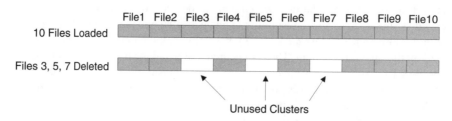

Figure 6.21   Illustration of disk cluster fragmentation caused by disk space allocation algorithm.

fast enough to keep up with the video, even if the rated speed is ostensibly adequate. To ensure maximum performance from a given disk drive, a *defragmentation* utility should be used before attempting to record video information from a real-time source. The defragmentation utility reorganizes existing data on the disk into contiguous sectors, leaving any free space also in contiguous sectors.

Helical-Scan Magnetic Tape

Magnetic tape has been used as a storage medium for both analog and digital information for many years. Recording-head and oxide-film coating technologies have advanced steadily over the years to the point where it is now possible to record two or more hours of sound and video on a tape that can be easily carried in one's pocket. The amount of information in a video signal dictates that for magnetic tape recording the recording head speed relative to the magnetic tape must be quite high in order to achieve the required signal bandwidth. One solution would be to use very long tapes and transport them at high speed past the recording head in a manner similar to audio tapes. The disadvantage of this approach is that the tape reels would have to be quite large to accommodate a reasonable length of tape and, therefore, fairly heavy. Starting and stopping a large mass of tape moving at high speeds presents serious technical and mechanical challenges and would have a tendency to stretch the mylar material of which magnetic tape is usually made. Stretching a magnetic tape seriously degrades the fidelity of any signal recorded on it. The alternative solution in widespread use today is the rotary-head tape transport. This scheme moves the magnetic tape at a relatively low speed but rotates the recording and playback heads to produce a high relative head-to-tape velocity. Figure 6.22 illustrates how in traditional recording methods the recorded tracks are linear, running the entire length of the tape, whereas in helical-scan recording the tracks are angular relative to the tape and broken up into short segments. This angular orientation of recording tracks is accomplished by routing the tape at an angle relative to the rotational axis of the drum which carries the recording heads.

To maximize recording head contact per revolution, the tape is wrapped around a portion of the recording rotor. Wrapping the tape at an angle relative to the rotational axis forms the tape into a partial helix, thus the name *helical* scan. A fairly common rotary head tape transport configuration is known as the C format. It gets this name from the fact that the tape wraps almost all the way around the recording drum as shown in Figure 6.23, forming the shape of the letter C.

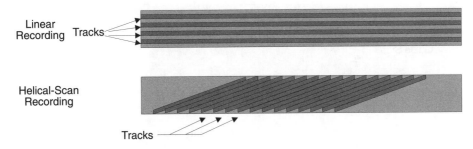

Figure 6.22   Relative arrangement of recorded tracks in linear versus helical-scan recording.

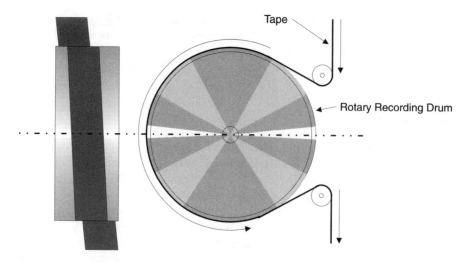

Figure 6.23   C-format rotary recording head-to-tape arrangement.

A common rotary-head configuration divides the head drum into a fixed part and a rotating part. The fixed part has a helical guide step which keeps the tape aligned properly as it slides around the drum. The rotating part carries the recording heads as shown in Figure 6.24.

The rotating drum assembly which carries the recording heads is referred to as the *scanner*. In a typical VCR the scanner is mounted at an angle so that the tape can be horizontal. When a VHS tape is loaded into a VCR for recording or playback the tape transport mechanism actually pulls the tape out of the cartridge and wraps it around the scanner as illustrated in Figure 6.25.

The scanner may carry two or four recording heads which are typically all mounted in the same plane of rotation. An alternative configuration is to mount the recording heads in pairs, in which case they are vertically staggered so they can follow two tracks on the tape simultaneously. These tape head arrangements for rotary scanners are illustrated in Figure 6.26.

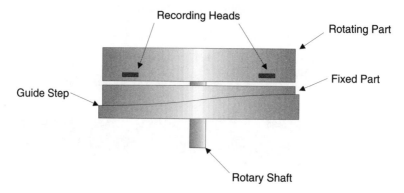

Figure 6.24   Rotating versus stationary portion of rotary, head tape scanner.

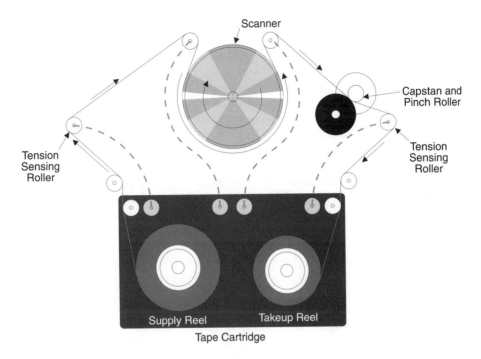

Figure 6.25   Routing of tape from cartridge to rotary-head tape scanner.

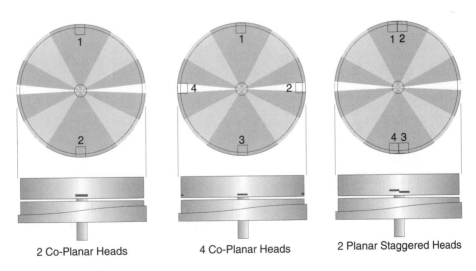

Figure 6.26   Various arrangements of recording heads in rotary-head tape scanners.

A major impact of the use of rotary head recording techniques is what happens as a result of variations in tape transport speed. For example, if an audio tape is slowed on playback the only result is a reduction in the frequency of signals read from the tape. In a rotary head recording, even if the tape stops moving, the scanner can continue to spin, providing a signal from the tape. This is how the freeze-frame feature works on most consumer-grade VCRs. However, tape-head tracking is different for forward, slow, stop, or reverse tape transport speeds. This is because the track angle is affected by the tape transport speed. During normal forward tape motion the track length and angle are the result of the rotational speed of the scanner, the helix angle of the tape, and the tape transport speed. Figure 6.27(a) shows that when the tape transport is stopped the track angle is perpendicular to the rotational axis of the scanner. Assuming scanner rotation is opposite the tape direction when the tape is moving, the horizontal component of the head velocity is added to the tape transport velocity, effectively changing the head tracking angle to something other than perpendicular to the rotational axis of the scanner. This is the normal operating mode for the mechanism. So as long as tape velocity and rotational speed are held constant the information can be recorded and played back reliably. However, if the tape motion is slowed, stopped, or reversed the effective head tracking angle changes accordingly as illustrated in Figure 6.27(b). This causes the playback track to cross several recorded tracks during each scan. The result of this in a typical low-cost, two-head VCR is a series of horizontal bands of static across the image. These bands of static correspond to points where the playback head is crossing from one recorded track to the next.

The picture seems to remain relatively intact between the static bars because for NTSC signals the decoder is able to lock onto the signal as the playback head enters the valid portion of each recorded track. For PAL format the situation is a bit more difficult because the decoder loses line synchronization as the playback head moves between tracks. Phase alternation of the color burst ref-

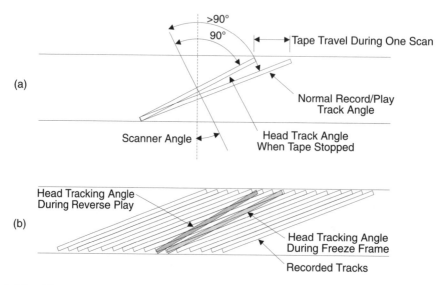

Figure 6.27   Affects of tape transport speed on rotary-head tracking angle.

erence then dictates that the decoder will have a 50% chance of locking onto the correct color burst phase when the playback head reenters the next valid recorded track. For analog recording formats such as VHS, each track on tape represents one field in the video sequence. Compact video format uses time compression which means that the time required to record the field on the track is less than the actual field time. This means that the scanner can be smaller but requires that at least part of the signal be buffered for time base correction. During slow, stop, or reverse operation there is a greater chance that at least one playback head will be in a valid track area at any given time if a four-head system is used. This accounts for the higher quality during these operating modes for a four-head versus a two-head machine. Given the approximately 0.9 micron minimum wavelength which can be recorded on magnetic tape using current technology, and the fact that the NTSC signal band-width is approximately 6 MHz, one field can be recorded on a track about 10 cm long. Because each track contains one field and NTSC specifies 60 fields per second, the tape speed for normal play-back must present 60 tracks per second to the scanner. A method of tracking is also required to ensure that the playback heads are properly positioned over the recorded tracks. A technique is used which is similar to the low frequency modulation tracking used in the laser disk. Within the scan-ner each individual recording head is mounted on an piezoelectric *bimorph*. A bimorph is a mechanical structure that bends in response to an electric current, similar to a bimetallic strip, which bends in response to heat. As shown in Figure 6.28, a counteropposing bimorph must be used to make small head position adjustments without degrading signal response due to angular errors.

A low-frequency sinusoid waveform in the range of 400 to 700 Hz is applied to the bimorph, causing the recording head to vibrate. The amplitude of vibration is slightly less than the track

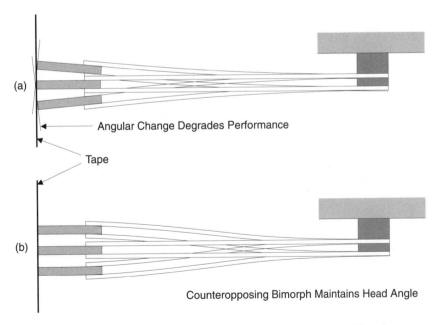

Figure 6.28   Illustration of the need for counteropposing bimorph head positioners.

width. This effectively modulates the low-frequency sinusoid onto the playback signal. By filtering out the modulated signal and checking its phase against the original it is possible to determine whether the recording head is above or below the target track as shown in Figure 6.29.

Digital Tape Formats

In addition to conventional analog video tape formats such as VHS there are a number of digital formats which also use helical-scan technology. Two of these, D1 and D2, will be discussed here. The D1 format records digital component video using the CCIR-601 specification and 4:2:2 subsampling. The D2 format records digital composite video. Each was developed in response to a different set of requirements but both have an advantage over analog video in that the video quality does not degrade after multiple generations of copying.

D1 Format

The D1 format records video component data sampled at 6.75 MHz for chrominance and 13.5 MHz for luminance. For each line, 360 of each chrominance sample (Cr and Cb) and 720 luminance samples are encoded, for a total of 1,440 samples per line. NTSC format records 250 lines per field while PAL format records 300 lines per field. With the 50 Hz versus 60 Hz field rates respectively, both formats result in 1,500 lines per second. The overall data rate is therefore 2.16 megabytes per second. To fit within the physical bandwidth limitations of magnetic recording medium, D1 machines use pairs of recording heads to record and play back two tracks simultaneously with each

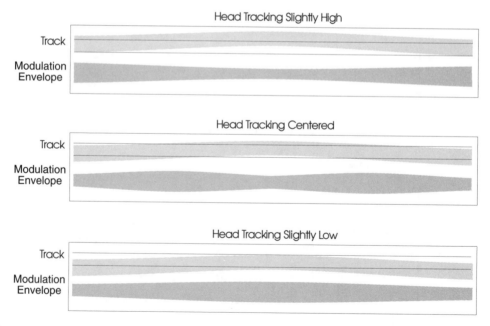

Figure 6.29   Mechanics of head position error signal generation via head positioner modulation.

rotation of the scanner. In addition to the helical-scan video tracks the tape format also incorporates linear audio, control, and time code tracks. The control track is used to generate feedback signals for controlling the capstan. The time code track is used to support linear editing by allowing specific frames in the video sequence to be identified. The linear audio track allows the audio portion of the recording to be played back over a range of tape transport speeds. This is a supplement to the primary audio channel which is four-channel stereo digitally recorded in the helical-scan format along with the video portion. Figure 6.30 illustrates how the helical video and audio tracks along with the linear tracks are laid out on tape. Figure 6.31 illustrates in greater detail how video and audio data are organized in the helical-scan tracks.

D2 Format

The D2 digital tape format was developed shortly after the D1 format. D2 format is created simply by sampling the composite video signal and storing the digitized samples on tape. While it can be argued that D1 has significant advantages over D2, the extra complexity added by the requirement for color subsampling and filtering on encode and decode processes tends to add significant expense. D2 was developed in response to the need for a system with the advantages of digital recording formats but at a price which would not make the cost of retrofitting a large automatic broadcast system prohibitive. A common technique used by broadcast studios is to record commercials and other elements of a day's programming on cassette tapes which are then automatically loaded in the correct sequence by robot equipment. The sampling rate is four times the frequency of the subcarrier, which amounts to oversampling. D1 and D2 formats both use the same type of cassette shell and both use ¾-inch tape. *Azimuth* recording is used for D2 because it allows elimination of *guard-band* between tracks on the tapes. Azimuth recording means that the angle of the record and playback heads is different for adjacent tracks. Signal strength on playback falls off rapidly if the angle of the playback head is different from that of the recording head. By using a different azimuth for adjacent tracks crosstalk is effectively eliminated. A channel-coding technique known

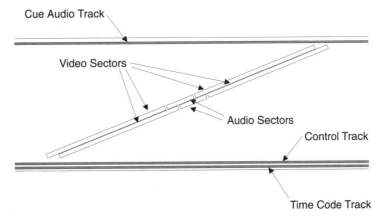

Figure 6.30 Organization of audio, video, and control tracks in D1 digital tape format.

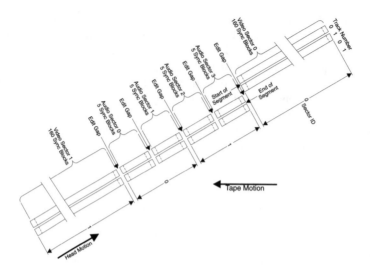

Figure 6.31   Detail diagram of single-field data track organization.

as *Miller code* (similar in concept to CCIR-656 coding) is used to ensure the flux transition frequency never drops below ⅓ the sample rate. This is necessary because the crosstalk immunity of azimuth recording falls off at low frequencies. At low frequencies the wavelengths are too long to produce any significant phase shift due to head angle. The high frequency of digital data makes it impractical to record an entire field on one track, so fields are split across two tracks. This does not create the kind of synchronization problems that it would in analog recording, however, because the discrete samples allow precise continuity. Unlike D1 format, audio information is recorded at the ends of the track rather than in the center. The arrangement of tracks on a D2 format tape is illustrated in Figure 6.32.

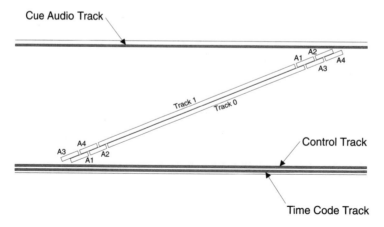

Figure 6.32   Organization of audio, video, and control tracks in D2 digital tape format.

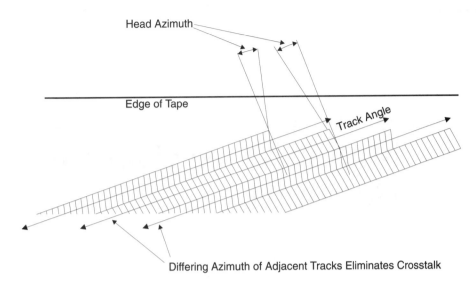

Figure 6.33 Illustration of recording head azimuth for adjacent tracks to eliminate track guard-band requirement.

The linear audio, control, and time code tracks have the same basic functions as in the D1 format. Figure 6.33 shows the approximate arrangement of head azimuth angles.

For NTSC format each field is recorded as three tracks of 85 lines each, for a total of 255 lines. For PAL format each field is recorded as four tracks with 76 lines in each track for a total of 304 lines. The head arrangement is slightly different for NTSC versus PAL format so the same machine cannot be used to record or playback both formats. Color burst and sync signals are not recorded because this information can be derived by counting samples. For NTSC format 768 samples per line are recorded, and 948 samples per line for PAL format.

7

Motion Video Capture Hardware

There are currently several options available to PC users who wish to work with video information. Faster, cheaper, and better capture systems are being introduced at a rapid pace as more companies enter the market. At the time of this writing more PC video capture cards had been introduced or announced than were practical to review given the allotted time. Therefore, this chapter will cover only three of the better-established video capture subsystems on the market. These are: The Video Spigot from Creative Labs, the Pro Movie Studio from Media Vision, and the Intel Smart Video Recorder. All three of these come bundled with Microsoft Video for Windows. Evidently, the marketers at each company understand human nature fairly well because each board comes packaged in a relatively large colorful box which is heavy enough to feel quite substantial when you lift it from the shelf. The weight, of course, comes from the software manuals packaged with the hardware. Besides Video for Windows, each capture card comes with one or more software application programs which can make use of the video information captured with the new toy. All three boards were tested on a 25 MHz 386SX PC with four megabytes of memory and a 212 megabyte hard disk drive. The hard disk drive was a Maxtor IDE drive with 15 mS access time. Nothing fancy.

Video Spigot

The Video Spigot from Creative Labs was one of the first PC video capture cards on the market. It does not contain any data compression or playback-assist hardware and is therefore one of the lowest-cost capture boards on the market. This does, however, place some limitations on its performance and makes it more dependent on the performance of the host system. The instruction manual that comes with the board is very short and simple and it even contains a little pep talk on the new, exciting, emerging PC video market, possibly so the manual doesn't seem *too* short and simple. Installation was fast and easy with no surprises. The board has an RCA jack for composite video input and a connector for S-Video input. The board plugs into the host system the same way as any

212

other PC add-in card. The package did not include a cable for connecting from the camera or VCR to the card, but fortunately one of the others did (the Intel board). With the camera connected, the hardware installation is complete. Software installation is equally simple. If Video for Windows is already installed (and it can be without any capture device) Video Spigot software installation consists simply in installing three drivers. There is one capture driver and two codec (encode/decode) drivers. The drivers are installed through the Windows control panel utility. When the capture driver is installed it automatically displays a dialog box which allows the interrupt level and base memory address to be modified, if necessary. If no unusual add-in cards are installed in the host system it is unnecessary to modify these parameters. As anyone who has installed a lot of PC add-in cards can tell you, it is no fun tracking down memory, I/O, interrupt, or DMA conflicts. To simplify the process in the event there is a conflict, the driver contains a utility for automatically scanning the memory and interrupt space to identify installed cards. There is a disclaimer that this operation could potentially hang the software. In most cases, however, this type of memory scan will not be necessary.

Video Spigot comes with a set of capture and compression software drivers that fit into the Video for Windows software framework (more details on this in Chapter 8). The software driver provides custom dialog boxes and controls specific to the capture hardware for which it was written. (This is the case for the other two capture boards as well.) Microsoft Video for Windows provides an application called *VidCap*, which is essentially a standard user interface for video capture hardware. Several items on the VidCap menu are modified by the installed capture driver. Under the Options menu, selecting Video Format produces a dialog box as illustrated in Figure 7.1.

This dialog box allows the user to select the scale of incoming video frames as well as the pixel data format. Selecting the button marked "Full" will cause the system to capture full resolution 640×480 video images. The other buttons reduce the scale accordingly with "½" producing 320×240 images, "⅜" producing 240×180 images, "¼" producing 160×120 images, and "⅛" producing 80×60 pixel images. The Image Format dialog box allows the user to select either 8-bit palletized, 8-bit dithered, 16-bit RGB 5:5:5, 24-bit RGB, Spigot Compression, or YUV 4:2:2. Spigot Compression is a proprietary compression algorithm developed for the Video Spigot, presumably to optimize the capture process. General descriptions of the other pixel formats are available in Chapters 2, 4, and 5. Exactly which is the best combination of image dimensions and pixel formats depends on the configuration of the machine being used. This evaluation was done on a 25 MHz

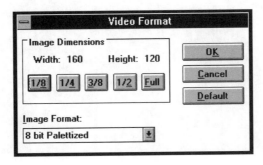

Figure 7.1 Video Format dialog box for the Video Spigot capture card.

386SX-based machine in spite of the fact that the Video Spigot installation guide specifies at least a 33 MHz 386DX machine with eight megabytes of memory. The results were really not too bad considering the host was slightly underpowered. Capturing motion video at full 640×480 resolution is really not practical because even at 15 frames per second, the data rate coming from the capture system is about 9.2 megabytes per second. To transfer this much data from the capture system into the PC memory buffers and then from there back out through the expansion bus to a disk drive is more than the PC expansion bus can handle. However, it is useful for capturing fairly high-resolution still images and does work even on the underpowered machine used for this evaluation. Figure 7.2 is a still image captured at 320×240 resolution with an 8-bit palettized pixel format.

The image was then saved as a *Windows device-independent bitmap* (DIB). This bitmap file was then imported into Corel Draw and printed directly on a 300 dpi laser printer. The same process works just as well at full resolution (640×480) but didn't produce any discernible improvement in picture quality on the printer, probably due to the limitation of the printer resolution. The full-resolution mode was a little more difficult to use because the system is more sensitive to timing aberrations resulting from user actions such as selecting menu items or clicking screen buttons. This occasionally results in a slightly skewed image but corrects itself after the CPU finishes whatever it was doing and can return its attention to the capture process again. This problem probably doesn't occur when using the recommended platform. Another item under the Options menu specific to the Video Spigot is the Video Source dialog box shown in Figure 7.3.

This allows the user to select which connector the incoming video signal should be received on and the signal standard to be used. There is also a checkbox to indicate whether or not the incoming signal is from a VCR or directly from a camera. It is important to set this checkbox correctly because it has an impact on the quality of the captured video. A VCR tends to produce less stable

Figure 7.2   Still image captured at 320×240 resolution with the Video Spigot capture card.

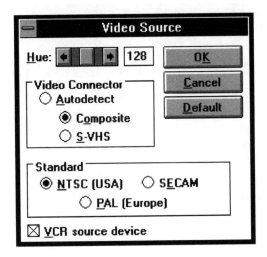

Figure 7.3   Video Source dialog box for the Video Spigot capture card.

sync signals than a direct camera input. Therefore, the genlock circuitry has to be a little more for-giving for a VCR signal. The result of this, however, is slightly lower quality in the captured image. The capture will still work if a camera is used and the VCR checkbox is selected. It *may* work if a VCR source is used and the VCR checkbox is *not* selected. However, there is a chance that the cap-ture process may lose synchronization at some point during recording, resulting in skewed images or vertical rolling. This, by the way, is not specific to the Video Spigot capture board and can be found in virtually any PC video capture system. To capture one or more individual images from a video sequence, the Capture Frames item from the Capture menu is used. The resulting dialog box is shown in Figure 7.4.

Each time the Capture button is clicked another image is added to the capture file. These may be saved as individual bitmap images or this feature may be used to produce animation. An exam-ple of this is provided in the video clip file named BEAR.VID. To capture a video sequence auto-matically the Video item in the Capture menu is used. This produces a dialog box as shown in Figure 7.5.

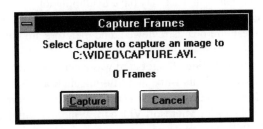

Figure 7.4   Capture Frames dialog box (common to all capture cards reviewed).

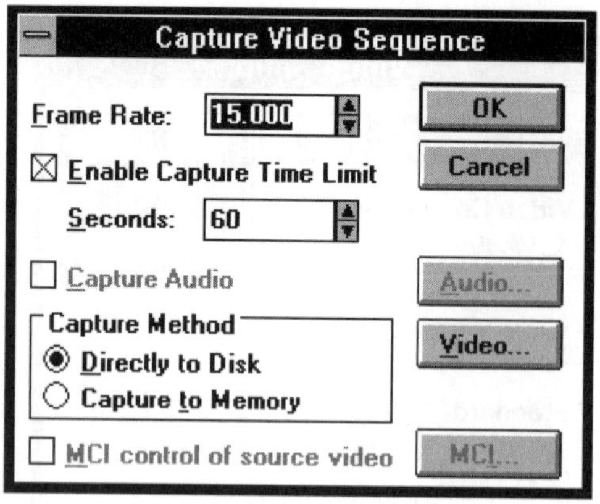

Figure 7.5   Capture Video dialog box (common to all capture cards reviewed).

The video frame rate is user-selectable although the practical frame rate achievable depends on the speed of the host machine. Using the 25 MHz 386SX machine with 15 frames per second as a target, most video sequences resulted in 10 to 15% of the frames being dropped. There is also a programmable time limit which will automatically stop the capture process after a given number of seconds. If the host system has enough memory and the video sequence to be captured is short enough it may be possible to capture the entire sequence directly to main memory. If a sound card is also installed in the system, audio information can be optionally captured simultaneous with the video. The Video button in this dialog box brings up the Video Format dialog box illustrated in Figure 7.1. A similar configuration is available for audio if audio hardware is installed and depends on the specific hardware installed, but is not covered here. The Media Control Interface (MCI) checkbox allows automatic control of the video source if the appropriate hardware and interface is installed. The primary advantage of MCI control is the ability to set automatic start and stop times and automatically step through video frames at lower than the normal playback rate, allowing a higher capture resolution. This option was not evaluated, however, as the appropriate equipment was not available. The last item in the capture menu brings up the Capture Palette dialog box as illustrated in Figure 7.6.

This allows an optimized color palette to be captured for playing video sequences on machines limited to 256 colors displayed simultaneously on the screen. This is a useful feature because, in fact, most PCs currently in use today have that limitation.

The Capture Palette, Capture Video, Capture Frames, and Single Frame dialog boxes are essentially the same for all capture boards reviewed, and therefore are not discussed further in the following sections.

Included in the box with the Video Spigot card was a copy of Microsoft Video for Windows as well as Multimedia Tool Box, Media Blitz, and Multimedia Make Your Point from Asymetrix, Inc. These products include a large number of prerecorded video clips stored on CD-ROM. There is also a CD-ROM video clip library for Microsoft Video for Windows with the Creative Labs logo on it. The content of these CD-ROMs was not reviewed because for one thing, that could take days, and besides, there ought to be some element of surprise when you open the box containing your latest

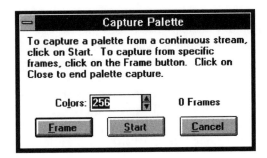

Figure 7.6   Capture Palette dialog box (common to all capture cards reviewed).

new gadget. There are also file converters to translate between Video for Windows and Quick Time video file formats. The Video Spigot capture board is based on the Philips Semiconductor SAA7191 NTSC decoder. The implementation is basically a simple frame grabber which operates fast enough to enable near full-motion video.

Media Vision Pro Movie Studio

Physical installation of the Pro Movie Studio board was essentially the same as that for the Video Spigot. The video inputs are also the same, with an RCA jack for composite video input and an S-Video connector. The Pro Movie Studio also uses the Phillips Semiconductor SAA7191 NTSC decoder. However, it also has a pair of custom integrated circuits which can be used for compressing the video information in real time as it is captured. Software installation is DOS-based and takes the user through a series of menus allowing selection of various configuration options including setting up an audio card. There are no DIP switches or jumpers and the installation software automatically detects the hardware configuration of the board. When monitoring live video from a camera using the preview video option the display frame update rate seems a little faster than for the Video Spigot. This could be due to differences in hardware or software driver implementation. There is, however, no way to measure that particular frame rate automatically. When capturing video in 160×120 format the video preview display frame update rate was about 5 frames per second. When the frame size was increased to 240×180 the frame rate dropped to about 2.5 frames per second. At 320×240 it dropped to about 1.5 frames per second. Again, this is due at least in part to limitations to the PC expansion bus.

Capturing video was a straightforward process similar in most respects to the process for the Video Spigot. There are, however, many more options available to the user through the hardware-specific dialog boxes for configuration. These will be discussed shortly. The installation manual specifies a minimum hardware configuration of a 386SX or better PC with at least two megabytes of memory, so the host platform used for the evaluation should not be a limiting factor in this case. Video captured at 15 frames per second was very smooth with no dropped frames. When capturing video at 30 frames per second about 2% of the frames were dropped but it was hardly noticeable. In both cases the video was captured at 160×120 using the Media Vision video compression option. This option uses 15-bit RGB as its basic image format and produces up to 16:1 compression. There is also an option to capture directly into 256-color mode using the VGA palette. This requires a two-step process: first, capturing a color palette for the video sequence, and then capturing the video sequence itself. The results are remarkably good when played back on a 256-color system. This mode is, however, uncompressed resulting in about eight megabytes of information for a 30 second video clip at 160×120 resolution. The Video Format dialog box for the Media Vision Pro Movie Studio is illustrated in Figure 7.7.

The Video Format item under the Options menu allows practically any image size and aspect ratio for capture to be selected by the user. There is, however, a pull-down selection box which makes it easier to select the standard image sizes, which probably work better anyway because scaling with odd aspect ratios tends to introduce visual artifacts and is less efficient. If the Media Vision Microsoft Video Compressor option is selected the image format is automatically switched to 32,768-color (15-bit RGB) mode. The compression settings control the amount of detail retained in each frame. If the Coarseness control is increased to maximum the image becomes very blocky. The Detail control didn't seem to produce any noticeable difference. It does, however, follow the Coarseness control whenever the Coarseness control is increased. In other words, the Detail control cannot be set lower than the Coarseness control. If the Advanced Compression Control check box is disabled, these two slider controls collapse into a single Quality control, presumably to make a trade-off between compression ratio and image quality. Unfortunately, the Compression Ratio enunciator just above the cancel button is only updated *after* the dialog box is dismissed using the OK button. This means that to see the effect on the compression ratio of a change in the compression setting it is necessary to dismiss the dialog box and then recall it. Playing around with these controls produced only two different compression ratios: 16:1 and 5.3:1. Perhaps future software development will add a little more granularity to this ostensibly sophisticated control. The worksheet section on the right-hand side of the dialog box apparently has no direct control over the oper-

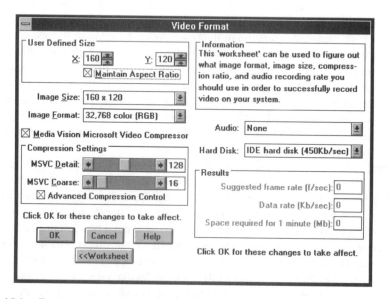

Figure 7.7   Video Format dialog box for the Pro Movie Studio capture card.

ation of the hardware but is essentially a calculation tool to help anticipate the parameters required for a given audio sampling rate and hard disk data rate. The Video Source control in the Option menu, shown in Figure 7.8, contains all the same basic controls as the equivalent control for the Video Spigot, plus a number of extras.

The Hue control can be used to compensate for chroma variations in the input source. The Horizontal and Vertical Start controls can be used to center the captured video horizontally or vertically to eliminate border areas resulting from incorrect video timing. All the controls on the right side are used to control how the Pro Movie Studio board processes incoming video signals. There is not a great deal of detail in the documentation about the effects or benefits of the Anti-Snow, Chroma AGC, or Vertical Noise controls; however, the Detail and Sharpness controls do have a noticeable impact on the output image. The checkbox options, Color Killer, Sensitivity, and Chroma Gain are likewise rather obscure in the documentation and it was difficult to notice any perceivable difference resulting from variations in these controls. The Input Filters are primarily useful for filtering out noise to improve the compression ratio. In this evaluation, use of the horizontal input filter did seem to produce a spurious visual bar on the right-hand side of the image approximately three or four pixels wide, probably resulting from the delay characteristics of the filter. The dialog boxes produced by the Capture menu items are essentially the same as those for Video Spigot with the exception that if capturing video in a 256-color palettized mode, a warning will appear if a palette has not been captured prior to capturing the video sequence. Still-frame and manual-frame capture operates in essentially the same way with the same capabilities as found in the Video Spigot board with the exception of the image enhancement and filtering capabilities defined in the Video Source menu item. Figure 7.9 is a 320×240 still-frame image captured using the Pro Movie Studio capture

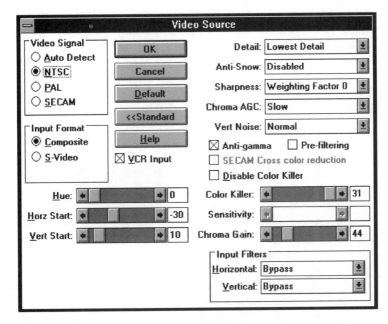

Figure 7.8   Video Source dialog box for the Pro Movie Studio capture card.

Figure 7.9   Still image captured at 320×240 resolution with the Pro Movie Studio capture card.

card with maximum image detail and contrast. Close examination will reveal slight visual artifacts along the extreme right and left edges of the image as well as around the vertical bars of the banister in the background. By adjusting the controls, these artifacts can be made to disappear, but the contrast and sharpness is reduced as a result. Being able to adjust the image characteristics, however, is definitely an advantage.

The Pro Movie Studio comes bundled with a copy of Microsoft Video for Windows and a CD-ROM containing a video clip library, as well as a program called Authorware Star, also produced by Media Vision. There are also file converters to translate between Video for Windows and Quick Time video file formats.

Intel Smart Video Recorder

The Intel Smart Video Recorder is built on a full-length PC add-in card with a daughter card which contains some of the electronics used for capture and compression of video. It incorporates the usual RCA jack for composite video input as well as an S-Video input connector. There is a bank of eight dip switches accessible through a slot in the mounting plate. These can be used to change the I/O base address in the event there is a conflict with another board in the system. The default factory setting is selected so that in most cases no change should be necessary. In the event there is a conflict with some other board in the system the installation software, through a series of menu selections, guides the user to select the correct setting. No conflicts or problems were encountered during installation for this evaluation. Software installation is via a DOS-based installed program and works by guiding the user through a series of menu choices. There are no difficult choices in the process, however. The installation program also installs the Video for Windows capture and compression drivers so the new hardware was available for use via Video for Windows immediately after running the install program. As usual, the Video Source and Video Format items in the options menu under VidCap are customized for the Smart Video Recorder. The Video Source dialog box, shown in Figure 7.10, incorporates the customary radio buttons and checkbox for selecting between composite or S-Video input and VCR or camera, respectively. It also contains slide-bar controls for contrast, tint, saturation, and brightness.

These are fairly intuitive adjustments and the effects are immediately visible in the preview capture window if preview is enabled. The Video Format dialog box, shown in Figure 7.11, appears when Video Format is selected from the Options menu. It is quite a bit simpler than the equivalent control on either Pro Movie Studio or Video Spigot, supporting only 160×120 or 320×240 screen resolutions for motion video, and 640×480 resolution for still-frame capture.

There are two compression options: Indeo™, which is Intel's proprietary compression algorithm, or YVU9, which is essentially uncompressed data, also a proprietary format. YVU9 actually means the color information is subsampled 16:1 bidirectionally. There are four different compressor settings, allowing a trade-off between quality and compression ratio. There is also an input box to allow selection of from one to five frames between key frames. A key frame is one which is not derived from another frame. To compare the effects of these settings, a ten-second video clip was captured at 160×120 resolution, 15 frames per second at maximum and minimum image quality settings without audio. At the maximum quality setting with three frames per key frame the ten-second video clip occupied 973K bytes of disk space with an estimated 254K bytes per second data rate. At the maximum compression setting with five frames per key frame the video clip occupied 768K bytes of disk space with an estimated data rate of 254K bytes per second. Evidently the estimated data rate is not actually calculated because in both cases the data rate for this test should have been under 100K bytes per second. Capturing still frames is not quite as straightforward as on the Pro Movie Studio because even though the capture frame menu item does capture a single frame, the image cannot be directly saved to disk as a bitmap file (.BMP). To save images as bitmap files it is necessary to load a video sequence into the VidEdit video editor, choose the desired frame using the

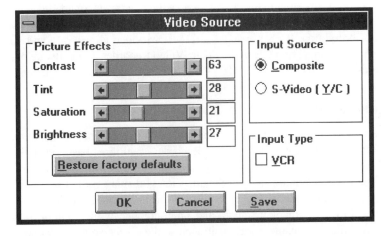

Figure 7.10   Video Source dialog box for the Intel Smart Video Recorder capture card.

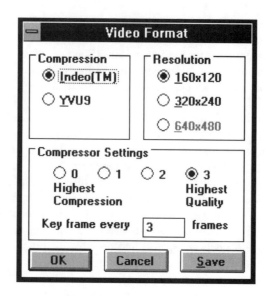

Figure 7.11   Video Format dialog box for the Intel Smart Video Recorder capture card.

edit controls, and select Edit Copy to copy the frame to the Windows clipboard. This can then be pasted into some other document capable of accepting bitmap information. While not exactly straightforward, this technique does get the job done, as illustrated in Figure 7.12.

This image, like the others, was captured at 320×240 resolution and pasted into a Corel Draw file. When YVU9 format is selected, images can be captured at 640×480 resolution. This mode is designated for still-frame capture only, however, and does not work for motion video. When capturing images at this resolution, it is a good idea to have plenty of available memory and as few applications running as possible. Otherwise you may get a message from the clipboard manager process saying there is insufficient memory. Again, like the others, the Smart Video Recorder comes bundled with Microsoft Video for Windows as well as Compel and Media Blitz software packages from Asymetrix Corporation. It also includes a CD-ROM video clip library and a six-foot RCA cable for connecting a camera or VCR to the Smart Video Recorder. For software playback of captured and compressed video clips, a 25 MHz 486SX or better machine is recommended.

Capture Resolution and Image Quality

To illustrate the visual differences in images captured with different spatial resolutions a "still-life" image was captured with the Intel Smart Video Recorder at all three basic resolutions (160×120, 320×240, and 640×480), and is shown here in (almost) full color in all three cases. The images were displayed on a VGA monitor using a Stealth VRAM display card at 640×480 resolution in 32,768 color mode, with the Media Player application from Microsoft Video for Windows. Each image was scaled to fill the display screen, and photographed with a 35mm SLR camera with ASA400 color slide film. The camera was positioned so the displayed image would completely fill the view finder. No doubt some image detail is lost in the four-color half-tone printing process, but

Figure 7.12   Still image captured at 320×240 resolution with the Intel Smart Video Recorder.

some of the more obvious visual artifacts should still be visible. In the 160×120 version shown in Figure 7.13, the most glaring artifact is graininess caused by the low image resolution. However, when shown in its native resolution on a 640×480 VGA screen, it doesn't look too bad; the image is just very small (about 2.5 inches across). Most PCs are not capable of updating an image larger than this fast enough to give the impression of smooth motion. The next image size, 320×240, shown in Figure 7.14, still carries some jagged edges in areas of high contrast where the edge is nearly vertical or horizontal. This is most noticeable among the branches above the brass vase. The full-resolution image, shown in Figure 7.15, is near-photographic quality. There are almost no high-contrast edge problems. The only obvious artifacts are slight color perturbations, again around the dark branches against the white background. This is probably due to the YVU9 color subsampling method used by the Indeo video capture format. Had the image been captured using CCIR-601 4:2:2 format or full-color sampling, these color variations would probably be less visible, although the image storage space would be larger. This image is provided in the file named VASE.PIC on the sample diskette.

When the images that make up a video sequence are compressed, there is inevitably some loss of image quality. Exactly what form this loss takes depends on the compression algorithm used, as discussed to some extent in Chapter 5. The compression techniques available with Video for Windows and the capture boards reviewed each produce different results, both in image quality and in the ability of a given CPU to decode the images on playback. Pictures in a book really cannot convey the impressions created by jerky video, so as a compromise a comparison of image quality relative to uncompressed data is given along with written descriptions of other phenomena.

To begin with, a 6.5-second video clip was captured using the Media Vision Pro Movie Studio with the Media Vision 4:2:2 Super Match compression, a modified CCIR-601 compatible format. This was then processed with VidEdit to produce a full-frame sequence, which simply means the color information was interpolated to generate a full set of luminance and chrominance information for each pixel. This full-frame sequence was then compressed using each available compression format (again using VidEdit). The original video clip (and therefore all subsequent versions) have a resolution of 160×120 pixels. For comparison, two instances of the Media Player application were started, with the full-frame version loaded into one instance, and each of the compressed versions alternately loaded into the other instance. The compressed clip was played at normal speed, and then both clips advanced to a position where a reasonable mix of motion, detail, and smooth contours are present in the image. The paused images were then scaled as large as possible while fitting side-by-side on the display, and photographed using the same technique described earlier. The full-frame image is shown on the left in each comparison. The display mode is 640×480 with 32,768 colors. Table 7.1 gives a few statistics comparing the various compression techniques.

The data rate using the Media Vision 4:2:2 format is really too high for software playback on a PC because it exceeds the transfer bandwidth of most common hard disk drives. The image quality, however, is quite high relative to full frame format, as illustrated in Figure 7.16. The frame labeled AUTHOR_F.AVI is a full-frame image, and that labeled AUTHOR_C.AVI is the 4:2:2 subsampled image. There is no discernible difference. The hardware compression option of the Pro Movie Studio appears the same as the Microsoft Video 1 format, as there was no other compression driver available to work with VidEdit for off-line compression, so it was assumed that compression format could be covered as part of Video 1. Video 1 is also the format used for off-line compression with the Video Spigot.

The Intel YVU9 format is also evidently not intended for software playback due to the relatively high data rate. If it were possible to simply copy the image data to the graphics frame buffer this format might make a good high-quality edit format, but unfortunately the color format must be converted to RGB, which consumes some CPU bandwidth. This combined with the disk access limitation tends to produce relatively jerky or slow (if frame-dropping is disabled) video playback. The image quality, however, remains fairly good as shown in Figure 7.17, with no gross degradation relative to full-frame images. The frame labeled AUTHOR_F.AVI is a full-frame image, and that labeled AUTHOR_9.AVI is the Intel YVU9 subsampled image.

The Indeo compression format produces fairly good compression (on the order of 9.5:1 for this sequence), and results in a fairly smooth playback. Stepping through the sequence frame by frame, the most noticeable artifact is the presence of shadows or "ghosts" wherever there is a com-

Table 7.1   6.5-Second Sample Video Clip Compression Statistics

File Size	Average Data Rate	Compression Format
5.7 MB	800 KB/Sec.	Full Frame
3.8 MB	580 KB/Sec.	4:2:2 Media Vision Super Match
2.1 MB	320 KB/Sec.	Intel YVU9
0.6 MB	92 KB/Sec.	Intel Indeo
0.3 MB	46 KB/Sec.	Microsoft Video 1

Figure 7.13 Still image captured at 160×120 resolution with the Intel Smart Video Recorder.

Figure 7.14 Still image captured at 320×240 resolution with the Intel Smart Video Recorder.

Figure 7.15 Still image captured at 640×480 resolution with the Intel Smart Video Recorder.

Figure 7.16 Sample video clip using Media Vision 4:2:2 Super Match compression.

Figure 7.17 Sample video clip using Intel YVU9 chroma subsampling.

Figure 7.18 Sample video clip using Intel Indeo and Microsoft Video 1 compression.

Figure 7.19 Intel Smart Video Recorder capture card.

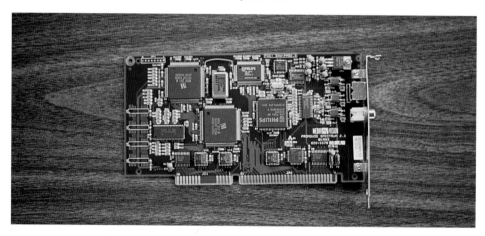

Figure 7.20 Media Vision Pro Movie Studio capture card.

Figure 7.21 Creative Labs Video Spigot capture card.

bination of rapid motion and high contrast. There is some blockiness, but overall the basic impression of the image is retained fairly well. The paused Indeo video is shown with maximum and minimum quality settings in Figure 7.18. The quality adjustment appears to have little effect on data rate or image quality.

The Microsoft Video 1 format was evidently designed specifically to run best on commonly available PCs, as the off-line compression time is faster than that of Indeo, and it seems less prone to drop frames during software playback. It does not exhibit the same tendency to produce ghosts as Indeo compression, but the color tends to be more blotchy. If the image is not viewed too closely the blotchiness is integrated by the eye, but unfortunately the distance at which this is most effective is too far away to see the image very well. The paused Microsoft Video 1 sample is shown with maximum and minimum quality settings in Figure 7.18. In this case, the quality adjustment has a significant effect on data rate and image quality, enough to be visible in the photograph.

The last three photographs, shown in Figures 7.19, 7.20, and 7.21, show the physical appearance of each of the capture cards reviewed.

Motion Video Software Environment

The evolution of motion video availability on IBM-compatible personal computers has been mainly within the context of Microsoft Windows. Much of the pioneering work that laid the groundwork for the introduction of video as a data type on the PC was done at Apple Computer, Silicon Graphics, and Intel's DVI group. However, because the bulk of the desktop personal computer market is made up of IBM-compatible PCs, that is the focus of this book. To understand how video works within the context of MicrosoftWindows it is first necessary to understand how Windows works. To understand this, it is useful to have some insight into how Windows evolved from DOS. This chapter includes discussions of how programs operate in the DOS environment, similarities and differences between the Windows environment and the DOS environment, an overview of how programs operate in the Windows environment, a detailed discussion of how Microsoft Video for Windows integrates into the Microsoft Windows graphical user interface, and a discussion of how Apple Computer's QuickTime for Windows interfaces to the programming environment. The concepts of device drivers and Dynamic Link Libraries (DLLs) are central to this discussion and, therefore, are covered in a fair amount of detail.

Programming Under DOS

One characteristic of the IBM-compatible PC that has been instrumental in developing the large sales volumes this product has enjoyed is the fact that each new generation of equipment has maintained a high level of backward compatibility with the original IBM PC. This can be viewed as either a blessing or a curse depending on your point of view. It is a blessing for software vendors selling into a large installed base of compatible equipment and for hardware vendors who can claim compatibility with a huge library of available software. It is a curse for anyone who has to develop the large performance increases constantly demanded by evolving technology, while carrying the baggage of longtime compatibility. In any case, the architecture is still with us and understanding its evolution will make its idiosyncrasies seem a bit more sensible. The original IBM PC was limited to a one-megabyte address space by the 20-bit address bus of the 8088 CPU. This megabyte of memory space is partitioned into various regions whose functions are dedicated, some by the architecture of the CPU and some by the system architecture, as illustrated in Figure 8.1.

The upper 64K-byte address space is dedicated to the system Basic I/O System (BIOS). The 192K-byte region just below that is reserved for BIOS extensions residing on add-in cards. The 128K-byte region just below that, starting at A0000(hex), is reserved for display memory, also usually residing on add-in cards. The first 1,024 bytes starting at address 00000h are reserved for the CPU interrupt vector table, and just above that is a small area reserved for use by the BIOS. The remainder of the memory space, which amounts to 640K bytes, is used for DOS and application programs. When DOS is first loaded into memory and gains control of the microprocessor it looks for a file named CONFIG.SYS in the root directory of the disk from which it was loaded. This file contains specifications for various operating system parameters and device-driver files. Device drivers are executable programs which remain in memory as long as DOS is operational. They are written according to strict specifications which allow them to be linked with the operating system to provide hardware-specific services to the operating system. These should not be confused with Terminate and Stay Resident (TSR) programs, which are not called by the operating system. When DOS loads an application program into memory, any memory references which involve segment registers are modified to reflect the location in memory at which the program is loaded. These modifications are called *segment fixups*. During the final stage of compiling an application program the linkage editor, or linker, stores special records in the executable file which define what areas in the program need to be fixed up when it is loaded into memory. This process is discussed here because a similar procedure occurs when a DLL is loaded under Windows. With the 80286 CPU, a new

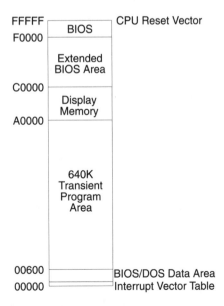

Figure 8.1   One-megabyte address space partitioning of the original IBM PC.

operating mode was introduced called *Protected Mode*. This involves the use of *selectors*, which are indirect memory reference mechanisms that allow programs and data to reside above the one-megabyte limit imposed by the 8086/8088. The 80286 can address up to 16 megabytes of memory.

A new type of driver called a *DOS extender* was developed to allow DOS programs to take advantage of this new extended address ability. To distinguish Protected Mode from the old operating mode, the old mode was named *Real Mode*. Unfortunately, when operating in Protected Mode there was no simple way to switch back to Real Mode, so a rather awkward technique was developed which involved resetting the CPU and then resuming execution at the appropriate place depending on a flag set in nonvolatile memory before the reset. This problem was solved with the introduction of the 80386 and later microprocessors. The 80386 also introduced a new operating mode known as *Enhanced Mode*. Of course, it also supported the operating modes of previous generations of microprocessors. The 80386 memory management technique uses data structures known as *descriptors*. These allow memory segments to be defined with a specified length, base address, and protection attributes, thus facilitating a true virtual memory operating system. This means that programs written for DOS using the conventional segment and offset memory addressing scheme can operate in a virtual 8086 environment protected from similar programs running on the same machine, effectively a preemptive multitask environment. Windows 3.1 supports this virtual 8086 operating environment for DOS programs but, oddly enough, does not use this technique for Windows applications. Windows applications use a cooperative multitask scheduling scheme, which presents an interesting dilemma for real-time applications such as motion video, as we will see.

Microsoft Windows

Early versions of Windows were capable of running in Real Mode, without benefit of any hardware multitask support or memory protection, which presented some difficult problems. Windows 3.1 no longer supports Real Mode but does support two operating modes known as *Standard Mode* and *Enhanced Mode*. Standard Mode is the default when Windows is operated on an 80286-based machine, and Enhanced Mode is the default when operated on an 80386 or higher machine. Standard Mode does not support the preemptive multitask operating mode for DOS applications as in Enhanced Mode, which explains why a DOS application cannot be run inside a window in Standard Mode. In Enhanced Mode, two or more DOS windows can be opened and two or more DOS applications run simultaneously in those windows. Control is passed among these processes and windows by an interrupt-driven preemption process. Among Windows applications, control of the CPU is transferred only when the currently executing application yields control to the windows scheduler. These applications actually all run within the context of a single virtual 8086 machine, unlike processes running in DOS windows. However, this one has the benefit of a DOS extender known as the DOS *Protected Mode Interface* (DPMI). Figure 8.2 is a simplified block diagram showing the relationships among the various functional units that make up Windows. The DPMI allows Windows to allocate memory as needed for Windows applications as well as any virtual 8086 machines that may need to be started.

Control and communication between Windows and its applications, and among the applications themselves, is accomplished by means of *messages*. Sometimes control of the CPU is passed at the same time a message is sent to a given process, and other times the message is simply posted to be processed at some later time, in which case CPU control immediately returns to the sender.

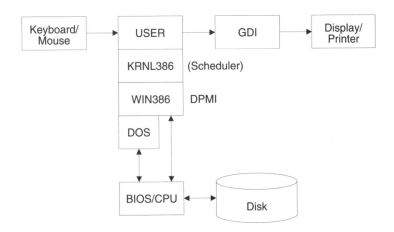

Figure 8.2   Simplified block diagram of major internal Windows components.

Each Windows application has a message queue and a message-processing loop. Windows receives input from the user via the keyboard or mouse (or possibly from other hardware events) and generates system messages which are placed into the message queue of the currently active application. The currently active application is said to have the *focus*, which is usually indicated by the window being on top of any other windows visible on the screen, and by different colors in the title bar and window frame. The message processing loop dispatches control to various message processing routines which carry out whatever actions are necessary according to the defined function of the application, based on an interpretation of the messages it receives. This flow of messages is illustrated in Figure 8.3.

If an event is something that needs to be processed right away, for example, a character being typed into a word processor, and no other process has current control of the CPU, the target process receives control of the CPU at the same time it receives a message indicating that the character was typed. The appropriate process within the application records the fact and possibly calls Windows system services to display the character on the screen or perform some other action. The flow of control for a typical scenario such as this is illustrated in Figure 8.4.

Each time a message is retrieved from the application's message queue, Windows may, if it chooses, transfer control to another application. If the currently executing application goes a long time without retrieving any messages it may be a long time before any other Windows application gets control. Ironically, this does not affect the availability of the processor for applications running in DOS Windows.

Dynamic Link Libraries (DLLs)

Essentially all Windows system services that involve access to hardware which is not standard on all PCs involves the use of DLLs. Additionally, a DLL may be used to modify the behavior of an application program without modifying the application itself. Microsoft Video for Windows is a good example of this use of DLLs. A DLL is an executable program that contains one or more sub-

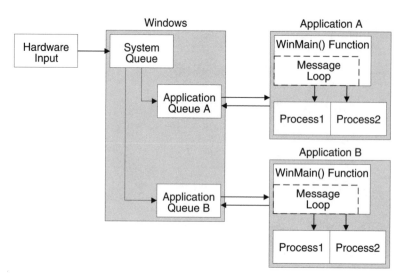

Figure 8.3 Illustration of message-processing flow within Microsoft Windows.

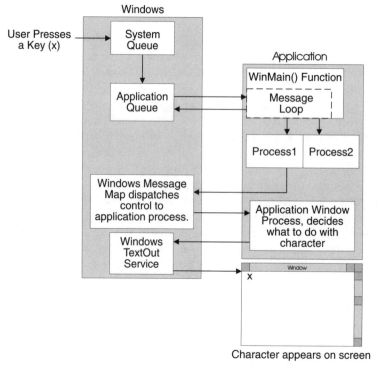

Character appears on screen

Figure 8.4 Example of message processing for a character typed into a Windows application.

routines that are dynamically loaded and linked to the calling application during runtime. The routines in a DLL may be linked by more than one application program, and if no applications require services of a DLL it may be released from memory. A DLL may also be moved to a different location in memory after being loaded if Windows is consolidating free memory space. The programmer can specify whether or not these actions can be taken by designating the DLL as movable and/or discardable. The process by which DLL functions are linked to application calls is similar to the fixups performed when DOS programs are loaded into memory. During compilation and linkage editing, functions are made available to external calling programs by *exporting* them. This involves writing fixup information in the header of the executable program file. This fixup information includes the names of the functions exported, to be made visible to the application program. Functions to be provided by a DLL must be *imported* into the calling program. This involves specifying the function name and possibly the name of the file containing the function. A DLL can also be made known to Windows by placing its name in a file named SYSTEM.INI. Examination of this file will reveal the names of virtually all device-dependent DLLs used by Windows on a particular system.

The advantage of using DLLs to modularize Windows applications is that they can be easily customized or modified without recompiling the entire application. Microsoft Video for Windows makes extensive use of this capability in the Windows operating environment. When a process attempts to access code that resides inside a DLL which has not been loaded, control of the CPU is diverted to the Windows memory manager. The name of the module file containing the required DLL may be incorporated into the client program that made the call to begin with. The memory manager then attempts to open the module file in the current default directory. Failing that, it looks in the information table provided by SYSTEM.INI. If the file is not available in the Windows or system directory, an error message is displayed indicating that the program cannot proceed because the DLL is not available. If, however, the module file is located, memory is allocated and the file is loaded. The appropriate far-call code is then inserted into the program that made the original attempt to access the DLL so that subsequent attempts will succeed without system intervention.

While dynamic linking may seem a bit arcane to the uninitiated, the basic elements of coding DLL interfaces are remarkably simple. Consider the case where you are developing an application program that requires certain hardware-specific functions to be placed inside a DLL so the application can be used with different types of hardware simply by providing a different DLL rather than a complete new application for each variety of hardware. Both the client application and the DLL have to understand the interface so they can communicate with each other. This understanding is achieved by exporting the names and addresses of the functions that make up the interface. This is done by using the _export qualifier keyword in the function declaration. All DLL interface functions must be declared FAR because there is no way to know where in memory they will be loaded. They must also be declared using the PASCAL calling convention because that is the convention used by Windows. The following function declaration illustrates the basic format for a DLL interface:

```
void FAR PASCAL _export FunctionName(Argument Declarations);
```

The void return data type is not required, and can be replaced by any valid return data type. Function arguments are ordinarily passed by reference rather than by value particularly if large amounts of data are involved. The DLL uses the stack of the application that called it. Large data buffers are best allocated using the global heap under Windows. By using an include file containing interface function declarations in the format shown above, included in both the client application and DLL source files, the connection can be easily established.

Another method is to include EXPORTS and IMPORTS statements in the respective module definition files for the DLL and the application. A module definition file is used to specify information that is included in the header of a module file about an executable program module. This is extended information beyond what is contained in the ordinary DOS-based executable file header. Besides exports and imports, the module definition file also defines whether or not a program must run under Windows, local heap size and stack size, and various memory management characteristics for code and data segments. The export statement is used for the DLL to define which function names should have external linkage information included in the program file header during the linkage edit process. In other words, it defines fixup information to be used by Windows and/or Windows client applications at runtime. The format of the EXPORTS statement in the Module Definition File is as follows:

```
EXPORTS FunctionName [=InternalName] [@Ordinal# [RESIDENTNAME]] [NODATA]
```

Items enclosed in brackets [] are optional. "FunctionName" is the name to be used by the calling application and need not necessarily match the internal function name of the given interface function. "InternalName" is the actual function name used inside the DLL source code file. The ordinal number is a numeric identification used by Windows for keeping track of dynamic linkage information in its memory management tables. For example, an ordinal of two would be specified as @2. If no ordinal number is specified the linkage editor assigns one automatically. If the keyword RESIDENTNAME is included it indicates that the name of this function should remain in memory at all times and cannot be discarded during the memory management process. The NODATA option specifies that the DLL will use the caller's data segment and, therefore, does not need to have its own data segment allocated. The following lines illustrate various ways to write the EXPORTS statement.

```
EXPORTS
WEP@0RESIDENTNAME
MyFunction
AliasName=MyAliasName
```

The IMPORTS statement is used with the application program to define external function references that must be resolved at runtime rather than at linkage edit time. It is the counterpart to the EXPORTS statement used in the DLL. The format of the IMPORTS statement is as follows:

```
IMPORTS [InternalName=]ModuleName.{FunctionName,Ordinal#}
```

"InternalName" is the actual function name used in the DLL source code. It is only necessary if it is different from the exported function name or if the import function is specified by ordinal number. "ModuleName" is the name of the executable file where the interface function is stored. ModuleName does not include the three-letter file extension. Following the period after ModuleName, either a function name or an ordinal number must be specified. "FunctionName," if specified, defines the name by which the interface function will be called inside the calling application. If an ordinal number is used it must match the ordinal number used in the corresponding EXPORTS statement for the DLL module definition file and the IMPORTS

InternalName must also be specified. The following lines illustrate various ways to write the EXPORTS statement.

```
IMPORTS
MYDLL.MyFunction
MyAliasName=MYDLL.AliasName
AliasByOrdinal=MYDLL.2
```

Including the _export specification in the interface function declaration is sufficient to cause the dynamic linkage fixup information to be stored in the binary output file after compiling and linking your DLL. As an alternative to including the IMPORTS statement in the module definition file for an application using a DLL you can generate an import library that contains the necessary linkage fixup information and then link that with the application. The functions residing inside the DLL must, of course, be declared external in this case. If the appropriate _export declarations are specified, and the import library is linked, the application program can refer to functions contained in a DLL as if they were statically linked. As another alternative, the application program can explicitly load the DLL into memory and link to specific functions. This is done using the LoadLibrary() and GetProcAddress() functions provided by Windows. If a DLL has to have its own main frame window or if it uses modeless dialog boxes it should incorporate a PreTranslateMessage() function and export this to the calling application. The reason for this is that a DLL does not have its own *message pump*. A message pump is a code loop that fetches messages from the application input message queue. If a DLL has to process user input, for example, to respond to user dialog boxes, the only rational source of input is the DLL's current client application. This way a DLL can service multiple clients and always respond to whichever client is currently active. One last important principle in understanding DLLs is the idea of *instance*. Object-oriented programming, as in C++, carries the idea of multiple instances of a given object. Whenever a new object instance is created, memory is allocated for its data members but code is shared. This means that code must be *reentrant*. In other words, it must be possible to reenter the code before the previous entry is finished executing. In the case of a DLL, automatic variables are allocated on the caller's stack. A DLL is allowed to have one 64K-byte segment for local heap storage. Any dynamically allocated memory beyond this must be requested from the Windows memory management system using the GlobalAlloc() function. Because the Windows memory manager may reorganize memory at any time there is no way for a DLL to be sure that memory allocated on a caller's stack or local heap will remain where it is after control is returned. Therefore, to support multiple instances a DLL must maintain a small amount of state information and configuration information which will be preserved from one call to the next. To allow the DLL to distinguish which client is calling it at any given moment, the concept of opening and closing a DLL or driver is established. When a DLL is opened, it returns a unique handle or identifier to the process that opened it. The caller then uses this handle on all subsequent calls so the DLL knows the history of each client process it works with.

Video for Windows

Video for Windows is essentially an extended application programmer interface (API). Its architecture is similar in many ways to the graphics device interface (GDI). The GDI provides a set of standard function calls that an application program can use to display graphics or text information on a display device or a printer. It also defines a set of functions, data structures, and protocols used to control physical graphics devices through device-specific software drivers. These drivers are implemented as DLLs. In the same way, the Video for Windows API defines a set of application function calls which the programmer can use to capture and playback video sequences. It also defines a driver interface to allow various types of capture-compression and video playback hardware to be used with any application written according to the API specification. The package also includes video capture, edit, and playback applications provided by Microsoft. Playing around with these three applications gives a pretty good idea of the general philosophy behind Video for Windows. With the capture program you can reserve file space for capturing video data, configure the capture hardware, select capture and compression options, preview captured video on the display, and trigger the simultaneous capture of video and audio information. If audio hardware is installed in the system it also can be configured through this application. The editing program allows video sequences to be compressed or decompressed or converted from one format to another, allows insertion or deletion of arbitrary-length video sequences, allows a separate sound file to be merged with a video file, and supports extraction of single-frame images. The playback utility allows a video sequence to be played in a window or in full-screen mode using the 320×200 VGA display mode (mode 13h) supporting 256 colors. The following sections give an overview of programming applications and drivers to work with Video for Windows. The intention is to provide a clear picture of the capabilities and potential offered by this software package. It would be impractical to provide a complete reference here as the subject is quite complex. Besides, a complete and detailed reference manual is available from Microsoft for anybody who seriously wants to program for this interface.

Video for Windows is included in the Windows system by inserting the name of the Video for Windows Media Control Interface AVI driver in the SYSTEM.INI file under the section labeled [mci]. The entry is:

```
AVIVideo=MCIAVI.DRV
```

Video compression or decompression drivers are made known to the system in the [drivers] section of SYSTEM.INI. Each compression or decompression driver is identified by an entry with the following form:

```
VIDC.<four letter code>= <file name>.DRV
```

The four-letter code following VIDC is a unique identifier which must be registered with Microsoft to avoid conflicts. The DRV file is the name of the DLL which actually contains the compression or decompression code. For example, the Microsoft video driver has an entry in the form:

```
VIDC.MSVC=msvidc.drv
```

There is a handy Windows utility named SYSEDIT.EXE in the WINDOWS\SYSTEM directory under Windows 3.1 which does not get installed automatically but is very useful for editing or looking at the SYSTEM.INI, WIN.INI, CONFIG.SYS, and AUTOEXEC.BAT files. Installing it will make it easier to poke around the Windows system and understand how Video for Windows works. It is easy to install using the Windows Program Manager FILE, NEW, Program Item, Browse commands.

Media Control Interface

The media control interface (MCI) was originally developed to support the concept of the *multimedia computer*. Initially, this simply meant adding sound capability to the PC. When video capability was added, a file protocol known as audio video interleave (AVI) was developed. The extended version of MCI therefore is called MCIAVI, or DVMCI (digital video media control interface). Video files use the extension AVI while strictly audio files use the extension WAV, presumably in reference to the wave format of an audio signal. The audio portion of MCI supports digitized audio signals at sample rates of 11 KHz, 22 KHz, and 44 KHz with sample sizes of 8 bits or 16 bits. Because audio was developed first, apart from video, and video capability was an add-on which needed to be compatible with existing audio protocols, there is no frame-by-frame synchronization of audio information with video. Synchronization is implicit in the interleave of audio and video information in an AVI file but the scheme is not bulletproof. Playing a strictly audio file is simply a matter of delivering a relatively low-bandwidth stream of audio samples to a D/A converter, which presents no difficulty within the PC architecture. Video streams, on the other hand, tend to saturate the CPU and internal data paths of the PC. The rate of playback is therefore often limited by the ability of the machine to keep up. For video, a subjective result of this is the tendency for motion to appear slower than normal; not desirable but not intolerable. It is, however, intolerable for any accompanying audio stream. The audio sample rate generally cannot be smoothly reduced because of the architecture of the audio playback conversion hardware. Therefore, if the average data rate for audio is lower than required, the result is a series of silent gaps in what would otherwise be a continuous audio stream. The only way to ensure that the audio portion of an AVI file is not broken up by an inadequate CPU is to drop video frames. This makes the apparent motion of the video sequence seem jerky. This tradeoff is necessitated by use of an underpowered computer regardless of how audio and video are synchronized. The most common problem resulting from the lack of explicit audio and video synchronization within AVI files is the tendency for audio to get slightly out of synchronization with the video as a result of video frames being buffered in the computer's memory. The longer the absolute delay between reading audio and video information from the disk and actually displaying it on the screen and playing it through the speaker, the more likely there will be an objectionable loss of synchronization.

There are two methods for an application program to control the playback of audio and video files: the string interface and the command interface. The same basic set of commands is available through both methods. Which method is used is presumably a matter of preference and the two methods can be intermixed. Commands are sent through the string interface by calling the function named MCISendString(). The arguments are a pointer to a command string, a pointer to a string buffer for return information, the length of the return string buffer, and an optional handle to a *callback* function for processing MCI messages. A callback function is a local function called by Windows in response to a specific event. The MCI command interface is used by calling a function named MCISendCommand(). The arguments are the device ID, which identifies the target of the command, a message code, a double-word flags parameter, and a pointer to a command-specific data structure. The basic procedure for playing an AVI file with MCI is as follows:

1. Open the AVI file.
2. Configure the playback window.

3. Play the video sequence. (Note: You can stop the sequence or seek to a given position at any time during the playback.)

4. Close the AVI file.

Table 8.1 shows the command strings and corresponding command codes used by the string interface and command interface respectively.

Each of the commands has a limited set of modifiers that define what the caller wishes to do. For example, the string "status media present" sent through the string interface is equivalent to a call to the command interface using the message MCI_STATUS and the qualifier MCI_DGV_STATUS_MEDIA_PRESENT. The total number of possible unique commands is fairly large and, therefore, beyond the scope of this discussion. The MCI command interface is only useful for player applications. In other words, it cannot be used to capture, compress, edit, or otherwise modify AVI files.

Installable Compression Manager

The installable compression manager (ICM) is basically the heart of Video for Windows. It is to PC video very similar to what the GDI is to graphics. The API consists of a set of function calls which the ICM processes and converts into calls to device drivers controlling capture, compression, and

Table 8.1 MCI String Commands and Corresponding Command Messages

String Command	Command Message
capability	MCI_GETDEVCAPS
close	MCI_CLOSE
configure	MCI_CONFIGURE
cue	MCI_CUE
info	MCI_INFO
open	MCI_OPEN
pause	MCI_PAUSE
play	MCI_PLAY
put	MCI_PUT
realize	MCI_REALIZE
resume	MCI_RESUME
seek	MCI_SEEK
set	MCI_SET
setaudio	MCI_SETAUDIO
setvideo	MCI_SETVIDEO
signal	MCI_SIGNAL
status	MCI_STATUS
step	MCI_STEP
stop	MCI_STOP
update	MCI_UPDATE
where	MCI_WHERE
window	MCI_WINDOW

decompression hardware. Compression and decompression may also be performed in software by the driver. Figure 8.5 illustrates roughly how an application connects through the GDI, Windows API, and ICM to the various hardware elements required to capture, compress, and playback video.

The names of the API functions of the ICM are listed in Table 8.2, along with a brief description of each.

The Video for Windows API also includes extensions to the GDI in the form of a set of functions designed to enhance the transfer of image frames to the display screen. The names of these functions are listed in Table 8.3, with a brief description of each.

Video Compression and Decompression Drivers

Compression and decompression of video information is actually done by drivers written as DLLs. There are three main functions performed by video drivers: capture, compression, and decompression. The decompression process may optionally include display of the decompressed images. All of these functions can be handled by a single driver, or by multiple drivers. Capture drivers define four channels for the transfer of video information. Figure 8.6 illustrates the conceptual organization of these channels. The four channels are referred to as External In, External Out, Video In, and Video Out.

External In refers to the path by which signals are received from a camera, VCR, TV tuner, or some other source. It is the path by which video information is received, processed, and stored by the capture hardware. External Out is the path by which video frames can be displayed if the capture hardware supports the display. This could be a video overlay device or an external monitor. The Video In channel is the path by which the host CPU transfers video information out of the capture device. The Video Out channel is the path through which the CPU transfers video information

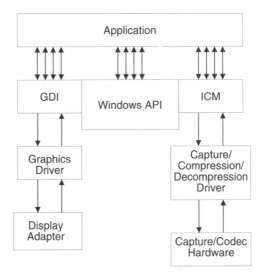

Figure 8.5   Interfaces of application and drivers to Windows internal structures.

Table 8.2   API Functions Defined in the Video for Windows ICM

`ICInfo()`	Returns information about the compression or decompression driver.
`ICOpen()`	Establishes a connection between the application and compression or decompression driver.
`ICClose()`	Closes the connection between the application and compression or decompression driver.
`ICLocate()`	Determines whether a specific compression or decompression driver is loaded or available.
`ICInstall()`	Installs a compression or decompression driver, generally not used by application programs.
`ICRemove()`	Removes an installed compression or decompression driver.
`ICQueryConfigure()`	Queries a driver to determine if a configuration dialog box is supported.
`ICConfigure()`	Triggers the display of the configuration dialog box supported by the compression or decompression driver.
`ICGetStateSize()`	Returns the buffer size needed to store the state of the driver.
`ICGetState()`	Causes the driver to store its current state data in a buffer supplied by the calling application.
`ICSetState()`	Restores state of the driver from a buffer supplied by the calling application.
`ICGetInfo()`	Returns information about the compression or decompression driver.
`ICGetDefaultKeyFrameRate()`	Returns the default key frame rate of the compression or decompression driver.
`ICGetDisplayFormat()`	Returns the preferred display format for a compression or decompression driver.
`ICGetDefaultQuality()`	Returns the default quality level created by the driver.
`ICQueryAbout()`	Returns a flag indicating whether the compression or decompression driver supports an about dialog box.
`ICAbout()`	Causes the compression or decompression driver to display its about dialog box.
`ICCompress()`	Causes the compression driver to compress a frame of data.
`ICCompressBegin()`	Prepares a compression driver for compressing data.
`ICCompressEnd()`	Informs a compression driver there will be no more frames compressed.
`ICCompressGetFormat()`	Returns an indication of the output format from a compression driver.
`ICCompressGetFormatSize()`	Returns the size of the buffer required to store the format definition data.
`ICCompressGetSize()`	Returns the size of the compressed data for a given frame.

`ICCompressQuery()`	Returns a flag indicating whether a compressor can compress given data format.
`ICDecompress()`	Causes the decompression driver to decompress a frame of data.
`ICDecompressBegin()`	Informs a decompression driver to prepare for decompressing images.
`ICDecompressEnd()`	Informs the decompression driver that no more frames will be decompressed.
`ICDecompressGetFormat()`	Returns the format of data generated by the decompressor.
`ICDecompressGetFormatSize()`	Returns the size of a buffer needed to store format information.
`ICDecompressGetPalette()`	Returns a palette to be used with data generated by the decompressor.
`ICDecompressQuery()`	Returns a flag indicating whether a decompression driver can decompress specific compression format.
`ICDrawBegin()`	Instructs a decompression driver to prepare for drawing images.
`ICDrawEnd()`	Informs the decompression driver that no more drawing operations will be required.
`ICDrawFlush()`	Causes the decompression driver's drawing buffers to be emptied.
`ICDrawQuery()`	Returns a flag indicating whether the compression driver can render drawings in a specific format.
`ICDrawStart()`	Starts the internal clock used by a decompression driver for drawing.
`ICDrawStop()`	Stops the internal clock used by a decompression driver for drawing.
`ICGetBuffersWanted()`	Returns a value indicating the amount of buffer space required by the compression or decompression driver.
`ICDrawGetTime()`	Returns the current time as stored by the decompression driver.
`ICDrawRealize()`	Causes the decompression driver to generate a palette used with images generated by the driver.
`ICDrawSetTime()`	Sets the value of the internal timer used by the decompression driver.
`ICDrawWindow()`	Causes the decompression driver to redraw the display window.

to the capture device for display if display is supported. The compression and decompression process may or may not involve specialized hardware. A conceptual model for the flow of video information through a compression driver is illustrated in Figure 8.7.

The client application program receives uncompressed video frames from the video source and passes them to the compression driver. After compression, the application program transfers

Table 8.3   Enhanced DIB Drawing Functions for Video Frames

`DrawDIBOpen()`	Establishes a device context for drawing.
`DrawDIBDraw()`	Draws a device independent bit map on the display.
`DrawDIBClose()`	Releases a drawing context.
`DrawDIBBegin()`	Notifies the driver that drawing is about the begin.
`DrawDIBEnd()`	Frees the resources allocated by the begin message.
`DrawDIBChangePalette()`	Loads the display palette with a new set of data used for drawing bit maps.
`DrawDIBGetPalette()`	Reads palette data used by the drawing context.
`DrawDIBRealize()`	Generates a set of palette data used for drawing.
`DrawDIBSetPalette()`	Loads the hardware palette with the data generated by the realize function.

the compressed data to its destination, which may be an AVI file or some other destination. If the capture device has built-in compression during capture, the client application may not actually get involved in handling the uncompressed video frames. Typically, the only indication of this to the application would be that no buffer space would be requested by the driver to be supplied by the application program. There is, however, a specific indication returned by the driver to indicate if it is capable of supporting its own display of video frames. The decompression process is essentially the reverse of the compression process in terms of the flow of data, as illustrated in Figure 8.8.

If there is a hardware video accelerator in the system that also supports display the decompression and display driver may take advantage of these hardware capabilities to bypass the conventional display data path going through the GDI. This is illustrated in Figure 8.9.

Along these lines, by the time this book is published there will probably be a new release of Microsoft Video for Windows with a special display API to address the specific needs of motion video. This has been a problem in the past because the GDI was specifically written for device independence somewhat at the expense of graphics display performance. Because of the differences in

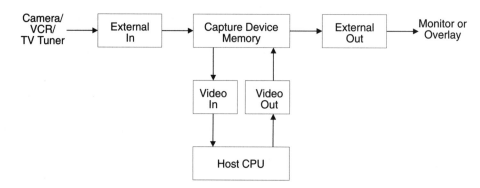

Figure 8.6   Illustration of the four major video data channels defined under Video for Windows.

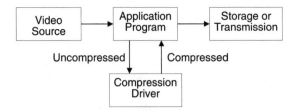

Figure 8.7 Flow of data through a compression driver.

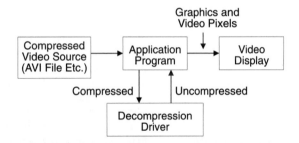

Figure 8.8 Flow of data through a decompression driver.

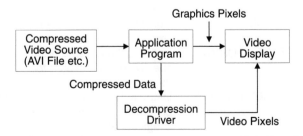

Figure 8.9 Flow of data through a decompression driver with hardware display support.

data types and the high sustained data rates required for motion video, the GDI has tended to be a bottleneck.

The video driver communicates with the system through a single entry point known as DriverProc(). This function takes five arguments: a double-word driver ID, a handle to the driver, an unsigned integer message code, and two long-word parameters, one of which usually carries flags information and the other of which usually carries a pointer to a data structure. The exact interpretation of the last two arguments depends on the type of message and the message code. The messages sent to the driver roughly correspond to the individual function calls defined in the ICM. These messages with a brief description of each are listed in Table 8.4.

If the driver supports video capture it must also handle a set of messages specifically related to capturing video information. The mechanism for passing these messages to the driver is the same as for the previously listed driver messages. Capture-specific driver messages are listed in Table 8.5, with a brief description of each.

Table 8.4   ICM Messages to Be Handled by Video Drivers

ICM_COMPRESS	Instructs the driver to compress a video frame and store it in the buffer provided by the calling application.
ICM_COMPRESS_BEGIN	Instructs the driver to prepare for compressing video frames.
ICM_COMPRESS_END	Instructs the driver that no more compression operations will be requested.
ICM_COMPRESS_GET_FORMAT	Fills a data structure with information defining the format of compressed frames.
ICM_COMPRESS_GET_SIZE	Requests the driver to return a number indicating the maximum size of one image frame after being compressed.
ICM_COMPRESS_QUERY	Interrogates the driver if it is capable of compressing using a specific input format.
ICM_DECOMPRESS	Instructs the driver to decompress the image frame and store it in the buffer provided by the calling application.
ICM_DECOMPRESS_BEGIN	Instructs the driver to prepare for decompressing image frames.
ICM_DECOMPRESS_END	Notifies the driver that no more video frames will be sent for the current sequence.
ICM_DECOMPRESS_GET_FORMAT	Instructs the driver to return a block of information specifying the optimum format for decompressed data.
ICM_DECOMPRESS_GET_PALETTE	Instructs the driver to fill a data structure with palette information to be used with decompressed image frames.
ICM_DECOMPRESS_QUERY	Returns a flag indicating whether or not the driver can decompress a specific input compressed data format.

ICM_DRAW	Instructs the driver to decompress a video frame and draw it on the display screen.
ICM_DRAW_BEGIN	Informs the driver that a sequence of video frames to be decompressed and drawn on the display screen is about to begin.
ICM_DRAW_END	Informs the driver that no more frames to be decompressed and displayed will be sent.
ICM_DRAW_GETTIME	Requests the driver to return the value stored in its internal clock.
ICM_DRAW_QUERY	Requests the driver to return a flag indicating whether it can display images in a specified format.
ICM_DRAW_REALIZE	Causes the driver to generate palette data based on the frames being processed.
ICM_DRAW_SETTIME	Resets the driver's internal clock which is used for timing video frames.
ICM_DRAW_START	Instructs the driver to stop its internal clock.
ICM_DRAW_WINDOW	Informs the driver that a window has been moved or obscured.
ICM_DRAW_FLUSH	Instructs the driver to flush any buffered frames that are awaiting display.
ICM_ABOUT	Instructs the driver to display a dialog box showing copyright information.
ICM_CONFIGURE	Instructs the driver to display a dialog box for user configuration of driver specific parameters.
ICM_GETBUFFERSWANTED	Requests the driver to return a number indicating how much memory buffer space the driver needs to perform decompression and display.
ICM_GETDEFAULTKEYFRAMERATE	Requests the driver to return a number indicating the optimum key frame rate for the driver.
ICM_GETDEFAULTQUALITY	Requests the driver to return a number corresponding to the default quality level used by the driver.
ICM_GETINFO	Requests the driver to return general information about itself.
ICM_GETQUALITY	Requests the driver to return information regarding the current setting of its quality levels for decompression.
ICM_GETSTATE	Causes the driver to fill a data structure provided by the calling application with data describing the compressor's current configuration and state.
ICM_SETQUALITY	Causes the driver to change its image compression quality level to that specified by the calling application.
ICM_SETSTATE	Restores the state information in the driver which was returned as a result of the GetState message.
DRV_OPEN	Informs the driver that it is about to be called upon by a client application and causes the driver to return the unique instance handle which will be used in subsequent calls by the application.

Table 8.5   ICM Messages Specifically for Video Capture Drivers

DVM_GETERRORTEXT	Causes the driver to return a character string containing the description of an error which occurred previously.
DVM_STREAM_GETERROR	Causes the driver to return a code indicating the error reported by a previous event.
DVM_DIALOG	Instructs the driver to display a dialog box which the user can control to set up capture specific parameters for a given channel.
DVM_DST_RECT	Causes the driver to either set or return the boundaries of the destination rectangle used by the video display.
DVM_FORMAT	Configures the format of a video device channel used by the driver.
DVM_GET_CHANNEL_CAPS	Requests the driver to return information defining the capabilities of a given channel to be used.
DVM_GETVIDEOAPIVER	Requests the driver to return the version number of the video API used by the driver.
DVM_PALETTE	Instructs the driver to either load or return the data for a palette used by a given video device channel.
DVM_PALETTERGB555	Informs the driver that an RGB555 palette is to be associated with a given video device channel.
DVM_SRC_RECT	Instructs the driver to set or return the boundaries of the source rectangle used by a given video device channel.
DVM_FRAME	Instructs the driver to process a single frame from the video capture device.
DVM_STREAM_ADDBUFFER	Notifies the driver that an input buffer is available to be filled with video information.
DVM_STREAM_FINI	Instructs the driver to terminate a stream of video information on a given channel.
DVM_STREAM_GETPOSITION	Requests the driver to return a number indicating the current position of a specified video input stream.
DVM_STREAM_INIT	Instructs to driver to initialize a given video device channel to receive a stream of video information.
DVM_STREAM_PREPAREHEADER	Writes header information to an input buffer used to receive video data from the video input stream.
DVM_STREAM_RESET	Instructs the driver to stop a currently active input stream and reset the current position counter to zero.
DVM_STREAM_START	Instructs the driver to start capturing a video stream.
DVM_STREAM_STOP	Instructs the driver to stop receiving a video stream.
DVM_STREAM_UNPREPAREHEADER	Instructs the driver to remove header information generated by a previous call to DVM_STREAM_PREPAREHEADER.

DVM_UPDATE	Informs the driver that the display needs to be updated. Usually used with the external out channel.
MM_DRVM_CLOSE	This is a video callback message used to indicate that a video channel has been closed.
MM_DRVM_DATA	This is a callback message used to inform the calling application that a specified data buffer is being returned for use by the application.
MM_DRVM_ERROR	This is a video callback message used to inform the calling application when an error has occurred.
MM_DRVM_OPEN	This is a video callback message which notifies the calling application that a video channel has been opened.

The following sample program code illustrates the basic framework for implementing a Video for Windows driver. The include files used with this program are provided in the Microsoft Video for Windows Software Developers Kit. The SDK contains complete sample programs and all necessary header and library files to create Video for Windows applications and drivers, so that information is not reproduced here.

Example Program Code for Video Driver

```
#include <windows.h>
#include <mmsystem.h>
#include <compddk.h>
#define SAMPLE_DRIVER_ID       1

LRESULT CALLBACK DriverProcVideo(
  DWORD dwDriverID,
  HDRVR hDriver,
  UINT uiMessage,
  LPARAM lParam1,
  LPARAM lParam2);

LRESULT CALLBACK _loadds DriverProc(
  DWORD dwDriverID,
  HDRVR hDriver,
  UINT uiMessage,
  LPARAM lParam1,
  LPARAM lParam2)
  {
INSTINFO *pi;
int i;
LRESULT dw;
if ( (dwDriverID == SAMPLE_DRIVER_ID) || (dwDriverID == 0)) pi = NULL;
else pi = (INSTINFO *)(UINT)dwDriverID;
switch (uiMessage)
  {
```

```
        case DRV_LOAD:
          return (LRESULT)1L;
        case DRV_FREE:
          return (LRESULT)1L;
        case DRV_OPEN:
          if (lParam2 == NULL) return SAMPLE_DRIVER_ID;
        case DRV_QUERYCONFIGURE:
          return (LRESULT)0L;
        case DRV_CONFIGURE:
          return DRV_OK;
        case DRV_DISABLE:
        case DRV_ENABLE:
          return (LRESULT)1L;
        case DRV_INSTALL:
        case DRV_REMOVE:
          return (LRESULT)DRV_OK;
        default:
          if (pi && pi->DriverProc) return
            pi->DriverProc(dwDriverID,hDriver,uiMessage,lParam1,lParam2);
          else return
            DefDriverProc(dwDriverID,hDriver,uiMessage,lParam1, lParam2);
      }
  }

LRESULT CALLBACK DriverProcVideo(
  DWORD dwDriverID,
  HDRVR hDriver,
  UINT uiMessage,
  LPARAM lParam1,
  LPARAM lParam2)
  {
  INSTINFO *pi = (INSTINFO *)(WORD)dwDriverID;
  switch (uiMessage)
    {
    case DRV_LOAD:
      return (LRESULT)Load();
    case DRV_FREE:
      Free();
      return (LRESULT)1L;
    case DRV_OPEN:
      return (LRESULT)(DWORD)(WORD)Open((ICOPEN FAR *) lParam2);
    case DRV_CLOSE:
      if (pi) Close(pi);
      return (LRESULT)1L;
    case ICM_CONFIGURE:
      if (lParam1 == -1)
        return QueryConfigure(pi) ? ICERR_OK : ICERR_UNSUPPORTED;
      else
        return Configure(pi, (HWND)lParam1);
    case ICM_ABOUT:
      if (lParam1 == -1)
        return QueryAbout(pi) ? ICERR_OK : ICERR_UNSUPPORTED;
      else
```

```
      return About(pi, (HWND)lParam1);
case ICM_GETSTATE:
  return GetState(pi, (LPVOID)lParam1, (DWORD)lParam2);
case ICM_SETSTATE:
  return SetState(pi, (LPVOID)lParam1, (DWORD)lParam2);
case ICM_GETINFO:
  return GetInfo(pi, (ICINFO FAR *)lParam1, (DWORD)lParam2);
case ICM_GETQUALITY:
case ICM_SETQUALITY:
case ICM_GETDEFAULTQUALITY:
  return ICERR_UNSUPPORTED;
case ICM_GETDEFAULTKEYFRAMERATE:
  return ICERR_UNSUPPORTED;
case ICM_COMPRESS_QUERY:
  return CompressQuery(pi,(LPBITMAPINFOHEADER)lParam1,
  (LPBITMAPINFOHEADER)lParam2);
case ICM_COMPRESS_BEGIN:
  return CompressBegin(pi,(LPBITMAPINFOHEADER)lParam1,
    (LPBITMAPINFOHEADER)lParam2);
case ICM_COMPRESS_GET_FORMAT:
  return CompressGetFormat(pi,(LPBITMAPINFOHEADER)lParam1,
    (LPBITMAPINFOHEADER)lParam2);
case ICM_COMPRESS_GET_SIZE:
  return CompressGetSize(pi,(LPBITMAPINFOHEADER)lParam1,
    (LPBITMAPINFOHEADER)lParam2);
case ICM_COMPRESS:
  return Compress(pi,(ICCOMPRESS FAR *)lParam1, (DWORD)lParam2);
case ICM_COMPRESS_END:
  return CompressEnd(pi);
case ICM_DECOMPRESS_QUERY:
  return DecompressQuery(pi,(LPBITMAPINFOHEADER)lParam1,
    (LPBITMAPINFOHEADER)lParam2);
case ICM_DECOMPRESS_BEGIN:
  return DecompressBegin(pi,(LPBITMAPINFOHEADER)lParam1,
    (LPBITMAPINFOHEADER)lParam2);
case ICM_DECOMPRESS_GET_FORMAT:
  return DecompressGetFormat(pi,(LPBITMAPINFOHEADER)lParam1,
    (LPBITMAPINFOHEADER)lParam2);
case ICM_DECOMPRESS_GET_PALETTE:
  return DecompressGetPalette(pi,
    (LPBITMAPINFOHEADER)lParam1,(LPBITMAPINFOHEADER)lParam2);
case ICM_DECOMPRESS:
  return Decompress(pi,(ICDECOMPRESS FAR *)lParam1, (DWORD)lParam2);
case ICM_DECOMPRESS_END:
  return DecompressEnd(pi);
case ICM_DRAW_QUERY:
  return DrawQuery(pi,
    (LPBITMAPINFOHEADER)lParam1) ? ICERR_OK : ICERR_UNSUPPORTED;
case ICM_DRAW_BEGIN:
  return DrawBegin(pi,(ICDRAWBEGIN FAR *)lParam1, (DWORD)lParam2);
case ICM_DRAW:
  return Draw(pi,(ICDRAW FAR *)lParam1, (DWORD)lParam2);
case ICM_DRAW_END:
```

```
          return DrawEnd(pi);
      }
    if (uiMessage < DRV_USER)
      return DefDriverProc(dwDriverID,hDriver,uiMessage,lParam1,Param2);
    else return ICERR_UNSUPPORTED;
    }

int NEAR PASCAL LibMain(
    HMODULE hModule,
    WORD wHeapSize,
    LPSTR lpCmdLine)
    {
    ghModule = hModule;
    return 1;
    }
```

AVI File Format

AVI stands for *audio video interleave*. AVI files use a format known as the RIFF file format. The RIFF form is characterized by its use of a concept known as a *chunk*. A chunk is a section of the file distinguished by a *chunk header*. All the data for a given video clip is contained in a section known as a RIFF "avi" chunk. A chunk is always preceded by an 8- or 12-byte tag which is organized as follows: The first four-bytes contain four ASCII characters. These letters are "RIFF" for the main file chunk. Following that is a 4-byte integer value indicating the length of the chunk. Optionally following that is another 4-character code further classifying the chunk. For example, the RIFF AVI chunk tag takes the form of the four characters "RIFF" followed by a 4-byte chunk length followed by the letters "AVI." The RIFF AVI chunk is composed of multiple "LIST" chunks optionally followed by an index chunk which uses the identifier "idx1." The basic structure of the hierarchy is shown below:

RIFF AVI File Structure

```
"RIFF" <length> "AVI "
    "LIST" <length> "hdrl"
        "avih" <length>
        <Main AVI Header Data>
        "LIST" <length> "strl"
            "strh" <length>
             <Stream Header Data>
            "strf" <length>
            <Stream Format Information>
            "srtd" <length>
            <Optional Extra Stream Data>
        "LIST" <length> "strl" (There may be any number of streams)
            "strh" <length>
            <Stream Header Data>
            "strf" <length>
            <Stream Format Information>
            "srtd" <length>
            <Optional Extra Stream Data>
```

```
etc.
"LIST" <length> "movi"
    "##dc" <length>
    <Compressed Frame Data>
    "##db" <length>
    <Uncompressed Frame Data>
    "##wb" <length>
    <Audio Wafeform Data>
    etc.
"idx1" <length>  (Optional index data chunk)
    <Index Data>
```

The first list chunk is classified as "hdrl" and contains header information for the file. The first subchunk in the header is an "avih" chunk which is a mixed data structure containing 14 double-word values. The organization of this structure is shown in Figure 8.10.

Microseconds per frame indicates the period between image frames. This is basically the reciprocal of the frame rate. **Maximum bytes per second** indicates the data rate that must be supported in order to play the video sequence at full speed. The **flags** field indicates whether the file has an index chunk, whether the index chunk should be used to determine the order of frames in the file, whether the file contains multiple interleaved streams, whether it's a capture file, and whether or not the file is copyrighted. **Total frames** indicates how many distinct frames there are in the file.

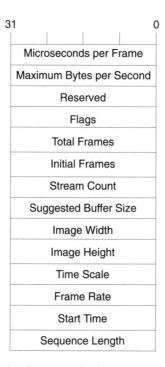

Figure 8.10   Main AVI file header data organization.

Initial frames specifies how many frames of audio information should be buffered before starting to play the video sequence synchronized with the audio sequence. This is done to ensure that the audio hardware does not run out of data while the video driver is trying to figure out what to do in the event it starts to get behind. **Streams** indicates how many separate data streams are contained in the file. For example, a file containing both audio and video information would consist of two streams. The streams are interleaved in the file, hence the name AVI. **Suggested buffer size** generally indicates what is the largest anticipated chunk in the file. This is to ensure that it is not necessary to allocate memory during playback which would reduce performance. The **height** and **width** fields define the size of the displayed image in pixels. The **scale** and **rate** fields effectively define the samples-per-second data rate of the file where rate is the number of samples and scale is the number of seconds. The **start** and **length** fields indicate starting time and the length of the file in units defined by rate and scale.

Following the main file header is a list of stream headers identified by the tag LIST "strl." Each stream header consists of two parts: a stream header chunk with the tag "strh" and a stream format chunk with the tag "strf." The "strh" chunk is a fixed data structure consisting of 12 doubleword values as illustrated in Figure 8.11.

The **type** field is a four-character code set to "vids" if it is a video stream or "auds" if an audio stream. The **handler** field contains a four-character code which identifies the compression or decompression driver to be used on this data. The fields that correspond to fields in the main file header with the same name have the same meanings and override the main header if set to different values. The "strf" chunk always follows the "strh" chunk and dictates the format of the data in the stream. The size and format of the "strf" chunk depends on what type of stream it refers to. For a

Figure 8.11   Stream format header data organization.

video stream this chunk consists of a BITMAPINFO structure which is defined in the Windows SDK documentation. The "strl" chunk may also contain a stream data chunk with the tag "strd" following the "strf" chunk. If present, this chunk contains data that is specific to the compression or decompression driver used with this stream and is passed to the driver. If an application encounters chunks it does not recognize it should ignore them. This is easily accomplished since each chunk tag contains a field defining the length of the chunk so the chunk can be easily skipped. Following the LIST "hdrl" chunk is a LIST "movi" chunk which actually contains the video frames. Each individual frame is contained in a subchunk with a four-character identifier tag. The first two characters of this tag are a stream number corresponding to the order in which the streams were defined in the LIST "hdrl" header chunk. "00" corresponds to the first stream, "01" to the second stream, and so on. The last two characters identify what type of stream chunk this is. For an audio waveform chunk these characters are "wb." For an uncompressed device-independent bitmap (DIB) these two characters are "db." If the frame data is compressed the two characters are "dc." If the chunk contains data for a palette update the two characters are "pc." The actual format of the data within the chunk varies accordingly. The format of these chunks can be discovered by looking at the source code for the video format translation sample program shown below. Finally, following the LIST "movi" chunk is an optional "idx1" chunk. If present, this is a list of structures, each 16 bytes long, each of which is an index entry referring to one of the video frames in the LIST "movi" chunk. The structure consists of four double-word fields as illustrated in Figure 8.12.

The **ID** field identifies the chunk tag for the frame it corresponds to. The **chunk offset** field defines the position of the chunk relative to the LIST "movi" chunk tag. The **chunk length** field defines the length of the video frame chunk minus the eight bytes required for the RIFF tag. For interleaved files (that is, files that contain both audio and video streams) the audio and video for each frame is combined into a record chunk using the tag "rec." This creates the implied synchronization between video and audio. The Video for Windows SDK provides a set of functions to simplify writing AVI files. These are listed in Table 8.6 with a brief description of each.

While these Video for Windows functions do simplify creation of RIFF files, the file format is simple enough so that it can be handled directly by a DOS-based program. In the interest of reaching the widest possible audience and enabling the lowest common denominator in terms of computing equipment a utility is included which converts a full-frame AVI motion video file into a special format designed for video playback on a machine containing a standard VGA display adapter. After all, what would be the use of providing sample programs and then requiring you to go out and

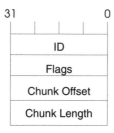

Figure 8.12   AVI file index chunk data format.

Table 8.6 RIFF File Management Functions

`mmioOpen()`	Opens a file for reading or writing and returns a handle.
`mmioCreateChunk()`	Creates a new chunk in the RIFF file.
`mmioWrite()`	Writes a specific number of bytes to an open RIFF file.
`mmioAscend()`	Closes the current RIFF file chunk and ascends to the next level in the hierarchy.
`mmioClose()`	Closes an open RIFF file.

buy Video for Windows to be able to try them out? The demonstrations provided here do not, of course, have all the features and capabilities of Microsoft Video for Windows, but the intent is to provide a detailed internal view of how PC motion video works.

AVI2VID Source Code

The following source code is from a program named AVI2VID.EXE, which is designed to convert a video file (AVI) into a simplified format using the file extension VID. The input file must be in full-frame 8-bit-per-pixel format. Any audio stream will be ignored. Data structures for the RIFF format are provided in file AVI_RIFF.H, which is included in Appendix B.

```
//————————————————————
// AVI2VID.CPP
//————————————————————
// Program:   Implementation code for AVI2VID.EXE
// Author:    Phil Mattison
// Compiler:  Borland Turbo C++ v1.01
//————————————————————

#include <stdlib.h>
#include <stdio.h>
#include <string.h>
#include <conio.h>
#include <dos.h>
#include "avi_riff.h"

int Compare4C(char *s1, char *s2) // Compare a pair of 4-char tags
  {
  if(s1[0]==s2[0] &&
     s1[1]==s2[1] &&
     s1[2]==s2[2] &&
     s1[3]==s2[3])return(1);
  return(0);
  }

void ExitError(int err)  // Exit with error message
  {
  printf("File Error %d \n",err);
  exit(0);
```

```
   }
//————————————————————————
void main(int argc, char* argv[])
  {

  FILE    *fi,*fo;
  DWORD   chunk_size;          // Current chunk length
  DWORD   main_chunk_length;   // Length of main RIFF chunk
  DWORD   main_header_length;  // Length of main RIFF header chunk
  DWORD   movi_length;         // Length of movi chunk
  char    sub_type[4];         // Chunk sub type ID
  int     x_size,y_size;       // Video frame size
  int     frame_count;         // Video frame count
  int     frame_size;          // Video frame data size
  int     palette_entrys;      // Number of palette locations used
  BYTE frame_out[IMAGE_SIZE];
  BYTE image_buffer[IMAGE_SIZE];

union                          // File input data buffer
  {
  TagT               tags;
  MainAVIHeader      main_header;
  AVIStreamHeader    stream_header;
  BitMapInfoHeader   dib_header;
  RGBQuad            palette[1024];
  unsigned char      buffer[IMAGE_SIZE];
  } data;

union                          // File output header buffer
  {
  vid vid_header;
  unsigned char buffer[sizeof(vid)];
  } output;

  strcpy(output.vid_header.file_ID,"BOOK_VID"); // Set file ID
  output.vid_header.compression=0;        // Write uncompressed file
  if(argc<3)      // Validate command line parameters
    {
    printf
    ("Please provide two file names: <input_file> <output_file>\n");
    exit(0);
    }
  fi=fopen(argv[1],"rb");
  fo=fopen(argv[2],"wb");
  if(fi==NULL)
    {
    printf("Could not open input file %s.\n",argv[1]);
    exit(0);
    }
  if(fo==NULL)
    {
    printf("Could not open output file %s.\n",argv[2]);
    exit(0);
```

```
    }

  fread(data.buffer,TAG_SIZE,1,fi);    // Read RIFF 'AVI ' tag
  if(!Compare4C(data.tags.chunk_type,"RIFF"))ExitError(1);
  fread(sub_type,ID_SIZE,1,fi);
  if(!Compare4C(sub_type,"AVI "))ExitError(2);

  fread(data.buffer,TAG_SIZE,1,fi);    // Read LIST 'hdrl' tag
  if(!Compare4C(data.tags.chunk_type,"LIST"))ExitError(3);
  fread(sub_type,ID_SIZE,1,fi);
  if(!Compare4C(sub_type,"hdrl"))ExitError(4);
  main_header_length=data.tags.chunk_size+0x14L;

  fread(data.buffer,TAG_SIZE,1,fi);    // Read 'avih' tag & data
  if(!Compare4C(data.tags.chunk_type,"avih"))ExitError(5);
  if(data.tags.chunk_size!=HDR_SIZE)ExitError(6);
  fread(data.buffer,HDR_SIZE,1,fi);
  frame_count=output.vid_header.frames=
  (int)data.main_header.TotalFrames;
  output.vid_header.x_size=(int)data.main_header.Width;
  output.vid_header.y_size=(int)data.main_header.Height;
  if(output.vid_header.x_size!=160)ExitError(7);
  if(output.vid_header.y_size!=120)ExitError(8);

  fread(data.buffer,TAG_SIZE,1,fi);    // Read LIST 'strl' tag
  if(!Compare4C(data.tags.chunk_type,"LIST"))ExitError(9);
  fread(sub_type,ID_SIZE,1,fi);
  if(!Compare4C(sub_type,"strl"))ExitError(10);

  fread(data.buffer,TAG_SIZE,1,fi);    // Read 'strh' tag
  if(!Compare4C(data.tags.chunk_type,"strh"))ExitError(11);
  chunk_size=data.tags.chunk_size;
  fread(data.buffer,(int)chunk_size,1,fi);

  fread(data.buffer,TAG_SIZE,1,fi);    // Read 'strf' tag
  if(!Compare4C(data.tags.chunk_type,"strf"))ExitError(12);
  fread(data.buffer,sizeof(BitMapInfoHeader),1,fi);
  palette_entrys=data.dib_header.ClrUsed;
  fread(data.buffer,4*palette_entrys,1,fi);
  for(int i=0;i<240;i++)
    {
    output.vid_header.palette[i][0] =(int)data.palette[i].Red>2;
    output.vid_header.palette[i][1] =(int)data.palette[i].Green>2;
    output.vid_header.palette[i][2] =(int)data.palette[i].Blue>2;
    }
  fseek(fi,main_header_length,SEEK_SET);// Seek to end of header
  fread(data.buffer,TAG_SIZE,1,fi);     // Read LIST 'movi' tag
  if(!Compare4C(data.tags.chunk_type,"LIST"))ExitError(13);
  fread(sub_type,ID_SIZE,1,fi);
  if(!Compare4C(sub_type,"movi"))ExitError(14);
  fwrite(output.buffer,sizeof(vid),1,fo); // Write VID file header

  for(i=0;i<frame_count;i++)              // Process all frames
```

```
            {
            fread(data.buffer,TAG_SIZE,1,fi);      // Read '00db' tag
            if(!Compare4C(data.tags.chunk_type,"00db"))ExitError(15);
            chunk_size=data.tags.chunk_size;
            fread(data.buffer,chunk_size,1,fi);   // Read image chunk
            for(int y=0;y<120;y++)                      // Un-invert DIB image
              {
              memmove(&frame_out[y*160],&(data.buffer[19040-(y*160)]),160);
              }
            for(y=0;y<IMAGE_SIZE;y++)                 // Adjust pixel base value
              {
              frame_out[y]=frame_out[y]+16;
              }
            fwrite(frame_out,IMAGE_SIZE,1,fo);    // Store frame in VID file
            }
        fclose(fi);
        fclose(fo);
        printf("Done.\n");
        }
```

VIEW_VID Source Code

The following C++ source code is for a program which plays VID files on a PC using a VGA display in 320×200 256-color mode (mode 13 hex). The program is mouse driven, and supports a file open menu and real-time play, stop, rewind, and fast forward controls. The main() program is contained in file VIEW_VID.CPP, and the bulk of the video player implementation code is contained in VID_FILE.CPP.

```cpp
#define  APP_TITLE "VID File Viewer"

#include <stdio.h>
#include <conio.h>
#include <dos.h>
#include "ctrl_256.h"
#include "disp_256.h"
#include "vid_file.h"


//————————————————————————————
// Program:   VID File viewer program
// Author:    Phil Mattison
// Compiler:  Borland Turbo C++ v1.01
//————————————————————————————

extern "C" void SetVmode(int);
extern "C" void WriteBlock(int,int,int,int,unsigned char far *);
extern "C" void DrawBlock(int,int,int,int,int);
extern "C" void DrawASCII(int,int,int,int);

extern int  PlayVideo(void);
extern int  FFVideo(void);
extern int  RewindVideo(void);
```

```
extern int  StopVideo(void);
extern int  OpenFile(void);
extern int  CloseFile(void);
extern int  StandardCallback(void);
extern void UserMessage(char *message);

void SignOn(void)
  {
  DrawBlock(0,0,320,200,DARKGRAY);      // Gray background
  DrawBlock(0,0,320,10,LIGHTBLUE);      // Title Bar
  DrawString(160-strlen(APP_TITLE)*4,2,APP_TITLE,WHITE);    // Title
  DrawBlock(0,10,320,1,BLUE);           // Title Bar Outline
  DrawBlock(319,0,1,10,BLUE);
  DrawBlock(0,0,320,1,CYAN);
  DrawBlock(0,0,1,10,CYAN);

  DrawBlock(0,186,320,14,LIGHTGRAY); // Message Bar
  DrawBlock(2,198,220,1,WHITE);
  DrawBlock(222,187,1,12,WHITE);
  DrawBlock(2,187,221,1,DARKGRAY);
  DrawBlock(2,187,1,12,DARKGRAY);
  }

int Quit()    //Exit via mouse click
  {
  return(RUN_DISABLED);
  }
//****************************************************

void main(void)
  {
  SetVmode(0x13);
  SignOn();
  TControl Mouse;
  Mouse.SetStandardCallback(&StandardCallback);
  Mouse.CreateButton(&Quit,226,187,90,11,"[Esc] Quit");

  DrawBlock(FRAME_POS,FRAME_SIZE,LIGHTGRAY);     // Control focus area
  DrawBlock(SCREEN_POS,SCREEN_SIZE,BLACK);       // Screen area
  Mouse.CreateButton(&CloseFile,B_POS_CLOSE,B_SIZE_FILE,"Close");
  Mouse.CreateButton(&OpenFile,B_POS_OPEN,B_SIZE_FILE,"Open");
  Mouse.CreateButton(&StopVideo,B_POS_STOP,B_SIZE_CTRL,"\x16");
  Mouse.CreateButton(&RewindVideo,B_POS_REW,B_SIZE_CTRL,"|\x11");
  Mouse.CreateButton(&FFVideo,B_POS_FF,B_SIZE_CTRL,"\x10\x10");
  Mouse.CreateButton(&PlayVideo,B_POS_PLAY,B_SIZE_CTRL,"\x10");
  Mouse.Run();
  SetVmode(3);
  }
```

VID_FILE.CPP Source Code

```
//————————————————————
//
// VID_FILE.CPP
//
//————————————————————
// Program:   VID file access implementation for VIEW_VID.EXE
// Author:    Phil Mattison
// Compiler:  Borland Turbo C++ v1.01
//————————————————————

#include <stdio.h>
#include <conio.h>
#include <string.h>
#include <time.h>
#include <dir.h>
#include <dos.h>
#include "ctrl_256.h"
#include "vid_file.h"

extern "C" void DrawBlock(int,int,int,int,int);
extern "C" void DrawASCII(int,int,int,int);
extern "C" void WriteEntry(int,int,int,int);
extern "C" void WriteBlock(int,int,int,int,char far *);
extern     void DrawString(int,int,char *,int);

TControl *Dialog;          // Pointer to dialog box mouse control object
header_t input;            // File header input structure
DWORD    f_file_pos;       // File seek pointer
DWORD    f_start_pos;      // File seek pointer
FILE     *f_stream;        // File stream pointer
long     previous_time;    // Time of last frame display
char     f_list[10][13];   // File name list
int      f_is_open;        // File open flag
int      f_index;          // Index to file name list
int      f_count;          // Number of files in list
int      f_select;         // File selection flag
int      f_play;           // File play flag
int      f_play_fast;      // File play fast forward flag
int      f_frame;          // Video frame counter
int      x_size,y_size;    // Video frame size
int      frame_count;      // Video frame count
int      palette_entrys;   // Number of palette locations used
int      compression;      // Compression flag
int      block_size;       // Compressed block size
int      block_number;     // Compressed block count

BYTE     image_buffer[IMAGE_SIZE];
BYTE     data_buffer[IMAGE_SIZE];

//————————————————————————--
void UserMessage(char *message)          // Display a message on the screen
```

```
    {
    DrawBlock(3,189,218,10,LIGHTGRAY);
    DrawString(6,189,message,WHITE);
    DrawBlock(2,198,220,1,WHITE);
    }

//————————————————————————————-
int Compare4C(char *s1, char *s2)      // Compare a pair of 4-char tags
    {
    if(s1[0]==s2[0] &&
       s1[1]==s2[1] &&
       s1[2]==s2[2] &&
       s1[3]==s2[3])return(1);
    return(0);
    }

//————————————————————————————-
int ShowNextFrame() // Show the next frame in a video sequence
    {
    int buffer_p; // Pointer to compressed data buffer
    int image_p;  // Pointer to decompressed image frame
    BYTE pixel;   // Pixel storage
    BYTE row;     // Pixel row counter

    if(compression && f_frame>0)
      {
      fread(&block_number,sizeof(int),1,f_stream);
      if(block_number!=f_frame)
        {
        DrawBlock(DLG_POS,DLG_SIZE,BLACK);
        DrawString(LIST_BAR_XPOS,LIST_BAR_YPOS,"File Error",WHITE);
        f_is_open=FALSE;
        f_play=FALSE;
        f_play_fast=FALSE;
        f_frame=0;
        }
      else
        {
        fread(&block_size,sizeof(int),1,f_stream);
        fread(data_buffer,block_size,1,f_stream);
        buffer_p=0;
        image_p=0;
        while(image_p<19200)
          {
          pixel=data_buffer[buffer_p++];
          if(pixel==0)image_p+=(int)data_buffer[buffer_p++];
          else image_buffer[image_p++]=pixel;
          }
        }
      WriteBlock(SCREEN_POS,160,120,(char far *)image_buffer);
      f_frame++;
      }
    else
```

```
      {
      fread(image_buffer,19200,1,f_stream);      // Read image
      WriteBlock(SCREEN_POS,160,120,(char far *)image_buffer);
      f_frame++;
      if(f_play_fast && f_frame<frame_count-1)
         {
         fseek(f_stream,19200,SEEK_CUR);
         fseek(f_stream,19200,SEEK_CUR);
         f_frame+=2;
         }
      }
   if(f_frame>=frame_count)UserMessage("End of Video.");
   return(1);
   }

//─────────────────────────────────────
int ReadHeaderInfo()   // Read video information file header
   {
   fpos_t  filepos;     // File position pointer
   fread(input.buffer,sizeof(vid_t),1,f_stream);
   if(!Compare4C(input.vid_header.file_ID,"BOOK"))return(0);
   for(int i=0;i<240;i++)     // Set palette for this video
      {
      int Red=  (int)input.vid_header.palette[i][0];
      int Green=(int)input.vid_header.palette[i][1];
      int Blue= (int)input.vid_header.palette[i][2];
      WriteEntry(i+16,Red,Green,Blue);
      }
   frame_count=input.vid_header.frames;
   compression=input.vid_header.compression;
   fgetpos(f_stream,&filepos);
   f_start_pos=(DWORD)filepos;     // Set start position for rewind
   f_frame=0;
   return(1);
   }

//─────────────────────────────────────
int SelectFile()     // User clicked on a file name in list box
   {
   int old=f_index;
   f_index=(Dialog->GetPositionY()-LIST_BAR_YPOS)/10;
   if(f_index<f_count)
      {
      Dialog->HideCursor();
      DrawBlock(LIST_BAR_XPOS,LIST_BAR_YPOS+old*10,LIST_BAR_SIZE,WHITE);
      DrawString
      (LIST_BAR_XPOS+1,LIST_BAR_YPOS+old*10+1,f_list[old],BLACK);
      DrawBlock
      (LIST_BAR_XPOS,LIST_BAR_YPOS+f_index*10,LIST_BAR_SIZE,LIGHTBLUE);
      DrawString
      (LIST_BAR_XPOS+1,LIST_BAR_YPOS+f_index*10+1,f_list[f_index],WHITE);
      Dialog->ShowCursor();
      }
```

```
      else f_index=old;
      return(RUN_ENABLED);
      }

//─────────────────────────────────────
int FileOK()          // User accepts selected file
   {
   f_select=F_SELECTED;
   return(RUN_DISABLED);
   }

//─────────────────────────────────────
int FileCancel()      // User cancels file open
   {
   f_select=F_CANCELED;
   return(RUN_DISABLED);
   }

//─────────────────────────────────────
int PlayVideo()          // User clicked the play button
   {
   f_play=TRUE;
   f_play_fast=FALSE;
   if(f_is_open)UserMessage("Playing.");
   return(RUN_ENABLED);
   }

//─────────────────────────────────────
int FFVideo()          // User clicked the fast forward button
   {
   f_play=TRUE;
   f_play_fast=TRUE;
   if(f_is_open)UserMessage("Playing Fast Forward.");
   return(RUN_ENABLED);
   }

//─────────────────────────────────────
int RewindVideo()        // User clicked the rewind button
   {
   f_frame=0;
   f_play=FALSE;
   f_play_fast=FALSE;
   fseek(f_stream,f_start_pos,SEEK_SET);
   if(f_is_open)ShowNextFrame();
   if(f_is_open)UserMessage("Video Rewound.");
   return(RUN_ENABLED);
   }

//─────────────────────────────────────
int StopVideo()          // User clicked the stop button
   {
   f_play=FALSE;
   f_play_fast=FALSE;
```

```
   if(f_is_open)UserMessage("Playback Stopped.");
   return(RUN_ENABLED);
   }


//————————————————————————————————
int OpenFile()          // User clicked the File Open button
   {
   struct ffblk file_parms;    // File directory search structure
   int headerOK;               // Return flag
   f_is_open=FALSE;
   Dialog=new TControl;
   Dialog->HideCursor();
   DrawBlock(DLG_POS,DLG_SIZE,LIGHTGRAY);
   DrawBlock(LIST_BOX_POS,LIST_BOX_SIZE,WHITE);
   Dialog->SetCallback(&SelectFile,LIST_BOX_POS,LIST_BOX_SIZE);
   Dialog->CreateButton(&FileOK,B_POS_OK,B_SIZE,"OK");
   Dialog->CreateButton(&FileCancel,B_POS_CANCEL,B_SIZE,"Skip");
   f_count=0;
   if(findfirst("*.vid",&file_parms,FA_ARCH)==0) // Get file list
      {
      strcpy(f_list[0],file_parms.ff_name);
      DrawString(LIST_BAR_XPOS+1,LIST_BAR_YPOS+1,f_list[0],BLACK);
      f_count++;
      while(f_count<10 && findnext(&file_parms)==0)
         {
         strcpy(f_list[f_count],file_parms.ff_name);
         DrawString(LIST_BAR_XPOS+1,LIST_BAR_YPOS+f_count*10+1,
         f_list[f_count],BLACK);
         f_count++;
         }
      }
   f_index=0;
   DrawBlock
   (LIST_BAR_XPOS,LIST_BAR_YPOS+f_index*10,LIST_BAR_SIZE,LIGHTBLUE);
   DrawString
   (LIST_BAR_XPOS+1,LIST_BAR_YPOS+f_index*10+1,f_list[f_index],WHITE);
   f_select=F_NOT_SELECTED;
   UserMessage("Select a file.");
   Dialog->ShowCursor();
   Dialog->Run();             // Select a file to open
   if(f_select==F_SELECTED)   // Open the file and read header info
      {
      f_stream=fopen(f_list[f_index],"rb");
      if(f_stream!=NULL)
         {
         f_is_open=TRUE;
         headerOK=ReadHeaderInfo();
         }
      }
   Dialog->HideCursor();
   DrawBlock(DLG_POS,DLG_SIZE,BLACK);
   if(!headerOK)
      {
```

```
      f_is_open=FALSE;
      DrawString(LIST_BAR_XPOS,LIST_BAR_YPOS,"File Error",WHITE);
      }
   else
      {
      if(f_is_open)ShowNextFrame();
      }
   f_play=FALSE;
   f_play_fast=FALSE;
   Dialog->ShowCursor();
   delete Dialog;
   if(f_is_open)UserMessage("File Opened.");
   return(RUN_ENABLED);
   }


//————————————————————————————————-
int CloseFile()              // User clicked the File Close button
   {
   f_play=FALSE;
   f_play_fast=FALSE;
   f_count=0;
   if(f_is_open)
      {
      fclose(f_stream);
      f_is_open=FALSE;
      DrawBlock(SCREEN_POS,SCREEN_SIZE,BLACK);
      UserMessage("File Closed.");
      }
   return(RUN_ENABLED);
   }


//————————————————————————————————-

int StandardCallback()       // Exit via Escape key (process KB input)
   {                         // or process a video frame if play active
   if(f_play && f_frame<frame_count && f_is_open)
      {
      long current_time=clock(); // Clock tick 18.2 per sec.
      if(f_play_fast || current_time>previous_time)
         {
         previous_time=current_time;
         ShowNextFrame();
         }
      }
   else
      {
      if(kbhit()!=0)
         {
         if(getch()==ESC_KEY)return(RUN_DISABLED);
         }
      }
   return(RUN_ENABLED);
   }
```

It is not obvious from the Video for Windows SDK documentation whether it is necessary for end users to purchase Video for Windows before being able to use applications written with the Video for Windows SDK. There may be a runtime package which can be shipped with an application to enable users who do not have Video for Windows, and serious software developers should contact Microsoft directly for details on that.

QuickTime for Windows

QuickTime for Windows is a version of the computer video software developed by Apple Computer to run on their Macintosh line of machines. QuickTime was actually introduced prior to Video for Windows. The overall structure of QuickTime for Windows is similar in many ways to that of Video for Windows. There is a media control interface driver named MCIQTW.DRV, which is specified under the [mci] section in the SYSTEM.INI file for Windows. The terminology in the QuickTime for Windows SDK documentation is somewhat different from that in the Video for Windows documentation, probably reflecting cultural differences between Microsoft and Apple, as well as software infrastructure differences. One very nice thing about the QuickTime SDK is that practically the entire developer's manual is provided as an on-line help utility, fully cross-indexed with sample source code included. At a low level, QuickTime for Windows obviously must conform to Windows programming conventions, however, there are some clear philosophical differences in how pictures and sound are conceived. QuickTime for Windows is built around a conceptual object known as a *movie controller*. Several important aspects of the movie controller are clearly spelled out in the QuickTime documentation:

1. QuickTime movies can only be played using the movie controller.
2. It is not possible to create a custom movie controller component.
3. The movie controller is functionally identical to that used under the QuickTime environment on the Macintosh.

QuickTime for Windows does support the same high-level MCI string- and command-oriented interfaces as Video for Windows. Each of the MCI commands defined under Video for Windows performs essentially the same function under QuickTime for Windows. QuickTime relies heavily on the concept of *components*. A component is a software object that acts as an extension to QuickTime for Windows. QuickTime provides a software framework known as the *Component Manager* which provides services to classify components by function. It is conceptually similar to the Video for Windows ICM. Components are typically implemented as DLLs. A typical component might be a video decompression driver. QuickTime for Windows does not have a facility for managing video capture hardware on a PC. QuickTime for Windows requires Windows version 3.1 to operate.

The Component Manager classifies components according to the type of service provided and the level of service. The component type is identified by a four-character code. All image compression components have a component code of "IMCO". All components of a given type are required to support the same set of API functions. The API for video decompression components is defined by Apple and documented in the QuickTime for Windows SDK programmer's manual.

Conceptual Model

Video sequences under QuickTime are called *movies*. Under Windows a QuickTime movie is stored in a standard DOS file with an extension of MOV. In order to be played, a movie must be associated with a movie controller. QuickTime movies may be played under Windows but cannot be edited or saved. The programming model of QuickTime is intended to insulate the programmer from any details of the actual data format of the stored movies. QuickTime defines time during movie play in terms of two values: *scale* and *rate*. Scale defines the number of intervals per second used as the basis for timing. Rate is a multiplier defining how many of these time units should pass per second. QuickTime contains an internal scheduler that allocates time slices to movies that are *active*. An active movie simply means one that is ready to be played. In order to be played a movie must be associated with a movie controller, which is the QuickTime-supplied user interface for controlling movies. A movie controller contains all the user interface elements you would expect: a start/stop button, fast forward, fast reverse, and a slider bar to position the movie at arbitrary points. A movie and its associated controller both descend from the same parent window, usually the application in whose client area they both appear.

QuickTime Application Programmer Interface

User control of QuickTime movies is accomplished by inserting a call to the function MCIsPlayerMessage() into the main application's message pump. There must be a separate call to this function for every movie controller created by the calling application. A movie controller is created by a call to NewMovieController() which can simultaneously associate a specific movie with the newly created controller. The movie associated with a given controller can be changed or disconnected by a call to MCSetMovie(). Movies can be played, stopped, rewound, and so forth, through calls to a function named MCDoAction(). Synchronization of sound and video are performed automatically by the movie controller. QuickTime for Windows supports a relatively large set of API functions. These are listed in Table 8.7 with a brief description of each.

MCDoAction()

The MCDoAction function is the primary interface through which the application program directs the actions of the movie controller. There are a number of different messages sent through this function to control movies. The messages used with mcDoAction are listed in Table 8.8, with a brief description of each.

Writing a Decompressor Component

A QuickTime for Windows video decompressor is implemented as a DLL similar to drivers under Video for Windows. Like a Video for Windows driver it communicates to its client application through a single entry point, named DriverProc(). Unlike Video for Windows the single entry point is rerouted through an index table to multiple internal entry points, and supports additional required direct entry points. The QuickTime specification requires a decompressor to support a specific set of internal entry points indexed by specific values. These are classified in two categories: required Component Manager functions and required QuickTime Toolbox functions. The Component

Table 8.7   Summary of QuickTime for Windows API Functions

AddTime()	Used to calculate timing using the time units defined in the context of a given movie.
ClearMoviesStickyError()	Clears the flag which indicates an error has occurred that has not yet been processed.
CloseMovieFile()	Closes an open movie file.
ClosePictureFile()	Closes an open picture file.
ConvertTimeScale()	Converts a time measurement defined in terms of one time scale into terms of another time scale.
CountUserDataType()	Returns the number of items of a given data type in a list.
DeleteMovieFile()	Deletes a movie file.
DisposeMovie()	Frees up memory currently in use by a movie.
DisposeMovieController()	Eliminates a given instance of a movie controller, freeing its memory to be used for other purposes.
DisposePicture()	Frees memory currently in use by a picture data structure.
DrawPicture()	Draws a QuickTime for Windows picture on the display.
DrawPictureFile()	Draws a picture stored in a file.
EnterMovies()	QuickTime for Windows initialization procedure. Allocates memory for QuickTime for Windows.
ExitMovies()	Releases memory previously allocated by a call to EnterMovies. QuickTime cannot run after calling ExitMovies.
GetMovieActive()	Returns a flag indicating whether or not a given movie can be played.
GetMovieActiveSegment()	Determines which segment of a movie is selected for playing.
GetMovieBox()	Returns a data structure containing the dimensions of a rectangle needed to play a movie.
GetMovieCreationTime()	Retrieves the date and time a movie was created.
GetMovieDataSize()	Returns the number of bytes required to store movie data.
GetMovieDuration()	Returns a value indicating the duration of a movie expressed in units of the movie's time scale.
GetMovieModificationTime()	Returns the date and time a movie was last modified.
GetMoviePict()	Returns an individual frame from a movie.
GetMoviePosterPict()	Returns the poster frame from a movie. A poster frame is an image used to graphically identify a movie while it is not being played.
GetMoviePosterTime()	Returns a value indicating at what point in a movie's duration the frame occurs which should be used as the movie poster.
GetMoviePreferredRate()	Returns the preferred rate at which the movie should be played.
GetMoviePreferredVolume()	Returns the preferred volume setting at which a movie's audio stream should be played.
GetMoviesError()	Returns an error code, if any, and resets the error code to zero.
GetMoviesStickyError()	Returns an error code indicating an error that occurred previously.
GetMovieStatus()	Checks a movie database for inconsistencies and reports an error if any are found.
GetMovieTime()	Returns the current time of a movie in play.

Table 8.7 *continued*

GetMovieTimeScale()	Returns the time scale of a specified movie.
GetMovieUserData()	Returns a handle to a data structure containing information such as copyright data, etc. about a movie.
GetNextUserDataType()	Retrieves a data item from a user data structure.
GetPictureFileHeader()	Returns the header from a file containing a picture.
GetPictureFileInfo()	Returns data structure containing detailed information about a picture file.
GetPictureFromFile()	Extracts a picture from a picture file.
GetSoundInfo()	Returns information about the movie's sound.
GetUserData()	Returns one item of data from a user data structure.
GetUserDataText()	Fills a color supplied buffer with text from a user data structure.
GetVideoInfo()	Returns information about the video and a movie file.
KillPicture()	Frees memory allocated for storing a picture.
MCActivate()	Activates or deactivates a movie controller.
MCDraw()	Redraws a video frame.
MCDrawBadge()	Displays a movie's badge.
MCGetController BoundsRect()	Returns the boundary rectangle for a movie display.
MCGetControllerInfo()	Returns a set of movie controller flags.
MCGetCurrentTime()	Returns the time indicated by the slider control bar on the movie controller.
MCGetMovie()	Returns a pointer to the movie object associated with a controller.
MCGetVisible()	Returns the flag indicating whether or not a movie controller is visible.
MCIdle()	Allocates CPU time to a movie controller.
MCIsControllerAttached()	Returns a flag indicating whether a movie controller is attached to a given movie.
MCIsPlayerMessage()	This is used to redirect Windows messages to a movie controller.
MCKey()	Passes a Windows key press message to a movie controller.
MCNewAttachedController()	Connects a movie to an existing movie controller.
MCPositionController()	Sets the size and position of a movie controller. If a movie is attached it also positions the movie.
MCSetController BoundsRect()	Changes the dimensions of a movie controller.
MCSetMovie()	Connects or disconnects a movie controller from a movie.
MCSetVisible()	Hides or shows a movie controller.
NewMovieController()	Creates a new movie controller and attaches it to a movie.
NewMovieFromFile()	Performs initialization tasks required to play a movie from a previously opened movie file.
NormalizeRect()	Adjusts the aspect ratio of a rectangle in order to make it compatible with a movie.
OpenMovieFile()	Opens a file containing a movie.

Table 8.7 *continued*

PrerollMovie()	Loads a specified number of initial video frames into buffers to enhance movie playback performance.
QTInitialize()	Binds the calling application to QuickTime for Windows. Initializes QuickTime in preparation for playing movies.
QTTerminate()	Closes the connection between the application and QuickTime for Windows.
SetMovieActive()	Changes a movie's status to either active or inactive.
UpdateMovie()	Displays the current video frame immediately rather than at its regularly scheduled time.

Table 8.8 Summary of MCDoAction() Messages

mcActionActivate	Activates the movie controller.
mcActionBadgeClick	Notifies a user-defined function that the user has clicked on a movie's badge. A badge is a small icon that distinguishes a paused movie from a still picture.
mcActionControllerSizeChanged	Notification sent to a caller-defined function that the user has resized the movie controller.
mcActionDeactivate	Deactivates the movie controller.
mcActionDraw	Draws or redraws the current video frame.
mcActionGetFlags	Returns a variable containing binary flags that define the behavior of the movie controller.
mcActionGetKeysEnabled	Returns a flag indicating whether the movie controller's keyboard interface is enabled.
mcActionGetLooping	Returns a flag indicating whether looping is enabled for a movie controller.
mcActionGetLoopIsPalindrome	Returns a flag indicating whether Palindrome looping is enabled.
mcActionGetPlayEveryFrame	Returns a flag indicating whether the controller has been instructed to play all frames in the video sequence.
mcActionGetPlayRate	Returns the rate for the video sequence.
mcActionGetPlaySelection	Returns a flag indicating whether a movie is limited to playing only a certain portion of the movie.
mcActionGetUseBadge	Returns a flag indicating whether a movie controller is capable of displaying a badge.
mcActionGetVolume	Returns the value of the movie's audio volume.
mcActionGoToTime	Positions the current frame pointer to a point in the movie specified by the caller.
mcActionIdol	Allocates CPU time for a movie controller.
mcActionKey	Sends a Windows key press message to the movie controller.
mcActionPlay	Starts playing a movie.

Table 8.8 *continued*

mcActionSetFlags	Sets the movie controller flags to define the controller's behavior.
mcActionSetGrowBoxBounds	Sets the maximum size to which the movie can be adjusted.
mcActionSetKeysEnabled	Enables or disables a movie controller's ability to receive input from the computer keyboard.
mcActionSetLooping	Enables or disables looping for a movie controller.
mcActionSetLoopIsPalindrome	Enables or disables Palindrome looping in a movie controller. Palindrome looping means the movie first plays forward and then backward continuously.
mcActionSetPlayEveryFrame	Causes a movie controller to play all frames in a video sequence.
mcActionSetPlaySelection	Sets or clears a flag which limits the movie controller to playing only a selected portion of the video sequence.
mcActionSetSelectionBegin	Sets the beginning point at which a constrained movie should start playing.
mcActionSetSelectionDuration	Sets the duration of a selected part of a movie to be played.
mcActionSetUseBadge	Controls a movie controller's ability to display a badge.
mcActionSetVolume	Controls the setting of the movie's audio volume.
mcActionStep	Instructs the movie controller to play a specific number of frames at one time.

Manager functions are required for any QuickTime component whether it is a decompressor or not. The Toolbox functions are only required for decompressor components. The Component Manager functions use negative index values to distinguish them from user-defined or Toolbox interface functions. The names of the required Component Manager functions with their corresponding index values and a brief description of each are shown in Table 8.9.

There are four required QuickTime Toolbox functions which are called directly by the Toolbox. These *must* be implemented in a decompressor. The names and a brief description of each function are listed in Table 8.10.

While QuickTime for Windows provides relatively good video playback performance and supports a relatively simple programmer interface, it also exemplifies the philosophy of setting strict limits on the visibility into the inner workings of the system. The QuickTime for Windows SDK is sufficient to develop an application incorporating a movie player or a decompression driver for playing movies using the QuickTime user interface, but does not provide support for full-featured video creation and editing. It is reasonable to assume that the Windows subset of QuickTime was primarily intended for Macintosh developers who wish to incorporate cross-platform capability into their applications.

Table 8.9   Required Component Manager Functions

Function	Index	Description
Open()	−1	Notifies the component that a request has been made to establish a new connection. The component should create a new instance of any relevant data structures in preparation for handling further requests from the caller.
Close()	−2	Notifies the component that no further calls relating to a specific instance will be made. The component can therefore release any memory allocated in support of the instance indicating a close operation.
CanDo()	−3	This is a query from the caller to determine whether or not a component can support a specific function.
Version()	−4	A request from the caller for the component to return its version number.
Register()	−5	Issued to a component upon registration to give the component an opportunity to determine whether it is capable of operating in the current environment.
Target()	−6	Requests a component to link to another component and pass along requests to the target component. This allows the target component to implement a super set of the functionality in the original component.

Table 8.10   Required Toolbox Functions

GetCodecInfo()	Requests the component to fill in a data structure supplied by the caller with information giving details on its capabilities.
PreDecompress()	Requests the component to fill in a data structure containing specific information about the capabilities of its decompression functions.
SequenceBusy()	A request from the caller to determine if the component is currently busy.
BandDecompress()	A request from the caller for the component to actually decompress data.

Conclusion

There is a broad range of options available to the programmer who wishes to investigate or develop PC motion video capabilities. For those who wish to focus on PC and MacIntosh cross-platform capability there is QuickTime for Windows. For those who wish to focus on the PC platform but provide a broad range of capability and build on the features provided in the Windows environment, there is Video for Windows. For those who wish to take a more detailed approach optimizing for size and speed as in an embedded application, for example, the Video for Windows documentation provides enough detail so that some of that infrastructure can be drafted on for less-sophisticated applications. This is a rapidly advancing technology and new developments are constantly occurring in the software operating environments as well as other areas. For example, at the time of this writing Microsoft is reportedly working on extensions to the GDI to improve video playback performance while retaining a high degree of hardware independence and software interface flexibility that characterizes Windows. Most of the software examples provided in this book are, out of necessity, designed to work with the lowest common denominator in terms of equipment. An attempt is made, however, to show the potential for developing powerful and elaborate video-based systems for use on more powerful machines. A full specification of the Video for Windows or QuickTime programmer interfaces would be well beyond the scope of this book. It is hoped, however, that the information provided here will be sufficient to enable an informed decision on which path to take.

Video Image Processing Techniques

While showing motion pictures on a computer may fascinate for about 15 minutes, the basic capability has relatively little to offer in the way of true utility. In the entertainment realm, moving pictures have been around for a long time. Viewers' expectations in terms of quality are very high and increasing all the time. The motion picture industry has developed the art of creating moving pictures to an amazing degree of sophistication. In this context, movies on a PC are almost pathetic. However, if you think of PC motion video as information rather than entertainment the potential is enormous. Bringing motion video as a data type to personal computers creates fertile ground for innovation. It is hoped that the possibilities presented here will spark some connection in the reader's mind, allowing all of us to enjoy the benefits of some ingenious new application of low-cost personal computing technology.

Filtering

Some of the theoretical basis for signal filtering was discussed in Chapter 2. Generally, the objective of filtering is to change the frequency characteristics of a given signal in some deterministic way. For example, filtering is used in an AM radio to separate audio frequency signals from the radio frequency carrier. As applied to images, filtering generally must take place in two dimensions. Ordinarily, a signal is thought of as having two dimensions: *amplitude* and *time*. A black-and-white image can be thought of as having three: amplitude and *X* and *Y spatial dimensions*. Frequency then refers to changes per unit of distance in either the *X* or *Y* direction. Color images consisting of three components per pixel can actually be thought of as three separate images or image planes. Filter operations or other processes may be applied differently to different image components. Generally, when processing color images it is a good idea to represent the image as separate luminance and chrominance components rather than RGB because the artifacts introduced by filtering operations can create very visible color distortions when applied to RGB data. This is because of the nonuniform contributions of the three primary colors to the overall image appearance. In YCrCb color space there are still some nonuniformities, but they are less pronounced. All examples and discussions in this chapter will assume YCrCb color space.

Low-Pass Spatial Filter

One of the most common applications of image filtering is simply to improve the general appearance of the image. For example, this is very useful for subsampled color components. It is also very useful after scaling or other spatial transformations. The most common filter for the removal of visual artifacts is a low-pass *finite impulse response (FIR)* filter. The mathematical basis for this was discussed in Chapter 2 along with a brief discussion of a simplified, although less accurate, integer implementation. Spatial filters typically employ a structure known as a *convolution kernel*. This kernel is a pattern of coefficients which are multiplied by the target pixel and other pixels in the immediate vicinity to produce a weighted average value to replace the target pixel. A reasonable approximation of the finite impulse response filter kernel in two dimensions is shown in Figure 9.1. Notice that the sum of the coefficients in the kernel is one.

The basic effect is to reduce the contrast of high frequency variations in the image while leaving low frequency variations relatively unchanged. The tendency to blur the image is minimized by the fact that pixels surrounding the target pixel contribute less to the result than the target pixel. Implementation is very efficient because all required division operations are powers of two and can be implemented as simple shift operations. Greater accuracy can be achieved by scaling all the coefficients by a factor of 16 and then dividing the result by 16 after summation as illustrated in Figure 9.2.

When applied before a video compression process, a low-pass spatial filter can also improve the compression ratio by eliminating signal noise and improving correlation between sequential frames. When applied *after* decompression of a video sequence the low-pass filter can improve the appearance of the display images by reducing the visual impact of artifacts produced by the compression and decompression processes.

High-Pass Spatial Filter

The convolution kernel for a high-pass spatial filter is typically characterized by a relatively large coefficient for the target pixel and predominantly negative coefficients for surrounding pixels immediately adjacent. The general effect of a high-pass filter is to increase the amplitude of high fre-

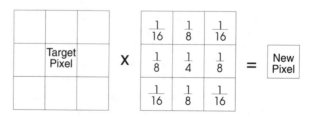

Figure 9.1 Basic low-pass spatial filter kernel.

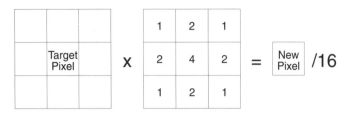

Figure 9.2 Optimized low-pass filter kernel for simple math operations.

quency variations while having little or no effect on the amplitude of low-frequency variations. Three examples of fairly typical high-pass filter kernels are shown in Figure 9.3. Note that in each case the sum of the coefficients is one. The reason this works is fairly simple. Consider a couple of examples using the kernel shown in Figure 9.3(a). If the filter is applied to a region where all the pixels are the same value the target pixel is multiplied by nine and all the immediately adjacent pixels are multiplied by -1. The net result is the same as the original pixel because there are only eight -1 coefficients, giving a net multiplier of one.

If the filter is applied to a high-frequency region, for example, vertical stripes with a frequency of one-half the sampling rate, the *difference* between the target pixel and the adjacent pixels will be increased. Figure 9.4 illustrates this with two different cases involving high-frequency vertical stripes alternating between pixel values of 100 and 200.

Note: If the target pixel is in the 200 column (the higher-intensity column) its value is increased to 800. If the target pixel is in the lower-intensity column with a value of 100 its intensity is decreased to minus 500. In both cases, the absolute delta from the original pixel value is 600. Because of the sampled nature of the data and the relatively small sample set processed by the filter kernel the response curve tends not to be very smooth and the cutoff frequency tends to be fairly high. In fact, spatial filter response is better represented as a surface rather than a two-dimensional curve; however, that is beyond the scope of this discussion. Suffice it to say that a high-pass filter can be used to sharpen a blurred image. A good application of high-pass and low-pass filters would be to apply a low-pass filter to subsampled chrominance data after it is resampled to full resolution and apply a high-pass filter to luminance data to enhance the image sharpness. Of course, you would probably want to use a less radical convolution kernel than the one depicted in Figure 9.3(a).

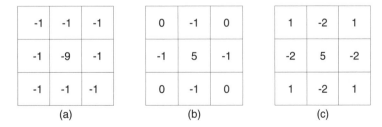

Figure 9.3 Several sample high-pass filter kernels.

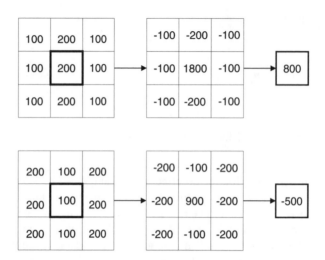

Figure 9.4   Illustration of high-pass filter kernel operation.

Filter Demonstration Programs

The following source code listings are for programs named LPF_DEMO.EXE and HPF_DEMO.EXE, which filter the images in a black-and-white video sequence, using a predetermined filter kernel. The program works only on black-and-white uncompressed files, so any of the video clips provided will have to be uncompressed and converted to black and white before processing with these filters. These are DOS-based, command-line driven programs which take an input file name and an output file name as command-line parameters.

LPF_DEMO.CPP Listing

```
//================================================================
// LPF_DEMO.CPP
//
// This program applies a Low Pass Filter (LPF) to every frame
// in a video sequence. The input file must be an uncompressed
// VID file of black and white images.
//————————————————————————
// Program:   Implementation file for LPF_DEMO.EXE
// Author:    Phil Mattison
// Compiler:  Borland Turbo C++ v1.01
//————————————————————————

#include <stdlib.h>
#include <stdio.h>
#include <string.h>
#include <conio.h>
#include <dos.h>
```

```
#include <math.h>

#define BYTE        unsigned char
#define WORD        unsigned int
#define DWORD       unsigned long

#define IMAGE_SIZE  19200
#define THRESHOLD   10

typedef struct
   {
   char        file_ID[8];
   int         x_size;
   int         y_size;
   int         frames;
   int         compression;
   int         palette[240][3];
   } vid_t;

typedef union
   {
   vid_t vid_header;
   unsigned char buffer[sizeof(vid_t)];
   } header_t;

//————————————————————
int Compare4C(char *s1, char *s2)          // Compare a pair of 4-char tags
   {
   if(s1[0]==s2[0] &&
   s1[1]==s2[1] &&
   s1[2]==s2[2] &&
   s1[3]==s2[3])return(1);
   return(0);
   }

int Addr(int x, int y)
   {
   return(y*160+x);
   }


//————————————————————

void ExitError(int n)
   {
   switch(n)
      {
      case 0:printf("ERROR — This is not a valid video file.\n");
      case 1:printf("ERROR — Input file must not be compressed.\n");
      case 2:
      printf("ERROR — Input file must be black and white images.\n");
      }
   exit(0);
   }
```

```
//————————————————————

void main(int argc, char* argv[])
  {
  FILE    *fi;                    // File stream pointer
  FILE    *fo;                    // File stream pointer
  int     frame_count;            // Video frame count
  int     f_frame;                // Video frame counter
  int     i,x,y,acc;              // General indices
  BYTE    image_buffer[IMAGE_SIZE];
  BYTE    new_image_buffer[IMAGE_SIZE];
  header_t input;                 // File header input structure

  if(argc<3)
    {
    printf
    ("Please provide two file names: <input_file> <output_file>\n");
    exit(0);
    }
  fi=fopen(argv[1],"rb");
  fo=fopen(argv[2],"wb");
  if(fi==NULL)
    {
    printf("Could not open input file %s.\n",argv[1]);
    exit(0);
    }
  if(fo==NULL)
    {
    printf("Could not open output file %s.\n",argv[2]);
    exit(0);
    }
  fread(input.buffer,sizeof(vid_t),1,fi);
  if(!Compare4C(input.vid_header.file_ID,"BOOK"))ExitError(0);
  if((input.vid_header.compression&1)==1)ExitError(1); // Compressed
  if((input.vid_header.compression&2)!=2)ExitError(2); // Not B/W
  frame_count=input.vid_header.frames;
  fwrite(input.buffer,sizeof(vid_t),1,fo);

  for(f_frame=0;f_frame<frame_count;f_frame++)
    {
    fread(image_buffer,19200,1,fi);          // Read image
    for(i=0;i<IMAGE_SIZE;i++)new_image_buffer[i]=image_buffer[i];
    for(y=1;y<119;y++)
      {
      for(x=1;x<159;x++)
        {
        acc=4*(int)image_buffer[Addr(x,y)];
        acc+=2*(int)image_buffer[Addr(x+1,y)];
        acc+=2*(int)image_buffer[Addr(x-1,y)];
        acc+=2*(int)image_buffer[Addr(x,y+1)];
        acc+=2*(int)image_buffer[Addr(x,y-1)];
        acc+=(int)image_buffer[Addr(x+1,y+1)];
```

```
            acc+=(int)image_buffer[Addr(x+1,y-1)];
            acc+=(int)image_buffer[Addr(x-1,y+1)];
            acc+=(int)image_buffer[Addr(x-1,y-1)];
            acc/=16;
            if(acc<16)acc=16;
            if(acc>255)acc=255;
            new_image_buffer[Addr(x,y)]=(BYTE)acc;
            }
        }
    fwrite(new_image_buffer,19200,1,fo);          // Write image
    printf("Frame %d.%c",f_frame,0xD);
    }
  fclose(fi);
  fclose(fo);
  printf("\nDone.\n");
  }
```

HPF_DEMO.CPP Listing

```
//===============================================================
// HPF_DEMO.CPP
//
// This program applies a High Pass Filter (HPF) to every frame
// in a video sequence. The input file must be an uncompressed
// VID file of black and white images.
//
//─────────────────────────────
// Program:   Implementation file for HPF_DEMO.EXE
// Author:    Phil Mattison
// Compiler:  Borland Turbo C++ v1.01
//─────────────────────────────

#include <stdlib.h>
#include <stdio.h>
#include <string.h>
#include <conio.h>
#include <dos.h>
#include <math.h>

#define BYTE        unsigned char
#define WORD        unsigned int
#define DWORD       unsigned long

#define IMAGE_SIZE  19200
#define THRESHOLD   10

typedef struct
  {
  char        file_ID[8];
  int         x_size;
  int         y_size;
  int         frames;
  int         compression;
```

```
    int        palette[240][3];
    } vid_t;

typedef union
    {
    vid_t vid_header;
    unsigned char buffer[sizeof(vid_t)];
    } header_t;

//————————————————————
int Compare4C(char *s1, char *s2)          // Compare a pair of 4-char tags
    {
    if(s1[0]==s2[0] &&
    s1[1]==s2[1] &&
    s1[2]==s2[2] &&
    s1[3]==s2[3])return(1);
    return(0);
    }

int Addr(int x, int y)
    {
    return(y*160+x);
    }

//————————————————————
void ExitError()
    {
    printf("File Error \n");
    exit(0);
    }

//————————————————————
void main(int argc, char* argv[])
    {
    FILE      *fi;              // File stream pointer
    FILE      *fo;              // File stream pointer
    int       frame_count;     // Video frame count
    int       f_frame;         // Video frame counter
    int       i,x,y,acc;       // General indices
    BYTE      image_buffer[IMAGE_SIZE];
    BYTE      new_image_buffer[IMAGE_SIZE];
    header_t input;            // File header input structure

    if(argc<3)
        {
        printf
        ("Please provide two file names: <input_file> <output_file>\n");
        exit(0);
        }
    fi=fopen(argv[1],"rb");
    fo=fopen(argv[2],"wb");
    if(fi==NULL)
        {
```

```
        printf("Could not open input file %s.\n",argv[1]);
        exit(0);
        }
    if(fo==NULL)
        {
        printf("Could not open output file %s.\n",argv[2]);
        exit(0);
        }
    fread(input.buffer,sizeof(vid_t),1,fi);
    if(!Compare4C(input.vid_header.file_ID,"BOOK"))ExitError();
    if((input.vid_header.compression&1)==1)ExitError(); // Compressed
    if((input.vid_header.compression&2)!=2)ExitError(); // Not B/W
    frame_count=input.vid_header.frames;
    fwrite(input.buffer,sizeof(vid_t),1,fo);
    for(f_frame=0;f_frame<frame_count;f_frame++)
        {
        fread(image_buffer,19200,1,fi);          // Read image
        for(i=0;i<IMAGE_SIZE;i++)new_image_buffer[i]=image_buffer[i];
        for(y=1;y<119;y++)
            {
            for(x=1;x<159;x++)
                {
                acc=5*(int)image_buffer[Addr(x,y)];
                acc-=(int)image_buffer[Addr(x+1,y)];
                acc-=(int)image_buffer[Addr(x-1,y)];
                acc-=(int)image_buffer[Addr(x,y+1)];
                acc-=(int)image_buffer[Addr(x,y-1)];
                if(acc<16)acc=16;
                if(acc>255)acc=255;
                new_image_buffer[Addr(x,y)]=(BYTE)acc;
                }
            }
        fwrite(new_image_buffer,19200,1,fo);  // Write image
        printf("Frame %d.%c",f_frame,0xD);
        }
    fclose(fi);
    fclose(fo);
    printf("\nDone.\n");
    }
```

Scaling

Very often the native size of a digital video image is not the desired size for viewing. Digital video images tend to be rather small because large high-resolution images contain far too much data to be handled effectively on existing computer systems when 15 to 30 images per second must be reproduced. Images of 160×120 or 320×240 resolution are fairly common sizes for PC motion video today. A 160×120 image displayed on a 14-inch monitor with 1024×768 resolution is only about 1.5 inches across. Therefore, it is not uncommon to want to expand the image to a larger size to make it easier to view. In any case, scaling can be thought of as a means for producing the desired image size for display from the native image size as it is stored internally. There are essentially two cases that must be dealt with in scaling an image. One is scaling to a higher resolution than the original and the other is scaling to a lower resolution. It may be necessary to deal with both cases in a single image, for example, the case where an image is stretched horizontally and squeezed vertically or vice versa. In the case of scaling up, there are more pixels in the destination image than in the source, requiring interpolation. In the case of scaling down, each destination pixel draws its value from more than one source pixel; therefore, a weighted average calculation is required. Generally, horizontal and vertical scaling processes can be applied separately. This simplifies the process if both upscaling and downscaling must be applied to the same image. In both cases, the preferred technique is known as *reverse mapping*. This involves calculating how each destination pixel maps to the source image. It ensures that a pixel value will be calculated for every pixel in the destination, thereby avoiding gaps or voids. Because horizontal and vertical scaling can be applied separately and in either order, this discussion will focus on one-dimensional scaling, assuming that it can be applied in either dimension. The discussion will focus on *linear* scaling where the same scale factor is applied over the entire range of the image in a given axis. The same techniques, however, can be applied in nonlinear scaling applications to create special effects such as image *warp*. In either case, the worse case for scaling is when it is done with some noninteger scale factor. Therefore, the cases illustrated will try to show a worse-case situation. The techniques shown will therefore work in all other simpler situations.

Scaling Up

Figure 9.5 illustrates a case where the source must be scaled up by a factor of approximately 2.9. From the diagram it would appear that some destination pixels need merely to be copied from the source while others are a weighted average of two source pixels.

This, however, is not a very good technique, especially for high-scale factors (above two, for example), because it tends to make the resulting image look blocky. A better technique is to interpolate the values of all destination pixels that do not exactly align with a source pixel. To facilitate this, it is better to imagine each pixel as a mathematical point separated from its neighbors by a known distance but having no size. This is illustrated in Figure 9.6. In this case, every destination pixel that does not exactly line up with the source pixel is calculated as a weighted average of two source pixels.

The weight factors used for interpolation are derived from the relative distance from the destination pixel to each of the nearest source pixels. The two factors, then, added together, will always equal one. All that remains is to figure out for each destination pixel which source pixel or pixels to

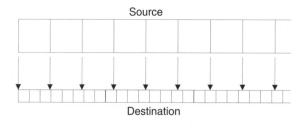

Figure 9.5   Example for scaling up an image in one dimension.

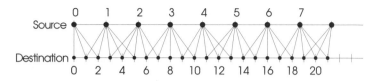

Figure 9.6   Improved conceptual model for scaling up in one dimension.

use in calculating its value and what the interpolation factors are. If we assume, for example, a scale factor of 2.9, the procedure would be as follows: Source and destination pixels have integer addresses starting at zero. For each destination pixel the address is divided by the scale factor, in this case 2.9. The integer part of the result is the address of one of the source pixels to be used for interpolation. That address plus one is the address of the other source pixel to be used for interpolation. The ratio of these two pixels is determined by the fractional part of the result. The first source pixel is multiplied by the fractional part of the result and the second source pixel is multiplied by one minus the fractional part of the result. Put in mathematical terms, the calculation is as follows:

```
SourceA = TRUNC(<destination>/<scale>)
SourceB = SourceA+1
WeightA = (<destination>/<scale>)-SourceA
WeightB = 1-WeightA
```

To avoid expensive division operations in support of arbitrary scale factors it may be desirable to use a *digital differential accumulator (DDA)*. This involves calculating the reciprocal of the scale factor once and adding that to an accumulator for each increment of the destination pixel address. Whenever the accumulator exceeds one in value, the source pixel address is incremented and one is subtracted from the accumulator. The value in the accumulator and its difference from one can then always be used as the weight factors in calculating interpolated pixel values for the destination. This technique can be implemented using strictly integer math requiring only addition and shift operations by scaling the DDA accumulator by some power of two, for example, 1,024. In this case, the source pixel address would increment each time the accumulator exceeds 1,024. Interpolation is accomplished by multiplying the two relevant source pixels by a pair of values that add up to 1,024. The result can then be divided by 1,024 simply by shifting right ten bits. The image scaling example provided in the program DDA_DEMO.C uses this technique.

Scaling Down

The simplest method of scaling an image to a smaller size is known as *decimation*. This means simply keeping only those source pixels that most closely correspond in position to the destination pixels. Again, while easy to do, it tends to introduce visual artifacts into the scaled image. These are exacerbated if the scaled image is stored and later scaled up to a larger size. This is most easily noticed in cases where the scale factor is close to one, for example 0.9. Decimation in this case would mean simply throwing away every tenth pixel. The result is an easily observable pattern of discontinuities with a frequency of nine pixels. A more accurate implementation is to calculate each destination pixel as a weighted average of source pixels. If the scale factor is between 0.5 and 1

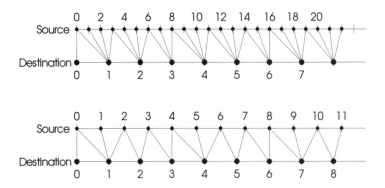

Figure 9.7   Conceptual model for scaling down in one dimension.

there will always be at most two source pixels contributing to each destination pixel. If the scale factor is less than .5 there may be more than two source pixels contributing to each destination pixel. The calculation can be performed using a DDA in a manner similar to that used for upscaling. In this case, the DDA constant is the actual scale factor rather than its reciprocal and the accumulator is initialized to one rather than zero. The scaling process is as follows: For each destination pixel the DDA constant is added to the accumulator and the pixel value accumulator is set to zero. If the DDA accumulator does not exceed one, the value of the currently addressed source pixel is added to the pixel accumulator and the source pixel address is incremented. This is repeated until the DDA accumulator exceeds one, keeping track of the number of source pixels added to the pixel accumulator. If the accumulator does exceed one, the difference between one and the previous accumulator value is multiplied by the current source pixel and added to the pixel accumulator. The pixel accumulator is then divided by the number of source pixels processed up to that point, yielding the new weighted average destination pixel value. A conceptual model for this process is illustrated in Figure 9.7.

DDA_DEMO Scaling Demonstration Program

The following source code listing is for a program named DDA_DEMO.EXE, which scales the images in a black-and-white video sequence, using a scale factor selected by the user. The program works only on uncompressed files, so any of the video clips provided will have to be uncompressed and converted to black and white before processing with these filters. This is a DOS-based, command-line driven program which takes an input file name, an output file name, and a scale factor as its command-line parameters.

DDA_DEMO.CPP Listing

```
//===========================================================
// DDA_DEMO.CPP
//---------------------------------------
// Program:  Implementation file for DDA_DEMO.EXE
// Author:   Phil Mattison
// Compiler: Borland Turbo C++ v1.01
//---------------------------------------
```

```
#include <stdlib.h>
#include <stdio.h>
#include <string.h>
#include <conio.h>
#include <dos.h>
#include <math.h>
#include "avi_riff.h"

//————————————————————

int Compare4C(char *s1, char *s2)          // Compare a pair of 4-char tags
  {
  if(s1[0]==s2[0] &&
  s1[1]==s2[1] &&
  s1[2]==s2[2] &&
  s1[3]==s2[3])return(1);
  return(0);
  }

//————————————————————
void ExitError(int n)
  {
  switch(n)
    {
    case 0:
    printf("ERROR — This is not a valid video file.\n");
    break;
    case 1:
    printf("ERROR — This video file must be decompressed first.\n");
    break;
    case 2:
    printf("ERROR — Input file must be black and white video.\n");
    break;
    case 3:
    printf("ERROR — Scale factor out of range. Must be 0.1 to 4.0\n");
    }
  exit(0);
  }

//————————————————————

void ScaleUp(BYTE in[], BYTE out[], float factor)
  {
  int     dda_const;       // DDA increment value
  int     accum;           // DDA accumulator
  int     dst;             // Destination index
  int     src;             // Source index
  long    w_left,w_right;  // Left and right pixel weights

  dst=0;
  src=0;
  accum=0;
```

```c
  dda_const=(int)(1024.0/factor);
  while(src<159)
    {
    w_left=1024L-(long)accum;
    w_right=(long)accum;
    out[dst++]=
    (BYTE)((w_left*(long)in[src]+w_right*(long)in[src+1])/1042L);
    accum+=dda_const;
    if(accum>1024)
      {
      src++;
      accum-=1024;
      }
    }
  }

//————————————————————
void ScaleDown(BYTE in[], BYTE out[], float factor)
  {
  int    dda_const;    // DDA increment value
  int    accum;        // DDA accumulator
  int    dst;          // Destination index
  int    src;          // Source index
  long   p_accum;      // Pixel Accumulator
  long   p_count;      // Pixel accumulation count

  dst=0;
  src=0;
  accum=0;
  p_accum=0L;
  p_count=0L;
  dda_const=(int)(1024.0*factor);
  while(src<159)
    {
    while(accum<1024 && src<160)          // Add up whole pixels
      {
      p_accum+=1024L*(long)in[src++];
      accum+=dda_const;
      p_count+=1024L;
      }
    accum=(src<160)?accum-1024:0;          // Calculate fractional pixels
    p_accum-=(long)accum*(long)in[src-1];
    p_count-=(long)accum;
    out[dst++]=(BYTE)(p_accum/p_count);
    p_count=1024L-(long)accum;
    p_accum=p_count*(long)in[src-1];
    }
  }

//————————————————————
void main(int argc, char* argv[])
  {
  FILE   *fi;                          // File stream pointer
```

```
FILE    *fo;                        // File stream pointer
int     frame_count;               // Video frame count
int     f_frame;                   // Video frame counter
float   x_scale,y_scale;           // Image scale factors
int     i,x,y,start,end;           // General indices
BYTE    image_buffer[IMAGE_SIZE];  // File input buffer
BYTE    old_line[160];             // Image pixel line buffer
BYTE    new_line[640];             // Image pixel line buffer
vid     vid_header;                // File header input structure

printf("VID file image scaling demonstration program.\n\n");
printf("Copyright (c) John Wiley & Sons, Inc., 1994.\n\n");

if(argc<5)
  {
  printf
  ("Please provide two file names: <input_file> <output_file>\n");
  printf("followed by an X and a Y scale factor from 0.1 to 4.0.\n");
  exit(0);
  }
fi=fopen(argv[1],"rb");
fo=fopen(argv[2],"wb");
if(fi==NULL)
  {
  printf("Could not open input file %s.\n",argv[1]);
  exit(0);
  }
if(fo==NULL)
  {
  printf("Could not open output file %s.\n",argv[2]);
  exit(0);
  }
fread(&vid_header,sizeof(vid),1,fi);
if(!Compare4C(vid_header.file_ID,"BOOK"))ExitError(0);
if((vid_header.compression&1)==1)ExitError(1);
if((vid_header.compression&2)!=2)ExitError(2);
x_scale=atof(argv[3]);
y_scale=atof(argv[4]);
if(x_scale<0.1 || x_scale>4.0)ExitError(3);
if(y_scale<0.1 || y_scale>4.0)ExitError(3);
frame_count=vid_header.frames;
fwrite(&vid_header,sizeof(vid),1,fo);
for(f_frame=0;f_frame<frame_count;f_frame++)
  {
  fread(image_buffer,19200,1,fi);         // Read image
  for(y=0;y<120;y++)
    {
    i=y*160;
    for(x=0;x<160;x++)old_line[x]=image_buffer[i++];
    i-=160;
    if(x_scale>=1.0)
      {
      ScaleUp(old_line,new_line,x_scale);
```

```
      start=(int)(x_scale*80.0)-80;
      for(x=start;x<start+160;x++)image_buffer[i++]=new_line[x];
      }
  else
     {
     ScaleDown(old_line,new_line,x_scale);
     start=80-(int)(x_scale*80.0);
     end=start+(int)(x_scale*160.0);
     for(x=0;x<start;x++)image_buffer[i++]=16;
     for(x=0;x<end-start;x++)image_buffer[i++]=new_line[x];
     for(x=end;x<160;x++)image_buffer[i++]=16;
     i=0;
     }
  }
for(x=0;x<160;x++)
  {
  i=x;
  for(y=0;y<120;y++)
     {
     old_line[y]=image_buffer[i];
     i+=160;
     }
  if(y_scale>=1.0)
     {
     ScaleUp(old_line,new_line,y_scale);
     i=x;
     start=(int)(y_scale*60.0)-60;
     for(y=start;y<start+120;y++)
        {
        image_buffer[i]=new_line[y];
        i+=160;
        }
     }
  else
     {
     ScaleDown(old_line,new_line,y_scale);
     i=x;
     start=60-(int)(y_scale*60.0);
     end=start+(int)(y_scale*120.0);
     for(y=0;y<start;y++)
        {
        image_buffer[i]=16;
        i+=160;
        }
     for(y=0;y<end-start;y++)
        {
        image_buffer[i]=new_line[y];
        i+=160;
        }
     for(y=end;y<120;y++)
        {
        image_buffer[i]=16;
        i+=160;
```

```
            }
         i=0;
         }
      }
   fwrite(image_buffer,19200,1,fo);     // Write image
   printf("Frame %d.%c",f_frame,0xD);
   }
fclose(fi);
fclose(fo);
printf("\nDone.\n");
}
```

Contrast Enhancement

For black-and-white images, contrast enhancement is a fairly simple matter of increasing the dynamic range of pixel values within the image. This can be done using a simple multiply with saturate (this means taking into account the maximum and minimum possible values of the result, as opposed to the concept of *color* saturation) on each pixel in the image, using the same intensity scale factor throughout. The same applies for color images if only the luminance is to be adjusted. If color contrast (i.e., saturation) needs to be adjusted, the problem gets a little more difficult. Recall that in YCrCb color-space color is represented as a Cartesian transformation of a vector in polar coordinate space. Color saturation corresponds to the magnitude of the color vector and hue corresponds to its angle. To adjust the length of the vector while retaining its angle requires adjustment of *both* Cr and Cb. You don't even want to *think* about how you would adjust color saturation in RGB color space. Because the angle of a vector is the ratio of its horizontal and vertical components, if both components are multiplied by the same scale factor the angle will not change. Recalling the distance formula we all learned in high school, the length of a vector is proportional to the sum of the squares of its horizontal and vertical components, so multiplying both components by a given scale factor is the same as multiplying the vector length by the same scale factor. Of course, in the real world we have to deal with such annoying things as the physical limitations of A/D converters, and so forth. If Cr and Cb are scaled so that one of them saturates (mathematically) and one doesn't, the hue will change. In that case, the component that didn't saturate needs to be adjusted to the same scale factor as the one that did, to retain the hue.

A critical element in correct contrast adjustment is finding the median brightness level of the image to be adjusted. The median brightness level of an image is the level at which half of all pixels are less than and the other half are brighter than the median. The median pixel value for a given image can be determined by using a *histogram*. A histogram is essentially an array of numbers giving the approximate probability of occurrence for each possible pixel value in a given image. The Huffman coding example in Chapter 5 used a histogram to determine the optimum code distribution for data compression. Finding the median pixel value involves a much simpler process. The histogram can be implemented as an array of integers provided each integer variable is capable of counting at least as high as the total number of pixels in the image. The number of elements in the array should equal the total number of possible pixel values. For example, a 320×200 grayscale image with 256 gray levels could use a histogram implemented as an array of 256 16-bit unsigned integers. For each pixel in the image the pixel value is used as an index into the histogram array and the selected element is incremented by one. Then, starting with the first element in the array, the histogram values are accumulated until the sum exceeds one-half the total number of pixels in the image. The histogram index at this point is the median pixel value of the image. This median value number is then subtracted from each pixel value in the image so that pixel values are evenly distributed above and below zero. A contrast scale value can then be applied to each pixel in turn as a simple multiplication. Adding the median value back to each pixel will then translate the dynamic range of the image back to the original range. The final step is checking for overflow, which means setting to zero any pixel values below zero and setting to the maximum, for example 255, any pixels that exceed the maximum. This effectively implements multiplication with saturation of the contrast scale value. Of course, this describes the process for adjusting the contrast on a single image. For a sequence of images, as in a motion video clip, there are two other factors to consider. First, if a given contrast scale factor is applied over time, what may have been an appropriate scale factor at the beginning of the sequence may cause excessive saturation of the dynamic range at various points in the sequence. Second, the median intensity is likely to change during the sequence and, therefore, using a single median intensity value over time would not be appropriate. One possible solution would be to recalculate the median and adjust the scale factor for each frame. Most commercial video cameras use a process similar to this to implement *automatic gain control (AGC)*. AGC action can be observed in a consumer camcorder by alternatively directing the camera lens at a relatively dark area and then a relatively bright area. On each transition, for a split second, the viewfinder becomes either totally dark or totally washed out until the image sensor gain amplifier is automatically adjusted. Therefore, it should ordinarily be unnecessary to apply luminance contrast adjustments simply to improve the subjective appearance of the video image. However, to bring out low-contrast details in a video sequence it may be desirable to apply contrast adjustments in a dynamically controlled manner. There are many ways this could be done, depending on the application and the degree of flexibility required. Because the focus here is on the inner workings of digital video and not on how to write fancy user interfaces, the sample program provided is implemented as a simple command line processor that applies a fixed contrast adjustment to all frames in a video sequence. The program is named CON_DEMO.EXE. It can be used to adjust either luminance contrast or color saturation. Because all the video sequences provided are palette-based, the program simply modifies the palette data. The C source code for doing this follows.

CON_DEMO Contrast Adjustment Demonstration Program

The source code listing is for a program named CON_DEMO.EXE, which adjusts the contrast of images in a black-and-white video sequence, using a fixed contrast scale factor. Contrast may be increased or decreased with each pass of the program. The program works only on uncompressed files, so any of the video clips provided will have to be uncompressed and converted to black and white before processing with this program. This is a DOS-based, command-line driven program which takes an input file name, an output file name, and a contrast direction ($+/-$) as its command-line parameters.

CON_DEMO.CPP Listing

```
//====================================================================
// CON_DEMO.CPP
//
// This program applies a contrast adjustment to every frame
```

```
// in a video sequence. The input file must be an uncompressed
// VID file of black and white images.
//
//─────────────────────────────
// Program:   Implementation file for CON_DEMO.EXE
// Author:    Phil Mattison
// Compiler:  Borland Turbo C++ v1.01
//─────────────────────────────

#include <stdlib.h>
#include <stdio.h>
#include <string.h>
#include <conio.h>
#include <dos.h>
#include <math.h>

#define BYTE    unsigned char
#define WORD    unsigned int
#define DWORD   unsigned long

#define IMAGE_SIZE  19200
#define THRESHOLD   10

typedef struct
  {
  char file_ID[8];
  int  x_size;
  int  y_size;
  int  frames;
  int  compression;
  int  palette[240][3];
  } vid_t;

typedef union
  {
  vid_t                  vid_header;
  unsigned char buffer[sizeof(vid_t)];
  } header_t;

//─────────────────────────────
int Compare4C(char *s1, char *s2)        // Compare a pair of 4-char tags
  {
  if(s1[0]==s2[0] &&
  s1[1]==s2[1] &&
  s1[2]==s2[2] &&
  s1[3]==s2[3])return(1);
  return(0);
  }
int Addr(int x, int y)
  {
  return(y*160+x);
  }
```

```
//————————————————
void ExitError()
  {
  printf("File Error \n");
  exit(0);
  }

//————————————————
void main(int argc, char* argv[])
  {

  FILE    *fi;          // File stream pointer
  FILE    *fo;          // File stream pointer
  int     frame_count;  // Video frame count
  int     f_frame;      // Video frame counter
  int     i,x,y,acc;    // General indices
  BYTE    image_buffer[IMAGE_SIZE];
  header_t input;       // File header input structure

  if(argc<4)
    {
    printf
    ("Please provide two file names: <input_file> <output_file>\n");
    printf("followed by either + or - for more or less contrast.\n");
    exit(0);
    }
  fi=fopen(argv[1],"rb");
  fo=fopen(argv[2],"wb");
  if(fi==NULL)
    {
    printf("Could not open input file %s.\n",argv[1]);
    exit(0);
    }
  if(fo==NULL)
    {
    printf("Could not open output file %s.\n",argv[2]);
    exit(0);
    }
  fread(input.buffer,sizeof(vid_t),1,fi);
  if(!Compare4C(input.vid_header.file_ID,"BOOK"))ExitError();
  if((input.vid_header.compression&1)==1)ExitError(); // Compressed
  if((input.vid_header.compression&2)!=2)ExitError(); // Not B/W
  frame_count=input.vid_header.frames;
  fwrite(input.buffer,sizeof(vid_t),1,fo);

  for(f_frame=0;f_frame<frame_count;f_frame++)
    {
    fread(image_buffer,19200,1,fi);           // Read image
    for(i=0;i<IMAGE_SIZE;i++)
      {
      acc=(int)image_buffer[i];
```

```
                acc-=136;
                if(*argv[3]=='+')acc=(int)(1.2*(float)acc);
                else            acc=(int)((float)acc/1.2);
                acc+=136;
                if(acc>255)acc=255;
                if(acc<16)acc=16;
                image_buffer[i]=(BYTE)acc;
                }
            fwrite(image_buffer,19200,1,fo);        // Write image
            printf("Frame %d.%c",f_frame,0xD);
            }
        fclose(fi);
        fclose(fo);
        printf("\nDone.\n");
        }
```

As a further illustration of why a median value must be found before adjusting image contrast, consider Figure 9.8. This diagram represents the cross-section of pixel intensity values for a hypothetical image.

The pixel median value is represented by the dotted line going approximately through the middle of the solid waveform. The dotted line waveform shows how the intensity profile might look after applying the contrast adjustment scale factor. Notice how the new waveform crosses the median line at all the same points as the original. This technique prevents the image from becoming brighter or darker overall as a result of contrast adjustment. If an intensity scale factor were simply applied to all pixels in the image without concern for the median intensity value, any increase in contrast would also produce a corresponding increase in brightness. There would also be a much greater tendency to saturate the brightest areas of the image.

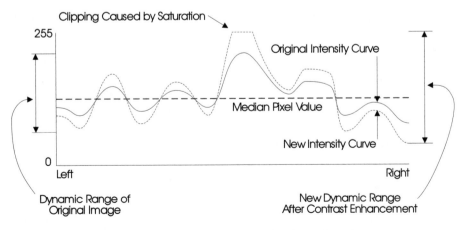

Figure 9.8 Image cross-section diagram showing median intensity value.

Negative Transformation

Generating a negative image requires conservation of a median pixel value to that for contrast enhancement. After normalizing the median to zero, conversion to a negative image is a simple matter of changing the sign of each pixel. After adding the median value back into all pixels of the image the result is a negative image with the same contrast ratio and average brightness as the original. Figure 9.9 illustrates how the image cross-section waveform is effectively a mirror of the original waveform.

Pixel-by-pixel addition of a positive and a negative image created this way will result in a uniform gray. Of course, if the median pixel intensity is near the maximum or minimum of the available dynamic range and the intensity curve has local extremes in the opposite direction, applying the technique just described could result in clipping of the intensities, as shown in Figure 9.10.

This can be avoided by translating the median pixel value to a level which will allow the entire intensity curve that was in the original dynamic range. The translation is performed by subtracting the median value from the maximum possible value in the dynamic range. For example, if the median was 200 and the range was zero to 255, the new median would be 255 minus 200, or 55. The result of this, when applied to the intensity curve shown in Figure 9.10, is illustrated in Figure 9.11.

Rather than go through the laborious process of calculating an image median, however, there is a much simpler, more direct way to translate an image to its negative. For intensity levels, each pixel need only be subtracted from the maximum value in the range. This automatically creates a negative image with the appropriate median intensity level. To create a color negative, a transformation also must be applied to the two color components of each pixel. Recall that in YCrCb color space the color component values are normalized to allow representation as unsigned integers. Values below 128, therefore, actually represent negative numbers. If the color component levels were centered about zero, translation of the color element to its negative would simply involve changing the sign of each color component. However, because the color components are normalized so that a value of 255 is equivalent to positive 127 and a value of zero is equivalent to negative 128, subtracting the component value from the maximum of 255 is equivalent to changing its sign. We see, therefore, that the same process can be applied to all three image components to create a negative color image. A sample program for converting images to their negative and back is provided in

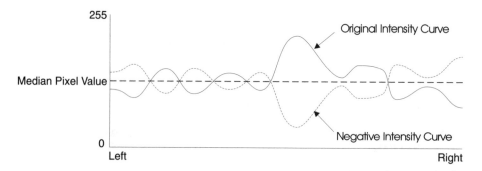

Figure 9.9   Illustration of negative image transformation about a median intensity value.

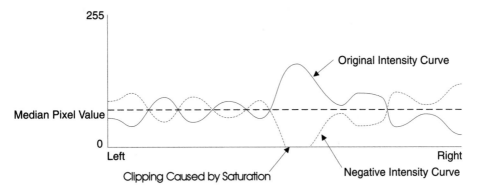

Figure 9.10 Illustration of signal clipping caused by incorrect negative median value.

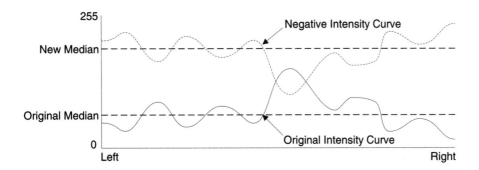

Figure 9.11 Transformation of both median and image data to negative domain through simple subtraction.

the file named NEG_DEMO.EXE. Because all the video sequences provided are palette-based, the program simply modifies the palette data. The source code follows.

NEG_DEMO Image Negative Demonstration Program

The source code listing is for a program named NEG_DEMO.EXE, which inverts the intensity (and color) of the images in a color or black-and-white video sequence. The program works on any VID file because it only modifies the palette. This is a DOS-based, command-line driven program which takes an input file name and an output file name as its command-line parameters.

NEG_DEMO.CPP Listing

```
//=========================================================
// NEG_DEMO.CPP
//
```

```
// This program inverts the brightness and color of every frame
// in a video sequence by changing the palette.
//————————————————————————
// Program:   Implementation file for NEG_DEMO.EXE
// Author:    Phil Mattison
// Compiler:  Borland Turbo C++ v1.01
//————————————————————————

#include <stdlib.h>
#include <stdio.h>
#include <string.h>
#include <conio.h>
#include <dos.h>
#include <math.h>

#define BYTE        unsigned char
#define WORD        unsigned int
#define DWORD       unsigned long

#define IMAGE_SIZE  19200
#define THRESHOLD   10

typedef struct
  {
  char file_ID[8];
  int  x_size;
  int  y_size;
  int  frames;
  int  compression;
  int  palette[240][3];
  } vid_t;

typedef union
  {
  vid_t vid_header;
  unsigned char buffer[sizeof(vid_t)];
  } header_t;

//————————————————————————
int Compare4C(char *s1, char *s2)  // Compare a pair of 4-char tags
  {
  if(s1[0]==s2[0] &&
  s1[1]==s2[1] &&
  s1[2]==s2[2] &&
  s1[3]==s2[3])return(1);
  return(0);
  }

//————————————————————————
void ExitError()
  {
  printf("File Error \n");
  exit(0);
```

```
    }

//————————————————————
void main(int argc, char* argv[])
  {
  FILE  *fi;              // File stream pointer
  FILE  *fo;              // File stream pointer
  int   frame_count;      // Video frame count
  int   f_frame;          // Video frame counter
  int   block_number;     // Compressed frame number
  int   block_size;       // Compressed frame size
  float R,G,B;            // Intermediate RGB values
  int   i;                // General indices
  BYTE  image_buffer[IMAGE_SIZE];
  BYTE  new_pixel[240];
  header_t input;         // File header input structure

  if(argc<3)
    {
    printf
    ("Please provide two file names: <input_file> <output_file>\n");
    exit(0);
    }
  fi=fopen(argv[1],"rb");
  fo=fopen(argv[2],"wb");
  if(fi==NULL)
    {
    printf("Could not open input file %s.\n",argv[1]);
    exit(0);
    }
  if(fo==NULL)
    {
    printf("Could not open output file %s.\n",argv[2]);
    exit(0);
    }
  fread(input.buffer,sizeof(vid_t),1,fi);
  if(!Compare4C(input.vid_header.file_ID,"BOOK"))ExitError();
  for(i=0;i<240;i++)          // Translate palette data
    {
    input.vid_header.palette[i][0]=63-input.vid_header.palette[i][0];
    input.vid_header.palette[i][1]=63-input.vid_header.palette[i][1];
    input.vid_header.palette[i][2]=63-input.vid_header.palette[i][2];
    }
  frame_count=input.vid_header.frames;
  fwrite(input.buffer,sizeof(vid_t),1,fo);
  if(input.vid_header.compression&1==1)
    {
    fread(image_buffer,IMAGE_SIZE,1,fi);
    fwrite(image_buffer,IMAGE_SIZE,1,fo);    // Write image
    for(f_frame=1;f_frame<frame_count;f_frame++)
      {
      fread(&block_number,sizeof(int),1,fi);
      fread(&block_size,sizeof(int),1,fi);
```

```
        fread(image_buffer,block_size,1,fi);
        fwrite(&block_number,sizeof(int),1,fo);
        fwrite(&block_size,sizeof(int),1,fo);
        fwrite(image_buffer,block_size,1,fo);      // Write image
        printf("Frame %d.%c",f_frame,0xD);
        }
    }
else
    {
    for(f_frame=0;f_frame<frame_count;f_frame++)
        {
        fread(image_buffer,IMAGE_SIZE,1,fi);
        fwrite(image_buffer,IMAGE_SIZE,1,fo);      // Write image
        printf("Frame %d.%c",f_frame,0xD);
        }
    }
fclose(fi);
fclose(fo);
printf("\nDone.\n");
}
```

Feature Extraction

One application of digital video that has been employed in industrial settings for a number of years is pattern recognition. This is useful for process control, automatic inspection, optical character recognition, and a wide variety of other activities. While there are many techniques for implementing pattern recognition, a critical element in many of them is *feature extraction*, or edge detection. An *edge* can be thought of as any relatively abrupt transition in image intensity associated with some linear direction. This distinction is made to distinguish an edge from a spot. Another definition of an edge is the boundary between two areas of differing pixel intensities. Edges can be detected using a technique similar to that described for filtering. A widely used technique for edge detection is known as *Sobel's algorithm*. The basic theory behind Sobel's algorithm is to detect differences in pixel intensity along every possible axis relative to a given target pixel. In two-dimensional space obviously there is no limit to the number of possible directions an edge might take. However, as always, we make a tradeoff between calculation workload and accuracy. The resulting implementation detects edges nearest one of four possible directions: horizontal, vertical, and two diagonals. To do this, a 3×3 filter kernel is defined in four different configurations. These are illustrated in Figure 9.12. Notice that each configuration effectively divides the kernel into two regions, one positive and one negative.

The row of three zeros defines the axis along which the nearest edge will be detected if it exists. When each pixel in the image is multiplied by its corresponding coefficient in the filter kernel and all the resulting products are added together, the absolute value of the sum is proportional to the *slope* of the edge. Each of the four kernel patterns is applied to each target pixel producing four possible slope coefficients. From these, the largest is selected based on the assumption that the largest absolute difference is produced by the kernel which most closely aligns with a given edge in the image. In any of the kernels the positive and negative values could easily be reversed with the same result because it is the absolute *difference* that is the object of concern. Figure 9.13 shows how each of the four kernel configurations would line up to detect the edges of a circle.

1	1	1
0	0	0
-1	-1	-1

-1	0	1
-1	0	1
-1	0	1

1	1	0
1	0	-1
0	-1	-1

0	1	1
-1	0	1
-1	-1	0

Figure 9.12   Filter kernel configurations for simple Sobel's algorithm implementation.

It can be seen from this example that the kernel in which the row of zeros most closely aligns with the edge in question is selected for any given pixel position. Obviously, it would be possible to create an infinite variety of more and more finely tuned kernel configurations to detect every conceivable edge angle. There is, however, the inevitable point of diminishing returns and four different configurations are generally adequate for an example. Figure 9.14(a) shows how a cross-section of an image can be plotted to show its relative pixel intensities. The same cross-section after processing with an edge detection filter would produce a profile something like that shown in Figure 9.14(b).

The abruptness and magnitude of pixel intensity variation over a given spatial distance is referred to as *edge energy*. Objects can be detected by setting the appropriate edge energy threshold as also shown in Figure 9.14(b). These energy levels are in fact the true indication of how much information is contained in a given image. The larger and more frequent these energy spikes the more information there is. The ratio of the amount of energy in an image before and after compres-

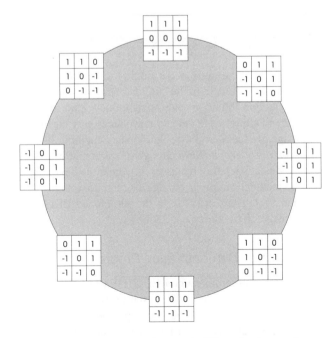

Figure 9.13   Illustration of how different kernels match different edge angles.

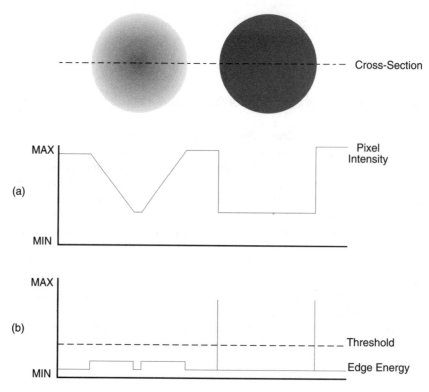

Figure 9.14   Illustration of edge energy versus edge intensity variation.

sion and decompression is a good measure of the fidelity of the compression and decompression processes. Edge detection is a key element in the automatic analysis of image data. When combined with motion, image edge detection should provide some unique opportunities for innovation. When viewed simply as an image transform, edge detection produces very curious effects. The edge energy pattern of a natural image produces an image that looks something like a bas-relief sculpture or perhaps a *scanning electron micrograph (SEM)* image of some microscopic protozoan. As the use of edge energy patterns to detect specific objects or movement is beyond the scope of this discussion, the example program included simply generates a new set of images showing edge energy patterns. The program demonstrating this effect is in the file named EDG_DEMO.EXE, and works only on black-and-white images. The source code follows.

EDG_DEMO Edge Detection Demonstration Program

The source code listing is for a program named EDG_DEMO.EXE, which detects edges of the images in a black-and-white video sequence. The program works only on uncompressed files, so any of the video clips provided will have to be uncompressed and converted to black and white before processing with this program. This is a DOS-based, command-line driven program which takes an input file name and an output file name as its command-line parameters.

EDG_DEMO.CPP Listing

```cpp
//==========================================================
// EDG_DEMO.CPP
//
// This program measures edge energy shown as gray levels
// for every frame in a video sequence. The input file
// must be an uncompressed VID file of black and white images.
//───────────────────────────────────
// Program:   Implementation file for EDG_DEMO.EXE
// Author:    Phil Mattison
// Compiler:  Borland Turbo C++ v1.01
//───────────────────────────────────

#include <stdlib.h>
#include <stdio.h>
#include <string.h>
#include <conio.h>
#include <dos.h>
#include <math.h>

#define BYTE        unsigned char
#define WORD        unsigned int
#define DWORD       unsigned long

#define IMAGE_SIZE  19200
#define THRESHOLD   10

typedef struct
  {
  char file_ID[8];
  int  x_size;
  int  y_size;
  int  frames;
  int  compression;
  int  palette[240][3];
  } vid_t;

typedef union
  {
  vid_t vid_header;
  unsigned char buffer[sizeof(vid_t)];
  } header_t;

//───────────────────────────────────
int Compare4C(char *s1, char *s2) // Compare a pair of 4-char tags
  {
  if(s1[0]==s2[0] &&
  s1[1]==s2[1] &&
  s1[2]==s2[2] &&
  s1[3]==s2[3])return(1);
  return(0);
  }
```

```
int Addr(int x, int y)
  {
  return(y*160+x);
  }

//————————————————
void ExitError()
  {
  printf("File Error \n");
  exit(0);
  }

//————————————————
void main(int argc, char* argv[])
  {
  FILE *fi;                  // File stream pointer
  FILE *fo;                  // File stream pointer
  int  frame_count;          // Video frame count
  int  f_frame;              // Video frame counter
  int  i,j,k,x,y,acc[4];     // General indices
  BYTE image_buffer[IMAGE_SIZE];
  BYTE new_image_buffer[IMAGE_SIZE];
  header_t input;            // File header input structure

  if(argc<3)
    {
    printf
    ("Please provide two file names: <input_file> <output_file>\n");
    exit(0);
    }
  fi=fopen(argv[1],"rb");
  fo=fopen(argv[2],"wb");
  if(fi==NULL)
    {
    printf("Could not open input file %s.\n",argv[1]);
    exit(0);
    }
  if(fo==NULL)
    {
    printf("Could not open output file %s.\n",argv[2]);
    exit(0);
    }
  fread(input.buffer,sizeof(vid_t),1,fi);
  if(!Compare4C(input.vid_header.file_ID,"BOOK"))ExitError();
  if((input.vid_header.compression&1)==1)ExitError(); // Compressed
  if((input.vid_header.compression&2)!=2)ExitError(); // Not B/W
  frame_count=input.vid_header.frames;
  fwrite(input.buffer,sizeof(vid_t),1,fo);

  for(f_frame=0;f_frame<frame_count;f_frame++)
    {
    fread(image_buffer,19200,1,fi);            // Read image
```

```c
  for(i=0;i<IMAGE_SIZE;i++)new_image_buffer[i]=136;
  for(y=1;y<119;y++)
    {
    for(x=1;x<159;x++)
      {
      for(i=0;i<4;i++)acc[i]=136;
      acc[0]+=(int)image_buffer[Addr(x-1,y+1)];
      acc[0]+=(int)image_buffer[Addr(x,  y+1)];
      acc[0]+=(int)image_buffer[Addr(x+1,y+1)];
      acc[0]-=(int)image_buffer[Addr(x-1,y-1)];
      acc[0]-=(int)image_buffer[Addr(x,  y-1)];
      acc[0]-=(int)image_buffer[Addr(x+1,y-1)];
      acc[1]+=(int)image_buffer[Addr(x-1,y+1)];
      acc[1]+=(int)image_buffer[Addr(x-1,  y)];
      acc[1]+=(int)image_buffer[Addr(x-1,y-1)];
      acc[1]-=(int)image_buffer[Addr(x+1,y+1)];
      acc[1]-=(int)image_buffer[Addr(x+1,  y)];
      acc[1]-=(int)image_buffer[Addr(x+1,y-1)];
      acc[2]-=(int)image_buffer[Addr(x-1,y+1)];
      acc[2]-=(int)image_buffer[Addr(x,  y+1)];
      acc[2]-=(int)image_buffer[Addr(x+1,y+1)];
      acc[2]+=(int)image_buffer[Addr(x-1,y-1)];
      acc[2]+=(int)image_buffer[Addr(x,  y-1)];
      acc[2]+=(int)image_buffer[Addr(x+1,y-1)];
      acc[3]-=(int)image_buffer[Addr(x-1,y+1)];
      acc[3]-=(int)image_buffer[Addr(x-1,  y)];
      acc[3]-=(int)image_buffer[Addr(x-1,y-1)];
      acc[3]+=(int)image_buffer[Addr(x+1,y+1)];
      acc[3]+=(int)image_buffer[Addr(x+1,  y)];
      acc[3]+=(int)image_buffer[Addr(x+1,y-1)];
      j=0;
      k=0;
      for(i=0;i<4;i++)
        {
        if(abs(136-acc[i])>k)
          {
          k=abs(136-acc[i]);
          j=i;
          acc[i]-=136;
          acc[i]/=2;
          acc[i]+=136;
          if(acc[i]<16)acc[i]=16;
          if(acc[i]>255)acc[i]=255;
          }
        }
      new_image_buffer[Addr(x,y)]=(BYTE)acc[j];
      }
    }
  fwrite(new_image_buffer,19200,1,fo);          // Write image
  printf("Frame %d.%c",f_frame,0xD);
  }
fclose(fi);
fclose(fo);
```

```
printf("\nDone.\n");
}
```

Threshold Representation

While there have been a number of references to the idea of a threshold in prior discussions, none of them have applied the concept directly to the image itself. The basic idea of a threshold does not require a lot of discussion. It is simply a limit that produces a binary decision (or decisions) from some continuously variable data, such as image data. One application in image processing might be to obliterate information from an image above or below a certain threshold thereby emphasizing what remains. This is quite a simplistic application and produces only marginally useful results. The approximate effects of one such possible application on an image profile cross-section is illustrated in Figure 9.15. Here, any pixels that fall below the established threshold are simply reduced to zero.

The visual effect would be a solid black image with only details showing in areas where pixel values are above the threshold. Pixels falling below the threshold could also just as well be changed to any other constant value from full-intensity white to any value in between. Another approach is to establish multiple thresholds, as shown in Figure 9.16. This effectively quantizes the image into a series of discrete intensity levels rather than a continuous tone.

The effect is to produce a sort of *contour map* of the image. In fact, contouring is a term sometimes used to describe the image artifacts caused by representing a continuous-tone image with an insufficient number of unique pixel values. If a series of bright colors which sharply contrast from

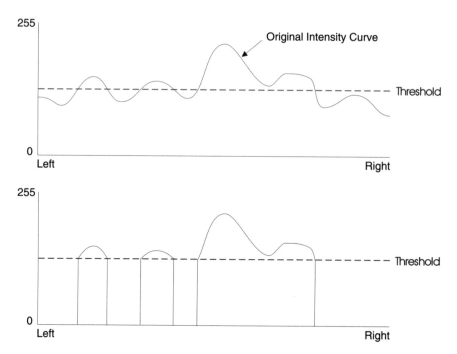

Figure 9.15   Illustration of a simple one-level threshold transformation.

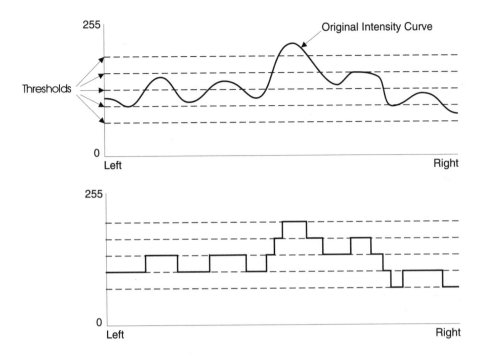

Figure 9.16 Illustration of multilevel threshold transformation.

one another are assigned to each of the different thresholds the effect can be quite striking in terms of the ability to detect objects that otherwise might be obscured. For a grayscale image in which the various gray levels are stored in a hardware palette, such as in a VGA display adapter, if the palette values are in numerical order the image threshold process can be accomplished very simply by writing different values to the palette. This technique is utilized in a demonstration program named THD_DEMO.EXE. The source code for this program follows.

THD_DEMO Threshold Demonstration Program

The source code listing is for a program named THD_DEMO.EXE, which maps intensity thresholds of the images in a black-and-white video sequence. The program works only on uncompressed files, so any of the video clips provided will have to be uncompressed and converted to black-and-white before processing with this program. This is a DOS-based, command-line driven program which takes an input file name and an output file name as its command-line parameters.

THD_DEMO.CPP Listing

```
//============================================================
// THD_DEMO.CPP
//
// This program adds color to a black and white VID file palette
```

```
// to distinguish among different quantized levels of pixel
// intensity. Only the palette is changed, so the program works
// on compressed files as well as uncompressed. The input file
// must, howevever, be black and white.
//─────────────────────────────
// Program:   Implementation file for THD_DEMO.EXE
// Author:    Phil Mattison
// Compiler:  Borland Turbo C++ v1.01
//─────────────────────────────

#include <stdlib.h>
#include <stdio.h>
#include <string.h>
#include <conio.h>
#include <dos.h>
#include <math.h>

#define BYTE        unsigned char
#define WORD        unsigned int
#define DWORD       unsigned long

#define IMAGE_SIZE  19200
#define THRESHOLD   10

typedef struct
  {
  char file_ID[8];
  int  x_size;
  int  y_size;
  int  frames;
  int  compression;
  int  palette[240][3];
  } vid_t;

typedef union
  {
  vid_t   vid_header;
  unsigned char buffer[sizeof(vid_t)];
  } header_t;

//─────────────────────────────
int Compare4C(char *s1, char *s2) // Compare a pair of 4-char tags
  {
  if(s1[0]==s2[0] &&
  s1[1]==s2[1] &&
  s1[2]==s2[2] &&
  s1[3]==s2[3])return(1);
  return(0);
  }

//─────────────────────────────
void ExitError()
```

```
    {
    printf("File Error \n");
    exit(0);
    }

//——————————————————————

void main(int argc, char* argv[])
    {
    FILE  *fi;          // File stream pointer
    FILE  *fo;          // File stream pointer
    int   frame_count;  // Video frame count
    int   f_frame;      // Video frame counter
    int   block_number; // Compressed frame number
    int   block_size;   // Compressed frame size
    float R,G,B;        // Intermediate RGB values
    int   i;            // General indices
    BYTE  image_buffer[IMAGE_SIZE];
    BYTE  new_pixel[240];
    header_t input;     // File header input structure

    if(argc<3)
       {
       printf
       ("Please provide two file names: <input_file> <output_file>\n");
       exit(0);
       }
    fi=fopen(argv[1],"rb");
    fo=fopen(argv[2],"wb");
    if(fi==NULL)
       {
       printf("Could not open input file %s.\n",argv[1]);
       exit(0);
       }
    if(fo==NULL)
       {
       printf("Could not open output file %s.\n",argv[2]);
       exit(0);
       }
    fread(input.buffer,sizeof(vid_t),1,fi);
    if(!Compare4C(input.vid_header.file_ID,"BOOK"))ExitError();
    if((input.vid_header.compression&2)!=2)
       {
       printf("ERROR — Input file must be black and white\n");
       ExitError();
       }
    for(i=0;i<40;i++)          // Translate palette data
       {
       input.vid_header.palette[i][0]=0;
       input.vid_header.palette[i][1]=63;
       input.vid_header.palette[i][2]=0;
       }
```

```
for(i=40;i<80;i++)          // Translate palette data
  {
  input.vid_header.palette[i][0]=0;
  input.vid_header.palette[i][1]=0;
  input.vid_header.palette[i][2]=63;
  }
for(i=80;i<120;i++)         // Translate palette data
  {
  input.vid_header.palette[i][0]=63;
  input.vid_header.palette[i][1]=0;
  input.vid_header.palette[i][2]=63;
  }
for(i=120;i<160;i++)        // Translate palette data
  {
  input.vid_header.palette[i][0]=63;
  input.vid_header.palette[i][1]=0;
  input.vid_header.palette[i][2]=0;
  }
for(i=160;i<200;i++)        // Translate palette data
  {
  input.vid_header.palette[i][0]=32;
  input.vid_header.palette[i][1]=32;
  input.vid_header.palette[i][2]=0;
  }
for(i=200;i<240;i++)        // Translate palette data
  {
  input.vid_header.palette[i][0]=64;
  input.vid_header.palette[i][1]=64;
  input.vid_header.palette[i][2]=0;
  }
frame_count=input.vid_header.frames;
fwrite(input.buffer,sizeof(vid_t),1,fo);
if(input.vid_header.compression&1==1)
  {
  fread(image_buffer,IMAGE_SIZE,1,fi);
  fwrite(image_buffer,IMAGE_SIZE,1,fo);      // Write image
  for(f_frame=1;f_frame<frame_count;f_frame++)
    {
    fread(&block_number,sizeof(int),1,fi);
    fread(&block_size,sizeof(int),1,fi);
    fread(image_buffer,block_size,1,fi);
    fwrite(&block_number,sizeof(int),1,fo);
    fwrite(&block_size,sizeof(int),1,fo);
    fwrite(image_buffer,block_size,1,fo);  // Write image
    printf("Frame %d.%c",f_frame,0xD);
    }
  }
else
  {
  for(f_frame=0;f_frame<frame_count;f_frame++)
    {
    fread(image_buffer,IMAGE_SIZE,1,fi);
    fwrite(image_buffer,IMAGE_SIZE,1,fo);      // Write image
```

```
        printf("Frame %d.%c",f_frame,0xD);
        }
    }
    fclose(fi);
    fclose(fo);
    printf("\nDone.\n");
    }
```

Graphics and Video

Some very interesting visual effects can be achieved by intermixing graphical information with motion video. This technique has been widely used for a long time to apply titles and other overlay information to video sequences, most commonly for television commercials. More recently, highly sophisticated graphics techniques have shown up as special effects in movies such as *Terminator II* and *The Abyss*. In fact, Video for Windows and the Video Player demonstration program included with this book both mix graphics and video in the sense that both are displayed on the screen simultaneously. However, for purposes of this discussion mixing graphics and video refers to putting graphics into the video sequence rather than playing a video sequence on a graphics display device.

One problem associated with dynamically merging video and graphics is sometimes referred to as *clobber*. This means that if you draw graphics on a region of the display which is showing motion video it will be clobbered when the next video frame comes along. That is, it will be overwritten. This can be observed in the VIEW_VID.EXE sample application provided by moving the mouse cursor into the active video region while it is playing. If graphical information is redrawn over every new frame of a video sequence the graphics will tend to flicker and the performance of the video sequence will be reduced because of the extra overhead introduced by graphics operations. The problem can be solved in hardware if the added expense is acceptable. One fairly common solution is the use of a *color key*. This is a method for merging two separate pixel streams where one stream or the other is selected based on a key color. The technique is often used for television weather reporting and is referred to as "blue screen." The meteorologist stands in front of a solid blue backdrop in view of a video camera. The video signal from this camera is fed into a merge circuit along with the video signal from a graphics device. Whenever the merge circuit detects the color blue in the video signal it substitutes the graphics signal. The color blue was chosen because it is one of the easier colors to distinguish from the others in YUV color space.

Probably the most significant attribute of hardware graphics merge is that it works in real time. If it is acceptable to process the video and graphics off-line, the same kind of effects can be achieved with software. In fact, it is possible to achieve even more dramatic effects because the capabilities are not limited by the hardware design. For example, you could overlay graphics on motion video so the video images move but the graphics don't, as in video titles. You could blend the graphics with the video images. You could use the graphics as a mask to apply other effects such as filtering or edge detection or contrast enhancement or image negation or color removal. The possibilities are almost limitless. As a simple demonstration of what is possible, the sample program named G_V_DEMO.EXE allows you to merge a text file with a video sequence causing the text to scroll from the bottom to the top of the video screen as the video plays in the background. Because of the low resolution of the video and graphics used for the demonstration, each line of text cannot be more than 20 characters, otherwise it will run off the right-hand side of the video screen. The number of lines of text that can be scrolled across the video as it plays also depends on the length of the video sequence and the speed at which the text scrolls. The text color and scrolling speed can be specified when the program is invoked. Source code for the graphics and video merge demonstration program follows.

G_V_DEMO Image Negative Demonstration Program

The source code listing is for a program named G_V_DEMO.EXE, which overlays graphics text on the images in a color or black-and-white video sequence. The program works only on uncompressed files, so any of the video clips provided will have to be uncompressed before processing with this program. This is a DOS-based, command-line driven program which takes two input file names and an output file name as its command-line parameters.

G_V_DEMO.CPP Listing

```
//=========================================================
// G_V_DEMO.CPP
//
// This program overlays a video sequence with scrolling
// text read from an ASCII file. The text may be applied
// over color or black and white images, and may be any
// of the 16 colors defined for a standard 16-color VGA.
// The input video file must be uncompressed. The order
// of command line parameters is:
//
// <video file> <output file> <text file> <text color #>
//
// Text beyond the 19th character on each line is truncated.
//
//--------------------------------------
// Program:    Implementation file for G_V_DEMO.EXE
// Author:     Phil Mattison
// Compiler:   Borland Turbo C++ v1.01
//--------------------------------------

#include <stdlib.h>
#include <stdio.h>
#include <string.h>
#include <conio.h>
#include <dos.h>
#include <math.h>

extern "C" SetVmode(int);
extern "C" WriteEntry(int,int,int,int);
extern "C" WriteBlock(int,int,int,int,char far *);
extern "C" DrawASCII(int,int,int,int);
extern "C" ReadPixel(int,int);

#define BYTE        unsigned char
#define WORD        unsigned int
```

```
#define DWORD        unsigned long

#define IMAGE_SIZE   19200
#define Y_ORG        40
#define X_ORG        80
#define FRAME_ORG    80,40
#define LINE_SP      10
#define FRAME_SIZE   160,120

typedef struct
  {
  char   file_ID[8];
  int    x_size;
  int    y_size;
  int    frames;
  int    compression;
  int    palette[240][3];
  } vid_t;

typedef union
  {
  vid_t vid_header;
  unsigned char buffer[sizeof(vid_t)];
  } header_t;

//————————————————————
int Compare4C(char *s1, char *s2) // Compare a pair of 4-char tags
  {
  if(s1[0]==s2[0] &&
  s1[1]==s2[1] &&
  s1[2]==s2[2] &&
  s1[3]==s2[3])return(1);
  return(0);
  }

int Addr(int x, int y)
  {
  return(y*160+x);
  }

//————————————————————
void ExitError(int n)
  {
  switch(n)
    {
    case 0:printf("ERROR — This is not a valid video file.\n");
    case 1:printf("ERROR — Input file must not be compressed.\n");
    case 2:printf("ERROR — Text color must be between 0 and 15.\n");
    }
  exit(0);
  }

//————————————————————
```

```c
void DrawString(int x_pos,int y_pos,char *string,int color)
  {
  while(*string!=0 && x_pos<312)
    {
    DrawASCII(x_pos,y_pos,(int)*string,color);
    x_pos+=8 ;
    string++;
    }
  }

//——————————————————————
void main(int argc, char* argv[])
  {
  FILE   *fi;                 // File stream pointer
  FILE   *fo;                 // File stream pointer
  FILE   *ft;                 // File stream pointer
  int    frame_count;         // Video frame count
  int    f_frame;             // Video frame counter
  int    text_color;          // Overlay text color
  int    y_org;               // Text Y origin
  int    text_start;          // Text list start index
  int    text_end;            // Text list end index
  int    i,j,x,y,R,G,B,lines; // General indices
  char   line_buffer[128];    // Read up to 128-char lines
  char   text_buffer[20][20]; // Store up to 20 lines of text
  BYTE   image_buffer[IMAGE_SIZE];
  header_t input;             // File header input structure

  if(argc<5)
    {
    printf
    ("Please provide two file names: <input_file> <output_file>\n");
    printf
    ("plus <text file> and <text color #> (in the range 0-15).\n");
    exit(0);
    }
  fi=fopen(argv[1],"rb");
  fo=fopen(argv[2],"wb");
  ft=fopen(argv[3],"rt");
  if(fi==NULL)
    {
    printf("Could not open input file %s.\n",argv[1]);
    exit(0);
    }
  if(fo==NULL)
    {
    printf("Could not open output file %s.\n",argv[2]);
    exit(0);
    }
  if(ft==NULL)
    {
    printf("Could not open text file %s.\n",argv[3]);
    exit(0);
```

```
  }
text_color=atoi(argv[4]);
if(text_color<0 || text_color>15)ExitError(2);        // Range error
fread(input.buffer,sizeof(vid_t),1,fi);
if(!Compare4C(input.vid_header.file_ID,"BOOK"))ExitError(0);
if((input.vid_header.compression&1)==1)ExitError(1); // Compressed
lines=0;
while(lines<20 && !feof(ft))
  {
  fgets(line_buffer,80,ft);
  line_buffer[strlen(line_buffer)-1]=0;  // Drop new-line char
  line_buffer[19]=0;                      // Truncate to 19 characters
  strcpy(text_buffer[lines],line_buffer);// Store in text buffer
  lines++;
  }
fclose(ft);
frame_count=input.vid_header.frames;
fwrite(input.buffer,sizeof(vid_t),1,fo); // Write file header
SetVmode(0x13);
for(i=0;i<240;i++)  // Set palette to avoid alarming the user
  {
  int R=(int)input.vid_header.palette[i][0];
  int G=(int)input.vid_header.palette[i][1];
  int B=(int)input.vid_header.palette[i][2];
  WriteEntry(i+16,R,G,B);
  }
y_org=Y_ORG+120;
text_start=0;
text_end=1;
for(f_frame=0;f_frame<frame_count;f_frame++)
  {
  fread(image_buffer,IMAGE_SIZE,1,fi);  // Read image
  WriteBlock(FRAME_ORG,FRAME_SIZE,(char far *)image_buffer);
  for(i=text_start;i<text_end;i++)      // Overlay text on screen
    {
    DrawString(X_ORG+4,(i-text_start)*LINE_SP+y_org,
    text_buffer[i],text_color);
    }
  if(y_org>Y_ORG-10)y_org—;               // Calculate text boundarys
  else                                    // for next frame
    {
    y_org+=9;
    if(text_start<text_end)text_start++;
    }
  text_end=(Y_ORG+129-y_org)/10+text_start;
  if(text_end>lines)text_end=lines;
  i=0;
  for(y=Y_ORG;y<Y_ORG+120;y++)            // Copy image from screen
    {
    for(x=X_ORG;x<X_ORG+160;x++)
      {
      image_buffer[i++]=ReadPixel(x,y);
      }
```

```
        }
    fwrite(image_buffer,IMAGE_SIZE,1,fo); // Write image to file
    printf("Frame %d.%c",f_frame,0xD);
    }
SetVmode(3);
fclose(fi);
fclose(fo);
printf("\nDone.\n");
}
```

10

JPEG Image Compression Standard

JPEG stands for *Joint Photographic Experts Group*. The standard was designed specifically for compression and recovery of still photographic images. However, numerous applications have used the technique for motion video compression as well, because it provides a fairly good compression ratio with fairly high-quality image recovery, and requires less computing power than MPEG compression. JPEG compression is based on the *discrete cosine transform*, or *DCT*. There are two classes of JPEG compression referred to as *lossless* and *lossy*. The lossless version will not be covered here because it is generally useful only for still pictures. A subset of the full JPEG specification, called *baseline sequential DCT-based coding*, will be covered here because it is the least complicated and least computationally expensive method in the specification. Details of how the DCT works are covered in Chapter 5, which covers various compression techniques. For JPEG encoding, the input image pixel samples are grouped into 8×8 blocks. Each block is transformed by the forward DCT (FDCT) into a set of 64 values known as DCT coefficients. The 64 coefficients are then quantized, which essentially means reducing their accuracy by some degree, usually resulting in some of them being reduced to zero. The coefficients are prepared for entropy encoding by converting them into what is known as a *zig-zag* sequence. This effectively takes a two-dimensional array of samples and converts it to a one-dimensional array ordered as nearly as possible in ascending order of frequency components. The first coefficient in the zig-zag sequence is known as the *DC* coefficient while the remainder are all *AC* coefficients. For DC coefficients, the difference between the current value and the previous value is calculated for encoding. The zig-zag sequence is then *entropy* encoded using one of two possible encoding schemes: *Huffman encoding* or *arithmetic encoding*. If Huffman encoding is used, a Huffman table specification must be provided. If arithmetic encoding is used, an arithmetic conditioning table must be provided. Figure 10.1 is a simplified block diagram showing the various procedures involved in JPEG encoding.

Decoding is essentially the inverse of the encoding process. All the same processes are carried out, but in reverse order. The table specifications used in the encoding process are carried along with

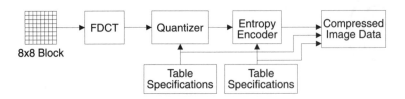

Figure 10.1   Sequence of JPEG encoding procedures.

the data stream after compression and used for decompression. The entropy decoder converts the compressed bit-stream into a new zig-zag table of DCT coefficients. These are then multiplied by dequantization coefficients and fed into the inverse DCT process (IDCT). The output of the process is a reconstructed 8×8 block of pixels. Of course, this 8×8 block of pixels may not precisely reproduce the original because some of the information was lost in the encoding process. This is why it is called lossy compression. Figure 10.2 is a simplified block diagram of the basic processes involved in JPEG decompression.

There are four different modes within which the JPEG compression and decompression process can operate: *sequential DCT-based*, *progressive DCT-based*, *lossless*, and *hierarchical*. As mentioned earlier, lossless encoding is not useful for motion video because it does not provide high enough compression ratios. Progressive DCT-based and hierarchical encoding are primarily used to provide rapid partial decoding of a compressed picture so that the general appearance of the picture can be determined before it is fully decoded. This also is not useful for motion video because motion video is constructed of a series of still pictures, each of which must be decoded and displayed at a very rapid pace. Of the two entropy encoding alternatives, arithmetic encoding is used only in extended DCT-based and lossless encoding processes. This discussion will only cover the baseline sequential process described in the JPEG specification, which uses Huffman coding. The baseline encoding process is defined for use with 8-bit samples although other processes can use 12-bit samples or up to 16 bits per sample. For encoding images that have multiple components, for example luminance and chrominance, the baseline process in sequential mode uses a noninterleaved format for the image components, that is, all of one component is processed first, then all of the next, and so forth, within what is called a *minimum coded unit (MCU)*. The JPEG specification provides a uniform structure and parameters for all classes and modes of encoding. Compressed image data is divided into sections that are identified by special 2-byte codes known as *markers*. Some of these are followed by special sequences such as table specifications and headers. Others mark the beginning and end of image data. Markers that identify blocks of parameters, together with those parameters, are referred to as *marker segments*. One special type of marker known as the *restart mark-*

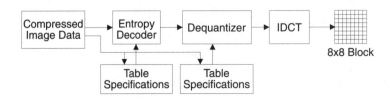

Figure 10.2   Sequence of JPEG decoding procedures.

$$\text{FDCT} \qquad S_{vu} = \frac{1}{4} C_U C_V \sum_{x=0}^{7} \sum_{y=0}^{7} S_{yx} \cos\left[\frac{(2x+1)u\pi}{16}\right] \cos\left[\frac{(2y+1)v\pi}{16}\right]$$

$$\text{IDCT} \qquad S_{yx} = \frac{1}{4} \sum_{U=0}^{7} \sum_{v=0}^{7} C_U C_V S_{vu} \cos\left[\frac{(2x+1)u\pi}{16}\right] \cos\left[\frac{(2y+1)v\pi}{16}\right]$$

Where:
C_U and $C_V = \frac{1}{\sqrt{2}}$ when $v,u = 0,0$ (DC component) .

C_U and $C_V = 1$ in all other cases.

S_{vu} = Target cell for DCT coefficient.

S_{yx} = Target cell for reconstructed pixel.

Figure 10.3 FDCT and IDCT equations.

er isolates blocks of entropy-coded data. These markers can be identified without decoding the compressed data, which allows isolation of corrupted data segments and random access in the entropy-encoded data. There are certain minimum requirements for entropy-coded segments and marker segments to ensure interchangeability of data from one application to the next. An abbreviated format is provided for table specification data that allows this information to be provided separately from the image data. For motion video applications, a common technique is to provide standardized quantization and Huffman tables that are used on all frames of the video sequence. This reduces the amount of data that has to be carried in the encoded bit-stream and also simplifies the decoding process, allowing a higher frame rate to be achieved. The mathematical definitions for the forward and inverse DCT processes are illustrated in Figure 10.3.

These are fairly formidable-looking equations, and in fact contain terms that cannot be computed with perfect accuracy in any real implementation. A more detailed explanation of how these equations operate is given in Chapter 5. Note that the *V* and the *U* used in these equations have no relationship to the V and the U in YUV color space. In this case they are simply an extra pair of two-dimensional index values, because *X* and *Y* are already used, and it is necessary to address each element in the 8×8 block for every DCT coefficient calculated. Figure 10.4 illustrates how quantization and dequantization is applied to the DCT coefficients.

$$\text{Quantization} \quad S_{qvu} = \text{round}\left(\frac{S_{vu}}{Q_{vu}}\right)$$

$$\text{Dequantization} \quad R_{vu} = S_{qvu} \times Q_{vu}$$

Where:
S_{vu} = DCT coefficient.

S_{qvu} = Quantized DCT coefficient.

Q_{vu} = Quantization coefficient.

R_{vu} = Dequantized DCT coefficient.

Figure 10.4 Quantization and dequantization equations.

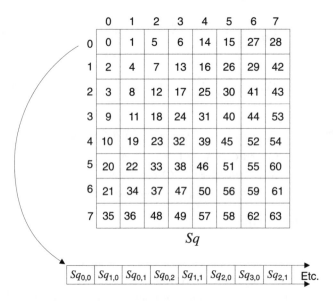

Figure 10.5 Order of DCT coefficients after zig-zag reordering.

The Q term in these equations is supplied by a quantization table defined later in this text. The so-called zig-zag sequence defines how the 8×8 two-dimensional block of DCT coefficients is unraveled to form a one-dimensional string of 64 DCT coefficients in quasi-ascending order in terms of frequency content. Figure 10.5 illustrates the order of the zig-zag sequence.

Compressed Data Formats

This section describes the various markers and parameters that make up the baseline DCT-based JPEG format using nondifferential Huffman coding. All markers are in the form of a 2-byte code: a 0xFF byte followed by a byte that is not equal to 0xFF or zero. Markers can be preceded by any number of fill bytes with a value of 0xFF. Table 10.1 summarizes the marker segments that will be discussed in the following paragraphs.

A marker segment is composed of a marker segment code followed by a number of parameters. The first parameter in a marker segment is a 2-byte value defining the length of the segment. This length value includes the length parameter but excludes the 2-byte marker. A marker segment identified by the *start of frame (SOF)* marker code is known as the *frame header*. Entropy-coded data segments contain the actual compressed image data for the picture. Each data segment is composed of an integer number of *bytes* regardless of whether the entropy coded bit-stream actually uses a number of *bits* that is an even multiple of eight. For Huffman coding, if the bit-stream does not fill out an even byte at the end, the last byte is padded with bits with a value of one. If a sequence of eight "one" bits occurs in a Huffman-encoded bit-stream, it is followed by a "zero" byte to disqualify it as a marker. The eight "one" bits are then decoded as part of the Huffman bit-stream, and the eight "zero" bits that follow are ignored. Figure 10.6 illustrates the compressed bit-stream data format for sequential DCT-based JPEG compressed images.

Table 10.1 Marker Segment Codes

0xFFC0	(SOF) Start of Frame Marker
0xFFC4	(DHT) Define Huffman Table
0xFFD0 to 0xFFD7	(RST) Restart Interval Termination
0xFFD8	(SOI) Start of Image
0xFFD9	(EOI) End of Image
0xFFDA	(SOS) Start of Scan
0xFFDB	(DQT) Define Quantization Table(s)
0xFFDC	(DNL) Define Number of Lines
0xFFDD	(DRI) Define Restart Interval
0xFFE0 to 0xFFEF	(APP) Application Segment Markers
0xFFFE	(COM) Start of Comment

It is important to note that the JPEG compression standard does not provide for any interframe coding. That is, each frame of a video sequence is a separate entity distinct from all the others. This means that the compression algorithm is not able to take advantage of any temporal correlation and, therefore, cannot achieve as high a compression rate as other standards that do. A single compressed frame begins with a *start of image (SOI)* marker and ends with an *end of image*

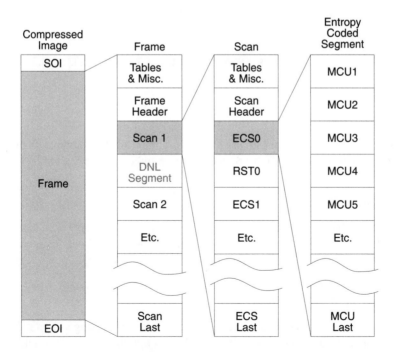

Figure 10.6 Compressed bit-stream data format for sequential DCT-based images.

(EOI) marker. The image data between is further subdivided into a number of logical segments. A frame begins with a frame header followed by a series of scans. A frame header may optionally be preceded by one or more table specification or miscellaneous marker segments. Recall that the table specifications define data tables of constants used in the DCT process and Huffman encoding. The formats of the various table specifications will be discussed in a later section. A *scan* contains one or more entropy-coded data segments each of which is comprised of one or more minimum coded units (MCU). The MCU is defined later. Excluding table specifications, each descending level of detail that makes up a single image will be discussed in the following paragraphs.

Frame Header

A frame header is made up of several fixed data fields of various sizes followed by one or more component specification parameter blocks. The fixed part of the frame header is composed of six fields. Each of these six fields is described in Table 10.2.

Start of Frame (SOF)

This marks the beginning of the frame header. The start of frame marker can take any one of several values to specify what type of coding is implemented in this particular frame. For purposes of this discussion, only the baseline DCT sequential encoding mode will be discussed, which uses an SOF marker value of 0xFFC0.

Frame Header Length (Lf)

This is a 16-bit number that indicates the length in bytes of the frame header, inclusive of the length field, but exclusive of the SOF marker.

Sample Precision (P)

This field specifies the number of bits used in each sample for the components that make up the frame. For baseline sequential DCT-based coding, this number is always eight.

Number of Lines (Y)

This field specifies the number of pixel rows that make up the component with the maximum number of vertical samples if subsampling is used. If subsampling is not used, this specifies the number of lines in each component. This field can have a value from zero to 65535.

Number of Samples per Line (X)

This defines the number of horizontal pixels in the image. If subsampling is used it defines the number of horizontal pixels in the component with the largest horizontal size. This field can have a value from 1 to 65535.

Number of Image Components in a Frame (Nf)

Typically this will be three. For a monochrome image, this would be one. The allowable range of values is 1 to 255. Table 10.2 summarizes the fields found at the beginning of a frame header.

Following the first six fields of the frame header is one or more frame component specification parameter blocks. Each block consists of four fields. There is one block for each image component defined in the frame (i.e., the Nf parameter specifies how many of these blocks will follow). The fields that make up the component specification parameter block are as follows:

Component Identifier (Ci)

This is used to assign a unique number to each image component and the sequence of components used in the frame. These numbers are used in scan headers to identify components used in the scan. A typical assignment of labels would be 0 for the first one, 1 for the second one, 2 for the third one, and so forth.

Horizontal Sampling Factor (Hi)

This defines the number of 8×8 blocks of the component that are used in each MCU horizontally.

Vertical Sampling Factor (Vi)

This defines the number of 8×8 blocks of the component that are used in each MCU vertically.

Quantization Table Selector (Tqi)

Up to four different quantization tables for use in dequantization of DCT coefficients can be defined for each image. This field selects which table is to be used. The table selection should not be changed until all scans containing the current component have been decoded.

Table 10.2 Fixed Header Fields

Parameter	Size (Bits)	Values	Description
SOF	16	0xFFC0	Start of Frame
Lf	16	3Nf+8	Frame Header Length
P	8	8	Sample Precision
Y	16	0–65535	Number of Lines
X	16	1–65535	Samples per Line
Nf	8	1–255	Number of Image Components

Table 10.3   Component Specification Header Fields

Parameter	Size (Bits)	Values	Description
C_i	8	0–255	Component Identifier
H_i	4	1–4	Horizontal Sampling Factor
V_i	4	1–4	Vertical Sampling Factor
Tq_i	8	0-3	Quantization Table Selector

Scan Header Syntax

Recall that a frame is made up of a frame header followed by one or more *scan blocks*. A scan block is made up of a *scan header* followed by one or more entropy-coded segments. Like the frame header, the scan header is made up of a mix of fixed and variable data fields. The first field is the *start of scan* marker that indicates the beginning of the scan header. The remaining fields are described in the following.

Scan Header Length (Ls)

Defines the length of the scan header including the length field but not including the start of scan marker.

Number of Image Components (Ns)

This field defines how many sets of scan component specification parameters are included in the scan header. Immediately following this field is a variable number of sets of scan component specification parameters. Each set consists of three elements as follows:

Scan Component Selector (Csj)   Recall that in the frame header there were a variable number of component definition parameter blocks. Each of those was assigned a unique identification number. This field in the scan header refers to one of those component identifiers from the frame header and must match at least one of them. Also, the ordering of components in the scan header must match the ordering of components in the frame header. If more than one component is included in the scan there is a restriction on the subsampling of the components: The sum of the products of the horizontal and vertical sampling factors for all the components within the scan cannot be greater than ten. For example, if three components are used and two of them are subsampled by a factor of two in both horizontal and vertical directions, the sum of the products is $1 \times 1 + 2 \times 2 + 2 \times 2$, which equals nine. If a sampling factor greater than two were used on either of the subsampled components, those components would have to be encoded in separate scan blocks.

DC Entropy Coding Table Selector (Tdj)   This selects one of the four possible DC entropy coding tables required to decode the DC coefficients for the component defined in the previous field. This refers to one of the tables defined in an earlier table specification marker segment.

AC Entropy Coding Table Selector (Taj) This field selects one of four possible AC entropy coding tables required for decoding the AC coefficients of the component defined for the scan. The AC entropy coding table must have been previously defined in a table definition marker segment. One set of the previous three fields must be present in the scan header for each component contained in the scan.

Start of Spectral Selection (Ss)

This field defines the first DCT coefficient in each block that is coded in the scan for sequential DCT processes. This field is set to zero for baseline sequential mode.

End of Spectral Selection (Se)

This field specifies the last DCT coefficient in each block to be coded in the scan. For baseline sequential DCT processing this field is set to 63 indicating the last DCT coefficient in the block.

Successive Approximation Bit Positions High and Low (Ah & Al)

These fields are set to zero for baseline sequential DCT processing. Table 10.4 summarizes the fields that make up the scan header and shows the appropriate range of values to be used in each field.

Quantization Table Specification Syntax

Quantization tables are defined in marker segments that begin with the *defined quantization table marker (DQT)* 0xFFDB. From one to four quantization tables can be defined within a single marker segment. A 16-bit field immediately following the table marker (Lq) defines the overall length of

Table 10.4 Scan Header Fields

Parameter	Size (Bits)	Values	Description
SOS	16	0xFFD8	Start of Scan
Ls	16	2Ns+6	Scan Header Length
Ns	8	1–4	Number of Image Components
Csj	8	0–255	Scan Component Selector
Tdj	4	0–1	DC Coding Table Selector
Taj	4	0–1	AC Coding Table Selector
Ss	8	0	Start of Spectral Selection
Se	8	63	End of Spectral Selection
Ah	4	0	Successive Approximation Bit High
Al	4	0	Successive Approximation Bit Low

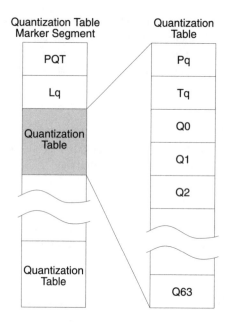

Figure 10.7 Organization of quantization table specification.

the specification table. Following this are one or more groups of fields each of which define one quantization table. Figure 10.7 illustrates the arrangement.

The first field in the quantization table (Pq) defines a precision of the quantization coefficients. If this field is zero, 8-bit quantization coefficients are used. If it is one, 16-bit quantization coefficients are used. For baseline sequential DCT mode, only 8-bit quantization coefficients are used. The next field (Tq) is the quantization table identifier, which assigns one of four possible quantization tables, into which the following data is to be loaded. The remainder of the table consists of the 64 quantization coefficients. Table 10.5 summarizes the fields included in a quantization table specification marker segment and the appropriate range of values for each field.

Table 10.5 Quantization Table Fields

Parameter	Size (Bits)	Values	Description
DQT	16	0xFFDB	Define Quantization Table Marker
Lq	16	$65n+2$ *	Quantization Table Length
Pq	4	0	Quantization Table Precision
Tq	4	0–3	Quantization Table Identifier
Qk	8	1–255	Quantization Table Element

*NOTE: n is the number of quantization tables defined.

Huffman Table Specification Syntax

This section describes how Huffman tables are defined within a *define Huffman table (DHT)* marker segment. Each marker segment can define from one to four Huffman tables. The segment begins with a 16-bit DHT marker (0xFFC4), which identifies the table, followed by a Huffman table length field (Lh), which defines the overall length of the segment. This is followed by one to four Huffman table definitions, each of which is made up of several fields. Figure 10.8 illustrates the arrangement.

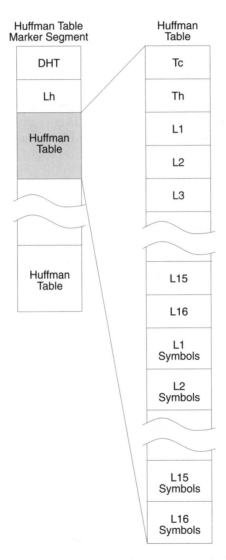

Figure 10.8   Organization of Huffman table marker segment data.

The fields that make up each Huffman table are as follows:

Table Class (Tc)

This defines whether the table is a DC table or an AC table. Zero indicates DC and one indicates AC.

Table Identifier (Th)

This is a value from zero to three that indicates which of the four possible Huffman tables the data following should be loaded into.

Huffman Code Counts (Li)

Each of the next sixteen fields specifies the number of Huffman codes for each of the sixteen possible lengths allowed by the JPEG specification. The first field specifies how many 1-bit codes there are; the second, how many 2-bit codes there are; the third, how many 3-bit codes there are; and so on.

Huffman Code Table (Vij)

Following the table of code length counts is the table of the actual values associated with each Huffman code. For example, if there are no 1-bit codes assigned but there are three 2-bit codes, then the first three values in this segment correspond to the three 2-bit codes. Table 10.6 summarizes the fields that make up the Huffman table specification marker segment and the appropriate values that can be assigned to each field.

Table 10.6   Huffman Table Fields

Parameter	Size (Bits)	Values	Description
DHT	16	0xFFC4	Define Huffman Table Marker
Lh	16	*	Huffman Table Definition Length
Tc	4	0,1	Table Class: 0=DC; 1=AC
Th	4	0,1	Huffman Table Identifier
Li	8	0–255	Huffman Code Length
Vij	8	0–255	Huffman Code Value

*NOTE: This value depends on the number of tables defined and the number of codes defined for each code length.

Restart Interval Definition Marker Syntax

Restart interval markers are used to break up the entropy encoded bit-stream into shorter segments to facilitate error recovery and improve reliability. The marker segment is made up of three fixed fields. The first is the *define restart interval marker (DRI)*, which has a value of 0xFFDD. The second field is the length of the marker segment (Lr), which always has a value of four. And the third is a 16-bit value (Ri), which defines the number of minimum coded units (MCU) in the interval; also referred to as an entropy-coded segment. The restart interval definition should not be confused with the restart marker itself, which has a value of 0xFFD0 through 0xFFD7 and is embedded in the encoded bit-stream. The restart interval simply defines how many MCUs are encoded before the next restart marker is inserted into the bit-stream. The least significant three bits of the restart marker code are cycled through a count from zero to seven to implement a sort of cyclic redundancy check to allow the decoder to periodically verify that it has not missed a restart marker. Table 10.7 summarizes the arrangement of the restart interval definition marker segment.

Application Data Segment

An *application data marker* (APP, 0xFFE0 to 0xFFEF) is included in the JPEG specification to allow application specific data to be embedded into the bit-stream of an encoded picture. The marker segment consists of three fields. The first is the application data marker, which identifies the segment; the second is the segment length (Lp), which specifies how many bytes of data are included in the segment. The third field is a variable-length field (Ap) containing the number of bytes specified in the length field. Table 10.8 summarizes how the fields are arranged for this segment and the appropriate values for each field.

Encoding Procedures

The following paragraphs describe in a top-down manner the procedures required for encoding a frame of video. The same procedure is repeated for each frame in the video sequence. The procedure is described using a successive refinement of flowcharts. The top-level flowchart, as shown in Figure 10.9, consists simply of writing a start of image and coding a frame and writing an end of image marker.

The frame and coding procedure consists of first writing any optional table data marker segments followed by a frame header and one or more scan segments. This is illustrated in Figure 10.10.

Table 10.7 Restart Marker Segment Fields

Parameter	Size (Bits)	Values	Description
DRI	16	0xFFDD	Define Reset Interval Marker
Lr	16	4	DRI Segment Length
Ri	16	0–65535	Number of MCU in Interval

Table 10.8 Application Data Table Fields

Parameter	Size (Bits)	Values	Description
APP	16	0xFFE0 to 0xFFEF	Application Information Marker
Lp	16	2–65535	APP Segment Length
Ap	8	0–255	Application Data Byte

A scan is made up of one row of minimum coded units (MCU). The MCUs that make up the scan can be subdivided into smaller groups known as *restart intervals*. A restart interval is made up of one or more MCUs. The restart interval can be defined in the miscellaneous optional table marker segments that occur before the frame header or before the scan header. If the scan is not subdivided into multiple reset intervals the entire scan is considered a single restart interval. In any case, the scan is always followed by a restart interval marker. The procedure for encoding a scan is shown in Figure 10.11.

Encoding a restart interval consists simply of encoding the number of MCUs defined in the restart interval. The diagram illustrating this is shown in Figure 10.12.

The significant element in the procedure is the fact that the encoder is reset. This means that during the decode procedure every time a restart interval is ended the decoder can also be reset, allowing recovery from any errors that may have been encountered during the decode of the previous restart interval. Encoding an MCU consists of encoding each of the 8×8 blocks of pixels that

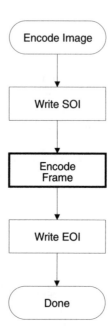

Figure 10.9 Image encoding procedure.

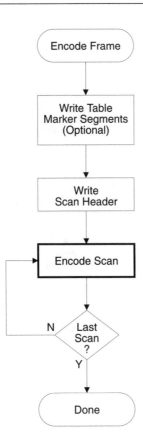

Figure 10.10 Frame encoding procedure.

make up the MCU in the sequence defined by the specification. The exact order of blocks to be processed in an MCU depends on the number of components in the image and the subsampling factors. In general, the blocks that make up an MCU are encoded from left to right, top to bottom. The blocks for the various image components, if there is more than one component in the image, are processed in the order defined in the frame header. For example, if an image is made up of three components, one luminance and two chrominance, and the chrominance components are subsampled by two in both horizontal and vertical directions, one MCU would consist of four blocks of luminance and one block from each of the chrominance components. Figure 10.13 illustrates this. The procedure for encoding an MCU is illustrated in Figure 10.14.

The procedure for coding a single 8×8 block of samples is the same for all components except that different quantization tables and Huffman encoding tables may be chosen for different components as defined in the frame header. The following steps are required: First, calculate the forward 8×8 discrete cosine transform for the block. Second, divide by the quantization table selected in the frame header. Third, calculate the difference between the current DC coefficient for the block and the previous DC coefficient. Fourth, encode the difference using the DC Huffman

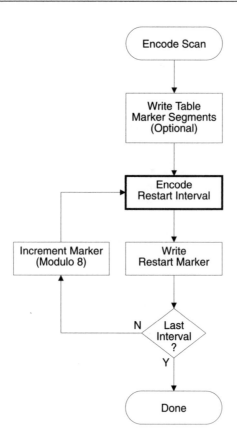

Figure 10.11   Procedure for encoding a single image scan.

table assigned in the scan header. Next, encode the AC coefficients from the 8×8 block in zig-zag order using the AC Huffman table assigned in the scan header. Because the mathematical formula for the discrete cosine transform is described in Chapter 5 along with the zig-zag sequence for the 8×8 pixel blocks, they will not be further discussed here. The theory and process for generating Huffman code tables is also described in Chapter 5. The JPEG specification describes a specific algorithm for generating Huffman code tables. This allows an optimum code table to be generated in order to maximize compression and image quality. While this feature has significant value for the encoding of still image pictures, it is less practical for encoding motion video sequences because of the large number of frames involved. The technique involves generating a histogram table showing the relative frequency of each possible value of the symbols within the image or images. The symbol values are then sorted according to probability. A symbol is actually a two-dimensional vector. One part is a value from the 8×8 table of frequency coefficients produced by the DCT. The other part is a run-length describing how many zeros precede the next nonzero value after reordering the 8×8 table of frequency coefficients into zig-zag order. It is clear then that the accumulation of statistics for generation of the Huffman tables requires the entire encode process up to, but not including, the Huffman encode. Because motion video involves a large number of separate images that

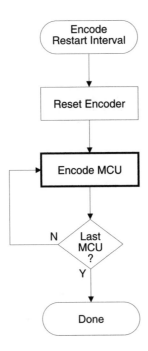

Figure 10.12 Procedure for encoding a restart interval.

may be considerably different from each other, the statistics generated from one image may not be optimum for another. Generating a new Huffman table for each frame would require a prohibitive amount of computing power. Generating statistics for the entire video sequence would not only require a great deal of computing power but also would make real-time encoding of a video stream impossible, because the entire stream would have to be processed *before* compression could be completed. The JPEG specification provides a set of Huffman encoding tables for luminance and chrominance based on a large statistical data set that is representative of typical video sequences. The programming examples provided with this book use the Huffman code tables provided by the JPEG specification. These tables are also included in the text for reference purposes.

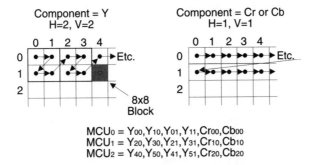

Figure 10.13 Ordering of image components in a minimum coded unit.

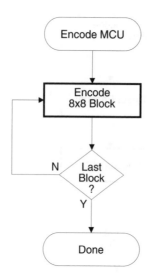

Figure 10.14 Procedure for encoding a minimum coded unit.

Magnitude Range Categories

Both AC and DC Huffman coding procedures use a signed magnitude range category scheme to encode the precise magnitudes of DCT coefficients using additional bits beyond the statistically generated Huffman codes. For DC coefficients the Huffman code represents a category for the difference between the current DC coefficient and the previous one for the same image component. For

Table 10.9 Predefined Magnitude Categories for AC and DC Coefficients

Category	Magnitude Range
0	0
1	−1, 1
2	−3, −2, 2, 3
3	−7... −4, 4... 7
4	−15... −8, 8... 15
5	−31... −16, 16... 31
6	−63... −32, 32... 63
7	−127... −64, 64... 127
8	−255... −128, 128... 255
9	−511... −256, 256... 511
A	−1023...−512, 512... 1023
B	−2047... −1024, 1024... 2047

AC coefficients the Huffman code represents a run-length/category pair for the current AC coefficient. In both cases, the Huffman code is followed by a variable number of bits that give the precise value for the coefficient within the selected category. Table 10.9 shows the range of values that can be represented by each category.

The number of bits defined by the selected category immediately follows the corresponding Huffman code in the bit-stream, most significant bit first. If the coefficient is a positive value, these bits directly reflect the corresponding number of low-order bits of the coefficient. If the coefficient is a negative value, these bits reflect the corresponding number of low-order bits of the coefficient minus one. For example, if the current DC coefficient minus the previous yields a value of -1, the corresponding Huffman code is "010," and the category is 1, for a 1-bit magnitude representation. Because the two's complement representation of -1 at 9-bit precision is 0x1FF, subtracting 1 gives 0x1FE. The low-order bit is then zero, giving a total sequence of "0100". If the value had been positive 1, the sequence would have been "0101".

Predefined Huffman Code Tables

A set of commonly used Huffman codes, determined through empirical testing and statistical analysis, is provided. These are not *recommended* as optimum for general use, but are adequate to get an initial application working. If the properties of the images to be encoded are known, it may be advantageous to create a new set of code tables optimized for the intended application.

AC Code Tables

The data in the Huffman tables shown here is organized into three columns. The first column is the run length and category. The first digit is a 4-bit value ranging from zero to 0xF that represents how many zero coefficients precede the encoded value in the zig-zag sequence. The second digit in the first column is a 4-bit value ranging from zero to 0xF that represents a category for the next nonzero value from the DCT block taken in zig-zag order. These two 4-bit values taken together form an 8-bit index to select a Huffman code from the table. There are two special cases for this 8-bit index: 0x00 indicates an end-of-block, meaning all remaining coefficients in the zig-zag sequence are zero. 0xF0 indicates a run of 15 zeros followed by another zero, for a total run of 16 zeros. None of the other symbols have zero in the lower 4 bits. The third column in the table is the code length that gives the number of bits in the corresponding Huffman code word. The last column is the actual code word. One complete table is provided for luminance coefficients and a second table for chrominance coefficients. The same chrominance table can be used for both Cr and Cb chrominance coefficients. These tables are shown sorted in the order of value and run length, not in the order they would occur in the Huffman table marker segment and the encoded bit-stream. The tables are used only for encoding AC coefficients. Tables 10.10 and 10.11 give the predefined Huffman codes provided in the JPEG specification for luminance and chrominance, respectively.

The AC and DC Huffman codes provided in these tables can be used in a real JPEG encode/decode application by placing them in the proper order in the required Huffman table marker segments. To do so the codes must be grouped by length. Table 10.12 gives the number of Huffman codes at each of the 16 possible lengths for AC and DC coefficients.

Table 10.10   Predefined Luminance AC Huffman Codes

Run/Cat.	Length	Code	
0x00	4	1010	(EOB)
0x01	2	00	
0x02	2	01	
0x03	3	100	
0x04	4	1011	
0x05	5	11010	
0x06	7	1111000	
0x07	8	11111000	
0x08	10	1111110110	
0x09	16	1111111110000010	
0x0A	16	1111111110000011	
0x11	4	1100	
0x12	5	11011	
0x13	7	1111001	
0x14	9	111110110	
0x15	11	11111110110	
0x16	16	1111111110000100	
0x17	16	1111111110000101	
0x18	16	1111111110000110	
0x19	16	1111111110000111	
0x1A	16	1111111110001000	
0x21	5	11100	
0x22	8	11111001	
0x23	10	1111110111	
0x24	12	111111110100	
0x25	16	1111111110001001	
0x26	16	1111111110001010	
0x27	16	1111111110001011	
0x28	16	1111111110001100	
0x29	16	1111111110001101	
0x2A	16	1111111110001110	
0x31	6	111010	
0x32	9	111110111	
0x33	12	111111110101	
0x34	16	1111111110001111	
0x35	16	1111111110010000	
0x36	16	1111111110010001	
0x37	16	1111111110010010	
0x38	16	1111111110010011	
0x39	16	1111111110010100	
0x3A	16	1111111110010101	
0x41	6	111011	
0x42	10	1111111000	
0x43	16	1111111110010110	
0x44	16	1111111110010111	

Run/Cat.	Length	Code
0x45	16	1111111110011000
0x46	16	1111111110011001
0x47	16	1111111110011010
0x48	16	1111111110011011
0x49	16	1111111110011100
0x4A	16	1111111110011101
0x51	7	1111010
0x52	11	11111110111
0x53	16	1111111110011110
0x54	16	1111111110011111
0x55	16	1111111110100000
0x56	16	1111111110100001
0x57	16	1111111110100010
0x58	16	1111111110100011
0x59	16	1111111110100100
0x5A	16	1111111110100101
0x61	7	1111011
0x62	12	111111110110
0x63	16	1111111110100110
0x64	16	1111111110100111
0x65	16	1111111110101000
0x66	16	1111111110101001
0x67	16	1111111110101010
0x68	16	1111111110101011
0x69	16	1111111110101100
0x6A	16	1111111110101101
0x71	8	11111010
0x72	12	111111110111
0x73	16	1111111110101110
0x74	16	1111111110101111
0x75	16	1111111110110000
0x76	16	1111111110110001
0x77	16	1111111110110010
0x78	16	1111111110110011
0x79	16	1111111110110100
0x7A	16	1111111110110101
0x81	9	111111000
0x82	15	111111111000000
0x83	16	1111111110110110
0x84	16	1111111110110111
0x85	16	1111111110111000
0x86	16	1111111110111001
0x87	16	1111111110111010
0x88	16	1111111110111011
0x89	16	1111111110111100
0x8A	16	1111111110111101
0x91	9	111111001

Table 10.10 *continued*

Run/Cat.	Length	Code
0x92	16	1111111110111110
0x93	16	1111111110111111
0x94	16	1111111111000000
0x95	16	1111111111000001
0x96	16	1111111111000010
0x97	16	1111111111000011
0x98	16	1111111111000100
0x99	16	1111111111000101
0x9A	16	1111111111000110
0xA1	9	111111010
0xA2	16	1111111111000111
0xA3	16	1111111111001000
0xA4	16	1111111111001001
0xA5	16	1111111111001010
0xA6	16	1111111111001011
0xA7	16	1111111111001100
0xA8	16	1111111111001101
0xA9	16	1111111111001110
0xAA	16	1111111111001111
0xB1	10	1111111001
0xB2	16	1111111111010000
0xB3	16	1111111111010001
0xB4	16	1111111111010010
0xB5	16	1111111111010011
0xB6	16	1111111111010100
0xB7	16	1111111111010101
0xB8	16	1111111111010110
0xB9	16	1111111111010111
0xBA	16	1111111111011000
0xC1	10	1111111010
0xC2	16	1111111111011001
0xC3	16	1111111111011010
0xC4	16	1111111111011011
0xC5	16	1111111111011100
0xC6	16	1111111111011101
0xC7	16	1111111111011110
0xC8	16	1111111111011111
0xC9	16	1111111111100000
0xCA	16	1111111111100001
0xD1	11	11111111000
0xD2	16	1111111111100010
0xD3	16	1111111111100011
0xD4	16	1111111111100100
0xD5	16	1111111111100101
0xD6	16	1111111111100110

Run/Cat.	Length	Code	
0xD7	16	1111111111100111	
0xD8	16	1111111111101000	
0xD9	16	1111111111101001	
0xDA	16	1111111111101010	
0xE1	16	1111111111101011	
0xE2	16	1111111111101100	
0xE3	16	1111111111101101	
0xE4	16	1111111111101110	
0xE5	16	1111111111101111	
0xE6	16	1111111111110000	
0xE7	16	1111111111110001	
0xE8	16	1111111111110010	
0xE9	16	1111111111110011	
0xEA	16	1111111111110100	
0xF0	11	11111111001	(ZRL)
0xF1	16	1111111111110101	
0xF2	16	1111111111110110	
0xF3	16	1111111111110111	
0xF4	16	1111111111111000	
0xF5	16	1111111111111001	
0xF6	16	1111111111111010	
0xF7	16	1111111111111011	
0xF8	16	1111111111111100	
0xF9	16	1111111111111101	
0xFA	16	1111111111111110	

Table 10.11   Predefined Chrominance AC Huffman Codes

Run/Cat.	Length	Code	
0x00	2	00	(EOB)
0x01	2	01	
0x02	3	100	
0x03	4	1010	
0x04	5	11000	
0x05	5	11001	
0x06	6	111000	
0x07	7	1111000	
0x08	9	111110100	
0x09	10	1111110110	
0x0A	12	111111110100	
0x11	4	1011	
0x12	6	111001	
0x13	8	11110110	
0x14	9	111110101	

Table 10.11 *continued*

Run/Cat.	Length	Code
0x15	11	11111110110
0x16	12	111111110101
0x17	16	1111111110001000
0x18	16	1111111110001001
0x19	16	1111111110001010
0x1A	16	1111111110001011
0x21	5	11010
0x22	8	11110111
0x23	10	1111110111
0x24	12	111111110110
0x25	15	111111111000010
0x26	16	1111111110001100
0x27	16	1111111110001101
0x28	16	1111111110001110
0x29	16	1111111110001111
0x2A	16	1111111110010000
0x31	5	11011
0x32	8	11111000
0x33	10	1111111000
0x34	12	111111110111
0x35	16	1111111110010001
0x36	16	1111111110010010
0x37	16	1111111110010011
0x38	16	1111111110010100
0x39	16	1111111110010101
0x3A	16	1111111110010110
0x41	6	111010
0x42	9	111110110
0x43	16	1111111110010111
0x44	16	1111111110011000
0x45	16	1111111110011001
0x46	16	1111111110011010
0x47	16	1111111110011011
0x48	16	1111111110011100
0x49	16	1111111110011101
0x4A	16	1111111110011110
0x51	6	111011
0x52	10	1111111001
0x53	16	1111111110011111
0x54	16	1111111110100000
0x55	16	1111111110100001
0x56	16	1111111110100010
0x57	16	1111111110100011
0x58	16	1111111110100100

Run/Cat.	Length	Code
0x59	16	1111111110100101
0x5A	16	1111111110100110
0x61	7	1111001
0x62	11	11111110111
0x63	16	1111111110100111
0x64	16	1111111110101000
0x65	16	1111111110101001
0x66	16	1111111110101010
0x67	16	1111111110101011
0x68	16	1111111110101100
0x69	16	1111111110101101
0x6A	16	1111111110101110
0x71	7	1111010
0x72	11	11111111000
0x73	16	1111111110101111
0x74	16	1111111110110000
0x75	16	1111111110110001
0x76	16	1111111110110010
0x77	16	1111111110110011
0x78	16	1111111110110100
0x79	16	1111111110110101
0x7A	16	1111111110110110
0x81	8	11111001
0x82	16	1111111110110111
0x83	16	1111111110111000
0x84	16	1111111110111001
0x85	16	1111111110111010
0x86	16	1111111110111011
0x87	16	1111111110111100
0x88	16	1111111110111101
0x89	16	1111111110111110
0x8A	16	1111111110111111
0x91	9	111110111
0x92	16	1111111111000000
0x93	16	1111111111000001
0x94	16	1111111111000010
0x95	16	1111111111000011
0x96	16	1111111111000100
0x97	16	1111111111000101
0x98	16	1111111111000110
0x99	16	1111111111000111
0x9A	16	1111111111001000
0xA1	9	111111000
0xA2	16	1111111111001001
0xA3	16	1111111111001010
0xA4	16	1111111111001011

Table 10.11   *continued*

Run/Cat.	Length	Code
0xA5	16	1111111111001100
0xA6	16	1111111111001101
0xA7	16	1111111111001110
0xA8	16	1111111111001111
0xA9	16	1111111111010000
0xAA	16	1111111111010001
0xB1	9	111111001
0xB2	16	1111111111010010
0xB3	16	1111111111010011
0xB4	16	1111111111010100
0xB5	16	1111111111010101
0xB6	16	1111111111010110
0xB7	16	1111111111010111
0xB8	16	1111111111011000
0xB9	16	1111111111011001
0xBA	16	1111111111011010
0xC1	9	111111010
0xC2	16	1111111111011011
0xC3	16	1111111111011100
0xC4	16	1111111111011101
0xC5	16	1111111111011110
0xC6	16	1111111111011111
0xC7	16	1111111111100000
0xC8	19	1111111111100001
0xC9	16	1111111111100010
0xCA	16	1111111111100011
0xD1	11	11111111001
0xD2	16	1111111111100100
0xD3	16	1111111111100101
0xD4	16	1111111111100110
0xD5	16	1111111111100111
0xD6	16	1111111111101000
0xD7	16	1111111111101001
0xD8	16	1111111111101010
0xD9	16	1111111111101011
0xDA	16	1111111111101100
0xE1	14	11111111100000
0xE2	16	1111111111101101
0xE3	16	1111111111101110
0xE4	16	1111111111101111
0xE5	16	1111111111110000
0xE6	16	1111111111110001
0xE7	16	1111111111110010
0xE8	16	1111111111110011

Run/Cat.	Length	Code	
0xE9	16	1111111111110100	
0xEA	16	1111111111110101	
0xF0	10	1111111010	(ZRL)
0xF1	15	111111111000011	
0xF2	16	1111111111110110	
0xF3	16	1111111111110111	
0xF4	16	1111111111111000	
0xF5	16	1111111111111001	
0xF6	16	1111111111111010	
0xF7	16	1111111111111011	
0xF8	16	1111111111111100	
0xF9	16	1111111111111101	
0xFA	16	1111111111111110	

Table 10.12 Predefined Length Counts for AC and DC Coefficients

Length	Luma Counts	Chroma Counts
1	0	0
2	2	2
3	1	1
4	3	2
5	3	4
6	2	4
7	4	3
8	3	4
9	5	7
10	5	5
11	4	4
12	4	4
13	0	0
14	0	1
15	1	2
16	125	119

Following the list of code lengths in the marker segment is a list of symbols in order of probability. This allows a one-to-one correspondence between each symbol and its assigned Huffman code. Table 10.13 shows the symbols defined above (from Tables 10.10 and 10.11) in the order they should appear in the table definition marker segment.

DC Code Tables

A separate set of tables is used for DC coefficients. The least significant 4 bits of the DC coefficient symbol are used to select a category. This category field defines a binary order of magnitude for the DC coefficient and selects a leading bit sequence for the corresponding Huffman code. Tables 10.14 and 10.15 give Huffman codes that can be used to encode DC luminance and chrominance values for JPEG encoding. These are not *recommended* as optimum for general use, but are adequate to get

Table 10.13   Probability Order of AC Symbols, Hexadecimal

Luminance AC Symbols

01	02	03	00	04	11	05	12	21	31	41	06	13	51	61	07
22	71	14	32	81	91	A1	08	23	42	B1	C1	15	52	D1	F0
24	33	62	72	82	09	0A	16	17	18	19	1A	25	26	27	28
29	2A	34	35	36	37	38	39	3A	43	44	45	46	47	48	49
4A	53	54	55	56	57	58	59	5A	63	64	65	66	67	68	69
6A	73	74	75	76	77	78	79	7A	83	84	85	86	87	88	89
8A	92	93	94	95	96	97	98	99	9A	A2	A3	A4	A5	A6	A7
A8	A9	AA	B2	B3	B4	B5	B6	B7	B8	B9	BA	C2	C3	C4	C5
C6	C7	C8	C9	CA	D2	D3	D4	D5	D6	D7	D8	D9	DA	E1	E2
E3	E4	E5	E8	E7	E8	E9	EA	F1	F2	F3	F4	F5	F8	F7	F8
F9	FA														

Chrominance AC Symbols

00	01	02	03	11	04	05	21	31	06	12	41	51	07	61	71
13	22	32	81	08	14	42	91	A1	B1	C1	09	23	33	52	F0
15	62	72	D1	0A	16	24	34	E1	25	F1	17	18	19	1A	26
27	28	29	2A	35	36	37	38	39	3A	43	44	45	46	47	48
49	4A	53	54	55	56	57	58	59	5A	63	64	65	66	67	68
69	6A	73	74	75	76	77	78	79	7A	82	83	84	85	86	87
88	89	8A	92	93	94	95	96	97	98	99	9A	A2	A3	A4	A5
A6	A7	A8	A9	AA	B2	B3	B4	B5	B6	B7	B8	B9	BA	C2	C3
C4	C5	C6	C7	C8	C9	CA	D2	D3	D4	D5	D6	D7	D8	D9	DA
E2	E3	E4	E5	E6	E7	E8	E9	EA	F2	F3	F4	F5	F6	F7	F8
F9	FA														

Table 10.14 Predefined Luminance DC Huffman Codes

Category	Code Length	Code
0	2	00
1	3	010
2	3	011
3	3	100
4	3	101
5	3	110
6	4	1110
7	5	11110
8	6	111110
9	7	1111110
A	8	11111110
B	9	111111110

an initial application working. If the properties of the images to be encoded are known it may be advantageous to create a new set of code tables optimized for the intended application.

The same method of appending a variable-length binary value to the Huffman code is used for DC symbols as for AC symbols. The difference is that for DC symbols the binary value represents the *difference* between the current DC coefficient and the previous one.

Table 10.15 Predefined Chrominance DC Huffman Codes

Category	Code Length	Code
0	2	00
1	2	01
2	2	10
3	3	110
4	4	1110
5	5	11110
6	6	111110
7	7	1111110
8	8	11111110
9	9	111111110
A	10	1111111110
B	11	11111111110

Predefined Quantization Tables

A set of quantization tables are provided for luminance and chrominance coefficients. These are not *recommended* as optimum for general use, but are adequate to get an initial application working. If the properties of the images to be encoded are known, it may be advantageous to create a new set of quantization tables optimized for the intended application. Table 10.16 shows luminance quantization coefficients, and Table 10.17 shows chrominance quantization coefficients.

JPEG Demonstration Software

A pair of sample programs named JPEG_CMP.EXE and JPEG_UNC.EXE are provided. These programs compress or decompress a video sequence using the baseline sequential DCT-based algorithm described in this chapter. This program does *not* capture a video sequence using one of the capture boards described in Chapter 7. It operates on a file created by one of the conversion utilities developed in Chapter 8. The speed of compression and decompression will depend on the complexity of the video images, the amount of motion, and the computing power of the host machine. No doubt much could be done to optimize the program code to improve speed, but rather than consume massive amounts of the publication schedule tweaking code, the endless process of optimization is

Table 10.16   Predefined Luminance Quantization Coefficients

16	11	10	16	24	40	51	61
12	12	14	19	26	58	60	55
14	13	16	24	40	57	69	56
14	17	22	29	81	87	80	62
18	22	37	56	68	109	103	77
24	35	55	64	81	104	113	92
49	64	78	87	103	121	120	101
72	92	95	98	112	100	103	99

Table 10.17   Predefined Chrominance Quantization Coefficients

17	18	24	47	99	99	99	99
18	21	26	66	99	99	99	99
24	26	56	99	99	99	99	99
47	66	99	99	99	99	99	99
99	99	99	99	99	99	99	99
99	99	99	99	99	99	99	99
99	99	99	99	99	99	99	99
99	99	99	99	99	99	99	99

left as an exercise for the reader. (I had to say that at least once, didn't I?) The main code segment for each program is relatively short, most of the work being done by subroutines. This tends to make the code less efficient but easier to read, which is the more important objective here. Each of the main program files is shown below, followed by a file named JPEG_SUB.CPP, which contains the subroutines used by both programs. An include file named JPEG_DEF.H is also shown.

Source File JPEG_CMP.CPP

```
//======================================================================
// JPEG_CMP.CPP JPEG compression utility
//—————————————————
// Program:  Implementation file for JPEG_CMP.EXE
// Author:   Phil Mattison
// Compiler: Borland Turbo C++ v1.01
//—————————————————

#include <stdlib.h>
#include <stdio.h>
#include <string.h>
#include <conio.h>
#include <dos.h>
#include <math.h>
#include "jpeg_def.h"

extern long PackBits(array_t *, BYTE *, long , int);
extern void CalculateFDCT(byte_block_t *, int_block_t *);
extern void Quantize(int_block_t *,int_block_t *,int);
extern void ZigZag(int_block_t *,int_block_t *,int);
extern long HuffEncode(int_block_t *, BYTE *, long, int);
extern long HuffDecode(BYTE *, int_block_t *, long, int);
extern int  Compare4C(char *, char *);
extern int  Saturate(int);


//—————————————————

void main(int argc, char* argv[])
  {
  FILE          *fi;          // File stream pointer
  FILE          *fo;          // File stream pointer
  int           blk_row;      // Block row counter
  int           blk,x,y;      // Block counter
  int           x_size,y_size; // Video frame size
  int           frame_count;  // Video frame count
  int           f_frame;      // Video frame counter
  long          src,idxY,idxCr,idxCb;  // Pixel buffer indices
  int           blk_len;      // Output block_length
  long          bit_count;    // Encoded bit count
  WORD          frame_size;   // Uncompressed frame size
  byte_block_t  pixels;       // 8x8 pixel block
  int_block_t   dct_data;     // 8x8 DCT data block
  int_block_t   zz_data;      // 8x8 zig-zag data block
```

```
array_t       output;          // Encoded block buffer
BYTE          *file_buffer;    // File input buffer pointer
BYTE          *Y_buffer;       // Y block row buffer pointer
BYTE          *Cr_buffer;      // Cr block row buffer pointer
BYTE          *Cb_buffer;      // Cb block row buffer pointer
vid_t         vid_header;      // File header structure
WORD          reset_marker=0xFFD0;

if(argc<3)
  {
  printf
  ("Please provide two file names: <input_file> <output_file>\n");
  exit(0);
  }
fi=fopen(argv[1],"rb");
fo=fopen(argv[2],"wb");
if(fi==NULL)
  {
  printf("Could not open input file %s.\n",argv[1]);
  exit(0);
  }
if(fo==NULL)
  {
  printf("Could not open output file %s.\n",argv[2]);
  exit(0);
  }
fread(&vid_header,sizeof(vid_t),1,fi);
if(!Compare4C(vid_header.file_ID,"BOOK"))
  {
  printf("ERROR - This is not a valid video file.\n");
  exit(0);
  }
if((vid_header.compression&4)!=4)
  {
  printf("ERROR - This file is not YCrCb format.\n");
  exit(0);
  }
if((vid_header.compression&1)!=0)
  {
  printf("ERROR - This file is already compressed.\n");
  exit(0);
  }

x_size=vid_header.x_size;
y_size=vid_header.y_size;
frame_size=x_size*y_size*2;
file_buffer=(BYTE *)malloc(frame_size);
Y_buffer=   (BYTE *)malloc(x_size*8);
Cr_buffer=  (BYTE *)malloc(x_size*4);
Cb_buffer=  (BYTE *)malloc(x_size*4);

if(file_buffer==NULL||Y_buffer==NULL||Cr_buffer==NULL||Cb_buffer==NULL)
  {
```

```
      printf("ERROR — Could not allocate sufficient buffer storage.\n");
      exit(0);
      }
frame_count=vid_header.frames; // Get frame count
vid_header.compression|=1;      // Set compression flag
vid_header.file_ID[0]='J';      // File type = JPEG
vid_header.file_ID[1]='P';
vid_header.file_ID[2]='E';
vid_header.file_ID[3]='G';
fwrite(&vid_header,sizeof(vid_t),1,fo);
for(f_frame=0;f_frame<frame_count;f_frame++)
  {
  fread(file_buffer,frame_size,1,fi);          // Read image
  src=0L;
  bit_count=0L;
  for(blk_row=0;blk_row<y_size/8;blk_row++)
    {
    idxY=idxCr=idxCb=0;
    while(idxY<x_size*8)
      {
      Y_buffer[idxY++]= file_buffer[src]; file_buffer[src++]=0;
      Cr_buffer[idxCr++]=file_buffer[src]; file_buffer[src++]=0;
      Y_buffer[idxY++]= file_buffer[src]; file_buffer[src++]=0;
      Cb_buffer[idxCb++]=file_buffer[src]; file_buffer[src++]=0;
      }
    for(blk=0;blk<x_size/8;blk++)  // Process Y pixels
      {
      for(y=0;y<8;y++)
        {
        for(x=0;x<8;x++)
          {
          pixels.block[y][x]=Y_buffer[blk*8+x_size*y+x];
          }
        }
      CalculateFDCT(&pixels, &dct_data);
      Quantize(&dct_data,&dct_data,LUMA);
      ZigZag(&dct_data,&zz_data,FORWARD);
      bit_count=HuffEncode(&zz_data,file_buffer,bit_count,LUMA);
      }
    for(blk=0;blk<x_size/16;blk++)  // Process Cr pixels
      {
      for(y=0;y<8;y++)
        {
        for(x=0;x<8;x++)
          {
          pixels.block[y][x]=Cr_buffer[blk*8+x_size/2*y+x];
          }
        }
      CalculateFDCT(&pixels, &dct_data);
      Quantize(&dct_data,&dct_data,CHROMA);
      ZigZag(&dct_data,&zz_data,FORWARD);
      bit_count=HuffEncode(&zz_data,file_buffer,bit_count,CHROMA);
      }
```

```
        for(blk=0;blk<x_size/16;blk++)   // Process Cb pixels
          {
          for(y=0;y<8;y++)
            {
            for(x=0;x<8;x++)
              {
              pixels.block[y][x]=Cb_buffer[blk*8+x_size/2*y+x];
              }
            }
          CalculateFDCT(&pixels, &dct_data);
          Quantize(&dct_data,&dct_data,CHROMA);
          ZigZag(&dct_data,&zz_data,FORWARD);
          bit_count=HuffEncode(&zz_data,file_buffer,bit_count,CHROMA);
          }
        }
      blk_len=1+(int)(bit_count/8L);
      fwrite(&reset_marker,sizeof(int),1,fo);
      fwrite(&blk_len,sizeof(int),1,fo);
      fwrite(file_buffer,blk_len,1,fo);
      printf("Frame %d.%c",f_frame,0xD);
      }
  fclose(fi);
  fclose(fo);
  printf("\nDone.\n");
  }
```

Source File JPEG_UNC.CPP

```
//==========================================================
// JPEG_UNC.CPP JPEG decompression utility
//--------------------------------------------------------
// Program:  Implementation file for JPEG_UNC.EXE
// Author:   Phil Mattison
// Compiler: Borland Turbo C++ v1.01
//--------------------------------------------------------

#include <stdlib.h>
#include <stdio.h>
#include <string.h>
#include <conio.h>
#include <dos.h>
#include <math.h>
#include "jpeg_def.h"

extern void Filter(byte_block_t *, byte_block_t *);
extern void CalculateIDCT(int_block_t *, byte_block_t *);
extern void Dequantize(int_block_t *,int_block_t *,int);
extern void ZigZag(int_block_t *,int_block_t *,int);
extern long HuffDecode(BYTE *, int_block_t *, long, int);
extern int  Compare4C(char *, char *);
extern int  Saturate(int);
```

```
//————————————————————
void main(int argc, char* argv[])
  {
  FILE       *fi;               // File stream pointer
  FILE       *fo;               // File stream pointer
  int        blk_row;           // Block row counter
  int        blk,x,y;           // Block counter
  long       bit_count;         // Bit counter
  int        blk_len;           // Compressed frame block length
  int        x_size,y_size;     // Video frame size
  int        frame_count;       // Video frame count
  int        f_frame;           // Video frame counter
  long       dst,idxY,idxCr,idxCb; // Pixel buffer indices
  WORD       frame_size;        // Uncompressed frame size
  byte_block_t pixels;          // 8x8 pixel block
  int_block_t  dct_data;        // 8x8 DCT data block
  int_block_t  zz_data;         // 8x8 DCT data block
  BYTE       *input;            // File input buffer pointer
  BYTE       *file_buffer;      // File output buffer pointer
  BYTE       *Y_buffer;         // Y block row buffer pointer
  BYTE       *Cr_buffer;        // Cr block row buffer pointer
  BYTE       *Cb_buffer;        // Cb block row buffer pointer
  vid_t      vid_header;        // File header structure

  if(argc<3)
    {
    printf
    ("Please provide two file names: <input_file> <output_file>\n");
    exit(0);
    }
  fi=fopen(argv[1],"rb");
  fo=fopen(argv[2],"wb");
  if(fi==NULL)
    {
    printf("Could not open input file %s.\n",argv[1]);
    exit(0);
    }
  if(fo==NULL)
    {
    printf("Could not open output file %s.\n",argv[2]);
    exit(0);
    }
  fread(&vid_header,sizeof(vid_t),1,fi);
  if(!Compare4C(vid_header.file_ID,"JPEG"))
    {
    printf("ERROR — This is not a valid video file.\n");
    exit(0);
    }
  if((vid_header.compression&4)!=4)
    {
    printf("ERROR — This file is not YCrCb format.\n");
    exit(0);
    }
```

```
if((vid_header.compression&1)!=1)
  {
  printf("ERROR - This file is already uncompressed.\n");
  exit(0);
  }
x_size=vid_header.x_size;
y_size=vid_header.y_size;
frame_size=x_size*y_size*2;
file_buffer=(BYTE *)malloc(frame_size);
input=      (BYTE *)malloc(frame_size/4);
Y_buffer=   (BYTE *)malloc(x_size*8);
Cr_buffer=  (BYTE *)malloc(x_size*4);
Cb_buffer=  (BYTE *)malloc(x_size*4);

if(input==NULL||file_buffer==NULL||
  Y_buffer==NULL||Cr_buffer==NULL||Cb_buffer==NULL)
  {
  printf("ERROR - Could not allocate sufficient buffer storage.\n");
  exit(0);
  }
frame_count=vid_header.frames;  // Get frame count
vid_header.compression&=6;      // Clear compression bit
vid_header.file_ID[0]='B';      // Reset file type to normal
vid_header.file_ID[1]='O';
vid_header.file_ID[2]='O';
vid_header.file_ID[3]='K';
fwrite(&vid_header,sizeof(vid_t),1,fo);

for(f_frame=0;f_frame<frame_count;f_frame++)
  {
  dst=0L;
  bit_count=0L;
  fread(&blk_len,sizeof(int),1,fi);
  if(blk_len!=0xFFD0)
    {
    printf("ERROR - Lost sync.\n");
    fclose(fi);
    fclose(fo);
    exit(0);
    }
  fread(&blk_len,sizeof(int),1,fi);    // Get block length
  fread(input,blk_len,1,fi);           // Get block
  for(blk_row=0;blk_row<y_size/8;blk_row++)
    {
    for(blk=0;blk<x_size/8;blk++)      // Process Y pixels
      {
      bit_count=HuffDecode(input,&zz_data,bit_count,LUMA);
      ZigZag(&zz_data,&dct_data,INVERSE);
      Dequantize(&dct_data,&dct_data,LUMA);
      CalculateIDCT(&dct_data,&pixels);
      Filter(&pixels,&pixels);
      for(y=0;y<8;y++)
        {
```

```
                  for(x=0;x<8;x++)
                    {
                    Y_buffer[blk*8+x_size*y+x]=pixels.block[y][x];
                    }
                  }
                }
          for(blk=0;blk<x_size/16;blk++)    // Process Cr pixels
            {
            bit_count=HuffDecode(input,&zz_data,bit_count,CHROMA);
            ZigZag(&zz_data,&dct_data,INVERSE);
            Dequantize(&dct_data,&dct_data,CHROMA);
            CalculateIDCT(&dct_data,&pixels);
            Filter(&pixels,&pixels);
            for(y=0;y<8;y++)
              {
              for(x=0;x<8;x++)
                {
                Cr_buffer[blk*8+x_size/2*y+x]=pixels.block[y][x];
                }
              }
            }
          for(blk=0;blk<x_size/16;blk++)    // Process Cb pixels
            {
            bit_count=HuffDecode(input,&zz_data,bit_count,CHROMA);
            ZigZag(&zz_data,&dct_data,INVERSE);
            Dequantize(&dct_data,&dct_data,CHROMA);
            CalculateIDCT(&dct_data,&pixels);
            Filter(&pixels,&pixels);
            for(y=0;y<8;y++)
              {
              for(x=0;x<8;x++)
                {
                Cb_buffer[blk*8+x_size/2*y+x]=pixels.block[y][x];
                }
              }
            }
        idxY=idxCr=idxCb=0;
        while(idxY<x_size*8)
          {
          file_buffer[dst++]=Y_buffer[idxY++];
          file_buffer[dst++]=Cr_buffer[idxCr++];
          file_buffer[dst++]=Y_buffer[idxY++];
          file_buffer[dst++]=Cb_buffer[idxCb++];
          }
      }
    fwrite(file_buffer,frame_size,1,fo);
    printf("Frame %d.%c",f_frame,0xD);
    }
  fclose(fi);
  fclose(fo);
  printf("\nDone.\n");
  }
```

Source File JPEG_SUB.CPP

```
//============================================================
// JPEG_SUB.CPP   JPEG compression utility subroutines
//------------------------------------------------------------
// Program:  Implementation file for JPEG_CMP.EXE & JPEG_UNC.EXE
// Author:   Phil Mattison
// Compiler: Borland Turbo C++ v1.01
//------------------------------------------------------------
#include <math.h>
#include "jpeg_def.h"


//------------------------------------------------------------
// Compare a pair of 4-char tags
//------------------------------------------------------------
int Compare4C(char *s1, char *s2)        // Compare a pair of 4-char tags
  {
  if(s1[0]==s2[0] &&
  s1[1]==s2[1] &&
  s1[2]==s2[2] &&
  s1[3]==s2[3])return(1);
  return(0);
  }


//------------------------------------------------------------
// Ensure number is >=0 and <=255
//------------------------------------------------------------
int Saturate(int n)
  {
  if(n>255)return(255);
  if(n<0)return(0);
  return(n);
  }


//------------------------------------------------------------
// Return a magnitude category according to JPEG specification
//------------------------------------------------------------
int GetCategory(int n)
  {
  int x=(n>0)?n:-n;      // Get absolute value
  int cat=11;            // Start with max. length
  int bit=0x400;         // Set mask bit for 1024+
  if(x==0)return(0);     // 0 is category 0
  while((x&bit)==0)      // Find high-order bit position
    {
    cat-;
    bit=bit>1;
    }
  return(cat);
  }


//------------------------------------------------------------
// Calculate a forward DCT on an 8x8 block of pixels
```

```
//─────────────────────────────
void CalculateFDCT(byte_block_t *input, int_block_t *output)
  {
  int  x,y,index,coeff; // General index
  long tmp1[8][8];       // Intermediate block buffer
  long tmp2[8][8];       // Intermediate block buffer
  long dct_coeff[8][8]=
    {
    +1448L,+1448L,+1448L,+1448L,+1448L,+1448L,+1448L,+1448L,
    +2008L,+1702L,+1137L, +399L, -399L,-1137L,-1702L,-2008L,
    +1892L, +783L, -783L,-1892L,-1892L, -783L, +783L,+1892L,
    +1702L, -399L,-2008L,-1137L,+1137L,+2008L, +399L,-1702L,
    +1448L,-1448L,-1448L,+1448L,+1448L,-1448L,-1448L,+1448L,
    +1137L,-2008L, +399L,+1702L,-1702L, -399L,+2008L,-1137L,
     +783L,-1892L,+1892L, -783L, -783L,+1892L,-1892L, +783L,
     +399L,-1137L,+1702L,-2008L,+2008L,-1702L,+1137L, -399L
    };

  for(y=0;y<8;y++)          // Convert block to long
    {
    for(x=0;x<8;x++)
      {
      tmp2[x][y]=(long)input->block[x][y];
      }
    }
  for(y=0;y<8;y++)          // Do 1-dimensional row FDCTs
    {
    for(coeff=0;coeff<8;coeff++)
      {
      tmp1[y][coeff]=0L;
      for(x=0;x<8;x++)
        {
        tmp1[y][coeff]+=
        dct_coeff[coeff][x]*(long)tmp2[y][x];
        }
      tmp1[y][coeff]=tmp1[y][coeff]>11;
      }
    }
  for(x=0;x<8;x++)          // Do 1-dimensional column FDCTs
    {
    for(coeff=0;coeff<8;coeff++)
      {
      tmp2[coeff][x]=0L;
      for(index=0;index<8;index++)
        {
        tmp2[coeff][x]+=
        tmp1[index][x]*dct_coeff[coeff][index];
        }
      output->block[coeff][x]=(int)(tmp2[coeff][x]>11);
      }
    }
  }
```

```
//————————————————————
// Calculate an inverse DCT on an 8x8 block of pixels
//————————————————————
void CalculateIDCT(int_block_t *input, byte_block_t *output)
  {
  int  x,y,index,coeff;  // General index
  long tmp1[8][8];        // Intermediate block buffer
  long tmp2[8][8];        // Intermediate block buffer
  int  tmp3;              // Intermediate buffer
  long dct_coeff[8][8]=
    {
    +1448L,+1448L,+1448L,+1448L,+1448L,+1448L,+1448L,+1448L,
    +2008L,+1702L,+1137L, +399L, -399L,-1137L,-1702L,-2008L,
    +1892L, +783L, -783L,-1892L,-1892L, -783L, +783L,+1892L,
    +1702L, -399L,-2008L,-1137L,+1137L,+2008L, +399L,-1702L,
    +1448L,-1448L,-1448L,+1448L,+1448L,-1448L,-1448L,+1448L,
    +1137L,-2008L, +399L,+1702L,-1702L, -399L,+2008L,-1137L,
     +783L,-1892L,+1892L, -783L, -783L,+1892L,-1892L, +783L,
     +399L,-1137L,+1702L,-2008L,+2008L,-1702L,+1137L, -399L
    };

  for(y=0;y<8;y++)       // Convert block to long
    {
    for(x=0;x<8;x++)
      {
      tmp2[x][y]=(long)input->block[x][y];
      }
    }
  for(x=0;x<8;x++)       // Do 1-dimensional column IDCT
    {
    for(coeff=0;coeff<8;coeff++)
      {
      tmp1[coeff][x]=0L;
      for(index=0;index<8;index++)
        {
        tmp1[coeff][x]+=
        tmp2[index][x]*dct_coeff[index][coeff];
        }
      tmp1[coeff][x]=tmp1[coeff][x]>11;
      }
    }
  for(y=0;y<8;y++)       // Do 1-dimensional row IDCT
    {
    for(coeff=0;coeff<8;coeff++)
      {
      tmp2[y][coeff]=0L;
      for(index=0;index<8;index++)
        {
        tmp2[y][coeff]+=
        tmp1[y][index]*dct_coeff[index][coeff];
        }
      tmp3=(int)(tmp2[y][coeff]>15);
      tmp3=(tmp3>255)?255:tmp3;
```

```
          tmp3=(tmp3<0)   ?0   :tmp3;
          output->block[y][coeff]=(BYTE)tmp3;
          }
      }
   }


//————————————————————
// Reorder a block of DCT coefficients by frequency content
//————————————————————
void ZigZag(int_block_t *input, int_block_t *output, int flag)
  {
  int index;
  int translate[64]=
    {
     0, 1, 8,16, 9, 2, 3,10,
    17,24,32,25,18,11, 4, 5,
    12,19,26,33,40,48,41,34,
    27,20,13, 6, 7,14,21,28,
    35,42,49,56,57,50,43,36,
    29,22,15,23,30,37,44,51,
    58,59,52,45,38,31,39,46,
    53,60,61,54,47,62,55,63
    };
  if(flag==FORWARD)         // Reorder normal -> zig-zag
    {
    for(index=0;index<64;index++)
      {
      output->linear[index]=input->linear[translate[index]];
      }
    }
  if(flag==INVERSE)         // Reorder zig-zag -> normal
    {
    for(index=0;index<64;index++)
      {
      output->linear[translate[index]]=input->linear[index];
      }
    }
  }


//————————————————————
// Divide a block of DCT coefficients by quantization factors
//————————————————————
void Quantize(int_block_t *input, int_block_t *output, int flag)
  {
  int index;
  BYTE luma_quantizer[64]=
  {
  16, 11, 10, 16, 24, 40,  51,  61,
  12, 12, 14, 19, 26, 58,  60,  55,
  14, 13, 16, 24, 40, 57,  69,  56,
  14, 17, 22, 29, 81, 87,  80,  62,
  18, 22, 37, 56, 68, 109, 103, 77,
  24, 35, 55, 64, 81, 104, 113, 92,
```

```
49, 64, 78, 87, 103, 121, 120, 101,
72, 92, 95, 98, 112, 100, 103, 99
};

BYTE chroma_quantizer[64]=
{
17, 18, 24, 47, 99, 99, 99, 99,
18, 21, 26, 66, 99, 99, 99, 99,
24, 26, 56, 99, 99, 99, 99, 99,
47, 66, 99, 99, 99, 99, 99, 99,
99, 99, 99, 99, 99, 99, 99, 99,
99, 99, 99, 99, 99, 99, 99, 99,
99, 99, 99, 99, 99, 99, 99, 99,
99, 99, 99, 99, 99, 99, 99, 99
};

if(flag==LUMA)          // Use luminance factors
  {
  for(index=0;index<64;index++)
    {
    output->linear[index]=input->linear[index]/luma_quantizer[index];
    }
  }
if(flag==CHROMA)              // Use chrominance factors
  {
  for(index=0;index<64;index++)
    {
    output->linear[index]=
    input->linear[index]/chroma_quantizer[index];
    }
  }
}

//————————————————————————
// Multiply a block of DCT coefficients by quantization factors
//————————————————————————
void Dequantize(int_block_t *input, int_block_t *output, int flag)
  {
  int index;
  BYTE luma_quantizer[64]=
  {
  16, 11, 10, 16, 24,  40,  51,  61,
  12, 12, 14, 19, 26,  58,  60,  55,
  14, 13, 16, 24, 40,  57,  69,  56,
  14, 17, 22, 29, 81,  87,  80,  62,
  18, 22, 37, 56, 68,  109, 103, 77,
  24, 35, 55, 64, 81,  104, 113, 92,
  49, 64, 78, 87, 103, 121, 120, 101,
  72, 92, 95, 98, 112, 100, 103, 99
  };

  BYTE chroma_quantizer[64]=
  {
```

```
  17, 18, 24, 47, 99, 99, 99, 99,
  18, 21, 26, 66, 99, 99, 99, 99,
  24, 26, 56, 99, 99, 99, 99, 99,
  47, 66, 99, 99, 99, 99, 99, 99,
  99, 99, 99, 99, 99, 99, 99, 99,
  99, 99, 99, 99, 99, 99, 99, 99,
  99, 99, 99, 99, 99, 99, 99, 99,
  99, 99, 99, 99, 99, 99, 99, 99
  };

  if(flag==LUMA)          // Use luminance factors
    {
    for(index=0;index<64;index++)
      {
      output->linear[index]=input->linear[index]*luma_quantizer[index];
      }
    }
  if(flag==CHROMA)        // Use chrominance factors
    {
    for(index=0;index<64;index++)
      {
      output->linear[index]=
      input->linear[index]*chroma_quantizer[index];
      }
    }
  }


//————————————————————————
// Store a variable-length Huffman code or magnitude in a buffer
//————————————————————————
long PackBits(WORD symbol, int length, BYTE *output, long bit_count)
  {
  long   output_index=bit_count/8L;       // Find buffer index
  int    bits_used=(int)(bit_count-8L*output_index);
  int    bits_remaining=8-bits_used;      // Available bits in this byte
  int    upper_bits;                      // # bits in upper byte
  int    lower_bits;                      // # bits in lower byte
  BYTE   upper_byte;                      // Data for upper byte
  BYTE   lower_byte;                      // Data for lower byte

  upper_byte=(BYTE)(symbol>8);
  lower_byte=(BYTE)(symbol&0xFF);
  lower_bits=0;
  upper_bits=length;
  if(upper_bits>8)
    {
    lower_bits=upper_bits-8;
    upper_bits=8;
    }
  *(output+output_index)|=(upper_byte>bits_used); // Store upper bits
  bits_used+=upper_bits;
  bit_count+=(long)upper_bits;
  if(bits_used>=8)
```

```
      {
      bits_used-=8;
      output_index++;
      *(output+output_index)|=(upper_byte<<bits_remaining);
      bits_remaining=8-bits_used;
      }
    if(lower_bits>0)                                    // Store lower bits
      {
      *(output+output_index)|=(lower_byte>bits_used);
      bit_count+=(long)lower_bits;
      bits_used+=lower_bits;
      if(bits_used>=8)
        {
        bits_used-=8;
        output_index++;
        *(output+output_index)|=(lower_byte<<bits_remaining);
        bits_remaining=8-bits_used;
        }
      }
    return(bit_count);
    }

//——————————————————————————
// Extract a variable-length DC Huffman symbol from a buffer
//——————————————————————————
int UnpackHuffBitsDC(BYTE *input, long *bit_count, int flag)
  {
  int  luma_DC_list[17]={0,0,0,1,6,7,8,9,10,11,0,0,0,0,0,0,0};
  int  luma_DC_cnt[17]={0,0,1,5,1,1,1,1,1,1,-1,0,0,0,0,0,0};
  WORD luma_DC_code[12]=
    {
    0x0000,0x4000,0x6000,0x8000,0xA000,0xC000,
    0xE000,0xF000,0xF800,0xFC00,0xFE00,0xFF00
    };
  int  chroma_DC_list[17]={0,0,0,3,4,5,6,7,8,9,10,11,0,0,0,0,0};
  int  chroma_DC_cnt[17]={0,0,3,1,1,1,1,1,1,1,1,1,-1,0,0,0,0};
  WORD chroma_DC_code[12]=
    {
    0x0000,0x4000,0x8000,0xC000,0xE000,0xF000,
    0xF800,0xFC00,0xFE00,0xFF00,0xFF80,0xFFC0
    };

  long  input_index=*bit_count/8L;         // Find buffer index
  int   bits_used=(int)(*bit_count-8L*input_index);
  BYTE  input_mask=0x80>bits_used;         // Set input bit position
  WORD  output_mask=0x8000;                // Set output bit position
  WORD  output_code=0;                     // Clear output buffer
  //—- We know no DC symbol is less than 2 bits, so get the first 2
  int   index,count,symbol;                // General purpose variables
  int   match=0;                           // Match flag
  int   length=2;                          // Initial length of symbol

  BYTE  input_data=*(input+input_index);
```

```
for(int i=0;i<2;i++)
  {
  if((input_data&input_mask)!=0)output_code|=output_mask;
  bits_used++;
  if(bits_used==8)
    {
    bits_used-=8;
    input_index++;
    input_data=*(input+input_index);
    input_mask=0x80;
    }
  else input_mask=input_mask>1;
  output_mask=output_mask>1;
  }
*bit_count+=2L;
if(flag==LUMA)           // Extract a luminance symbol
  {
  while(match==0)
    {
    index=luma_DC_list[length];
    count=luma_DC_cnt[length];
    if(count<0)
      {
      match=-1;          // Error: no match found
      }
    else
      {
      while(count>0) // See if any patterns of this length match
        {
        if(output_code==luma_DC_code[index])
          {
          match=1;
          symbol=index;
          }
        index++;
        count-;
        }
      }
    if(match==0)    // No match was found, get another bit
      {
      if((input_data&input_mask)!=0)output_code|=output_mask;
      length++;
      bits_used++;
      *bit_count+=1L;
      if(bits_used==8)
        {
        bits_used-=8;
        input_index++;
        input_data=*(input+input_index);
        input_mask=0x80;
        }
      else input_mask=input_mask>1;
      output_mask=output_mask>1;
```

```
          }
        }
      }
  if(flag==CHROMA)              // Extract a chrominance symbol
    {
    while(match==0)
      {
      index=chroma_DC_list[length];
      count=chroma_DC_cnt[length];
      if(count<0)
        {
        match=-1;             // Error: no match found
        }
      else
        {
        while(count>0)
          {
          if(output_code==chroma_DC_code[index])
            {
            match=1;
            symbol=index;
            }
          index++;
          count--;
          }
        }
      if(match==0)             // No match was found, get another bit
        {
        if((input_data&input_mask)!=0)output_code|=output_mask;
        length++;
        bits_used++;
        *bit_count+=1L;
        if(bits_used==8)
          {
          bits_used-=8;
          input_index++;
          input_data=*(input+input_index);
          input_mask=0x80;
          }
        else input_mask=input_mask>1;
        output_mask=output_mask>1;
        }
      }
    }
  return(symbol);
  }


//------------------------------
// Extract a variable-length AC Huffman symbol from a buffer
//------------------------------
WORD UnpackHuffBitsAC(BYTE *input, long *bit_count, int flag)
  {
  int luma_AC_list[17]={0,0,0,2,3,6,9,11,15,18,23,28,32,0,0,36,37};
```

```
int luma_AC_cnt[17]={0,0,2,1,3,3,2,4,3,5,5,4,4,0,0,1,125};
int luma_AC_code[162]=
  {
  0x0000,0x4000,0x8000,0xa000,0xb000,0xc000,0xd000,0xd800,0xe000,
  0xe800,0xec00,0xf000,0xf200,0xf400,0xf600,0xf800,0xf900,0xfa00,
  0xfb00,0xfb80,0xfc00,0xfc80,0xfd00,0xfd80,0xfdc0,0xfe00,0xfe40,
  0xfe80,0xfec0,0xfee0,0xff00,0xff20,0xff40,0xff50,0xff60,0xff70,
  0xff80,0xff82,0xff83,0xff84,0xff85,0xff86,0xff87,0xff88,0xff89,
  0xff8a,0xff8b,0xff8c,0xff8d,0xff8e,0xff8f,0xff90,0xff91,0xff92,
  0xff93,0xff94,0xff95,0xff96,0xff97,0xff98,0xff99,0xff9a,0xff9b,
  0xff9c,0xff9d,0xff9e,0xff9f,0xffa0,0xffa1,0xffa2,0xffa3,0xffa4,
  0xffa5,0xffa6,0xffa7,0xffa8,0xffa9,0xffaa,0xffab,0xffac,0xffad,
  0xffae,0xffaf,0xffb0,0xffb1,0xffb2,0xffb3,0xffb4,0xffb5,0xffb6,
  0xffb7,0xffb8,0xffb9,0xffba,0xffbb,0xffbc,0xffbd,0xffbe,0xffbf,
  0xffc0,0xffc1,0xffc2,0xffc3,0xffc4,0xffc5,0xffc6,0xffc7,0xffc8,
  0xffc9,0xffca,0xffcb,0xffcc,0xffcd,0xffce,0xffcf,0xffd0,0xffd1,
  0xffd2,0xffd3,0xffd4,0xffd5,0xffd6,0xffd7,0xffd8,0xffd9,0xffda,
  0xffdb,0xffdc,0xffdd,0xffde,0xffdf,0xffe0,0xffe1,0xffe2,0xffe3,
  0xffe4,0xffe5,0xffe6,0xffe7,0xffe8,0xffe9,0xffea,0xffeb,0xffec,
  0xffed,0xffee,0xffef,0xfff0,0xfff1,0xfff2,0xfff3,0xfff4,0xfff5,
  0xfff6,0xfff7,0xfff8,0xfff9,0xfffa,0xfffb,0xfffc,0xfffd,0xfffe
  };
int luma_AC_sym[162]=
  {
  0x01,0x02,0x03,0x00,0x04,0x11,0x05,0x12,
  0x21,0x31,0x41,0x06,0x13,0x51,0x61,0x07,
  0x22,0x71,0x14,0x32,0x81,0x91,0xA1,0x08,
  0x23,0x42,0xB1,0xC1,0x15,0x52,0xD1,0xF0,
  0x24,0x33,0x62,0x72,0x82,0x09,0x0A,0x16,
  0x17,0x18,0x19,0x1A,0x25,0x26,0x27,0x28,
  0x29,0x2A,0x34,0x35,0x36,0x37,0x38,0x39,
  0x3A,0x43,0x44,0x45,0x46,0x47,0x48,0x49,
  0x4A,0x53,0x54,0x55,0x56,0x57,0x58,0x59,
  0x5A,0x63,0x64,0x65,0x66,0x67,0x68,0x69,
  0x6A,0x73,0x74,0x75,0x76,0x77,0x78,0x79,
  0x7A,0x83,0x84,0x85,0x86,0x87,0x88,0x89,
  0x8A,0x92,0x93,0x94,0x95,0x96,0x97,0x98,
  0x99,0x9A,0xA2,0xA3,0xA4,0xA5,0xA6,0xA7,
  0xA8,0xA9,0xAA,0xB2,0xB3,0xB4,0xB5,0xB6,
  0xB7,0xB8,0xB9,0xBA,0xC2,0xC3,0xC4,0xC5,
  0xC6,0xC7,0xC8,0xC9,0xCA,0xD2,0xD3,0xD4,
  0xD5,0xD6,0xD7,0xD8,0xD9,0xDA,0xE1,0xE2,
  0xE3,0xE4,0xE5,0xE6,0xE7,0xE8,0xE9,0xEA,
  0xF1,0xF2,0xF3,0xF4,0xF5,0xF6,0xF7,0xF8,
  0xF9,0xFA
  };
int chroma_AC_list[17]={0,0,0,2,3,5,9,13,16,20,27,32,36,0,40,41,43};
int chroma_AC_cnt[17]={0,0,2,1,2,4,4,3,4,7,5,4,4,0,1,2,119};
int chroma_AC_code[162]=
  {
  0x0000,0x4000,0x8000,0xa000,0xb000,0xc000,0xc800,0xd000,0xd800,
  0xe000,0xe400,0xe800,0xec00,0xf000,0xf200,0xf400,0xf600,0xf700,
  0xf800,0xf900,0xfa00,0xfa80,0xfb00,0xfb80,0xfc00,0xfc80,0xfd00,
```

```
    0xfd80,0xfdc0,0xfe00,0xfe40,0xfe80,0xfec0,0xfee0,0xff00,0xff20,
    0xff40,0xff50,0xff60,0xff70,0xff80,0xff84,0xff86,0xff88,0xff89,
    0xff8a,0xff8b,0xff8c,0xff8d,0xff8e,0xff8f,0xff90,0xff91,0xff92,
    0xff93,0xff94,0xff95,0xff96,0xff97,0xff98,0xff99,0xff9a,0xff9b,
    0xff9c,0xff9d,0xff9e,0xff9f,0xffa0,0xffa1,0xffa2,0xffa3,0xffa4,
    0xffa5,0xffa6,0xffa7,0xffa8,0xffa9,0xffaa,0xffab,0xffac,0xffad,
    0xffae,0xffaf,0xffb0,0xffb1,0xffb2,0xffb3,0xffb4,0xffb5,0xffb6,
    0xffb7,0xffb8,0xffb9,0xffba,0xffbb,0xffbc,0xffbd,0xffbe,0xffbf,
    0xffc0,0xffc1,0xffc2,0xffc3,0xffc4,0xffc5,0xffc6,0xffc7,0xffc8,
    0xffc9,0xffca,0xffcb,0xffcc,0xffcd,0xffce,0xffcf,0xffd0,0xffd1,
    0xffd2,0xffd3,0xffd4,0xffd5,0xffd6,0xffd7,0xffd8,0xffd9,0xffda,
    0xffdb,0xffdc,0xffdd,0xffde,0xffdf,0xffe0,0xffe1,0xffe2,0xffe3,
    0xffe4,0xffe5,0xffe6,0xffe7,0xffe8,0xffe9,0xffea,0xffeb,0xffec,
    0xffed,0xffee,0xffef,0xfff0,0xfff1,0xfff2,0xfff3,0xfff4,0xfff5,
    0xfff6,0xfff7,0xfff8,0xfff9,0xfffa,0xfffb,0xfffc,0xfffd,0xfffe
    };
int chroma_AC_sym[162]=
    {
    0x00,0x01,0x02,0x03,0x11,0x04,0x05,0x21,
    0x31,0x06,0x12,0x41,0x51,0x07,0x61,0x71,
    0x13,0x22,0x32,0x81,0x08,0x14,0x42,0x91,
    0xA1,0xB1,0xC1,0x09,0x23,0x33,0x52,0xF0,
    0x15,0x62,0x72,0xD1,0x0A,0x16,0x24,0x34,
    0xE1,0x25,0xF1,0x17,0x18,0x19,0x1A,0x26,
    0x27,0x28,0x29,0x2A,0x35,0x36,0x37,0x38,
    0x39,0x3A,0x43,0x44,0x45,0x46,0x47,0x48,
    0x49,0x4A,0x53,0x54,0x55,0x56,0x57,0x58,
    0x59,0x5A,0x63,0x64,0x65,0x66,0x67,0x68,
    0x69,0x6A,0x73,0x74,0x75,0x76,0x77,0x78,
    0x79,0x7A,0x82,0x83,0x84,0x85,0x86,0x87,
    0x88,0x89,0x8A,0x92,0x93,0x94,0x95,0x96,
    0x97,0x98,0x99,0x9A,0xA2,0xA3,0xA4,0xA5,
    0xA6,0xA7,0xA8,0xA9,0xAA,0xB2,0xB3,0xB4,
    0xB5,0xB6,0xB7,0xB8,0xB9,0xBA,0xC2,0xC3,
    0xC4,0xC5,0xC6,0xC7,0xC8,0xC9,0xCA,0xD2,
    0xD3,0xD4,0xD5,0xD6,0xD7,0xD8,0xD9,0xDA,
    0xE2,0xE3,0xE4,0xE5,0xE6,0xE7,0xE8,0xE9,
    0xEA,0xF2,0xF3,0xF4,0xF5,0xF6,0xF7,0xF8,
    0xF9,0xFA
    };


long    input_index=*bit_count/8L;
int     bits_used=(int)(*bit_count-8L*input_index);
BYTE    input_mask=0x80>bits_used;
WORD    output_mask=0x8000;
WORD    output_code=0;
//-- We know no AC symbol is less than 2 bits, so get the first 2
int     index,count,symbol;  // General purpose variables
int     match=0;             // Symbol match flag
int     length=2;            // Set initial length == 2

BYTE        input_data=*(input+input_index);
for(int i=0;i<2;i++)
```

```
   {
   if((input_data&input_mask)!=0)output_code|=output_mask;
   bits_used++;
   if(bits_used==8)
     {
     bits_used-=8;
     input_index++;
     input_data=*(input+input_index);
     input_mask=0x80;
     }
   else input_mask=input_mask>1;
   output_mask=output_mask>1;
   }
*bit_count+=2L;

if(flag==LUMA)          // Extract a luminance symbol
  {
  while(match==0)
    {
    index=luma_AC_list[length];
    count=luma_AC_cnt[length];
    if(length>16)
      {
      match=-1;         // Error: no match found
      }
    else
      {
      while(count>0)  // See if any patterns of this length match
        {
        if(output_code==luma_AC_code[index])
          {
          match=1;
          symbol=luma_AC_sym[index];
          }
        index++;
        count-;
        }
      }
    if(match==0)        // No match was found, get another bit
      {
      if((input_data&input_mask)!=0)output_code|=output_mask;
      length++;
      bits_used++;
      *bit_count+=1L;
      if(bits_used==8)
        {
        bits_used-=8;
        input_index++;
        input_data=*(input+input_index);
        input_mask=0x80;
        }
      else input_mask=input_mask>1;
      output_mask=output_mask>1;
```

```
                 }
               }
             }
        if(flag==CHROMA)              // Extract a chrominance symbol
          {
          while(match==0)
            {
            index=chroma_AC_list[length];
            count=chroma_AC_cnt[length];
            if(length>16)
              {
              match=-1;              // Error: no match found
              }
            else
              {
              while(count>0)
                {
                if(output_code==chroma_AC_code[index])
                  {
                  match=1;
                  symbol=chroma_AC_sym[index];
                  }
                index++;
                count-;
                }
              }
            if(match==0)                  // No match was found, get another bit
              {
              if((input_data&input_mask)!=0)output_code|=output_mask;
              length++;
              bits_used++;
              *bit_count+=1L;
              if(bits_used==8)
                {
                bits_used-=8;
                input_index++;
                input_data=*(input+input_index);
                input_mask=0x80;
                }
              else input_mask=input_mask>1;
              output_mask=output_mask>1;
              }
            }
          }
      return(symbol);
      }

//——————————————————————
// Extract a variable-length magnitude field from a buffer
//——————————————————————
int UnpackMagBits(BYTE *input, long *bit_count, int bits)
  {
  int bit_mask[17]=
```

```
    {
    0x0000,
    0x0001,0x0002,0x0004,0x0008,0x0010,0x0020,0x0040,0x0080,
    0x0100,0x0200,0x0400,0x0800,0x1000,0x2000,0x4000,0x8000
    };
  int sign_bits[17]=
    {
    0x0000,
    0xFFFE,0xFFFC,0xFFF8,0xFFF0,0xFFE0,0xFFC0,0xFF80,0xFF00,
    0xFE00,0xFC00,0xF800,0xF000,0xE000,0xC000,0x8000,0x0000
    };
  long   input_index=*bit_count/8L;       // Find input buffer index
  int    bits_used=(int)(*bit_count-8L*input_index);
  BYTE   input_mask=0x80>bits_used;       // Set input bit position
  WORD   output_mask=bit_mask[bits];      // Set output bit position
  WORD   output_code=0;                   // Clear output buffer
  int    magnitude;                       // Final result buffer

  BYTE   input_data=*(input+input_index);
  for(int i=0;i<bits;i++)   // Accumulate the correct # of bits
    {
    if((input_data&input_mask)!=0)output_code|=output_mask;
    output_mask=output_mask>1;
    *bit_count+=1L;
    bits_used++;
    if(bits_used==8)
      {
      bits_used-=8;
      input_index++;
      input_data=*(input+input_index);
      input_mask=0x80;
      }
    else input_mask=input_mask>1;
    }
  if((output_code&bit_mask[bits])==0)
    {
    output_code|=sign_bits[bits];
    magnitude=((int)output_code)+1;
    }
  else magnitude=(int)output_code;
  return(magnitude);
  }


//————————————————
// Encode a block of DCT coefficients using Huffman coding
//————————————————
long HuffEncode(int_block_t *input, BYTE *output, long bit_count, int flag)
  {
  int luma_AC_len[256]=
    {
     4, 2, 2, 3, 4, 5, 7, 8,10,16,16, 0, 0, 0, 0, 0,
     0, 4, 5, 7, 9,11,16,16,16,16,16, 0, 0, 0, 0, 0,
     0, 5, 8,10,12,16,16,16,16,16,16, 0, 0, 0, 0, 0,
```

```
     0,  6,  9,12,16,16,16,16,16,16,16,  0,  0,  0,  0,  0,
     0,  6,10,16,16,16,16,16,16,16,16,  0,  0,  0,  0,  0,
     0,  7,11,16,16,16,16,16,16,16,16,  0,  0,  0,  0,  0,
     0,  7,12,16,16,16,16,16,16,16,16,  0,  0,  0,  0,  0,
     0,  8,12,16,16,16,16,16,16,16,16,  0,  0,  0,  0,  0,
     0,  9,15,16,16,16,16,16,16,16,16,  0,  0,  0,  0,  0,
     0,  9,16,16,16,16,16,16,16,16,16,  0,  0,  0,  0,  0,
     0,  9,16,16,16,16,16,16,16,16,16,  0,  0,  0,  0,  0,
     0,10,16,16,16,16,16,16,16,16,16,  0,  0,  0,  0,  0,
     0,10,16,16,16,16,16,16,16,16,16,  0,  0,  0,  0,  0,
     0,11,16,16,16,16,16,16,16,16,16,  0,  0,  0,  0,  0,
     0,16,16,16,16,16,16,16,16,16,16,  0,  0,  0,  0,  0,
    11,16,16,16,16,16,16,16,16,16,16,  0,  0,  0,  0,  0,
    };
WORD luma_AC_code[256]=
    {
    0xa000,0x0000,0x4000,0x8000,0xb000,0xd000,0xf000,0xf800,
    0xfd80,0xff82,0xff83,0x0000,0x0000,0x0000,0x0000,0x0000,
    0x0000,0xc000,0xd800,0xf200,0xfb00,0xfec0,0xff84,0xff85,
    0xff86,0xff87,0xff88,0x0000,0x0000,0x0000,0x0000,0x0000,
    0x0000,0xe000,0xf900,0xfdc0,0xff40,0xff89,0xff8a,0xff8b,
    0xff8c,0xff8d,0xff8e,0x0000,0x0000,0x0000,0x0000,0x0000,
    0x0000,0xe800,0xfb80,0xff50,0xff8f,0xff90,0xff91,0xff92,
    0xff93,0xff94,0xff95,0x0000,0x0000,0x0000,0x0000,0x0000,
    0x0000,0xec00,0xfe00,0xff96,0xff97,0xff98,0xff99,0xff9a,
    0xff9b,0xff9c,0xff9d,0x0000,0x0000,0x0000,0x0000,0x0000,
    0x0000,0xf400,0xfee0,0xff9e,0xff9f,0xffa0,0xffa1,0xffa2,
    0xffa3,0xffa4,0xffa5,0x0000,0x0000,0x0000,0x0000,0x0000,
    0x0000,0xf600,0xff60,0xffa6,0xffa7,0xffa8,0xffa9,0xffaa,
    0xffab,0xffac,0xffad,0x0000,0x0000,0x0000,0x0000,0x0000,
    0x0000,0xfa00,0xff70,0xffae,0xffaf,0xffb0,0xffb1,0xffb2,
    0xffb3,0xffb4,0xffb5,0x0000,0x0000,0x0000,0x0000,0x0000,
    0x0000,0xfc00,0xff80,0xffb6,0xffb7,0xffb8,0xffb9,0xffba,
    0xffbb,0xffbc,0xffbd,0x0000,0x0000,0x0000,0x0000,0x0000,
    0x0000,0xfc80,0xffbe,0xffbf,0xffc0,0xffc1,0xffc2,0xffc3,
    0xffc4,0xffc5,0xffc6,0x0000,0x0000,0x0000,0x0000,0x0000,
    0x0000,0xfd00,0xffc7,0xffc8,0xffc9,0xffca,0xffcb,0xffcc,
    0xffcd,0xffce,0xffcf,0x0000,0x0000,0x0000,0x0000,0x0000,
    0x0000,0xfe40,0xffd0,0xffd1,0xffd2,0xffd3,0xffd4,0xffd5,
    0xffd6,0xffd7,0xffd8,0x0000,0x0000,0x0000,0x0000,0x0000,
    0x0000,0xfe80,0xffd9,0xffda,0xffdb,0xffdc,0xffdd,0xffde,
    0xffdf,0xffe0,0xffe1,0x0000,0x0000,0x0000,0x0000,0x0000,
    0x0000,0xff00,0xffe2,0xffe3,0xffe4,0xffe5,0xffe6,0xffe7,
    0xffe8,0xffe9,0xffea,0x0000,0x0000,0x0000,0x0000,0x0000,
    0x0000,0xffeb,0xffec,0xffed,0xffee,0xffef,0xfff0,0xfff1,
    0xfff2,0xfff3,0xfff4,0x0000,0x0000,0x0000,0x0000,0x0000,
    0xff20,0xfff5,0xfff6,0xfff7,0xfff8,0xfff9,0xfffa,0xfffb,
    0xfffc,0xfffd,0xfffe,0x0000,0x0000,0x0000,0x0000,0x0000,
    };
int chroma_AC_len[256]=
    {
     2,  2,  3,  4,  5,  5,  6,  7,  9,10,12,  0,  0,  0,  0,  0,
     0,  4,  6,  8,  9,11,12,16,16,16,16,  0,  0,  0,  0,  0,
```

```
      0,  5,  8,10,12,15,16,16,16,16,16,  0,  0,  0,  0,  0,
      0,  5,  8,10,12,16,16,16,16,16,16,  0,  0,  0,  0,  0,
      0,  6,  9,16,16,16,16,16,16,16,16,  0,  0,  0,  0,  0,
      0,  6,10,16,16,16,16,16,16,16,16,  0,  0,  0,  0,  0,
      0,  7,11,16,16,16,16,16,16,16,16,  0,  0,  0,  0,  0,
      0,  7,11,16,16,16,16,16,16,16,16,  0,  0,  0,  0,  0,
      0,  8,16,16,16,16,16,16,16,16,16,  0,  0,  0,  0,  0,
      0,  9,16,16,16,16,16,16,16,16,16,  0,  0,  0,  0,  0,
      0,  9,16,16,16,16,16,16,16,16,16,  0,  0,  0,  0,  0,
      0,  9,16,16,16,16,16,16,16,16,16,  0,  0,  0,  0,  0,
      0,  9,16,16,16,16,16,16,19,16,16,  0,  0,  0,  0,  0,
      0,11,16,16,16,16,16,16,16,16,16,  0,  0,  0,  0,  0,
      0,14,16,16,16,16,16,16,16,16,16,  0,  0,  0,  0,  0,
     10,15,16,16,16,16,16,16,16,16,16,  0,  0,  0,  0,  0,
    };
WORD chroma_AC_code[256]=
    {
    0x0000,0x4000,0x8000,0xa000,0xc000,0xc800,0xe000,0xf000,
    0xfa00,0xfd80,0xff40,0x0000,0x0000,0x0000,0x0000,0x0000,
    0x0000,0xb000,0xe400,0xf600,0xfa80,0xfec0,0xff50,0xff88,
    0xff89,0xff8a,0xff8b,0x0000,0x0000,0x0000,0x0000,0x0000,
    0x0000,0xd000,0xf700,0xfdc0,0xff60,0xff84,0xff8c,0xff8d,
    0xff8e,0xff8f,0xff90,0x0000,0x0000,0x0000,0x0000,0x0000,
    0x0000,0xd800,0xf800,0xfe00,0xff70,0xff91,0xff92,0xff93,
    0xff94,0xff95,0xff96,0x0000,0x0000,0x0000,0x0000,0x0000,
    0x0000,0xe800,0xfb00,0xff97,0xff98,0xff99,0xff9a,0xff9b,
    0xff9c,0xff9d,0xff9e,0x0000,0x0000,0x0000,0x0000,0x0000,
    0x0000,0xec00,0xfe40,0xff9f,0xffa0,0xffa1,0xffa2,0xffa3,
    0xffa4,0xffa5,0xffa6,0x0000,0x0000,0x0000,0x0000,0x0000,
    0x0000,0xf200,0xfee0,0xffa7,0xffa8,0xffa9,0xffaa,0xffab,
    0xffac,0xffad,0xffae,0x0000,0x0000,0x0000,0x0000,0x0000,
    0x0000,0xf400,0xff00,0xffaf,0xffb0,0xffb1,0xffb2,0xffb3,
    0xffb4,0xffb5,0xffb6,0x0000,0x0000,0x0000,0x0000,0x0000,
    0x0000,0xf900,0xffb7,0xffb8,0xffb9,0xffba,0xffbb,0xffbc,
    0xffbd,0xffbe,0xffbf,0x0000,0x0000,0x0000,0x0000,0x0000,
    0x0000,0xfb80,0xffc0,0xffc1,0xffc2,0xffc3,0xffc4,0xffc5,
    0xffc6,0xffc7,0xffc8,0x0000,0x0000,0x0000,0x0000,0x0000,
    0x0000,0xfc00,0xffc9,0xffca,0xffcb,0xffcc,0xffcd,0xffce,
    0xffcf,0xffd0,0xffd1,0x0000,0x0000,0x0000,0x0000,0x0000,
    0x0000,0xfc80,0xffd2,0xffd3,0xffd4,0xffd5,0xffd6,0xffd7,
    0xffd8,0xffd9,0xffda,0x0000,0x0000,0x0000,0x0000,0x0000,
    0x0000,0xfd00,0xffdb,0xffdc,0xffdd,0xffde,0xffdf,0xffe0,
    0xffe1,0xffe2,0xffe3,0x0000,0x0000,0x0000,0x0000,0x0000,
    0x0000,0xff20,0xffe4,0xffe5,0xffe6,0xffe7,0xffe8,0xffe9,
    0xffea,0xffeb,0xffec,0x0000,0x0000,0x0000,0x0000,0x0000,
    0x0000,0xff80,0xffed,0xffee,0xffef,0xfff0,0xfff1,0xfff2,
    0xfff3,0xfff4,0xfff5,0x0000,0x0000,0x0000,0x0000,0x0000,
    0xfe80,0xff86,0xfff6,0xfff7,0xfff8,0xfff9,0xfffa,0xfffb,
    0xfffc,0xfffd,0xfffe,0x0000,0x0000,0x0000,0x0000,0x0000,
    };
int luma_DC_len[12]={2,3,3,3,3,3,4,5,6,7,8,9};
WORD luma_DC_code[12]=
    {
```

```
  0x0000,0x4000,0x6000,0x8000,0xA000,0xC000,
  0xE000,0xF000,0xF800,0xFC00,0xFE00,0xFF00
  };
int chroma_DC_len[12]={2,2,2,3,4,5,6,7,8,9,10,11};
WORD chroma_DC_code[12]=
  {
  0x0000,0x4000,0x8000,0xC000,0xE000,0xF000,
  0xF800,0xFC00,0xFE00,0xFF00,0xFF80,0xFFC0
  };
WORD bit_mask[12]=
  {
  0x0000,0x0001,0x0003,0x0007,0x000F,0x001F,
  0x003F,0x007F,0x00FF,0x01FF,0x03FF,0x07FF
  };
int  src=0;   // Source index
int  end;     // End of buffer pointer
int  run;     // Run length
int  cat;     // Category
int  mag;     // Magnitude

//-- Transfer DC Huffman code
cat=GetCategory(input->linear[src]);
if(flag==LUMA)bit_count=
PackBits(luma_DC_code[cat],luma_DC_len[cat],output,bit_count);
if(flag==CHROMA)bit_count=
PackBits(chroma_DC_code[cat],chroma_DC_len[cat],output,bit_count);

//-- Transfer DC magnitude
mag=input->linear[src++];
if(mag<0)mag-=1;
mag&=bit_mask[cat];
mag=mag<<(16-cat);
bit_count=PackBits(mag,cat,output,bit_count);

//-- Find end of Zig-Zag ordered block
end=63;
while(end>1 && input->linear[end]==0)end--;
while(src<end)
  {
  //-- Count zeroes if any
  run=0;
  while(src<end && input->linear[src]==0 && run<16)
    {
    run++;
    src++;
    }

  //-- Get symbol for AC code
  if(run==16)cat=0xF0;
  else
    {
    cat=GetCategory(input->linear[src]);
    cat|=((run&0xF)<<4);
```

```
        }

    //-- Transfer AC Huffman code
    if(flag==LUMA)bit_count=
    PackBits(luma_AC_code[cat],luma_AC_len[cat],output,bit_count);
    if(flag==CHROMA)bit_count=
    PackBits(chroma_AC_code[cat],chroma_AC_len[cat],output,bit_count);

    //-- Transfer AC magnitude
    if(cat!=0xF0)
      {
      cat&=0xF;
      mag=input->linear[src++];
      if(mag<0)mag-=1;
      mag&=bit_mask[cat];
      mag=mag<<(16-cat);
      bit_count=PackBits(mag,cat,output,bit_count);
      }
    }

  //-- Transfer EOB symbol
  if(flag==LUMA)bit_count=
  PackBits(luma_AC_code[0],luma_AC_len[0],output,bit_count);
  if(flag==CHROMA)bit_count=
  PackBits(chroma_AC_code[0],chroma_AC_len[0],output,bit_count);
  return(bit_count);
  }


//-------------------------------
// Decode a block of DCT coefficients using Huffman coding
//-------------------------------
long HuffDecode(BYTE *input, int_block_t *output, long bit_count, int flag)
  {
  int term=0;    // Process termination flag
  int dst=0;     // Destination index
  int end;       // End of block pointer
  int run;       // Run length
  int cat;       // Category
  int run_cat;   // Magnitude

  //-- Store zeros in output block
  for(end=0;end<64;end++)output->linear[end]=0;

  //-- Get DC coefficient
  cat=UnpackHuffBitsDC(input,&bit_count,flag);
  output->linear[dst++]=UnpackMagBits(input,&bit_count,cat);

  //-- Decode coefficients till EOB found
  while(term==0)
    {
    run_cat=UnpackHuffBitsAC(input,&bit_count,flag);
    run=(run_cat&0xF0)>4;
    cat=run_cat&0xF;
```

```
        switch(run_cat)
          {
          case 0x00:          // EOB symbol
            {
            term=1;
            break;
            }
          case 0xF0:          // Run of 16 zeros
            {
            dst+=16;
            break;
            }
          default:            // Run/Value pair decoded, get magnitude
            {
            dst+=run;
            output->linear[dst++]=UnpackMagBits(input,&bit_count,cat);
            break;
            }
          }
        }
      return(bit_count);
      }


//———————————————————————
// Remove noise introduced by compression/decompression process
//———————————————————————
void Filter(byte_block_t *input, byte_block_t *output)
  {
  byte_block_t  temp;        // Temporary block storage
  int           x,y,pixel;   // General purpose variables

  //—- Filter center pixels
  for(y=1;y<7;y++)
    {
    for(x=1;x<7;x++)
      {
      pixel=4*(int)(input->block[y][x]);
      pixel+=(int)(input->block[y+1][x]);
      pixel+=(int)(input->block[y-1][x]);
      pixel+=(int)(input->block[y][x+1]);
      pixel+=(int)(input->block[y][x-1]);
      pixel/=8;
      if(abs(pixel-(int)(input->block[y][x]))<THRESHOLD)
        {
        temp.block[y][x]=(BYTE)pixel;
        }
      else
        {
        temp.block[y][x]=input->block[y][x];
        }
      }
    }
```

```
//—- Filter left and right edges
for(y=1;y<7;y++)
   {
   pixel=4*(int)(input->block[y][0]);
   pixel+=2*(int)(input->block[y+1][0]);
   pixel+=2*(int)(input->block[y-1][0]);
   pixel/=8;
   if(abs(pixel-(int)(input->block[y][0]))<THRESHOLD)
      {
      temp.block[y][0]=(BYTE)pixel;
      }
   else
      {
      temp.block[y][0]=input->block[y][0];
      }
   pixel=4*(int)(input->block[y][7]);
   pixel+=2*(int)(input->block[y+1][7]);
   pixel+=2*(int)(input->block[y-1][7]);
   pixel/=8;
   if(abs(pixel-(int)(input->block[y][7]))<THRESHOLD)
      {
      temp.block[y][7]=(BYTE)pixel;
      }
   else
      {
      temp.block[y][7]=input->block[y][7];
      }
   }

//—- Filter top and bottom edges
for(x=1;x<7;x++)
   {
   pixel=4*(int)(input->block[0][x]);
   pixel+=2*(int)(input->block[0][x+1]);
   pixel+=2*(int)(input->block[0][x-1]);
   pixel/=8;
   if(abs(pixel-(int)(input->block[0][x]))<THRESHOLD)
      {
      temp.block[0][x]=(BYTE)pixel;
      }
   else
      {
      temp.block[0][x]=input->block[0][x];
      }
   pixel=4*(int)(input->block[7][x]);
   pixel+=2*(int)(input->block[7][x+1]);
   pixel+=2*(int)(input->block[7][x-1]);
   pixel/=8;
   if(abs(pixel-(int)(input->block[7][x]))<THRESHOLD)
      {
      temp.block[7][x]=(BYTE)pixel;
      }
   else
```

```
      {
      temp.block[7][x]=input->block[7][x];
      }
   }

//-- Filter upper left corner
pixel=4*(int)(input->block[0][0]);
pixel+=2*(int)(input->block[0][1]);
pixel+=2*(int)(input->block[1][0]);
pixel/=8;
if(abs(pixel-(int)(input->block[0][0]))<THRESHOLD)
   {
   temp.block[0][0]=(BYTE)pixel;
   }
else
   {
   temp.block[0][0]=input->block[0][0];
   }

//-- Filter upper right corner
pixel=4*(int)(input->block[0][7]);
pixel+=2*(int)(input->block[1][7]);
pixel+=2*(int)(input->block[0][6]);
pixel/=8;
if(abs(pixel-(int)(input->block[0][7]))<THRESHOLD)
   {
   temp.block[0][7]=(BYTE)pixel;
   }
else
   {
   temp.block[0][7]=input->block[0][7];
   }

//-- Filter lower left corner
pixel=4*(int)(input->block[7][0]);
pixel+=2*(int)(input->block[7][1]);
pixel+=2*(int)(input->block[6][0]);
pixel/=8;
if(abs(pixel-(int)(input->block[7][0]))<THRESHOLD)
   {
   temp.block[7][0]=(BYTE)pixel;
   }
else
   {
   temp.block[7][0]=input->block[7][0];
   }

//-- Filter lower right corner
pixel=4*(int)(input->block[7][7]);
pixel+=2*(int)(input->block[6][7]);
pixel+=2*(int)(input->block[7][6]);
pixel/=8;
if(abs(pixel-(int)(input->block[7][7]))<THRESHOLD)
```

```
      {
      temp.block[7][7]=(BYTE)pixel;
      }
   else
      {
      temp.block[7][7]=input->block[7][7];
      }

   for(x=0;x<64;x++)output->linear[x]=temp.linear[x];
   }
```

Source File JPEG_DEF.H

```
//===========================================================
// JPEG_DEF.CPP
//————————————————————————————
// Program:  Definition file for JPEG_CMP.EXE and JPEG_UNC.EXE
// Author:   Phil Mattison
// Compiler: Borland Turbo C++ v1.01
//————————————————————————————

#define BYTE    unsigned char
#define WORD    unsigned int
#define DWORD   unsigned long

#define FORWARD    0
#define INVERSE    1
#define LUMA       0
#define CHROMA     1
#define THRESHOLD 15

typedef union
   {
   BYTE block[8][8];
   BYTE linear[64];
   } byte_block_t;

typedef union
   {
   int block[8][8];
   int linear[64];
   } int_block_t;

typedef union
   {
   int  code[128];
   BYTE data[256];
   } array_t;

typedef struct
   {
   char file_ID[8];
```

```
int   x_size;
int   y_size;
int   frames;
int   compression;
int   palette[240][3];
} vid_t;
```

These programs implement the essential features of the JPEG specification: block organization, DCT encoding, zig-zag ordering of coefficients, quantization, and Huffman encoding. They do not strictly adhere to the structural hierarchy of the JPEG bit-stream definition, for reasons of readability. The intention is to illustrate how to implement the critical elements of the compression algorithm. The programs can be used to compress and decompress any of the video sequences provided as examples. If it is necessary to implement the full specification in all its details, a copy of the JPEG specification should be obtained from the International Organization for Standardization.

11

MPEG Video
Compression Standard

This chapter describes a motion picture encoding standard known as *ISO1172*. The *ISO* is the *International Organization for Standardization*. *MPEG* is an acronym for *Moving Picture Experts Group*, a committee formed by the ISO to develop this standard. The MPEG specification was developed specifically to allow the transmission of broadcast standard images at a data rate of approximately 1 to 1.5 megabits per second. ISO1172 is also sometimes referred to as *MPEG1*. Another specification known as *MPEG2* has been developed to support higher-resolution images and higher data rates. It represents an evolution from MPEG1 and is similar in most respects and, therefore, will not be covered here. The MPEG specification itself is quite terse and assumes a significant level of background knowledge on the part of the reader. This chapter does not presume to be a complete working-level document of the standard, but rather seeks to provide enough background knowledge to assist the reader in understanding the standard. The ISO is the same organization that developed the JPEG standard. MPEG is similar to JPEG in many respects, but extends the techniques to take advantage of the temporal aspects of motion video. Many of the same techniques used in MPEG are also used in the H.261 standard described in Chapter 12.

Overview

The fact that MPEG was designed to support a series of pictures rather than individual pictures imposes significant complexity above and beyond the JPEG specification. The MPEG data stream is designed specifically to allow such features as forward play, fast-forward play, slow-forward play, and fast-reverse play. This allows the viewer to control the video stream in much the same way as he or she is accustomed to with conventional video sources such as a VCR. Because of the real-time nature of the decoding process it is necessary to introduce the concept of buffers and buffer-level management to ensure that the decoder never runs out of data and that the data buffers never overflow. The color representation chosen for MPEG is YCrCb. The chrominance information is subsampled by half in both horizontal and vertical directions so there is one set of chrominance data for each 2×2 block of luminance pixels. Chrominance and luminance pixels are organized into 8×8 blocks in a manner similar to the JPEG specification, but with less flexibility. Pixel blocks are transformed into the frequency domain via the DCT and quantized to eliminate some low-amplitude high-frequency components. This is essentially the same technique as used in JPEG but the suggested quantization coefficients tend to be less radical, allowing more information to be retained. Probably one of the most significant advantages of MPEG is the concept of *predictive coding*. This simply means calculating how and how much the next image changes from the previous one and transmitting code that indicates the difference rather than the picture itself.

The images in a sequence can be classified into four types. A complete image which is coded without reference to any other images is known as an *intra*picture, or *I frame*. An image that is coded relative to another image is called a *predicted* picture or *P frame*. Predicted frames can be generated relative to intraframes or other predicted frames. An image that is derived from *two* other images, one before and one after, is called a *bidirectional* picture, or *B frame*. Bidirectional frames can be derived from intra- or predicted frames but not other bidirectional frames. The fourth type, which is a special format not used for ordinary playback, is called a *DC picture* or *D frame*. This is a very-low-resolution image consisting of only the DC terms of the constituent pixel blocks and is used only for fast-forward search operations. A typical frequency for intraframes is one intraframe for every 12 to 15 other frames. Typically, two bidirectional frames are inserted between each pair of intra- and predicted frames so the number of frames per intraframe would always be a multiple of three.

Because bidirectional frames are derived from images which come after the derived image, encoded images cannot be sent in the order in which they are displayed. For example, in a case where there are 12 images transmitted, the first of which is an intraframe, the order in which images are derived is shown by the arrows in Figure 11.1. Looking at the first two bidirectional frames, it is obvious that each is derived at least in part from the first predicted frame which follows them in the sequence. This means that in the encoded bit-stream the first predicted frame must immediately follow the intraframe so that the two intermediate bidirectional frames can be interpolated from the intra- and predicted frames. After the bidirectional frames have been decoded and displayed the predicted frame can be displayed.

Each image is subdivided into units called *slices*. This way, if an error occurs in the bit-stream it affects only the slice in which it occurs and does not propagate throughout the entire image. A slice is made up of one or more *macro blocks*. A macro block consists of four 8x8 blocks of luminance pixels and one each 8x8 blocks of the two chroma components. Because the decoder must derive bidirectional frames from intraframes and other predicted frames, the encoder must accurately model the decoder in order to correctly predict the decoded values from which subsequent

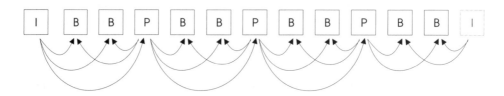

Figure 11.1   Order of image decoding in an MPEG picture group.

frames will be derived. This also places a minimum accuracy requirement on the calculations used to decode the bit-stream. Because of the potential number of bidirectional frames and predicted frames derived from each intraframe, an inadequate accuracy level could produce significant deterioration of image quality by the end of the sequence derived from a given intraframe. As the decode process may have to calculate several images before it can arrive at the next image to be displayed, the decoder typically must be implemented in a pipeline fashion. That is, a certain number of image frames must be already decoded and stored in buffers waiting to be displayed at any given time. Given the bidirectional image prediction capability, at least two frames must be stored by the decoder. Figure 11.2 illustrates the conceptual data flow for an MPEG decoder.

To decode an intraframe, the *variable length code (VLC)* decoder extracts the frequency coefficients for each block in the image and sends them on to the dequantization process which multiplies each coefficient by the appropriate quantization factor. These are then reordered appropriately from the zig-zag sequence and processed through the inverse DCT to generate the appropriate pixel values for each block. These are then transferred to the previous image buffer until the entire image has been constructed. It remains there until the appropriate time to be displayed. The intraframe is not displayed immediately because the following predicted frame must be decoded before the bidirectional frame immediately following the just-decoded intraframe can be decoded. For predicted frames and bidirectional frames the initial sequence of decoding a block of pixels is essentially the same as for intraframes up through the inverse DCT. For predicted frames, however, the values coming out of the inverse DCT process represent differences from the previous image rather than absolute image values. Also, the VLC decoder may detect motion vectors which are not processed through the dequantization and inverse DCT processes. For a predicted image, a motion vector specifies an offset from the block position of the current block at which pixels are to be extracted from the previous image to be used as a reference to which the pixel difference values are added to produce the new image. As each predicted frame pixel block is decoded and added with

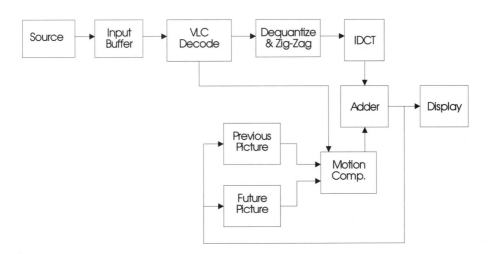

Figure 11.2　MPEG decoder image data flow diagram.

the appropriate motion-compensated block from the previous image it is then stored in the future image buffer. Once the entire predicted frame has been decoded and stored in the future image buffer the image currently in the previous image buffer can be displayed. The future and previous images are then available for bidirectional motion compensation in the calculation of subsequent bidirectional frames. A bidirectional frame is decoded in essentially the same way as a predicted frame except that motion compensation vectors may draw on either the previous image or the future image buffers for motion-compensation pixel blocks. The decision as to which image is the best source for motion compensation blocks is made during the encode process. While decoding bidirectional frames, if the next frame encountered in the data stream is an intra- or predicted frame, the image stored in the future image buffer is moved to the previous image buffer and the new intra- or predicted frame is decoded and stored in the future image buffer. By waiting until both the previous and future image buffers are filled before displaying the first frame, the decoder ensures that it will never have to decode more than one frame before displaying the next one. The thing to remember is that the next frame decoded is not necessarily the next frame displayed.

Target Image Characteristics

MPEG is designed to operate on a specific class of images and, therefore, is not nearly as flexible in this respect as JPEG. For the intended data rate of 1 to 1.5 megabits per second, supporting a frame rate of 20 to 30 frames per second, the optimum spatial resolution is either 352×240 or 352×288, depending on whether the source is NTSC or PAL. Assuming digital pixel values according to the CCIR-601 specification, the resolution of the raw incoming image is 720×480 for NTSC or 720×576 for PAL. An image at this resolution is called a *Source Input Format (SIF)* image. Typically, the chrominance data is subsampled by 2:1 in the horizontal direction only. To reduce this resolution in a way that will avoid introducing noise artifacts or spatial alias artifacts it is important to filter the data appropriately. A fairly common method of achieving the desired frame rate is simply to use only the even or odd fields from the input video. This will reduce a 60 Hz NTSC signal to 30 frames per second or reduce a 50 Hz PAL signal to 25 frames per second. Best results are obtained by capturing both fields for each frame and applying filter and scale operations to the resulting full-resolution image. This of course requires more memory and computing power but produces noticeably better results. Reducing the spatial resolution of images can introduce visual artifacts which result from the presence of spatial frequencies higher than the new effective sampling rate of the reduced image. To prevent this from happening, a low-pass filter should be used which is tuned to filter out frequencies above one-half the effective sample rate of the new image resolution. Figure 11.3 illustrates a pair of one-dimensional filter kernels which are tuned to achieve the necessary cutoff frequency to accomplish this for luminance and chrominance pixels.

Note that there are an odd number of taps for the luminance filter kernel and an even number of taps for the chrominance filter kernel. The luminance filter will produce a new filtered sample aligned with the original sample in the image whereas the chrominance filter will produce a one-half pixel phase shift. This is necessary because of the chrominance subsampling technique used for MPEG. A further discussion on filter theory can be found in Chapter 2. These filters are designed to decimate an original image in CCIR-601 4:4:2 format. Figure 11.4 illustrates the transformation from the original format to the decimated, scaled-down format using these filters.

Note that the 4:1 ratio of luminance sites to chrominance sites corresponds to the 4:1 ratio of luminance blocks to chrominance blocks. When a raw source image of 720 pixels across is scaled to

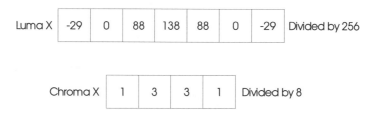

Figure 11.3 Luminance and chrominance decimation filter kernels for MPEG image scaling.

one-half size the resulting frame is 360 pixels across. Unfortunately, this is not evenly divisible by 16, which is the size of the macro block. To remedy this, the right and left edges of the image are simply clipped to produce a resulting size of 352 horizontally. If the raw input image is decimated vertically by simply extracting a single field, the vertical resolution of 480 is automatically reduced to 240, which is evenly divisible by 16. For a PAL image the native vertical resolution of 576 divided by two is 288, which also is evenly divisible by 16. The fact that the original input image chrominance data is already subsampled by 2:1 in the horizontal direction simplifies the scaling process. If a single field is extracted from the original image the resulting unfiltered chrominance image is 360×240. The chrominance decimation filter can then be applied both horizontally and vertically to reduce the image to 180×120, which is then clipped to 176×120. A diagram of this process for luminance and chrominance frames is shown in Figure 11.5.

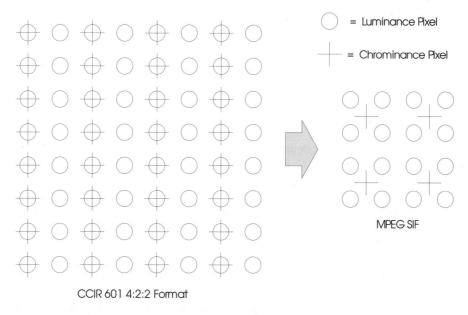

Figure 11.4 MPEG luminance image scaling and filtering process.

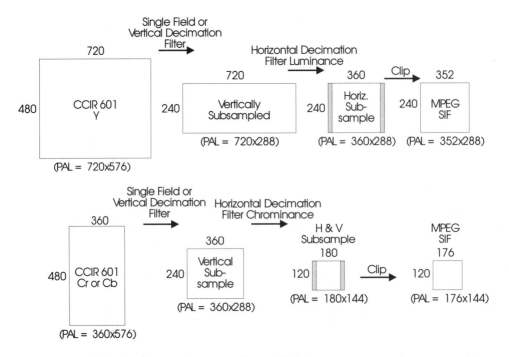

Figure 11.5 MPEG chrominance image scaling and filtering process.

The image size to be encoded does not necessarily have to be exactly 352×240 or 352×288. If it is desirable not to clip the left and right edges of the picture the image can be padded to the next even multiple of 16, which would be 368. If this is necessary, however, the padding should be done by duplicating the last column of pixels to avoid introducing a sharp edge into the image. This would result in large DCT coefficients when those blocks were encoded, reducing the efficiency of the encoder.

Encoded Bit-Stream Syntax

An MPEG-encoded bit-stream is organized as a *sequence*. A sequence begins with a sequence header and ends with a sequence end code. Logically, it is a sequence of images, as you would expect. Within the sequence, images can be further subdivided into *groups*. This further subdivision is provided to allow certain parameters to be modified within the sequence as applied to a given group or groups of images. Other parameters are defined in the sequence header and applied to all images in the sequence. There are certain limitations which may be placed on these parameters, which, if conformed to in the encoder, results in what is called a *constrained bit-stream*. This is the baseline for compatibility across applications. Encoders and decoders which conform to these constraints should be able to operate together even though produced by different manufacturers. Within the bit-stream, certain key information is identified by special header codes. These codes are characterized by a relatively long series of zero bits followed by a specific code identifying the data to follow. Table 11.1 summarizes these codes and their meanings.

Table 11.1 MPEG Bit-Stream Start Codes

Sequence Header	000001B3
Start Group of Pictures	000001B8
Extension Data	000001B5
User Data	000001B2
Picture Start	00000100
Slice Start	00000101 — 000001AF

The sections that follow define the data segments identified by these codes, the data contained in each, and the formats.

Sequence Header

A sequence header begins with a sequence header code and is followed by a series of variable-length bit fields describing certain parameters for the sequence. Figure 11.6 illustrates the organization of a sequence header.

Following the sequence header code, the horizontal and vertical size fields are each 12-bit unsigned integer numbers representing the size of the image in pixels. A value of zero is not allowed, so the range of numbers is from 1 to 4095. The aspect ratio field is a 4-bit code selecting one of 14 possible values for the aspect ratio of the images. Table 11.2 shows the aspect ratio values associated with each possible code. The frame-rate code is likewise a 4-bit value, which selects a predefined frame rate from a table of eight different possibilities. These are listed in Table 11.3.

The bit-rate field is an 18-bit unsigned integer, which, when multiplied by 400, is the actual bit rate for the data stream. To indicate variable bit-rate operation all 18 of these bits are set to one. The marker bit follows the bit-rate field and is always set to one to prevent confusion of the decoder

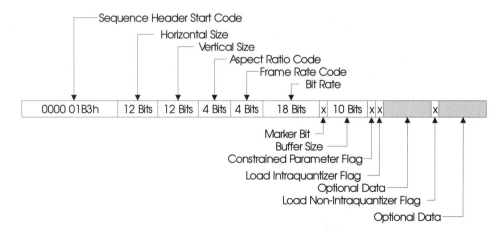

Figure 11.6 MPEG sequence header organization.

Table 11.2   Encoding of Image Aspect Ratio

Code	Aspect Ratio
0000	Undefined, not to be used
0001	1.0 (Square Pixels)
0010	0.6735
0011	0.7175
0100	0.7615
0101	0.8055
0110	0.8495
0111	0.8935
1000	0.9375 (720×576 at 4:3)
1001	0.9815
1010	1.0255
1011	1.0695
1100	1.1135 (720×485 at 4:3)
1101	1.1535
1110	1.2015
1111	Undefined, reserved

(recall the start codes all begin with a long string of zeros). The buffer size field is a 10-bit unsigned integer which, when multiplied by 16,384, gives the minimum required size for the input buffer of the decoder. The constrained parameter flag bit, if set to one, indicates that the bit-stream conforms to the constrained parameter requirements to make it compatible with other conforming decoders or devices. Some of the constraints are: a maximum of 720×576 pixel image size, a maximum total

Table 11.3   Encoding of Frame Rate

CODE	Frame Rate
0000	Do not use
0001	23.976
0010	24
0011	25
0100	29.97
0101	30
0110	50
0111	59.94
1000	60
1001	Reserved
1010	Reserved
1011	Reserved
1100	Reserved
1101	Reserved
1110	Reserved
1111	Reserved

number of macro blocks no more than 396, and a maximum pixel rate of 2,534,400 pixels per second. A load-intraquantizer-matrix flag bit, if set to one, indicates that a set of 64 8-bit integer values are to follow. These represent an 8×8 intraquantizer set of coefficients. All 64 coefficients must be nonzero. If the flag bit is set to zero, the intraquantization matrix should be set to a default table, which is shown in Table 11.4.

The load-nonintraquantization-matrix flag bit operates in essentially the same way, except that the default quantization matrix has all coefficients set to a value of 16. The overall organization of an MPEG bit-stream sequence is illustrated in Figure 11.7. It begins with a sequence header and ends with a sequence end code.

Between these are one or more *picture groups*. A picture group is a logical subdivision of an MPEG sequence. There may be extra sequence headers embedded among the picture groups if it is necessary to change any global parameters in the process of a sequence.

Picture Group

A picture group is a sequence of encoded images which starts with an intraimage and may contain any number of intra-, predicted, or bidirectional pictures in any order. The images are decoded in the order in which they occur in the bit-stream. The order in which they are displayed is determined by sequence codes embedded within each image. There are two classes of picture groups: *opened* and *closed*. A closed group implies that no images outside the group are required for the calculation of motion compensation. An open group implies that there are one or more bidirectional images that require the presence of the last image from the previous group in order to be fully decoded. A picture group begins with a picture group header as illustrated in Figure 11.8.

Following the picture group start code in the picture group header is a time code which conforms to a format defined by the *Society for Motion Picture and Television Engineers (SMPTE)*. This field indicates the elapsed time since the beginning of the sequence. The time code field is further subdivided as shown in Table 11.5.

Note that seconds are subdivided in terms of images rather than milliseconds or some other conventional measurement. The exact meaning of the image number field in the time code depends on the frame rate encoded in the sequence header. Following the time code are two single-bit flags. The first is the closed-group flag, which, if set, indicates the group is closed as described earlier in this section. The second is the broken-link flag, which indicates that the sequence has been edited and the group preceding the current group is not the original preceding group. The implication is

Table 11.4 Default Quantization Matrix for Intrablocks

8	16	19	22	26	27	29	34
16	16	22	24	27	29	34	37
19	22	26	27	29	34	34	38
22	22	26	27	29	34	37	40
22	26	27	29	32	35	40	48
26	27	29	32	35	40	48	58
26	27	29	34	38	46	56	69
27	29	35	38	46	56	69	83

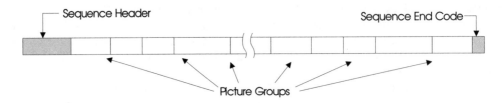

Figure 11.7   MPEG sequence organization.

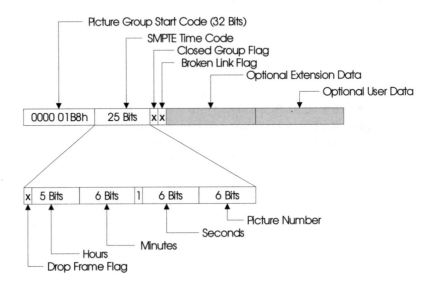

Figure 11.8   MPEG picture group header organization.

Table 11.5   SMPTE Time Code Format

Field	Bits	Values
Drop-Frame Flag	1	0 or 1
Hours	5	0 to 23
Minutes	6	0 to 59
Fixed	1	1
Seconds	6	0 to 59
Image Number	6	0 to 60

that if the current group is an open group needing images from a previous group to decode bidirectional images they will not be decoded properly. If the decoder detects a broken link it must attempt to gracefully recover the affected images. Following the broken-link flag there may be two optional data fields inserted into the header. These are *extension data* and *user data*. These can occur at the end of a sequence header and other places in the bit-stream as well and therefore are discussed separately later in this chapter. Figure 11.9 illustrates how a picture group is organized. A picture group header is followed by one or more encoded images. Note that there is nothing in the group header to indicate how many images are encoded within the current group. The primary purpose of group organization is to maintain synchronization of the decoder with the overall timing of the sequence.

Encoded Image

Each encoded image within a group begins with a picture header as illustrated in Figure 11.10.

The picture header start code is followed by a 10-bit temporal reference number. This is an unsigned integer ranging from zero to 1023 indicating the order in which images in a group are to be displayed. If there are more than 1,024 images in a group the temporal reference simply rolls over to zero after the 1,024th image and continues counting. The picture type is a 3-bit field indicating whether the image has an intra-, predicted, bidirectional or DC picture. The meanings of the possible code combinations are shown in Table 11.6.

Following the picture type is a 16-bit unsigned integer field called the *virtual buffer verifier delay*. This number defines the time in units of 1/90,000 of a second required to fill the decoder's input buffer from empty to the current required state. This effectively defines how many bits should be in the input buffer at the beginning of the image decode process. The number of bits can be determined by multiplying this value by the defined channel bit rate for the sequence and dividing the product by 90,000. Following the virtual buffer verifier delay are two pairs of fields defining the range and precision of motion vectors to be used in the image. The first is a precision bit indicating, if set, that the precision of the motion vectors is in terms of a full pixel. If zero, it indicates the precision is half a pixel. The second part is a 3-bit code indicating the range of motion vectors, effectively defining the number of bits used to represent motion vectors. The codes used in this field and their meanings are listed in Table 11.7.

There is a vector precision bit and an F-code for use with *forward motion vectors* and a pair for use with *backward motion vectors*. A forward motion vector refers to motion relative to a previous frame. A backward motion vector refers to motion relative to a subsequent frame. Following

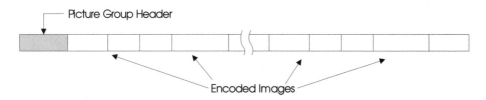

Figure 11.9 MPEG picture group overall organization.

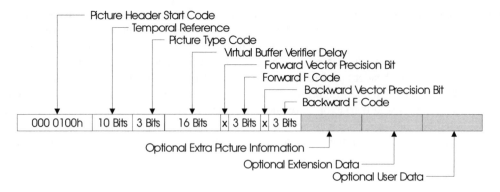

Figure 11.10   MPEG picture header organization.

Table 11.6   Encoding of MPEG Image Type Identifier

Code	Picture Type
000	Do not use
001	I Picture
010	P Picture
011	B Picture
100	D Picture
101	Reserved
110	Reserved
111	Reserved

Table 11.7   Motion Vector Range and Precision Control Codes

Forward F Code or Backward F Code	Precision Bit = 0	Precision Bit = 1
1	−8 to 7.5	−16 to 15
2	−16 to 15.5	−32 to 31
3	−32 to 31.5	−64 to 63
4	−64 to 63.5	−128 to 127
5	−128 to 127.5	−256 to 255
6	−256 to 255.5	−512 to 511
7	−512 to 511.5	−1024 to 1023

these fixed information fields are possibly three optional data fields. The first optional field is called *extra picture information* and may consist or any number of bytes. Each byte is preceded by a flag bit set to one. The last byte is followed by a flag bit set to zero. Following this is an optional extension data block and a possible optional user data block, both of which are described later in this chapter. The overall organization of an image is shown in Figure 11.11. It consists of a picture header followed by one or more image slices.

Image Slice

Encoded images may be subdivided into multiple slices to improve bit-stream error recovery characteristics. An image may contain only a single slice in one extreme or there may be a separate slice for every macro block at the other extreme. The number of slices to be used depends on the amount of overhead that can be tolerated in the encoded bit-stream. Each slice header comprises 40 bits. The format of a slice header is illustrated in Figure 11.12.

The first 32 bits are a slice header start code. The last eight bits of the start code may have a value ranging from 01h to AFh. This number represents the position of the beginning of the slice in terms of macro blocks vertically. For example, a value of 01 indicates the slice starts in the first row of macro blocks and the image. The quantizer scale is a 5-bit unsigned integer ranging in value from one to 31. The quantizer scale may be used to dynamically adjust the degree of quantization applied to transmitted DCT coefficients. The final field in the slice header is an optional extra-slice-information block. The format of this is the same as the extra picture information in the picture header. If no extra information is included, that fact is indicated by a single zero bit. These extra information blocks are reserved for use by future revisions of the specification and should not be used for application specific purposes. Overall organization of a picture slice is illustrated in Figure 11.13. It consists of a slice header followed by one or more macro blocks.

Macro Block

A macro block is the first level in the hierarchy of bit-stream organization that cannot be further subdivided into a variable number of autonomous logical units. The overall size of a macro block, however, is variable because the entire macro block is made up of variable-size codes. There are various types of macro blocks and the types of macro blocks that can be encountered depend on the type of image being encoded. Recall that the bulk of the information contained in a macro block is the DCT coefficients for four 8×8 blocks of luminance pixels and one 8×8 block for each of two

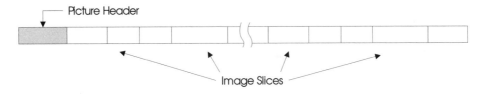

Figure 11.11 MPEG encoded image overall organization.

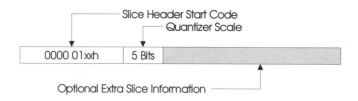

Figure 11.12   MPEG slice header organization.

chrominance coefficient pixels. These may be accompanied by forward or backward motion vectors. The first item in an encoded macro block is a variable-length code called an *address increment*. Macro blocks are numbered sequentially throughout an image starting at the upper-left corner of the image. The macro block address increment specifies the position of the current macro block relative to the previously decoded macro block. Whenever the decoder starts a new image it sets the macro block address to minus one. The smallest possible increment is one so the first macro block in the image can start with an address of zero. The address increment is encoded using variable length codes as shown in Table 11.8.

Note that there are two special codes in the table: *Escape* and *Stuffing*. The escape code is used to encode address increments above 33. The escape code essentially means: "Add 33 to the address plus the increment indicated by the following code." Any number of escape codes can be included effectively allowing any number of macro blocks to be skipped in a decoding sequence. The stuffing code is essentially nothing more than filler that is used to synchronize buffer fullness according to buffer levels anticipated by the encode process. The address increment is followed by another variable-length code indicating the macro-block-type. The codes indicating the macro-block-type differ depending on the type of image in which the macro block is contained. Macro blocks are differentiated by whether or not they contain forward or backward motion vectors, whether they contain an adjustment to the quantization scale factor, whether or not they are coded as intrablocks, and whether or not a coded pattern is included. Tables 11.9, 11.10, and 11.11 show the macro-block-type codes that can appear in intrapictures, predicted pictures, and bidirectional pictures, respectively.

If a new quantizer scale is included, it follows the macro-block-type code. If motion vectors are included, they follow the type code or quantizer scale in the following order: Horizontal forward, horizontal backward, vertical forward, and vertical backward. These are signed integer values represented by a number of bits specified by the vector precision bit and F-code as included in the image header. These are optionally followed by a decoded block pattern consisting of six bits, each

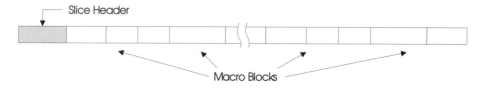

Figure 11.13   MPEG picture slice overall organization.

Table 11.8   MPEG Macro Block Address Increment Encoding

Increment	Variable-Length Code
1	1
2	011
3	010
4	0011
5	0010
6	00011
7	00010
8	0000111
9	0000110
10	00001011
11	00001010
12	00001001
13	00001000
14	00000111
15	00000110
16	0000010111
17	0000010110
18	0000010101
19	0000010100
20	0000010011
21	0000010010
22	00000100011
23	00000100010
24	00000100001
25	00000100000
26	00000011111
27	00000011110
28	00000011101
29	00000011100
30	00000011011
31	00000011010
32	00000011001
33	00000011000
Escape	00000001000
Stuffing	00000001111

of which corresponds to one of the 8×8 blocks that make up the macro block. This 6-bit code is not directly inserted into the bit-stream. Because certain combinations of patterns are more common than others, the 6-bit code is translated into a variable-length code, the shortest of which is three bits and the longest of which is nine bits. Finally, the encoded blocks themselves are included. Motion vectors are encoded as a difference relative to the motion vector of the previous macro block. The prediction vectors are set to zero at the beginning of each slice.

Table 11.9 Macro-Block-Type Codes Appearing in Intrapictures

Quantizer Scale	Variable-Length Code
No	1
Yes	01

Table 11.10 Macro-Block-Type Codes Appearing in Predicted Pictures

Intra Coding	Forward Motion	Coded Pattern	Quantizer Scale	Variable-Length Code
No	Yes	Yes	No	1
No	No	Yes	No	01
No	Yes	No	No	001
Yes	No	No	No	00011
No	Yes	Yes	Yes	00010
No	No	Yes	Yes	00001
Yes	No	Yes	No	000001

Table 11.11 Macro-Block-Type Codes Appearing in Bidirectional Pictures

Intra Coding	Forward Motion	Backward Motion	Coded Pattern	Quantizer Scale	Variable-Length Code
No	Yes	Yes	No	No	10
No	Yes	Yes	Yes	No	11
No	No	Yes	No	No	010
No	No	Yes	Yes	No	011
No	Yes	No	No	No	0010
No	Yes	No	Yes	No	0011
Yes	No	No	No	No	00011
No	Yes	Yes	Yes	Yes	00010
No	Yes	No	Yes	Yes	000011
No	No	Yes	Yes	Yes	000010
Yes	No	No	No	Yes	000001

Block Encoding

Blocks of luminance and chrominance pixels are encoded in a manner very similar to that used for JPEG encoding. The primary difference is that if motion vectors are involved the encoded block represents a difference relative to some other block rather than an absolute set of DCT coefficients. For each 8×8 block to be transmitted within a macro block the encode process begins with a forward DCT as shown in Figure 11.14.

The decision whether or not to encode a block depends on whether or not the macro block is an intra-type, whether there are nonzero motion vectors, and whether the difference between the current block and the previous block in the same position is significant. If after transformation and quantization all DCT coefficients are zero, the block is not transmitted. If all six blocks within a macro block don't need to be transmitted, then the macro block is not transmitted. If a block is a predicted or bidirectional type then there is a coding decision to be made based on what will produce the best image quality and lowest transmitted bit rate. In fact, the motion estimation process is part of the input into the macro-block-type selection decision. That is, within an intrapicture all macro blocks are intra types. Within a predicted picture macro blocks may be predicted types or intra-types. Within a bidirectional picture macro blocks may be any of those three types (intra-, predicted, or bidirectional). A detailed description of how the DCT works is given in Chapter 5. The ordering of blocks within a macro block relative to their positions in the image is shown in Figure 11.15.

After transformation via DCT each of the resulting coefficients is divided by its corresponding quantization coefficient. These may be the default values described earlier in this chapter or may be customized values loaded by way of the sequence header. Under MPEG1 the value of the quantization coefficient for the DC term is always defined as eight and should not be modified. The value of the DC coefficient is always encoded relative to the previous DC coefficient within an image and within an image component. That is, DC values for luminance are always coded relative to other luminance values, and DC values for chrominance are always coded relative to corresponding chrominance values. Because there are four luminance blocks within each macro block, the DC term of block zero is always coded relative to the DC term of block three in the previous

$$\text{FDCT} \qquad S_{vu} = \frac{1}{4} C_u C_v \sum_{x=0}^{7} \sum_{y=0}^{7} S_{yx} \cos\left[\frac{(2x+1)u\pi}{16}\right] \cos\left[\frac{(2y+1)v\pi}{16}\right]$$

$$\text{IDCT} \qquad S_{yx} = \frac{1}{4} \sum_{u=0}^{7} \sum_{v=0}^{7} C_u C_v S_{vu} \cos\left[\frac{(2x+1)u\pi}{16}\right] \cos\left[\frac{(2y+1)v\pi}{16}\right]$$

Where:

C_u and $C_v = \frac{1}{\sqrt{2}}$ when $v,u = 0,0$ (DC component).

C_u and $C_v = 1$ in all other cases.

S_{vu} = Target cell for DCT coefficient.

S_{yx} = Target cell for reconstructed pixel.

Figure 11.14 Forward and inverse DCT equations used in MPEG encode and decode.

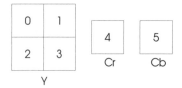

Figure 11.15   Order of 8×8 pixel blocks within an MPEG macro block.

macro block for luminance. At the beginning of each image slice all three DC predictors are set to 128. (A predictor is a variable holding the value of the previous coefficient). As under JPEG, the DC coefficient difference is categorized according to the absolute value of its magnitude. A variable-length code is used to signify the category followed by the corresponding number of bits to carry magnitude information. Table 11.12 gives the categories and corresponding variable length codes for both luminance and chrominance DC difference coefficients.

The quantized coefficients are reordered in a zig-zag sequence in a similar manner as under JPEG. Zero runs are then accumulated and paired with their successive nonzero coefficients and translated through a table into variable-length codes. Unlike JPEG, the run-length and the value of the coefficient can be directly encoded into a single variable-length code. The run-length and value pairs with their corresponding variable-length codes used in MPEG are shown in Table 11.13.

For a run of zero and a value of one, the code is 1x if it is the first coefficient in the block, otherwise it is 11x. Obviously this table is not large enough to accommodate all possible combinations and contains only those combinations which have been found through statistical analysis to occur most frequently. For combinations that do not map to this table an escape code is used. Note that the escape code is the last variable-length code in Table 11.13. The last bit in each code (denoted by "x") is the sign bit and indicates the sign of the corresponding coefficient magnitude. If the escape code is required it is immediately followed by a fixed-length 6-bit code indicating the run length. With six bits, of course, this code can accommodate any possible run length within a block. Following this is an 8- or 16-bit code giving the sign and magnitude of the DCT coefficient as shown in Table 11.14.

Table 11.12   Variable-Length Codes for MPEG DC Difference Coefficients

DC Difference	Length	Luma Code	Chroma Code
0	0	100	00
1	1	00	01
2 to 3	2	01	10
4 to 7	3	101	110
8 to 15	4	110	1110
16 to 31	5	1110	11110
32 to 63	6	11110	111110
64 to 127	7	111110	1111110
128 to 255	8	1111110	11111110

Table 11.13 Variable-Length Codes for MPEG Run-Value Coefficient Pairs

Run	Value	Variable-Length Code
EOB	N/A	10
0	1	1x or 11x
0	2	0100x
0	3	00101x
0	4	0000110x
0	5	00100110x
0	6	00100001x
0	7	0000001010x
0	8	000000011101x
0	9	000000011000x
0	10	000000010011x
0	11	000000010000x
0	12	0000000011010x
0	13	0000000011001x
0	14	0000000011000x
0	15	0000000010111x
0	1d	00000000011111x
0	17	00000000011110x
0	18	00000000011101x
0	19	00000000011100x
0	20	00000000011011x
0	21	00000000011010x
0	22	00000000011001x
0	23	00000000011000x
0	24	00000000010111x
0	25	00000000010110x
0	26	00000000010101x
0	27	00000000010100x
0	28	00000000010011x
0	29	00000000010010x
0	30	00000000010001x
0	31	00000000010000x
0	32	000000000011000x
0	33	000000000010111x
0	34	000000000010110x
0	35	000000000010101x
0	36	000000000010100x
0	37	000000000010011x
0	38	000000000010010x
0	39	000000000010001x
0	0	000000000010000x
1	0	011x
1	2	000110x
1	3	00100101x
1	4	0000001100x

Table 11.13 *continued*

Run	Value	Variable-Length Code
1	5	000000011011x
1	6	0000000010110x
1	7	0000000010101x
1	8	000000000011111x
1	9	000000000011110x
1	10	000000000011101x
1	11	000000000011100x
1	12	000000000011011x
1	13	000000000011010x
1	14	000000000011001x
1	15	0000000000010011x
1	16	0000000000010010x
1	17	0000000000010001x
1	18	0000000000010000x
2	1	0101x
2	2	0000100x
2	3	0000001011x
2	4	000000010100x
2	5	0000000010100x
3	1	00111x
3	2	00100100x
3	3	000000011100x
3	4	0000000010011x
4	1	00110x
4	2	0000001111x
4	3	000000010010x
5	1	000111x
5	2	0000001001x
5	3	0000000010010x
6	1	000101x
6	2	000000011110x
6	3	0000000000010100x
7	1	000100x
7	2	000000010101x
8	1	0000111x
8	2	000000010001x
9	1	0000101x
9	2	0000000010001x
10	1	00100111x
10	2	0000000010000x
11	1	00100011x
11	2	0000000000011010x
12	1	00100010x
12	2	0000000000011001x
13	1	00100000x

Run	Value	Variable-Length Code
13	2	0000000000011000x
14	1	0000001110x
14	2	0000000000010111x
15	1	0000001101x
15	2	0000000000010110x
16	1	0000001000x
16	2	000000000010101x
17	1	000000011111x
18	1	000000011010x
19	1	000000011001x
20	1	000000010111x
21	1	000000010110x
22	1	0000000011111x
23	1	0000000011110x
24	1	0000000011101x
25	1	0000000011100x
26	1	0000000011011x
27	1	0000000000011111x
28	1	0000000000011110x
29	1	0000000000011101x
30	1	0000000000011100x
31	1	0000000000011011x
Escape	N/A	000001

For each macro block in a predicted or bidirectional image a decision must be made whether to code it directly as an intrablock or relative to a corresponding block in another image. A common technique is to encode the block both ways, decode it, and then calculate an error relative to the original and determine which method produces the smallest error. If it is determined that the block can be encoded as a relative block, the DCT coefficients are examined after quantization to determine if any of them are nonzero. If all of them are zero it means there was not enough difference between the current block and the previous corresponding block to show up after the quantization process. In this case, there is no need to transmit the block; the old one can be used. If the block is transmitted, regardless of whether it is an intrablock or a relative block, the decision whether to modify the quantization scale is a matter of buffer management. If the buffer level is tending toward overflow the quantization scale factor may be increased. If tending toward underflow it may be decreased. If the buffer level is within reasonable limits the quantization scale factor is generally not modified.

Summary

The MPEG specification does not define how encoders or decoders should be designed. The bitstream format and encoding specification are concise enough so that it should be fairly straightforward to design a decoder. As long as the accuracy requirements of the mathematics are met, a con-

Table 11.14 Magnitude Encoding for Escaped DCT Coefficients

Value	Variable-Length Code
−256	Do not use
−255	1000000000000001
−254	1000000000000010
...	...
−130	1000000001111110
−129	1000000001111111
−128	1000000010000000
−127	10000001
−126	10000010
−125	10000011
...	...
−3	11111101
−2	11111110
−1	11111111
0	Do not use
1	00000001
2	00000010
3	00000011
...	...
125	01111101
126	01111110
127	01111111
128	0000000010000000
129	0000000010000001
130	0000000010000010
...	...
253	0000000011111101
254	0000000011111110
255	0000000011111111

forming bit-stream can be adequately decoded. A more difficult task is determining how much compute power is required to adequately decode a conforming bit-stream. There is enough flexibility in the encode process to allow a wide latitude of techniques to be used. The amount of computing power that could be expended on this task is almost unlimited. It is even more true for encode than for decode that the difficulty lies in determining how much compute power is adequate at one extreme, and necessary at the other. Numerous specialized hardware solutions have been developed for both encode and decode of MPEG video streams. Prices have fallen rapidly and there is a great deal of interest in using MPEG for commercial satellite and cable broadcast.

12

H.261 Video
Compression Standard

The *H.261 standard* is similar in many respects to MPEG. Both are based on much of the same research and statistical analysis. While MPEG is designed for full-motion video transmission within a fairly constrained range of data rates, H.261 is designed to be more flexible in terms of the data rates it can support. H.261 is intended specifically for two-way telecommunications applications. As such, the encode process is greatly simplified over MPEG in order to bring it more in line with the decode process in terms of complexity and computing power required. This is because in a two-way communications environment it is critical to encode the video in real time, same as the decode process. It is also important that as little delay as possible be introduced into the video stream. That is, if the time from an action in front of the camera at one end until it is seen at the other end is more than a small fraction of a second it will create an annoying disruption in the communication process. H.261 is part of a larger umbrella specification called *H.320*. This includes specifications for audio signal compression and decompression, audio, video and data channel framing and error correction, and communication channel signaling protocols. H.320 and all its component specifications was developed by the *International Telegraph and Telephone Consultative Committee (CCITT)*. H.261 is DCT-based, uses predictive encoding, macro blocks, and other concepts similar to the MPEG slice organization. This chapter is an overview of the H.261 specification which will point out its particular differences from and similarities to MPEG.

Encoder Structure

An H.261 encoder can be visualized as a serial transform and quantization structure with a feedback loop that models the decoder. The feedback loop is required because the decoder reconstructs predicted images based on previously decoded images. The errors introduced by the encode and decode process would accumulate rapidly, causing serious loss of image quality if the encode process did not use decoded pictures in calculating the prediction coefficients. Figure 12.1 illustrates the flow of

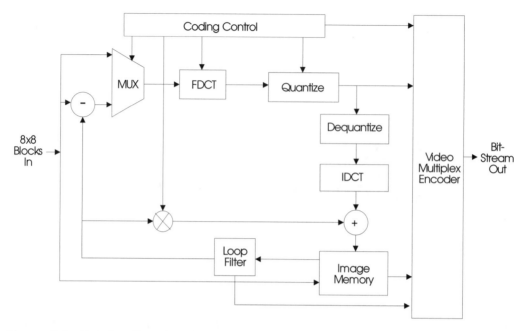

Figure 12.1   Data flow through an H.261 encoder.

8×8-pixel blocks through an H.261 encoder. These blocks may be fed directly into the forward DCT and quantization sections to be encoded and sent to the output stream. They can also be dequantized and inverse-transformed and stored in an image memory.

These decoded blocks are then filtered and used as the basis for delta calculations in subsequent predicted frames. In creating multiple generations of predicted images the previous image blocks must be added back together with the newly decoded blocks in the model decoder, thus the addition symbol between the inverse DCT block and the image memory. The video multiplex encoder has responsibility for calculating run lengths and generating variable-length code symbols. The specification is designed to work with images using a *common intermediate format (CIF)*. The CIF is defined as 352×288 pixels. Recall from the MPEG discussion that this is a scaled-down aspect ratio from a PAL format source image. Evidently, while drafting the specification there was some bickering between the Americans and Europeans over which broadcast standard should be used as the basis for the CIF. A compromise was reached where the standard frame rate would be specified at 30 frames per second and the standard image size at 352×288. Of course, the frame rate is variable so European systems can easily run at 25 frames per second (half the standard 50 frames per second PAL frame rate) without a problem. American systems using NTSC cameras have to somehow scale a 480-line image down, or a 240-line image up, to 288 lines. It seems the Europeans drove a hard bargain in this case. An alternative image format known as *quarter CIF (QCIF)* is 176×144 pixels. The color format and subsampling scheme are the same as those used in MPEG. Chrominance data is subsampled 2:1 both horizontally and vertically for an overall 4:1 subsampling ratio. Alignment of luminance and chrominance samples are as illustrated in Figure 12.2.

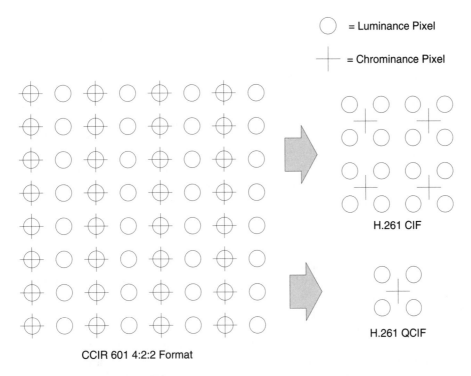

Figure 12.2 Alignment of luminance and chrominance samples in an H.261 image.

Frame rate can be controlled by dropping one, two, or three frames between transmitted frames. Motion compensation is also supported in the specification but is not required. The range of motion vectors is restricted to plus or minus 15 pixels horizontally and vertically. Each image is subdivided into 8×8-pixel blocks organized into macro blocks the same as in MPEG. The content and organization of macro blocks is illustrated in Figure 12.3.

The loop filter operates on separate 8×8 blocks. The horizontal and vertical filter processes can be applied separately with a filter kernel defined as illustrated in Figure 12.4. Edge pixels are filtered only in one direction parallel to the edge.

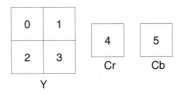

Figure 12.3 Macro-block organization.

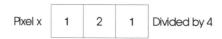

Pixel x	1	2	1	Divided by 4

Figure 12.4 Loop filter kernel definition.

The forward and inverse DCT is performed using the same equation as used in MPEG and JPEG, as shown in Figure 12.5. All of the quantization coefficients used on a given block are the same except for the DC quantizer which has a value of eight. The AC quantization coefficient may vary from a value of two up to a maximum of 62. After decoding, any pixels with a value less than zero or greater than 255 are clipped to a range of zero to 255. The bit-stream produced by an H.261 compliant encoder is organized in a four-level hierarchy similar in some respects to that used with MPEG. The following paragraphs describe the various levels of the H.261 bit-stream organization.

Picture

A picture or image begins with a picture header as illustrated in Figure 12.6. The first field in the picture header is a picture start code which comprises 20 bits. This is followed by a 5-bit unsigned integer temporal reference.

When images are being transmitted at the full-rated frame rate, the temporal reference simply counts frames, rolling over back to zero after every 32 frames. If images are dropped from the sequence the temporal reference also indicates how many were dropped. For example, if the previous image transmitted was number five and three frames were dropped, the next frame would have a temporal reference number of nine. The picture-type field is composed of a sequence of single-bit indicators. These may optionally be followed by a series of extra data bytes using the same scheme as outlined in MPEG for extra data headers. If the flag bit is set to zero it means no further data follows. If it is a one then the next eight bits represent a data byte and the next bit after that indicates whether more data is to follow, and so on. The overall structure of an image is illustrated in Figure 12.7. A picture header is followed by several groups of blocks.

$$\text{FDCT} \qquad S_{vu} = \tfrac{1}{4}\, C_u\, C_v \sum_{x=0}^{7} \sum_{y=0}^{7} S_{yx}\, \cos\left[\tfrac{(2x+1)u\pi}{16}\right] \cos\left[\tfrac{(2y+1)v\pi}{16}\right]$$

$$\text{IDCT} \qquad S_{yx} = \tfrac{1}{4} \sum_{u=0}^{7} \sum_{v=0}^{7} C_u\, C_v\, S_{vu}\, \cos\left[\tfrac{(2x+1)u\pi}{16}\right] \cos\left[\tfrac{(2y+1)v\pi}{16}\right]$$

Where: C_u and $C_v = \dfrac{1}{\sqrt{2}}$ when $v,u = 0,0$ (DC component).

C_u and $C_v = 1$ in all other cases.

S_{vu} = Target cell for DCT coefficient.

S_{yx} = Target cell for reconstructed pixel.

Figure 12.5 DCT and IDCT equations for H.261.

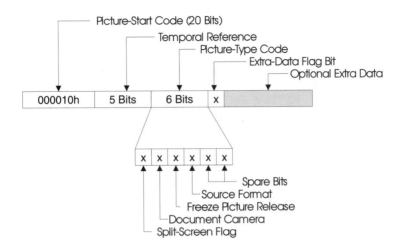

Figure 12.6   H.261 picture header organization.

Group of Blocks

Unlike MPEG, the next level of logical subdivision has a fixed organization. A group of blocks is similar to an MPEG slice but the number of macro blocks in an H.261 group of blocks is fixed. Each group of blocks in the bit-stream is preceded by a group-of-blocks header as shown in Figure 12.8.

The first field in a group-of-blocks header is the group-of-blocks start code. This is followed by a 4-bit number that indicates the group number. This field can take values from one to 12, inclusive. In a CIF image there are 12 groups of blocks. In a QCIF image there are three groups of blocks. Each group of blocks is composed of three rows of 11 macro blocks each. A CIF picture is arranged as two groups of blocks horizontally and six groups of blocks vertically. A QCIF picture has a single group of blocks horizontally and three groups of blocks vertically. Group-of-blocks spatial organization for CIF and QCIF images is illustrated in Figure 12.9.

Following the group number is a 5-bit group quantizer which is the AC quantization coefficient applied to all macro blocks that do not have an explicit quantizer defined. Following this is an extra-data flag bit optionally followed by data bytes in the same format used in the picture header. The overall organization of a group of blocks in the bit-stream is shown in Figure 12.10. A group-of-blocks header is followed by 33 macro blocks.

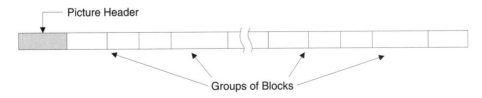

Figure 12.7   H.261 image structure.

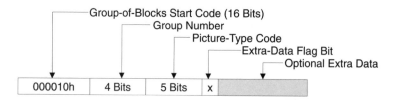

Figure 12.8   H.261 group-of-blocks header organization.

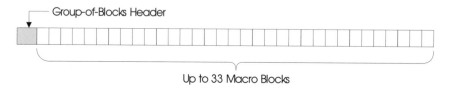

Figure 12.9   Group-of-locks organization within an encoded bit-stream.

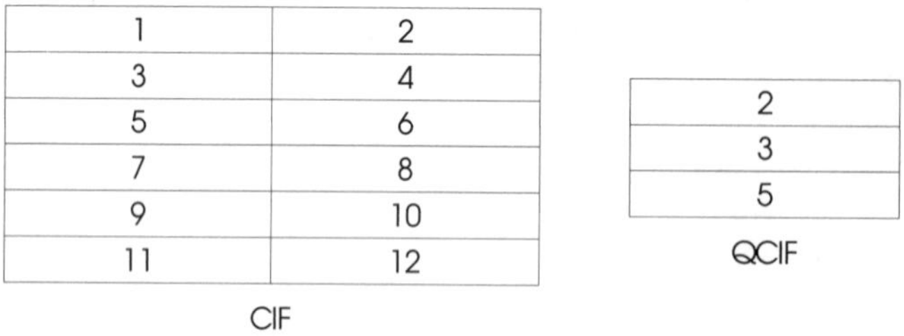

1	2
3	4
5	6
7	8
9	10
11	12

CIF

2
3
5

QCIF

Figure 12.10   Group-of-blocks spatial organization for CIF and QCIF images.

Macro Blocks

Macro blocks are organized spatially within a group of blocks as shown in Figure 12.11. Each macro block starts with a macro-block header as shown in Figure 12.12.

The first field in the macro-block header is the macro-block address increment. This is a variable-length code defining the difference between the address of the current macro block and that of

1	2	3	4	5	6	7	8	9	10	11
12	13	14	15	16	17	18	19	20	21	22
23	24	25	26	27	28	29	30	31	32	33

Figure 12.11   Organization of macro blocks within an H.261 group-of-blocks.

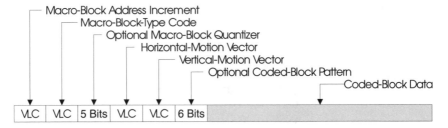

Figure 12.12   H.261 macro-block header organization.

the previous one in the bit-stream. The address increment field for the first macro block in a group of macro blocks contains the actual address of the macro block rather than an increment value. If all macro blocks are present in a group of blocks this field will have a value of one for every macro block. The possible values and their corresponding variable length codes are shown in Table 12.1.

Following the macro-block address increment field is another variable-length code indicating the macro-block type. The block type is determined by the presence or absence of a macro-block quantizer, motion vectors, a coded-block pattern, and transmitted DCT coefficients. Table 12.2 shows the variable-length block-type codes and their corresponding conditions.

Table 12.1   Variable-Length Codes for Macro-Block Address Increment

Increment	Variable-Length Code
1	1
2	011
3	010
4	0011
5	0010
6	00011
7	00010
8	0000111
9	0000110
10	00001011
11	00001010
12	00001001
13	00001000
14	00000111
15	00000110
16	0000010111
17	0000010110
18	0000010101
19	0000010100
20	0000010011

Table 12.1 *continued*

Increment	Variable-Length Code
21	0000010010
22	00000100011
23	00000100010
24	00000100001
25	00000100000
26	00000011111
27	00000011110
28	00000011101
29	00000011100
30	00000011011
31	00000011010
32	00000011001
33	00000011000
Stuffing	00000001111

Table 12.2 Variable-Length Block-Type Codes

Quantizer Sent	Motion Vector	Coded Pattern	Transmitted Coefficients	Variable-Length Code
No	No	Yes	Yes	1
No	Yes	Yes	Yes	01
No	Yes	No	No	001
No	No	No	Yes	0001
Yes	No	Yes	Yes	00001
Yes	Yes	Yes	Yes	000001
Yes	No	No	Yes	0000001
No	Yes	Yes	Yes	00000001
No	Yes	No	No	000000001
Yes	Yes	Yes	Yes	0000000001

Following this is a 5-bit field which is a macro-block quantization coefficient. This modifies any value that was set in the group-of-blocks header. The new value remains in effect until changed again by another macro-block quantizer. Motion vectors are included in every macro block and represent the difference between the current macro-block motion vector and the previous macro-block motion vector. That is, the values given in the motion vectors for a given macro block are added to the motion vectors of the previous macro block. There are three cases in which the motion vectors from the previous macro block are reset to zero before calculating the relative displacement of the new motion vector. The first is calculating the relative displacement of motion vectors for macro blocks numbered one, 12, and 23 within a group of blocks. This is because these are the leftmost blocks in each of the three rows that make up a group of blocks. The second case is calculating the relative displacement for macro blocks which are not spatially adjacent to the previous macro blocks, that is, if the block-address increment is greater than one. The third case is if the previous macro block was not motion compensated. In this case, the motion vectors from the previous block would be meaningless. Each motion vector is represented by a variable-length code. Because motion vectors are limited to an absolute magnitude no greater than 15, the absolute difference can never exceed 30. All but three of the motion-vector codes represent two possible values. For any given existing motion-vector value only one of the two possible deltas will produce a new motion vector that does not fall outside the permitted range. Thus ambiguity is eliminated. The variable-length codes and the motion-vector difference values they represent are listed in Table 12.3.

Table 12.3   Variable-Length Codes for Motion-Vector Difference Values

Motion Vector	Variable-Length Code
−16 or 16	00000011001
−15 or 17	00000011011
−14 or 18	00000011101
−13 or 19	00000011111
−12 or 20	00000100001
−11 or 21	00000100011
−10 or 22	0000010011
−9 or 23	0000010101
−8 or 24	0000010111
−7 or 25	00000111
−6 or 26	00001001
−5 or 27	00001011
−4 or 28	0000111
−3 or 29	00011
−2 or 30	0011
−1	011
0	1
1	010
2 or −30	0010
3 or −29	00010
4 or −28	0000110
5 or −27	00001010
6 or −26	00001000
7 or −25	00000110
8 or −24	0000010110
9 or −23	0000010100
10 or −22	0000010010
11 or −21	00000100010
12 or −20	00000100000
13 or −19	00000011110
14 or −18	00000011100
15 or −17	00000011010

Following the motion vectors is an optional 6-bit field. Each bit defines whether or not one of the six possible blocks within a macro block is actually encoded. If there is no change in a given block from the previous frame then there is no need to transmit any information about that block. The technique for encoding block data is similar to that used for MPEG. A set of variable-length codes are defined for the most commonly occurring run-value pairs. These codes are shown in Table 12.4.

Table 12.4 Variable-Length Codes for Run-Value Pairs in H.261

Run	Value	Variable-Length Code
EOB	N/A	10
0	1	1x or 11x
0	2	0100x
0	3	00101x
0	4	0000110x
0	5	00100110x
0	6	00100001x
0	7	0000001010x
0	8	000000011101x
0	9	000000011000x
0	10	000000010011x
0	11	000000010000x
0	12	0000000011010x
0	13	0000000011001x
0	14	0000000011000x
0	15	0000000010111x
0	1d	00000000011111x
0	17	00000000011110x
0	18	00000000011101x
0	19	00000000011100x
0	20	00000000011011x
0	21	00000000011010x
0	22	00000000011001x
0	23	00000000011000x
0	24	00000000010111x
0	25	00000000010110x
0	26	00000000010101x
0	27	00000000010100x
0	28	00000000010011x
0	29	00000000010010x
0	30	00000000010001x
0	31	00000000010000x
0	32	000000000011000x
0	33	000000000010111x
0	34	000000000010110x
0	35	000000000010101x
0	36	000000000010100x
0	37	000000000010011x

Run	Value	Variable-Length Code
0	38	000000000010010x
0	39	000000000010001x
0	0	000000000010000x
1	0	011x
1	2	000110x
1	3	00100101x
1	4	0000001100x
1	5	000000011011x
1	6	000000000010110x
1	7	000000000010101x
1	8	00000000000011111x
1	9	00000000000011110x
1	10	00000000000011101x
1	11	00000000000011100x
1	12	00000000000011011x
1	13	00000000000011010x
1	14	00000000000011001x
1	15	000000000000010011x
1	16	000000000000010010x
1	17	000000000000010001x
1	18	000000000000010000x
2	1	0101x
2	2	0000100x
2	3	0000001011x
2	4	000000010100x
2	5	0000000010100x
3	1	00111x
3	2	00100100x
3	3	000000011100x
3	4	0000000010011x
4	1	00110x
4	2	0000001111x
4	3	000000010010x
5	1	000111x
5	2	0000001001x
5	3	000000000010010x
6	1	000101x
6	2	000000011110x
6	3	0000000000010100x
7	1	000100x
7	2	000000010101x
8	1	0000111x
8	2	000000010001x
9	1	0000101x
9	2	0000000010001x
10	1	00100111x
10	2	0000000010000x

Table 12.4   *continued*

Run	Value	Variable-Length Code
11	1	00100011x
11	2	0000000000011010x
12	1	00100010x
12	2	0000000000011001x
13	1	00100000x
13	2	0000000000011000x
14	1	0000001110x
14	2	0000000000010111x
15	1	0000001101x
15	2	0000000000010110x
16	1	0000001000x
16	2	000000000010101x
17	1	000000011111x
18	1	000000011010x
19	1	000000011001x
20	1	000000010111x
21	1	000000010110x
22	1	0000000011111x
23	1	0000000011110x
24	1	0000000011101x
25	1	0000000011100x
26	1	0000000011011x
27	1	0000000000011111x
28	1	0000000000011110x
29	1	0000000000011101x
30	1	0000000000011100x
31	1	0000000000011011x
Escape	N/A	000001

For a run of zero and a value of one, the code is 1x if it is the first coefficient in the block, otherwise it is 11x. If a particular run-value pair cannot be represented by one of these codes, an escape code is transmitted followed by the 6-bit run length and an 8-bit value. The 6-bit run length is a simple unsigned integer. The codes used to represent quantized DCT coefficients are given in Table 12.5. An end-of-block code is transmitted following the last nonzero DCT coefficient from the zig-zag order block.

Forward Error Correction

Because H.261 is designed for transmission over a medium which may be subject to data errors, an error detection and correction scheme is incorporated. This involves dividing the encoded bit-stream into regular blocks for each of which a parity signature is generated. The block size is 492 bits and the parity signature is 18 bits. Each block is preceded by a frame-sequence bit and a fill-

Table 12.5   Encoding Scheme for Escaped DCT Coefficients

Value	Fixed-Length Code
−127	10000001
−126	10000010
−125	10000011
...	...
−3	11111101
−2	11111110
−1	11111111
0	Do Not Use
1	00000001
2	00000010
3	00000011
...	...
125	01111101
126	01111110
127	01111111

indicator bit, and followed by the parity signature. The frame-sequence bit is used to verify and maintain error-correction frame synchronization. These bits are transmitted with a regular repeating pattern of 00011011, so that the sequence bit pattern repeats for every eight error-correction framing blocks. The fill-indicator bit set to one indicates that the following 492 bits represent encoded image data. If set to zero, the following 492 bits are simply bit-stream filler data. Figure 12.13 illustrates the organization of error-correction framing bits. The fill-indicator bit is included in the parity signature calculation.

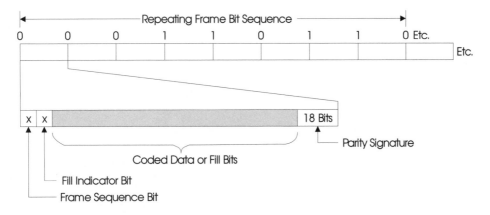

Figure 12.13   Error-correction block structure imposed on encoded bit-stream.

Summary

H.261 has many structures and techniques in common with MPEG. It is optimized to support a wider range of encoded data rates from 40 kilobits to two megabits per second. It is designed specifically with telecommunications applications in mind. The simpler encoding technique of H.261 allows a more symmetrical implementation of encoding and decoding than MPEG. It also helps reduce the delays introduced by the encoder. An error-detection and correction scheme is incorporated to facilitate real-time transmission over digital media having various levels of signal integrity.

APPENDIX A

Motion Video and Still Image File Formats

Because the focus of this book is on computer processing of video on a PC, the storage medium chosen for all the software video examples is disk files. All of the video sequences used as examples for this book were captured using Video for Windows capture hardware. This Appendix describes the relevant Video for Windows file formats and the simplified video and image formats used for the sample material provided with this book. The Video for Windows file format was adapted from earlier multimedia file formats created by Microsoft. As such, they require a much higher level of flexibility than is needed for demonstration purposes here, as well as bring along some multimedia baggage. The file formats used for the demonstration videos are greatly simplified from this. They are not designed to carry audio information along with video, for example. A program is provided to convert from Video for Windows format into the demonstration file format. The demonstration files can be compressed but the conversion program cannot convert a compressed Video for Windows file directly. There are many different Video for Windows file compression formats but it is necessary to have the appropriate compression or decompression driver in order to use one of these compressed files with Windows applications. The uncompressed files can take the form of 24-bit, 16-bit, or 15-bit RGB, or 8-bit-per-pixel color index format. This is also sometimes referred to as *color look up table (CLUT)* format. The conversion program supports 24-bit RGB and 8-bit color index formats. The conversion process for 8-bit color index formats does little more than remove most of the file header information and simplify the frame format. When reading 24-bit RGB video files the conversion program creates either 4:2:2 subsampled YCrCb format or can convert them to 8-bit-per-pixel color index format. To do this it is necessary to create a color palette with no more than 240 entries (this reserves 16 entries for the standard VGA colors). The technique for doing this can be examined in the source code provided later in this Appendix. Essentially, the technique used here is to reduce the total number of possible colors by using quantization and then grouping those colors based on the statistics of their use, creating a table of the 240 most-used colors. The table is then searched to find the nearest match to each 24-bit pixel from the original image. The following sections describe the relevant file formats and the programs used to convert between them.

Eight-Bit and 24-Bit AVI Files

An *AVI file* is a variant on a more generic file-type known as the *RIFF file*. This was originally evolved to support multimedia data types. It is built around the concept of parallel data streams and can support virtually any number of them. Of course, there are practical limitations on how many streams can be handled by an ordinary computer, as well as actual limitations on the number of streams that can be represented in a file header. However, the former is bound to become a limitation much sooner than the latter. Logically, a RIFF file is subdivided into units known as *chunks*. Each chunk has a very simple format which is shown in Figure A.1. See also Chapter 8 for a further discussion of RIFF files.

The chunk length defines the number of bytes in the chunk following the chunk-length field and including the optional chunk-subtype field. An AVI file is essentially just a RIFF chunk stored in a DOS file as shown in Figure A.2. The data segment of the RIFF chunk is subdivided into two or three subsections. The first section is the header chunk, which is shown in Figure A.3. The data field of the header chunk is further subdivided into a main header chunk followed by one or more stream header chunks. The format of the main header chunk is shown in Figure A.4.

Notice this is the first level of logical subdivision that does not have the optional chunk-subtype field because the data in the chunk has a fixed format. Following the main header chunk is one or more stream header chunks, the number of which depends on how many data streams are present in the file. Each stream header chunk has the format shown in Figure A.5.

The stream header chunk is divided into two or three subchunks. The first is the main stream header chunk, which is very similar in format to the main AVI header chunk. The second is the stream format chunk which defines how data in the actual stream is formatted. The third is an optional chunk which contains extra information used by the decoder. The exact format of this data is not defined under the AVI specification. The main stream header chunk format is illustrated in Figure A.6.

The fields within the data structures contained in this and the main AVI header structure are described in Chapter 8. Following the header chunk is a stream format chunk. This contains the data structure defined under Windows which carries certain stream-specific parameters to regulate the playback of the stream. The format of this chunk is illustrated in Figure A.7.

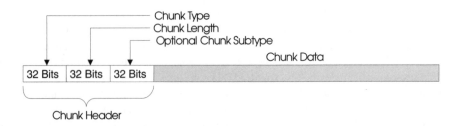

Figure A.1   Elementary Microsoft file chunk format.

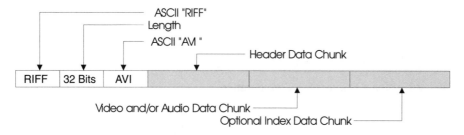

Figure A.2 RIFF AVI file format illustration.

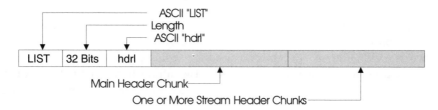

Figure A.3 RIFF AVI file header organization.

Figure A.4 RIFF AVI main header chunk organization.

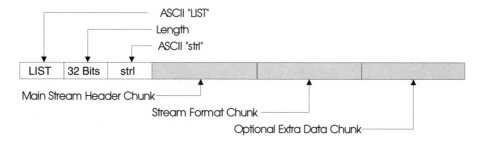

Figure A.5 Stream header chunk organization.

Figure A.6   Main stream header chunk organization.

Figure A.7   Stream format definition chunk organization.

The structures contained in the data segment of this chunk are defined in the Windows Software Developer's Kit documentation. The BITMAPINFO structure is used for image streams and the two WAVEFORMAT structures are used for audio streams. The format of the optional stream-specific data chunk is shown in Figure A.8. The information found in these structures can also be seen in the source code for the include file named AVI_RIFF.H shown in Appendix B. This include file is used in many of the demonstration programs.

Applications typically just pass this data along to the format-specific driver under Video for Windows. Following the main header section of the AVI file is the chunk that contains the actual audio and/or video data for which the file was created. Figure A.9 shows how this chunk is organized. It is simply a chunk header followed by one or more subordinate chunks.

Typically, one of these subordinate chunks is used for each frame in a video sequence. If there is only one data stream in the file, as in the case of video with no audio, each of these chunks consists simply of a chunk header followed by the actual image data as illustrated in Figure A.10.

Figure A.8   Optional stream data chunk organization.

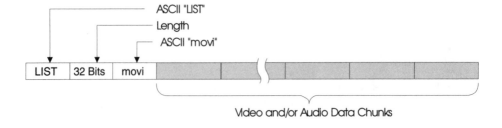

Figure A.9   AVI file data chunk containing the actual video frames.

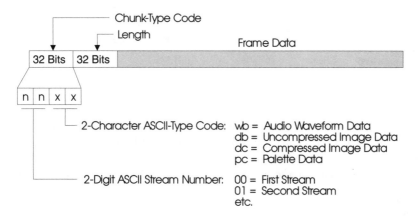

Figure A.10 Frame chunk organization.

The chunk type code defines what kind of data is contained in the chunk. If there are multiple streams within the file each of these subordinate chunks may be further subdivided. In this case the format of the subordinate chunk is as shown in Figure A.11. This chunk is typically subdivided into a number of subordinate chunks equal to the number of currently active streams. If there are multiple streams they do not all necessarily start at the same point in the file. For example, if there is a video stream and an audio stream there might be several frames of video data in the file before the audio stream starts. In this case there would be several record chunks as shown in Figure A.11 which contain only video followed by a series of record chunks which contain both video and audio. Typically this is done to allow buffering of video frames to facilitate synchronization of audio and video. When record chunks of this type are used, the subordinate chunks take the form shown in Figure A.10. The final chunk in the file, if present, is the optional index chunk as shown in Figure A.12.

This chunk is not further subdivided into subordinate chunks. In the data field it contains a series of data structures, each 16 bytes long, one for each frame in the main data chunk. The contents of this structure are defined in Chapter 8. The index chunk is provided to support random access to the video file. This is useful for reverse play or editing of the video sequence.

If the uncompressed video data is in 24-bit RGB format, each pixel is represented by three successive bytes: one for red, one for green, and one for blue. These proceed from the top-left corner of the image in scanning order left to right, top to bottom. The number of bytes in the image is therefore three times the height times the width. For 8-bit pixels each pixel occupies one byte in the

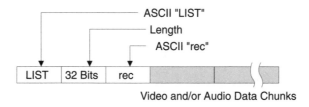

Figure A.11 Frame record chunk organization.

Figure A.12   Optional index chunk organization.

file following the same order as the 24-bit format. In Windows parlance these are called *device-independent bitmaps (DIBs)*. There are several other types of DIBs but they will not be discussed here because they are not supported by the conversion program for demonstration purposes. For a full description of DIB formats refer to the Windows Software Developer's Kit documentation.

VID File Format

The VID file format was created specifically to support a series of images for use as motion video. The format is quite simple, consisting of a small file header followed by a series of images. The format of the file header is shown in Figure A.13, while Figure A.14 shows how the file is organized.

Following the file header the images are stored contiguously in sequential order. For uncompressed video files the boundaries between sequential images are determined simply by calculating the size of the image. For example, a 160×120 video using 8-bit color lookup format would consist of a series of frames each containing 19,200 bytes. The format flags in the file header contain three significant bits. These control whether the file is compressed or uncompressed, whether it is a color or monochrome image, and whether it is in 8-bit lookup format or in 4:2:2 YCrCb format. The arrangement of these flag bits is illustrated in Figure A.15.

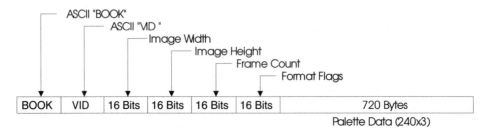

Figure A.13   VID file header organization.

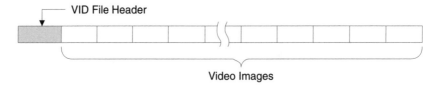

Figure A.14   Overall VID file organization.

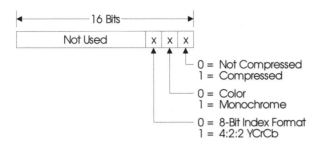

Figure A.15 Flag bit assignments in VID file header.

VID files can be compressed if they are stored in 8-bit color index format. These compressed files can be played back the same as uncompressed files. In fact, playback of compressed files tends to be smoother because it is not as constrained by disk access time and latency. A distinction was made between color and monochrome because some of the filtering and other processing demonstration programs cannot operate on color index pixels. The monochrome format defines the pixels to represent luminance only, ranging from 16 to 255. This allows math operations to be performed on them. The YCrCb format was devised to allow the JPEG demonstration programs to compress and decompress full-color images. Files with this format can be played back using the viewer program but the viewer only shows the luminance portion of the data so the file appears as a monochrome image. This was done because the disk data rate and the time required to perform color space conversion in real time produces an unacceptably slow frame rate on many less powerful machines.

Compressed Color Index Format

A very simple compression algorithm is used for color index format video files. It works simply by eliminating redundancy between sequential images in the file. Redundancy simply means that if the value of a pixel is the same in the current image as it was in the previous image there is no need to store it in the file. The previous one can simply be used instead. A threshold level is defined to allow pixels to be compared on the basis of their RGB values rather than their index values. This way, a pixel does not have to be an exact match to be classified as redundant. To reduce sensitivity to signal noise the threshold is set at a level below which any difference in pixel values is assumed to be irrelevant. Each row of pixels in the image is analyzed to find groups of pixels which do not need to be changed relative to the previous image. These groups are stored as an escape code and a count value which indicates to the viewer program how many pixels to skip before storing the next valid pixels. Recall that 16 colors in the VGA palette are reserved for standard VGA colors. This means that all valid image pixels have an index value of 16 or higher. Therefore, zero is used as the escape code. Whenever zero is detected, the next byte indicates the number of pixels to be skipped before storing any pixels to follow. Of course, this means the size of an image frame in the file can no longer be determined simply by multiplying the width times the height. Therefore, two 16-bit integers are stored at the beginning of each image frame in a compressed file as shown in Figure A.16.

The frame number is used to maintain frame synchronization while decompressing. The viewer program always knows the number of the next frame to be played, so if the correct frame

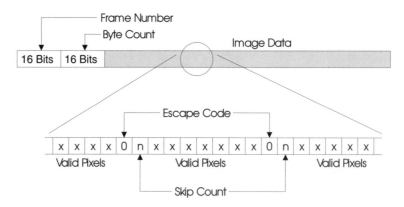

Figure A.16   Illustration of 8-bit-per-pixel compression in VID file.

number is not found in the correct location in the file, it knows an error has occurred or the input file is corrupted. The block length indicates how many bytes to read for the current frame before decompression.

YCrCb Format

VID files can store images in YCrCb format, also sometimes called YUV format. In this case luminance and chrominance data are stored separately and chrominance is subsampled 2:1 horizontally. Each frame, therefore, requires twice the number of bytes as the equivalent color lookup image format. Each pair of pixels requires four bytes to represent. Two bytes represent luminance information for the two pixels and the remaining two bytes carry chrominance information which is applied to both pixels. Figure A.17 illustrates how data is stored in this case. For display, only the Y pixels are extracted and truncated to a minimum value of 16 before being displayed with a standardized monochrome palette. Otherwise, overall organization is the same as for an 8-bit color lookup video file. The number of bytes per frame is two times the height times the width.

JPEG File Format

For demonstration purposes the JPEG file format was adapted from the VID file format. The JPEG specification defines a bit-stream format for a single-image frame but not for anything outside of the image frame. A video sequence requires a series of images and, therefore, JPEG compression is applied to images independently. These are then stored within the VID file format in a manner sim-

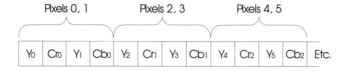

Figure A.17   Illustration of color component storage order in YCrCb VID file format.

Figure A.18 Organization of JPEG compressed VID file image frame.

ilar to the other formats. The same file header is used except that instead of the letters BOOK in the first four bytes, the letters JPEG are used. To delineate between frames a technique is used similar to that used for compressed color lookup images. Each frame starts with a reset marker as defined in the JPEG specification. This is followed by a block-length field which specifies how many bytes are occupied by the frame. The remaining bytes constitute a compressed bit-stream conforming for the most part to the JPEG specification. This scheme is illustrated in Figure A.18.

The qualification "for the most part" is used because the compressed bit-stream does not conform fully to the JPEG specification. Some features of the JPEG bit-stream sequence were omitted in order to simplify the demonstration program source code to allow a clearer focus on the fundamental elements of JPEG. Those elements omitted include: differential encoding of DC frequency coefficients, quantization table marker segments, and Huffman table marker segments. The quantization tables and Huffman code tables are simply embedded in the program source code rather than in the image file. The block ordering does not exactly follow the JPEG specification, either. Again, this was just a matter of simplifying the source code for better readability.

Alternate AVI-to-VID Conversion Program Source Code

The following source code is a more complex implementation of a conversion program which can accept both 8-bit and 24-bit full-frame AVI file formats. It is also designed to accommodate a range of image resolutions rather than being restricted to 160×120 as AVI2VID.EXE is. A debug switch option is included to allow the contents of the various AVI header structures to be dumped to the display for inspection. The output format can be either 8-bit or 4:2:2 YCrCb format. The latter is needed for the JPEG demonstration programs. None of the video files included on the sample diskettes are in YCrCb form because it takes too much space. The following program, named AVI_READ.EXE, is included mainly to provide a deeper understanding of AVI file structure, and a basis for explicit AVI file decoding if the reader so desires. The program is DOS based and command-line oriented. Invocation syntax is as follows:

```
AVI_READ <input file> <output file> <optional switch>
```

The optional switch can be either /d or /8. If /d is used, the program will not convert the input file, but will display the information contained in the AVI file header structures. If /8 is used, and the input file is 24-bit format, an optimized palette will be generated and the 24-bit AVI file converted to 8-bit VID format. Otherwise, 8-bit AVI files produce 8-bit VID files, and 24-bit AVI files produce 4:2:2 YCrCb VID files. The source code follows:

```
//============================================================
// AVI_READ.CPP
```

```
//————————————————————
// Program:  Implementation code for AVI_READ.EXE
// Author:   Phil Mattison
// Compiler: Borland Turbo C++ v1.01
//————————————————————

#include <stdlib.h>
#include <stdio.h>
#include <conio.h>
#include <string.h>
#include <alloc.h>
#include <math.h>
#include <dos.h>
#include "avi_riff.h"


//————————————————————
// Global program variables
//————————————————————

MainAVIHeader      main_header;              // AVI main header
AVIStreamHeader    stream_header;            // AVI stream header
BitMapInfoHeader   stream_format;            // AVI DIB stream format
RGBQuad            palette[256];             // VGA palette data
int                color_count[9];           // Color classification
vid                vid_header;               // Output file header
BYTE               local_palette[240][3];    // Local palette storage
BYTE               *frame_buffer;            // Frame buffer pointer
BYTE               color_table[4096];        // Palette generation table
FILE               *output;                  // File output buffer pointer
int                stream_number;            // Stream number storage
int                frame;                    // Frame counter
int                clut_flag;                // 8-Bit or 24-Bit flag

struct ColorInfo                             // Color classification
  {
  BYTE        Blue;
  BYTE        Green;
  BYTE        Red;
  BYTE        palette_index;
  long        count;
  ColorInfo   *next;
  } *color_list[9];


//————————————————————
int CMP4(char *s1, char *s2)   // Compare a pair of 4-char tags
  {
  if(s1[0]==s2[0] && s1[1]==s2[1]
  && s1[2]==s2[2] && s1[3]==s2[3])return(1);
  return(0);
  }


//————————————————————
```

```
void ExitError(int n)
  {
  switch(n)
    {
    case 0:printf("ERROR — This is not a RIFF file.\n"); break;
    case 1:printf("ERROR — This is not an AVI file.\n"); break;
    case 2:printf("ERROR — Invalid file format.\n");      break;
    case 3:printf("ERROR — Invalid header length.\n");    break;
    case 4:printf("ERROR — File must have DIB frame format.\n");break;
    case 5:
    printf("ERROR — Can only read 8-bit or 24-bit pixels.\n");break;
    case 6:
    printf("ERROR — Insufficient frame buffer memory.\n");break;
    default:printf("PROGRAM ERROR — Undefined error number.\n");
    }
  exit(0);
  }


//————————————————————————
// Classify a color into one of 8 categories or gray (0 saturation)
//————————————————————————
int GetListIndex(BYTE R, BYTE G, BYTE B)
  {
  int index,Y,Cr,Cb;
  if(R==G && G==B)return(8);
  else
    {
    Y=(int)((76L*(long)R + 150L*(long)G + 29L*(long)B)/256L);
    Cr=R-Y;
    Cb=B-Y;
    index=0;
    if(Cr>0)index|=1;
    if(Cb>0)index|=2;
    if(abs(Cr)>abs(Cb))index|=4;
    }
  return(index);
  }



//————————————————————————
// Add a color to the appropriate category list
//————————————————————————
void AddColor(BYTE R, BYTE G, BYTE B)
  {
  int                index;
  int                flag=0;
  struct ColorInfo   *color,*head;
  index=GetListIndex(R,G,B);
  color=color_list[index];
  head=color;

  while(flag==0 && color!=NULL)
    {
```

```
         if(color->Red==R && color->Green==G && color->Blue==B)
           {
           flag=1;
           }
         else
           {
           color=color->next;
           }
       }
     if(flag==1)
       {
       color->count++;
       }
     else
       {
       color_count[index]++;
       if(head==NULL)
         {
         color_list[index]=new ColorInfo;
         color=color_list[index];
         }
       else
         {
         color=head;
         while(color->next!=NULL)color=color->next;
         color->next=new ColorInfo;
         color=color->next;
         }
       color->Red   =R;
       color->Green=G;
       color->Blue =B;
       color->count=1L;
       color->palette_index=0;
       color->next =NULL;
       }
   }

//————————————————————
// Construct an optimized palette of 240 entries
//————————————————————
void BuildPalette(void)
   {
   int             i,index=0;
   int             flag=0;
   struct ColorInfo *color,*selection;
   long            max;

   while(index<240 && flag==0)    // For each palette entry,
     {
     max=0L;
     selection=NULL;
     for(i=0;i<9;i++)             // For each color category,
       {
```

```
      color=color_list[i];
      while(color!=NULL)          // Search for the most-used color;
        {
        if(color->count>max)
          {
          max=color->count;
          selection=color;
          }
        color=color->next;
        }
      }
    if(selection!=NULL)          // Add this color to the palette
      {
      selection->palette_index=(BYTE)index+16;
      selection->count=0L;
      vid_header.palette[index][0]=selection->Red;
      vid_header.palette[index][1]=selection->Green;
      vid_header.palette[index][2]=selection->Blue;
      index++;
      }
    else flag=1;
    }

  for(i=0;i<9;i++)              // Delete unused color entries
    {
    color=color_list[i];
    while(color!=NULL && color->next!=NULL)
      {
      if(color->next->palette_index==0)
        {
        selection=color->next;
        color=selection->next;
        delete selection;
        }
      else
        {
        color=color->next;
        }
      }
    }
  }


//————————————————————
// Find the best match in the palette for an RGB color
//————————————————————
BYTE GetPaletteIndex(BYTE R, BYTE G, BYTE B)
  {
  struct ColorInfo *list,*selection;
  int              error;
  int              min_error;
  BYTE             index;

  min_error=64*3;
```

```
      selection=NULL;
      list=color_list[GetListIndex(R,G,B)];
      while(list!=NULL)
        {
        if(list->palette_index>0)
          {
          error=abs(R-list->Red)+abs(G-list->Green)+abs(B-list->Blue);
          if(error<min_error)
            {
            selection=list;
            min_error=error;
            }
          }
        list=list->next;
        }
      index=selection->palette_index;
      return(index);
      }


//——————————————————————
// Convert an input AVI frame to an output VID frame
//——————————————————————
long ProcessFrame(FILE *stream, TagT *RIFF_tag)
  {
  char   chunk_type[4];           // RIFF type ID
  long   bytes_read;              // Main AVI header block length
  long   block_length;            // Main AVI header block length
  BYTE   line_buffer[1024];       // Temporary line buffer
  BYTE   R,G,B;                   // RGB storage
  int    R1,G1,B1,R2,G2,B2;       // RGB storage
  int    Y1,Y2,Cr1,Cr2,Cb1,Cb2;  // YCrCb storage
  WORD   i;                       // General counter
  int    src,dst;                 // Buffer pointers

  chunk_type[0]='0';              // Construct stream chunk ID
  chunk_type[1]='0'+(BYTE)stream_number;
  chunk_type[2]='d';
  chunk_type[3]='b';

  bytes_read=RIFF_tag->chunk_size;
  printf("Frame %d%c",frame,0x0d);

  if(stream_format.BitCount==8)   // *** Process an 8-bit frame ***
    {
    fread(frame_buffer,bytes_read,1,stream);
    if(CMP4(RIFF_tag->chunk_type,chunk_type))
      {
      int x_size=vid_header.x_size;
      int y_size=vid_header.y_size;

      if(frame==0)fwrite(&vid_header,sizeof(vid),1,output);

      for(int y=0;y<y_size/2;y++) // Un-invert DIB image
```

```
          {
      memmove(line_buffer,
              &frame_buffer[bytes_read-((y+1)*x_size)],x_size);
      memmove(&frame_buffer[bytes_read-((y+1)*x_size)],
              &frame_buffer[y*x_size],x_size);
      memmove(&frame_buffer[y*x_size],line_buffer,x_size);
          }
    for(int i=0;i<bytes_read;i++) // Adjust pixel base value
        {
        frame_buffer[i]=frame_buffer[i]+16;
        }
    fwrite(frame_buffer,bytes_read,1,output);
    frame++;
        }
    }

if(stream_format.BitCount==24)    // *** Process a 24-bit frame ***
    {
    fread(frame_buffer,bytes_read,1,stream);
    if(CMP4(RIFF_tag->chunk_type,chunk_type))
        {
        int x_size=vid_header.x_size;
        int y_size=vid_header.y_size;
        src=0;
        dst=0;
        if(frame==0)
            {
            printf("Building color palette.\n");
            for(i=0;i<9;i++)
                {
                color_list[i]=NULL;
                color_count[i]=0;
                }
            for(i=0;i<x_size*y_size;i++) // Create a palette on frame 0
                {
                B=frame_buffer[src++];
                G=frame_buffer[src++];
                R=frame_buffer[src++];
                R=(R/4)&0xFC;
                G=(G/4)&0xFC;
                B=(B/4)&0xFC;
                AddColor(R,G,B);
                }
            BuildPalette();
            fwrite(&vid_header,sizeof(vid),1,output);
            }
        src=0;
        dst=0;
        if(clut_flag==1)                    // Convert to 8-bit CLUT
            {
            for(i=0;i<x_size*y_size;i++)  // Map RGB to palette
                {
                B=frame_buffer[src++]/4;
```

```
                  G=frame_buffer[src++]/4;
                  R=frame_buffer[src++]/4;
                  frame_buffer[dst++]=GetPaletteIndex(R,G,B);
                  }
              bytes_read/=3;
              for(int y=0;y<y_size/2;y++)    // Un-invert DIB image
                  {
                  memmove(line_buffer,
                          &frame_buffer[bytes_read-((y+1)*x_size)],x_size);
                  memmove(&frame_buffer[bytes_read-((y+1)*x_size)],
                          &frame_buffer[y*x_size],x_size);
                  memmove(&frame_buffer[y*x_size],line_buffer,x_size);
                  }
              fwrite(frame_buffer,bytes_read,1,output);
              bytes_read*=3;
              }
          else
              {
              for(i=0;i<x_size*y_size/2;i++)    // Save as 4:2:2 YCrCb
                  {
                  B1=(int)frame_buffer[src++];
                  G1=(int)frame_buffer[src++];
                  R1=(int)frame_buffer[src++];
                  Y1=(int)((76L*(long)R1+150L*(long)G1+29L*(long)B1)/256L);
                  Cr1=(R1-Y1)/2+128;
                  Cb1=(B1-Y1)/2+128;
                  B2=(int)frame_buffer[src++];
                  G2=(int)frame_buffer[src++];
                  R2=(int)frame_buffer[src++];
                  Y2=(int)((76L*(long)R2+150L*(long)G2+29L*(long)B2)/256L);
                  Cr2=(R2-Y2)/2+128;
                  Cb2=(B2-Y2)/2+128;
                  frame_buffer[dst++]=(BYTE)Y1;
                  frame_buffer[dst++]=(BYTE)((Cr1+Cr2)/2);
                  frame_buffer[dst++]=(BYTE)Y2;
                  frame_buffer[dst++]=(BYTE)((Cb1+Cb2)/2);
                  }
              bytes_read=bytes_read/3*2;
              for(int y=0;y<y_size/2;y++)    // Un-invert DIB image
                  {
                  memmove(line_buffer,
                          &frame_buffer[bytes_read-((y+1)*x_size*2)],x_size*2);
                  memmove(&frame_buffer[bytes_read-((y+1)*x_size*2)],
                          &frame_buffer[y*x_size*2],x_size*2);
                  memmove(&frame_buffer[y*x_size*2],line_buffer,x_size*2);
                  }
              fwrite(frame_buffer,bytes_read,1,output);
              bytes_read=bytes_read/2*3;
              }
          frame++;
          }
      }
  return(bytes_read);
```

```
    }

//————————————————————
// Process a "rec" chunk to extract appropriate frame data
//————————————————————
long ReadRecord(FILE *stream, long chunk_size)
    {
    TagT   RIFF_tag;      // RIFF file tag structure
    long   bytes;         // Main AVI header block length
    long   bytes_read;    // Main AVI header block length
    long   block_length;  // Main AVI header block length
    long   header_length; // Main AVI header length

    block_length=chunk_size-ID_SIZE;
    bytes_read=0;
    while(block_length>0L)
        {
        fread(&RIFF_tag.chunk_type,TAG_SIZE,1,stream); // Get chunk tag
        block_length-=TAG_SIZE;
        bytes_read+=TAG_SIZE;
        bytes=ProcessFrame(stream,&RIFF_tag);
        block_length-=bytes;
        bytes_read+=bytes;
        }
    return(bytes_read);
    }

//————————————————————
// Scan through a LIST "movi" chunk, processing frames
//————————————————————
int ReadFrames(FILE *stream)
    {
    TagT   RIFF_tag;      // RIFF file tag structure
    char   RIFF_type[4];  // RIFF type ID
    long   bytes;         // Main AVI header block length
    long   bytes_read;    // Main AVI header block length
    long   block_length;  // Main AVI header block length
    long   header_length; // Main AVI header length

    fread(&RIFF_tag.chunk_type,TAG_SIZE,1,stream); // Get chunk tag
    fread(&RIFF_type,ID_SIZE,1,stream);
    if(!CMP4(RIFF_tag.chunk_type,"LIST"))ExitError(2);
    if(!CMP4(RIFF_type,"movi"))ExitError(2);
    block_length=RIFF_tag.chunk_size-ID_SIZE;
    bytes_read=TAG_SIZE+ID_SIZE;

    frame=0;
    while(frame<(int)main_header.TotalFrames)
        {
        fread(&RIFF_tag.chunk_type,TAG_SIZE,1,stream);
        block_length-=TAG_SIZE;
        bytes_read+=TAG_SIZE;
```

```
  if(CMP4(RIFF_tag.chunk_type,"LIST"))
    {
    fread(&RIFF_type,ID_SIZE,1,stream);
    if(!CMP4(RIFF_type,"rec "))ExitError(2);
    block_length-=ID_SIZE;
    bytes_read+=ID_SIZE;
    bytes=ReadRecord(stream,RIFF_tag.chunk_size);
    }
  else
    {
    bytes=ProcessFrame(stream,&RIFF_tag);
    }
  block_length-=bytes;
  bytes_read+=bytes;
  }
return(0);
}


//—————————————————————————
// Read a stream format chunk from the AVI file
//—————————————————————————
long ReadStreamFormat(FILE *stream, int debug)
  {
  TagT  RIFF_tag;        // RIFF file tag structure
  char  RIFF_type[4];    // RIFF type ID
  long  bytes_read;      // Stream header block length
  long  format_length;   // Stream format length

  fread(&RIFF_tag.chunk_type,TAG_SIZE,1,stream); // Get block tag
  bytes_read=TAG_SIZE;
  if(!CMP4(RIFF_tag.chunk_type,"strf"))ExitError(2);
  format_length=RIFF_tag.chunk_size;             // Save length
  bytes_read+=format_length;
  fread(&stream_format,DIB_HDR_SIZE,1,stream);   // Read format data
  if(debug)
    {
    printf("\n");
    printf("Stream Format Header: %ld bytes.\n\n",format_length);
    printf("Size         : %ld\n",stream_format.Size);
    printf("Width        : %ld\n",stream_format.Width);
    printf("Height       : %ld\n",stream_format.Height);
    printf("Planes       : %d \n",stream_format.Planes);
    printf("BitCount     : %d \n",stream_format.BitCount);
    printf("Compression  : %ld\n",stream_format.Compression);
    printf("SizeImage    : %ld\n",stream_format.SizeImage);
    printf("XPelsPerMeter : %ld\n",stream_format.XPelsPerMeter);
    printf("YPelsPerMeter : %ld\n",stream_format.YPelsPerMeter);
    printf("ClrUsed      : %ld\n",stream_format.ClrUsed);
    printf("ClrImportant : %ld\n",stream_format.ClrImportant);
    getch();
    }
  if(stream_format.BitCount!=8 && stream_format.BitCount!=24)
  ExitError(5);
```

```
    format_length-=(long)DIB_HDR_SIZE;
    fread(&palette[0],format_length,1,stream);    // Read palette data
    return(bytes_read);
    }

//——————————————————————————
// Read a stream header chunk from the AVI file
//——————————————————————————
long ReadStreamHeader(FILE *stream, int debug, int n)
    {
    TagT    RIFF_tag;              // RIFF file tag structure
    char    RIFF_type[4];          // RIFF type ID
    long    block_length;          // Stream header block length
    long    bytes_read;            // Stream header block length
    long    header_length;         // Stream header length
    AVIStreamHeader local_header;  // Local header data buffer

    fread(&RIFF_tag.chunk_type,TAG_SIZE,1,stream); // Get header block tag
    fread(&RIFF_type,ID_SIZE,1,stream); // Get stream length tag
    bytes_read=TAG_SIZE+ID_SIZE;

    if(!CMP4(RIFF_tag.chunk_type,"LIST"))ExitError(2);
    if(!CMP4(RIFF_type,"strl"))ExitError(2);
    block_length=RIFF_tag.chunk_size-ID_SIZE;      // Save header length

    fread(&RIFF_tag.chunk_type,TAG_SIZE,1,stream); // Get header tag
    if(!CMP4(RIFF_tag.chunk_type,"strh"))ExitError(2);
    header_length=RIFF_tag.chunk_size;             // Save header length
    bytes_read+=TAG_SIZE;
    block_length-=TAG_SIZE;
    if(header_length!=STR_HDR_SIZE)ExitError(3);
    fread(&local_header,STR_HDR_SIZE,1,stream);    // Read header data
    block_length-=header_length;
    bytes_read+=header_length;

    if(debug)
      {
      printf("\n");
      printf("AVI Stream Header    : %ld bytes.\n\n",header_length);
      printf("Type                 : %s\n",local_header.Type);
      printf("Handler              : %s\n",local_header.Handler);
      printf("Flags                : %ld\n",local_header.Flags);
      if(local_header.Flags&RIFF_HASINDEX)       printf("HASINDEX\n");
      if(local_header.Flags&RIFF_MUSTUSEINDEX) printf("MUSTUSEINDEX\n");
      if(local_header.Flags&RIFF_ISINTERLEAVED)printf("ISINTERLEAVED\n");
      if(local_header.Flags&RIFF_COPYRIGHTED)  printf("COPYRIGHTED\n");
      printf("Priority             : %ld\n",local_header.Priority);
      printf("InitialFrames        : %ld\n",local_header.InitialFrames);
      printf("Scale                : %ld\n",local_header.Scale);
      printf("Rate                 : %ld\n",local_header.Rate);
      printf("Start                : %ld\n",local_header.Start);
      printf("Length               : %ld\n",local_header.Length);
      printf("SuggestedBufferSize  : %ld\n",local_header.SuggestedBufferSize);
```

```
        printf("Quality                : %ld\n",local_header.Quality);
        printf("SampleSize             : %ld\n",local_header.SampleSize);
        getch();
        }

    if(CMP4(local_header.Type,"vids") &&
       CMP4(local_header.Handler,"DIB "))
       {
       memcpy(&stream_header,&local_header,STR_HDR_SIZE);  // Save header
       long bytes=ReadStreamFormat(stream,debug);          // Get format
       block_length-=bytes;
       bytes_read+=bytes;
       stream_number=n;
       }
    if(block_length>0L)
       {
       fseek(stream,block_length,SEEK_CUR);
       bytes_read+=block_length;
       }
    return(bytes_read);
    }

//─────────────────────────────
// Read a main AVI header chunk from the AVI file
//─────────────────────────────
int ReadHeader(FILE *stream, int debug)
    {
    TagT    RIFF_tag;          // RIFF file tag structure
    char    RIFF_type[4];      // RIFF type ID
    long    bytes_read;        // Main AVI header block length
    long    block_length;      // Main AVI header block length
    long    header_length;     // Main AVI header length

    fread(&RIFF_tag.chunk_type,TAG_SIZE,1,stream); // Get "LIST....hdrl"
    fread(&RIFF_type,ID_SIZE,1,stream);
    bytes_read=TAG_SIZE+ID_SIZE;

    if(!CMP4(RIFF_tag.chunk_type,"LIST"))ExitError(2);
    if(!CMP4(RIFF_type,"hdrl"))ExitError(2);
    block_length=RIFF_tag.chunk_size-ID_SIZE;          // Account for "hdrl"

    fread(&RIFF_tag.chunk_type,TAG_SIZE,1,stream); // Get header tag
    if(!CMP4(RIFF_tag.chunk_type,"avih"))ExitError(2);
    bytes_read+=TAG_SIZE;
    block_length-=TAG_SIZE;
    header_length=RIFF_tag.chunk_size;                 // Save header length
    if(header_length!=MAIN_HDR_SIZE)ExitError(3);
    fread(&main_header,MAIN_HDR_SIZE,1,stream);     // Read header data
    bytes_read+=header_length;
    block_length-=header_length;

    if(debug)
```

```
      {
      printf("\n");
      printf("Main AVI Header     : %ld bytes.\n\n",header_length);
      printf("MicroSecPerFrame    : %ld\n",main_header.MicroSecPerFrame);
      printf("MaxBytesPerSec      : %ld\n",main_header.MaxBytesPerSec);
      printf("Flags               : %ld\n",main_header.Flags);
      if(main_header.Flags&RIFF_HASINDEX)      printf("HASINDEX\n");
      if(main_header.Flags&RIFF_MUSTUSEINDEX) printf("MUSTUSEINDEX\n");
      if(main_header.Flags&RIFF_ISINTERLEAVED)printf("ISINTERLEAVED\n");
      if(main_header.Flags&RIFF_COPYRIGHTED)  printf("COPYRIGHTED\n");
      printf("TotalFrames         : %ld\n",main_header.TotalFrames);
      printf("InitialFrames       : %ld\n",main_header.InitialFrames);
      printf("Streams             : %ld\n",main_header.Streams);
      printf
      ("SuggestedBufferSize : %ld\n",main_header.SuggestedBufferSize);
      printf("Width               : %ld\n",main_header.Width);
      printf("Height              : %ld\n",main_header.Height);
      getch();
      }

  for(int i=0;i<main_header.Streams;i++) // Read the stream headers
    {
    long bytes=ReadStreamHeader(stream,debug,i);
    block_length-=bytes;
    bytes_read+=bytes;
    }
  if(!CMP4(stream_header.Type,"vids") ||
     !CMP4(stream_header.Handler,"DIB "))
    {
    ExitError(4);                          // Validate AVI file type
    }
  if(block_length>0L)                      // Seek past any junk data
    {
    fseek(stream,block_length,SEEK_CUR);
    bytes_read+=block_length;
    }
  return(0);
  }

//————————————————————————
// Process a RIFF AVI file chunk
//————————————————————————
int ReadRIFF(FILE *stream,int debug)
  {
  TagT    RIFF_tag;               // RIFF file tag structure
  char    RIFF_type[4];           // RIFF type ID
  long    main_header_length;     // Main RIFF header length

  fread(&RIFF_tag.chunk_type,TAG_SIZE,1,stream);
  if(!CMP4(RIFF_tag.chunk_type,"RIFF"))ExitError(0);
  fread(&RIFF_type,ID_SIZE,1,stream);
  if(!CMP4(RIFF_type,"AVI "))ExitError(1);  // Verify this is AVI file
```

```
    ReadHeader(stream,debug);                    // Read the file header

    frame_buffer=(BYTE *)malloc(stream_format.SizeImage);
    if(frame_buffer==NULL)ExitError(6);

    strcpy(vid_header.file_ID,"BOOK_VID");    // Set file ID
    vid_header.compression=0;                 // Write uncompressed file
    if(stream_format.BitCount==24 && clut_flag==0)
      {
      vid_header.compression|=YCRCB;          // Set flag if YCrCb
      }

    vid_header.frames=(int)main_header.TotalFrames;
    vid_header.x_size=(int)main_header.Width;
    vid_header.y_size=(int)main_header.Height;

    for(int i=0;i<stream_format.ClrUsed;i++)    // Use palette from file
      {
      vid_header.palette[i][0]=(int)palette[i].Red>2;
      vid_header.palette[i][1]=(int)palette[i].Green>2;
      vid_header.palette[i][2]=(int)palette[i].Blue>2;
      }

    if(debug==0)ReadFrames(stream);
    return(0);
    }

//————————————————————————
// Main program segment
//————————————————————————
void main(int argc, char* argv[])
  {
  FILE           *fi,*fo;
  int            debug=0;

  clut_flag=0;
  printf("AVI to VID file conversion program.\n\n");
  printf("Copyright (c) John Wiley & Sons, Inc., 1994.\n\n");
  if(argc<3)          // Validate command line parameters
    {
    printf
    ("Please provide two file names: <input_file> <output_file>\n");
    printf("followed by '8' for 24-bit to 8-bit conversion, or 'd' \n");
    printf("for a dump of AVI file header information. \n");
    exit(0);
    }
  fi=fopen(argv[1],"rb");
  fo=fopen(argv[2],"wb");
  if(fi==NULL)
    {
    printf("Could not open input file %s.\n",argv[1]);
    exit(0);
```

```
   }
if(fo==NULL)
   {
   printf("Could not open output file %s.\n",argv[2]);
   exit(0);
   }
output=fo; // Use global output pointer

if(argc==4 && argv[3][0]=='8')clut_flag=1; // Convert 24-bit to 8-bit
if(argc==4 && argv[3][0]=='d')debug=1;      // Set debug display
if(argc==4 && argv[3][0]=='D')debug=1;

ReadRIFF(fi,debug);

fclose(fi);
fclose(fo);
printf("Done.\n");
   }
```

Still Image File Formats

Still images are used for many of the demonstration programs illustrating various compression techniques in Chapter 5. These images are available in two forms: color and black-and-white. Both use the VGA 256-color lookup table mode for display. The color images use an optimized palette. The palette data for all 256 entries is stored at the beginning of the file as illustrated in Figure A.19. Following this is data for a 320×240 image.

Because each image occupies the full screen, all 256 color palette entries are used. In other words, no palette entries need be reserved because nothing else is displayed on the screen simultaneously with the picture. For color images, an optimal color set is selected using the same technique as for color 8-bit video files. For black-and-white images, the palette is filled with a linear number sequence so that index zero is black, and index 255 is white. Because the VGA RAMDAC actually supports only six bits per A/D converter, only 64 gray levels can be displayed. This means that index locations zero through three all have the value 0, 0, 0, four through seven have 1, 1, 1, and so on. This automatically quantizes the 256 gray levels represented by the eight-bit pixels when they are displayed, and math operations can be performed with 8-bit accuracy instead of 6-bit.

Figure A.19   Organization of PIC 8-bit-per-pixel still image file data.

AVI-to-PIC File Conversion Program Source Code

The following program source code is a utility used to extract the first image from an AVI file image sequence and store it as a PIC file. The input AVI file must be in 8-bit format, with 320×240 resolution. Because the PIC file is designed for use with Mode 13h of the VGA display adapter (320×200 with 256 colors), the top 10 rows of pixels and the last 30 rows are cropped to make the image fit on screen. The aspect ratio does not match perfectly, so the images appear stretched a little vertically when viewed on the computer screen. Several images captured with Video for Windows hardware and converted with this program are included on the sample diskettes and listed in Appendix C. The program source code follows:

```
//==========================================================
// AVI2PIC.CPP
//----------------------------------------
// Program:    Implementation code for AVI2PIC.EXE
// Author:     Phil Mattison
// Compiler:   Borland Turbo C++ v1.01
//----------------------------------------

#include <stdlib.h>
#include <stdio.h>
#include <string.h>
#include <conio.h>
#include <dos.h>

#include "avi_riff.h"

//----------------------------------------
int Compare4C(char *s1, char *s2) // Compare a pair of 4-char tags
  {
  if(s1[0]==s2[0] &&
  s1[1]==s2[1] &&
  s1[2]==s2[2] &&
  s1[3]==s2[3])return(1);
  return(0);
  }

//----------------------------------------
void ExitError(int err)            // Exit with error message
  {
  printf("File Error %d \n",err);
  exit(0);
  }

//----------------------------------------
void main(int argc, char* argv[])
  {
  FILE    *fi,*fo;
  DWORD   chunk_size;              // Current chunk length
```

```
    DWORD    main_chunk_length;   // Length of main RIFF chunk
    DWORD    main_header_length;  // Length of main RIFF header chunk
    DWORD    movi_length;         // Length of movi chunk
    char     sub_type[4];         // Chunk sub type ID
    int      x_size,y_size;       // Video frame size
    int      palette_entrys;      // Number of palette locations used
    int      i,j;
    BYTE     frame_out[320];      // File output buffer
    BYTE     palette[256][3];     // VGA palette storage

  union                           // File input data buffer
    {
    TagT                tags;
    MainAVIHeader       main_header;
    AVIStreamHeader     stream_header;
    BitMapInfoHeader    dib_header;
    RGBQuad             palette[1024];
    BYTE                buffer[1024*sizeof(RGBQuad)];
    } data;

  //─────────────────────────────
    printf("AVI to PIC file conversion program\n\n");
    printf("Copyright (c) John Wiley & Sons, Inc., 1994.\n\n");

    if(argc<3)        // Validate command line parameters
      {
      printf
      ("Please provide two file names: <input_file> <output_file>\n");
      exit(0);
      }
    fi=fopen(argv[1],"rb");
    fo=fopen(argv[2],"wb");
    if(fi==NULL)
      {
      printf("Could not open input file %s.\n",argv[1]);
      exit(0);
      }
    if(fo==NULL)
      {
      printf("Could not open output file %s.\n",argv[2]);
      exit(0);
      }

    fread(data.buffer,TAG_SIZE,1,fi);        // Read RIFF 'AVI ' tag
    if(!Compare4C(data.tags.chunk_type,"RIFF"))ExitError(1);
    fread(sub_type,ID_SIZE,1,fi);
    if(!Compare4C(sub_type,"AVI "))ExitError(2);

    fread(data.buffer,TAG_SIZE,1,fi);        // Read LIST 'hdrl' tag
    if(!Compare4C(data.tags.chunk_type,"LIST"))ExitError(3);
    fread(sub_type,ID_SIZE,1,fi);
    if(!Compare4C(sub_type,"hdrl"))ExitError(4);
```

```
main_header_length=data.tags.chunk_size+0x14L;

fread(data.buffer,TAG_SIZE,1,fi);          // Read 'avih' tag & data
if(!Compare4C(data.tags.chunk_type,"avih"))ExitError(5);
if(data.tags.chunk_size!=HDR_SIZE)ExitError(6);
fread(data.buffer,HDR_SIZE,1,fi);

x_size=(int)data.main_header.Width;
y_size=(int)data.main_header.Height;
if(x_size!=320 || y_size!=240)ExitError(8);

fread(data.buffer,TAG_SIZE,1,fi);          // Read LIST 'strl' tag
if(!Compare4C(data.tags.chunk_type,"LIST"))ExitError(9);
fread(sub_type,ID_SIZE,1,fi);
if(!Compare4C(sub_type,"strl"))ExitError(10);

fread(data.buffer,TAG_SIZE,1,fi);          // Read 'strh' tag
if(!Compare4C(data.tags.chunk_type,"strh"))ExitError(11);
chunk_size=data.tags.chunk_size;
fread(data.buffer,(int)chunk_size,1,fi);

fread(data.buffer,TAG_SIZE,1,fi);          // Read 'strf' tag
if(!Compare4C(data.tags.chunk_type,"strf"))ExitError(12);
fread(data.buffer,sizeof(BitMapInfoHeader),1,fi);
palette_entrys=data.dib_header.ClrUsed;
fread(data.buffer,4*palette_entrys,1,fi);

for(i=0;i<16;i++)          // Zero out reserved palette entries
   {
   palette[i][0]=0;
   palette[i][1]=0;
   palette[i][2]=0;
   }                        // Load optimum colors
for(i=0;i<240;i++)
   {
   palette[i+16][0]=data.palette[i].Red;
   palette[i+16][1]=data.palette[i].Green;
   palette[i+16][2]=data.palette[i].Blue;
   }
fseek(fi,main_header_length,SEEK_SET);   // Seek to end of AVI header
fread(data.buffer,TAG_SIZE,1,fi);          // Read LIST 'movi' tag
if(!Compare4C(data.tags.chunk_type,"LIST"))ExitError(13);
fread(sub_type,ID_SIZE,1,fi);
if(!Compare4C(sub_type,"movi"))ExitError(14);

fwrite(&(palette[0][0]),768,1,fo);  // Write PIC file header

fread(data.buffer,TAG_SIZE,1,fi);   // Read '00db' tag (DIB stream 0)
if(!Compare4C(data.tags.chunk_type,"00db"))ExitError(15);
chunk_size=data.tags.chunk_size;

for(i=0;i<210;i++)                    // Skip 210 lines
   {
```

```
      fread(frame_out,320,1,fi);
      }
for(i=0;i<200;i++)                      // Uninvert DIB
   {
   fseek(fi,-640,SEEK_CUR);
   fread(frame_out,320,1,fi);           // Read image scan line
   for(j=0;j<320;j++)frame_out[j]+=16;
   fwrite(frame_out,320,1,fo);          // Store pixels in PIC file
   }
fclose(fi);
fclose(fo);
printf("Done.\n");
}
```

APPENDIX B

DOS-Based C++ Source Files

The software and source code provided on the sample diskettes is organized into three separate subdirectories. The first is SW_GEN, which contains assembly code routines for the few hardware-specific or highly performance-critical code segments, C++ include files, some commonly used C++ subroutines, and a few demonstration programs that are not file related. That is, they do not operate on image files. The second is SW_PIC, which contains programs that operate on still image files. The third is SW_VID, which contains programs that operate on motion-video files. Most of the programs provided with this book are command-line oriented. They process files, taking one input file and producing one output file. A few programs, including the non-file-related ones, are interactive, and operate with a mouse. Most of these operate in VGA mode 13h (320×200 with 256 colors) to allow display of natural images on a broad range of PC equipment. No advantage is taken of advanced Super VGA adapters' capabilities for higher resolution and color depth because that would tend to divert the focus of this book. Many fine books have been written on programming Super VGA adapters, and Microsoft Windows takes much of the drugery out of that task as well. The shell programs from which the interactive programs were derived are included in the SW_GEN directory. There is one for mode 13h as well as one for mode 12h (640×480 with 16 colors). These shell programs and a few of the demonstration programs use the object-oriented capability of C++. This was used only where it made the code simpler and smaller, and otherwise was avoided for the sake of those not already conversant with C++. The three primary advantages available from C++ utilized here are the ability to associate data with specific executable code, the ability to better segregate and classify data, and the improved ease of dynamic memory allocation. A nice thing about C++ is that if you don't want to use object classes, you don't have to. If you don't already understand C++, it is worth learning. Enough said.

Because this book focuses more on *how* than on *what*, the path from camera to computer display tends to be rather convoluted. To make that process easier to navigate, diagrams are provided in Figures B.1 and B.2 which illustrate in graphic form how each of the relevant file formats relates to each of the demonstration programs provided.

All of these programs were created using a Borland C++ compiler, and where project files are used, the path is set up to find include files and assembly and C++ library files in the appropriate directory if the directory structure from the diskettes is maintained. The directory path under the options menu of the Integrated Development Environment should also be set to reflect the location of the include files (the SW_GEN\INCLUDE directory). Table B.1 outlines the programs provided on the software diskette.

Within the SW_GEN directory are several subdirectories which contain assembly language code, include files, and C++ library code. Tables B.2, B.3 and B.4 outline the files contained there.

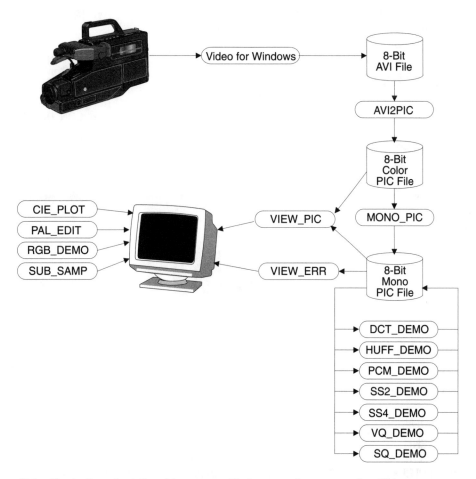

Figure B.1   Illustration of relationships among file types and programs for still images.

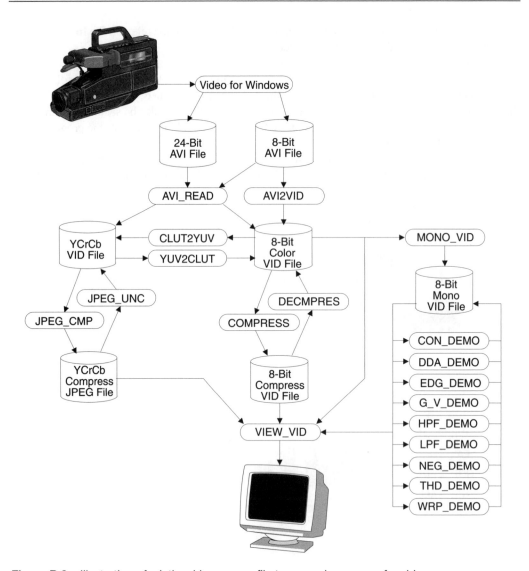

Figure B.2   Illustration of relationships among file types and programs for video.

Table B.1   Outline of Programs Provided

Program Name	Description
SW_GEN:	
CIE_PLOT.EXE	Demonstration of CIE color diagram coordinate system.
PAL_EDIT.EXE	Demonstration of VGA palette organization and access.
RGB_DEMO.EXE	Demonstration of RGB vs. YCrCb color space calculation.
SUB_SAMP.EXE	Demonstration of color subsampling visual effects.

Program Name	Description
SW_PIC:	
AVI2PIC.EXE	Extracts first image frame from AVI file and stores in PIC format.
MONO_PIC.EXE	Converts a color PIC file into a monochrome PIC file.
HUFFDEMO.EXE	Demonstration of generic Huffman encoding of image data.
DCT_DEMO.EXE	Demonstration of the effects of DCT coding on image data.
PCM_DEMO.EXE	Demonstration of the effects of DPCM coding on image data.
SS2_DEMO.EXE	Demonstration of 2×2 subsampling of image data.
SS4_DEMO.EXE	Demonstration of 4×4 subsampling of image data.
VQ_DEMO.EXE	Demonstration of vector quantization coding of image data.
SQ_DEMO.EXE	Demonstration of simple quantization of image data.
VIEW_PIC.EXE	Program to view PIC files.
VIEW_ERR.EXE	Program to view errors introduced by image processing.
SW_VID:	
AVI2VID.EXE	Simple 8-bit AVI to VID format conversion utility.
AVI_READ.EXE	More versatile AVI to VID format conversion utility.
CLUT2YUV.EXE	8-bit CLUT to 4:2:2 YCrCb format conversion utility.
YUV2CLUT.EXE	4:2:2 YCrCb to 8-bit CLUT format conversion utility.
COMPRESS.EXE	Compression utility for 8-bit VID format files.
DECMPRES.EXE	Decompression utility for 8-bit VID format files.
MONO_VID.EXE	Converts an 8-bit color video file into 8-bit monochrome.
JPEG_CMP.EXE	Demonstration of JPEG compression process on 4:2:2 YCrCb.
JPEG_UNC.EXE	Demonstration of JPEG decompression process on 4:2:2 YCrCb.
CON_DEMO.EXE	Demonstration of contrast adjustment on monochrome VID files.
DDA_DEMO.EXE	Demonstration of scaling on monochrome VID files.
EDG_DEMO.EXE	Demonstration of edge detection on monochrome VID files.
G_V_DEMO.EXE	Demonstration of graphics overlay on 8-bit VID files.
HPF_DEMO.EXE	Demonstration of high-pass filtering on monochrome VID files.
LPF_DEMO.EXE	Demonstration of low-pass filtering on monochrome VID files.
NEG_DEMO.EXE	Demonstration of negative translation on 8-bit VID files.
THD_DEMO.EXE	Demonstration of thresholding on monochrome VID files.
WRP_DEMO.EXE	Demonstration of image warping on monochrome VID files.
VIEW_VID.EXE	VID file viewer program.

Table B.2   Outline of C++ Include Files

File Name	Description
INCLUDE:	
AVI_RIFF.H	Data structures and constants for reading AVI files.
MOUSE.H	Object class definitions for 640×480 mouse interface.
CONTROL.H	Object class definitions for 640×480 mouse control.
DISPLAY.H	Object class definitions for 640×480 display interface.
MOUSE256.H	Object class definitions for 320×200 mouse interface.
CTRL_256.H	Object class definitions for 320×200 mouse control.
DISP_256.H	Object class definitions for 320×200 display interface.

Table B.3   Outline of C++ Library Files

File Name	Description
CPP_LIB:	
MOUSE.CPP	Implementation code for 640×480 mouse interface.
CONTROL.CPP	Implementation code for 640×480 mouse control.
DISPLAY.CPP	Implementation code for 640×480 display interface.
MOUSE256.CPP	Implementation code for 320×200 mouse interface.
CTRL_256.CPP	Implementation code for 320×200 mouse control.
DISP_256.CPP	Implementation code for 320×200 display interface.

Table B.4   Outline of Assembly Language Files

File Name	Description
ASM_LIB:	
SETVMODE.ASM	Subroutine to set the video display mode.
VPALETTE.ASM	Subroutines to read and write the VGA hardware palette.
DRAW_BLK.ASM	Subroutines to draw color blocks on mode 13h display.
DRWASCII.ASM	Subroutines to draw ASCII charaters on mode 13h display.
WRITEBLK.ASM	Subroutines to read and write pixel blocks on mode 13h display.

Include File Source Code Listings

Each of the following include files is used with one or more of the programs provided with this book. Where appropriate, a brief description of the contents is given along with the code listing.

AVI_RIFF.H Source Code

```
//=========================================================
// AVI_RIFF.H
//————————————————————
// Program:   Data Structures and constants for AVI2VID.EXE
// Author:    Phil Mattison
// Compiler:  Borland Turbo C++ v1.01
//————————————————————

#define BYTE         unsigned char
#define WORD         unsigned int
#define DWORD        unsigned long

#define ESC_KEY      27
#define IMAGE_SIZE   19200
#define TAG_SIZE     sizeof(TagT)
```

```
#define MAIN_HDR_SIZE   sizeof(MainAVIHeader)
#define STR_HDR_SIZE    sizeof(AVIStreamHeader)
#define DIB_HDR_SIZE    sizeof(BitMapInfoHeader)
#define ID_SIZE         4

#define COMPRESSED      1
#define MONOCHROME      2
#define YCRCB           4
#define COMPRESSED_X    6
#define MONOCHROME_X    5
#define YCRCB_X         3

// flags for use in <dwFlags> in AVIFileHdr

#define RIFF_HASINDEX       0x00000010   // Index at end of file?
#define RIFF_MUSTUSEINDEX   0x00000020
#define RIFF_ISINTERLEAVED  0x00000100
#define RIFF_COPYRIGHTED    0x00020000

// flags for use in <dwFlags> in AVIStreamHdr

#define AVI_DISABLED         0x00000001   // User rendering control
#define AVI_VIDEO_PALCHANGES 0x00010000   // Embedded palette changes

typedef struct              // RIFF tag structure
  {
  char chunk_type[4];
  long chunk_size;
  } TagT;

typedef struct              // Main AVI File Header
  {
  DWORD MicroSecPerFrame;    // frame display rate (or 0L)
  DWORD   MaxBytesPerSec;    // max. transfer rate
  DWORD   Reserved1;
  DWORD   Flags;             // RIFF flags
  DWORD   TotalFrames;       // # frames in file
  DWORD   InitialFrames;     // For interleaved files
  DWORD   Streams;           // Stream count
  DWORD   SuggestedBufferSize;// Chunk buffer size
  DWORD   Width;             // Frame Size
  DWORD   Height;
  DWORD   Reserved[4];
  } MainAVIHeader;

typedef struct              // Stream header
  {
  char    Type[4];           // Should be "vids"
  char    Handler[4];        // Driver code
  DWORD   Flags;             // Contains AVI_* flags
  DWORD   Priority;
  DWORD   InitialFrames;
```

```
     DWORD     Scale;
     DWORD     Rate;                 // dwRate/dwScale == samples/second
     DWORD     Start;
     DWORD     Length;               // In units above...
     DWORD     SuggestedBufferSize;
     DWORD     Quality;
     DWORD     SampleSize;
     DWORD     Reserved[2];
     } AVIStreamHeader;

  typedef struct               // Bitmap Information Header
     {
     DWORD  Size;                    // Size of this structure
     long   Width;                   // Bitmap width
     long   Height;                  // Bitmap Height
     WORD   Planes;                  // Bitmap bit planes
     WORD   BitCount;                // Bits per pixel
     DWORD  Compression;             // Compression type
     DWORD  SizeImage;               // # of bytes in image
     long   XPelsPerMeter;           // H resolution
     long   YPelsPerMeter;           // V resolution
     DWORD  ClrUsed;                 // # of palette entrys used; 0=all
     DWORD  ClrImportant;            // # of important entrys
     } BitMapInfoHeader;

  typedef struct               // RGB Quad Structure
     {
     BYTE          Blue;
     BYTE          Green;
     BYTE          Red;
     BYTE          Reserved;
     } RGBQuad;

  typedef struct   // Bitmap Structure for Stream Format Header
     {
     BitMapInfoHeader Header;
     RGBQuad          Colors[256];
     } BitMapInfo;

  typedef struct   // VID file header structure
     {
     char   file_ID[8];
     int    x_size;
     int    y_size;
     int    frames;
     int    compression;
     int    palette[240][3];
     } vid;
```

MOUSE.H Source Code

```
  #include <dos.h>
  #include <stdlib.h>
```

```
//****************************************************************
//        Class TMouse
//
//        This class defines a group of functions and data structures
//        which allow a DOS-based program to set up mouse-operated
//        controls. A call-back mechanism allows regions of the
//        screen to be defined which trigger calls to user-defined
//        functions when the left mouse button is pressed and the
//        cursor is within the defined region.
//
//****************************************************************

#ifndef __MOUSE_H
#define __MOUSE_H
#endif

#define MOUSE_INT         51
#define BUTTON_DOWN        1
#define BUTTON_UP          0
#define BUTTON_LEFT        1
#define BUTTON_RIGHT       2
#define STANDARD_SET       1
#define NO_STANDARD        0
#define BUTTON_ENABLED     1
#define BUTTON_DISABLED    0
#define RUN_ENABLED        0
#define RUN_DISABLED       1

#define MC_RESET           0
#define MC_SHOWCURSOR      1
#define MC_HIDECURSOR      2
#define MC_GETSTATUS       3
#define MC_SETXLIMIT       7
#define MC_SETYLIMIT       8
#define MC_SETMICKEYS     15

class TMouse
  {
private:
  struct coord_t
    {
    int current_position;
    int down_position;
    int up_position;
    int limit_min;
    int limit_max;
    } x,y;
  struct button_t
    {
    int status;
    int down_interval;
    int up_interval;
    } left,right;
```

```
    struct list_t
      {
      int x_pos,y_pos;
      int x_size,y_size;
      int enable_flag;
      int (*callback)();
      struct list_t *next;
      } list_head,*current_call,*list_tail;

    union REGS inregs,outregs;
    int standard_flag,run_flag,callback_count;
    enum {TRUE,PROCESSED,FALSE} press_pending;

  public:
    TMouse();
    ~TMouse();
    virtual void HideCursor();
    virtual void ShowCursor();
    virtual void SetMouseLimits(int,int,int,int);
    virtual void SetStandardCallback(int(near*)());
    virtual void SetCallback(int(near*)(),int,int,int,int);
    virtual void DeleteCallback(int(near*)());
    virtual void Run();
  private:
    void FlagReset();
    void GetStatus();
    void SetMickeysPerPixel(int,int);
    };
```

CONTROL.H Source Code

```
    #ifndef __MOUSE_H
    #include "mouse.h"
    #endif

    #ifndef __CONTROL_H
    #define __CONTROL_H
    #endif

    //*****************************************************************
    //          Class TControl
    //
    //          This class defines a group of functions and data structures
    //          which allow a DOS-based program to set up mouse-operated
    //          controls. A call-back mechanism allows buttons on the
    //          screen to be defined which trigger calls to user-defined
    //          functions when the left mouse button is pressed and the
    //          cursor is within the defined button. This class is derived
    //          from class TMouse.
    //
    //*****************************************************************

    #include <stdio.h>
```

```
#include <string.h>
#include <graphics.h>
#include <conio.h>

#define LABEL_SIZE        16
#define BUTTON_ENABLED    1
#define BUTTON_DISABLED   0
#define TRUE              1
#define FALSE             0

class TControl : public TMouse
   {
public:
  TControl();
  ~TControl();
  virtual int  CreateButton(int(near*)(),int,int,int,int,char*);
  virtual void DeleteButton(int);
  virtual void EnableButton(int);
  virtual void DisableButton(int);

// Functions inherited from TMouse
//
// void HideCursor();
// void ShowCursor();
// void SetMouseLimits(int,int,int,int);
// void SetStandardCallback(int(near*)());
// void SetCallback(int(near*)(),int,int,int,int);
// void Run();

private:

  struct button_list_t
    {
    char        label[LABEL_SIZE];
    void        *background,*bitmap;
    int         x_pos,y_pos;
    int         x_size,y_size;
    int         (*callback)();
    int         handle,status;
    struct button_list_t *next;
    } *button_list_head,*button_list_tail,*button_list_ptr,*temp;

  int         handle;
  int         error_flag;
  };
```

DISPLAY.H Source Code

```
#ifndef __DISPLAY_H
#define __DISPLAY_H
#endif

#include <graphics.h>
```

```
#include <string.h>
#include <stdlib.h>
#include <stdio.h>

//****************************************************************
//        Class TDisplay
//
//        This class defines a group of functions and data structures
//        which allow a DOS-based program to set up display windows
//        on the user screen for numbers or text. The Show() function
//        is overloaded to work with int, long, float, or char[] data
//        types.
//
//****************************************************************

#define BUFFER_SIZE        80
#define DEFAULT_XSIZE      96
#define DEFAULT_YSIZE      22
#define DEFAULT_MAX_X      639-DEFAULT_XSIZE
#define DEFAULT_MAXLEN     (96-16)/8
#define DEFAULT_FG         BLACK
#define DEFAULT_BG         WHITE
#define BORDER             1
#define NOBORDER           0

class TDisplay
   {
public:
  struct display_t
    {
    int                x_pos,y_pos;
    int                x_size,y_size;
    int                x1,y1,x2,y2;
    int                bg_color,fg_color;
    int                max_length;
    int                border_flag;
    } *parms;
  char                 buffer[BUFFER_SIZE];

  TDisplay(int,int,int,int,int,int,int);
  TDisplay(int,int,int);
  ~TDisplay();
  virtual void Show(int);
  virtual void Show(long int);
  virtual void Show(char *,float);
  virtual void Show(char *);
  };
```

MOUSE256.H Source Code

```
#include <dos.h>
#include <stdlib.h>
```

```
//****************************************************************
//        Class TMouse
//
//        This class defines a group of functions and data structures
//        which allow a DOS-based program to set up mouse-operated
//        controls. A call-back mechanism allows regions of the
//        screen to be defined which trigger calls to user-defined
//        functions when the left mouse button is pressed and the
//        cursor is within the defined region.
//
//****************************************************************

#ifndef __MOUSE256_H
#define __MOUSE256_H
#endif

#define MOUSE_INT         51
#define BUTTON_DOWN       1
#define BUTTON_UP         0
#define BUTTON_LEFT       1
#define BUTTON_RIGHT      2
#define STANDARD_SET      1
#define NO_STANDARD       0
#define BUTTON_ENABLED    1
#define BUTTON_DISABLED   0
#define RUN_ENABLED       0
#define RUN_DISABLED      1

#define MC_RESET          0
#define MC_SHOWCURSOR     1
#define MC_HIDECURSOR     2
#define MC_GETSTATUS      3
#define MC_SETXLIMIT      7
#define MC_SETYLIMIT      8
#define MC_SETMICKEYS     15

class TMouse
  {
private:
  struct coord_t
    {
    int current_position;
    int down_position;
    int up_position;
    int limit_min;
    int limit_max;
    } x,y;
  struct button_t
    {
    int status;
    int down_interval;
    int up_interval;
```

```
        } left,right;
    struct list_t
      {
      int x_pos,y_pos;
      int x_size,y_size;
      int enable_flag;
      int (*callback)();
      struct list_t *next;
      } list_head,*current_call,*list_tail;

    union REGS inregs,outregs;
    int standard_flag,run_flag,callback_count;
    enum {TRUE,PROCESSED,FALSE} press_pending;

  public:
    TMouse();
    ~TMouse();
    virtual int  GetPositionX(void) {return(x.current_position);};
    virtual int  GetPositionY(void) {return(y.current_position);};
    virtual void HideCursor();
    virtual void ShowCursor();
    virtual void SetMouseLimits(int,int,int,int);
    virtual void SetStandardCallback(int(near*)());
    virtual void SetCallback(int(near*)(),int,int,int,int);
    virtual void DeleteCallback(int(near*)());
    virtual void Run();
  private:
    void FlagReset();
    void GetStatus();
    void SetMickeysPerPixel(int,int);
    };
```

CTRL_256.H Source Code

```
    #ifndef __MOUSE256_H
    #include "mouse256.h"
    #endif

    #ifndef __CONTROL256_H
    #define __CONTROL256_H
    #endif

    //*****************************************************************
    //        Class TControl
    //
    //        This class defines a group of functions and data structures
    //        which allow a DOS-based program to set up mouse-operated
    //        controls. A call-back mechanism allows buttons the
    //        screen to be defined which trigger calls to user-defined
    //        functions when the left mouse button is pressed and the
    //        cursor is within the defined button. This class is derived
    //        from class TMouse.
```

```
//
//****************************************************************

#include <stdio.h>
#include <string.h>
#include <conio.h>

#define LABEL_SIZE          16
#define BUTTON_ENABLED      1
#define BUTTON_DISABLED     0
#define TRUE                1
#define FALSE               0

#ifndef __BASIC_COLORS
#define __BASIC_COLORS
#define BLACK               0
#define BLUE                1
#define GREEN               2
#define CYAN                3
#define RED                 4
#define MAGENTA             5
#define BROWN               6
#define LIGHTGRAY           7
#define DARKGRAY            8
#define LIGHTBLUE           9
#define LIGHTGREEN          10
#define LIGHTCYAN           11
#define LIGHTRED            12
#define LIGHTMAGENTA        13
#define YELLOW              14
#define WHITE               15
#endif

void DrawString(int,int,char *,int);

class TControl : public TMouse
  {
public:
  TControl();
  ~TControl();
  virtual int  CreateButton(int(near*)(),int,int,int,int,char*);
  virtual void DeleteButton(int);
  virtual void EnableButton(int);
  virtual void DisableButton(int);

// Functions inherited from TMouse
//
// void HideCursor();
// void ShowCursor();
// void SetMouseLimits(int,int,int,int);
// void SetStandardCallback(int(near*)());
// void SetCallback(int(near*)(),int,int,int,int);
// void Run();
```

```
  private:

    struct button_list_t
      {
      char   label[LABEL_SIZE];
      void   *background,*bitmap;
      int    x_pos,y_pos;
      int    x_size,y_size;
      int    (*callback)();
      int    handle,status;
      struct button_list_t *next;
      } *button_list_head,*button_list_tail,*button_list_ptr,*temp;

    int handle;
    int error_flag;
    };
```

DISP_256.H Source Code

```
  #ifndef __DISPLAY256_H
  #define __DISPLAY256_H
  #endif

  #include <string.h>
  #include <stdlib.h>
  #include <stdio.h>

  //****************************************************************
  //        Class TDisplay
  //
  //        This class defines a group of functions and data structures
  //        which allow a DOS-based program to set up display windows
  //        on the user screen for numbers or text. The Show() function
  //        is overloaded to work with int, long, float, or char[] data
  //        types.
  //
  //****************************************************************

  #ifndef __BASICCOLORS
  #define __BASICCOLORS
  #define BLACK          0
  #define BLUE           1
  #define GREEN          2
  #define CYAN           3
  #define RED            4
  #define MAGENTA        5
  #define BROWN          6
  #define LIGHTGRAY      7
  #define DARKGRAY       8
  #define LIGHTBLUE      9
  #define LIGHTGREEN     10
  #define LIGHTCYAN      11
```

```
#define LIGHTRED        12
#define LIGHTMAGENTA    13
#define YELLOW          14
#define WHITE           15
#endif

#define BUFFER_SIZE     80
#define DEFAULT_XSIZE   96
#define DEFAULT_YSIZE   14
#define DEFAULT_MAX_X   319-DEFAULT_XSIZE
#define DEFAULT_MAXLEN  (96-16)/8
#define DEFAULT_FG      BLACK
#define DEFAULT_BG      WHITE
#define BORDER          1
#define NOBORDER        0

class TDisplay
  {
public:
  struct display_t
    {
    int x_pos,y_pos;
    int x_size,y_size;
    int x1,y1,x2,y2;
    int bg_color,fg_color;
    int max_length;
    int border_flag;
    } *parms;
  char buffer[BUFFER_SIZE];

  TDisplay(int,int,int,int,int,int,int);
  TDisplay(int,int,int);
  ~TDisplay();
  virtual void Show(int);
  virtual void Show(long int);
  virtual void Show(char *,float);
  virtual void Show(char *);
  };
```

C++ Library Source Code Listings

Each of the following C++ files is used with one or more of the programs provided with this book. These are the implementation files for mouse and display controls for the interactive programs. Where appropriate, a brief description of the contents is given along with the code listing.

MOUSE.CPP Source Code

```
#include "mouse.h"

//****************************************************************
```

```
//          Class TMouse
//
//          This class defines a group of functions and data structures
//          which allow a DOS-based program to set up mouse-operated
//          controls. A call-back mechanism allows regions of the
//          screen to be defined which trigger calls to user-defined
//          functions when the left mouse button is pressed and the
//          cursor is within the defined region.
//
//***************************************************************

void TMouse::FlagReset()
  {
  inregs.x.ax=MC_RESET;
  int86(MOUSE_INT,&inregs,&outregs);
  }

void TMouse::HideCursor(void)
  {
  inregs.x.ax=MC_HIDECURSOR;
  int86(MOUSE_INT,&inregs,&outregs);
  }

void TMouse::ShowCursor(void)
  {
  inregs.x.ax=MC_SHOWCURSOR;
  int86(MOUSE_INT,&inregs,&outregs);
  }

void TMouse::GetStatus(void)
  {
  int status;
  inregs.x.ax=MC_GETSTATUS;
  int86(MOUSE_INT,&inregs,&outregs);
  status=outregs.x.bx;
  left.status=status&BUTTON_LEFT;
  right.status=(status&BUTTON_RIGHT)>1;
  if(left.status==BUTTON_DOWN &&
    press_pending==FALSE)press_pending=TRUE;
  if(left.status==BUTTON_UP &&
    press_pending==PROCESSED)press_pending=FALSE;
  x.current_position=outregs.x.cx;
  y.current_position=outregs.x.dx;
  }

void TMouse::SetMouseLimits(int xmin,int xmax,int ymin,int ymax)
  {
  inregs.x.ax=MC_SETXLIMIT;
  inregs.x.cx=xmin;
  inregs.x.dx=xmax;
  int86(MOUSE_INT,&inregs,&outregs);
  inregs.x.ax=MC_SETYLIMIT;
  inregs.x.cx=ymin;
```

```
    inregs.x.dx=ymax;
    int86(MOUSE_INT,&inregs,&outregs);
    }

void TMouse::SetMickeysPerPixel(int x,int y)
    {
    inregs.x.ax=MC_SETMICKEYS;
    inregs.x.cx=x;
    inregs.x.dx=y;
    int86(MOUSE_INT,&inregs,&outregs);
    }

TMouse::TMouse()
    {
    list_head.next=NULL;
    list_head.callback=NULL;
    list_tail=&list_head;
    current_call=&list_head;
    standard_flag=NO_STANDARD;
    run_flag=RUN_DISABLED;
    callback_count=0;
    press_pending=FALSE;
    FlagReset();
    }

TMouse::~TMouse()
    {
    run_flag=RUN_DISABLED;
    HideCursor();
    list_tail=list_head.next;
    while(callback_count>0 && list_tail!=NULL)
      {
      current_call=list_tail->next;
      delete list_tail;
      list_tail=current_call;
      current_call-;
      }
    }

void TMouse::SetStandardCallback(int (*callback)())
    {
    list_head.callback=callback;
    standard_flag=STANDARD_SET;
    run_flag=RUN_ENABLED;
    }

void TMouse::SetCallback(int (*callback)(),
    int x_pos,int y_pos,int x_size,int y_size)
    {
    list_tail->next=new struct list_t;
    list_tail=list_tail->next;
    list_tail->callback=callback;
    list_tail->x_pos=x_pos;
```

```
      list_tail->y_pos=y_pos;
      list_tail->x_size=x_size;
      list_tail->y_size=y_size;
      list_tail->enable_flag=BUTTON_ENABLED;
      list_tail->next=NULL;
      run_flag=RUN_ENABLED;
      callback_count++;
      }

void TMouse::DeleteCallback(int (*callback)())
  {
  struct list_t *temp;
  temp=&list_head;
  current_call=list_head.next;
  while(current_call!=NULL && current_call->callback!=callback)
    {
    temp=current_call;
    current_call=current_call->next;
    }
  if(current_call!=NULL && current_call->callback==callback)
    {
    temp->next=current_call->next;  // Unlink structure
    delete current_call;            // Delete it
    callback_count-;
    }
  }

void TMouse::Run()
  {
  int x_min,x_max;
  int y_min,y_max;
  int (*callback)();
  ShowCursor();
  while(run_flag==RUN_ENABLED)
    {
    GetStatus();
    if(press_pending==TRUE)
      {
      press_pending=PROCESSED;
      if(callback_count>0)
        {
        current_call=list_head.next;
        while(current_call!=NULL)
          {
          x_min=current_call->x_pos;
          y_min=current_call->y_pos;
          x_max=x_min+current_call->x_size;
          y_max=y_min+current_call->y_size;
          if(x.current_position>x_min && x.current_position<x_max)
          if(y.current_position>y_min && y.current_position<y_max)
            {
            callback=current_call->callback;
            run_flag|=callback();
```

```
              }
            current_call=current_call->next;
            }
          }
        }
      if(standard_flag==STANDARD_SET)
        {
        callback=list_head.callback;
        run_flag|=callback();
        }
      }
    }
```

CONTROL.CPP Source Code

```
#include "control.h"

//*****************************************************************
//          Class TControl
//
//          This class defines a group of functions and data structures
//          which allow a DOS-based program to set up mouse-operated
//          controls. A call-back mechanism allows buttons on the
//          screen to be defined which trigger calls to user-defined
//          functions when the left mouse button is pressed and the
//          cursor is within the defined button. This class is derived
//          from class TMouse.
//
//*****************************************************************

TControl::TControl()
  {
  button_list_head=NULL;
  button_list_tail=NULL;
  button_list_ptr=NULL;
  error_flag=FALSE;
  handle=1;
  }

TControl::~TControl()
  {
  button_list_ptr=button_list_head;
  while(button_list_head!=NULL)
    {
    button_list_ptr=button_list_head->next;
    delete button_list_head;
    button_list_head=button_list_ptr;
    }
  }

//*****************************************************************
// CreateButton defines a button on the screen, and returns its
```

```
// handle. If the create operation failed, it returns zero.
// An alternate "hot-key" can also be assigned to the screen
// button, and a callback function triggered whenever the
// screen button is clicked with the mouse, or the hot-key
// is pressed.
//****************************************************************

int  TControl::CreateButton(int(*callback)(),
  int x_pos,int y_pos,int x_size,int y_size,
  char *label)
  {
  if(button_list_head==NULL)
    {
    if(!(button_list_head=new button_list_t))error_flag=TRUE;
    button_list_tail=button_list_head;
    }
  else
    {
    if(!(button_list_tail->next=new button_list_t))error_flag=TRUE;
    button_list_tail=button_list_tail->next;
    }
  if(!error_flag)
    {
    strcpy(button_list_tail->label,label);
    button_list_tail->x_pos=x_pos;
    button_list_tail->y_pos=y_pos;
    button_list_tail->x_size=x_size;
    button_list_tail->y_size=y_size;
    button_list_tail->status=BUTTON_ENABLED;
    button_list_tail->handle=handle++;
    button_list_tail->callback=callback;
    button_list_tail->next=NULL;
    setfillstyle(SOLID_FILL,LIGHTGRAY);
    setcolor(BLACK);
    setlinestyle(SOLID_LINE,0,NORM_WIDTH);
    bar3d(x_pos,y_pos,x_pos+x_size,y_pos+y_size,0,0);
    setcolor(DARKGRAY);
    line(x_pos+1,y_pos+y_size-1,x_pos+x_size-1,y_pos+y_size-1);
    line(x_pos+x_size-1,y_pos+1,x_pos+x_size-1,y_pos+y_size-1);
    setcolor(WHITE);
    line(x_pos+1,y_pos+1,x_pos+x_size-1,y_pos+1);
    line(x_pos+1,y_pos+1,x_pos+1,y_pos+y_size-1);
    settextjustify(CENTER_TEXT,CENTER_TEXT);
    outtextxy(x_pos+x_size/2,y_pos+y_size/2,label);
    SetCallback(callback,x_pos,y_pos,x_size,y_size);
    return(button_list_tail->handle);
    }
  else
    {
    return(0);
    }
  }

void TControl::DeleteButton(int handle)
```

```
    {
    temp=NULL;
    button_list_ptr=button_list_head;
    while(button_list_ptr->handle!=handle && button_list_ptr->next!=NULL)
      {
      temp=button_list_ptr;
      button_list_ptr=button_list_ptr->next;
      }
    if(button_list_ptr->handle==handle)
      {
      if(temp==NULL)          //Delete first entry
        {
        button_list_head=button_list_ptr->next;
        }
      else                    //Delete other entry
        {
        temp->next=button_list_ptr->next;
        }
      delete button_list_ptr;
      }
    }

void TControl::EnableButton(int handle)
  {
  button_list_ptr=button_list_head;
  while(button_list_ptr->handle!=handle && button_list_ptr->next!=NULL)
    {
    temp=button_list_ptr;
    button_list_ptr=button_list_ptr->next;
    }
  if(button_list_ptr->handle==handle)
    {
    button_list_ptr->status=BUTTON_ENABLED;
    }
  }

void TControl::DisableButton(int handle)
  {
  button_list_ptr=button_list_head;
  while(button_list_ptr->handle!=handle && button_list_ptr->next!=NULL)
    {
    temp=button_list_ptr;
    button_list_ptr=button_list_ptr->next;
    }
  if(button_list_ptr->handle==handle)
    {
    button_list_ptr->status=BUTTON_DISABLED;
    }
  }
```

DISPLAY.CPP Source Code

```
#include <display.h>
```

```
//****************************************************************
//        Class TDisplay
//
//        This class defines a group of functions and data structures
//        which allow a DOS-based program to set up display windows
//        on the user screen for numbers or text. The Show() function
//        is overloaded to work with int, long, float, or char[] data
//        types.
//
//****************************************************************

TDisplay::TDisplay(int x_pos,int y_pos,int x_size,int y_size,
  int bg,int fg,int border)
  {
  parms=new display_t;
  parms->x_pos=x_pos;
  parms->y_pos=y_pos;
  parms->x_size=x_size;
  parms->y_size=y_size;
  parms->x1=x_pos+3;
  parms->y1=y_pos+3;
  parms->x2=x_pos+x_size-3;
  parms->y2=y_pos+y_size-3;
  parms->bg_color=bg;
  parms->fg_color=fg;
  parms->max_length=(x_size-16)/8;
  if(parms->max_length<0)parms->max_length=0;
  parms->border_flag=border;
  if(border==BORDER)
    {
    setfillstyle(SOLID_FILL,LIGHTGRAY);
    setcolor(BLACK);
    setlinestyle(SOLID_LINE,0,NORM_WIDTH);
    bar3d(x_pos,y_pos,x_pos+x_size,y_pos+y_size,0,0);
    setcolor(WHITE);
    line(x_pos+1,y_pos+1,x_pos+x_size-1,y_pos+1);
    line(x_pos+2,y_pos+y_size-2,x_pos+x_size-2,y_pos+y_size-2);
    line(x_pos+1,y_pos+1,x_pos+1,y_pos+y_size-1);
    line(x_pos+x_size-2,y_pos+2,x_pos+x_size-2,y_pos+y_size-2);
    setfillstyle(SOLID_FILL,bg);
    setcolor(BLACK);
    bar3d(parms->x1,parms->y1,parms->x2,parms->y2,0,0);
    }
  else
    {
    setfillstyle(SOLID_FILL,bg);
    setcolor(BLACK);
    setlinestyle(SOLID_LINE,0,NORM_WIDTH);
    bar3d(x_pos,y_pos,x_pos+x_size,y_pos+y_size,0,0);
    }
  }

TDisplay::TDisplay(int x_pos,int y_pos,int border) // Def. size & color
```

```
      {
      parms=new display_t;
      if(x_pos>DEFAULT_MAX_X)x_pos=DEFAULT_MAX_X;
      parms->x_pos=x_pos;
      parms->y_pos=y_pos;
      parms->x_size=DEFAULT_XSIZE;
      parms->y_size=DEFAULT_YSIZE;
      parms->x1=x_pos+3;
      parms->y1=y_pos+3;
      parms->x2=x_pos+DEFAULT_XSIZE-3;
      parms->y2=y_pos+DEFAULT_YSIZE-3;
      parms->bg_color=DEFAULT_BG;
      parms->fg_color=DEFAULT_FG;
      parms->max_length=DEFAULT_MAXLEN;
      parms->border_flag=border;
      if(border==BORDER)
         {
         setfillstyle(SOLID_FILL,LIGHTGRAY);
         setcolor(BLACK);
         setlinestyle(SOLID_LINE,0,NORM_WIDTH);
         bar3d(x_pos,y_pos,x_pos+parms->x_size,y_pos+parms->y_size,0,0);
         setcolor(WHITE);
         line(x_pos+1,y_pos+1,x_pos+parms->x_size-1,y_pos+1);
         line(x_pos+2,y_pos+parms->y_size-2,
            x_pos+parms->x_size-2,y_pos+parms->y_size-2);
         line(x_pos+1,y_pos+1,x_pos+1,y_pos+parms->y_size-1);
         line(x_pos+parms->x_size-2,y_pos+2,
            x_pos+parms->x_size-2,y_pos+parms->y_size-2);
         setfillstyle(SOLID_FILL,parms->bg_color);
         setcolor(BLACK);
         bar3d(parms->x1,parms->y1,parms->x2,parms->y2,0,0);
         }
      else
         {
         setfillstyle(SOLID_FILL,parms->bg_color);
         setcolor(BLACK);
         setlinestyle(SOLID_LINE,0,NORM_WIDTH);
         bar3d(x_pos,y_pos,x_pos+parms->x_size,y_pos+parms->y_size,0,0);
         }
      }

TDisplay::~TDisplay()
   {
   delete parms;
   }

void TDisplay::Show(char *string)
   {
   setfillstyle(SOLID_FILL,parms->bg_color);
   setcolor(BLACK);
   setlinestyle(SOLID_LINE,0,NORM_WIDTH);
   bar(parms->x1+1,parms->y1+1,parms->x2-1,parms->y2-1);
   strcpy(buffer,string);
```

```
  if(strlen(buffer)>parms->max_length)buffer[parms->max_length+1]=0;
  settextjustify(LEFT_TEXT,CENTER_TEXT);
  outtextxy(parms->x_pos+8,parms->y_pos+(parms->y_size/2),buffer);
  }

void TDisplay::Show(int value)
  {
  setfillstyle(SOLID_FILL,parms->bg_color);
  setcolor(BLACK);
  setlinestyle(SOLID_LINE,0,NORM_WIDTH);
  bar(parms->x1+1,parms->y1+1,parms->x2-1,parms->y2-1);
  itoa(value,buffer,10);
  if(strlen(buffer)>parms->max_length)
    {
    strnset(buffer,'#',parms->max_length);
    buffer[parms->max_length]=0;
    }
  settextjustify(RIGHT_TEXT,CENTER_TEXT);
  outtextxy(parms->x_pos+parms->x_size-8,
  parms->y_pos+(parms->y_size/2),buffer);
  }

void TDisplay::Show(long int value)
  {
  setfillstyle(SOLID_FILL,parms->bg_color);
  setcolor(BLACK);
  setlinestyle(SOLID_LINE,0,NORM_WIDTH);
  bar(parms->x1+1,parms->y1+1,parms->x2-1,parms->y2-1);
  ltoa(value,buffer,10);
  if(strlen(buffer)>parms->max_length)
    {
    strnset(buffer,'#',parms->max_length);
    buffer[parms->max_length]=0;
    }
  settextjustify(RIGHT_TEXT,CENTER_TEXT);
  outtextxy(parms->x_pos+parms->x_size-8,
  parms->y_pos+(parms->y_size/2),buffer);
  }

void TDisplay::Show(char *format,float value)
  {
  setfillstyle(SOLID_FILL,parms->bg_color);
  setcolor(BLACK);
  setlinestyle(SOLID_LINE,0,NORM_WIDTH);
  bar(parms->x1+1,parms->y1+1,parms->x2-1,parms->y2-1);
  sprintf(buffer,format,value);
  if(strlen(buffer)>parms->max_length)
    {
    strnset(buffer,'#',parms->max_length);
    buffer[parms->max_length]=0;
    }
  settextjustify(RIGHT_TEXT,CENTER_TEXT);
  outtextxy(parms->x_pos+parms->x_size-8,
```

```
        parms->y_pos+(parms->y_size/2),buffer);
        }
```

MOUSE256.CPP Source Code

```
    #include "mouse256.h"

    void TMouse::FlagReset()
        {
        inregs.x.ax=MC_RESET;
        int86(MOUSE_INT,&inregs,&outregs);
        }

    void TMouse::HideCursor(void)
        {
        inregs.x.ax=MC_HIDECURSOR;
        int86(MOUSE_INT,&inregs,&outregs);
        }

    void TMouse::ShowCursor(void)
        {
        inregs.x.ax=MC_SHOWCURSOR;
        int86(MOUSE_INT,&inregs,&outregs);
        }

    void TMouse::GetStatus(void)
        {
        int status;
        inregs.x.ax=MC_GETSTATUS;
        int86(MOUSE_INT,&inregs,&outregs);
        status=outregs.x.bx;
        left.status=status&BUTTON_LEFT;
        right.status=(status&BUTTON_RIGHT)>1;
        if(left.status==BUTTON_DOWN &&
          press_pending==FALSE)press_pending=TRUE;
        if(left.status==BUTTON_UP &&
          press_pending==PROCESSED)press_pending=FALSE;
        x.current_position=outregs.x.cx/2;
        y.current_position=outregs.x.dx;
        }

    void TMouse::SetMouseLimits(int xmin,int xmax,int ymin,int ymax)
        {
        inregs.x.ax=MC_SETXLIMIT;
        inregs.x.cx=xmin;
        inregs.x.dx=xmax;
        int86(MOUSE_INT,&inregs,&outregs);
        inregs.x.ax=MC_SETYLIMIT;
        inregs.x.cx=ymin;
        inregs.x.dx=ymax;
        int86(MOUSE_INT,&inregs,&outregs);
        }
```

```
void TMouse::SetMickeysPerPixel(int x,int y)
   {
   inregs.x.ax=MC_SETMICKEYS;
   inregs.x.cx=x;
   inregs.x.dx=y;
   int86(MOUSE_INT,&inregs,&outregs);
   }

TMouse::TMouse()
   {
   list_head.next=NULL;
   list_head.callback=NULL;
   list_tail=&list_head;
   current_call=&list_head;
   standard_flag=NO_STANDARD;
   run_flag=RUN_DISABLED;
   callback_count=0;
   press_pending=FALSE;
   FlagReset();
   }

TMouse::~TMouse()
   {
   run_flag=RUN_DISABLED;
   list_tail=list_head.next;
   while(callback_count>0 && list_tail!=NULL)
      {
      current_call=list_tail->next;
      delete list_tail;
      list_tail=current_call;
      current_call-;
      }
   }

void TMouse::SetStandardCallback(int (*callback)())
   {
   list_head.callback=callback;
   standard_flag=STANDARD_SET;
   run_flag=RUN_ENABLED;
   }

void TMouse::SetCallback(int (*callback)(),
   int x_pos,int y_pos,int x_size,int y_size)
   {
   list_tail->next=new struct list_t;
   list_tail=list_tail->next;
   list_tail->callback=callback;
   list_tail->x_pos=x_pos;
   list_tail->y_pos=y_pos;
   list_tail->x_size=x_size;
   list_tail->y_size=y_size;
   list_tail->enable_flag=BUTTON_ENABLED;
   list_tail->next=NULL;
```

```
      run_flag=RUN_ENABLED;
      callback_count++;
      }

void TMouse::DeleteCallback(int (*callback)())
   {
   struct list_t *temp;
   temp=&list_head;
   current_call=list_head.next;
   while(current_call!=NULL && current_call->callback!=callback)
      {
      temp=current_call;
      current_call=current_call->next;
      }
   if(current_call!=NULL && current_call->callback==callback)
      {
      temp->next=current_call->next;          // Unlink structure
      delete current_call;                    // Delete it
      callback_count—;
      }
   }

void TMouse::Run()
   {
   int x_min,x_max;
   int y_min,y_max;
   int (*callback)();
   ShowCursor();
   while(run_flag==RUN_ENABLED)
      {
      GetStatus();
      if(press_pending==TRUE)
         {
         press_pending=PROCESSED;
         if(callback_count>0)
            {
            current_call=list_head.next;
            while(current_call!=NULL)
               {
               x_min=current_call->x_pos;
               y_min=current_call->y_pos;
               x_max=x_min+current_call->x_size;
               y_max=y_min+current_call->y_size;
               if(x.current_position>x_min && x.current_position<x_max)
               if(y.current_position>y_min && y.current_position<y_max)
                  {
                  callback=current_call->callback;
                  run_flag|=callback();
                  }
               current_call=current_call->next;
               }
            }
         }
```

```
      if(standard_flag==STANDARD_SET)
        {
        callback=list_head.callback;
        run_flag|=callback();
        }
    }
  }
```

CTRL_256.CPP Source Code

```
#include "ctrl_256.h"

extern "C" void DrawBlock(int,int,int,int,int);
extern "C" void DrawASCII(int,int,int,int);

void DrawString(int x_pos,int y_pos,char *string,int color)
  {
  while(*string!=0 && x_pos<312)
    {
    DrawASCII(x_pos,y_pos,(int)*string,color);
    x_pos+=8 ;
    string++;
    }
  }

TControl::TControl()
  {
  button_list_head=NULL;
  button_list_tail=NULL;
  button_list_ptr=NULL;
  error_flag=FALSE;
  handle=1;
  }

TControl::~TControl()
  {
  button_list_ptr=button_list_head;
  while(button_list_head!=NULL)
    {
    button_list_ptr=button_list_head->next;
    delete button_list_head;
    button_list_head=button_list_ptr;
    }
  }

// CreateButton defines a button on the screen, and returns its
// handle. If the create operation failed, it returns zero.
// An alternate "hot-key" can also be assigned to the screen
// button, and a callback function triggered whenever the
// screen button is clicked with the mouse, or the hot-key
// is pressed.
```

```
int  TControl::CreateButton(int(*callback)(),
  int x_pos,int y_pos,int x_size,int y_size,
  char *label)
  {
  if(button_list_head==NULL)
    {
    if(!(button_list_head=new button_list_t))error_flag=TRUE;
    button_list_tail=button_list_head;
    }
  else
    {
    if(!(button_list_tail->next=new button_list_t))error_flag=TRUE;
    button_list_tail=button_list_tail->next;
    }
  if(!error_flag)
    {
    strcpy(button_list_tail->label,label);
    button_list_tail->x_pos=x_pos;
    button_list_tail->y_pos=y_pos;
    button_list_tail->x_size=x_size;
    button_list_tail->y_size=y_size;
    button_list_tail->status=BUTTON_ENABLED;
    button_list_tail->handle=handle++;
    button_list_tail->callback=callback;
    button_list_tail->next=NULL;

    DrawBlock(x_pos,y_pos,x_size,y_size,LIGHTGRAY);
    DrawBlock(x_pos,y_pos+y_size,x_size+1,1,DARKGRAY);
    DrawBlock(x_pos+x_size,y_pos,1,y_size,DARKGRAY);
    DrawBlock(x_pos,y_pos,x_size,1,WHITE);
    DrawBlock(x_pos,y_pos,1,y_size,WHITE);
    DrawString(1+x_pos+x_size/2-strlen(label)*4,
    1+y_pos+y_size/2-4,label,WHITE);

    SetCallback(callback,x_pos,y_pos,x_size,y_size);
    return(button_list_tail->handle);
    }
  else
    {
    return(0);
    }
  }

void TControl::DeleteButton(int handle)
  {
  temp=NULL;
  button_list_ptr=button_list_head;
  while(button_list_ptr->handle!=handle && button_list_ptr->next!=NULL)
    {
    temp=button_list_ptr;
    button_list_ptr=button_list_ptr->next;
    }
```

```
      if(button_list_ptr->handle==handle)
        {
        if(temp==NULL)          //Delete first entry
          {
          button_list_head=button_list_ptr->next;
          }
        else                    //Delete other entry
          {
          temp->next=button_list_ptr->next;
          }
        delete button_list_ptr;
        }
    }

void TControl::EnableButton(int handle)
    {
    button_list_ptr=button_list_head;
    while(button_list_ptr->handle!=handle && button_list_ptr->next!=NULL)
        {
        temp=button_list_ptr;
        button_list_ptr=button_list_ptr->next;
        }
    if(button_list_ptr->handle==handle)
        {
        button_list_ptr->status=BUTTON_ENABLED;
        }
    }

void TControl::DisableButton(int handle)
    {
    button_list_ptr=button_list_head;
    while(button_list_ptr->handle!=handle && button_list_ptr->next!=NULL)
        {
        temp=button_list_ptr;
        button_list_ptr=button_list_ptr->next;
        }
    if(button_list_ptr->handle==handle)
        {
        button_list_ptr->status=BUTTON_DISABLED;
        }
    }
```

DISP_256.CPP Source Code

```
#include <disp_256.h>

//******************************************************************
//          Class TDisplay
//
//          This class defines a group of functions and data structures
//          which allow a DOS-based program to set up display windows
//          on the user screen for numbers or text. The Show() function
```

```
//          is overloaded to work with int, long, float, or char[] data
//          types.
//
//*****************************************************************

extern "C" void DrawBlock(int,int,int,int,int);
extern "C" void DrawASCII(int,int,int,int);
extern void DrawString(int,int,char *,int);

TDisplay::TDisplay(int x_pos,int y_pos,int x_size,int y_size,
  int bg,int fg,int border)
  {
  parms=new display_t;
  parms->x_pos=x_pos;
  parms->y_pos=y_pos;
  parms->x_size=x_size;
  parms->y_size=y_size;
  parms->x1=x_pos;
  parms->y1=y_pos;
  parms->x2=x_pos+x_size;
  parms->y2=y_pos+y_size;
  parms->bg_color=bg;
  parms->fg_color=fg;
  parms->max_length=(x_size-16)/8;
  if(parms->max_length<0)parms->max_length=0;
  parms->border_flag=border;
  if(border==BORDER)
    {
    DrawBlock(x_pos-1,y_pos-1,x_size+2,y_size+2,BLACK);
    }
  DrawBlock(x_pos,y_pos,x_size,y_size,bg);
  }

TDisplay::TDisplay(int x_pos,int y_pos,int border) // Def. size & color
  {
  parms=new display_t;
  if(x_pos>DEFAULT_MAX_X)x_pos=DEFAULT_MAX_X;
  parms->x_pos=x_pos;
  parms->y_pos=y_pos;
  parms->x_size=DEFAULT_XSIZE;
  parms->y_size=DEFAULT_YSIZE;
  parms->x1=x_pos;
  parms->y1=y_pos;
  parms->x2=x_pos+DEFAULT_XSIZE;
  parms->y2=y_pos+DEFAULT_YSIZE;
  parms->bg_color=DEFAULT_BG;
  parms->fg_color=DEFAULT_FG;
  parms->max_length=DEFAULT_MAXLEN;
  parms->border_flag=border;
  if(border==BORDER)
    {
    DrawBlock(x_pos-1,y_pos-1,parms->x_size+2,parms->y_size+2,BLACK);
```

```
    }
  DrawBlock(x_pos,y_pos,parms->x_size,parms->y_size,parms->bg_color);
  }

TDisplay::~TDisplay()
  {
  delete parms;
  }

void TDisplay::Show(char *string)
  {
  DrawBlock(parms->x_pos,parms->y_pos,
            parms->x_size,parms->y_size,parms->bg_color);
  strcpy(buffer,string);
  if(strlen(buffer)>parms->max_length)buffer[parms->max_length+1]=0;
  DrawString(parms->x_pos+8,
  parms->y_pos+(parms->y_size/2)-3,buffer,parms->fg_color);
  }

void TDisplay::Show(int value)
  {
  DrawBlock(parms->x_pos,parms->y_pos,
            parms->x_size,parms->y_size,parms->bg_color);
  itoa(value,buffer,10);
  if(strlen(buffer)>parms->max_length)
    {
    strnset(buffer,'#',parms->max_length);
    buffer[parms->max_length]=0;
    }
  DrawString(parms->x_pos+parms->x_size-strlen(buffer)*8-8,
  parms->y_pos+(parms->y_size/2)-3,buffer,parms->fg_color);
  }

void TDisplay::Show(long int value)
  {
  DrawBlock(parms->x_pos,parms->y_pos,
            parms->x_size,parms->y_size,parms->bg_color);
  ltoa(value,buffer,10);
  if(strlen(buffer)>parms->max_length)
    {
    strnset(buffer,'#',parms->max_length);
    buffer[parms->max_length]=0;
    }
  DrawString(parms->x_pos+parms->x_size-strlen(buffer)*8-8,
  parms->y_pos+(parms->y_size/2)-3,buffer,parms->fg_color);
  }

void TDisplay::Show(char *format,float value)
  {
  DrawBlock(parms->x_pos,parms->y_pos,
            parms->x_size,parms->y_size,parms->bg_color);
  sprintf(buffer,format,value);
  if(strlen(buffer)>parms->max_length)
```

```
    {
    strnset(buffer,'#',parms->max_length);
    buffer[parms->max_length]=0;
    }
DrawString(parms->x_pos+parms->x_size-strlen(buffer)*8-8,
parms->y_pos+(parms->y_size/2)-3,buffer,parms->fg_color);
    }
```

Assembly Language Module Source Code Listings

Each of the following source files is used with one or more of the programs provided with this book. Where appropriate, a brief description of the contents is given along with the code listing.

SETVMODE.ASM Source Code

```
                .MODEL          small
                .CODE

;
; Name:         SetVmode
;
; Function:     Call IBM PC ROM BIOS to set a video display mode.
;
; Caller:       Turbo C:
;
;               void SetVmode(n);
;
;               int n;          /* video mode */
;
;====================================================================

FLAGS           EQU     byte ptr ds:[10h] ; (in Video Display Data Area)

CGAflag         EQU     00100000b       ; bits for FLAGS
MDAflag         EQU     00110000b

                PUBLIC  SetVmode
_SetVmode       PROC    NEAR
                ARG     v_mode:WORD

                push    bp              ; preserve caller registers
                mov     bp,sp
                push    ds

                mov     ax,40h
                mov     ds,ax           ; DS -> Display Data Area
                mov     bl,CGAflag      ; BL := Detect CGA
                mov     ax,[v_mode]     ; AL := Mode number
                mov     ah,al           ; Monochrome?
                and     ah,7
                cmp     ah,7
```

```
                jne         L01             ; Mode not 7 or 0Fh
                mov         bl,MDAflag      ; Set MDA

L01:            and         FLAGS,11001111b
                or          FLAGS,bl
                xor         ah,ah   ; AH := 0 (INT 10h function number)
                push        bp
                int         10h             ; Set the video mode
                pop         bp

                pop         ds
                mov         sp,bp
                pop         bp
                ret

_SetVmode       ENDP

                END
```

VPALETTE.ASM Source Code

```
                TITLE       'Access 256 Color Palette'
                .MODEL      small
                .CODE

PelMask         EQU         3c6h
PelReadPort     EQU         3c7h
PelWritePort    EQU         3c8h
PelData         EQU         3c9h
PelMax          EQU         3*256


;
; Name:         WritePalette
;
; Function:     Copy Data Into 256-Color Palette
;
; Caller:       Turbo C:
;
;               void WritePalette(src);
;
;               unsigned char far *src   /* Pointer to Source Block */
;===================================================================

                PUBLIC      _WritePalette
_WritePalette   NEAR        PROC
                ARG         src:FAR PTR BYTE

                push        bp          ; preserve caller registers
                mov         bp,sp
                push        ds
                push        es
                push        si
```

```
                push       di
                push       ax
                push       bx
                push       cx
                push       dx

                lds        si,[src]      ; Set source pointer (ds:si)

                mov        dx,PelMask
                mov        al,0ffh
                out        dx,al         ; Enable all bit planes
                mov        dx,PelWritePort
                xor        al,al
                out        dx,al         ; Start at color #0
                mov        cx,PelMax
                mov        dx,PelData
                mov        bx,0
                cli
L5:             mov        al,ds:[si]
                out        dx,al      ; Load palette data
                inc        si
                loop       L5
                sti

                pop        dx
                pop        cx
                pop        bx
                pop        ax
                pop        di          ; restore registers and exit
                pop        si
                pop        es
                pop        ds
                mov        sp,bp
                pop        bp
                ret

_WritePalette   ENDP


;
; Name:          ReadPalette
;
; Function:      Copy Data Into 256-Color Palette
;
; Caller:        Turbo C:
;
;                void ReadPalette(dst);
;
;                unsigned char far *dst  /* Pointer to Source Block */
;

                PUBLIC     _ReadPalette
_ReadPalette    PROC       NEAR
```

```
                    ARG           dst:FAR PTR BYTE

                    push          bp          ; preserve caller registers
                    mov           bp,sp
                    push          ds
                    push          es
                    push          si
                    push          di
                    push          ax
                    push          bx
                    push          cx
                    push          dx

                    lds           di,[dst]    ; Set dest. pointer (ds:di)

                    mov           dx,PelMask
                    mov           al,0ffh
                    out           dx,al       ; Enable all bit planes
                    mov           dx,PelReadPort
                    xor           al,al
                    out           dx,al       ; Start at color #0
                    mov           cx,PelMax
                    mov           dx,PelData
                    mov           bx,0
                    cli
L6:                 in            al,dx       ; Get palette data
                    mov           ds:[di],al
                    inc           si
                    loop          L6
                    sti

                    pop           dx
                    pop           cx
                    pop           bx
                    pop           ax
                    pop           di          ; restore registers and exit
                    pop           si
                    pop           es
                    pop           ds
                    mov           sp,bp
                    pop           bp
                    ret

_ReadPalette        ENDP




;
; Name:        WriteEntry
;
; Function:    Copy Data Into 256-Color Palette
;
; Caller:      Turbo C:
```

```
;
;                  void WriteEntry(windex,r,g,b);
;
;                  int windex;   /* Palette Index */
;                  int r,g,b;    /* Palette Data */


                   PUBLIC     _WriteEntry
_WriteEntry        PROC       NEAR
                   ARG        windex:WORD,rdata:WORD,gdata:WORD,bdata:WORD

                   push       bp      ; preserve caller registers
                   mov        bp,sp
                   push       ds
                   push       es
                   push       si
                   push       di
                   push       ax
                   push       bx
                   push       cx
                   push       dx

                   mov        dx,PelMask
                   mov        al,0ffh
                   out        dx,al          ; Enable all bit planes
                   mov        dx,PelWritePort
                   mov        ax,[windex]
                   out        dx,al          ; Point to color @windex
                   mov        dx,PelData
                   cli
                   mov        ax,[rdata]
                   out        dx,al   ; Load palette data
                   mov        ax,[gdata]
                   out        dx,al   ; Load palette data
                   mov        ax,[bdata]
                   out        dx,al   ; Load palette data
                   sti

                   pop        dx
                   pop        cx
                   pop        bx
                   pop        ax
                   pop        di      ; restore registers and exit
                   pop        si
                   pop        es
                   pop        ds
                   mov        sp,bp
                   pop        bp
                   ret

_WriteEntry        ENDP

;
```

```
; Name:           ReadEntry
;
; Function:       Copy Data Into 256-Color Entry
;
; Caller:         Turbo C:
;
;                 void ReadEntry(rindex,dst);
;
;                 int rindex;              /* Palette Index */
;                 unsigned char far *dst   /* Pointer to Source Block */
;

                  PUBLIC    _ReadEntry
_ReadEntry        PROC      NEAR
                  ARG       rindex:WORD,dst:FAR PTR BYTE

                  push      bp                  ; preserve caller registers
                  mov       bp,sp
                  push      ds
                  push      es
                  push      si
                  push      di
                  push      ax
                  push      bx
                  push      cx
                  push      dx

                  lds       di,[dst]     ; Set dest. pointer (ds:di)

                  mov       dx,PelMask
                  mov       al,0ffh
                  out       dx,al        ; Enable all bit planes
                  mov       dx,PelReadPort
                  mov       ax,[windex]
                  out       dx,al        ; Point to color @windex
                  mov       dx,PelData
                  cli
                  in        al,dx    ; Get palette data
                  mov       ds:[di],al
                  inc       di
                  in        al,dx    ; Get palette data
                  mov       ds:[di],al
                  inc       di
                  in        al,dx    ; Get palette data
                  mov       ds:[di],al
                  inc       di
                  sti

                  pop       dx
                  pop       cx
                  pop       bx
                  pop       ax
                  pop       di           ; restore registers and exit
```

```
                pop        si
                pop        es
                pop        ds
                mov        sp,bp
                pop        bp
                ret

_ReadEntry      ENDP

                END
```

DRAW_BLK.ASM Source Code

```
                TITLE       'Draw a Block of Pixels in 256 Color Mode'
                .MODEL      small
                .CODE
;
; Name:          DrawBlock
;
; Function:      Copy an Image in 320x200 Graphics Mode Frame Buffer
;
; Caller:        Turbo C:
;
;                void DrawBlock(x,y,width,height,color);
;
;                int x;         /* X Location - Bytes */
;                int y;         /* Y Location - Lines */
;                int width;     /* Width - Pixels */
;                int height;    /* Height - Pixels */
;                int color;     /* Color Index 0-255 */
;
;====================================================================

                PUBLIC      _DrawBlock
_DrawBlock      PROC        NEAR
                ARG         x_loc:WORD,y_loc:WORD,x_size:WORD,y_size:WORD,col-
or:WORD

                push        bp          ; preserve caller registers
                mov         bp,sp
                push        ds
                push        es
                push        si
                push        di
                push        ax
                push        bx
                push        cx
                    push        dx

                mov         ax,320
                mul         [y_loc]
                add         ax,[x_loc]   ; Calculate Frame Buffer Start
```

```
                         mov       di,ax          ; DI —> block start
                         mov       ax,0a000h
                         mov       es,ax          ; Set frame buff segment (es:di)

; routine for byte-aligned bit blocks

                         mov       ax,[x_size]
                         mov       cx,ax
                         mov       ax,[y_size]
                         mov       bx,ax
                         mov       ax,[color]
                         cld                      ; set direction forward
L10:                     push      di             ; preserve Destination
                         push      cx             ; preserve width

L12:                     mov       es:[di],al     ; update display memory
                         inc       di             ; increment output pointer
                         loop      L12

                         pop       cx
                         pop       di
                         add       di,320         ; ES:DI -> next pixel row
                         dec       bx             ; Decrement row count
                         jnz       L10            ; loop down pixel rows

                         pop       dx
                         pop       cx
                         pop       bx
                         pop       ax
                         pop       di             ; restore registers and exit
                         pop       si
                         pop       es
                         pop       ds
                         mov       sp,bp
                         pop       bp
                         ret

_DrawBlock       ENDP

;=====================================================================
;
; Name:          DrawPixel
;
; Function:      Draw a Pixel in 320x200 Graphics Mode Frame Buffer
;
; Caller:        Turbo C:
;
;                void DrawPixel(x,y,color);
;
;                int x;     /* X Location - Bytes */
;                int y;     /* Y Location - Lines */
;                int color; /* Color Index 0-255 */
;
```

```
                PUBLIC      _DrawPixel
_DrawPixel      PROC        NEAR
                ARG         x_loc:WORD,y_loc:WORD,color:WORD

                push        bp      ; preserve caller registers
                mov         bp,sp
                push        es
                push        di

                mov         ax,320
                mul         [y_loc]
                add         ax,[x_loc] ; Calculate Frame Buffer Start
                mov         di,ax      ; DI -> block start
                mov         ax,0a000h
                mov         es,ax      ; Set frame buffer segment (es:di)

; routine for byte-aligned bit blocks

                mov         ax,[color]
                mov         es:[di],al ; update display memory

                pop         di         ; restore registers and exit
                pop         es
                mov         sp,bp
                pop         bp
                ret

_DrawPixel      ENDP

;====================================================================
;
; Name:         ReadPixel
;
; Function:     Read a Pixel in 320x200 Graphics Mode Frame Buffer
;
; Caller:       Turbo C:
;
;               int ReadPixel(x,y);
;
;               int x; /* X Location - Bytes */
;               int y; /* Y Location - Lines */
;

                PUBLIC      _ReadPixel
_ReadPixel      PROC        NEAR
                ARG         x_loc:WORD,y_loc:WORD

                push        bp      ; preserve caller registers
                mov         bp,sp
                push        es
                push        di

                mov         ax,320
```

```
                    mul       [y_loc]
                    add       ax,[x_loc]    ; Calculate Frame Buffer Start
                    mov       di,ax         ; DI -> block start
                    mov       ax,0a000h
                    mov       es,ax         ; Set frame buff. segment (es:di)
                    mov       al,es:[di]    ; Read display memory
                    mov       ah,0

                    pop       di            ; restore registers and exit
                    pop       es
                    mov       sp,bp
                    pop       bp
                    ret

_ReadPixel          ENDP

                    END
```

DRWASCII.ASM Source Code

```
                    TITLE     'Draw an ASCII character in 256 Color Mode'
                    .MODEL    small
                    .CODE
;
; Name:         DrawASCII
;
; Function:     Draw an ASCII character in 256 Color Mode
;
; Caller:       Turbo C:
;
;                 void DrawASCII(x,y,char,color);
;
;                 int x;     /* X Location - Bytes */
;                 int y;     /* Y Location - Lines */
;                 int char;  /* Character Index 0-127 */
;                 int color; /* Color Index 0-255 */
;
;======================================================================

                    PUBLIC    _DrawASCII
_DrawASCII          PROC      NEAR
                    ARG       x_loc:WORD,y_loc:WORD,char:WORD,color:WORD

                    push      bp      ; preserve caller registers
                    mov       bp,sp
                    push      ds
                    push      es
                    push      si
                    push      di
                    push      ax
                    push      bx
                    push      cx
```

```
                push      dx

                mov       ax,320
                mul       [y_loc]
                add       ax,[x_loc]  ; Calculate Frame Buffer Start
                mov       di,ax       ; DI -> block start
                mov       ax,0a000h
                mov       es,ax       ; Set frame buffer segment (es:di)


                mov       si,OFFSET _VideoFont
                mov       ax,SEG _VideoFont
                mov       ds,ax       ; DS:SI -> Font Table
                mov       ax,[char]
                and       ax,7fh
                shl       ax,1        ; Calculate font offset
                shl       ax,1
                shl       ax,1
                add       si,ax

                mov       ax,8
                mov       bx,ax
                mov       cx,ax
                mov       ax,[color]
                xchg      ah,al
                mov       al,[si]     ; Get bit map row
                cld                   ; set direction forward
L10:            push      di          ; preserve Destination
                push      cx          ; preserve width
                push      ax          ; preserve color/bitmap

L12:            and       al,80h
                jz        L14
                xchg      ah,al
                mov       es:[di],al  ; update display memory
                xchg      ah,al
L14:            pop       ax

                shl       al,1
                push      ax
                inc       di          ; increment output pointer
                loop      L12

                pop       ax
                pop       cx
                pop       di
                inc       si
                mov       al,[si]     ; Get next bit map row
                add       di,320      ; ES:DI -> next pixel row
                dec       bx          ; Decrement row count
                jnz       L10         ; loop down pixel rows

                pop       dx
```

```
            pop         cx
            pop         bx
            pop         ax
            pop         di      ; restore registers and exit
            pop         si
            pop         es
            pop         ds
            mov         sp,bp
            pop         bp
            ret

_VideoFont      label       byte

;           These are the bit-mapped characters for graphics mode.

            db          000h,000h,000h,000h,000h,000h,000h,000h ; 00 - nul
            db          07eh,081h,0a5h,081h,0bdh,099h,081h,07eh ; 01 - ^A
            db          07eh,0ffh,0dbh,0ffh,0c3h,0e7h,0ffh,07eh ; 02 - ^B
            db          06ch,0feh,0feh,0feh,07ch,038h,010h,000h ; 03 - ^C
            db          010h,038h,07ch,0feh,07ch,038h,010h,000h ; 04 - ^D
            db          038h,07ch,038h,0feh,0feh,07ch,038h,07ch ; 05 - ^E
            db          010h,010h,038h,07ch,0feh,07ch,038h,07ch ; 06 - ^F
            db          000h,000h,018h,03ch,03ch,018h,000h,000h ; 07 - ^G
            db          0ffh,0ffh,0e7h,0c3h,0c3h,0e7h,0ffh,0ffh ; 08 - ^H
            db          000h,03ch,066h,042h,042h,066h,03ch,000h ; 09 - ^I
            db          0ffh,0c3h,099h,0bdh,0bdh,099h,0c3h,0ffh ; 0A - ^J
            db          00fh,007h,00fh,07dh,0cch,0cch,0cch,078h ; 0B - ^K
            db          03ch,066h,066h,066h,03ch,018h,07eh,018h ; 0C - ^L
            db          03fh,033h,03fh,030h,030h,070h,0f0h,0e0h ; 0D - ^M
            db          07fh,063h,07fh,063h,06eh,067h,0e6h,0c0h ; 0E - ^N
            db          099h,05ah,03ch,0e7h,0e7h,03ch,05ah,099h ; 0F - ^O
            db          080h,0e0h,0f8h,0feh,0f8h,0e0h,080h,000h ; 10 - ^P
            db          002h,00eh,03eh,0feh,03eh,00eh,002h,000h ; 11 - ^Q
            db          018h,03ch,07eh,018h,018h,07eh,03ch,018h ; 12 - ^R
            db          066h,066h,066h,066h,066h,000h,066h,000h ; 13 - ^S
            db          07fh,0dbh,0dbh,07bh,01bh,01bh,01bh,000h ; 14 - ^T
            db          03eh,063h,038h,06ch,06ch,038h,0cch,078h ; 15 - ^U
            db          000h,000h,000h,000h,07eh,07eh,07eh,000h ; 16 - ^V
            db          018h,03ch,07eh,018h,07eh,03ch,018h,0ffh ; 17 - ^W
            db          018h,03ch,07eh,018h,018h,018h,018h,000h ; 18 - ^X
            db          018h,018h,018h,018h,07eh,03ch,018h,000h ; 19 - ^Y
            db          000h,018h,00ch,0feh,00ch,018h,000h,000h ; 1A - ^Z
            db          000h,030h,060h,0feh,060h,030h,000h,000h ; 1B - ^[
            db          000h,000h,0c0h,0c0h,0c0h,0feh,000h,000h ; 1C - ^\
            db          000h,024h,066h,0ffh,066h,024h,000h,000h ; 1D - ^]
            db          000h,018h,03ch,07eh,0ffh,0ffh,000h,000h ; 1E - ^6
            db          000h,0ffh,0ffh,07eh,03ch,018h,000h,000h ; 1F - ^-
            db          000h,000h,000h,000h,000h,000h,000h,000h ; 20 - spc
            db          030h,078h,078h,030h,030h,000h,030h,000h ; 21 - !
            db          06ch,06ch,06ch,000h,000h,000h,000h,000h ; 22 - "
            db          06ch,06ch,0feh,06ch,0feh,06ch,06ch,000h ; 23 - #
            db          030h,07ch,0c0h,078h,00ch,0f8h,030h,000h ; 24 - $
            db          000h,0c6h,0cch,018h,030h,066h,0c6h,000h ; 25 - %
```

```
db      038h,06ch,038h,076h,0dch,0cch,076h,000h ; 26 - &
db      060h,060h,0c0h,000h,000h,000h,000h,000h ; 27 - `
db      018h,030h,060h,060h,060h,030h,018h,000h ; 28 - (
db      060h,030h,018h,018h,018h,030h,060h,000h ; 29 - )
db      000h,066h,03ch,0ffh,03ch,066h,000h,000h ; 2A - *
db      000h,030h,030h,0fch,030h,030h,000h,000h ; 2B - +
db      000h,000h,000h,000h,000h,030h,030h,060h ; 2C - ,
db      000h,000h,000h,0fch,000h,000h,000h,000h ; 2D - -
db      000h,000h,000h,000h,000h,030h,030h,000h ; 2E - .
db      006h,00ch,018h,030h,060h,0c0h,080h,000h ; 2F - /
db      07ch,0c6h,0ceh,0deh,0f6h,0e6h,07ch,000h ; 30 - 0
db      030h,070h,030h,030h,030h,030h,0fch,000h ; 31 - 1
db      078h,0cch,00ch,038h,060h,0cch,0fch,000h ; 32 - 2
db      078h,0cch,00ch,038h,00ch,0cch,078h,000h ; 33 - 3
db      01ch,03ch,06ch,0cch,0feh,00ch,01eh,000h ; 34 - 4
db      0fch,0c0h,0f8h,00ch,00ch,0cch,078h,000h ; 35 - 5
db      038h,060h,0c0h,0f8h,0cch,0cch,078h,000h ; 36 - 6
db      0fch,0cch,00ch,018h,030h,030h,030h,000h ; 37 - 7
db      078h,0cch,0cch,078h,0cch,0cch,078h,000h ; 38 - 8
db      078h,0cch,0cch,07ch,00ch,018h,070h,000h ; 39 - 9
db      000h,030h,030h,000h,000h,030h,030h,000h ; 3A - :
db      000h,030h,030h,000h,000h,030h,030h,060h ; 3B - ;
db      018h,030h,060h,0c0h,060h,030h,018h,000h ; 3C - <
db      000h,000h,0fch,000h,000h,0fch,000h,000h ; 3D - =
db      060h,030h,018h,00ch,018h,030h,060h,000h ; 3E - >
db      078h,0cch,00ch,018h,030h,000h,030h,000h ; 3F - ?
db      07ch,0c6h,0deh,0deh,0deh,0c0h,078h,000h ; 40 - @
db      030h,078h,0cch,0cch,0fch,0cch,0cch,000h ; 41 - A
db      0fch,066h,066h,07ch,066h,066h,0fch,000h ; 42 - B
db      03ch,066h,0c0h,0c0h,0c0h,066h,03ch,000h ; 43 - C
db      0f8h,06ch,066h,066h,066h,06ch,0f8h,000h ; 44 - D
db      0feh,062h,068h,078h,068h,062h,0feh,000h ; 45 - E
db      0feh,062h,068h,078h,068h,060h,0f0h,000h ; 46 - F
db      03ch,066h,0c0h,0c0h,0ceh,066h,03eh,000h ; 47 - G
db      0cch,0cch,0cch,0fch,0cch,0cch,0cch,000h ; 48 - H
db      078h,030h,030h,030h,030h,030h,078h,000h ; 49 - I
db      01eh,00ch,00ch,00ch,0cch,0cch,078h,000h ; 4A - J
db      0e6h,066h,06ch,078h,06ch,066h,0e6h,000h ; 4B - K
db      0f0h,060h,060h,060h,062h,066h,0feh,000h ; 4C - L
db      0c6h,0eeh,0feh,0feh,0d6h,0c6h,0c6h,000h ; 4D - M
db      0c6h,0e6h,0f6h,0deh,0ceh,0c6h,0c6h,000h ; 4E - N
db      038h,06ch,0c6h,0c6h,0c6h,06ch,038h,000h ; 4F - O
db      0fch,066h,066h,07ch,060h,060h,0f0h,000h ; 50 - P
db      078h,0cch,0cch,0cch,0dch,078h,01ch,000h ; 51 - Q
db      0fch,066h,066h,07ch,06ch,066h,0e6h,000h ; 52 - R
db      078h,0cch,0e0h,070h,01ch,0cch,078h,000h ; 53 - S
db      0fch,0b4h,030h,030h,030h,030h,078h,000h ; 54 - T
db      0cch,0cch,0cch,0cch,0cch,0cch,0fch,000h ; 55 - U
db      0cch,0cch,0cch,0cch,0cch,078h,030h,000h ; 56 - V
db      0c6h,0c6h,0c6h,0d6h,0feh,0eeh,0c6h,000h ; 57 - W
db      0c6h,0c6h,06ch,038h,038h,06ch,0c6h,000h ; 58 - X
db      0cch,0cch,0cch,078h,030h,030h,078h,000h ; 59 - Y
db      0feh,0c6h,08ch,018h,032h,066h,0feh,000h ; 5A - Z
```

```
        db      078h,060h,060h,060h,060h,060h,078h,000h ; 5B - [
        db      0c0h,060h,030h,018h,00ch,006h,002h,000h ; 5C - \
        db      078h,018h,018h,018h,018h,018h,078h,000h ; 5D - ]
        db      010h,038h,06ch,0c6h,000h,000h,000h,000h ; 5E - ^
        db      000h,000h,000h,000h,000h,000h,000h,0ffh ; 5F - _
        db      030h,030h,018h,000h,000h,000h,000h,000h ; 60 - `
        db      000h,000h,078h,00ch,07ch,0cch,076h,000h ; 61 - a
        db      0e0h,060h,060h,07ch,066h,066h,0dch,000h ; 62 - b
        db      000h,000h,078h,0cch,0c0h,0cch,078h,000h ; 63 - c
        db      01ch,00ch,00ch,07ch,0cch,0cch,076h,000h ; 64 - d
        db      000h,000h,078h,0cch,0fch,0c0h,078h,000h ; 65 - e
        db      038h,06ch,060h,0f0h,060h,060h,0f0h,000h ; 66 - f
        db      000h,000h,076h,0cch,0cch,07ch,00ch,0f8h ; 67 - g
        db      0e0h,060h,06ch,076h,066h,066h,0e6h,000h ; 68 - h
        db      030h,000h,070h,030h,030h,030h,078h,000h ; 69 - i
        db      00ch,000h,00ch,00ch,00ch,0cch,0cch,078h ; 6A - j
        db      0e0h,060h,066h,06ch,078h,06ch,0e6h,000h ; 6B - k
        db      070h,030h,030h,030h,030h,030h,078h,000h ; 6C - l
        db      000h,000h,0cch,0feh,0feh,0d6h,0c6h,000h ; 6D - m
        db      000h,000h,0f8h,0cch,0cch,0cch,0cch,000h ; 6E - n
        db      000h,000h,078h,0cch,0cch,0cch,078h,000h ; 6F - o
        db      000h,000h,0dch,066h,066h,07ch,060h,0f0h ; 70 - p
        db      000h,000h,076h,0cch,0cch,07ch,00ch,01eh ; 71 - q
        db      000h,000h,0dch,076h,066h,060h,0f0h,000h ; 72 - r
        db      000h,000h,07ch,0c0h,078h,00ch,0f8h,000h ; 73 - s
        db      010h,030h,07ch,030h,030h,034h,018h,000h ; 74 - t
        db      000h,000h,0cch,0cch,0cch,0cch,076h,000h ; 75 - u
        db      000h,000h,0cch,0cch,0cch,078h,030h,000h ; 76 - v
        db      000h,000h,0c6h,0d6h,0feh,0feh,06ch,000h ; 77 - w
        db      000h,000h,0c6h,06ch,038h,06ch,0c6h,000h ; 78 - x
        db      000h,000h,0cch,0cch,0cch,07ch,00ch,0f8h ; 79 - y
        db      000h,000h,0fch,098h,030h,064h,0fch,000h ; 7A - z
        db      01ch,030h,030h,0e0h,030h,030h,01ch,000h ; 7B - {
        db      018h,018h,018h,000h,018h,018h,018h,000h ; 7C - |
        db      0e0h,030h,030h,01ch,030h,030h,0e0h,000h ; 7D - }
        db      076h,0dch,000h,000h,000h,000h,000h,000h ; 7E - ~
        db      000h,010h,038h,06ch,0c6h,0c6h,0feh,000h ; 7F -

_DrawASCII      ENDP

                ENDS

                END


WRITEBLK.ASM Source Code

                TITLE   'Display Block of Pixels in 256 Color Mode'
                .MODEL  small
                .CODE
;
; Name:         WriteBlock
;
```

```
; Function:      Copy an Image in 320x200 Graphics Mode Frame Buffer
;
; Caller:        Turbo C:
;
;                void WriteBlock(x,y,width,height,src);
;
;                int x;                    /* X Location - Bytes */
;                int y;                    /* Y Location - Lines */
;                int width;                /* Width - Pixels */
;                int height;               /* Height - Pixels */
;                unsigned char far *src    /* Pointer to Source Block */
;
;====================================================================
                PUBLIC     _WriteBlock
_WriteBlock     PROC       NEAR
                ARG
x_loc:WORD,y_loc:WORD,x_size:WORD,y_size:WORD,src:FAR PTR BYTE

                push       bp      ; preserve caller registers
                mov        bp,sp
                push       ds
                push       es
                push       si
                push       di
                push       ax
                push       bx
                push       cx
                push       dx

                mov        ax,320
                mul        [y_loc]
                add        ax,[x_loc] ; Calculate Frame Buffer Start Address
                mov        di,ax      ; DI —> block start
                mov        ax,0a000h
                mov        es,ax      ; Set frame buff. segment (es:di)
                lds        si,[src]   ; Set source pointer (ds:si)

                mov        ax,[x_size]
                mov        cx,ax
                mov        ax,[y_size]
                mov        bx,ax
                cld                   ; set direction forward
L10:            push       di         ; preserve Destination
                push       cx         ; preserve width

L12:            lodsb                 ; AL := pixel @DS:SI
                mov        es:[di],al ; update display memory
                inc        di         ; increment output pointer
                loop       L12
                pop        cx
                pop        di
```

```
              add        di,320      ; ES:DI -> next pixel row
              dec        bx          ; Decrement row count
              jnz        L10         ; loop down pixel rows
              pop        dx
              pop        cx
              pop        bx
              pop        ax
              pop        di          ; restore registers and exit
              pop        si
              pop        es
              pop        ds
              mov        sp,bp
              pop        bp
              ret
_WriteBlock   ENDP
              END
```

Utility Program Source Code Listings

A number of utility programs not included in earlier chapters are included in the sample program disk to facilitate translation between image file formats. The source code for these programs is listed below, with specific comments or remarks where appropriate.

VIEW_PIC.CPP Source Code

```cpp
//====================================================================
// VIEW_PIC.CPP
//------------------------------------
// Program:  Implementation code for VIEW_PIC.EXE
// Author:   Phil Mattison
// Compiler: Borland Turbo C++ v1.01
//------------------------------------

#include <stdlib.h>
#include <stdio.h>
#include <conio.h>
#include <dos.h>

extern "C" void SetVmode(int);
extern "C" void DrawBlock(int,int,int,int,int);
extern "C" void WriteBlock(int,int,int,int,char far *);
extern "C" void WriteEntry(int,int,int,int);

void main(int argc, char* argv[])
  {
  FILE *fi;          // Input file pointer
  int x,y,r,g,b;     // General purpose variables
  unsigned char buf[32000];
  printf("256-Color Picture Viewing Program\n\n");
  printf("Copyright (c) John Wiley & Sons, Inc., 1994.\n\n");
```

```
 if(argc<2)
   {
   printf
 ("Please provide a file name. Example: VIEW_PIC <file>.PIC\n");
   exit(0);
   }
 fi=fopen(argv[1],"rb");
 if(fi==NULL)
   {
   printf("Could not open file %s\n",argv[1]);
   exit(0);
   }
 SetVmode(0x13);
 DrawBlock(0,0,319,199,0);
 for(y=0;y<256;y++)
   {
   fread(buf,3,1,fi);
   r=(int)buf[0]>2;
   g=(int)buf[1]>2;
   b=(int)buf[2]>2;
   WriteEntry(y,r,g,b);
   }
 for(y=0;y<2;y++)
   {
   fread(buf,32000,1,fi);
   WriteBlock(0,y*100,320,100,(char far *)buf);
   }
 getch();
 SetVmode(3);
 }
```

VIEW_ERR.CPP Source Code

```
//=====================================================================
// VIEW_ERR.CPP
//————————————————————————
// Program:  Implementation code for VIEW_ERR.EXE
// Author:   Phil Mattison
// Compiler: Borland Turbo C++ v1.01
//————————————————————————

#include <stdlib.h>
#include <stdio.h>
#include <conio.h>
#include <math.h>
#include <dos.h>

#include "avi_riff.h"

extern "C" void SetVmode(int);
extern "C" void DrawBlock(int,int,int,int,int);
extern "C" void DrawPixel(int,int,int);
```

```
extern "C" void WriteEntry(int,int,int,int);

void main(int argc, char* argv[])
  {
  FILE    *f1,*f2;        // File access pointers
  int     x,y,r,g,b;      // General purpose variables
  int     error;          // Pixel error
  double  accumulator;    // MSE accumlator
  BYTE    buf1[320];      // Image pixel row input buffers
  BYTE    buf2[320];

  printf("Monochrome Image Difference Viewing Program\n\n");
  printf("Copyright (c) John Wiley & Sons, Inc., 1994.\n\n");

  if(argc<3)
    {
    printf("Please provide two monochrome image file names.\n");
    printf("Example: VIEW_ERR <file1>.B_W <file2>.B_W\n");
    exit(0);
    }
  f1=fopen(argv[1],"rb");
  f2=fopen(argv[2],"rb");
  if(f1==NULL)
    {
    printf("Could not open file %s\n",argv[1]);
    exit(0);
    }
  if(f2==NULL)
    {
    printf("Could not open file %s\n",argv[2]);
    exit(0);
    }
  SetVmode(0x13);
  DrawBlock(0,0,319,199,BLACK);
  for(y=0;y<256;y++)    // Initialize Palette
    {
    r=g=b=y>2;
    WriteEntry(y,r,g,b);
    }
  accumulator=0.0;
  for(y=0;y<3;y++)      // Read past palette data in input files
    {
    fread(buf1,256,1,f1);
    fread(buf2,256,1,f2);
    }
  for(y=0;y<200;y++)    // Display the image difference
    {
    fread(buf1,320,1,f1);
    fread(buf2,320,1,f2);
    for(x=0;x<320;x++)
      {
      error=(int)buf1[x]-(int)buf2[x];
      accumulator+=(double)error*(double)error;
```

```
        error/=2;
        error+=128;
        error=(error>255)?255:error;
        error=(error<0)?0:error;
        DrawPixel(x,y,error);
        }
    }
  accumulator/=64000.0;
  accumulator=sqrt(accumulator);
  getch();
  SetVmode(3);
  printf("Mean Square Error = %f\n",accumulator);
  }
```

MONO_PIC.CPP Source Code

```
//===================================================================
// MONO_PIC.CPP
//————————————————————————————
// Program:  PIC file color to monochrome conversion
// Author:   Phil Mattison
// Compiler: Borland Turbo C++ v1.01
//————————————————————————————

#include <stdlib.h>
#include <stdio.h>
#include <conio.h>
#include <dos.h>
#include "avi_riff.h"

void main(int argc, char* argv[])
  {
  FILE *fi,*fo;               // File input and output pointers
  BYTE image[320];            // Image line buffer
  BYTE palette[256][3];       // VGA palette data storage
  int  row,pel,index,r,g,b;   // General purpose variables

  printf("PIC file color to monochrome conversion program\n");
  printf("Copyright (c) John Wiley & Sons, Inc., 1994.\n\n");

  if(argc<3)
    {
    printf
    ("Please provide two file names: <input_file> <output_file>\n");
    exit(0);
    }
  fi=fopen(argv[1],"rb");
  fo=fopen(argv[2],"wb");
  if(fi==NULL)
    {
    printf("Could not open input file %s.\n",argv[1]);
    exit(0);
```

```
      }
  if(fo==NULL)
    {
    printf("Could not open output file %s.\n",argv[2]);
    exit(0);
    }

  for(index=0;index<256;index++)  // Genreate a monochrome palette
    {
    palette[index][0]=(BYTE)index;
    palette[index][1]=(BYTE)index;
    palette[index][2]=(BYTE)index;
    }
  fwrite(&palette[0][0],768,1,fo);      // Write palette to file
  fread(&palette[0][0],768,1,fi);       // Get original color palette
  for(row=0;row<200;row++)
    {
    fread(image,320,1,fi);              // For each pixel in the image
    for(pel=0;pel<320;pel++)
      {
      index=(int)image[pel];            // Convert color to luminance
      r=(int)palette[index][0];
      g=(int)palette[index][1];
      b=(int)palette[index][2];
      image[pel]=(BYTE)((r*77)/256+(g*75)/256+(g*75)/256+(b*29)/256);
      }
    fwrite(image,320,1,fo);
    }

  fclose(fi);
  fclose(fo);
  printf("Done.\n");
  }
```

CLUT2YUV.CPP Source Code

```
//===================================================================
// CLUT2YUV.CPP
//-------------------------------------------------------------
// Program:  Implementation file for CLUT2YUV.EXE
// Author:   Phil Mattison
// Compiler: Borland Turbo C++ v1.01
//-------------------------------------------------------------

#include <stdlib.h>
#include <stdio.h>
#include <string.h>
#include <conio.h>
#include <dos.h>
#include <math.h>
#include "avi_riff.h"
```

```
//————————————————————
int Compare4C(char *s1, char *s2) // Compare a pair of 4-char tags
  {
  if(s1[0]==s2[0] &&
  s1[1]==s2[1] &&
  s1[2]==s2[2] &&
  s1[3]==s2[3])return(1);
  return(0);
  }

//————————————————————
int Saturate(int n)
  {
  if(n>255)return(255);
  if(n<0)return(0);
  return(n);
  }

//————————————————————
void main(int argc, char* argv[])
  {
  FILE  *fi;                      // File stream pointer
  FILE  *fo;                      // File stream pointer
  int   frame_count;              // Video frame count
  int   f_frame;                  // Video frame counter
  int   R[240],G[240],B[240];     // Local palette data storage
  int   pel_index;                // Pixel index
  int   count;                    // Pixel counter
  int   row,i;                    // General indices
  BYTE  image_buffer_i[IMAGE_SIZE]; // Input file buffer
  BYTE  image_buffer_o[320];      // Output file buffer
  vid   vid_header;               // File header input structure

  printf("VID file 8-bit CLUT to 4:2:2 YCrCb conversion program.\n\n");
  printf("Copyright (c) John Wiley & Sons, Inc., 1994.\n\n");

  if(argc<3)
    {
    printf
    ("Please provide two file names: <input_file> <output_file>\n");
    exit(0);
    }
  fi=fopen(argv[1],"rb");
  fo=fopen(argv[2],"wb");
  if(fi==NULL)
    {
    printf("Could not open input file %s.\n",argv[1]);
    exit(0);
    }
  if(fo==NULL)
    {
    printf("Could not open output file %s.\n",argv[2]);
    exit(0);
```

```
    }
fread(&vid_header,sizeof(vid),1,fi);
if(!Compare4C(vid_header.file_ID,"BOOK"))
    {
    printf("ERROR - This is not a valid video file.\n");
    exit(0);
    }
if((vid_header.compression&COMPRESSED)==COMPRESSED)
    {
    printf("ERROR - This file is compressed; decompress first.\n");
    exit(0);
    }

for(i=0;i<240;i++)   // Get palette data
    {
    R[i]=Saturate((int)vid_header.palette[i][0]<<2);
    G[i]=Saturate((int)vid_header.palette[i][1]<<2);
    B[i]=Saturate((int)vid_header.palette[i][2]<<2);
    }

frame_count=vid_header.frames;
vid_header.compression|=YCRCB;          // Set YUV flag
fwrite(&vid_header,sizeof(vid),1,fo);

for(f_frame=0;f_frame<frame_count;f_frame++)
    {
    fread(image_buffer_i,IMAGE_SIZE,1,fi); // Read image
    for(row=0;row<120;row++)
        {
        pel_index=row*160;                 // Set start-of-row pointer
        int data_index=0;
        for(count=0;count<160;count+=2)     // Get current RGB values
            {
            int index1=(int)image_buffer_i[pel_index]-16;
            int R1=R[index1];
            int G1=G[index1];
            int B1=B[index1];
            pel_index++;
            int index2=(int)image_buffer_i[pel_index]-16;
            int R2=R[index2];
            int G2=G[index2];
            int B2=B[index2];
            pel_index++;
            int Y1=(R1*77)/256+(G1*75)/256+(G1*75)/256+(B1*29)/256;
            int V1=Saturate((R1-Y1)/2+128);
            int U1=Saturate((B1-Y1)/2+128);
            int Y2=(R2*77)/256+(G2*75)/256+(G2*75)/256+(B2*29)/256;
            int V2=Saturate((R2-Y2)/2+128);
            int U2=Saturate((B2-Y2)/2+128);
            image_buffer_o[data_index++]=(BYTE)Y1;
            image_buffer_o[data_index++]=(BYTE)((V1+V2)/2);
            image_buffer_o[data_index++]=(BYTE)Y2;
            image_buffer_o[data_index++]=(BYTE)((U1+U2)/2);
```

```
      }
    fwrite(image_buffer_o,320,1,fo); // Write converted data for row
    }
  printf("Frame %d.%c",f_frame,0xD);
  }
fclose(fi);
fclose(fo);
printf("\nDone.\n");
}
```

YUV2CLUT.CPP Source Code

```cpp
//===================================================================
// YUV2CLUT.CPP
//-------------------------------------
// Program:  Implementation file for YUV2CLUT.EXE
// Author:   Phil Mattison
// Compiler: Borland Turbo C++ v1.01
//-------------------------------------

#include <stdlib.h>
#include <stdio.h>
#include <string.h>
#include <conio.h>
#include <dos.h>
#include <math.h>
#include "avi_riff.h"

int R[240],G[240],B[240];   // Local palette data storage
int category[240];          // Color category

//-------------------------------------
int Compare4C(char *s1, char *s2) // Compare a pair of 4-char tags
  {
  if(s1[0]==s2[0] &&
  s1[1]==s2[1] &&
  s1[2]==s2[2] &&
  s1[3]==s2[3])return(1);
  return(0);
  }

//-------------------------------------
int GetCategory(int R, int G, int B)
  {
  int index,Y,Cr,Cb;
  Y=(int)((76L*(long)R + 150L*(long)G + 29L*(long)B)/256L);
  Cr=R-Y;
  Cb=B-Y;
  index=0;
  if(Cr>0)index|=1;
  if(Cb>0)index|=2;
  if(abs(Cr)>abs(Cb))index|=4;
```

```
       return(index);
       }

//—————————————————————
BYTE MatchColor(int Rx, int Gx, int Bx)
   {
   int i,cat,err,delta,index;
   err=256*3;
   cat=GetCategory(Rx,Gx,Bx);
   for(i=0;i<240;i++)
      {
      if(cat==category[i])
         {
         delta=abs(Rx-R[i])+abs(Gx-G[i])+abs(Bx-B[i]);
         if(err>delta)
            {
            err=delta;
            index=i;
            }
         }
      }
   return((BYTE)index+16);
   }

//—————————————————————
int Saturate(int n)
   {
   if(n>255)return(255);
   if(n<0)return(0);
   return(n);
   }

//—————————————————————
void main(int argc, char* argv[])
   {
   FILE      *fi;                       // File stream pointer
   FILE      *fo;                       // File stream pointer
   int       frame_count;               // Video frame count
   int       f_frame;                   // Video frame counter
   int       Red,Green,Blue;            // RGB storage
   int       pel_index;                 // 8-Bit Pixel index
   int       data_index;                // YUV Pixel index
   int       count;                     // Pixel counter
   int       i;                         // General index
   int       Y1,Y2,Cr,Cb;               // YCrCb storage
   BYTE      image_buffer_i[IMAGE_SIZE]; // Input file buffer
   BYTE      image_buffer_o[IMAGE_SIZE]; // Output file buffer
   vid       vid_header;                // VID file header structure

//—————————————————————
   printf("VID file YCrCb to 8-bit CLUT format conversion program.\n\n");
   printf("Copyright (c) John Wiley & Sons, Inc., 1994.\n\n");
```

```
if(argc<3)
  {
  printf
  ("Please provide two file names: <input_file> <output_file>\n");
  exit(0);
  }
fi=fopen(argv[1],"rb");
fo=fopen(argv[2],"wb");
if(fi==NULL)
  {
  printf("Could not open input file %s.\n",argv[1]);
  exit(0);
  }
if(fo==NULL)
  {
  printf("Could not open output file %s.\n",argv[2]);
  exit(0);
  }
fread(&vid_header,sizeof(vid),1,fi);
if(!Compare4C(vid_header.file_ID,"BOOK"))
  {
  printf("ERROR — This is not a valid video file.\n");
  exit(0);
  }
if((vid_header.compression&YCRCB)!=YCRCB)
  {
  printf("ERROR — This file is not YCrCb format.\n");
  exit(0);
  }

for(i=0;i<240;i++)          // Get palette data
  {
  R[i]=(int)vid_header.palette[i][0]*4;
  G[i]=(int)vid_header.palette[i][1]*4;
  B[i]=(int)vid_header.palette[i][2]*4;
  category[i]=GetCategory(R[i],G[i],B[i]);
  }
frame_count=vid_header.frames;
vid_header.compression&=YCRCB_X;  // Clear YUV flag
fwrite(&vid_header,sizeof(vid),1,fo);

for(f_frame=0;f_frame<frame_count;f_frame++)
  {
  pel_index=0;
  for(i=0;i<2;i++)                   // Process in 2 parts
    {
    fread(image_buffer_i,IMAGE_SIZE,1,fi);   // Read first half image
    data_index=0;
    while(data_index<IMAGE_SIZE)
      {
      Y1=(int)image_buffer_i[data_index++];  // Get a pixel pair
      Cr=(int)image_buffer_i[data_index++];
```

```
            Y2=(int)image_buffer_i[data_index++];
            Cb=(int)image_buffer_i[data_index++];
            Cr=2*(Cr-128);
            Cb=2*(Cb-128);
            Red=  Saturate(Cr+Y1);                    // Convert to RGB
            Blue= Saturate(Cb+Y1);
            Green=Saturate(Y1-(int)((130L*(long)Cr+50L*(long)Cb)/256L));
            image_buffer_o[pel_index++]=MatchColor(Red,Green,Blue);
            Red=  Saturate(Cr+Y2);
            Blue= Saturate(Cb+Y2);
            Green=Saturate(Y2-(int)((130L*(long)Cr+50L*(long)Cb)/256L));
            image_buffer_o[pel_index++]=MatchColor(Red,Green,Blue);
            }
        }
    fwrite(image_buffer_o,IMAGE_SIZE,1,fo); // Write converted data
    printf("Frame %d.%c",f_frame,0xD);
    }
fclose(fi);
fclose(fo);
printf("\nDone.\n");
}
```

COMPRESS.CPP Source Code

```
//=====================================================================
// COMPRESS.CPP
//-------------------------------------
// Program:  Implementation file for COMPRESS.EXE
// Author:   Phil Mattison
// Compiler: Borland Turbo C++ v1.01
//-------------------------------------


#define   THRESHOLD  3

#include <stdlib.h>
#include <stdio.h>
#include <string.h>
#include <conio.h>
#include <dos.h>
#include <math.h>
#include "avi_riff.h"


//-------------------------------------
int Compare4C(char *s1, char *s2) // Compare a pair of 4-char tags
  {
  if(s1[0]==s2[0] &&
  s1[1]==s2[1] &&
  s1[2]==s2[2] &&
  s1[3]==s2[3])return(1);
  return(0);
  }
```

```
//————————————————

void main(int argc, char* argv[])
  {
  FILE       *fi;                   // File stream pointer
  FILE       *fo;                   // File stream pointer
  int        x_size,y_size;         // Video frame size
  int        frame_count;           // Video frame count
  int        f_frame;               // Video frame counter
  int        R[240],G[240],B[240];  // Local palette data storage
  int        pel_index;             // Pixel index
  int        count;                 // Pixel counter
  int        z_count;               // Zero counter
  int        row,i;                 // General indices

  BYTE       image_buffer_i[IMAGE_SIZE];
  BYTE       image_buffer_o[IMAGE_SIZE];
  BYTE       data_buffer[IMAGE_SIZE];
  BYTE       flag_buffer[160];
  BYTE       count_buffer[160];
  vid        vid_header;

//————————————————
  printf("VID file compression program.\n\n");
  printf("Copyright (c) John Wiley & Sons, Inc., 1994.\n\n");

  if(argc<3)
    {
    printf
    ("Please provide two file names: <input_file> <output_file>\n");
    exit(0);
    }
  fi=fopen(argv[1],"rb");
  fo=fopen(argv[2],"wb");
  if(fi==NULL)
    {
    printf("Could not open input file %s.\n",argv[1]);
    exit(0);
    }
  if(fo==NULL)
    {
    printf("Could not open output file %s.\n",argv[2]);
    exit(0);
    }
  fread(&vid_header,sizeof(vid),1,fi);
  if(!Compare4C(vid_header.file_ID,"BOOK"))
    {
    printf("ERROR — This is not a valid video file.\n");
    exit(0);
    }
  if((vid_header.compression&1)==1)
    {
```

```
    printf("ERROR — This file is already compressed.\n");
    exit(0);
    }
for(i=0;i<240;i++)  // Get palette data
  {
  R[i]=(int)vid_header.palette[i][0];
  G[i]=(int)vid_header.palette[i][1];
  B[i]=(int)vid_header.palette[i][2];
  }

frame_count=vid_header.frames;
vid_header.compression|=COMPRESSED;        // Set compression flag
fwrite(&vid_header,sizeof(vid),1,fo);
fread(image_buffer_o,IMAGE_SIZE,1,fi);  // Transfer full frame 0
fwrite(image_buffer_o,IMAGE_SIZE,1,fo);

for(f_frame=1;f_frame<frame_count;f_frame++)
  {
  fread(image_buffer_i,IMAGE_SIZE,1,fi);// Read image
  int data_index=0;
  for(row=0;row<120;row++)
    {
    pel_index=row*160;                  // Set start-of-row pointer
    for(count=0;count<160;count++) // Get prev & current RGB values
      {
      int index1=(int)image_buffer_i[pel_index]-16;
      int index2=(int)image_buffer_o[pel_index]-16;
      int R1=(int)R[index1];
      int G1=(int)G[index1];
      int B1=(int)B[index1];
      int R2=(int)R[index2];
      int G2=(int)G[index2];
      int B2=(int)B[index2];
      int delta=abs(R1-R2)+abs(G1-G2)+abs(B1-B2);
      if(delta>THRESHOLD)
        {                                   // Retain big changes
        flag_buffer[count]=1;
        image_buffer_o[pel_index]=image_buffer_i[pel_index];
        }
      else flag_buffer[count]=0;        // Ignore small changes
      pel_index++;
      }
    z_count=0;
    count=159;
    for(i=0;i<160;i++)     // Count runs of unchanged pixels
      {
      if(flag_buffer[count]==0)
        {
        z_count++;
        count_buffer[count]=z_count;
        }
      else
        {
```

```
                    count_buffer[count]=0;
                    z_count=0;
                    }
                count-;
                }
            pel_index=row*160;
            count=0;
            while(count<160)
                {
                if(count_buffer[count]>2) // Encode zero runs longer than 2
                    {
                    data_buffer[data_index++]=0;
                    data_buffer[data_index++]=(BYTE)count_buffer[count];
                    pel_index+=(int)count_buffer[count];
                    count+=(int)count_buffer[count];
                    }
                else  // Otherwise just copy pixels
                    {
                    if(image_buffer_i[pel_index]==0)
                        {
                        printf("Zero pixel error.\n");
                        exit(0);
                        }
                    data_buffer[data_index++]=image_buffer_i[pel_index++];
                    count++;
                    }
                }
            }
        fwrite(&f_frame,sizeof(int),1,fo);            // Write frame number
        fwrite(&data_index,sizeof(int),1,fo);        // Write compressed size
        fwrite(data_buffer,data_index,1,fo);         // Write compressed data
        printf("Frame %d.%c",f_frame,0xD);
        }
    fclose(fi);
    fclose(fo);
    printf("\nDone.\n");
    }
```

DECMPRES.CPP Source Code

```cpp
//====================================================================
// DECMPRES.CPP
//---------------------------------
// Program:  Implementation file for DECMPRES.EXE
// Author:   Phil Mattison
// Compiler: Borland Turbo C++ v1.01
//---------------------------------

#include <stdlib.h>
#include <stdio.h>
#include <string.h>
#include <conio.h>
```

```
#include <dos.h>
#include <math.h>
#include "avi_riff.h"

//————————————————————————————
int Compare4C(char *s1, char *s2) // Compare a pair of 4-char tags
  {
  if(s1[0]==s2[0] &&
  s1[1]==s2[1] &&
  s1[2]==s2[2] &&
  s1[3]==s2[3])return(1);
  return(0);
  }


//————————————————————————————
void main(int argc, char* argv[])
  {
  FILE  *fi;               // File stream pointer
  FILE  *fo;               // File stream pointer
  int   x_size,y_size;     // Video frame size
  int   frame_count;       // Video frame count
  int   f_frame;           // Video frame counter
  int   block_size;        // Compressed block size
  int   block_number;      // Compressed block count
  int   buffer_p;          // Pointer to compressed data buffer
  int   image_p;           // Pointer to decompressed image frame
  BYTE  pixel;             // Pixel storage
  BYTE  row;               // Pixel row counter
  BYTE  image_buffer[IMAGE_SIZE];
  BYTE  data_buffer[IMAGE_SIZE];
  vid   vid_header;

//————————————————————————————
  printf("VID file decompression program.\n\n");
  printf("Copyright (c) John Wiley & Sons, Inc., 1994.\n\n");


  if(argc<3)
    {
    printf
    ("Please provide two file names: <input_file> <output_file>\n");
    exit(0);
    }
  fi=fopen(argv[1],"rb");
  fo=fopen(argv[2],"wb");
  if(fi==NULL)
    {
    printf("Could not open input file %s.\n",argv[1]);
    exit(0);
    }
  if(fo==NULL)
    {
```

```
    printf("Could not open output file %s.\n",argv[2]);
    exit(0);
    }
  fread(&vid_header,sizeof(vid),1,fi);
  if(!Compare4C(vid_header.file_ID,"BOOK"))
    {
    printf("ERROR — This is not a valid video file.\n");
    exit(0);
    }
  if((vid_header.compression&COMPRESSED)==0)
    {
    printf("ERROR — This file is not compressed.\n");
    exit(0);
    }
  frame_count=vid_header.frames;
  vid_header.compression&=COMPRESSED_X;  // Set compression flag off
  fwrite(&vid_header,sizeof(vid),1,fo);
  fread(image_buffer,IMAGE_SIZE,1,fi);    // Read and write frame 0
  fwrite(image_buffer,IMAGE_SIZE,1,fo);

  for(f_frame=1;f_frame<frame_count;f_frame++)  // For each frame,
    {
    fread(&block_number,sizeof(int),1,fi); // Get block number & size
    fread(&block_size,sizeof(int),1,fi);
    fread(data_buffer,block_size,1,fi);     // Get compressed data
    buffer_p=0;
    image_p=0;
    while(image_p<IMAGE_SIZE)               // Decompress
      {
      pixel=data_buffer[buffer_p++];
      if(pixel==0)image_p+=(int)data_buffer[buffer_p++];
      else image_buffer[image_p++]=pixel;
      }
    fwrite(image_buffer,IMAGE_SIZE,1,fo);  // Write decompressed frame
    printf("Frame %d.%c",f_frame,0xD);
    }
  fclose(fi);
  fclose(fo);
  printf("\nDone.\n");
  }
```

MONO_VID.CPP Source Code

```
//====================================================================
// MONO_VID.CPP
//—————————————————————————————
// Program:  Implementation file for MONO_VID.EXE
// Author:   Phil Mattison
// Compiler: Borland Turbo C++ v1.01
//—————————————————————————————

#include <stdlib.h>
```

```
#include <stdio.h>
#include <string.h>
#include <conio.h>
#include <dos.h>
#include <math.h>
#include "avi_riff.h"

//————————————————————
int Compare4C(char *s1, char *s2)  // Compare a pair of 4-char tags
  {
  if(s1[0]==s2[0] &&
  s1[1]==s2[1] &&
  s1[2]==s2[2] &&
  s1[3]==s2[3])return(1);
  return(0);
  }

//————————————————————
void ExitError(int n)
  {
  switch(n)
    {
    case 0:printf("ERROR — This is not a valid video file.\n");
    case 1:printf("ERROR — Input file must not be compressed.\n");
    }
  exit(0);
  }

//————————————————————
void main(int argc, char* argv[])
  {
  FILE   *fi;                      // File stream pointer
  FILE   *fo;                      // File stream pointer
  int    frame_count;             // Video frame count
  int    f_frame;                 // Video frame counter
  float  R,G,B;                   // Intermediate RGB values
  int    i;                       // General indices
  BYTE   image_buffer[IMAGE_SIZE]; // Input image buffer
  BYTE   new_pixel[240];          // Pixel translation buffer
  vid    vid_header;              // VID file header structure

//————————————————————
  printf("VID file color to monochrome conversion program.\n\n");
  printf("Copyright (c) John Wiley & Sons, Inc., 1994.\n\n");

  if(argc<3)
    {
    printf
    ("Please provide two file names: <input_file> <output_file>\n");
    exit(0);
    }
  fi=fopen(argv[1],"rb");
  fo=fopen(argv[2],"wb");
```

```
  if(fi==NULL)
    {
    printf("Could not open input file %s.\n",argv[1]);
    exit(0);
    }
  if(fo==NULL)
    {
    printf("Could not open output file %s.\n",argv[2]);
    exit(0);
    }
  fread(&vid_header,sizeof(vid),1,fi);
  if(!Compare4C(vid_header.file_ID,"BOOK"))ExitError(0);
  if((vid_header.compression&COMPRESSED)==COMPRESSED)ExitError(1);
  vid_header.compression|=MONOCHROME;

  for(i=0;i<240;i++)  // Translate palette data
    {
    R=(float)(vid_header.palette[i][0]<<2);
    G=(float)(vid_header.palette[i][1]<<2);
    B=(float)(vid_header.palette[i][2]<<2);
    float gray_level=0.299*R+0.587*G+0.114*B;
    gray_level=(gray_level*240.0)/256.0;
    new_pixel[i]=16+(BYTE)gray_level;
    vid_header.palette[i][0]=((BYTE)((255.0*(float)i)/240.0))>2;
    vid_header.palette[i][1]=((BYTE)((255.0*(float)i)/240.0))>2;
    vid_header.palette[i][2]=((BYTE)((255.0*(float)i)/240.0))>2;
    }
  frame_count=vid_header.frames;
  fwrite(&vid_header,sizeof(vid),1,fo);

  for(f_frame=0;f_frame<frame_count;f_frame++)  // For each frame,
    {
    fread(image_buffer,IMAGE_SIZE,1,fi);         // Read image
    for(i=0;i<IMAGE_SIZE;i++)                    // Translate
      {
      image_buffer[i]=new_pixel[(int)image_buffer[i]-16];
      }
    fwrite(image_buffer,IMAGE_SIZE,1,fo);        // Write image
    printf("Frame %d.%c",f_frame,0xD);
    }
  fclose(fi);
  fclose(fo);
  printf("\nDone.\n");
  }
```

WRP_DEMO.CPP Source Code

```
//====================================================================
// WRP_DEMO.CPP
//------------------------------
// Program:  Implementation file for WRP_DEMO.EXE
// Author:   Phil Mattison
```

```
// Compiler: Borland Turbo C++ v1.01
//————————————————————

#include <stdlib.h>
#include <stdio.h>
#include <math.h>
#include "avi_riff.h"

//————————————————————
int Compare4C(char *s1, char *s2)  // Compare a pair of 4-char tags
  {
  if(s1[0]==s2[0] &&
  s1[1]==s2[1] &&
  s1[2]==s2[2] &&
  s1[3]==s2[3])return(1);
  return(0);
  }

//————————————————————

void ExitError(int n)
  {
  switch(n)
    {
    case 0:
    printf("ERROR — This is not a valid video file.\n");
    case 1:
    printf("ERROR — This video file must be decompressed first.\n");
    case 2:
    printf("ERROR — Input file must be black and white video.\n");
    case 3:
    printf("ERROR — Scale factor out of range. Must be 0.1 to 4.0\n");
    }
  exit(0);
  }

//————————————————————

int Warp(BYTE in[], BYTE out[], float factor[], int count)
  {
  int    dda_const;              // DDA increment value
  int    accum;                  // DDA accumulator
  int    dst;                    // Destination index
  int    src;                    // Source index
  long   w_left,w_right;         // Left and right pixel weights

  dst=0;
  src=0;
  accum=0;
  while(src<count)
    {
    dda_const=(int)(1024.0/factor[dst]);
    w_left=1024L-(long)accum;
```

```
      w_right=(long)accum;
      out[dst++]=
      (BYTE)((w_left*(long)in[src]+w_right*(long)in[src+1])/1042L);
      accum+=dda_const;
      if(accum>1024)
        {
        src++;
        accum-=1024;
        }
      }
  return(dst);
  }

//————————————————————————
void ScaleDown(BYTE in[], BYTE out[], float factor, int count)
  {
  int       dda_const;   // DDA increment value
  int       accum;       // DDA accumulator
  int       dst;         // Destination index
  int       src;         // Source index
  long      p_accum;     // Pixel Accumulator
  long      p_count;     // Pixel accumulation count

  dst=0;
  src=0;
  accum=0;
  p_accum=0L;
  p_count=0L;
  dda_const=(int)(1024.0*factor);
  while(src<count)
    {
    while(accum<1024 && src<count)        // Add up whole pixels
      {
      p_accum+=1024L*(long)in[src++];
      accum+=dda_const;
      p_count+=1024L;
      }
    accum=(src<count)?accum-1024:0;       // Calculate fractional pixels
    p_accum-=(long)accum*(long)in[src-1];
    p_count-=(long)accum;
    out[dst++]=(BYTE)(p_accum/p_count);
    p_count=1024L-(long)accum;
    p_accum=p_count*(long)in[src-1];
    }
  }

//————————————————————————
void main(int argc, char* argv[])
  {
  FILE      *fi;                         // File stream pointer
  FILE      *fo;                         // File stream pointer
  int       frame_count;                 // Video frame count
  int       f_frame;                     // Video frame counter
```

```
float      x_scale,y_scale;            // Image scale factors
float x_factor[1024];
float y_factor[1024];
int        i,x,y,start,end;            // General indices
BYTE       image_buffer[IMAGE_SIZE];
BYTE       old_line[160];
BYTE       mid_line[1024];
BYTE       new_line[1024];
vid        vid_header;                 // File output header

printf("VID file image warp filter demonstration program.\n\n");
printf("Copyright (c) John Wiley & Sons, Inc., 1994.\n\n");

if(argc<3)
  {
  printf
  ("Please provide two file names: <input_file> <output_file>\n");
  exit(0);
  }
fi=fopen(argv[1],"rb");
fo=fopen(argv[2],"wb");
if(fi==NULL)
  {
  printf("Could not open input file %s.\n",argv[1]);
  exit(0);
  }
if(fo==NULL)
  {
  printf("Could not open output file %s.\n",argv[2]);
  exit(0);
  }
fread(&vid_header,sizeof(vid),1,fi);
if(!Compare4C(vid_header.file_ID,"BOOK"))ExitError(0);
if((vid_header.compression&COMPRESSED)==COMPRESSED)ExitError(1);
if((vid_header.compression&MONOCHROME)!=MONOCHROME)ExitError(2);
frame_count=vid_header.frames;
fwrite(&vid_header,sizeof(vid),1,fo);

printf("Calculating warp factors.\n");
for(i=0;i<1024;i++)
  {
  x_factor[i]=2.0+(float)cos((double)i/50.995);
  y_factor[i]=2.0+(float)cos((double)i/38.186);
  }

for(f_frame=0;f_frame<frame_count;f_frame++)
  {
  fread(image_buffer,IMAGE_SIZE,1,fi);            // Read image
  for(y=0;y<120;y++)
    {                                             // Warp pixel rows
    i=y*160;
    for(x=0;x<160;x++)old_line[x]=image_buffer[i++];
    i-=160;
```

```
        x=Warp(old_line,mid_line,x_factor,160);
        ScaleDown(mid_line,new_line,160.0/(float)x,x);
        for(x=0;x<160;x++)image_buffer[i++]=new_line[x];
        }
      for(x=0;x<160;x++)                            // Warp pixel columns
        {
        i=x;
        for(y=0;y<120;y++)
          {
          old_line[y]=image_buffer[i];
          i+=160;
          }
        y=Warp(old_line,mid_line,y_factor,120);
        ScaleDown(mid_line,new_line,120.0/(float)y,y);
        i=x;
        for(y=0;y<120;y++)
          {
          image_buffer[i]=new_line[y];
          i+=160;
          }
        }
      fwrite(image_buffer,IMAGE_SIZE,1,fo);  // Write modified image
      printf("Frame %d.%c",f_frame,0xD);
      }
    fclose(fi);
    fclose(fo);
    printf("\nDone.\n");
    }
```

DOSSHELL.CPP Source Code

```
    #include "control.h"
    #include "display.h"
    #include <stdio.h>
    #include <string.h>
    #include <graphics.h>
    #include <conio.h>

    #define APP_TITLE "DOS Application Shell"

    void SignOn(void)
      {
      setfillstyle(SOLID_FILL,WHITE);
      bar(0,0,639,479);                            // White background
      setfillstyle(SOLID_FILL,LIGHTBLUE);
      setcolor(BLUE);
      setlinestyle(SOLID_LINE,0,THICK_WIDTH);
      bar3d(0,0,639,20,0,0);                       // Title Bar
      setcolor(WHITE);                             // Title
      settextjustify(CENTER_TEXT,CENTER_TEXT);
      outtextxy(320,10,APP_TITLE);
      setcolor(CYAN);                              // Title Bar Outline
```

```
    line(0,0,639,0);
    line(0,0,0,20);
    setfillstyle(SOLID_FILL,LIGHTGRAY);
    setcolor(BLACK);
    setlinestyle(SOLID_LINE,0,NORM_WIDTH);
    bar3d(0,455,639,479,0,0);                        // Message Bar
    rectangle(4,457,532,476);
    setcolor(WHITE);
    line(4,476,532,476);
    line(532,457,532,476);
    setfillstyle(SOLID_FILL,LIGHTGRAY);
    setcolor(BLACK);
    setlinestyle(SOLID_LINE,0,THICK_WIDTH);
    bar3d(80,100,560,280,0,0);                       // Signon Message Bar
    settextjustify(CENTER_TEXT,CENTER_TEXT);
    setcolor(WHITE);
    outtextxy(320,110,"Copyright (c) John Wiley & Sons, Inc., 1994.");
    setfillstyle(SOLID_FILL,WHITE);
    bar(70,90,570,290);                  // Erase Signon Message Bar
    }

int EscExit()      //Exit via Escape key (process KB input)
  {
  int st;
  st=kbhit();
  if(st!=0)
    {
    st=getch();
    if(st==27)return(RUN_DISABLED);
    }
  return(RUN_ENABLED);
  }

int Quit()         //Exit via mouse click
  {
  return(RUN_DISABLED);
  }

void UserMessage(char *message)
  {
  setfillstyle(SOLID_FILL,LIGHTGRAY);
  bar(5,458,530,474);
  setcolor(WHITE);
  settextjustify(LEFT_TEXT,CENTER_TEXT);
  outtextxy(12,468,message);
  }

//****************************************************
// User functions here (Process mouse input)
//****************************************************

int DoSomething()
```

```
    {
    UserMessage("OK, I did something.");
    return(RUN_ENABLED);
    }

//***************************************************
void main(void)
    {
    int        gdriver=VGA;
    int    gmode=VGAHI;

    initgraph(&gdriver,&gmode,"");
    SignOn();
    TControl Mouse;
    Mouse.SetStandardCallback(&EscExit);
    Mouse.CreateButton(&Quit,536,457,98,20,"[Esc] Quit");

    // Insert new user controls here

    Mouse.CreateButton(&DoSomething,270,320,120,24,"Do Something");
    Mouse.Run();
    closegraph();
    }
```

SHELL256.CPP Source Code

```
    #define APP_TITLE "DOS Application Shell"

    #include <stdio.h>
    #include <conio.h>
    #include <dos.h>
    #include "ctrl_256.h"
    #include "disp_256.h"

    extern "C" void SetVmode(int);
    extern "C" void WriteBlock(int,int,int,int,unsigned char far *);
    extern "C" void DrawBlock(int,int,int,int,int);
    extern "C" void DrawASCII(int,int,int,int);

    void SignOn(void)
      {
      DrawBlock(0,0,320,200,WHITE);              // White background
      DrawBlock(0,0,320,10,LIGHTBLUE);           // Title Bar
      DrawString(160-strlen(APP_TITLE)*4,2,APP_TITLE,WHITE);     // Title

      DrawBlock(0,10,320,1,BLUE);                // Title Bar Outline
      DrawBlock(319,0,1,10,BLUE);
      DrawBlock(0,0,320,1,CYAN);
      DrawBlock(0,0,1,10,CYAN);

      DrawBlock(0,186,320,14,LIGHTGRAY);         // Message Bar
```

```
    DrawBlock(2,198,220,1,WHITE);
    DrawBlock(222,187,1,12,WHITE);
    DrawBlock(2,187,221,1,DARKGRAY);
    DrawBlock(2,187,1,12,DARKGRAY);

    DrawBlock(5,15,310,122,DARKGRAY);      // SignOn Message Bar
    DrawBlock(6,16,308,120,LIGHTGRAY);
    DrawBlock(5,15,310,122,WHITE);         // Erase SignOn Message Bar
    }

int EscExit()         //Exit via Escape key (process KB input)
    {
    int st;
    st=kbhit();
    if(st!=0)
      {
      st=getch();
      if(st==27)return(RUN_DISABLED);
      }
    return(RUN_ENABLED);
    }

int Quit()         //Exit via mouse click
    {
    return(RUN_DISABLED);
    }

void UserMessage(char *message)
    {
    DrawBlock(3,189,218,10,LIGHTGRAY);
    DrawString(6,189,message,WHITE);
    DrawBlock(2,198,220,1,WHITE);
    }

//****************************************************
// User functions here (Process mouse input)
//****************************************************

int DoSomething()
    {
    UserMessage("OK, I did something.");
    return(RUN_ENABLED);
    }

//****************************************************

void main(void)
    {
    SetVmode(0x13);
    SignOn();
    TControl Mouse;
    Mouse.SetStandardCallback(&EscExit);
```

```
    Mouse.CreateButton(&Quit,226,187,90,11,"[Esc] Quit");

    // Insert new user controls here

    Mouse.CreateButton(&DoSomething,100,100,120,12,"Do Something");
    Mouse.Run();
    SetVmode(3);
    }
```

APPENDIX C

About the Software

What Is on the Companion Diskettes?

These diskettes contain executable programs and source code for all the example programs described in the book. They also contain several still image and motion video files for use with the programs. The programs can be classified into two groups: those that involve multiple source files, and those than require only one. For programs that require multiple source files, a Borland project file is included. The project file can be used with the Borland Integrated Development Environment (IDE) to build the executable program from the source files provided. The project files are set up to look for component files in the directories established by the default installation procedure. If the path names are modified during installation, the project files and include path names must be modified to reflect those changes before attempting to build the programs. For programs that require only a single source file, a batch file named MAKE.BAT is included for each source file. This MAKE file should not be confused with the MAKE utility provided by Borland or Microsoft; it simply invokes the compiler to compile and link the program. Each MAKE file contains one or more commands to compile a source file. These commands specify a path name for include files. Again, if the path names are modified during installation, the MAKE file must be modified to reflect those changes before attempting to build the programs.

System Requirements

The only absolute requirement for using these programs is a PC with at least a standard VGA display adapter and at least a 286 CPU. The executable programs were compiled to generate 286 object code, and therefore might not run correctly on an earlier machine. They could be recompiled for an earlier CPU, but the performance of many of the programs would probably be unacceptable. Some of the programs are relatively slow even on a 386 or 486SX machine, so you should expect to exercise some patience if running them on a 286 machine. The speed of the motion video playback can also be affected by disk speed and disk fragmentation. You should have at least five megabytes of disk space available for installation. If possible, it is a good idea to run a disk defragmentation utility before installing the sample programs and files. All these programs were developed on a 25 MHz 486SX machine with an IDE hard drive with 15 mS access time. The video display program is designed to show frames at a rate no faster than the 18 Hz internal system timer, but will slow down if the system cannot keep up that pace. For programs that use the mouse for input, it is necessary to have a DOS-based mouse driver installed. If no mouse driver is installed, all you can do is exit by pressing the Escape key.

Making a Backup Copy

Before you start to use the enclosed diskettes, we strongly recommend that you make a backup copy of the originals. Remember, however, that backup diskettes are for your own personal use only. Any other use of the backup diskettes violates copyright law. Please take the time now to make the backup, using the instructions below:

1. Insert your DOS disk into drive "A" of your computer, (assuming your floppy drive is "A").
2. At the A:>, type DISKCOPY A: A: and press Return.
   You will be prompted by DOS to place Disk 1 into drive A.
3. Place the disk into drive A.

Follow the directions on the screen to complete the copy. Repeat these steps to copy Disk 2. When you are through, remove the new diskettes and label them immediately. Remove the original diskettes and store them in a safe place.

Installing the Diskettes

The enclosed diskettes contain 160 individual files in compressed format. In order to use the files, you must run the installation program from the diskettes.
   You can install the diskettes onto your computer by following these simple steps:

1. Assuming your floppy drive is "A", insert the Disk 1 into your computers "A" drive.
2. At the A:> type INSTALL and press Return.

The installation program will be loaded. After the title screen appears, you will be given the options shown in Figure C.1.
   To change any of the default settings, type the highlighted letter or move the menu bar to the desired option and press Enter.

3. To start the installation type "S" or move the menu bar to the Start installation option and press Enter. Follow the instructions to complete the installation.

After the installation is complete, remove your original diskettes and store them in a safe place.

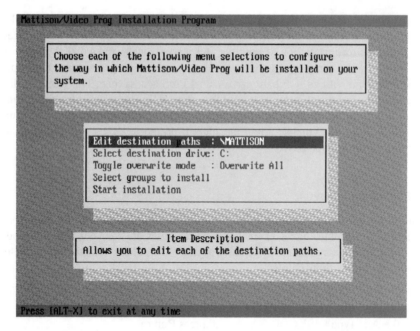

Figure C.1 Installation program startup screen.

Summary of Sample Video and Still Image Files

Tables C.1 and C.2 summarize the still images and moving pictures provided on the software diskettes for use with the demonstration programs. All the files are designed to be viewed using a standard VGA adapter with 256 colors.

Table C.1 320×200 Still Images

BALLOONS.PIC	Picture of hot-air balloons.
VASE.PIC	Still life; a vase on an onyx table.
AUTHOR.PIC	Picture of a guy who writes technical books.
GIRLS.PIC	Picture of girls in Halloween costumes.
FLAGS.PIC	Picture of a flag-team member in parade costume.
LANDING.PIC	Picture of an airliner landing.
KITTEN.PIC	Picture of a small fuzzy animal.

Table C.2   160×120 Motion Pictures

KITTEN.VID	Moving picture of a small fuzzy animal.
TENNIS.VID	Moving picture of a woman hitting a tennis ball.
BEAR.VID	Animated picture of a toy bear wandering on a desk.
FLAG.VID	Moving picture of the American flag in the wind.
FLAGS.VID	Moving picture of a girl in parade costume twirling flags.
JET.VID	Moving picture of an airliner flying overhead.
WHEELIE.VID	Moving picture of a van doing a wheel-stand at a race track.

User Assistance and Information

John Wiley & Sons, Inc., is pleased to provide assistance to users of this package. If you have questions regarding the use of this package, please call our technical support number at (212) 850-6194 weekdays between 9 A.M. and 4 P.M. Eastern Standard Time.

To place additional orders or to request information about other Wiley products, please call (800) 879-4539.

Further Reading

Books: Video Fundamentals

Prentiss, Stan, *Television from Analog to Digital*, Tab Books, Blue Ridge Summit, PA, 1985.

Herrick, Clyde N., *Color Television: Theory and Servicing*, Reston Publishing Company, Reston, VA, 1977.

Lenk, John D., *Lenk's Video Handbook, Operation and Troubleshooting*, McGraw-Hill, New York, 1991.

Davidson, Homer L., *Troubleshooting and Repairing Camcorders*, Tab Books, Blue Ridge Summit, PA, 1990.

Benson, K. Blair (ed.), *Television Engineering Handbook*, McGraw-Hill, New York, 1986.

Books: Digital Electronics Fundamentals

Bouwhuis, G., *Principles of Optical Disk Systems*, Adam Hilger, Bristol, UK, 1985.

Sherman, C. (ed.), *The CD ROM Handbook*, McGraw-Hill, New York, 1988.

Luther, Arch C., *Digital Video in the PC Environment*, McGraw-Hill, New York, 1991.

Books: Image Data Compression

Gonzalez, R. C. and Wintz, P., *Digital Image Processing*, 2nd edition, Addison-Wesley, Reading, MA, 1987.

Jain, A. K., *Fundamentals of Digital Image Processing*, Prentice-Hall, Englewood Cliffs, NJ, 1989.

Jones, Paul W. and Rabbani, Majid, *Digital Image Compression Techniques*, International Society for Optical Engineering, Bellingham, WA, 1991.

Books: Programming

Klein, Mike, *DLLs and Memory Management*, Sams Publishing, Carmel, IN, 1992.

Norton, Daniel A., *Writing Windows Device Drivers*, Addison-Wesley, New York, 1992.

Pietrek, Matt, *Windows Internals*, Addison-Wesley, New York, 1993.

Articles:

Blinn, Jim, "NTSC: Nice Technology, Super Color," *IEEE Computer Graphics and Applications*, March 1993.

Quinnel, Richard A., "Image Compression, Parts 1, 2, and 3," *EDN Magazine*, January, March, May 1993.

Music, John D., *U.S. Patent, Number 5,164,819,* April 1991.

Prater, J. and Williams, R., "Digital Filtering: The Right Stuff for Video," *Electronic Systems Design Magazine*, January 1988.

INDEX

A

Active Matrix LCD, 85
Adaptive Linear Interpolation, 54
Additive Primaries, 101
Address Increment, 386
AGC, 288
Aliasing, 42
Amplitude, 271
Analog CRT, 75
Application Data Marker, 325
Arithmetic Coding, 313
Artifacts, Visible, 49
Astigmatic Lens, 192
Audio/Video Interleave, 248
Automatic Gain Control, 288
AVI, 248
Azimuth Recording, 209

B

B Frame, 374
Back Porch, 36
Backward Motion Vector, 383
Bandwidth Video, 41
Baseband, 42
Baseline Sequential DCT Based Coding, 313
Basic IO System, 227
Bidirectional Picture, 374
Bimorph, 207

B (continued)

BIOS, 227
Bit Planar, 58
Bit Rate, 379
Bitmap File, 221
BITMAPINFO, 408, 442
Blanking Frequency, 32
Block Decode, 166
Block Encode, 166
Blocks, 201
Blooming, 23
BMT, 221

C

C Format, 203
Camera, Television, 16
Capture, 215
Capture Pallette, 216
Cathode Ray Tube, 71
CCD, 21,23,24,26,29
CCIR, 107
CCIR 601, 124
CCIR 656 Serial Video Code, 196
CCITT, 395
CD, 184
CD ROM, 184
CDS, 28
CGA, 74
Character Generator, 71
Charge couple device, 21

Charge Coupled, 81
Chromaticity Diagram, 89,93,100,110
Chunk, 248
CIE, 88
CIF, 396
Clusters, 201
CLUT, 409
Code Book, 145
Code Table Building, Huffman, 138
Coding Decision, 393
Color Burst, 28,35
Color Difference Signal, 20
Color Graphics Adapter, 56
Color Lookup, 59,66
Color Lookup Table, 409
Color Pallette, 60
Color Subcarrier, 33
Comb Filter, 35
Common Intermediate Format, 396
Compact Disc, 184
Component Manager, 263
Components, 263
Composite video, 19
Compression, Lossy, 143
Compression Control, 218
Computer, Electronic, Invention of, 6
Config.sys, 227
Constrained Bit Stream, 378
Contour Map, 302
Contrast Enhancement, 287
Controller, Movie, 263
Conversion, Color Space, 112
Convolution Kernel, 272
Correlation, 145
Correlated Double Sampling, 28
Cosine Wave, 159
CRT, 71
Current Mirrors, 49
Cutoff Frequency, 49
Cylinder, 199

D

D Frame, 374
D1 Format, 208
D2 Format, 209
Data Format, 194
DC Picture, 374
DCT, 158,313

DDA, 281
Decimation, 281
Defect Skipping, 202
Define Huffman Table, 323
Defragmentation, 202
Descriptor, 228
Device Independent Bit Map, 214
DHT, 323
DIB, 214
Differential Pulse Code Modulation, 153
Diffraction, 187
Digital Differential Accumulator, 281
Digital to Analog, 46
Digital Video Media Control Interface, 235
Direct Color, 66
Discrete Cosine Transform, 158,313
Display Refresh, 69
Distortion, 44
Dithering, 44
DLL, 226
DOS Extender, 228
DOS Protected Mode Interface, 228
DPCM, 153
DPMI, 228
DRAM, 68
DriverProc(), 242
Dual Scan LCD, 82
Dumb Terminal, 72
DVMCI, 235
Dynamic Focus, 192
Dynamic Link Library, 226

E

Edge Detection, 296
Edge Energy, 297
Electricity and Magnetism, Early
        Developments, 4
Electromagnetic Waves, Discovery of, 5
End of Image, 317
Energy Level, 125
Enhanced Graphics Adapter, 57,74
Enhanced Mode, 228
Entropy, 123,137
Entropy Coding, 313
EOI, 317
Escape, 386
Expansion Slot, 70
Export, 231

Extension Data, 383
Extra Picture Information, 385

F

FAT, 201
FDCT, 160
Feature Extraction, 296
FEC, 406
Fidelity, 173
Field Integration., 22
File Access Table, 201
Filtering, 271
Filtering, Digital, 41
Filtering, Two Dimensional, 52
Finite Impulse Response Filter, 49,272
FIR Filter, 49,272
Flash Convertor, 44
FM Coding, 195
Focus, 229
Focus Mechanism, 190
Format, 194
Forward Error Correction, 406
Forward Motion Vector, 383
Four Square Transform, 152
Frame Buffer, 58
Frame Header, 316,318
Frequency Domain, 165
Front Porch, 36
FST, 152

G

GDI, 240
GetProcAddress(), 233
Graphic Controller, 68
Graphics, Vector, 72
Graphics Device Interface, 240
Gray Code, 137
Gray Scale, 83
Group Delay, 49
Group of Blocks, 399
Groups, 378

H

H.261, 395
H.320, 395
Header, Frame, 316

Hielical Scan, 203
Hierarchical Encoding, 314
High Level Format, 201
Histogram, 287
HSV Model, 104
Huffman Code Table, Building, 138
Huffman Code Tables, 331
Huffman Coding, 137,313
Huffman Table, 323

I

I Frame, 374
ICM, 236
Iconoscope, 6,16
IDCT, 160
Illuminant C, 90
Image Quality, 222
Image Sensing, 24
Image Sensor, 20
Image Slice, 374
Image Warp, 280
Import, 231
Indeo, 221
Installable Compression Manager, 236
Instance, 233
Institute of Radio Engineers, 35
Intel Smart Video Recorder, 220
Interlaced Video, 27
Interleaving, 33
International Organization for
        Standardization, 373
International Telegraph and Telephone
        Consultative Commitee, 395
Intra Picture, 374
IQ, 35
IRE, 35,76
ISA Bus, 70
ISO, 373
ISO1172, 373

J

Joint Photographic Experts Group, 313
JPEG, 313

K

Kiniscope, 6,16

L

LCD, 80
Line Interlace, 36
Linear Scaling, 280
Lip Sync, 181
Liquid Crystal, 80
LoadLibrary(), 233
Lossy Compression, 143
Low Level Format, 200
Luma Subsampling, 132
Luminance Signal, 20

M

Macro Block, 374
Macro Block, H.261, 400
Manchester Coding, 195
Maréchal Criterion, 188
Marker Segments, 314
Markers, 314
MCI, 235
MCIAVI, 235
MCU, 314
Media Control Interface, 235
Message Pump, 233
Messages, 228
Microprocessor, Invention of, 7
Microsoft Windows, 228
Miller Code, 209
Minimum Coded Unit, 314
Modulation, Quatrature, 21
Monochrome Display Adapter, 56
Motion Compensation, 179
Motion Estimation, 178
Motion Vector, 383,403
Movie Controller, 263
MPEG, 373
Munsel Book of Color, 102
Munsel Color Space, 102

N

Negative Image, 292
Negative Modulation, 36
Noise, 44
Non-Return to Zero, 195
Non-Spectral Colors, 90
NRZ, 195

NTSC, 26,28,31,35
Numerical Aperature, 188
Nyquest Theorm, 42

O

Optical Data Pick-up, 190
Optical Integration., 25

P

P Frame, 374
Packed Pixel, 58
PAL, 35,37
Palette, 60,94,216
Particle Theory, 185
Passive Matrix, 81
PCM, 153
Phosphor, 76,79,93
Photo Lithography, 199
PIC File Format, 431
Picture Group, 381
Pixel Block, 167
Polarization, 81
Predicted Picture, 374
Printing, Invention of, 3
Pro Movie Studio, 219
Progressive DCT Encoding, 314
Projection Display, 79
Protected Mode, 228
Public Education, 4
Pulse Code Modulation, 153

Q

QCIF, 396
Quadrature Modulation, 21,35
Quantization, 43,150
Quantization Table, 321
Quantization Vector 143
Quantize, 164
Quarter CIF, 396
Quarter Wave Plate, 189
Quick Time, 264

R

Re-entrant, 233
Real Mode, 228

Refraction, 186
Refractive Index, 186
Refresh Pulses, 83,85
Restart Interval, 326
Restart Interval Marker, 325
Restart Marker, 314
Reverse Mapping, 280
RGB Conversion Tube, 93
RIFF, 248,410
RLE, 136
RLL, 196
RMSE, 123,173,179
Root Mean Square Error, 123,179
Run Length Encoding, 136
Run Length Limited, 196

S

Sample Set, 160
Sampling, 41
Saturation, 33
Scaling, 279
Scan Header, 320
Scanner, 204
SECAM, 35,37
Sector Skipping, 202
Sectors, 200
Segment Fixup, 227
Sequence, 378
Serial Video Code, 196
Shadow Mask, 76
SIF, 376
Slices, 374
Slope Overload, 154
Smart Video Recorder, 220
SMPTE, 381
Sobel's Algorithm, 296
Society for Motion Picture and Television
        Engineers, 381
SOF, 316
SOI, 317
Source Input Format, 376
Spatial Dimensions, 271
Spatial Dithering, 74
Spatial Filter, 272
Spectral Colors, 89
Spectral Distribution, 93
Standard Mode, 228
Start of Frame, 316

Start of Image, 317
Statistical Coding, 137
Striping, 23
Stripe filter, 19
Stuffing, 386
Subcarrier Frequency, 32
Subsample, 124
Subsampling Color, 123
Subtractive Primaries, 101
Super VGA, 57
SuperMatch Compression, 224
Sync Frequency, 32
SYSEDIT.EXE, 234
SYSTEM.INI, 231,234,263

T

Tearing Artifacts, 76
Telegraph, Invention of, 5
Telephone, Invention of, 5
TFT, 85
Thin Film, 199
Thin Film Transistor, 85
Threshold Process, 303
Tracking, 207
Transistor, Invention of, 7
True Color, 66
Twisted Nematic, 80
Two Dimensional Array, 161

U

User Data, 383

V

Variable Length Code, 375
Vector Graphics, 72
Vector Motion, 383
Vector Quantization, 143
VGA, 68
VGA LCD, 82
VID File Format, 414
VidCap, 213
Video, Composite, 19
Video Capture, 215
Video Graphics Array, 57
Video Spigot, 212
Virtual Buffer Verifier Delay, 383

Visible Spectrum, 88
Visual Acuity, 75
VLC, 375
VRAM, 68

W

Wave Theory, 185
Windows, 228

Y

YCrCb, 107
YIQ Color Space, 107
YUV Color Space, 104
YVU9, 221

Z

ZigZag Order, 328